This second edition of Peter Hajnal's book is timely and welcome, as the G20 enters its second decade in increasingly turbulent times. As always, his work is meticulous, authoritative, wise in its judgments and indispensable for all G20-watchers.

Sir Nicholas Bayne, *KCMG, London School of Economics and Political Science, UK*

This book is the essential authoritative reference for all scholars, students and professionals seeking to understand the G20 and global governance as a whole now. All should have a copy close at hand. It describes in careful detail the key features and growth of the G20 as an international institution and points to its centrality and effectiveness in today's complex, uncertain world.

John Kirton, *Munk School of Global Affairs, University of Toronto, Canada*

Peter Hajnal's book is an encyclopedia of the evolving G20 system. It provides readers with a deep and comprehensive analysis of the G20's role in the system of global governance. The book is essential reading for anyone seeking to understand informal summit institutions and look into their future.

Dr. Marina Larionova, *Russian Presidential Academy of National Economy and Public Administration, Moscow*

Peter Hajnal has written an account of the G20 that is informative, comprehensive, authoritative and up-to-date. He traces the origins of the G20, describes its workings and relationship to other inter- and non-governmental institutions, and offers an assessment of its significance, accomplishments and shortcomings.

Ramesh Thakur, *The Australian National University*

Peter Hajnal is a rare scholar of the history of contemporary 'club diplomacy'. His work on the G20 is uniquely knowledgeable and invaluable for the study of informal cooperation between great powers.

Karoline Postel-Vinay, *FNSP Research Professor, Sciences Po, France*

The G20

This revised and updated edition presents detailed analysis of the history and current state of the G20, and the challenges it faces.

The emergence of the G20 was the result of calls for full inclusion of major developing and other systemically important countries and to reflect new global economic and political realities. The growth of Chinese power, growing significance of other major developing countries and new concerns concerning anti-globalization and rising protectionism in the West have all resulted in important changes to the dynamics of the institution. The suspension of Russia's membership in the G8 has also necessitated a change in G7/G20 dynamics and the G20's processes, agenda priorities and role in global governance. Providing a historical overview and analysis of the evolving agenda, methods of performance evaluation, relationship with structured international organizations and other external actors, Hajnal's text is an authoritative work of history, analysis and reference on the G20 and also G7/G8/G20 reform.

This book is an essential source for researchers and students focusing on the G20, international organizations and global governance, and more generally for scholars in the fields of political science, economics and finance.

Peter I. Hajnal is Fellow of Senior College; Research Associate, Munk School of Global Affairs; and Emeritus Librarian, all at the University of Toronto. He was Adjunct Professor, Faculty of Information, University of Toronto for 11 years, and was a librarian, specializing in international organization information, for over 30 years. He has been a member of the G7/G8/G20 Research Groups since 1988; he attended 14 G7/G8/G20 summits as media correspondent and was Library Advisor to the Research Groups for 24 years. He is also a member of the Academic Council on the United Nations System, the International Studies Association, the Union of International Associations and the American Library Association. He served as consultant at the United Nations, in post-Yugoslavia Macedonia, in the Civil G8 project in 2006 in Russia, and in the Graham Library, Trinity College, University of Toronto.

Global Governance

Series Editor:
John J. Kirton,
University of Toronto, Canada

Global governance is growing rapidly to meet the compounding challenges of a globalized 21st-century world. Many issues once dealt with largely at the local, national or regional level are now going global, in the economic, social and political-security domains. In response, new and renewed intergovernmental institutions are arising and adapting, multi-level governance is expanding, and sub-national actors are playing a greater role, and create complex combinations and private-partnerships to this end.

This series focuses on the new dynamics of global governance in the 21st century by:

- Addressing the changes in the structure, operation and impact of individual intergovernmental institutions, above all their innovative responses to the growing global challenges they confront.
- Exploring how they affect, are affected by and relate to non-state actors of global relevance and reach.
- Examining the processes of cooperation, competition and convergence among international institutions and the many global governance gaps where global challenges such as terrorism, transnational crime and energy do not confront powerful international institutions devoted to their control.
- Dealing with how global institutions govern the links among key issues such as climate change and health.

In all cases, it focuses on the central questions of how global governance institutions and processes generate the effective, legitimate, accountable results required to govern today's interconnected, complex, uncertain and crisis-ridden world.

BRICS and Global Governance
John Kirton and Marina Larionova

The G7, Anti-Globalism and the Governance of Globalization
Edited by Chiara Oldani and Jan Wouters

Social Closure and International Society
The Politics of Clubs from the Family of Civilised Nations to the G20
Tristen Naylor

The G20
Evolution, Interrelationships, Documentation
2nd edition
Peter I. Hajnal

The Politics of Global Tax Governance
Henning Schmidtke

For more information about this series, please visit: www.routledge.com/Global-Governance/book-series/ASHSER1420

The G20

Evolution, Interrelationships, Documentation

Second, revised edition

Peter I. Hajnal
University of Toronto, Canada

Routledge
Taylor & Francis Group
LONDON AND NEW YORK

An electronic version of this book is freely available, thanks to the support of libraries working with Knowledge Unlatched (KU). KU is a collaborative initiative designed to make high quality books Open Access for the public good. The Open Access ISBN for this book is 9781351266802. More information about the initiative and links to the Open Access version can be found at www.knowledgeunlatched.org.

First edition published by Routledge 2014

Second edition published 2019
byRoutledge
2 Park Square, Milton Park, Abingdon, Oxon, OX14 4RN

and by Routledge
605 Third Avenue, New York, NY 10017

First issued in paperback 2021

Routledge is an imprint of the Taylor & Francis Group, an informa business

First edition published by Routledge 2014

British Library Cataloguing-in-Publication Data
A catalogue record for this book is available from the British Library

Library of Congress Cataloging-in-Publication Data
Names: Hajnal, Peter I., 1936- author.
Title: The G20 : evolution, interrelationships, documentation / Peter I. Hajnal.
Description: 2nd Edition. | New York : Routledge, 2019. | Series: Global governance | Revised edition of the author's The G20, [2014] | Includes bibliographical references and index.
Identifiers: LCCN 2018054216 | ISBN 9781138577503 (hardback)
Subjects: LCSH: Group of Twenty. | International economic relations. | Economic policy. | Summit meetings.
Classification: LCC HF1359 .H3445 2019 | DDC 337.1—dc23
LC record available at https://lccn.loc.gov/2018054216

ISBN 13: 978-1-03-207333-0 (pbk)
ISBN 13: 978-1-138-57750-3 (hbk)

DOI: 10.4324/9781351266802

Publisher's Note
The publisher has gone to great lengths to ensure the quality of this reprint but points out that some imperfections in the original copies may be apparent.

Contents

Tables

Preface and acknowledgements

The Group of 7 and the Group of 20 (G7 and G20) have undergone many changes, and global governance has also changed since the publication of my two previous books, *The G8 System and the G20*, in 2007, and *The G20: Evolution, Interrelationships, Documentation*, in 2014. These changes have included major developments in the G7/G8-G20 galaxy of institutions. The G7 (previously G8) has evolved further as an institution, but has faced increasing challenges to its composition, its relations with the G20, its values and its future. One of the two most significant changes was the emergence of the G20 at the Finance Ministers' level in 1999 and at the leaders' level in 2009 – both came about in response to calls for full inclusion of major developing and other systemically important countries in diplomatic deliberations, to reflect new global economic and political realities. The other major change was the suspension of Russia's membership in the G8 in 2014, turning it once again into the G7. Yet another challenge (especially for the G7) comes from the recent rise of populism internationally and US attitudes and actions under the Trump administration – on climate, trade, security and other issues. On a more positive note, the G7 and the G20, despite the challenges, are surviving as key institutions of global governance and it is hoped that setbacks will be temporary.

This book aspires to be an authoritative work of reference on the G20 as well as on the reform and potential future trajectory of the G7 and G20. It is, first, a historical survey of the G20, including the Finance Ministers' and Central Bank Governors' meetings which preceded and have coexisted with the G20 leaders' summits. Second, it analyzes agenda evolution, problems of membership, the broadening G20 system, and the increasingly significant G20 relationship with international governmental organizations, the business sector and civil society. Third, it examines the challenges and advances of monitoring and evaluating G20 performance. Fourth, it discusses the documentation of G20 summits and sub-summit groups, and reviews other sources of information about the G20. The book includes an extensive bibliography. Most of the material is up to date as of summer 2018.

It is my hope that this book will serve as a useful work of reference for analysts and students in the fields of economics, finance, political science and other disciplines, as well as officials of governments and international organizations, financial institutions, non-state actors and the media. Beyond these, this work may be of interest to a wider audience of the informed public.

For this second edition, I acknowledge with special appreciation the continuing encouragement and generously shared insights of the Right Honourable Paul Martin, former Prime Minister and Finance Minister of Canada. My thanks go also to Sir Nicholas Bayne, scholar and former diplomat, who was my mentor and whose rich experience, analytical mind and constructive suggestions have benefited me throughout many years of research and writing about the G7/G8 and G20. My colleague, Professor John Kirton of the University of Toronto, prominent G7/G8 and G20 scholar, Founder/Director of the G7/G8 Research Group and Founder and Co-director of the G20 Research Group, has given me continual encouragement, guidance and other valuable support. I thank Madeline Koch, Executive Director of the G20 Research Group, as well as Julia Kulik, Alissa Wang, Brittaney Warren and other past and current members of the G20 Research Group for their assistance. My thanks are due to the Munk School of Global Affairs and Public Policy, and to Trinity College at the University of Toronto for material support and use of office space. I express my gratitude to Senior College, University of Toronto, for a research grant to support the study of G7/G8/G20 reform and the challenges facing these institutions.

I wish to thank the many civil society and academic friends and colleagues, and government and international organization officials, who have shared their insight, observations and perspectives. Not all can be named here, but I wish to acknowledge the following: Thomas Bernes, former Director of the Centre for International Government Innovation; Nancy Alexander, Director, Economic Governance Programme, Heinrich Böll Foundation; Maggie Murphy of Transparency International; Steve Price-Thomas, Advocacy Director, Oxfam International; Zhu Jiejin of Fudan University, Shanghai; John Ruthrauff, Director, Center for Democratic Education (former Director of International Advocacy, InterAction); Andrew Cooper of the University of Waterloo; Jan Aart Scholte, School of Global Studies, Gothenburg University; Lou Pauly, University of Toronto; Sherrie Steiner of Purdue University, Fort Wayne; Edwin Truman, formerly of the Peterson Institute of International Economics; Gordon Smith, Barry Carin and Peter Heap – all formerly of the Centre for Global Studies (Gordon Smith, former Canadian sherpa and Centre Director), University of Victoria; Xu Ting, formerly at the School of International Relations, University of International Business and Economics, Beijing; and Kel Currah, CEO of What World Strategies.

Gillian Clinton, my excellent long-time research assistant, deserves my special thanks. She was instrumental in putting together this book. I thank her for careful fact-checking, a keen eye and meticulous editorial help, and for researching and preparing the section on social media in Chapter 10. I thank Routledge, and in particular Robert Sorsby and Claire Maloney, for encouraging and facilitating the publication of this revised second edition, as well as Gordon Matchado of Apex CoVantage for shepherding the book into print. Last, but certainly not least, I want to thank my wife, Edna, and son, Mark, for their support and patience.

I am grateful to all of them for their help in improving this work. Any inaccuracies or omissions are entirely mine.

Peter Hajnal
Toronto, August 2018

Abbreviations and acronyms

#eSkills4Girls	G20 initiative promoting the participation of women in the global economy
3G	Global Governance Group
ACWG	Anti-Corruption Working Group
ADB	Asian Development Bank
AfDB	African Development Bank
AFI	Alliance for Financial Inclusion
AIDS	Acquired immunodeficiency syndrome
AIIB	Asian Infrastructure Investment Bank
AMIS	Agricultural Market Information System
APEC	Asia-Pacific Economic Cooperation (forum)
ASEAN	Association of Southeast Asian Nations
ATIP	Access to Information and Privacy (Canada)
AU	African Union
B7	Business Engagement Group
B20	Business Summit (Business 20)
BCBS	Basel Committee on Banking Supervision (of BIS)
BCE	Before Common Era
BIS	Bank for International Settlements
BRIC	Brazil, Russia, India and China
BRICS	(Group of) Brazil, Russia, India, China and South Africa
C7	Civil Society 7
C20	Civil Society 20
CAR	Comprehensive Accountability Report
CARICOM	Caribbean Community
CCFD	Comité Catholique Contre la Faim et Pour le Développement
CEO	Chief executive officer
CFGS	Centre for Global Studies
CFR	Council on Foreign Relations
CGAP	Consultative Group to Assist the Poor
CGFS	Committee on the Global Financial System
Chatham House	Royal Institute of International Affairs
CIGI	Centre for International Governance Innovation

Coordination SUD	Coordination Solidarité, Urgence, Développement
CPMI	Committee on Payments and Market Infrastructures
CPSS	Committee on Payment and Settlement Systems
CRA	Contingent Reserve Arrangement
CRS	Creditor Reporting System (OECD)
CSO	Civil society organization
DAC	Development Assistance Committee (OECD)
DATA	Debt, AIDS, Trade, Africa (now merged with ONE)
DWG	G20 Development Working Group
EBRD	European Bank for Reconstruction and Development
EC	European Community (-ies)
ECB	European Central Bank
ECOWAS	Economic Community of Western African States
EEFTG	Energy Efficiency Finance Task Group
EIB	European Investment Bank (EU)
EMDC	Emerging-market developing countries
EU	European Union
F20	F20 Foundations Platform
F20	Faith 20
FAO	Food and Agriculture Organization of the United Nations
FATF	Financial Action Task Force
FIAP	Financial Inclusion Action Plan
FIM	Forum international de Montréal (now FIM Forum for Democratic Global Governance)
FRIDE	Fundación para las Relaciones Internacionales y el Diálogo Exterior
FSB	Financial Stability Board
FSF	Financial Stability Forum
FTT	Financial transaction tax
G2A2	Green Growth Action Alliance (B20)
G5 or 'Outreach 5'	(Group of) Brazil, China, India, Mexico and South Africa
G6	Group of Six
G7	Group of Seven
G8	Group of Eight
G20	Group of 20
G20YEA	Young Entrepreneurs' Alliance
G20YES	Young Entrepreneurs' Summit (aka YESG20)
G22	Group of 22 (aka Willard Group)
G33	Group of 33
GCAP	Global Call to Action against Poverty
GCC	Gulf Cooperation Council (Cooperation Council for the Arab States of the Gulf)
GDP	Gross domestic product
GFIA	Global Federation of Insurance Associations
GFSG	Green Finance Study Group

GMEP	Global Marine Environment Protection
GPFI	Global Partnership for Financial Inclusion
G-Science	National Academies of Brazil, Canada, China, France, Germany, India, Indonesia, Italy, Japan, Mexico, Morocco, Russia, South Africa, UK & US
HAP	Heiligendamm/L'Aquila Process
HLDWG	G20 High-Level Development Working Group
HP	Heiligendamm Process
HSE	Higher School of Economics, National Research University (Moscow)
IAIS	International Association of Insurance Supervisors
IASB	International Accounting Standards Board
IATA	International Air Transport Association
IBSA	[Trading bloc of] India, Brazil and South Africa dialogue forum
ICAO	International Civil Aviation Organization
ICC	International Chamber of Commerce
ICT	Information and communication technology
IDB	Inter-American Development Bank
IEA	International Energy Agency (OECD)
IFAD	International Fund for Agricultural Development
IFIs	International financial institutions
IGO	International governmental organization
IHT	*International Herald Tribune*
IIF	Institute of International Finance
ILO	International Labour Organization
IMF	International Monetary Fund
IMFC	International Monetary and Financial Committee (IMF)
INFE	International Network on Financial Education
IOM	International Organization for Migration
IORI	International Organisations Research Institute, Higher School of Economics, National Research University (Moscow)
IOSCO	International Organization of Securities Commissions
ISIS	Islamic State of Iraq and Syria or Daesh
ITUC	International Trade Union Confederation
J8	Junior 8 youth forum
L7	Labour-7
L20	Labour 20 (Labour Summit)
LatinDADD	Latin American Network on Debt and Development
MAP	Mutual Assessment Process (G20, IMF and other IGOs)
MDB	Multilateral development bank
MDG	Millennium Development Goals (UN)
MEDEF	Mouvement des Entreprises de France
MEF	Major Economies Forum on Energy and Climate (earlier MEM)

MEM	Major Economies Meeting (later MEF)
MITKA	Mexico, Indonesia, Turkey, Korea and Australia
MYAP	Multi-Year Action Plan on Development (Seoul G20 summit)
NAB	New Arrangement to Borrow (IMF)
NAFTA	North American Free Trade Agreement
NATO	North Atlantic Treaty Organization
NDB	New Development Bank
NEPAD	New Partnership for Africa's Development
NGO	Non-governmental organization
NPGL	National Perspectives on Global Leadership
O5	Outreach 5 (Brazil, China, India, Mexico and South Africa)
ODA	Official development assistance
ODF	Official development finance
OECD	Organisation for Economic Co-operation and Development
OPEC	Organization of the Petroleum Exporting Countries
OSF	Open Society Foundations
P5	Security Council's 'Permanent Five' members (UN)
PCD	Policy coherence in development
PPP	Public-private partnership
RANEPA	Russian Presidential Academy of National Economy and Public Administration
Rio+20	United Nations Conference on Sustainable Development (2012)
S7	Science 7
S20	Science 20
SDGs	Sustainable Development Goals
SDR	Special Drawing Rights (IMF)
SDSN	Sustainable Development Solutions Network
SIIA	Singapore Institute of International Affairs
SMART	Sustainable innovation, Massive public platform, Accessible network, Revolutionary reform, and Technological innovation (B20)
SMEs	Small- and medium-sized enterprises
SSB	Strong, Sustainable, and Balanced Growth Working Group (G20)
T7	Think Tank 7
T20	Think20
T20	G20 Tourism Ministers
TI	Transparency International
TUAC	Trade Union Advisory Committee to the OECD
TUMSIAD	All Industrialists and Businessmen Association (Turkish)
UK	United Kingdom
UN	United Nations
UNCTAD	United Nations Conference on Trade and Development
UNDP	United Nations Development Programme

UNFCCC	UN Framework Convention on Climate Change
UNHCR	United Nations High Commissioner for Refugees
UNICEF	United Nations Children's Fund
UNIDO	United Nations Industrial Development Organisation
UNSC	United Nations Security Council
UNWTO	United Nations World Tourism Organization
US	United States of America
W7	Women 7
W20	Women 20
WEF	World Economic Forum
WFP	World Food Programme
WHO	World Health Organization
WTO	World Trade Organization
WWF	World Wide Fund for Nature (formerly World Wildlife Fund)
Y7	Youth 7
Y20	Youth 20
YEA20	Young Entrepreneurs' Alliance

Introduction

This introduction sets the stage for exploring the evolving complex Group of 20 (G20) forum. It begins with outlining the characteristics of this forum and proceeds to review various models of the G20 as a global governance institution. It then covers the objectives and structure of the work. Finally, it provides chapter summaries.

The G20: what it is and what it is not

The G20, like its creator institution, the Group of 7/Group of 8 (G7/G8), is an informal entity. Traditional, formally structured international governmental organizations are established by and based on a founding charter or international treaty, such as the Charter of the United Nations (UN) or the Articles of Agreement of the International Monetary Fund (IMF). Formal international organizations have permanent secretariats charged with implementing policies, decisions and directives of the governing body of the organization. By contrast, neither the G7/G8 nor the G20 is founded on a constitutional document, nor do they have permanent secretariats, although in the G20's case the country holding the rotating Presidency forms a temporary secretariat during its term in order to coordinate work and organize meetings. G7/G8 and G20 declarations carry no legal obligations and cannot be enforced. But this tells us only what the G20 is not.

It is more difficult to answer the question 'What is the G20?' The communiqué of the inaugural meeting of the G20 at the level of Finance Ministers and Central Bank Governors in 1999 declares,

> The G-20 was established to provide a new mechanism for informal dialogue in the framework of the Bretton Woods institutional system, to broaden the discussions on key economic and financial policy issues among systemically significant economies and promote co-operation to achieve stable and sustainable world economic growth that benefits all.
>
> (G20, 1999)

The French government, as host of the 2011 Cannes summit of G20 leaders, simply stated that the G20 'operates with an annually rotating chair under a

DOI: 10.4324/9781351266802-1

relatively informal system' (G20, 2011g). The Mexican host government of the 2012 Los Cabos summit characterized the G20 as the premier forum for international co-operation on the most important international economic and financial issues and emphasized that the forum brings together the world's major advanced and emerging economies. Further, the host government summarized the G20's objectives as follows: policy co-ordination in order to achieve global economic stability and sustainable growth; promotion of financial regulations to reduce risks and prevent future crises; and creation of a new international financial architecture. The 2017 German Presidency defined the G20 simply as 'the central forum for international cooperation on financial and economic issues' (B20, 2017b).

The G20 is a plurilateral forum of discussion and policy debate at the highest political level, composed of countries across regions of the world (contrasted with multilateral organizations with universal membership). 'The G8 summit had three distinct but interlocking objectives: political leadership; reconciling the domestic and external pressures of interdependence, now globalization; and collective management of the international system' (Bayne, 2011a, p. 249). Others have used the term 'minilateral' rather than 'plurilateral' (Hampson and Heinbecker, 2011, p. 301). The G20 can achieve (and in many cases has achieved) policy coordination and can launch (and has launched) policy initiatives in an increasing range of economic and some other issues. The G20 brings together the older group of democratic, market-economy countries with other systemically important countries of diverse political systems (some of which are also democratic). In addition to G7/G8 countries (Canada, France, Germany, Italy, Japan, Russia [whose membership in the G8 was suspended in 2014], the UK and the US), the G20 includes Argentina, Australia, Brazil, China, India, Indonesia, Mexico, Saudi Arabia, South Africa, the Republic of Korea and Turkey, and the European Union as the twentieth member. Like the G7/G8, the G20 can also be viewed as a club of (more or less) equal members. Several scholars, among them Gnath and Schmucker (2011) and Kirton (2013e, pp. 46–47), explore this concept.

The G20 countries account for 85 per cent of gross world product, three-quarters of global trade and two-thirds of the world's population. Its decisions are influential and help to bring about reform at national and multinational levels. Like the G7, the G20 is an informal forum. This is why each G20 Presidency plays a particularly important role. The Presidency is responsible for organizing the summit, setting its agenda and inviting guests (G20, 2018a). The group has become a major actor in global governance, particularly since the September 2009 Pittsburgh summit, where the leaders declared it to be 'the premier forum for our international economic cooperation' (G20, 2009c).

The annually rotating chair is one of the three-member 'troika' of the past, current and next year's chairs. The rotation is not strictly by calendar year; each member country on rotation for the following year usually assumes the G20 Presidency on 1 December and continues until November of the following year. The troika was established by G20 finance deputies in 2002 in order to ensure continuity and to give the current and succeeding chair access to the experience of the previous

Table I.1 Regional Groups for G20 Rotating Presidencies

Group 1	*Group 2*	*Group 3*	*Group 4*	*Group 5*
Australia	India	Argentina	France	China
Canada	Russia	Brazil	Germany	Indonesia
Saudi Arabia	South Africa	Mexico	Italy	Japan
United States	Turkey	–	United Kingdom	South Korea

Source: G20 (2018a).

year's chair (G20, 2007, pp. 22–23). The three are from the regional groups specified by the G20 (see Table I.1). The troika in 2018 comprises Germany as 2017 chair, Argentina as 2018 chair and Japan as 2019 chair.

Each member country creates a temporary secretariat for the duration of its G20 Presidency; this secretariat co-ordinates the work and organizes the various meetings of the G20. The first G20 summits had not yet applied the troika rotation: the initial summit was held in the US (Washington, November 2008), the second in the UK (London, April 2009), the third again in the US (Pittsburgh, September 2009) and the fourth in Canada (Toronto, June 2010 – hosted by Canada but under the 2010 Korean Presidency). Writing in 2010, John Kirton perceived a possible 'move for internal leadership from a rotating troika to a pentarchy composed of all democratic polities' (Kirton, 2010b, p. 31). This, however, raises a question: Would such a step risk loosening the G20's embrace of members from the North and from the South, with diverse political systems? Would it place China and some other emerging countries outside the leadership of global economic governance? In the event, the November 2010 summit was held in Korea under that country's Presidency and the Cannes G20 summit reaffirmed the troika principle. This reinforces the equal leadership role of all G20 members, not just the G7. It is indicative of the rotating presidencies of the G20 according to regional groupings.

The G20's relative informality has enabled its leaders to understand one another's domestic political and economic circumstances and constraints. As Hampson and Heinbecker (2011, p. 305) put it, while the 'greater diversity of membership of the G-20 . . . means less commonality of interest . . . there are offsetting advantages in terms of the breadth of support behind any agreement reached, and the capacity of the group to deliver on it'.

The G20 has provided the leaders with a forum to achieve policy coordination and to co-operate on policy initiatives on a growing number and variety of issues. During its 19 years of existence on the ministerial level and 10 years at the leaders' level, it has achieved important results on financial, economic, environmental, health and other global issues, although its performance has not been consistently high. It continues to draw criticism because of its perceived inefficiency and lack of universal representativeness and therefore full legitimacy, notwithstanding the fact that the G20 is much more representative of global economic and political realities than the more restrictive G7/G8.

Yet, according to former Canadian G20 sherpa Len Edwards, writing on the eve of the Cannes summit,

> The G20 represents the future of global economic governance. It provides emerging countries, led by the powerhouses of China, India and Brazil, with the opportunity to engage advanced economies and each other to create a new compact around effective governance and international economic behaviour. (Edwards, 2011, p. A19)

The G20 as a global governance institution

Drawing on several analyses of the G20, John Kirton (2013c) discusses the following schools of thought about the G20:

- *Redundant G20*. This view holds that the G20 is headed for redundancy due to its informal nature and large and diverse membership. It also regards the G20 as an unnecessary rival to the G7/G8 and the Bretton Woods institutions in the financial and economic realms. Some of this school even consider the G20 dangerous because it usurps power over financial governance and excludes the majority of UN member states (Åslund, 2009, p. 11).
- *Rejectionists*. This school rejects the G20's pre-eminence but accepts the G20's contributions and continued existence (Beeson and Bell, 2009). Others of this school point to the G20's institutional and performance problems (e.g., Duncan, 2008; Giles, 2009; Payne, 2010).
- *The G20 as reinforcement for the G7/G8*. This school argues that the G20 ought to be restricted to its core mission of promoting financial stability, sustained growth and globalization for the benefit of all (Alexandroff and Kirton, 2010; Griesgraber, 2009). Others point to the benefit of broader representation in the G20 compared with the G7/G8. Still others argue that 'the G7 will become an executive committee while the G20 will assume the role of an assembly' (Penttilä, 2009, p. 42). Another variation of this school is the idea of 'co-operative co-dependence' of the G20 and the G7/G8 (Cooper, 2010a).
- *Replacement of the G7/G8 by the G20*. Kirton (2013c, p. 10) cites various schools of 'replacers': those that consider that with the emergence of the G20 the G7/G8 would 'fade away as an effective central forum'. This alternative is explored in detail in Chapter 7.

Kirton goes on to argue that 'the G20 has emerged as a systemic hub with a performance at the ministerial and now leaders' level that has generally grown across a widening agenda and array of global governance dimensions . . . [moving towards] the hub of a growing global governance network' (Kirton, 2013c, p. 14). In fleshing out this concept of the G20, he acknowledges prior work on global economic governance as a network, notably Anne-Marie Slaughter's (1997) contribution. Kirton (2013e) conceptualizes G20 governance performance as having six dimensions: domestic political management, deliberation, direction-setting, decision-making, delivery and development of global governance.

A different method of assessing the G20 and other international institutions was developed by Bayne (2011b), using nine indices:

- *Political and economic*. How far can an institution reconcile politics and economics? The G20 summit still is predominantly an economic forum but it arose for political reasons.
- *Departmental intensity*. This index assesses institutions from the point of view of involvement of individual governments: how many ministries or other branches of a government are involved in interacting with international institutions? The G20, being primarily economic, (initially did not require) the involvement of many government departments apart from finance ministries (but with the expansion of its agenda, more ministries have become involved).
- *Domestic versus external issues on the agenda*. The G20 has strong domestic as well as strong international dimensions. (This is not dissimilar to Kirton's 'domestic political management' dimension of G20 governance.)
- *Voluntary cooperation versus a rule-making approach*. The G20 relies on voluntary cooperation among its members and lacks the capacity to enforce rules. (The G20 has this in common with the G7/G8.)
- *Accountability to member governments and their citizens*. Bayne deems the G20 strongly accountable. (See, however, Chapter 8 of the present work, which asserts that the G20's democratic accountability is weak. In addition, this book views transparency – Bayne's separate index factor – as a dimension of accountability.)
- *Degree of business-friendliness*. The G20 is business-friendly but at a distance.
- *Transparency towards the wider world, including civil society*. The G20 is only moderately transparent (and its ties with civil society are not consistently strong).
- *Staff resources versus reliance on member states*. Lacking its own staff, the G20 is necessarily member-driven.
- *Multi-level involvement*. Does the institution pursue its objectives beyond its own members? The G20 is strongly involved in multi-level diplomacy.

The G20 at the leaders' level has been called a 'crisis committee' since its original task was to deal with the financial and economic crisis at its inception in 2008. Once that immediate crisis eased, observers (and possibly the G20 itself) have pondered the modalities of turning it into a 'global steering committee' (see, e.g., Bradford and Lim, 2010). This is not a smooth transition. To illustrate this uncertain progression: the Cannes summit found itself suddenly in the midst of the euro-area sovereign debt crisis to which it was forced to pay central attention, to the detriment of its prearranged broader agenda. The argument, however, has been made that the crisis committee/steering committee framework is an unnecessary dichotomy. In practice, the G7/G8 as well as the G20 have evolved to be both: dealing with crises as they occur and attempting crisis management, and also acting as a steering committee on many issues; see, for example, Paul Martin (2009, p. 24), Merkel (2015, p. A15) and Martin (telephone interview with the author, 10 January 2018). Chapter 7 explores this theme further.

Objectives of this book

The purpose of this book is to provide an authoritative work of reference on the G20 and on G7/G8/G20 reform. The book traces the origins and predecessors of the G20; surveys the G20 Finance Ministers' meetings since 1999 and the series of G20 summits since 2008; reviews the evolution of their agenda; discusses the question of G20 membership; surveys the components of the G20 system; analyzes the relationship of the G20 with international governmental organizations (IGOs), the business sector, and civil society organizations and coalitions; surveys and analyses reform proposals and reforms already achieved; looks at the relationship between, and challenges confronting, the G7 and the G20; examines the question of evaluating G20 performance; surveys the pattern of documentation of G20 summits and sub-summit groups; and reviews other sources of information (writings about the G20, think-tanks focusing on G20 research, memoirs of prominent G20 participants, creative works, and websites and social media).

Chapter summaries

Following this introduction, Chapter 1 tracks the developments leading to the creation of the G20 Finance Ministers' and Central Bank Governors' forum (including a discussion of predecessor bodies) and the subsequent establishment of the G20 leaders' summits. It concludes that: the G20 arose, at both the Finance Ministers' and leaders' levels, in response to the economic and financial crises which existing institutions were unable to address adequately; the shift of the balance of power from advanced market-economy countries to major emerging countries made it imperative to include both kinds of actors as equals; and political leadership and commitment at the highest level were necessary in establishing and developing the G20 as a powerful institution with growing potential.

Chapter 2 examines the issue of G20 membership and invited non-member countries; surveys the G20 summits since they began in 2008; and traces the evolution of their agenda. It concludes that while the G20's composition, based on the membership of systemically significant countries, has remained constant, membership has been a contentious issue, with the persistent dichotomy of representativeness versus effectiveness. The chapter further shows the transformation of the G20 into a more permanent institution with an incrementally growing agenda characterized by both continuity and innovation as well as a recurring debate on whether the agenda should expand or remain narrowly focused. Agenda expansion is reflected in summit deliberations and in the creation of an increasing number of working groups and similar sub-summit groups.

Chapter 3 surveys and comments on the components of the evolving G20 system: ministerial fora, the Financial Stability Board, working groups and other sub-summit entities, and the leaders' personal representatives (sherpas). The chapter concludes that sub-summit entities are essential in supporting and supplementing the leaders' forum by working on specific issues and tasks. Changing priorities necessitate appropriate structures to investigate, plan, recommend and promote the required action.

The next three chapters focus on G20 relations with other types of actors: international organizations, the business sector and civil society. Chapter 4 discusses the characteristics, evolution, benefits and challenges of the relationship of the G20 with international governmental organizations: the Bretton Woods institutions, the United Nations, the Organisation for Economic Co-operation and Development, the Bank for International Settlements and other IGOs. The chapter also gives an account of the Mutual Assessment Process led by the IMF. It concludes that this connection is necessary and mutually beneficial; that collaboration has been established in G20 practice; and that the Bretton Woods institutions and a few other select IGOs enjoy a privileged relationship with the G20. IGOs provide analysis, policy proposals and performance evaluation, and may give greater legitimacy to the G20.

Chapter 5 discusses the nexus of the G20 with the business sector – a relationship of major importance to both actors. It examines the World Economic Forum, the International Chamber of Commerce, the Business 20 (B20), the Young Entrepreneurs' Summit (G20 YEA) and private philanthropies. It concludes that the G20's close relationship with this influential constituency has resulted in mutual benefit to both of these actors.

Chapter 6 examines and analyzes the evolving relationship of the G20 with not-for-profit civil society organizations and coalitions. It gives a brief history of this relationship; identifies modes of interaction; considers the motivations for, and range of, civil society engagement with the G20; and provides a review of factors helping or hindering the success of this relationship and civil society's impact on G20 processes, accountability and (to a limited extent) agenda. It concludes that this interaction has had some mutual benefits both for civil society and for the G20; but mere official G20 acknowledgement of civil society's role has not meant major impact on G20 outcomes. Thus, civil society's influence on G20 processes, accountability and agenda has not yet reached its full potential.

Chapter 7 surveys and analyzes proposals to reform the G7/G8 and G20, and reforms already achieved. It examines reform proposals on membership in the two groups, agenda development, institutional restructuring and improvement of processes. It then assesses the relationship between the G7/G8 and the G20, as well as groups and initiatives closely related to the G7/G8 and G20. It takes account of the continuing debate on the dichotomy of representativeness versus efficiency, and on the G20's function as a crisis committee and a steering committee. Further, it outlines potential trajectories of the G7/G8 and the G20, and analyzes challenges for the G7/G8 and the G20. The chapter notes that the G7-G20 coexistence as parallel institutions has prevailed until now. It argues that complex relationships of the G7/G8 and G20 with formal IGOs having major roles in global governance must be part of the future the G7/G8 and G20, and that the G7 and the G20 should continue to define and develop their mutual relationship.

Chapter 8 reviews and analyzes the monitoring and evaluation of the G20's performance. It examines the role of civil society (including think-tanks), IGOs and the G20 itself in monitoring and evaluating performance and fulfilment of G20 promises. The chapter concludes that monitoring and evaluation have a crucial accountability role in gauging the G20's progress and building its legitimacy. It argues that the diverse ways of evaluation all play a role in exposing the strengths and weaknesses of the G20.

The next two chapters discuss information by and about the G20. Chapter 9 examines the pattern, subject matter, preparation and dissemination of documents of the G20 summits, the G20 Finance Ministers' and Central Bank Governors' forum as well as other G20 ministerial meetings and working groups and other sub-summit entities. It illustrates how documents reflect G20 deliberations and initiatives, and indicates how lower-level documents feed into higher levels of the G20 hierarchy. The chapter also includes a survey of documents submitted to the G20 by external actors, and a discussion of the issue of transparency of the G20. It discusses briefly the (often fickle) official websites. The chapter concludes that while public documents released by G20 summits, ministerial fora and other sub-summit bodies are the principal source of information on the G20 and its activities, much remains out of bounds to the public, due either to the confidential nature of diplomatic negotiations or to inadvertent or overzealous custodians of information. Transparency of the G20 has increased on the whole, but there are persistent as well as new obstacles that need to be remedied whenever possible.

Chapter 10 reviews and analyzes several other types of information sources about the G20: writings about the G20; think-tanks and foundations concerned with G20 research; memoirs of prominent G20 participants; academic theses and dissertations; creative works; websites other than those of G20 governments; and social media. The chapter concludes that although public documents released by the G20 summits and ministerial and other sub-summit bodies are the main primary sources of public information on that forum, they must be supplemented by other important information sources about the G20. These sources constitute, to a greater or smaller extent, important additional information and dimensions about the G20, and they need to be incorporated in research in order to gain fuller understanding of the G20 and its activities. The final chapter presents the book's conclusions.

The bibliography includes not only references in the body of the book but also an extensive listing of reports and documents issued by the G20 (and the G7/G8 where relevant) as well as of works about the G20 and about G7/G8 reform. It is arranged as follows: books and shorter writings; book chapters; articles in periodicals; official (governmental and IGO) publications; and websites. Bibliographic entries provide web addresses when applicable.

References

Alexandroff, A.S. and Kirton, J., 2010. The 'great recession' and the emergence of the G20 leaders' summit. In: A. Alexandroff and A. F. Cooper, eds. *Rising States, Rising*

Institutions: Can the World Be Governed? Washington: Brookings Institution Press. pp. 177–195.

Åslund, A., 2009. The Group of 20 must be stopped. *Financial Times*, 27 November, p. 11.

B20, 2017b. *About the G20*. www.b20germany.org/the-b20/about-g20/ [Accessed: 17 July 2018].

Bayne, N., 2011a. The decline of the G8 summit and lessons for the G20. In: N. Bayne and S. Woolcock, eds. *The New Economic Diplomacy: Decision-Making and Negotiation in International Economic Relations*. 3rd ed. Global Finance Series. Farnham: Ashgate. pp. 249–262.

Bayne, N., 2011b. Plurilateralism and multilateralism: Comparing institutions. In: N. Bayne and S. Woolcock, eds. *The New Economic Diplomacy: Decision-Making and Negotiation in International Economic Relations*. 3rd ed. Global Finance Series. Farnham: Ashgate. pp. 205–230.

Beeson, M. and Bell, S., 2009. The G-20 and international economic governance: Hegemony, collectivism, or both? *Global Governance: A Review of Multilateralism and International Organizations*, 15(1), pp. 67–86.

Bradford, C.I. and Lim, W.H., 2010. *Toward the Consolidation of the G20 Summits: From Crisis Committee to Global Steering Committee*. Seoul and Washington, DC: Korea Development Institute and Brookings Institution. www.cigionline.org/articles/toward-consolidation-g20-summits-crisis-committee-global-steering-committee [Accessed: 27 March 2018].

Cooper, A.F., 2010a. The G8-G20 partnership. In: J.J. Kirton and M. Koch, eds. *G8-G20: The 2010 Canadian Summits: Recovery and New Beginnings*. London: Newsdesk. pp. 306–307.

Duncan, R., 2008. Bring back the link between gold and the dollar. *Financial Times*, 24 November, p. 11.

Edwards, L., 2011. Missing in action, the G20 must step up at Cannes. *The Globe and Mail*, 3 November, p. A19.

G20, 1999. *Communiqué of G-20 Finance Ministers and Central Bank Governors: Berlin, Germany*. 15–16 December. www.g20.utoronto.ca/1999/1999communiqué.pdf [Accessed: 18 January 2018].

G20, 2007. *The Group of Twenty: A History*. www.g20.utoronto.ca/docs/g20history.pdf [Accessed: 18 October 2017].

G20, 2009c. *Leaders Statement: The Pittsburgh Summit*; and Annexes: *Core Values for Sustainable Economic Activity; G20 Framework for Strong, Sustainable, and Balanced Growth*. 25 September. www.g20.utoronto.ca/2009/2009communiqué0925.html [Accessed: 24 October 2017].

G20, 2011g. *What Is the G20?* www.g20-g8.com/g8-g20/g20/english/what-is-the-g20-/what-is-the-g20-/what-is-the-g20.70.html [Accessed: 23 March 2012].

G20, 2018a. *About the G20: Frequently Asked Questions*. www.g20.org/en/g20/faqs [Accessed: 17 July 2018].

Giles, C., 2009. G20 yet to deliver on early promise. *Financial Times*, 9 November, p. 2.

Gnath, K. and Schmucker, C., 2011. *L'Allemagne et les 'clubs G'* [Germany and the 'G Clubs']. Note du Cerfa, 85. Paris: Comité d'études des relations franco-allemandes. May. www.g20.utoronto.ca/biblio/IFRI_noteducerfa85clubsgfr.pdf [Accessed: 14 April 2018]. Also available in German: *Deutschland und die G-Clubs*. www.g20.utoronto.ca/biblio/IFRI_noteducerfa85gclubsde.pdf [Accessed: 14 April 2018].

Griesgraber, J.M., 2009. Reforms for major new roles of the International Monetary Fund? The IMF post-G-20 summit. *Global Governance: A Review of Multilateralism and International Organizations*, 15(2), pp. 179–185.

Hampson, F.O. and Heinbecker, P., 2011. The 'new' multilateralism of the twenty-first century. *Global Governance: A Review of Multilateralism and International Organizations*, 17(3), pp. 299–310.

Kirton, J.J., 2010b. The G8-G20 partnership. *The Future of the G8 and G20*, special issue of *Studia Diplomatica*, 63(2), pp. 23–34.

Kirton, J.J., 2013c. Introduction. In: J.J. Kirton, ed. *G20 Governance for a Globalized World*, Farnham: Ashgate. pp. 3–26.

Kirton, J.J., 2013e. The systemic hub model of G20 governance. In: J.J. Kirton, ed. *G20 Governance for a Globalized World*. Farnham: Ashgate. pp. 27–52.

Martin, P., 2009. Key challenges. In: J.J. Kirton and M. Koch, eds. *The London Summit 2009: Growth, Stability, Jobs*. London: Newsdesk Media Group. pp. 24–25. www.g20.utoronto.ca/g20london2009.html [Accessed: 22 February 2018].

Merkel, A., 2015. Why the G7 Summit must go beyond crisis diplomacy. *The Globe and Mail*, 3 June, p. A15.

Payne, A., 2010. How many Gs are there in 'global governance' after the crisis? The perspectives of the 'marginal majority' of the world's states. *International Affairs*, 86(3), pp. 729–740.

Penttilä, R., 2009. *Multilateralism Light: The Rise of Informal International Governance*. London: Centre for European Reform. www.cer.eu/sites/default/files/publications/attachments/pdf/2011/penttila_essay_july09-1334.pdf [Accessed: 18 July 2018].

Slaughter, A.-M., 1997. The real new world order. *Foreign Affairs*, 76(5), pp. 183–197.

1 The origins of the G20

Introduction

Both the Group of 20 (G20) and its creator, the Group of 7/Group of 8 (G7/G8), were born of crises. The group of seven industrialized democracies (in its first incarnation as the G6, with France, [West] Germany, Italy, Japan, the UK and the US as members) emerged in response to the twin exchange rate and oil crises in the early 1970s. (For a detailed account of the origins and evolution of the G7/G8, see Putnam and Bayne, 1987, and Hajnal, 2007a.) Canada became a member in 1976, forming the G7; Russia was accepted as a full member in 1998, thus transforming the group into the G8. In 2014, in response to its action in Ukraine, Russia's membership was suspended, thus reverting the group back to the G7.

Finance Ministers and Central Bank Governors of the G7/G8 have been meeting regularly since 1986; this forum survived as the only remaining G7 component of the broader G8 system while it existed as the Group of 8 – although occasionally, usually just prior to leaders' G8 summits, they included their Russian counterparts. The Finance Ministers' and Central Bank Governors' G20 arose in 1999 in the aftermath of the Asian/Latin American financial crisis and in response to the growing recognition that some significant emerging-economy countries were not adequately represented in global economic discussions and governance.

This chapter tracks the developments leading to the creation of the G20 Finance Ministers' and Central Bank Governors' forum (including a discussion of predecessor bodies) and the subsequent emergence of the G20 leaders' summits. For a review of the series of G20 summits since their inception and the evolution of the G20 agenda, as well as a discussion of the G20's composition and invited non-member countries, see Chapter 2. Chapter 3 reviews the components of the broader G20 system: leaders' summits and supporting structures and officials, ministerial fora and other sub-summit groups. Chapter 7 surveys and analyzes proposals to reform the G7/G8 and G20, discusses reforms already achieved and examines the relationship between the G7/G8 and the G20.

Predecessors

The 1995 Halifax G7 summit expressed support for including important emerging-economy countries in the international financial system, stating that

DOI: 10.4324/9781351266802-2

'[g]reater resources and attention should be devoted to those countries of global significance, including both industrial countries and emerging economies'. Following up on that lead, the International Monetary Fund (IMF) established the New Arrangement to Borrow (NAB) in 1997 (it came into force in 1998), which provided for emergency credit lines among 26 participating governments. As the Asian financial crisis erupted and spread to Russia and Latin America, NAB led, successively, to two main groupings that preceded the formation of the G20 Finance Ministers' and Central Bank Governors' forum: the Group of 22 and the Group of 33.

John Kirton (2013b, pp. 58–63) conceptualizes the emergence of the G20 Finance Ministers' and Central Bank Directors' forum as occurring in several steps:

1 the 1988 Toronto G7 summit's recognition of the growing role of newly industrializing economies in the Asia-Pacific region;
2 creation of APEC (Asia-Pacific Economic Cooperation) forum at the Finance and Foreign Ministers' level in 1989;
3 creation of NAB in 1998;
4 establishment of the G22;
5 expansion of the G22 into the G33;
6 the convening of the Financial Stability Forum (FSF) by the G7 Finance Ministers in 1999 (G7 Finance Ministers, 1999a);
7 creation of the IMF's 24-member International Monetary and Financial Committee (IMFC), which was welcomed at the 1999 Cologne G8 summit; and
8 formation of the financial G20 itself in December 1999.

The Group of 22 (G22)

Also known as the Willard Group after the Washington, DC, hotel where the group first met, the G22 was set up in April 1998 as a result of a US initiative announced by President Bill Clinton at the meeting of APEC countries in Vancouver in November 1997. The leaders who were present reached an agreement to convene a meeting of Finance Ministers and Central Bank Governors to move forward the reform of global financial architecture. The resulting group – which characterized itself as 'Finance Ministers and Central Bank Governors from a number of systemically significant economies' – was originally conceived as a one-time meeting to resolve global aspects of the financial crisis in emerging-market economies (IMF, 1998).

A second meeting was called on 5 October 1998 on the margin of meetings of the World Bank and the IMF in Washington, DC, adding four more countries to the group. Represented at the first meeting were the G7 plus 15 other countries or economies: Argentina, Australia, Brazil, China, Hong Kong, India, Indonesia, Malaysia, Mexico, Poland, Russia, Singapore, South Africa, the Republic of Korea and Thailand. The second meeting was also attended by Belgium, the Netherlands, Sweden and Switzerland (G22, 1998; G20, 2007).

The Group of 33 (G33)

An even more inclusive group, the G33, was convened on the initiative of the G7, succeeding the G22 in early 1999. Its members were the Finance Ministers and Central Bank Governors of the G7 countries as well as the rest of the G22, plus Belgium, Chile, Côte d'Ivoire, Egypt, Morocco, the Netherlands, Saudi Arabia, Spain, Sweden, Switzerland and Turkey (IMF, 2006; G20, 2007).

The G33 met twice, in March and April 1999, to discuss reforms of the global economy and the international financial system. But '[d]issatisfaction with the *ad hoc* nature of both the G-22 and G-33 processes by both advanced and emerging economies was an important reason behind the establishment of the G-20'. The other, arguably more significant, impetus came from 'the wariness of G-7 countries of the merit in engaging systemically important emerging-market economies in a regular informal dialogue' (G20, 2007). Such a regular dialogue took shape with the creation of the G20 Finance Ministers' and Central Bank Governors' forum in 1999.

The Finance Ministers' and Central Bank Governors' G20

The G20 Finance Ministers' and Central Bank Governors' forum was established following the recommendation of the G7 Finance Ministers in their report to the Cologne G8 summit on strengthening the international financial architecture. This, as noted earlier, was motivated by the Asian/Latin American financial crisis and the recognition that the most important emerging-economy countries had to be included as full partners in global economic governance (Smith, 2011a). It had become clear that the G8 countries alone could not tackle economic and financial problems without the full participation of other systemically important economies.

Former Canadian Prime Minister and, previously, Finance Minister Paul Martin, together with former US Treasury Secretary Lawrence Summers, pushed for the expansion of the Finance Ministers' and Central Bank Governors' forum to 20 members. Cooper and Thakur (2013, p. 37) state,

> The champion of this new model was Martin, the finance minister of Canada. However, when Martin called on Lawrence Summers, the Clinton nominee for treasury secretary, in April 1999, there was instant buy-in. In a classic variation of informal 'back of the envelope' diplomacy, Martin and Summers put together a framework that constituted the basic ingredients of G20 Finance.

Summers (2008), recalling these beginnings, acknowledged Martin's role in recognizing the need to move the global financial system from various *ad hoc* groupings, such as the G22 and G33, onto a more regularized path. That was the germ of the idea of creating a more permanent group of Finance Ministers and Central Bank Governors, one that was to include systemically important emerging countries in discussions on a political level. Former UK Prime Minister Gordon Brown also credits Martin for his strong role in bringing this forum into being (Brown, 2010). Thus, the inspiration and initiative came from Martin and Summers, but the formal creator of the G20 was the G7. Samans, Uzan and Lopez-Carlos (2007a) review and analyze these beginnings in detail.

In addition to G8 countries, the G20 includes Argentina, Australia, Brazil, China, India, Indonesia, Mexico, Saudi Arabia, South Africa, the Republics of Korea and Turkey, and the European Union as the twentieth member. This number and composition were and continue to be seen as striking a balance between representativeness and efficiency.

The new forum was confirmed by the G7 Finance Ministers and Central Bank Governors in their joint communiqué in September 1999. The communiqué stated,

> We propose to establish a new mechanism for informal dialogue in the framework of the Bretton Woods institutional system, to broaden the dialogue on key economic and financial policy issues among systemically significant economies and promote cooperation to achieve stable and sustainable world economic growth that benefits all. We believe that discussions held in this group will prove useful to complement and reinforce the role of the governing bodies of the Bretton Woods institutions. Accordingly, in December in Berlin, we will invite our counterparts from a number of systemically important countries from regions around the world to launch this new group.
>
> (G7 Finance Ministers, 1999b)

The IMFC of the IMF was already in place in 1999, with 15 of its 24 members also G20 members – a significant overlap. A major distinction between the two bodies is that, while the IMFC represents its constituencies and functions under the IMF Articles of Agreement, the G20 ministers are independent of the IMF and do not take positions on behalf of a larger body. Samans, Uzan and Lopez-Carlos (2007b, p. xvii) note that

> [w]hile the International Monetary Fund's Board remains the formal locus of decision-making on immediate questions of Fund policy, the [Finance Ministers' and Central Bank Governors'] G-20 appears to be evolving into the most influential forum for exploration of longer-term issues and institutional reform, by virtue of the greater legitimacy conferred by its more representative character.

Paul Martin (2005), in advocating the transformation of the Finance Ministers' and Central Bank Governors' G20 into a leaders'-level forum, reviews and analyzes the circumstances of the emergence and functioning of the G20. The official history of the first nine years, published by the G20 (*The Group of Twenty*, 2007), documents and describes the historical background, establishment, structure, objectives, work programme and evolution of the G20 forum of Finance Ministers and Central Bank Governors, and discusses the relationship of the G20 to other international institutions and groups, particularly the G7 Finance Ministers' and Central Bank Governors' forum; it also comments on the operational and institutional effectiveness of the G20. Others analysing these issues include, for example, Porter (2000), Helleiner (2000), Culpeper (2003) and Kirton (2005a).

Following a preparatory meeting of G20 Finance and Central Bank Deputies in Vancouver in November 1999, the inaugural meeting of the G20 Finance Ministers and Central Bank Governors was convened in Berlin on 15–16 December 1999. Its joint hosts were Finance Ministers Hans Eichel of Germany and Paul Martin of Canada. According to Nancy Alexander (2011c) of the Heinrich Böll Foundation, Larry Summers, Martin and Eichel jointly chose the membership of the G20.

The G20 at the leaders' level

Earlier proposals to create a G20 leaders' forum, championed by Paul Martin, had not at first found enough support among some of his fellow leaders, despite the fact that 'the practical disadvantages occasioned by the unrepresentative nature of G7/G8 membership were becoming clearer' (Smith, 2011a, p. 5). An interim measure to address this anomaly came from UK Prime Minister Tony Blair, who, in 2005, invited five major developing countries to participate in some specific parts of the 2005 Gleneagles G8 summit: Brazil, China, India, Mexico and South Africa. This 'G8+5' formula, under various names, continued at the following G8 summits: 2006 in St Petersburg, 2007 in Heiligendamm (where host Chancellor Angela Merkel rechristened the '+5' the 'Outreach 5') and 2008 at Hokkaido (where the five formed their own 'G5').

The Heiligendamm G8 summit created the so-called Heiligendamm Process (HP), which, following a two-year extension of its life by the 2009 L'Aquila G8 summit, was renamed the Heiligendamm/L'Aquila Process (HAP). The HAP was mandated to present a substantive report to the Muskoka G8 summit in 2010 and its concluding report to the Deauville G8 summit in 2011 (G8, 2009). The four main pillars of HAP were: promoting and protecting innovation; enhancing freedom of investments by means of a transparent investment regime; energy, particularly energy efficiency and technological cooperation; and better cooperation and coordination in the field of sustainable development, especially in Africa.

The G8+5 formula and HAP failed to address the problem of lack of representation of key emerging countries in summit-centred governance, indeed in global governance. Paul Martin (2008, pp. 358–359), recalling the Gleneagles summit in his memoir, expressed his concern at the exclusion of major emerging countries:

> [T]he image of Hu Jintao, the president of China, and Manmohan Singh, the prime minister of India – leaders of the two most populous countries on earth, quite possibly destined to be the largest economies on earth within our lifetimes – waiting outside while we held our G8 meetings, coming in for lunch, and then being ushered from the room, so that we could resume our discussions. . . . How long will the emerging titans of the developing world

> be prepared to kowtow to the G8? . . . Either the developed world will reform its institutions, including the G8, to embrace these new economic giants, or they will go ahead and establish their own institutions, and perhaps one day we will be the ones waiting in the corridor for lunch to begin.

It was the financial and economic crisis that became global in 2008 that finally spurred the creation of the G20 leaders' summit. In response to the crisis and following an initial call for such a step from Nicolas Sarkozy, the French President, and Gordon Brown, the British Prime Minister, George W. Bush convened the first G20 meeting at the leaders' level in Washington, DC, on 14–15 November 2008, in one of his final acts as US President (Bayne and Woolcock, 2011). The underlying reason was that leaders realized that 'the G8 was not sufficiently influential on its own to stabilize a crisis on this scale' (Bronnert, 2011, p. 84). Bush (2010) acknowledged that Sarkozy had urged him to convene an international summit on the economic crisis but claimed that it was his (Bush's) decision to make this a summit of the 20, rather than of the G7, which would have been the preference of some European countries.

In his memoir, Gordon Brown (2010, pp. 44–45) recounts the impromptu meeting of leaders (some G20 members, others from non-G20 countries) that he called together on 25 September 2008, taking advantage of their presence at the UN General Assembly in New York. Their discussion centred on the economic crisis and the concerted action necessary to fight it:

> We all agreed that the G8 was too limited, because it excluded all the main emerging markets that were at the heart of the crisis. President Sarkozy and I had previously considered proposing jointly that we model a leaders' meeting on the G20 group of finance ministers.

This happened earlier in 2008, when Brown met Sarkozy at the latter's official country house; there, the two concluded that 'a G20 would be best' and that they would push for G20 membership for Spain and the Netherlands. After consultations with Sarkozy, Brown and European Commission President Manuel Barroso, on 22 October, Bush issued invitations to the Washington summit. Cooper and Thakur (2013, p. 48) argue that 'the logic of extending G20 Finance to encompass a leaders' summit, as opposed to replacing it, was building up prior to the 2008 global financial crisis'. The same logic that led to the creation of the Finance G20 applies to the G20 leaders' forum as well.

The leaders' summits are qualitatively different from the 'finance G20'. Cooper and Thakur (2013, pp. 44, 49, 75) note that while the 'finance G20' had a technical orientation, the leaders' G20 is characterized by a policy-driven agenda; and while the emphasis in the 'finance G20' is on norms, the leaders focus on process and delivery.

Nicholas Bayne (2015) raises issues of the coexistence of the G7/G8 and the G20 once the latter began meeting at the leaders' level. These issues are explored in more detail in Chapter 7.

The first G20 summit (the 'Summit on Financial Markets and the World Economy') took place shortly after the G20 Finance Ministers' annual meeting in São Paulo, Brazil – the country that held the G20 Presidency that year. In addition to the 20 members, the heads of the IMF, the World Bank and the United Nations were invited, together with Spain and the Netherlands as agreed. Bayne and Woolcock (2011, p. 76) note that '[a]lthough the G7 countries accepted [the G20] reluctantly, emerging countries had finally acquired the political power that matched their economic advances' at the G20 leaders' summits. Another aspect of this development is that '[p]ower sharing has to mean burden sharing . . . [b]ut burden sharing also has to mean benefit sharing' (Hampson and Heinbecker, 2011, p. 300).

The new summit format led the leaders to decide to meet again the following year, but in November 2008 the status of the G20 summit as a continuing forum was not yet firm. Chapter 2 reviews the evolution of the leaders' G20 as an established institution.

Conclusion

This review of the process that culminated in the emergence of the G20 – both at the Finance Ministers' and Central Bank Governors' level and at the leaders' level – demonstrates the threefold impetus for this major development in global governance. First, the G20, at both levels, arose in response to the economic and financial crises which existing institutions were unable to address adequately. Second, the shift of the balance of power from advanced market-economy countries to emerging giants – especially China, India and Brazil – made clear the need to include both kinds of actors as full equals. Whatever the reluctance of some of the old G7 or G8 countries, this development was inevitable and necessary for effective global governance. Beyond *realpolitik*, this shift also has to do with equity, if only by implication.

Lastly, political leadership and commitment at the highest level – that of heads of state and government – were needed to make the G20 a reality and the powerful institution that it has become. The G20's potential has begun to grow, albeit slowly, in areas beyond strictly economic and financial issues. This phenomenon will be examined later, particularly in Chapters 2 and 7.

References

Alexander, N., 2011c. *Introduction to the G20*. Washington, DC: Heinrich Böll Stiftung North America. June. www.boell.org/web/group_of_20-651.html [Accessed: 21 May 2012].

Bayne, N., 2015. 40 years of summits: Addressing global challenges. In: J.J. Kirton, M. Koch and A.S. Freitag, eds. *G7 Germany: The Schloss Elmau Summit, June 2015*. London: Newsdesk Media. Special Supplement, pp. 1–7, 10–15.

Bayne, N. and Woolcock, S. eds., 2011. *The New Economic Diplomacy: Decision-Making and Negotiation in International Economic Relations*. 3rd ed. Global Finance Series. Farnham: Ashgate.

Bronnert, D., 2011. Making government policy: The G8 and G20 in 2010. In: N. Bayne and S. Woolcock, eds. *The New Economic Diplomacy: Decision-Making and Negotiation in International Economic Relations*. 3rd ed. Global Finance Series. Farnham: Ashgate. pp. 81–91.

Brown, G., 2010. *Beyond the Crash: Overcoming the First Crisis of Globalization*. New York and London: Free Press.

Bush, G.W., 2010. *Decision Points*. New York: Crown Publishers.

Cooper, A.F. and Thakur, R., 2013. *The Group of Twenty (G20)*. Global Institutions Series. New York: Routledge.

Culpeper, R., 2003. Systemic reform at a standstill: A flock of 'Gs' in search of global financial stability. In: A. Berry and G. Indart, eds. *Critical Issues in International Financial Reform*. New Brunswick, NJ and London: Transaction Publishers. pp. 203–236.

G7, 1995. *The Halifax Summit Review of the International Financial Institutions: Background Document, 5: Promoting Financial Stability in a Globalized Economy*. 16 June. www.g8.utoronto.ca/summit/1995halifax/financial/5.html [Accessed: 18 October 2017].

G7 Finance Ministers and Central Bank Governors, 1999a. *Communiqué*. 20 February. www.g8.utoronto.ca/finance/fm022099.htm [Accessed: 18 October 2017].

G7 Finance Ministers and Central Bank Governors, 1999b. *Statement of G-7 Finance Ministers and Central Bank Governors*. Washington, DC. 25 September. www.g8.utoronto.ca/finance/fm992509state.htm [Accessed: 18 October 2017].

G8, 2009. *The Agenda of the Heiligendamm/L'Aquila Process (HAP)*. 9 July. www.g8.utoronto.ca/summit/2009laquila/2009-g5-g8-2-hap.html [Accessed: 18 October 2017].

G20, 2007. *The Group of Twenty: A History*. www.g20.utoronto.ca/docs/g20history.pdf [Accessed: 18 October 2017].

G22, 1998. *Summary of Reports on the International Financial Architecture*. Washington, DC. www.imf.org/external/np/g22/summry.pdf [Accessed: 18 October 2017].

Hajnal, P.I., 2007a. *The G8 System and the G20: Evolution, Role and Documentation*. Global Finance Series. Aldershot: Ashgate.

Hampson, F.O. and Heinbecker, P., 2011. The 'new' multilateralism of the twenty-first century. *Global Governance: A Review of Multilateralism and International Organizations*, 17(3), pp. 299–310.

Helleiner, G.K. 2000. *Markets, Politics and Globalization: Can the Global Economy Be Civilized?* 10th Raúl Prebisch Lecture: Delivered at the Palais des Nations, Geneva. 11 December. www.unctad.org/en/docs/prebisch10th.en.pdf [Accessed: 18 October 2017]. Abridged version published 2001 in *Global Governance: A Review of Multilateralism and International Organizations*, 7(3), pp. 243–263.

International Monetary Fund, 1998. *Reports on the International Financial Architecture*. October. www.imf.org/external/np/g22/ [Accessed: 7 September 2017].

International Monetary Fund, 2006. *A Guide to Committees, Groups, and Clubs: Factsheet*. www.imf.org/external/np/exr/facts/groups.htm [Accessed: 18 October 2017].

Kirton, J.J., 2005a. From G7 to G20: Capacity, leadership and normative diffusion in global financial governance. In: ISA (International Studies Association), *Dynamics of World Politics: Capacity, Preferences and Leadership*. Honolulu, Hawaii. 1–5 March. www.g8.utoronto.ca/scholar/kirton2005/kirton_isa2005.pdf [Accessed: 18 October 2017].

Kirton, J.J., 2013b. *G20 Governance for a Globalized World*. Farnham: Ashgate.

Martin, P., 2005. A global answer to global problems: The case for a new leaders' forum. *Foreign Affairs*, 84(3), pp. 2–6.

Martin, P., 2008. *Hell or High Water: My Life in and out of Politics*. Toronto: McClelland & Stewart.

Porter, T., 2000. The G-7, the Financial Stability Forum, the G-20, and the politics of international financial regulation. In: ISA (International Studies Association), *Reflection, Integration, Cumulation: International Studies Past and Future*. Los Angeles, CA. 15 March. www.g20.utoronto.ca/biblio/porter-isa-2000.pdf [Accessed: 18 October 2017].

Putnam, R.D. and Bayne, N., 1987. *Hanging Together: Cooperation and Conflict in the Seven-Power Summits*. rev. ed. Cambridge, MA: Harvard University Press.

Samans, R., Uzan, M. and Lopez-Carlos, A. eds., 2007a. *The International Monetary System, the IMF, and the G20: A Great Transformation in the Making?* World Economic Forum. Basingstoke: Palgrave Macmillan.

Samans, R., Uzan, M. and Lopez-Carlos, A., 2007b. Introduction: The international monetary convention project. In: R. Samans, M. Uzan and A. Lopez-Carlos, eds. *The International Monetary System, the IMF, and the G20: A Great Transformation in the Making?* World Economic Forum. Basingstoke: Palgrave Macmillan. pp. xiii–xxvii.

Smith, G.S., 2011a. *G7 to G8 to G20: Evolution in Global Governance*. CIGI G20 Papers, No. 6. Waterloo, Canada: Centre for International Governance Innovation. 25 May. www.cigionline.org/sites/default/files/g20no6-2.pdf [Accessed: 7 September 2017].

Summers, L., 2008. The birth of the G20. In: J.J. Kirton and M. Koch, eds. *G20 São Paulo/Brazil Summit 2008: Growth, Innovation, Inclusion: The G20 at Ten*. London: Newsdesk Communications. pp. 29–31.

2 Members, invitees, summit meetings, agenda

This chapter examines the issue of G20 membership and invited non-member countries, surveys the series of G20 summits since they began in 2008 and traces the evolution of the agenda. For a related discussion regarding G20 ministers as well as task forces and similar sub-summit groups, see Chapter 3. Aspects of membership are also covered in Chapter 7.

Members and invitees

The G20 consists of the G7 countries (Canada, France, Germany, Italy, Japan, the UK and the US), plus Argentina, Australia, Brazil, China, India, Indonesia, Mexico, the Republic of Korea, Russia, Saudi Arabia, South Africa and Turkey, and the European Union as the twentieth member. G20 membership, albeit not universal as in the United Nations and other global IGOs, represents developed as well as systemically important emerging countries from all regions. It also represents two-thirds of the world's population, 80 per cent of the world's gross domestic product in terms of purchasing power parity and 75 per cent of global trade (G20, 2017e).

The G20 leaders initially invited the Netherlands and Spain to attend their meetings. The 2010 Seoul summit decided that from then on only Spain would attend as a 'permanent guest'. Also at Seoul, the leaders decided to invite no more than five non-member countries in future, at least two of them from Africa (G20, 2010d). Germany, the host of the 2017 Hamburg summit, invited the leaders of the following countries: Spain in accordance with the Seoul decision, Norway, the Netherlands and Singapore 'as partner countries to the G20 process', Guinea (as chair of the African Union), Vietnam (representing the Asia-Pacific Economic Cooperation forum, APEC) and Senegal (representing the New Partnership for African Development, NEPAD) (G20, 2017e).

Administrative heads of the IMF and the World Bank are always invited, and the United Nations and the OECD often attend part of the summits, so the actual number present is larger, at times considerably larger, than 20. The 2017 German Presidency invited, in addition to the IMF and the World Bank, the UN, the OECD, the ILO, the WTO, the Financial Stability Board and the WHO to the Hamburg summit. Invitations to certain non-G20 countries and IGOs are a partial answer to the persistent question of representation in the forum.

DOI: 10.4324/9781351266802-3

There are no formal criteria for G20 membership. The principal consideration, when the G20 was first established in 1999 at the Finance Ministers' and Central Bank Governors' level, was to include systemically significant countries 'able to contribute to global economic and financial stability'. It was further stipulated that membership should reflect regional balance and that the G20 'be small enough to facilitate frank and open discussion' (G20, 2007, p. 20). Membership has not changed since, either at the ministerial level or at the leaders' level. The G20 thus does not include all of the 20 largest economies; for example, non-member (but 'permanent guest') Spain in 2011 was in around thirteenth place while South Africa, a member, was in twenty-fifth place (Giles, 2011, p. 2). Another concern is that the poorest developing countries are missing from the regular membership, as are 'capable smaller countries of the UN, such as Norway, Switzerland, Chile, Singapore and New Zealand, . . . effectively depriving G-20 deliberations of these countries' generally constructive and frequently innovative diplomacy' (Hampson and Heinbecker, 2011, p. 306).

The EU-G20 relationship

As noted previously, the European Union's G7/G8 connection and G20 membership differ from the membership of states; they thus deserve somewhat more detailed treatment here. The history of the EU's relationship with the G7/G8 had begun before the G7 itself was formed in 1975. During the years 1973–75, when the G5 (France, Germany, Japan, the UK and the US) Finance Ministers held a series of secret meetings, the then European Community (EC) voiced its discontent at being excluded from the discussions as a single body, rather than being represented separately by only three of its member states. Italy's last-minute admission as a member of the G6 club of leaders, starting with the 1975 Rambouillet summit (the group became G7 only in 1976, when Canada joined), was a partial solution to this problem. Beginning with the 1977 London G7 summit, the EC (later EU) became an official participant, albeit one occupying an unusual position in the G7. Some consider the EU as an observer, others as a full member – although not a member state (Hajnal, 2007a; Huigens and Niemann, 2009; Hajnal and Panova, 2012). The EU cannot chair nor normally host a summit, and hence it cannot shape the summit agenda the way member countries' leaders have when assuming the annual G8 Presidency. Exceptionally, the EU hosted (but did not chair) the revived G7 summit in Brussels on 4–5 June 2014 instead of the previously scheduled Sochi G8 summit, which was cancelled with Russia's suspension as a member of the G8.

The EU has its own sherpa and takes part in the preparation and conduct of the G7/G8 summits, participating in all discussions with fellow leaders. It also takes part in the meetings of ministerial fora and other subsidiary G7 and G8 bodies. The EU is represented at G7/G8 summits by the Commission President; with the Lisbon Treaty in force, the EU is represented by both the Commission President and the permanent EU President. Marina Larionova (2012a) and her collaborators explore various aspects of the EU-G8 connection in detail.

The EU has been a full member of the G20 since the latter's inception (although, as with the G7/G8, the EU does not participate in the rotating G20 presidencies and thus cannot chair or host G20 summits). This applies both to the G20 leaders' summits and meetings of other G20 bodies. At summits, the EU is represented by the Commission President (in 2017 Jean-Claude Juncker of Luxembourg) and the President of the European Council (in 2017 Donald Tusk of Poland). Among the Finance Ministers, the EU is represented by the member of the European Commission responsible for economic and monetary affairs, and by the President of the European Central Bank (currently Mario Draghi).

Peter Debaere (2010) analyzes the EU's performance and effectiveness in the G20 and the extent to which EU countries that are not members of the G20 are involved in developing EU positions in the G20 context. He concludes that while the aim of the EU is to deliver a coherent message to the G20, their agreed language is non-binding on EU member countries, thus putting coherence at risk. Many G8/G20 reform proposals have involved the EU; some of these have called for a single representation for the EU as a whole or for the euro zone. (Reform efforts are discussed in Chapter 7.)

Phases of development of the G20

G20 meetings at the ministerial and summit levels may be divided into distinct phases:

- Phase 1 (December 1999–October 2008): G20 Finance Ministers' and Central Bank Governors' meetings. (These continue parallel with the leaders' summits after November 2008.)
- Phase 2 (November 2008–October 2009): beginning of G20 leaders' summit meetings.
- Phase 3 (September 2009–October 2010): at the September 2009 Pittsburgh summit the leaders declared the G20 to be 'the premier forum for [their] international economic cooperation' (G20, 2009c), placing the G8-G20 relationship into a new framework.
- Phase 4 (November 2010–March 2014): the Seoul summit added development to the agenda, marking the beginning of expansion from the G20's theretofore strictly economic and financial focus.
- Phase 5 (March 2014–present): with Russia's suspension as a member of the G8, the latter has reverted to G7, changing the dynamic of the G7-G20 relationship. A major impact of this change on the G20 can be discerned in terms of agenda development, further institutionalization of the broader G20 system, relations with international organizations and other areas (Kirton, 2017).

In 2013, Kirton (2013b, pp 374–378) posited the following three phases of G20 development:

- Phase 1 (1999–2001): generating the group. This is the first period of G20 Finance Ministers' and Central Bank Governors' meetings. During this phase, the G20 agenda grew from the original focus on the Asian financial crisis to take on the fight against the financing of terrorism, reform of international financial institutions and other financial and economic issues.

- Phase 2 (2002–2007): equalizing the influence. During this period the G20 Finance Ministers' and Central Bank Governors' forum became a group of equals of advanced and emerging countries. Indicative of this change were the rotation of Presidency and the establishment of the troika system (see ahead), as well as agenda expansion, with each host country focusing on its major issues of concern.
- Phase 3 (2008–10): creating the G20 summit 'club'. This was a major step in the institutionalization of the G20 at the highest level, deepening the equality of its members.

Paul Martin (2011b, p. 13) also distinguishes three phases in the G20's evolution up to 2010:

- the founding of the Finance Ministers' and Central Bank Governors G20 in 1999;
- the emergence of the leaders' G20 in 2008; and
- the decision, taken in 2009, to hold the second 2010 G20 summit for the first time in a country outside of Europe and North America.

The G20 summits and their agenda

This section gives a brief history of G20 summit meetings convened beginning with 2008, indicating their main achievements. The discussion shows the gradual but uneven evolution of the forum's agenda. Each G20 summit has had its motto and distinctive logo. For example, the logo of the Seoul summit featured the *Cheongsachorong*, a traditional lantern; that of the Los Cabos summit was a pyramid somewhat resembling the Pyramid of the Sun in Teotihuacán, Mexico, built in the first century BCE (Mexico. President, 2012b; Kim, 2010). The logo of the 2013 St Petersburg summit, according to the Russian host government, is

> rooted in the traditions of Russian avant-garde art, pioneered by the great Russian artists Wassily Kandinsky and Kazimir Malevich . . . [Its] colors are the colors of the Russian flag, while its graphic element of the logo is an expression of will, progress, transformation, a commitment to innovation, candor, and bold ideas – the values personified by the Group of Twenty. The combination of logo elements, with various shapes and colors coexisting harmoniously in one space, is also a testament to a core idea behind the G20.
> (G20, 2013g)

Australia's logo of the 2014 Brisbane summit

> was designed by Indigenous creative agency Gilimbaa with logo artwork created by . . . Indigenous artist . . . Riki Salam. [It] represents a weaving together

> of nations, a gathering of leaders and the journeys they . . . embark[ed] upon throughout 2013–14. The triangle shapes represent the members, invited guests and international organisations that attend[ed] the G20.
>
> (G20, 2014d)

The logo of the 2015 Antalya summit represents Turkey's cultural heritage and includes the tulip, which symbolizes 'beauty, elegance and perfection. . . . [It] has been one of the main symbols of Istanbul and it was widely used in classic Turkish arts' (G20, 2015c). The 2016 Hangzhou summit logo

> incorporates a stylized bridge consisting of 20 layered lines, symbolizing the 20 members of the [G20] Group, the pattern of 'G20 2016 CHINA' and a seal with the characters [for China] in traditional Chinese font. The bridge signifies that the G20 is a bridge for global economic growth, international cooperation and a win-win future. The layered lines are reminiscent of fiber-optic cables, representing an inter-connected world in the information age. The letter 'O' highlighted in the image of 'G20' embodies unity and coordination among G20 members. The seal is a representation of traditional Chinese culture.
>
> (G20, 2016q)

Germany chose as the logo of the 2017 Hamburg summit a seafaring image reflecting the maritime character of the city: a reef knot. 'As the tension increases, the reef knot becomes tighter', said host leader Angela Merkel (G20, 2017k).

Table 2.1 identifies the Presidency, venue and date of each G20 summit.

Table 2.1 G20 Summit Meetings, 2008–2020

G20 Presidency	*Summit venue*	*Summit date*
Brazil	Washington, DC, US	15–16 November 2008
United Kingdom	London, UK	2–3 April 2009
United Kingdom	Pittsburgh, US	24–25 September 2009
Republic of Korea	Toronto, Canada	26–27 June 2010
Republic of Korea	Seoul, Korea	11–12 November 2010
France	Cannes, France	3–4 November 2011
Mexico	Los Cabos, Mexico	18–19 June 2012
Russia	St. Petersburg, Russia	5–6 September 2013
Australia	Brisbane, Australia	15–16 November 2014
Turkey	Antalya, Turkey	15–16 November 2015
China	Hangzhou, China	4–5 September 2016
Germany	Hamburg, Germany	6–9 July 2017
Argentina	Buenos Aires, Argentina	30 November–1 December 2018
Japan	Osaka, Japan	28–29 June 2019
Saudi Arabia	*To be announced*	2020

Source: G20 Information Centre (2018b).

Washington, DC, 15–16 November 2008

The first summit of G20 leaders, named 'Summit on Financial Markets and the World Economy', met in Washington, DC. It was called in response to the financial and economic crisis that became a full-fledged global crisis in 2008. The circumstances of the emergence of the summit-level G20 are described in detail in Chapter 1. The Washington summit:

- identified the root causes of the financial crisis and reviewed national actions already taken;
- agreed on economic stimulus measures still needed;
- set forth common principles for financial market reform and regulation;
- pledged to increase resources of the IMF, World Bank and other multilateral development banks (MDBs);
- reaffirmed commitment to the reform of the Bretton Woods institutions;
- expressed the G20's commitment to an open global economy; and
- charged ministers and experts with the elaboration of action plans.

The leaders indicated their desire to expand and strengthen the Financial Stability Forum. The summit's *Declaration*, with an annexed *Action Plan to Implement Principles for Reform*, fully documents these undertakings (G20, 2008).

London, 2–3 April 2009

Encouraged by the Washington summit's initiatives, and having built up enough peer support, UK Prime Minister Gordon Brown convened the second G20 summit in London, with the motto 'Stability, Growth, Jobs'. This summit achieved more substantial results in tackling the continuing economic and financial crisis, urging coordinated fiscal stimulus measures by member countries, and agreeing to treble financial resources available to the IMF (to US$750 billion) and to other important steps, including new Special Drawing Rights (SDR) allocations and trade finance support. In total, the summit came up with a '$1 trillion rescue plan for the world's economy . . . the biggest economic support program ever agreed on' (Brown, 2010, p. 113). The summit finalized its decision to expand and strengthen the Financial Stability Forum to reflect wider G20 membership and renamed it the Financial Stability Board – an important institutional development (G20, 2009d).

Pittsburgh, 24–25 September 2009

The London summit, in turn, led to the convening of the third meeting of G20 leaders in Pittsburgh, Pennsylvania, US, by President Barack Obama. Significantly, the Pittsburgh summit proclaimed the G20 to be 'the premier forum for our international economic cooperation' (G20, 2009c), thereby taking over this core function of the G8. The leaders at Pittsburgh launched a new 'Framework for Strong, Sustainable and Balanced Growth', called for the strengthening of the international financial regulatory system and for reforming the mandate, mission and governance of the IMF and the development banks, 'putting quality jobs at the heart of the recovery' and, once again, for an open global economy. Signalling an expansion of the G20 agenda, the leaders also pronounced on energy security and climate change, 'strengthening support for the most vulnerable', and core values and principles of sustainable economic activity (G20, 2009c). The leaders also signalled the institutionalization of the G20 summits, agreeing to hold two meetings in 2010 (Toronto in June and Seoul in November), and their expectation to meet once a year, beginning with the French-hosted summit in 2011.

Toronto, 26–27 June 2010

By the time the fourth G20 summit met in Toronto (immediately after the 25–26 June G8 summit, held in Muskoka, north of Toronto), recovery from the 2008 global economic crisis was underway and 'sentiment had shifted to fiscal consolidation' (Giles, 2011, p. 2). Thus the leaders committed 'to taking concerted actions to sustain the recovery, create jobs and to achieve stronger, more sustainable and more balanced growth. These will be differentiated and tailored to national circumstances' – the last sentence illustrating one of the ways in which the G20 gets around lack of unanimity. The leaders also agreed (but only for advanced member countries) to 'at least halve deficits by 2013 and stabilize or reduce government debt-to-GDP ratios by 2016' (G20, 2010a). (In a little more than a year, at the 2011 Cannes summit, it became clear – and the leaders at Cannes acknowledged this – that slow growth and other economic factors rendered the 2013 deadline unrealistic.)

In addition to following up on the Pittsburgh 'Framework for Strong, Sustainable and Balanced Growth', leaders at the Toronto summit continued calling for financial sector reform resting on four pillars: a strong regulatory framework, effective supervision, resolution and addressing of the issue of systemic institutions, and transparent international assessment and peer review (G20, 2010a). They created a Development Working Group (DWG), also known as Working Group on Development, looking towards the Seoul summit with development prominently on the agenda there. They also expressed their commitment to strengthen international financial institutions (IFIs), fight protectionism, and promote trade and investment. In a separate document, the Toronto summit spelled out *Principles for Innovative Financial Inclusion* (G20, 2010c). To support this, the summit launched the G20 Financial Inclusion Experts Group.

Seoul, 11–12 November 2010

The Seoul G20 summit, the leaders' fifth meeting, marked the further institutionalization of the G20. Its motto was 'Shared Growth beyond Crisis'. Significantly, this was the first time that such a summit was held in a non-G8 member country of the G20. Furthermore, Seoul marked an important expansion of the agenda by embracing development, financial safety nets and cross-border capital flows as well as, more tentatively, climate. On development, the leaders produced the *Seoul Development Consensus for Shared Growth* and the *Multi-year Action Plan on Development*. The summit also endorsed and enhanced the Mutual Assessment Process (MAP), an important process of G20 accountability (International Monetary Fund, 2011a). Reforming international financial institutions (particularly the IMF) and reforming financial systems, both carried over from previous summits, remained prominent on the agenda. The leaders also endorsed the agreement by the Basel Committee on Banking Supervision (BCBS) on a new bank capital and liquidity framework.

Cannes, 3–4 November 2011

Unexpected, fast-breaking events can have a major impact on the summit agenda. Just such an event intruded on the Cannes summit (whose motto was 'New World, New Ideas'). Although the major financial problems of Greece had been known for about two years, the sudden call by Greek Prime Minister George Papandreou three days before the summit for a referendum on the Greek debt bailout offer (and, indeed, on whether Greece was to stay in the euro zone) was a bolt from the blue. Responding to demands by the G20 and demonstrating the depth of Greece's financial and political crisis, he just as promptly retracted the referendum call and then lost his prime ministerial post. Nonetheless, Greece continued to be of serious concern for the euro area, and Italy's debt crisis loomed large.

The euro zone crisis remained a central preoccupation at Cannes, but other agenda items – most of them carefully prepared for the leaders in advance – were dealt with: growth and jobs; social inclusion; international monetary system reform; financial sector reform; commodity prices and the promotion of agriculture; energy markets and climate change; development; trade and protectionism; corruption; and global governance. These issues are reflected in the summit's *Communiqué*, in which the leaders prominently noted their *Cannes Action Plan for Growth and Jobs* (G20, 2011c, 2011a). This ambitious action plan aimed to address short-term vulnerabilities, restore financial stability and strengthen growth in the medium term.

The Cannes summit set a longer-term course for the G20. It welcomed a report to the leaders on global governance by UK Prime Minister David Cameron (2011), and agreed with him that the G20 should remain an informal group (UK. Prime Minister, 2011; G20, 2011b). The leaders decided to convene subsequent summits as follows: in June 2012 in Los Cabos, Baja California, Mexico; in September 2013 in Russia; in 2014 in Australia; and in 2015 in Turkey. Thereafter, G20 presidencies were to be chosen from rotating regional groups, starting in 2016 with a country in the Asian group comprising China, Indonesia, Japan and the Republic of Korea (G20, 2011c). (Since the G20's establishment at the summit level, the rotation of the Presidency has not coincided exactly with calendar years; rather, the new host country tends to assume the Presidency soon after the previous summit; Russia assumed the G20 Presidency on 1 December 2012, and 1 December remains the changeover date.)

Los Cabos, 18–19 June 2012

After the Seoul summit, the Los Cabos gathering was the second G20 leaders' meeting in a non-G8 developing country. The agenda included: economic stabilization and structural reforms; financial inclusion; reform of the international financial architecture; sustainable development, green growth and climate change. Food security and commodity price volatility were an important part of the discussions. All of these reflected the Mexican government's priorities as previously announced, and much of the agenda was carried over from previous summits, although with different emphasis. Inevitably, the euro area crisis again took up much of the leaders' attention; the previous year's concerns had not been alleviated, and there was some risk of global implications of the crisis. Notably, some of these issues, in particular the euro crisis and food security, were also on the agenda of the Camp David G8 summit in 2012 (US DoS, 2012).

The leaders' final *Declaration* (G20, 2012j) reflects most of these issues, focusing on: economic stabilization and global recovery; employment and social protection; trade (with the obligatory G20 nod to the moribund Doha Development Agenda); international financial architecture (including a reiteration of commitment to IMF quota and governance reform by 2012); financial sector reform and financial inclusion (on the latter, the leaders welcomed progress made by the Global Partnership for Financial Inclusion (GPFI) and endorsed the G20 Basic Set of financial inclusion indicators developed by the GPFI); food security and commodity price volatility; green growth; and corruption. Another important result of the summit was *The Los Cabos Growth and Jobs Action Plan* (G20, 2012m), designed to address fiscal and financial imbalances, and their effect on growth, employment and confidence. Also a significant result was the issuance of the document *Policy Commitments by G20 Members* (G20, 2012r). In terms of institutional innovation, for the first time in G20 summitry, the Mexicans publicized the division of work (operative since the Washington summit) into a finance track (focusing on financial and economic issues) and a sherpas' track, with its focus 'on political, non-financial issues, such as: employment, agriculture, energy, the fight against corruption and development, among others' (G20, 2012w). This division has continued.

Kirton and Kulik (2012a, 2012b), despite their earlier characterization of the Los Cabos summit as 'A Summit of Significant Success', identify several shortcomings of the summit: failure to fulfil the Pittsburgh undertaking to phase out fossil fuel subsidies; insufficient recognition of the contribution of the academic community to G20 governance (Kirton and Kulik do not mention here the important contribution of the Think-20 group of think-tanks from various G20 countries; see Chapter 6); lack of attention to human health; scant references to youth and young entrepreneurship; and the absence of women, girls and gender issues.

St Petersburg, 5–6 September 2013

On the day that Russia assumed the G20 Presidency, 1 December 2012, President Vladimir Putin announced the main objectives for the St Petersburg summit:

'developing measures to stimulate economic growth and create jobs . . . [involving] investment incentives, trust and transparency in markets, and effective regulation' (Russia. President, 2012). Thus, he signalled both continuity and some new approaches for the evolving G20 agenda. Within this framework, the ambitious agenda at St Petersburg was composed of the following:

- global economy and G20 framework for strong, sustainable and balanced growth;
- growth through quality jobs;
- financing for investment;
- multilateral trade;
- base erosion, tax avoidance and tax transparency;
- reform of the international financial architecture (including IMF quotas, and government borrowing and the sustainability of public debt);
- strengthening financial regulation;
- financial inclusion, financial education and consumer protection;
- promoting development for all;
- sustainable energy policy and global commodity market resilience;
- fight against climate change; and
- anti-corruption.

(G20, 2013f)

The *Declaration* was amplified by several annexes, notably those on the *St Petersburg Action Plan* (on supporting the recovery and addressing near-term risks; strengthening the Foundations for Strong, Sustainable and Balanced Growth and enhancing Fiscal Sustainability; and structural Reforms) (G20, 2013j), on the Global Partnership for Financial Inclusion (G20 GPFI, 2013), and the one containing the *Saint Petersburg Accountability Report on G20 Development Commitments* (G20, 2013k). The leaders also issued a *G20 5th Anniversary Vision Statement* (G20, 2013e), reaffirming the role of the G20 as their premier forum for international economic cooperation, and reviewing the forum's main achievements.

In the event, the Syrian crisis, particularly the use of chemical weapons – although not on the announced agenda – inevitably preoccupied the participating leaders who discussed it during the summit; as well, the Foreign Ministers held a hastily called meeting on Syria. Eleven of the attending leaders (Australia, Canada, France, Italy, Japan, South Korea, Saudi Arabia, Turkey, the UK and the US, plus 'permanent guest' Spain) produced a *Joint Statement on Syria* (US. White House OPS, 2013). The rest of the leaders participated in the discussion but did not join these 11 as authors of the statement.

Brisbane, 15–16 November 2014

The Brisbane summit centred on two agenda clusters: promoting stronger economic growth and employment outcomes, and making the global economy more resilient to deal with future shocks (G20, 2014g). Under the first cluster, the following detailed agenda was adopted: creating growth strategies outlining country-specific reforms and measures to address common challenges; attracting private infrastructure investment; raising employment and workforce participation; removing obstacles to trade and competition; and growth and development. Under the second cluster, the summit dealt with reform of the global financial system (a long-standing goal carried over from many previous summits); strengthening the international tax system; strengthening global institutions; strengthening energy markets; and fighting corruption.

Antalya, 15–16 November 2015

The Antalya summit set out three 'I's': inclusiveness on the domestic and international fronts, implementation of policy frameworks, and investment as a strong driver of growth (G20, 2015a). Detailed agenda items under the three 'I's' were: strengthening the global recovery and increasing potential; improving macroeconomic policy cooperation (investment, employment and trade; enhancing resilience in areas of the international financial architecture, international taxation and anti-corruption measures); and buttressing sustainability in development, energy and climate change financing.

(G20, 2014i)

Hangzhou, 4–5 September 2016

The Hangzhou summit referred to four 'I's': innovative, invigorated, interconnected and inclusive world economy (the last 'I' resembles one at the previous summit) (G20, 2016n). Within those parameters, the three agenda baskets were: the breaking of a new path for growth, robust international trade and investment, and inclusive and interconnected development. Significantly, this indicates the emphasis China placed on development, building on earlier summits, especially since the 2010 Seoul summit.

Detailed agenda items within the first basket were: maintaining the momentum of world economic recovery, lifting mid- to long-term growth potential, bringing about more effective and efficient global economic and financial governance, improving the international financial architecture, continuing financial sector reform, developing green finance, improving the international tax regime, and implementing consensus on anti-corruption; within the second basket, the agenda dealt with reinforcing trade and investment cooperation mechanisms, supporting the multilateral trading system, promoting the growth of global trade, promoting inclusive and integrated global value chains, and enhancing cooperation and coordination on global investment policy. And within the third basket: implementing the 2030 Agenda for Sustainable Development, optimizing the G20 development cooperation agenda, building infrastructure and connectivity, promoting an accessible, affordable and sustainable energy supply, increasing employment, improving food security and nutrition, mobilizing climate finance, eradicating poverty, and supporting industrialization in African and other developing countries.

Hamburg, 7–8 July 2017

The three main pillars of the German hosts' Hamburg summit agenda were: building resilience, improving sustainability and assuming responsibility (G20, 2017g). The detailed agenda focused on a number of issues: sharing the benefits of globalization (including a prosperous global economy; trade and investment; excess capacities; sustainable global supply chains; digital transformation; and boosting employment); building resilience (open and resilient financial system; enhancing the international financial architecture; working for international tax cooperation and financial transparency; safeguarding against health crises, strengthening health systems; and combating antimicrobial resistance); improving sustainable livelihoods (energy and climate issues – the most contentious section – sustainable development; women's empowerment; food security, water sustainability and rural youth employment; and resource efficiency and marine litter); and assuming responsibility, including launching the G20 Africa Partnership, stepping up coordination and cooperation on displacement and migration, and fighting corruption.

A few days after the summit, the German host government asserted that the 'G20 format has proved its worth, within the scope of both formal and informal talks . . . and stated that "[t]angible progress" was made on issues relating to global health, the G20 Africa Partnership and on measures to empower women'. Germany listed the following ten achievements at Hamburg:

1 supporting free trade and the WTO;
2 affirming that the Paris Agreement is irreversible (here, reflecting the open break with G20 consensus, all member states except the US 'reasserted their intention to resolutely implement the Paris Agreement on climate change . . . [and] adopted the G20 Hamburg Climate and Energy Action Plan for Growth')
3 launching a new G20 Africa Partnership based on the African Union's Agenda 2063 and accompanied by three initiatives focusing on Africa: the G20 Rural Youth Employment initiative, the '#eSkills4Girls' initiative to help women and girls acquire digital skills and the African Renewable Energy Initiative;
4 fighting terrorism;
5 promoting digitalization;
6 ensuring the stability of the international financial market, working to improve the international financial architecture and adoption of the *Hamburg Action Plan*;
7 supporting the UN's 2030 Agenda for Sustainable Development, issuing the *Hamburg Update*, which gives a summary of efforts of G20 countries to achieve the UN's Sustainable Development Goals (SDGs);
8 fighting pandemics and antimicrobial resistance;
9 supporting women entrepreneurs in developing countries, including the launching of the Women Entrepreneurs Finance Initiative; and
10 addressing the root causes of displacement and expulsion.

(G20, 2017l)

Significantly, the 2018 Buenos Aires summit (30 November–1 December 2018) will be the first G20 summit held in the South American half of the western hemisphere. The Argentine hosts have indicated the following agenda priorities: the future of work, infrastructure for development, and a sustainable food future. For a fuller discussion, see G20 (2017b, 2017m).

Leaders' meetings on the sidelines of summits

G20 summits are good opportunities for two, three or more assembled leaders to meet privately to discuss common concerns and, at times, come to mutual understanding or agreement. These meetings are not part of the summits. Some examples of bilateral and other such meetings follow:

- During the Los Cabos summit, President Obama met with his Russian counterpart, Vladimir Putin.
- Australian Prime Minister Tony Abbott met with the leaders of Spain, Italy, Brazil and Indonesia during the Brisbane summit.
- At the Antalya summit, Turkish host leader Recep Tayyip Erdoğan met with US President Barack Obama and German Chancellor Angela Merkel met with Vladimir Putin to discuss Ukraine and Syria.
- The following year in Hangzhou, Obama again met Putin (on Syria), and Merkel met Erdoğan (on migration, Syria and German-Turkish relations) and French President François Hollande (on the future of the EU, among other concerns).
- At the Hamburg summit, there was a much-discussed two-hour bilateral meeting between US President Donald Trump and Putin – the first meeting of the two. Reportedly, Trump questioned Putin about Russian meddling in the 2016 US election, which the latter denied; Putin, on his part, wanted an end to or the easing of Western sanctions against Russia. Syria was another topic of the meeting (Davis, Sanger and Thrush, 2017).

Conclusion

The composition of the G20, based on the selection of systemically significant countries as members and on geographical representation, continues to remain constant. Yet, the issue of G20 membership has been contentious, with arguments for and against broadening the forum, and the perceived need for including the excluded in the interest of fuller representativeness. This, however, runs up against the objective of efficiency, contrasted with representativeness. Invitations extended to leaders of non-member countries (as representatives of regional organizations and to enhance regional representation of individual countries chosen by the host leader) as well as to administrative heads of intergovernmental organizations are a partial solution to this dilemma.

The short history of G20 summit meetings held so far pinpoints the crisis-based emergence of the forum, and its transformation into a more permanent institution with an incrementally – albeit reluctantly – growing agenda characterized by both continuity and innovation. Although the G20 retains its core economic and financial focus, other global issues, particularly development, have inevitably claimed the leaders' attention. Other examples are anti-corruption, food security, digitalization, women's empowerment and terrorism and pandemics, all reflected in summit deliberations as well as in the launching of action plans and the creation of working groups and expert groups dealing with these issues on a technical level and reporting back to their principals.

Some observers have questioned the G20's capacity to expand its agenda further, or even whether it should have ventured beyond the economic and financial core. A mid-2011 conference co-hosted by the Stanley Foundation, CIGI and the China Institutes of Contemporary International Relations examined these challenges. They identified types of issues unlikely to be embraced by the G20: 'the local, the fuzzy, and the prickly', meaning subjects that are too local (applicable to a single region), those to which a collective policy response would be unclear, and those that are 'too geopolitically sensitive' (Stanley Foundation, 2011, p. 6). Thus, constraints on agenda growth flow from limits of capacity as well as political and other considerations.

A new, 2017 challenge for the G20 is the withdrawal of the US leadership role on some issues and the diverging priorities of the Donald Trump–led US administration, notably on climate change and action needed to combat it. This became crystal clear at the Hamburg summit. It is to the credit of the G20 that despite this challenge, the forum has found a way to continue as a powerful instrument of global governance.

References

Brown, G., 2010. *Beyond the Crash: Overcoming the First Crisis of Globalization*. New York and London: Free Press.

Davis, J.H., Sanger, D.E. and Thrush, G., 2017. Trump questions Putin on election meddling at eagerly awaited encounter. *The New York Times*, 7 July, p. A1.

Debaere, P., 2010. The output and input dimension of the European representation in the G20. *The Future of the G8 and G20*, special issue of *Studia Diplomatica*, 63(2), pp. 141–154.

G20, 2007. *The Group of Twenty: A History*. www.g20.utoronto.ca/docs/g20history.pdf [Accessed: 18 October 2017].

G20, 2008. *Declaration: Summit on Financial Markets and the World Economy* and *Action Plan to Implement Principles for Reform*. Washington, DC. 15 November. www.g20.utoronto.ca/2008/2008declaration1115.html [Accessed: 24 October 2017].

G20, 2009c. *Leaders Statement: The Pittsburgh Summit*; and Annexes: *Core Values for Sustainable Economic Activity; G20 Framework for Strong, Sustainable, and Balanced Growth*. 25 September. www.g20.utoronto.ca/2009/2009communique0925.html [Accessed: 24 October 2017].

G20, 2009d. *London Summit: Leaders' Statement*. 2 April. www.g20.utoronto.ca/2009/2009communique0402.pdf [Accessed 24 October 2017].

G20, 2010a. *The G-20 Toronto Summit Declaration*. 27 June. www.g20.utoronto.ca/2010/to-communique.html [Accessed 24 October 2017].

G20, 2010c. *Principles for Innovative Financial Inclusion*. 27 June. www.g20.utoronto.ca/2010/to-principles.html [Accessed: 26 September 2017].

G20, 2010d. *Seoul Summit Document*. www.g20.utoronto.ca/2010/g20seoul-doc.pdf [Accessed: 24 October 2017].

G20, 2011a. *The Cannes Action Plan for Growth and Jobs*. 4 November. www.g20.utoronto.ca/2011/2011-cannes-action-111104-en.html [Accessed: 24 October 2017].

G20, 2011b. *Cannes Summit Final Declaration: Building Our Common Future: Renewed Collective Action for the Benefit of All*. 4 November. www.g20.utoronto.ca/2011/2011-cannes-declaration-111104-en.html [Accessed: 24 October 2017].

G20, 2011c. *Final Communiqué [of the] G20 Leaders' Summit, Cannes*. 4 November. www.g20.utoronto.ca/2011/2011-cannes-communique-111104-en.html [Accessed: 24 October 2017].

G20, 2012j. *G20 Leaders Declaration*. 19 June. www.g20.utoronto.ca/2012/2012-0619-loscabos.pdf [Accessed: 26 September 2017].

G20, 2012m. *The Los Cabos Growth and Jobs Action Plan*. 19 June. www.g20.utoronto.ca/2012/2012-0619-loscabos-actionplan.pdf [Accessed: 24 October 2017].

G20, 2012r. *Policy Commitments by G20 Members*. 19 June. www.g20.utoronto.ca/2012/2012-0619-loscabos-commitments.pdf [Accessed: 24 October 2017].

G20, 2013e. *G20 5th Anniversary Vision Statement*. September. www.g20.utoronto.ca/2013/G20_5th_Anniversary_Vision_Statement.pdf [Accessed: 29 September 2017].

G20, 2013f. *G20 Leaders' Declaration*. 6 September. www.g20.utoronto.ca/2013/Saint_Petersburg_Declaration_ENG.pdf [Accessed: 8 September 2017].

G20, 2013g. [Official logo of the] *Leaders' Summit 2013*. en.g20russia.ru/docs/summit/summit_2013.html [Accessed: 24 October 2013].

G20, 2013j. *St. Petersburg Action Plan*. www.g20.utoronto.ca/2013/St_Petersburg_Action_Plan.pdf [Accessed: 8 September 2017].

G20, 2013k. *Saint Petersburg Accountability Report on G20 Development Commitments*. www.g20.utoronto.ca/2013/Saint_Petersburg_Accountability_Report_on_G20_Development_Commitments.pdf [Accessed: 29 September 2017].

G20, 2014d. *The G20 Australia 2014 Logo*. www.g20australia.org/sites/default/files/g20_resources/library/Factsheet-G20%20Logo.pdf [Accessed: 5 September 2017].

G20, 2014g. *Preparing the G20 Brisbane Summit Agenda: An Overview from the Australian Presidency*. www.g20.utoronto.ca/2014/2014-policy-notes.html [Accessed: 20 January 2017].

G20, 2014i. *Turkish G20 Presidency Priorities for 2015*. www.g20.utoronto.ca/2015/141201-turkish-priorities.html [Accessed: 21 January 2017].

G20, 2015a. *G20 Leaders' Communiqué*. 15–16 November. www.g20.utoronto.ca/2015/151116-communique.pdf [Accessed: 3 October 2017].

G20, 2015c. *Logo*. g20.org.tr/logo-2/ [Accessed: 5 September 2017].

G20, 2016n. *G20 Summit 2016: China*. www.g20.utoronto.ca/2016/xi-151en.pdf [Accessed: 21 January 2017].

G20, 2016q. *Logo*. www.g20chn.org/English/China2016/Logo/index.html [Accessed: 6 September 2017].

G20, 2017b. *Argentina's Priorities for the G20 2018 Agenda*. 13 December. www.g20.org/en/news/argentinas-priorities-g20-2018-agenda [Accessed: 20 December 2017].

G20, 2017e. *G20: A Meeting at the Highest Level*. www.g20.org/Webs/G20/EN/G20/Participants/participants_node.html;jsessionid=7B39207FA25D764A07156CB149DF27CD.s4t2 [Accessed: 5 September 2017].

G20, 2017k. *Introductory Statement*. www.g20.org/Content/EN/Artikel/2017/07_en/2017-07-07-eingangsstatement-merkel-g20-en.html [Accessed: 26 September 2017].

G20, 2017l. *The Outcomes of the G20 Summit: Tangible Progress Made*. www.bundesregierung.de/Content/EN/Artikel/2017/07_en/2017-07-11-g20-10-erfolge_en.html?nn=709674 [Accessed: 30 January 2018].

G20, 2017m. *Overview of Argentina's G20 Presidency: Building Consensus for Fair and Sustainable Development*. 1 December. g20.org/sites/default/files/docs/Marco-Conceptual-english.pdf [Accessed: 29 July 2018].

G20, 2017g. *G20 Leaders' Declaration*. 8 July. www.g20.utoronto.ca/2017/2017-G20-leaders-declaration.html [Accessed: 4 October 2017].

G20 Global Partnership for Financial Inclusion, 2013. *Report to the Leaders*. www.g20.utoronto.ca/2013/GPFI_Report_to_the_Leaders.pdf [Accessed: 29 September 2017].

G20 Information Centre, 2018b. *G20 Summits*. www.g20.utoronto.ca/summits/index.html [Accessed: 8 August 2018].

Giles, C., 2011. Meetings yet to reach the peak of achievement. *Financial Times*, 3 November, p. 2.

Hajnal, P.I., 2007a. *The G8 System and the G20: Evolution, Role and Documentation*. Global Finance Series. Aldershot: Ashgate.

Hajnal, P.I. and Panova, V., 2012. The future role and reform of the G8. In: M. Larionova, ed. *The European Union in the G8: Promoting Consensus and Concerted Actions for Global Public Goods*. Farnham: Ashgate. pp. 65–81.

Hampson, F.O. and Heinbecker, P., 2011. The 'new' multilateralism of the twenty-first century. *Global Governance: A Review of Multilateralism and International Organizations*, 17(3), pp. 299–310.

Huigens, J. and Niemann, A., 2009. *The EU within the G8: A Case of Ambiguous and Contested Actorness*. EU Diplomacy Papers, 5/2009. Bruges: College of Europe. www.g8.utoronto.ca/scholar/huigensneimann.pdf [Accessed: 24 October 2017].

International Monetary Fund, 2011a. *G-20 Mutual Assessment Process: From Pittsburgh to Cannes: IMF Umbrella Report*. IMF Staff Reports for the G-20 Mutual Assessment Process. www.imf.org/external/np/g20/pdf/110411.pdf [Accessed: 24 October 2017].

Kim, C.J., 2010. Special G20 Stamps Released. *Korea.net*, 10 November. www.korea.net/NewsFocus/Policies/view?articleId=97687 [Accessed: 14 September 2012].

Kirton, J.J., 2013b. *G20 Governance for a Globalized World*. Farnham: Ashgate.

Kirton, J.J. and Kulik, J., 2012a. *The Shortcomings of the G20 Los Cabos Summit*. Toronto: G20 Research Group. 27 June. www.g20.utoronto.ca/analysis/120627-kirton-kulik-shortcomings.html [Accessed: 24 October 2017].

Kirton, J.J. and Kulik, J., 2012b. *A Summit of Significant Success: G20 Los Cabos Leaders Deliver the Desired Double Dividend*. Los Cabos: G20 Research Group. 19 June. www.g20.utoronto.ca/analysis/120619-kirton-success.html [Accessed: 24 October 2017].

Larionova, M. ed., 2012a. *The European Union in the G8: Promoting Consensus and Concerted Actions for Global Public Goods*. Farnham: Ashgate.

Martin, P., 2011b. The G20: From global crisis responder to global steering committee. In: C.I. Bradford and W.H. Lim, eds. *Global Leadership in Transition: Making the G20 More Effective and Responsive*. Washington, DC: Brookings Institution Press with Korean Development Institute. pp. 13–15.

Mexico. President, 2012b. *Remarks Made by the President of Mexico, Felipe Calderón Hinojosa, during the G20 Ministers of Foreign Affairs Informal Meeting*. 20 February. www.g20mexico.org/index.php/en/speeches/221-mensaje-al-grupo-del-g20-por-parte-del-presidente-felipe-calderon [Accessed: 24 July 2012].

Russia. President, 2012. *Address by Vladimir Putin on Russia Assuming the G20 Presidency*. 1 December. www.g20.utoronto.ca/2012/2012-putin-1201.html [Accessed: 26 October 2017].

Stanley Foundation, 2011. *How Are Key 21st-Century Powers Arranging Themselves: For Competition, Coexistence, or Cooperation?* Policy Dialogue Brief. Muscatine, IA: Stanley Foundation. 6–8 June. www.stanleyfoundation.org/publications/pdb/21st CenturyPowersPDB811.pdf [Accessed: 26 September 2017].

United Kingdom. Prime Minister, 2011. *Governance for Growth: Building Consensus for the Future*. November. webarchive.nationalarchives.gov.uk/20130109092234/www.number10.gov.uk/wp-content/uploads/2011/11/GovernanceForGrowth_acc.pdf [Accessed: 26 September 2017].

United States. Department of State, 2012. *G8 Summit 2012*. https://2009-2017.state.gov/e/eb/ecosum/2012g8/index.htm [Accessed: 26 September 2017].

United States. White House. Office of the Press Secretary, 2013. *Joint Statement on Syria*. 6 September. www.whitehouse.gov/the-press-office/2013/09/06/joint-statement-syria [Accessed: 6 October 2017].

3 The evolving G20 system

This chapter surveys and comments on the following components of the G20 system: ministerial fora, the Financial Stability Board (FSB) and the Heiligendamm/L'Aquila Process; working groups, task forces and experts' groups; and the leaders' personal representatives (sherpas). It then gives a brief account of G20-organized seminars, workshops and conferences. The chapter aims, beyond a summary of these meetings, to show how the work of sub-summit entities feeds into the leaders' summits or the ministerial fora. Leaders' summits are reviewed in Chapter 2, and Chapter 9 discusses the documentation of the G20 at all levels: summits, ministerial fora, working groups and other sub-summit entities.

The G20 Finance Ministers' and Central Bank Governors' forum was the first component of the G20 system, preceding the leaders' summits (which, as the term 'summit' implies, are at the peak of the G20 pyramid) by almost a decade and continuing to run alongside the summits. This ministers' forum is a creation of the G8 leaders, following the recommendation of the G7 Finance Ministers. Since the establishment of the G20 at the summit level, an increasing number of other ministerial fora have been convened and working groups and similar sub-summit entities have been created, marking the gradual evolution of a broader G20 system. Some have regular periodic meetings while others have been convened on an *ad hoc* basis. In a practical sense, the work of these sub-summit entities may well be more important than the summit meetings in moving initiatives forward, notwithstanding the fact that the leaders' political input is essential. The role of the FSB in financial regulation is a case in point.

Finance Ministers and Central Bank Governors

The G20 Finance Ministers' and Central Bank Governors' forum was created on the recommendation of the G7 Finance Ministers in their report to the 1999 Cologne G8 summit on strengthening the international financial architecture, and in response to the 1997–98 Asian/Latin American financial crisis and the recognition that the most important emerging-economy countries had to be included as full partners in global economic governance (Smith, 2011a). It had become clear that the G8 countries alone could not tackle economic and financial problems without the full participation of other systemically important economies. As detailed in Chapter 1, Paul Martin, former Canadian Prime Minister and previously Finance

DOI: 10.4324/9781351266802-4

Minister, together with US Treasury Secretary Lawrence Summers, was instrumental in expanding the Finance Ministers' and Central Bank Governors' forum to 20 members (Summers, 2008; Cooper and Thakur, 2013, p. 37).

The G20 Finance Ministers and Central Bank Governors have had regular meetings, initially annually, and since 2008, two to four times a year. Table 3.1 lists those meetings held during 1999–2017. The ministers and governors have also communicated with one another without face-to-face meetings, by teleconferencing or email; for example, they participated in a conference call on 8 August 2011 and then issued a short statement on financial stability and economic growth. The Finance (Ministers') Deputies have their own series of meetings feeding into the ministerial meetings. The Finance Ministers are charged by the leaders to flesh out and develop various initiatives and programmes, as was the case at the 2011 Cannes G20 summit, where the ministers were asked:

- to work on options to strengthen the G20's capacity to cope with financial crises;
- for greater involvement in strategic guidance of the IMF;
- to review progress on the regulation and supervision of the financial sector;
- to work on reforms of the energy sector and report back to the leaders at the 2012 summit; and
- to report to the leaders at the 2012 summit on climate financing.

(G20, 2011b)

The ministers' meeting in Mexico City on 4–5 November 2012 had as its objective 'to assess progress on the fulfillment of the mandates given to us by our Leaders, to promote robust growth and job creation and to address ongoing economic and financial challenges' (G20, 2012e). Meetings took place again in countries holding the G20 Presidency: Russia in 2013, Australia in 2014, Turkey in 2015, China in 2016 and Germany in 2017. These meetings take place in addition to the usual meetings at the time of the IMF spring and fall meetings. (Table 3.1 gives a full list.)

Table 3.1 Meetings of G20 Finance Ministers and Central Bank Governors, 1999–July 2018

Date	*Venue*	*Date*	*Venue*
15–16 Dec. 1999	Berlin, Germany	25–26 Feb. 2012	Mexico City, Mexico
24–25 Oct. 2000	Montreal, Canada	19–20 Apr. 2012	Washington, DC, US (IMF/WBG Spring Meetings)
16–17 Nov. 2001	Ottawa, Canada	18–19 Jun. 2012	Los Cabos, Mexico (Leaders' Summit)
22–23 Nov. 2002	New Delhi, India	4–5 Nov. 2012	Mexico City, Mexico
26–27 Oct. 2003	Morelia, Mexico	15–16 Feb. 2013	Moscow, Russia
20–21 Nov. 2004	Berlin, Germany	18–19 Apr. 2013	Washington, DC, US (IMF/WBG Spring Meetings)
15–16 Oct. 2005	Xianghe, Hebei, China	19–20 Jul. 2013	Moscow, Russia (18–19 Jul. with Labour & Employment Ministers)

Table 3.1 Continued

Date	*Venue*	*Date*	*Venue*
18–19 Nov. 2006	Melbourne, Australia	5–6 Sep. 2013	St Petersburg, Russia (Leaders' Summit)
17–18 Nov. 2007	Kleinmond, South Africa	10–11 Oct. 2013	Washington, DC, US (IMF/WBG Annual Meetings)
13 Oct. 2008	Washington, DC, US (IMF/WBG Annual Meetings)	21–23 Feb. 2014	Sydney, Australia
14–15 Nov. 2008	Washington, DC, US (Leaders' Summit)	10–11 Apr. 2014	Washington, DC, US (IMF/WBG Spring Meetings)
8–9 Nov. 2008	São Paulo, Brazil	20–21 Sept. 2014	Cairns, Australia
14–15 Mar. 2009	Horsham, UK	19–10 Oct. 2014	Washington, DC, US (IMF/WBG Annual Meetings)
1–2 Apr. 2009	London, UK	15 Nov. 2014	Brisbane, Australia (Leaders' Summit)
24 Apr. 2009	Washington, DC, US (IMF/WBG Spring Meetings)	9–10 Feb. 2015	Istanbul, Turkey
4–5 Sept. 2009	London, UK	15–17 Apr. 2015	Washington, DC, US (IMF/WBG Spring Meetings)
24–25 Sept. 2009	Pittsburgh, US	4–5 Sept. 2015	Ankara, Turkey (4 Sept. with Labour Ministers)
6–7 Nov. 2009	St Andrews, Scotland	26–27 Feb. 2016	Shanghai, China
22–23 Apr. 2010	Washington, DC, US (IMF/WBG Spring Meetings)	14–15 Apr. 2016	Washington, DC, US (IMF/WBG Spring Meetings)
4–5 Jun. 2010	Busan, South Korea	23–24 Jul. 2016	Chengdu, China
26–27 Jun. 2010	Toronto, Canada (Leaders' Summit)	4–5 Sep. 2016	Hangzhou, China (Leaders' Summit)
9–10 Oct. 2010	Washington, DC, US (IMF/WBG Annual Meetings)	6 Oct. 2016	Washington, DC, US (IMF/WBG Annual Meetings)
22–23 Oct. 2010	Gyeongju, South Korea	17–18 Mar. 2017	Baden-Baden, Germany
11–12 Nov. 2010	Seoul, South Korea (Leaders' Summit)	20–21 Apr. 2017	Washington, DC, US (IMF/WBG Spring Meetings)
18–19 Feb. 2011	Paris, France	7 Jul. 2017	Hamburg, Germany (Leaders' Summit)
14–15 Apr. 2011	Washington, DC, US (IMF/WBG Spring Meetings)	12–13 Oct. 2017	Washington, DC, US (IMF/WBG Annual Meetings)
22–23 Sept. 2011	Washington, DC, US (IMF/WBG Annual Meetings)	19–20 Mar. 2018	Buenos Aires, Argentina
14–15 Oct. 2011	Paris, France	20 Apr. 2018	Washington, DC, US (IMF/WBG Spring Meetings)
3–4 Nov. 2011	Cannes, France (Leaders' Summit)	21–22 Jul. 2018	Buenos Aires, Argentina

Sources: G20 Information Centre (2018a); Finance Canada (2017).

At their meeting in Chengdu, China, on 24 July 2016, the Finance Ministers and Central Bank Governors reviewed 'their efforts in responding to key economic challenges, as well as the progress made since the beginning of [2016] . . . and achieved tangible outcomes on [their] agenda, which will be delivered for our Leaders' review at their Hangzhou Summit' (G20 FM&CBG, 2016). In Baden-Baden on 18 March 2017, the ministers and governors focused on 'strong, sustainable, balanced and inclusive growth, while enhancing economic and financial resilience' (G20 FM&CBG, 2017).

G20 leaders' summits, in addition to the heads of state, usually also include Finance Ministers as participants. This is in contrast to the G8, where Finance Ministers ceased attending the leaders' summits beginning with the 1998 Birmingham summit. As the G20 agenda broadens, ministers with other portfolios may also attend when their issues are discussed at the summits and additional ministerial fora will convene as necessary. IGOs and non-G20 countries are sometimes also invited to participate in G20 ministerial meetings.

Agriculture Ministers

G20 Agriculture Ministers met on 22–23 June 2011 in Paris, to discuss the volatility of agricultural commodity prices. On 11–12 April 2012, G20 Vice-Ministers of agriculture convened in Mexico City in the lead-up to the Los Cabos G20 summit, to arrive at agreements to coordinate action on economic, social and environmental aspects of agriculture and food. Several international organizations also participated, including the Food and Agriculture Organization of the UN (FAO), the International Fund for Agricultural Development (IFAD) and the World Food Programme (WFP). Agriculture Vice-Ministers and their deputies met in Mexico City on 17–18 May 2012.

The ministers met subsequently on 7–8 May 2015 in Istanbul, focusing on food security, nutrition and agricultural productivity. On 2–3 June 2016 in Xi'an they revisited food security and nutrition, and added to their agenda sustainable agricultural growth and rural development. On 22 January 2017 in Berlin they dealt with food and water security, climate change, information and communication technology in agriculture, aspects of antimicrobial resistance, and agricultural trade and investment.

Ministers of culture and intellectual property

A so-called Cultural G8-G20 of 19 Ministers of Culture and Intellectual Property (from a selection of G20 and non-G20 countries) was held after the Cannes G20 summit, on 17–18 November 2011 in Avignon, France (France held the Presidency of both the G8 and G20 in 2011). The meeting dealt with prospects of 'creation in the digital age' (France, MCC, 2011).

Development and International Cooperation Ministers

G20 Development and International Cooperation Ministers held a joint meeting with the Finance Ministers and Central Bank Governors on 23 September 2011 in Washington, DC, 'to address development challenges as part of the global economic agenda' (France, MEFI, 2011, para. 1). The IMF, World Bank, OECD and FAO were also represented.

Ministers responsible for digitalization

These ministers met, for the first time in G20 history, on 6–7 April 2017 in Düsseldorf, before the Hamburg summit. Their motto was 'Digitalisation: Policies for a Digital Future'. This meeting was called to support the digitalization agenda of the summit itself.

Foreign Ministers

For the first time, G20 Foreign Ministers held an informal meeting on 19–20 February 2012 in Los Cabos, Mexico. Ten additional countries were invited: Benin (representing the African Union), Cambodia (representing the Association of Southeast Asian Nations, ASEAN), Chile, Colombia and Spain, as well as Algeria, Azerbaijan, Norway, Singapore and the United Arab Emirates. President Calderón attended the meeting on 20 February and used the occasion to elaborate on Mexico's five priorities for the Los Cabos summit: economic stabilization and structural reforms as foundations for growth and employment; strengthening the financial system and fostering financial inclusion; improving the international financial architecture; enhancing food security and addressing commodity price volatility; promoting sustainable development, and green growth and action against climate change.

The meeting discussed the G20's role in addressing major challenges in global governance and preventing future crises. Participants covered the issues of reforming multilateral institutions; making use of existing international mechanisms and monitoring compliance with commitments; using preventive rather than reactive diplomacy; and developing comprehensive approaches embracing economic, political and security issues together. Some participants proposed a follow-up of this meeting. Although not a planned follow-up, another meeting of Foreign Ministers on the Syrian crisis was convened hastily on 6 September 2013 in St Petersburg, Russia. Canada, Kazakhstan, South Korea, Senegal, Mexico, Brazil, Germany, Turkey, France and some other countries participated, but not the US (Kazakhstan and Senegal are not G20 members). UN Envoy Lakhdar Brahimi also talked with the Foreign Ministers. Foreign Ministers met again on 15 November 2015 in Antalya and on 16–17 February 2017 in Bonn.

Health Ministers

For the first time in G20 history, Health Ministers met on 19–20 May 2017 in Berlin. They discussed economic aspects of global health issues, health crisis management, strengthening of health systems and antimicrobial resistance. This tied in with various health issues also on the German agenda of the Hamburg summit.

Labour and Employment Ministers

G20 Labour and Employment Ministers first met on 20–21 April 2010 in Washington, DC (on job creation, social protection and inclusive labour markets), and then on 26–27 September 2011 in Paris (on employment policies focusing on youth employment, social protection, and social and labour rights) and on 17–18 May 2012 in Guadalajara, Mexico, where their agenda included quality employment, particularly for youth, and 'green growth' as a factor in generating employment. Heads of the OECD and International Labour Organization (ILO) were also invited. The ministers' declaration was submitted to Mexican President Felipe Calderón, to share with his fellow leaders at the 2012 Los Cabos G20 summit. Another meeting was held on 18–19 July 2013 in Moscow (on 19 July jointly with Finance Ministers). Its focus was on job creation, labour activation and inclusion.

In Melbourne on 10–11 September 2014 the ministers discussed preventing structural unemployment, creating better jobs and boosting labour force participation of women and youth. In Ankara on 3–4 September 2015 the agenda centred on quality jobs, investing in skills and reducing inequality. In Beijing on 11–13 July 2016 the ministers concentrated on generating job opportunities, enhancing employability and promoting decent work and social protection. In Bad Neuenahr, Germany, on 18–19 May 2017 the focus was on reducing gender gaps and promoting labour market integration of migrants and refugees – all in support of the German Hamburg summit agenda, which also dealt prominently with women's empowerment and migrants and refugees.

Tourism Ministers

G20 Tourism Ministers (T20) first met on 22–24 February 2010 in Johannesburg, South Africa. The second meeting convened on 11–13 October 2010 in Buyeo, Republic of Korea; the third meeting followed on 24–25 October 2011 in Paris. The fourth meeting took place on 15–16 May 2012 in Merida on the Yucatan peninsula, Mexico, with a working meeting at the archaeological site of the Mayan city of Chichen Itza. In addition to G20 Tourism Ministers, the following countries were invited as guests: Denmark, Spain, Chile, Colombia, Cambodia, El Salvador, Guatemala, Jamaica and Peru. The World Tourism Organization (UNWTO), the Organisation for Economic Co-operation and Development (OECD), the ILO, the International Air Transport Association (IATA) and the International Civil Aviation Organization (ICAO) participated as well. T20 meetings have taken place with the assistance of UNWTO and each issued recommendations for the leaders at their subsequent G20 summit. For example, the 2012 meeting produced recommendations for the G20 leaders to support tourism and its role in job creation (UNWTO, 2012). Tourism Ministers convened again on 2 October 2015 in Antalya, Turkey (also the venue of the 2015 G20 summit).

Trade Ministers

G20 Trade Ministers met in April 2012 in Puerto Vallarta, Mexico. Ministers of Singapore, Chile, Spain, Cambodia, Peru and Colombia also attended, and the administrative heads of OECD and WTO participated as well. Representatives of the Business 20 (B20, which is discussed in detail in Chapter 5) were also present. The ministers met again on 19 July 2014 in Sydney, 6 October 2015 in Istanbul and 9–10 July 2016 in Shanghai.

The sherpas

The G20 leaders have their own personal representatives (known as sherpas), who in turn are supported by their teams. They are responsible for preparing – in consultation with their other G20 counterparts – for the upcoming summit and conducting a post-summit wrap-up. The preparatory process also includes sherpa consultations with non-government stakeholders, such as the business sector, think-tanks and civil society groups. Some G7/G8 members of the G20 have the same person as sherpa for both the G7/G8 and the G20.

The sherpas are assisted by Deputy Finance Ministers ('Finance Deputies'). This stands in contrast with the more elaborate sherpa structure of the G7/G8, where sherpa teams include: political directors who prepare the foreign policy portions of the G8 communiqués or declarations; foreign affairs sous-sherpas who are responsible for most of the remainder of the final summit documents; and – up to the 2009 L'Aquila G8 summit and again briefly at the 2011 Deauville G8 summit – finance sous-sherpas whose task was the preparation of the macroeconomic and financial portions of the final G8 documents. With the institutionalization of the G20 summit as 'the premier forum for our international economic cooperation' at the Pittsburgh summit in September 2009, the need for a G8 finance sous-sherpa had ceased (Bronnert, 2011, pp. 83, 85). If the gradual broadening of the G20 agenda continues, the G20 sherpa apparatus could grow. Table 3.2 lists G20 sherpas as of January 2018 and their positions in their governments.

Sherpas meet three or four or more times a year. The following sherpa meetings took place under the German G20 Presidency in December 2016–November 2017: a pre-summit meeting on 2–13 December 2016; and subsequent meetings in 2017 on 23–24 March, 18–19 May, and July, just before the Hamburg summit (this included a joint meeting with the finance deputies). The host leader, German Chancellor Angela Merkel, publicly thanked the sherpas for the quality of their preparatory work for the summit (G20, 2017c, 2017k, 2017o). A final follow-up meeting under the German Presidency was held on 9–10 November 2017.

Financial Stability Board

The Board's predecessor, the Financial Stability Forum (FSF), was created by the G7 Finance Ministers and Central Bank Governors at their meeting in February 1999 in Bonn. It held its first meeting in Washington, DC, in April of that year. Its mandate was to enhance cooperation among national and international supervisory bodies and international financial institutions and, to that end, to recommend appropriate new structures. The overall objective of FSF was to promote stability in the international financial system.

Table 3.2 G20 Sherpas as of January 2018

G20 member	*Name*	*Position*
Argentina	Pedro Raúl Villagra Delgado	Ambassador
Australia	David Gruen	Deputy Secretary, Economic, Department of the Prime Minister and Cabinet
Brazil	Carlos Márcio Cozendey	Undersecretary-General for Economic & Financial Affairs, Ministry of External Relations
Canada	Jonathan Fried	Coordinator, International Economic Relations, Global Affairs Canada
China	Xiaolong Wang	Special Envoy on G20 Affairs of the Foreign Ministry
France	Aurélien LeChevallier	Foreign Policy Advisor
Germany	Gesa Miehe-Nordmeyer	Head of G7/G20 Sherpa Team, German Chancellery
India	Shaktikanta Das	Former Secretary of the Department of Economic Affairs
Indonesia	Rizal Affandi Lukman	Deputy for International Economic Cooperation
Italy	Alessandro Motta	Head of G7/G20 Sherpa Unit & Consul General of Italy in Chicago, US
Japan	Kazuyuki Yamazaki	Senior Deputy Minister for Foreign Affairs
Mexico	Carlos de Icaza	Undersecretary of Foreign Affairs
Republic of Korea	Kyong Lim Choi	Ambassador
Russia	Svetlana Lukash	Deputy Chief of Presidential Experts' Directorate, Executive Office of the President
Saudi Arabia	Hamad Albazai	Deputy Minister of Finance
South Africa	Anil Sooklal	Deputy Director General: Asia & Middle East Department of International Relations and Cooperation
Turkey	Osman Çelik	Undersecretary of the Turkish Treasury
United Kingdom	Creon Butler	Director, European & Global Issues Secretariat, Cabinet Office
United States	Everett Eissenstat	Deputy Assistant to the President for International Economic Affairs, Deputy Director of the National Economic Council
European Union	Antoine Kasel	Legal Advisor of President Juncker, European Commission (Sherpa to both EU President and Commission President)

At their first summit (Washington 2008), the G20 leaders signalled their wish to expand and strengthen the FSF. The 2009 London summit finalized the decision to do so, in order to reflect wider G20 membership, and renamed the FSF the Financial Stability Board (FSB). On 4 November 2011, the last day of the Cannes G20 summit, the FSB appointed then-Bank of Canada governor Mark Carney as its new chair, to succeed Mario Draghi of Italy, who assumed leadership of the European Central Bank (ECB). The leaders in Cannes also expanded the mandate of the FSB, to:

- assess vulnerabilities affecting the financial system and identify and oversee action needed to address them;
- promote coordination and information exchange among authorities responsible for financial stability;
- monitor and advise on market developments and their implications for regulatory policy;
- advise on and monitor best practice in meeting regulatory standards;
- undertake joint strategic reviews of the policy development work of the international standard-setting bodies to ensure their work is timely, coordinated and focused on priorities and addressing gaps;
- set guidelines for and support the establishment of supervisory colleges;
- manage contingency planning for cross-border crisis management, particularly with respect to systemically important firms; and
- collaborate with the IMF to conduct Early Warning Exercises (FSB, 2012a).

The FSB's members are the highest financial officials (Finance Ministers and/or Central Bank Governors; in some cases other officials) of the G20 countries (and the EU) plus Hong Kong, the Netherlands, Singapore, Spain and Switzerland. The following international organizations are also members: Bank for International Settlements (BIS), IMF, OECD and World Bank; as well as these international standard-setting bodies: Basel Committee on Banking Supervision (BCBS), Committee on the Global Financial System (CGFS), Committee on Payments and Market Infrastructures (CPMI), International Association of Insurance Supervisors (IAIS), International Accounting Standards Board (IASB) and International Organization of Securities Commissions (IOSCO). The FSB's secretariat is located in Basel, hosted by the BIS. Although the FSB has become more independent of the G20, it remains very closely related to the latter and is therefore treated here as part of the G20 system.

The FSB held its inaugural plenary meeting in Basel in June 2009 and has met in plenary generally five or six times a year since. In addition, the FSB organizes regional and other types of meetings.

The FSB has done well, but it has opportunities to play a greater role. Paul Martin (2013, p. 12) would like to see the Board evolve into an effective international coordinating body to monitor national financial regulation. He argues that the Board needs to become treaty-based and 'must have the capacity to enforce its rules'. Along similar lines, the Cannes summit had already 'agreed to reform the FSB to improve its capacity to coordinate and monitor our financial regulation agenda. This reform includes giving it legal personality and greater financial autonomy' (G20, 2011c). Using this mandate, the FSB created a High-Level Working Group on FSB Capacity, Resources and Governance, which presented recommendations for major changes, including a revised Charter. The Los Cabos summit

> endorse[d] the recommendations and the revised FSB Charter for placing the FSB on an enduring organizational footing, with legal personality, strengthened governance, greater financial autonomy and enhanced capacity to coordinate the development and implementation of financial regulatory policies, while maintaining strong links with the BIS.
>
> (G20, 2012j, p. 8)

Following this, on 28 January 2013 the FSB established itself as a not-for-profit association under Swiss law.

Working groups, expert groups and other sub-summit bodies

The G20 leaders and ministers have established various working groups, task forces and expert groups. These groups support leaders, ministers and sherpas as needed. As a rule, they are co-chaired by one advanced and one emerging country member of the G20 (Canada DFAIT, 2012). A brief description of these groups follows (not a comprehensive list).

- *Agricultural Market Information System (AMIS).* Established by the G20 Agriculture Ministers, June 2011. Mandate: to strengthen policy dialogue and cooperation among major producing, exporting and importing countries, IGOs and commercial enterprises.
- *G20 Anti-Corruption Working Group.* Established by the 2010 Toronto summit. Mandate: to promote UN and OECD tools for fighting corruption, preventing access of corrupt officials to the financial system, fighting money laundering and tax havens, strengthening agreements on mutual aid, extradition and confiscation of assets, improving the protection of whistle-blowers and exchanging best practices.
- *Clean Energy and Energy Efficiency Working Group.* Established by the 2012 Mexican Presidency.
- *Climate Finance Study Group.* Established April 2012 by the G20 Finance Ministers and Central Bank Governors. Mandate: 'to consider ways to . . . mobilize resources and support . . . operationalization . . . of the Green Climate Fund' (G20 CFSG, 2016a, p. 2).
- *G20 Study Group on Commodities.* Established in March 2011 under the French Presidency.
- G20 *Development Working Group (Working Group on Development, DWG).* Also called G20 High-Level Development Working Group (HLDWG).

Established by the 2010 Toronto summit. The Development Working Group has the following subgroups or 'pillars':

- Infrastructure
- Human Resource Development
- Trade
- Private Investment and Job Creation
- Food Security
- Growth with Resilience
- Domestic Resource Mobilization
- Knowledge Sharing
- Financial Inclusion

- *Disaster Risk Management Working Group.* Established within the finance track by the G20 Mexican Presidency.
- *G20 Economic Impact Panel.* Established by the Cannes summit.
- *G20 Task Force on Employment.* Established September 2011 by the G20 Labour and Employment Ministers. Focuses on youth employment.
- *G20 Employment and Social Dimension of Globalization Working Group.* Established by the 2009 London summit.
- *Energy Experts Group.* Established by the Pittsburgh summit. Participants included all 20 countries and the group functioned under the supervision of the Finance and Energy Ministers. Mandate: to review fossil fuel subsidy programmes and develop strategies and timelines for phasing out inefficient fossil fuel subsidies. It had a Global Marine Environment Protection (GMEP) Experts Sub-Group.
- *Working Group on Energy and Commodities Markets* (overlaps with and replaces Energy Experts Group and Study Group on Commodities) and its Commodity Markets Subgroup and Energy and Growth Subgroup.
- *Energy Efficiency Finance Task Group (EEFTG).* Established March 2015 under the Turkish Presidency.
- *Energy Sustainability Working Group.* Established by the Russian Presidency.
- *G20 Financial Inclusion Experts Group.* Established by the Pittsburgh summit.
- *Global Partnership for Financial Inclusion (GPFI).* Established by the 2010 Seoul summit.
- *Reinforcing International Co-operation and Promoting Integrity in Financial Markets Working Group.* Established by the Washington summit.
- *Working Group on Financial Safety Nets.* Established by the Toronto summit. Builds on the Expert Group on Financial Safety Nets that was created by the Pittsburgh Summit.
- *G20 Study Group on Financing for Investment.* Established by the G20 Finance Ministers and Central Bank Governors in March 2013. Mandate: to identify the role of country-specific factors, domestic capital markets, and official and private sources in long-term financing. The group's concerns also include global financial regulatory reform.

- *Framework for Strong, Sustainable, and Balanced Growth Working Group (Framework Working Group)*. Established by the Pittsburgh summit. The group was tasked with developing the Los Cabos Action Plan for strong, sustainable and balanced growth. It has continued its work.
- *G20 Green Finance Study Group (GFSG)*. Established in 2016 under the Chinese Presidency.
- *Working Group on Green Growth.* An informal subgroup on inclusive green growth, established in 2012 by the Mexican Presidency.
- *Health Working Group*. Established by the German Presidency in 2017.
- *G20 High Level Panel on Infrastructure*. Established by the Seoul summit as part of the Multi-year Action Plan on Development, for a period of one year. Mandate: to work with multilateral development banks for scaling up and diversifying the financing for infrastructure, especially in low-income countries. Its recommendations were endorsed by the Cannes summit.
- *International Financial Architecture Working Group*. Established under the Mexican G20 Presidency.
- *International Monetary System Reform Working Group*. Established under the French Presidency.
- *Task Force to Advance the G20 Agenda on Innovation, the New Industrial Revolution and the Digital Economy*. Established 2016 by the Chinese Presidency.
- *Investment and Infrastructure Working Group*. Established under the Australian Presidency.
- *Working Group on Enhancing Sound Regulation and Strengthening Transparency*. Established by the Washington summit.
- *Trade and Investment Working Group*. Established in 2016 under the Chinese Presidency.
- *Trade Finance Experts Group*. Established by the Pittsburgh summit. Cf. WTO Experts Group on Trade Finance.
- *World Bank and Other Multilateral Development Banks Working Group*. Established by the Washington summit.

The Heiligendamm/L'Aquila Process

The 2007 Heiligendamm G8 summit created the Heiligendamm Process, which, following its extension by the L'Aquila G8 summit, was renamed the Heiligendamm/L'Aquila Process (HAP). Although it was a G8-related body, its active period overlapped with the early period of the G20 and has some relevance here because it brought selected emerging countries into the purview of the G20.

HAP rested on four main pillars: promoting and protecting innovation; enhancing freedom of investments by means of a transparent investment regime, including encouragement of socially responsible behaviour of business; energy, especially through increasing energy efficiency and fostering technological cooperation in order to reduce CO_2 emissions; and better co-operation and coordination in the field of sustainable development, particularly in Africa. The main purpose of the sustainable development pillar was to reach the Millennium Development Goals (MDGs), with the major focus on increased efficiency of aid to Africa in order to advance its sustainable development and to eradicate poverty (Cooper and Antkiewicz, 2008; Hajnal and Panova, 2012). By 2010 the HAP had run its course.

Workshops, conferences and seminars

The G20 and its sub-bodies have organized a number of workshops, seminars and conferences, often with the participation of other stakeholders – for example, IGOs, banks, experts, the business sector, think-tanks, civil society organizations and others. Even before the emergence of the G20 leaders' summits, many such workshops and conferences were called under the authority of the G20 Finance Ministers' and Central Bank Governors' forum. They tend to reflect the host country's G20 agenda priorities in any given year. Illustrative examples follow, for both earlier and recent years:

- Workshop on Globalization, Living Standards and Inequality: Recent Progress and Continuing Challenges, 18–27 May 2002.
- Workshop on Developing Strong Domestic Financial Markets, Ottawa, 26–27 April 2004. Co-hosted by the Deutsche Bundesbank and the Bank of Canada.
- Workshop on Regional Economic Integration in a Global Framework, Beijing, 22–23 September 2004.
- Workshop on Demographic Challenges and Migration, Sydney, Australia, 27–28 August 2005. Hosted by the Australian government.
- Conference on Demography and Financial Markets, Sydney, Australia, 23–25 July 2006. Hosted by the Australian government.
- G20 Workshop on Competition in the Financial Sector, Bali, 16–17 February 2008. Organized by the Bank of Indonesia and the Banco de Mexico.
- G20 Workshop on the Global Economy: Causes of the Crisis, Mumbai, India, 24–26 May 2009. Co-hosted by the Reserve Bank of India and the Bank of England.
- G-20 Workshop on Securing Sustainable Economic Recovery, Seoul, 15–16 November 2009.
- Effective Financial Market Regulation after Pittsburgh: Achievements and Challenges: International Conference, Berlin, 19–20 May 2010. Hosted by the German Federal Ministry of Finance.
- Korea – World Bank High-Level Conference on Post-Crisis Growth and Development, 11 June 2010.
- Korea-FSB (Financial Stability Board) Financial Reform Conference: An Emerging Market Perspective, 2–3 September 2010, Seoul, Republic of Korea. Co-hosted by the (Korean) Presidential Committee for the G20 Summit and the Financial Stability Board.
- Seminar on the Reform of the International Monetary System, Nanjing, China, 31 March 2011.

- G20-OECD Conference: Joining Forces against Corruption: G20 Business and Government, Paris, 21 October 2011. Co-organized by France and the OECD.
- G20 Seminar 'Current Challenges for Global Economic Growth'. 12–13 December 2011. Co-hosted by the Mexican Ministry of Finance and Public Credit and the Banco de México.
- Seminar 'Giving International Finance an Adequate Architecture' 18 January 2012. Co-hosted by the Mexican government and the Reinventing Bretton Woods Committee.
- High-Level Public-Private Sector IIF G-20 Seminar 'The G-20 Agenda under the Mexican Chairmanship', Mexico City, 24–25 February 2012. Co-organized by the Mexican government and the Institute of International Finance.
- Seminar 'Mexico and the G20: Rethinking Global Economic Balance'. Mexico City, 13 March 2012. Co-organized by the Americas Society/Council of the Americas and ProMéxico.
- Seminar 'The Priorities of Latin America and the Caribbean for the Group of Twenty'. Montevideo, Uruguay, 17 March 2012. Co-hosted by the Mexican Secretary of Finance and Public Credit and the Uruguay Minister of Economy and Finance.
- Financial Inclusion: From Principles to Action. Hosted by the World Bank. Washington, DC, 22 April 2012.
- G-20 Commodities Seminar, Los Cabos, Mexico, 5–6 May 2012. Co-organized by the Mexican government and the World Bank.
- G20 Seminar on Green Growth, Paris, 22 May 2012. Co-organized by the Mexican government and the OECD.
- Seminar 'Investment and Investment Finance: The Supply and Demand of Long-Term Finance'. Moscow, 13–14 February 2013. Organized by the Reinventing Bretton Woods Committee and the Ministry of Finance of Russia.
- Conference on 'Fostering Economic Growth and Sustainability', Moscow, 13 December 2012. Hosted by the Russian G20 Presidency.
- High-level seminar 'Public Debt Management under Non-Conventional Conditions on Debt Markets', Moscow, 2–3 April 2013.
- Seminar on Global Value Chains, Paris, 29 May 2013. Organized jointly by the Russian G20 Presidency and the OECD.
- Conference on commodity and energy markets 'Sustainable Energy: Designing Policy for G20', St Petersburg, 8 July 2013.
- International conference 'Comprehensive Approach to Social Protection and Food Security for Sustainable Development', 21–22 October 2013. Hosted by the Russian G20 Presidency in cooperation with the World Bank.
- G20 Anti-corruption Roundtable, Sydney, 28 February 2014.
- G20 Small and Medium Enterprises (SME) Workshop, Riadh, Saudi Arabia, 11–12 March 2014. Hosted by the Kingdom of Saudi Arabia as part of the Australia 2014 G20 Presidency.
- Commonwealth and La Francophonie dialogue (with the G20), Washington, DC, 7 April 2014.

- G-20 International Tax Symposium, Istanbul, 6–8 May 2014. Organized by the Turkish Ministry of Finance. Australian Presidency roundtable with engagement groups, Canberra, 12 May 2014.
- G20-OECD High-Level Anti-corruption Conference, Rome, 11 June 2014.
- Global Partnership for Financial Inclusion and Financial Stability Institute Conference, Basel, Switzerland, 30–31 October 2014.
- G20 – Global Forum on Migration and Development – Global Migration Group Joint Event, Izmir, Turkey, 3 June 2015.
- The International Monetary and Financial System – Short-Term Challenges, Long-Term Solutions, Bodrum, Turkey, 14 June 2015. Organized in collaboration with the Central Bank of Turkey and the Bank of England.
- G20 Workshop on Silver Economy and Active Ageing, Rome, 24 June 2015. Hosted by the Italian Ministry of Foreign Affairs and International Cooperation.
- G20-IAT-GFIA Conference on 'Insurance and the G20 Agenda', Istanbul, 29 July 2015. Organized in collaboration with G20 Turkish Presidency, the Undersecretariat of Turkish Treasury, the Insurance Association of Turkey (IAT) and the Global Federation of Insurance Associations (GFIA).
- G20's Contribution to the Implementation of the SDGs: High-Level Side Event on the margins of the UN Sustainable Development Summit 2015. Hosted by the G20 Turkish Presidency in collaboration with the United Nations Development Programme (UNDP), New York, 25 September 2015.
- High-Level Conference on Access to Energy in Sub-Saharan Africa, Istanbul, 1 October 2015.
- OECD-G20 Global Forum on International Investment, Istanbul, 5 October 2015. Organized by the OECD in partnership with the G20 and hosted by the Turkish Ministry of the Economy.
- International SME Conference: Leveraging Islamic Finance for SMEs, Istanbul 23–24 October 2015. Jointly hosted by the G20 Turkish presidency, World Bank, Islamic Development Bank and TUMSIAD (All Industrialists and Businessmen Association).
- Macroprudential Policy: Effectiveness and Implementation Challenges, Istanbul, 26–27 October 2015. Jointly organized by the Central Bank of Turkey, International Monetary Fund and the Bank for International Settlements.
- Forum on Tax Administration, Beijing, 11–13 May 2016.
- Workshop 'Brown to Green: Low-Carbon Development of the G20 and China', Beijing, 1 September 2016. Hosted by the Energy Research Institute of the National Development and Reform Commission, the Energy Foundation of China, WWF China and Climate Transparency.
- Conference 'Key Issues for Digital Transformation in the G20', Berlin, 12 January 2017. Hosted jointly by the German Presidency and the OECD.
- Workshop on the update of the Financial Inclusion Action Plan (FIAP), Wiesbaden, Germany, 23–24 January 2017. Hosted by the German G20 presidency.

- G20 Workshop 'Helping SMEs Go Global – Moving Forward in SME Finance', Frankfurt, 24 February 2017. Hosted by the German G20 Presidency.
- High-Level Symposium 'Global Economic Governance in a Multipolar World', Baden-Baden, 17 March 2017. Organized by the G20 finance ministers and Central Bank governors with the participation of experts, practitioners and representatives of academic institutions.
- Multi-stakeholder Conference on Digital Economy, Düsseldorf, 6 April 2017. Organized by the German Federal Ministry for Economic Affairs and Energy.
- High-Level Forum on Financial Inclusion of Forcibly Displaced Persons, Berlin, 26 April 2017. Hosted jointly by the German G20 presidency and the Alliance for Financial Inclusion (AFI), as part of the 2017 priorities of the GPFI (Global Partnership for Financial Inclusion).
- International Conference on the Prevention of Radicalisation, 13–15 November 2017.

Conclusion

The leaders' summits are at the peak of the G20 system but they are supported and supplemented by a growing body of ministerial fora, working groups, task forces and other sub-summit entities. They are devoted to particular issue areas and draw on inside or outside expertise as needed. They are generally tasked by and report back to the body that appointed them: the ministers to the leaders; and the task forces and expert groups to the ministers or directly to the leaders. These sub-summit entities perform important preparatory work and follow-up, helping the G20 leaders when the latter are willing to exercise their political input. As the G20 agenda evolves, the resulting new areas will call for appropriate structures to investigate, plan, recommend and promote implementation of required action.

References

Bronnert, D., 2011. Making government policy: The G8 and G20 in 2010. In: N. Bayne and S. Woolcock, eds. *The New Economic Diplomacy: Decision-Making and Negotiation in International Economic Relations*. 3rd ed. Global Finance Series. Farnham: Ashgate. pp. 81–91.

Canada. Department of Foreign Affairs and International Trade, 2012. *How the G20 Works*. www.canadainternational.gc.ca/g20/about-a_propos/howworks-g20-fonctionnement.aspx?lang=eng&view=d [Accessed: 14 July 2012].

Cooper, A.F. and Antkiewicz, A. eds., 2008. *Emerging Powers in Global Governance: Lessons from the Heiligendamm Process*. Waterloo, Canada: Wilfrid Laurier University Press and Centre for International Governance Innovation. Also available in Chinese 2009: *Quan Qiu Zhi Li Zhong De Xin Xing Guo Jia*. Shanghai: Shanghai People's Publishing House.

Cooper, A.F. and Thakur, R., 2013. *The Group of Twenty (G20)*. Global Institutions Series. New York: Routledge.

Finance Canada, 2017. *G20 Finance Ministers' and Central Bank Governors' Meetings.* [email] Message to P.I. Hajnal. Sent 6 December.

Financial Stability Board, 2012a. *Mandate.* www.fsb.org/about/ [Accessed: 3 October 2017].

France. Ministère de la Culture et de la Communication, 2011. *Cultural Summit Avignon, 17 and 18 November.* https://ifacca.org/en/news/2011/11/18/cultural-summit-avignon-17-and-18-november-2011/ and www.culturecommunication.gouv.fr/Ministere/L-histoire-du-ministere/Archives/Frederic-Mitterrand-2009-2012/Articles-2009-2012/Sommet-culturel-sur-la-creation-a-l-ere-numerique/(language)/fre-FR [Accessed: 27 November 2017].

France. Ministère de l'Économie, des Finances et de l'Industrie, 2011. *G20 Ministerial Meeting on Development: Communiqué.* Washington, DC. 23 September. http://proxy-pubminefi.diffusion.finances.gouv.fr/pub/document/18/11572.pdf [Accessed: 27 November 2017].

G20, 2011b. *Cannes Summit Final Declaration: Building Our Common Future: Renewed Collective Action for the Benefit of All.* 4 November. www.g20.utoronto.ca/2011/2011-cannes-declaration-111104-en.html [Accessed: 24 October 2017].

G20, 2012e. *Communiqué of Ministers of Finance and Central Bank Governors of the G20.* 5 November. www.g20.utoronto.ca/2012/2012-121105-finance-en.html [Accessed: 27 November 2017].

G20, 2012j. *G20 Leaders Declaration.* 19 June. www.g20.utoronto.ca/2012/2012-0619-loscabos.pdf [Accessed: 26 September 2017].

G20, 2017c. *First Day of the Summit.* www.bundesregierung.de/Content/EN/Artikel/2017/07_en/2017-07-07-gipfel-freitag_en.html?nn=709674 [Accessed: 30 January 2018].

G20, 2017k. *Introductory Statement.* www.g20.org/Content/EN/Artikel/2017/07_en/2017-07-07-eingangsstatement-merkel-g20-en.html [Accessed: 26 September 2017].

G20, 2017o. *Speech by Federal Chancellor Angela Merkel at the G20 Dialogue Forum with Non Governmental Organisations (C20) in Hamburg on 19 June 2017.* www.bundesregierung.de/Content/EN/Reden/2017/2017-06-19-bk-merkel-c20_en.html?nn=709674 [Accessed: 30 January 2018].

G20. Climate Finance Study Group, 2016a. *Report.* www.g20.utoronto.ca/2016/2016-promoting-efficient-transparent-provision.pdf [Accessed: 5 October 2017].

G20 Finance Ministers and Central Bank Governors, 2016. *Communiqué.* www.g20.utoronto.ca/2016/160724-finance.html [Accessed: 15 September 2017].

G20 Finance Ministers and Central Bank Governors, 2017. *Communiqué.* www.g20.utoronto.ca/2017/170318-finance-en.html [Accessed: 15 September 2017].

G20 Information Centre, 2018a. *G20 Meetings of Finance Ministers and Central Bank Governors and Deputies Official Documents.* www.g20.utoronto.ca/ministerials.html [Accessed: 7 February 2017].

Hajnal, P.I. and Panova, V., 2012. The future role and reform of the G8. In: M. Larionova, ed. *The European Union in the G8: Promoting Consensus and Concerted Actions for Global Public Goods.* Farnham: Ashgate. pp. 65–81.

Martin, P., 2013. The G20: From global crisis responder to steering committee. In: A.F. Cooper et al., eds. *The Oxford Handbook of Modern Diplomacy.* Oxford: Oxford University Press.

Smith, G.S., 2011a. *G7 to G8 to G20: Evolution in Global Governance.* CIGI G20 Papers, No. 6. Waterloo, Canada: Centre for International Governance Innovation. 25 May. www.cigionline.org/sites/default/files/g20no6-2.pdf [Accessed: 7 September 2017].

Stern, N., 2007. *The Economics of Climate Change: The Stern Review*. Cambridge; New York: Cambridge University Press.

Summers, L., 2008. The birth of the G20. In: J.J. Kirton and M. Koch, eds. *G20 São Paulo/Brazil Summit 2008: Growth, Innovation, Inclusion: The G20 at Ten*. London: Newsdesk Communications. pp. 29–31.

United Nations World Tourism Organization, 2012. *T.20 Initiative*. http://t20.unwto.org/en [Accessed: 27 November 2017].

4 Relations with international governmental organizations

This chapter discusses the characteristics, evolution, benefits and challenges of the relationship of the G20 with international governmental organizations (IGOs), in particular the United Nations (UN), the Bretton Woods institutions (the International Monetary Fund, IMF and the World Bank), the Organisation for Economic Co-operation and Development (OECD), and the Bank for International Settlements (BIS) and its Basel Committee (BCBS). Some informal groups that have been created as a reaction to the G7/G8 and G20 or are closely related to those two fora are discussed in Chapter 7: the BRICS group (Brazil, Russia, India, China and South Africa), the G5 or 'Outreach 5' (Brazil, China, India, Mexico and South Africa), the MEF (Major Economies Forum on Energy and Climate) and the Global Governance Group (3G). The European Union (EU) has had a direct relationship with the G7/G8, and the G20 as a non-state member; it is, therefore, examined in Chapter 2. The Financial Stability Board (FSB) is covered in Chapter 3 as part of the broader G20 system.

Introduction

In addition to leaders of G20 countries and of other invited countries, several IGOs participate in summits as invited observers. The administrative heads of the IMF and the World Bank are 'permanent invitees' and the UN Secretary-General has attended all G20 summits. At Hamburg in 2017, the heads of the following IGOs were present: International Labour Organization (ILO), OECD, World Trade Organization (WTO), Food and Agriculture Organization of the United Nations (FAO) and the World Health Organization (WHO). The head of the FSB also participated. It is, however, important to keep in mind that administrative heads of IGOs are public servants, without the stature of G20 leaders, who are elected officials of their countries.

The leaders of countries holding the rotating chair of certain regional IGOs participate as well; at Hamburg the leaders of Guinea (representing the African Union, AU), Vietnam (representing the Asia-Pacific Economic Cooperation, APEC) and Senegal (representing the New Partnership for Africa's Development, NEPAD). The AU's 15th General Assembly, held in July 2010, called for permanent AU membership in the G20, and specifically requested that the chair of the AU and the chair of NEPAD both be present at G20 summits (Kwami, 2010; GCAP email to

DOI: 10.4324/9781351266802-5

author, 9 August). Both have attended as observers but the G20 has not accepted the AU as a regular member on the pattern of the EU. Inviting participating IGOs is the prerogative of the leader of the country holding each year's G20 Presidency. Therefore, regional invitees vary from summit to summit. Argentina, for example, has included the Caribbean Community (CARICOM) among the IGOs invited to the Buenos Aires summit; it will be represented by Jamaica.

The relationship between the G20 and invited IGOs is not confined to the summit. They are present throughout the preparatory process, and sit in at ministerial and – as appropriate – other sub-summit meetings. Each IGO has its own sherpa.

Public documents of the G20 summits regularly acknowledge the role of IGOs in global governance. For example, the Hamburg *G20 Leaders Declaration* cites a number of IGOs:

> [I]t commends the WTO, UNCTAD and OECD for their monitoring activities; asks the OECD, WTO, World Bank Group and IMF to report back to G20 leaders in 2018 on trade and investment co-operation; promises co-operation with the WTO to improve its functioning; promising to foster the implementation of UN and ILO guidelines and principles; undertakes to work for achieving the UN's 2030 Agenda for Sustainable Development; promises to help finalize the Basel III framework (of the Basel Committee on Banking Supervision) on financial sector reform; looks forward to the completion of the next (15th) general review of IMF quotas and the new quota formula; anticipates the work of OECD on tax transparency and digitalization; calls on the UN to keep global health high on the political agenda and for support for WHO's role in this area; welcomes co-operation and financing of sustainable and clean energy by multilateral development banks; stresses the importance of implementing the UN Framework Convention on Climate Change (UNFCCC) commitments to the Paris climate agreement; commits to support famine relief work by UN agencies; offers to help African Union initiatives on infrastructure and investment; and anticipates the outcome of the work of the UN, IOM (International Organization for Migration) and UNHCR (United Nations High Commissioner on Refugees) on refugees and migrants.
> (G20, 2017g)

A symbolic recognition of the role of IGOs came prior to the Los Cabos G20 summit, when President Calderón awarded the Mexican Order of the Aztec Eagle to Margaret Chan, then-Director General of the World Health Organization (WHO); Rajendra Kumar Pachauri, former Director General of the Institute of Energy and Resources and President of the United Nations Intergovernmental Panel on Climate Change; Robert Zoellick, former President of the World Bank, along with Lord Nicholas Stern, President of the Grantham Research Institute on Climate Change and the Environment in the United Kingdom and author of the influential Stern Report (Stern, 2007).

Some observers hold that the G20 is 'a steering committee. It raises the profile of issues and prepares the ground for decisions by commissioning work. The G20 influences events by calling for action and reports from a variety of actors: international organizations, ministers and groups of officials'. Indeed, the G20 remits an increasing range of tasks to other actors. The 2011 Cannes summit, for example, asked the following organizations to develop ideas and action plans (and in some cases, report back to the G20): the IMF, the OECD, the World Bank, the BIS and others (Carin, 2011b). More recently, the *G20 Hamburg Action Plan* (G20, 2017f) asked the Financial Stability Board and the OECD to prepare a progress report on tax transparency and information exchange to the G20 Finance Ministers and Central Bank Governors by early 2018; and the FSB to deliver a stocktaking report to the G20 Finance Ministers and Central Bank Governors by October 2017.

UK Prime Minister David Cameron asserts that

> [l]eaders should commit the G20 to becoming much more structured and transparent in its engagement with other actors in the global system . . . [by] improving the G20's overarching relationship with other actors . . . and facilitating more subject-specific involvement in the G20's work . . . and by welcoming the effective participation of non-members, international institutions and others in its work . . . [when the] interests and views [of those actors] are pertinent to the outcome of particular discussions on a subject.
>
> (UK. PM, 2011, p. 12)

Certain civil society organizations (CSOs) and other groups have expressed reservations about these arrangements; for example, the Center of Concern (2012, p. 2), a US-based Roman Catholic group focused on financial institutions and regulation, notes that such remits to IGOs

> have . . . tremendous potential to determine the behavior of those organizations, to the point of displacing or pre-empting formal channels for decision-making in them . . . [A case in point is that in 2011] the Group [of 20] moved to commission plenty of papers from intergovernmental organizations. The papers competed for the time of staff in the organizations with other tasks given by their own political bodies. In several cases, at least, the papers were not even supposed to receive discussion or clearance in the formal organization to which the staff belonged, before being discussed at the G20.

The relationship of the G20 with IGOs is an indispensable element of global governance. This nexus offers mutual benefits to both types of actors, although it is not without its problems and concerns. The following sections focus on these key IGO interlocutors of the G20: the UN, the IMF, the World Bank, the OECD and the BIS.

The United Nations (UN)

The UN Secretary-General has been present at all G20 summits, supported by his own sherpa. As of 2018, Zhenmin Liu, Under-Secretary-General for economic and social affairs, holds that post.

Secretary-General Ban Ki-moon spoke at the opening working dinner of the first G20 summit, in Washington, DC, on 14 November 2008, about the impact of the financial crisis; he expressed his view that a global stimulus package was needed and voiced his concern that the financial crisis carried a risk of leading to a human crisis. The next day he attended the morning meeting of the leaders. At the end of the summit he welcomed the *Declaration of the Summit on Financial Markets and the World Economy*, emphasizing the leaders' undertakings on coordinating stimulus measures, moving towards inclusive economic governance and avoiding protectionism (UN. DPI, 2008).

Prior to the 2009 London summit, Ban met the UK Foreign Secretary. On the eve of the summit, on 1 April, he attended both a Buckingham Palace reception along with G20 leaders and the subsequent working dinner. In a statement at the end of the summit, he welcomed the leaders' pledge to provide $1.1 trillion in resources to the IMF (UN. DPI, 2009a, 2009c).

Before the 2009 Pittsburgh summit, on 25 September, Ban issued a statement outlining his priorities: assistance to the poorest, including $50 billion pledged in London and continuing stimulus measures; official development assistance, meeting the Gleneagles targets; and economic recovery strategies, including jobs, health, education, infrastructure and food security. He reminded the leaders of the need to deal with the challenge of the absence from the G20 of 85 per cent of countries and a third of the world population, and expressed hope that the G20 will 'see the United Nations as a key partner that can participate fully at all stages of [its] deliberations . . . [including] meetings of finance ministers and sherpas' (UN. DPI, 2009b).

At the 2010 Toronto summit, Ban emphasized the need to invest in jobs and global health, 'to build the global economic recovery from the ground up' and to promote green recovery. He appreciated the leaders' expression of support for the Millennium Development Goals (MDGs) (UN. DPI, 2010c, 2010a). At the 2010 Seoul summit, Ban praised the focus on development and emphasized that '[p]romises made must be promises kept' on funding commitments and accountability, particularly on the MDGs (UN. DPI, 2010b).

Before the Cannes summit, Ban weighed in with an opinion piece in the *International Herald Tribune* (2011), calling on the G20 leaders to show the same ambitious leadership and sense of responsibility that they exhibited at the London summit. He asked for a pro-poor, pro-growth agenda, for remedying inequality and protecting the environment. At the summit itself, he participated in working sessions on 'Growth and Jobs' and on development and trade (UN. DPI, 2011).

In 2012 Ban once again participated in the G20 summit in Los Cabos. He welcomed the summit's *Action Plan for Growth and Jobs* (which includes an Accountability Assessment Framework); called on donor countries to comply with their prior commitments and not to allow austerity to the detriment of poverty reduction; advocated continuing attention to food security and commodity price volatility; and emphasized the synergies of the Rio+20 summit and the G20, particularly on issues of green growth (UN. DPI, 2012). Ban was present at the 2013 St Petersburg summit as well, participating in some of the discussions and addressing the G20 at their working dinner on 5 September. He called on the leaders of the UN Security Council Permanent Five to discharge their responsibilities to find a solution to the Syrian crisis. He also asked the G20 leaders 'to fill the nearly $4.4 billion gap for humanitarian and refugee efforts in Syria and neighbouring countries' (UN News Service, 2013).

At a press conference held on the margins of the 2014 Brisbane summit, Ban remarked, 'G-20 countries possess not only the political power to set us on a better course, but a political responsibility to do so'. Specifically, he stated that '[t]he world looks to the G20 to lead on climate finance', adding that 'the G20 must continue efforts to reform the global financial system, strengthen tax systems, fight corruption and reaffirm their commitment to meeting the target of 0.7 per cent of gross national income for official development assistance' (UN News Service, 2014).

At the 2015 Antalya summit Ban asserted that 'the global response to terrorism needs to be robust, but always within the rule of law and with respect to human rights' (UN Secretary-General, 2015a).

. At a working lunch of leaders on 15 November, he commended the G20 for submitting their climate action plans ahead of the Paris climate conference and urged the leaders 'to look beyond national horizons and work in the common interest' (UN Secretary-General, 2015).

At the 2016 Hangzhou summit (his last as Secretary-General), Ban welcomed the summit's focus on the UN's Sustainable Development Goals (SDGs) and commended 'the outstanding leadership demonstrated by President Xi Jinping of China and President Barack Obama of the United States on officially joining the Paris agreement on climate change' (a stance that was reversed a year later by Obama's successor, Donald Trump) (UN. S-G, 2016). On the eve of the summit, Ban stated that he would engage G20 leaders across the breadth of the agenda.

The 2017 Hamburg summit was the first one for new Secretary-General António Guterres, Ban's successor. He participated in the working lunch on global growth and trade, another working lunch on digitalization, women's empowerment and employment, and in a working session on Partnership with Africa, migration and health (UN. S-G, 2017).

Some observers maintain that the UN relationship with the G7/G8/G20 is competitive or even mutually exclusive. John Kirton (2013c, pp. 10–12) cites some adherents of this school of thought: those who stress 'the failure of the G8 and UN in response to crisis, and assume . . . the advantages of a more representative L20 [leaders' level G20]'; and those who

> suggest . . . that a G20 summit could not only replace the G7/8 but also revitalize an otherwise immobilized UN, or even replace in practice its ineffective central command institutions such as the Security Council's Permanent Five (P5) . . . When in August 2010 French President Nicolas Sarkozy first announced his plans for the sixth G20 summit, which he would host in November 2011, he suggested more modestly that it would be used to reform the UNSC.

The Stanley Foundation (2010b, pp. 2, 17), in contrast, emphasizes that the UN-G20 relationship is more complementary than competitive. The UN's role is both at 'the "front end" and "back end" of the "G-x" process, helping to shape [the latter's] agenda and assisting with follow-through'; it asserts that 'the G-20 has much to offer the United Nations as a policy catalyst. By discussing initiatives and forming an initial consensus, the G-20 can push the UN agenda forward on critical issues'. The UN, in turn, can support G20 initiatives.

Hampson and Heinbecker (2011, pp. 306–307) argue that agreements reached in the G20 between emerging and developed countries can benefit the UN by carrying forward this North-South consensus into UN deliberations. They note that many UN members are apprehensive of the more restrictive G20, but they also recognize that the G20 'is capable of circumventing the UN when disagreements prevent effective action'. They quote Singapore's permanent UN representative, Vanu Gopala Menon, on the desirable dynamics between the UN and the G20: 'We firmly believe that the G-20 process should enhance and not undermine the UN'. One way to promote this objective would be for the UN Secretary-General to attend G20 summits 'as a matter of right, as would the heads of the IMF and . . . the World Bank when economic issues [are] on the agenda'. Yet,

> there is a risk that if the expected benefits of small group dynamics are too slow to materialize in the G-20, it will become more of a mini-UN than a macro-G8. In that case, both the UN and the G-20 as well as the world itself would be the poorer.

Heinbecker (2011b, pp. 237–239) expands on this idea by asserting that 'the UN remains a necessary but not sufficient response to the world's issues. The G20 is a further necessary but not sufficient response. Effective global governance depends considerably on the success of both institutions'. He points out that despite its weaknesses, '[t]he UN retains its unique legitimacy' and 'the UN and its Charter provide the rule book for the conduct of international relations, which all states, including G20 states, see . . . as in their interest to respect'. But the G20 has its own legitimacy because of its early record of dealing with the 2008 financial and economic crisis, and because it represents 85 per cent of the world's GNP, 67 per cent of the world's population and 80 per cent of world trade. Heinbecker describes ways in which the UN and the G20 can help each other and concludes that both entities can succeed better if they co-operate.

The Cameron report (UK. PM, 2011, p. 13), cited earlier, also notes that 'the UN and the G20 play complementary roles in the global system' and offers specific proposals to strengthen this relationship: using 'a variety of channels that provide a steady stream of information and opportunities for productive exchange', including G20 briefings and consultations with UN members; tasking a senior G20 official with oversight of this engagement; and using UN processes, such as informal debates devoted to specific issues.

The relationship with the UN continues to be crucial for the G20. This is shown, for example, in the Hangzhou summit's *G20 Action Plan on the 2030 Agenda for Sustainable Development*, where

> [t]he G20 acknowledges that the global follow-up and review process on the 2030 Agenda is a UN-led process and countries themselves may only be in the preliminary planning stages in 2016. The G20 supports these UN processes and recognizes that the UN High Level Political Forum has a central role in follow-up and review processes at the global level. G20 members will avoid duplicating individual reporting within the UN, in regard to their collective and national actions.
>
> (G20, 2016d, p. 15)

The International Monetary Fund (IMF)

The very first communiqué of the G20 Finance Ministers and Central Bank Governors stated that the group

> was established to provide a new mechanism for informal dialogue in the framework of the Bretton Woods institutional system, to broaden the discussions on key economic and financial policy issues among systemically significant economies and promote co-operation to achieve stable and sustainable world economic growth that benefits all.
>
> (G20, 1999)

The G20 has indeed had a particularly strong relationship with the IMF and the World Bank. Both sides consider this important, beneficial and mutually reinforcing. This connection predates the existence of the G20; the relationship between Finance Ministers and the Bretton Woods institutions predates the G7 itself. The G7, from its earliest days, relied on and called on the IMF on various matters; for example, on the IMF's role in surveillance (the IMF is mandated to oversee the international monetary system and to monitor its member states' financial and economic policies; see www.imf.org/external/about/econsurv.htm).

Reform of the Bretton Woods institutions has long been a concern of the G7, G8 and G20, including quota and governance reform. As these institutions, particularly the IMF, serve as crucial interlocutors, advisors and monitoring agents for the G20, their relationship is a significant test for both the G20 and the IMF. It presents challenges and as yet unsolved dilemmas (Truman, 2012). One proposal to solve the problems of legitimacy, representation and efficiency in both institutions was elaborated by Kharas and Lombardi (2012). Separately, Lombardi (2012, p. 8) argues that 'the G-20 is now the forum for political leaders to discuss critical IMF-related issues'. Payne (2014, p. 82) similarly calls for establishing 'clearly understood lines of influence over the major global economic institutions' (the IMF, the World Bank, the WTO plus a notional new global environmental organization).

The G20 initiative on quota and governance reform is especially important and challenging. This issue already emerged at the 2009 Pittsburgh summit. It became more explicit when the G20 Finance Ministers and Central Bank Governors, at their meeting in Gyeongju, Republic of Korea, on 23 October 2010, called for the doubling of quotas in favour of greater voting weight for emerging-market countries and for an increase in the representation of those countries on the IMF's Executive Board. On 15 December 2010 the IMF Board of Governors approved a package of reforms of quotas and governance. According to the IMF (2017a, p. 2), these reforms represent 'a major realignment of quota shares'. The reform package finally became effective on 26 January 2016, representing the doubling of total quotas and a major realignment of quota shares. China became the third largest IMF member country, and three other emerging-economy countries (Brazil, India and Russia) are now also among the ten largest shareholders in the IMF (the remaining shareholders are the US, Japan, France, Germany, Italy and the UK). As to governance reform, changes have been made in the Executive Board, reducing heavy European representation by two seats. The G20 also called for the next (fifteenth) quota review to be completed by January 2014. In the event, there was a delay: on 5 December 2016 the IMF Board of Governors called on the Executive Board to aim for completing this review by spring (or fall at the latest) of 2019. It remains to be seen whether current major shareholder countries will allow this further reform to take effect.

Bernes (2011, pp. 219–220) recalls that 'the G20 has described itself as the premier forum for international economic co-operation [and states that t]he IMF sees itself as the premier institution for international economic co-operation'; he asks what the difference is 'between the premier forum and the premier institution'. He asserts that before the 2008 financial crisis the future of the IMF came into question, but when the crisis erupted 'the G20 became the coordinating body and . . . provided the intellectual leadership while the IMF largely implemented what it was asked to do'. The IMF subsequently launched initiatives to improve its position. The challenge for the G20 is 'to clarify the role of the IMF and its [the G20's] relationship to it'.

The Managing Director of the IMF has been invited to all G20 summits. He or she also participates in meetings of the G20 Finance Ministers and Central Bank Governors, so that their mutual input proceeds throughout the year. The following have been Managing Directors since the establishment of the G20 at the ministerial level in 1999: Michel Camdessus of France (16 January 1987–14 February 2000), Horst Köhler of Germany (1 May 2000–4 March 2004), Rodrigo de Rato of Spain (7 June 2004–31 October 2007), Dominique Strauss-Kahn of France (1 November 2007–18 May 2011) and Christine Lagarde of France (since 5 July 2011). All are citizens of Western European countries. The IMF sherpa, as of 2018, is Martin Muhleisen.

The G20 has commissioned many IMF reports and studies, including a series of reports for the G20 Mutual Assessment Process (MAP), with the World Bank and other IGOs also playing a role (IMF, 2010a; World Bank, 2010). MAP was launched by the Pittsburgh G20 summit as a crucial component of the *Framework for Strong, Sustainable and Balanced Growth* (G20, 2009c). MAP was envisioned as an essential part of broader G20-IMF cooperation.

Before the Seoul summit, the IMF (2010b) issued a report assessing G20 policies under MAP. Seoul enhanced MAP, calling for indicative guidelines to identify and assess major imbalances in G20 countries, and self-identifying (by G20 members themselves) policy commitments made. In April 2011, G20 Finance Ministers and Central Bank Governors, at their meeting in Washington, DC, accepted a set of indicative guidelines, marking a further advance for MAP (G20, FM&CBG, 2011).

The IMF (in collaboration with the OECD, World Bank, ILO and UNCTAD) prepared several MAP-related analyses and assessments as input for the G20 Action Plan launched at the Cannes summit: an 'umbrella report' that summarizes the component reports and offers a scenario for collective action by the G20; an accountability report on G20 members' progress in implementing policy commitments since the Seoul summit; a MAP report analysing member countries' medium-term macroeconomic and policy frameworks; and sustainability reports for seven G20 countries (China, France, Germany, India, Japan, the UK and the US) (IMF, 2011a). The *Cannes Action Plan for Growth and Jobs* 'draws on the IMF Staff's independent assessments of the root causes of . . . imbalances and recommended policies to address them' (G20, 2011a).

The MAP report prepared for the Los Cabos summit, *Toward Lasting Stability and Growth: Umbrella Report for G-20 Mutual Assessment Process*, assesses the G20's global risks, policies and progress, and provides an 'upside' scenario for the Los Cabos summit. The report asserts that '[t]o attain their growth objectives, G-20 members must effectively manage rising risks, deliver on past commitments, and enact more complete and collective policies'. This calls for effective crisis and risk management, implementing previous commitments and undertaking additional steps for the mutual benefit of all members. Annexes to the *Umbrella Report* deal with global risk analysis and euro area imbalances, and provide 'enhanced accountability assessments' (IMF, 2012d, p. 8) (see also www.imf.org/external/np/g20/map2012.htm, which lists annexes and other information). In 2013, *MAP Policy Templates* for G20 countries were annexed to the *St Petersburg Action Plan* (G20, 2013c, 2013j). The IMF also issued *2013 Update of Staff Sustainability Assessments for G-20 Mutual Assessment Process (MAP)*, focusing on imbalances and growth (IMF, 2013b), and *Imbalances and Growth: Update of Staff Sustainability Assessments for G-20 Mutual Assessment Process* (IMF, 2015). Some examples of other G20-related or commissioned reports follow:

- *Note by the Staff of the International Monetary Fund on Stocktaking of the G-20 Responses to the Global Banking Crisis*. 13–14 March 2009 (IMF, 2009).
- *Supporting the Development of More Effective Tax Systems: A Report to the G-20 Development Working Group by the IMF, OECD, UN and World Bank*. 2011 (IMF, 2011c).
- *Progress Report on the G-20 Data Gaps Initiative: Status, Action Plans, and Timetables*. Prepared by the Staff of the IMF and the FSB Secretariat. September 2012 (IMF, 2012c).

- *Update on Global Prospects and Policy Challenges*. St Petersburg, 5–6 September 2013 (IMF, 2013b).
- *Growth-Friendly Fiscal Policy*. Cairns, Australia, 20–21 September 2014.
- *Time to Act on the G-20 Agenda: The Global Economy Will Thank You*. Blog by Managing Director Christine Lagarde. 2015 (IMF, 2014)
- *Global Prospects and Policy Challenges*. Group of Twenty IMF Surveillance Note: G-20 Finance Ministers and Central Bank Governors' Meetings in Shanghai, China: *IMF Note*. 26–27 February 2016 (IMF, 2016c).
- *G-20 Report on Strong, Sustainable and Balanced Growth*. Prepared by the staff of the IMF with input from the OECD. October 2017 (IMF, 2017b).
- *Technology and the Future of Work*. IMF Staff Note. 11 April 2018.

Not all these studies are purely financial. There is a growing body on other issues, such as trade and investment.

The IMF maintains a web page devoted to its relationship with the G20: www.imf.org/external/np/g20. It includes references to principal documents of G20 summits and Finance Ministers and Central Bank Governors; IMF's own related activities, with links to relevant documents such as the Managing Director's statements to summits; staff reports under the Mutual Assessment Process (see Chapter 8 for details) and pre-summit surveillance notes on global economic prospects.

The World Bank

Like the IMF, the World Bank is in the 'inner circle' of observers at the G20. It provides technical input into G20 processes and deliberations. The President of the World Bank has been invited to all G20 summits, as has also been the case with the Managing Director of the IMF. He is also a regular participant in meetings of the G20 Finance Ministers and Central Bank Governors. The following have filled the post of President since the establishment of the G20 at the ministerial level in 1999: James D. Wolfensohn (June 1995–May 2005), Paul Wolfowitz (June 2005–June 2007) and Robert B. Zoellick (July 2007–June 2012). Jim Yong Kim assumed Presidency in July 2012. All are United States citizens.

Nancy Alexander (2017) takes an astute view of the G20 relationship with the Bretton Woods institutions. She notes, 'The individual G20 member countries hold the overwhelming majority of votes at the IMF and World Bank, so it is not surprising that G20 priorities are often identical to those of the institutions they dominate'. She cites, as an example, infrastructure financing: the 2014 Brisbane G20 summit launched the G20 Global Infrastructure Hub; in the same year the World Bank launched the Global Infrastructure Facility. Further, '[w]hile the World Bank is tasked with expanding private investment in infrastructure, the IMF's Infrastructure Policy Support Initiative provides tools to help countries assess the macroeconomic and financial implications of various investment programs and improve their institutional capacity'. On another issue, 'The G20 will measure the performance of each MDB [multilateral development bank] by the extent to which it leverages private investment and, in turn, the MDBs will measure the performance of many countries by how effectively they leverage private investment' (Alexander, 2017).

The World Bank supports the G20 on various issues within its expertise, often in joint undertakings with the IMF and other IGOs. The following are some examples of World Bank reports prepared for the G20:

- World Bank Group (2011). *Mobilizing Climate Finance: A Paper Prepared at the Request of G20 Finance Ministers*. Coordinated by the World Bank Group, the IMF, the OECD and the regional development banks; and background papers:
    1. IMF, *Promising Domestic Fiscal Instruments for Climate Finance*;
    2. IMF, *Market-Based Instruments for International Aviation and Shipping as a Source of Climate Finance*;
    3. OECD, *Fossilfuel Support*;
    4. Shilpa Patel, *Climate Finance: Engaging the Private Sector*;
    5. Philippe Ambrosi, *How to Keep Momentum Up in Carbon Markets?*;
    6. World Bank Group, *The Scope for MDB Leverage and Innovation.*
- World Bank (2012d). *Restoring and Sustaining Growth, Prepared by World Bank Staff for the G20 Framework for Strong, Sustainable and Balanced Growth.*
- World Bank (2012a). *Boosting Jobs and Living Standards in G20 Countries: A Joint Report by the ILO, OECD, IMF and the World Bank.*
- World Bank (2013). *Press Statement from Dr Jim Yong Kim, President of the World Bank Group, at the End of Group of 20 Summit in St Petersburg, Russia.*
- *G20 Labour Markets: Outlook, Key Challenges and Policy Responses*. Report Prepared by ILO, OECD and the World Bank Group (2014).
- World Bank (2014). *Report on the Remittance Agenda of the G20*. Prepared for the G20 Australian presidency.
- World Bank (2015). *Addressing Rising Inequality in G20 Economies*. Let's Talk Development. Blog by Zia Qureshi (2015), 11 June.
- *Towards a G20 Strategy for Promoting Inclusive Global Value Chains*. Prepared by the OECD, WBG and the International Trade Centre for submission to the G20 Trade Ministers Meeting, Shanghai, China, 9–10 July 2016.
- *New World Bank Group Facility to Enable More than $1 Billion for Women Entrepreneurship*. Press release, 8 July 2017.
- *Cross-Border Spillover Effects of the G20 Financial Regulatory Reforms: Results from a Pilot Survey*. Policy Research Working Paper No. 8300. 2018.

As well, the Bank co-organized several G20 conferences and seminars – for example:

- Korea – World Bank High-Level Conference on Post-Crisis Growth and Development, 11 June 2010;

- G20 Commodities Seminar jointly with the Mexican government on 5–6 May 2012 in Los Cabos;
- International Conference 'Comprehensive Approach to Social Protection and Food Security for Sustainable Development', 21–22 October 2013, hosted jointly with the Russian G20 presidency;
- International SME Conference: Leveraging Islamic Finance for SMEs, Istanbul 23–24 October 2015, hosted jointly with the G20 Turkish presidency, Islamic Development Bank and TUMSIAD (All Industrialists and Businessmen Association).

The Development Research Group of the World Bank has created a public database, 'Global Financial Inclusion Indicators', with the help of an $11 million, ten-year grant from the Bill and Melinda Gates Foundation. The database, also called *Global Findex*, documents 'financial access across gender, age, geographic regions, national income levels and other indicators'. The Bank envisaged it as 'an important annual indicator for the G20 Financial Inclusion Experts Group' (World Bank, 2012b). It is characterized as 'the world's most comprehensive database on financial inclusion'. Data are collected 'in partnership with the Gallup World Poll and funded by the Bill and Melinda Gates Foundation' (World Bank Group, 2015).

Two new financial institutions

Two important new financial institutions emerged in 2016, the year of China's G20 Presidency: the New Development Bank (NDB) and the Asian Infrastructure Investment Bank (AIIB). This reflects China's increasing economic clout as well as a BRICS response to the slow and inadequate progress of reform of the Bretton Woods institutions. The AIIB is a Chinese initiative and the NDB has been established by BRICS. The Hangzhou summit's *G20 Action Plan on the 2030 Agenda for Sustainable Development* states, 'China will . . . promote the Asian Infrastructure Investment Bank and the New Development Bank and other institutions to play greater roles with a view to making contribution to global development' (G20, 2016d, p. 24). At present, the IMF does not regard these two institutions as competition. However, Alexander (2017) argues that if the World Bank's 'Maximizing Finance for Development' approach which 'would create greater reliance on commercial financing and reduce the need for World Bank lending to governments . . . [were to be] implemented, the World Bank could shrink as the Asian Infrastructure Investment Bank (and others) expand'. It should be noted that the G20 also maintains relations with the regional development banks: the African Development Bank (AfDB), Asian Development Bank (ADB), European Bank for Reconstruction and Development (EBRD) and Inter-American Development Bank (IDB).

The Organisation for Economic Co-operation and Development (OECD)

The OECD has participated in all G20 summits since they began in 2008, represented by the Secretary-General. The organization is also regularly represented at the G20 Finance Ministers' and Central Bank Governors' meetings and in several G20 working groups. Since the Pittsburgh summit, OECD has had its own sherpa (as of 2017, it is Gabriela Ramos, Special Counsellor to the Secretary-General, Chief of Staff), assisted by a finance deputy. The report (OECD, 2011a) *Beating the Crisis: The Role of the OECD and G20* describes the complementary role of the two entities in responding to the 2007–2008 economic and financial crisis.

OECD offers free use of premises and other facilities to G20 working groups and other sub-summit entities. Some consider the OECD a quasi-secretariat for the G20 – which lacks one – but this is not supported widely, particularly by those G20 countries that are not OECD members (by contrast, all G7 members are also in the OECD). So, OECD is not appropriate as a potential G20 secretariat. Yet, there is some merit in the assertion that OECD acts as a quasi-secretariat on certain G20 issues within its competence, as do some other IGOs in their appropriate sectors.

The OECD has supported the G20's work on a whole spectrum of issues, often in collaboration with the IMF, World Bank, FAO, ILO and other relevant IGOs: on growth and jobs; social responses to economic challenges; financial regulation; taxation; international financial system reform; fight against corruption; agriculture, price volatility and food security; development; and fossil fuel subsidies (OECD, 2018). On all such issues, the G20 regularly commissions OECD reports and policy recommendations. In fact,

> OECD's expertise . . . [is] increasingly recognized and relied upon for identifying the world's most pressing policy challenges and finding way to address them . . . [T]he OECD has broadened it support and become a recognised partner of the [G20].
>
> (OECD, 2017a)

The Hamburg *G20 Leaders' Declaration* singles out as notable the report *Investing in Climate, Investing in Growth* (cited ahead).

The following OECD reports were prepared for the Hamburg summit (some jointly with other IGOs – a trend particularly in recent years):

- *The Next Production Revolution: A Report for the G20.* Prepared at the request of the G20 New Industrial Revolution Task Force by the OECD with input from the United Nations Conference on Trade and Development (UNCTAD) and the United Nations Industrial Development Organisation (UNIDO). 2017 (OECD, 2017f).
- *G20 Global Displacement and Migration Trends Report 2017* (OECD, 2017c).
- *Integrity in Customs: Taking Stock of Good Practices*. Prepared at the request of the G20 Anti-Corruption Working Group (OECD, 2017d).
- OECD. Secretary-General (2017). [Tax] *Report to G20 Leaders*. Hamburg, July 9 (OECD, 2017b).
- *A Policy Framework to Help Guide the G20 in Its Development of Policy Options to Foster More Inclusive Growth.* Prepared by the OECD and the World Bank Group. July 2017 (OECD, 2017g).

- OECD and International Monetary Fund (2017). *Quantifying the Implementation and Impact of G-20 Members' Growth Strategies.* 2017 (OECD, 2017).
- *Compendium of Good Practices on the Publication and Reuse of Open Data for Anti-corruption across G20 Countries: Towards Data-Driven Public Sector Integrity and Civic Auditing.* 2017 (OECD, 2017b).
- *Investing in Climate, Investing in Growth.* Produced in the context of the German G20 Presidency. June 2017 (OECD, 2017e).

The OECD devotes a dedicated web page, www.oecd.org/g20, to its relations with, and work for, the G20. The page includes a brief history of OECD-G20 relations as well as links to major recent reports that the organization prepared for the G20, related other reports, speeches and articles, and further information.

Bank for International Settlements (BIS)

The mission of BIS is 'to serve central banks in their pursuit of monetary and financial stability, to foster international cooperation in those areas and to act as a bank for central banks' (BIS, 2012). The Basel Committee of BIS 'provides a forum for regular cooperation on banking supervisory matters . . . [in order] to enhance understanding of key supervisory issues and improve the quality of banking supervision worldwide'. It engages in information exchange on such issues and develops guidelines, principles and standards (BIS. BCBS, 2012a).

Basel III, the committee's important initiative, is an international framework for liquidity risk measurement, standards and monitoring. It sets out rules for 'global regulatory standards on bank capital adequacy and liquidity . . . [Its aim is] to protect financial stability and promote sustainable economic growth' (BIS. BCBS, 2010). Basel III was released in response to the Pittsburgh G20 summit; the G20 leaders endorsed it in Seoul. The Cannes summit called for timely and full implementation of Basel III; the Basel Committee submitted an interim report on Basel III implementation to the G20 leaders in time for their Los Cabos summit (BIS. BCBS, 2012c). Later in 2012, the Basel Committee released its new report to the G20 Finance Ministers (BIS. BCBS, 2012b). In 2013 the Basel Committee issued its latest *Progress Report on Implementation of the Basel Regulatory Framework* (BIS. BCBS, 2013), followed by additional annual progress reports, the latest one for 2017. These are all accessible on the committee's web page at www.bis.org/bcbs/publications.htm.

A fair amount of the work of BIS and the Basel Committee has been taken over by the Financial Stability Board, an entity which is part of the G20 system. The FSB is discussed in Chapter 3.

Conclusion

This review of the relationship of the G20 with international governmental organizations leads to the conclusion that the nexus is necessary and is of strong mutual benefit to both classes of actors. Collaboration has been well established as G20 practice. Certain IGOs, in particular the Bretton Woods institutions, enjoy a privileged relationship with the G20 as participant observers at summits, ministerial meetings and task forces. These and other IGOs (especially the UN, OECD, BIS and the Basel Committee) provide analysis, policy proposals, performance evaluation and, arguably, greater legitimacy to the G20. The G20 values their contributions but it cannot direct their work; only their own shareholders or constituents can. These IGOs, most of all the UN, can make the universal voice of the unrepresented heard in the G20. On the other hand, the G20, when it is able to reach consensus, supplies the political impetus on the highest level that facilitates progress in IGOs. The G20 has approved new resources, for example, to the IMF. Mutual information-sharing has aided process and progress in both the G20 and the IGOs. OECD, IMF, the World Bank and other IGOs' reports and studies have filled the capacity gap of the G20, which lacks its own secretariat.

References

Alexander, N. 2017. *IMF and World Bank: Marching to a G20 Tune?* 24 October. us.boell.org/2017/10/24/imf-and-world-bank-marching-g20-tune [Accessed: 15 December 2017].

Ban, K.-M., 2011. The clock is ticking. *International Herald Tribune*, 1 November.

Bank for International Settlements, 2012. *About BIS*. www.bis.org/about/index.htm [Accessed: 19 January 2018].

Bank for International Settlements. Basel Committee on Banking Supervision, 2010. *Basel III: International Framework for Liquidity Risk Measurement, Standards and Monitoring*. December. www.bis.org/publ/bcbs188.htm [Accessed: 19 January 2018].

Bank for International Settlements. Basel Committee on Banking Supervision, 2012a. *About the Basel Committee*. www.bis.org/bcbs/about.htm [Accessed: 19 January 2018].

Bank for International Settlements. Basel Committee on Banking Supervision, 2012b. *Report to G20 Finance Ministers and Central Bank Governors on Basel III Implementation*. October. www.bis.org/publ/bcbs234.pdf [Accessed: 19 January 2018].

Bank for International Settlements. Basel Committee on Banking Supervision, 2012c. *Report to G20 Leaders on Basel III Implementation*. June. www.bis.org/publ/bcbs220.pdf [Accessed: 19 January 2018].

Bank for International Settlements. Basel Committee on Banking Supervision, 2013. *Progress Report on Implementation of the Basel Regulatory Framework*. www.bis.org/publ/bcbs247.pdf [Accessed: 18 January 2018].

Bernes, T.A., 2011. IMF legitimacy and governance reform: Will the G20 help or hinder? In: C.I. Bradford and W.H. Lim, eds. *Global Leadership in Transition: Making the G20 More Effective and Responsive*. Washington, DC: Brookings Institution Press with Korean Development Institute. pp. 219–223.

Carin, B., 2011b. *No Fairy Tale at the Cannes G20 Summit*. Waterloo, Canada: Centre for International Governance Innovation. 7 November. www.cigionline.org/publications/no-fairy-tale-cannes-g20-summit [Accessed: 16 January 2018].

Center of Concern, 2012. A bottom-up approach to righting financial regulation. *The Group of 20, Financial Regulation and Human Rights*, (4). www.cesr.org/sites/default/files/G20_and_Financial_Regulation_0.pdf [Accessed: 23 November 2018].

G20, 1999. *Communiqué of G-20 Finance Ministers and Central Bank Governors: Berlin, Germany*. 15–16 December. www.g20.utoronto.ca/1999/1999communiqué.pdf [Accessed: 18 January 2018].

G20, 2009c. *Leaders Statement: The Pittsburgh Summit*; and Annexes: *Core Values for Sustainable Economic Activity; G20 Framework for Strong, Sustainable, and Balanced Growth*. 25 September. www.g20.utoronto.ca/2009/2009communiqué0925.html [Accessed: 24 October 2017].

G20, 2011a. *The Cannes Action Plan for Growth and Jobs*. 4 November. www.g20.utoronto.ca/2011/2011-cannes-action-111104-en.html [Accessed: 24 October 2017].

G20, 2013c. *Annex 3: MAP Policy Templates for all G20 Countries*. en.g20russia.ru/load/783046978 and www.g20.utoronto.ca/2013/Annex_3_MAP_Policy_Commitments_by_Members_September_5.pdf [Accessed: 28 November 2017].

G20, 2013j. *St. Petersburg Action Plan*. September. www.g20.utoronto.ca/2013/St_Petersburg_Action_Plan.pdf [Accessed: 8 September 2017].

G20, 2016d. *G20 Action Plan on the 2030 Agenda for Sustainable Development*. 8 September. www.g20.utoronto.ca/2016/g20-action-plan-on-2030-agenda.pdf [Accessed: 5 February 2017].

G20, 2017f. *G20 Hamburg Action Plan*. 8 July. www.g20.utoronto.ca/2017/2017-g20-hamburg-action-plan-en.pdf [Accessed: 17 October 2017].

G20, 2017g. *G20 Leaders' Declaration*. 8 July. www.g20.utoronto.ca/2017/2017-G20-leaders-declaration.html [Accessed: 4 October 2017].

G20 Finance Ministers and Central Bank Governors, 2011. *Communiqué [of the] Meeting, Washington, DC*. 14–15 April. www.g20.utoronto.ca/2011/2011-finance-110415-en.html [Accessed: 18 January 2018].

Hampson, F.O. and Heinbecker, P., 2011. The 'new' multilateralism of the twenty-first century. *Global Governance: A Review of Multilateralism and International Organizations*, 17(3), pp. 299–310.

Heinbecker, P., 2011b. The United Nations and the G20: Synergy or dissonance? In: C.I. Bradford and W.H. Lim, eds. *Global Leadership in Transition: Making the G20 More Effective and Responsive*. Washington, DC: Brookings Institution Press with Korean Development Institute. pp. 236–245.

International Monetary Fund, 2009. *Note by the Staff of the International Monetary Fund on Stocktaking of the G-20 Responses to the Global Banking Crisis*. 13–14 March. www.imf.org/external/np/g20/pdf/031909b.pdf [Accessed: 15 November 2017].

International Monetary Fund, 2010a. *G-20 Mutual Assessment Process: Alternative Policy Scenarios*. www.imf.org/external/np/g20/pdf/062710a.pdf [Accessed: 18 January 2018].

International Monetary Fund, 2010b. *G-20 Mutual Assessment Process: IMF Staff Assessment of G-20 Policies*. www.imf.org/external/np/g20/pdf/111210.pdf [Accessed: 18 January 2018].

International Monetary Fund, 2011a. *G-20 Mutual Assessment Process: From Pittsburgh to Cannes: IMF Umbrella Report*. IMF Staff Reports for the G-20 Mutual Assessment Process. www.imf.org/external/np/g20/pdf/110411.pdf [Accessed: 24 October 2017].

International Monetary Fund, 2011c. *Supporting the Development of More Effective Tax Systems: A Report to the G-20 Development Working Group by the IMF, OECD, UN and World Bank*. www.imf.org/external/np/g20/pdf/110311.pdf [Accessed: 15 November 2017].

International Monetary Fund, 2012c. *Progress Report on the G-20 Data Gaps Initiative: Status, Action Plans, and Timetables*. Prepared by the Staff of the IMF and the FSB Secretariat. September. www.imf.org/external/np/g20/pdf/093012.pdf [Accessed: 15 November 2017].

International Monetary Fund, 2012d. *Toward Lasting Stability and Growth: Umbrella Report for G-20 Mutual Assessment Process*. www.imf.org/external/np/g20/pdf/map2012/umbrella.pdf [Accessed: 24 October 2017].

International Monetary Fund, 2013b. *Update on Global Prospects and Policy Challenges*. St. Petersburg. 5–6 September. www.imf.org/external/np/g20/pdf/2013/090513.pdf [Accessed: 15 November 2017].

International Monetary Fund, 2014. *Growth-Friendly Fiscal Policy*. Cairns, Australia. 20–21 September. www.imf.org/external/np/g20/pdf/2014/fiscpolnote.pdf [Accessed: 15 November 2017].

International Monetary Fund, 2015. *Imbalances and Growth: Update of Staff Sustainability Assessments for G-20 Mutual Assessment Process*. October. www.imf.org/external/np/g20/pdf/map2015/map2015.pdf [Accessed: 14 November 2017].

International Monetary Fund, 2016c. *Global Prospects and Policy Challenges: G-20 Finance Ministers and Central Bank Governors' Meetings*. 26–27 February. www.imf.org/external/np/g20/pdf/2016/022616.pdf [Accessed: 15 November 2017].

International Monetary Fund, 2017a. *Factsheet: IMF Quotas*. 13 October. www.imf.org/About/Factsheets/Sheets/2016/07/14/12/21/IMF-Quotas?pdf=1 [Accessed: 19 January 2018].

International Monetary Fund, 2017b. *G-20 Report on Strong, Sustainable and Balanced Growth: IMF Annual Meetings*. Prepared with input from the OECD. October. www.imf.org/external/np/g20/pdf/2017/100617.pdf [Accessed: 15 November 2017].

Kharas, H. and Lombardi, D., 2012. *The Group of Twenty: Origins, Prospects and Challenges for Global Governance*. Global Economy and Development. Washington, DC: Brookings Institution. www.brookings.edu/wp-content/uploads/2016/06/g20-global-governance-kharas-lombardi.pdf [Accessed: 30 January 2018].

Kirton, J.J., 2013c. Introduction. In: J.J. Kirton, ed. *G20 Governance for a Globalized World*. Farnham: Ashgate. pp. 3–26.

Lagarde, C., 2015. Time to act on the G-20 agenda: The global economy will thank you. *IMFBlog*. 6 February. blogs.imf.org/2015/02/06/time-to-act-on-the-g-20-agenda-the-global-economy-will-thank-you/ [Accessed: 30 January 2018].

Lombardi, D., 2012. The G-20, the IMF and the European debt crisis. In: *The G-20 Los Cabos Summit 2012: Bolstering the World Economy amid Growing Fears of Recession*. Washington, DC: Brookings Institution. pp. 7–8. www.brookings.edu/~/media/research/files/reports/2012/6/g20/g20_lombardi.pdf [Accessed: 18 January 2018].

Organisation for Economic Co-operation and Development, 2011a. *Beating the Crisis: The Role of the OECD and G20*. www.oecd.org/document/0/0,3746,en_2649_201185_48964973_1_1_1_1,00.html [Accessed: 19 January 2018].

Organisation for Economic Co-operation and Development, 2012a. *Boosting Jobs and Living Standards in G20 Countries: A Joint Report by the ILO, OECD, IMF and the World Bank*. June. www.oecd.org/eco/productivityandlongtermgrowth/Boosting%20jobs%20and%20living%20standards%20in%20G20%20countries.pdf [Accessed: 18 January 2018].

Organisation for Economic Co-operation and Development, 2014. *G20 Labour Markets: Outlook, Key Challenges and Policy Responses*. Report Prepared by ILO, OECD and the World Bank Group. www.oecd.org/g20/topics/employment-and-social-policy/G20-labour-markets-outlook-key-challenges-and-policy-responses.pdf [Accessed: 10 November 2017].

Organisation for Economic Co-operation and Development, 2017a. *2017 G20 Hamburg Summit: OECD's Contributions*. Hamburg. 7–8 July. www.oecd.org/g20/ [Accessed: 21 November 2017].

Organisation for Economic Co-operation and Development, 2017b. *Compendium of Good Practices on the Publication and Reuse of Open Data for Anti-Corruption across G20*

Countries: Towards Data-Driven Public Sector Integrity and Civic Auditing. www.oecd.org/gov/digital-government/g20-oecd-compendium.pdf [Accessed: 11 November 2017].

Organisation for Economic Co-operation and Development, 2017c. *G20 Global Displacement and Migration Trends Report 2017*. www.oecd.org/g20/summits/hamburg/G20-OECD-migration.pdf [Accessed: 11 November 2017].

Organisation for Economic Co-operation and Development, 2017d. *Integrity in Customs: Taking Stock of Good Practices*. Prepared at the request of the G20 Anti-Corruption Working Group. www.oecd.org/gov/ethics/G20-integrity-in-customs-taking-stock-of-good-practices.pdf [Accessed: 11 November 2017].

Organisation for Economic Co-operation and Development, 2017e. *Investing in Climate, Investing in Growth*. Produced in the context of the German G20 presidency. June. www.oecd.org/environment/cc/g20-climate/synthesis-investing-in-climate-investing-in-growth.pdf [Accessed: 21 November 2017].

Organisation for Economic Co-operation and Development, 2017f. *The Next Production Revolution: A Report for the G20*. Prepared at the request of the G20 New Industrial Revolution Task Force by the OECD with input from the United Nations Conference on Trade and Development (UNCTAD) and the United Nations Industrial Development Organisation (UNIDO). www.oecd.org/g20/summits/hamburg/the-next-production-revolution-G20-report.pdf [Accessed: 11 November 2017].

Organisation for Economic Co-operation and Development, 2017g. *A Policy Framework to Help Guide the G20 in Its Development of Policy Options to Foster More Inclusive Growth*. Prepared by the OECD and the World Bank Group. July. www.oecd.org/g20/summits/hamburg/OECD-WBG-Policy-Framework-to-help-Gguide-the-G20-in-its-development.pdf [Accessed: 11 November 2017].

Organisation for Economic Co-operation and Development, 2018. *OECD and the G20: About*. www.oecd.org/g20/about.htm [Accessed: 31 January 2018].

Organisation for Economic Co-operation and Development. Secretary-General, 2017b. *Report to G20 Leaders*. Hamburg. July. www.oecd.org/g20/summits/hamburg/oecd-secretary-general-tax-report-g20-leaders-july-2017.pdf [Accessed: 11 November 2017].

Organisation for Economic Co-operation and Development and International Monetary Fund, 2017. *Quantifying the Implementation and Impact of G-20 Members' Growth Strategies*. www.oecd.org/g20/summits/hamburg/Quantifying-the-Implementation-of-Growth-Strategies-2017.pdf [Accessed: 11 November 2017].

Payne, A., 2014. Steering into the great uncertainty: The G20 as global governance. *Caribbean Journal of International Relations & Diplomacy*, 2(3), pp. 73–85.

Qureshi, Z., 2015. Addressing rising inequality in G20 economies. *Let's Talk Development Blog*. 11 June. blogs.worldbank.org/developmenttalk/addressing-rising-inequality-g20-economies [Accessed: 18 January 2018

Stanley Foundation, 2010b. *The United Nations and the G-20: Ensuring Complementary Efforts*. 41st United Nations Issues Conference. Tarrytown, NY. 26–28 March. www.stanleyfoundation.org/publications/report/Issues2010.pdf [Accessed: 16 January 2018].

Stern, N., 2007. *The Economics of Climate Change: The Stern Review*. Cambridge: Cambridge University Press.

Truman, E.M., 2012. The G-20 is failing. *Foreign Policy*, 12 April. foreignpolicy.com/2012/04/12/the-g-20-is-failing/ [Accessed: 30 January 2018].

United Kingdom. Prime Minister, 2011. *Governance for Growth: Building Consensus for the Future*. November. webarchive.nationalarchives.gov.uk/20130109092234/www.number10.gov.uk/wp-content/uploads/2011/11/GovernanceForGrowth_acc.pdf [Accessed: 26 September 2017].

United Nations. Department of Public Information, 2008. *Activities of the Secretary-General in Washington, DC*. 14–15 November. (SG/T/2633). www.un.org/News/Press/docs/2008/sgt2633.doc.htm [Accessed: 15 January 2018].

United Nations. Department of Public Information, 2009a. *Activities of the Secretary-General in United Kingdom*. 1–3 April. (SG/T/2665). www.un.org/News/Press/docs/2009/sgt2665.doc.htm [Accessed: 16 January 2018].

United Nations. Department of Public Information, 2009b. *Premature Exit from Stimulus Efforts Could Put Global Recovery at Risk, Secretary-General Warns in Remarks to G-20 Summit*. 25 September. (SG/SM/12491-ECO/171). www.un.org/News/Press/docs/2009/sgsm12491.doc.htm [Accessed: 16 January 2018].

United Nations. Department of Public Information, 2009c. *Secretary-General Welcomes Pledge of G-20 Leaders to $1.1 Trillion Aid Package*. (SG/SM/12165-ECO/148). www.un.org/News/Press/docs/2009/sgsm12165.doc.htm [Accessed: 16 January 2018].

United Nations. Department of Public Information, 2010a. *Daily Press Briefing by the Office of the Spokesperson for the Secretary-General*. 24 June. www.un.org/press/en/2010/db100624.doc.htm [Accessed: 16 January 2018].

United Nations. Department of Public Information, 2010b. *In Seoul, Secretary-General Says Development Not Side Issue: 'Investing in Development Is Investing in Everyone's Recovery'*. 12 November. (SG/SM/13244-DEV/2848). www.un.org/News/Press/docs/2010/sgsm13244.doc.htm [Accessed: 16 January 2018].

United Nations. Department of Public Information, 2010c. *Secretary-General, in Remarks to Economic and Social Council, Reports Uneven Progress on Millennium Development Goals*. 28 June. (SG/SM/12977-ECOSOC/6431). www.un.org/News/Press/docs/2010/sgsm12977.doc.htm [Accessed: 16 January 2018].

United Nations. Department of Public Information, 2011. *Daily Press Briefing by the Office of the Spokesperson for the Secretary-General*. 3 November. www.un.org/press/en/2011/db111103.doc.htm [Accessed: 16 January 2018].

United Nations. Department of Public Information, 2012. *Secretary-General Outlines Messages He Took to G-20 Summit in Los Cabos, Introduces Mexico's Vice-Minister to Brief General Assembly in Detail*. 31 July. (SG/SM/14438-GA/11265). www.un.org/News/Press/docs/2012/sgsm14438.doc.htm [Accessed: 16 January 2018].

United Nations News Service, 2013. *At G20 Summit, Ban, UN-Arab League Envoy Push for Political Solution to Syria Crisis*. 5 September. www.un.org/apps/news/story.asp?NewsID=45780&Cr=syria&Cr1=g20#.UnUiORBcyBZ [Accessed: 16 January 2018].

United Nations News Service, 2014. *G-20 Countries Have Political Responsibility to Tackle World's Greatest Challenges: Ban*. 15 November. www.un.org/apps/news/story.asp?NewsID=49348#.WgHs1IhOk2w [Accessed: 7 November 2017].

United Nations. Secretary-General, 2015. *Secretary-General's Remarks at G20 Working Lunch on Development and Climate Change*. 15 November. www.un.org/sg/statements/index.asp?nid=9247 [Accessed: 7 November 2017].

United Nations. Secretary-General, 2015a. *Secretary-General's Press Conference at G20 Summit in Turkey*. 15 November. https://www.un.org/sg/en/content/sg/press-encounter/2015-11-15/secretary-general%E2%80%99s-press-conference-g20-summit-turkey-qa [Accessed: 21 November 2018].

United Nations. Secretary-General, 2016. *Opening Remarks at Press Conference at G20 Summit in China*. 4 September. www.un.org/sg/en/content/sg/speeches/2016-09-04/opening-remarks-press-conference-g20-summit-china [Accessed: 7 November 2017].

United Nations. Secretary-General, 2017. *Activities of Secretary-General in Germany, 7–8 July*. 13 July. (SG/T/3183). www.un.org/press/en/2017/sgt3183.doc.htm [Accessed: 7 November 2017].

World Bank, 2010. *G20 and Global Development: Report Prepared by Staff of the World Bank for G20 Growth Framework and Mutual Assessment Process*. siteresources.worldbank.org/DEC/Resources/G20Framework&MAP-WBReport-TorontoSummit-2.pdf [Accessed: 18 January 2018].

World Bank, 2012a. *G20 Commodities Seminar: Summary*. Los Cabos, Mexico, 5–6 May. G20russia.ru/load/780990537 [Accessed: 21 August 2018].

World Bank, 2012b. *Measuring Financial Inclusion: The Global Financial Inclusion Indicators (GFII)*. go.worldbank.org/MXB6HOJ5U0 [Accessed: 18 January 2018].

World Bank, 2012d. *Restoring and Sustaining Growth*. 8 June. siteresources.worldbank.org/DEC/Resources/84797–1320153303397/World_Bank_Repor_for_G20_Framework_June_8_2012.pdf [Accessed: 30 January 2018].

World Bank, 2014. *Report on the Remittance Agenda of the G20*. Prepared for the G20 Australian Presidency. siteresources.worldbank.org/EXTFINANCIALSECTOR/Resources/282884–1400093105293/GPFI_Remittances_Report_Final072014.pdf [Accessed: 10 November 2017].

World Bank, 2016. *Towards a G20 Strategy for Promoting Inclusive Global Value Chains*. Prepared by the OECD, WBG, and the International Trade Centre for submission to the G20 Trade Ministers Meeting, Shanghai, China, 9–10 July. documents.worldbank.org/curated/en/736471473258884274/pdf/108169-WP.pdf [Accessed: 10 November 2017].

World Bank, 2017. *New World Bank Group Facility to Enable More Than $1 Billion for Women Entrepreneurship*. 8 July. www.worldbank.org/en/news/press-release/2017/07/08/new-world-bank-group-facility-to-enable-more-than-1-billion-for-women-entrepreneurship [Accessed: 10 November 2017].

World Bank Group, 2011. *Mobilizing Climate Finance: A Paper Prepared at the Request of G20 Finance Ministers*. 6 October. www.imf.org/external/np/g20/pdf/110411c.pdf [Accessed: 30 January 2018].

World Bank Group, 2015. *Global Findex: Measuring Financial Inclusion around the World*. www.worldbank.org/en/programs/globalfindex [Accessed: 17 November 2017].

5 Relations with the business sector

This chapter discusses the relationship of the G20 with the business sector – of crucial importance to both parties. It then reviews the following special groups and fora: the World Economic Forum (WEF), the International Chamber of Commerce (ICC), the Business 20 or 'Business Summit' (B20), the Young Entrepreneurs' Summit and private philanthropies.

The business community is more closely related to the G20 than to the G7/G8. As discussed in Chapter 6, inclusion of the business sector under the broad umbrella of civil society is problematic, and even misplaced. The interests, *modus operandi* and influence of business are fundamentally different from those of civil society organizations (CSOs). G7/G8 and G20 officials have distinguished between business players and non-profit CSOs, as has the business sector itself. The intensity of the business-G20 relationship far exceeds that between G20 government officials and non-profit CSOs (Alexander, 2012; email to author, 30 July).

The World Economic Forum (WEF)

G8/G20 connections with the WEF go back a number of years; for example, in 2005, UK Prime Minister Tony Blair chose this exclusive annual business gathering in Davos, Switzerland, to flesh out his agenda for the Gleneagles G8 summit that year. With some exceptions (e.g., Russian President Vladimir Putin in 2006), this has become an annual tradition, now embracing both the G7/G8 and G20 summits. The G20-WEF relationship also extends to WEF regional meetings, such as the one held in Puerto Vallarta, Mexico, in April 2012, where Mexican President Felipe Calderón Hinojosa received the recommendations of the task forces of the B20 (B20, 2012b).

In his keynote address to the WEF on 28 January 2010, South Korean then-President Lee Myung-bak announced that development would be his country's priority for the Seoul G20 summit. That summit not only delivered on his promise but also included certain aspects of climate change in its final agenda (WEF, 2010). Canada's then-Prime Minister, Stephen Harper, Chair of the June 2010 G8 and G20 summits, also spoke at Davos to the WEF on 28 January about his priorities (Canada PMO, 2010). On 27 January 2011, then-President Nicolas Sarkozy

DOI: 10.4324/9781351266802-6

of France fleshed out his vision for the Cannes G20 summit for the WEF. Mexican President Felipe Calderón Hinojosa (2012a), host of the 2012 Los Cabos G20 summit, gave his keynote address to the 2012 annual meeting of WEF with the title *Global Economic Crisis: Role and Challenges of the G20*. At WEF's 2013 annual meeting, it was Russian Prime Minister Dmitry Medvedev, rather than President Putin, who represented his country, the host of the year's G20 summit. He addressed WEF on 23 January (Russia. PM, 2013).

Continuing this tradition, Australian Prime Minister Tony Abbott, holder of the G20 Presidency in 2014, outlined Australia's priorities for the Brisbane summit at the World Economic Forum held in January that year (Australia PM, 2014). Similarly, Turkish Prime Minister Ahmet Davutoglu presented Turkey's vision for its 2015 G20 summit (Turkey PM, 2014). Chinese leader Xi Jinping did not attend the 2016 annual meeting of WEF but on 17 January 2017, only a few months after his year of G20 Presidency ended, he addressed, in a keynote speech at the opening plenary meeting, the advances and problems of economic globalization and global governance; he also discussed the achievements of the 2016 Hangzhou summit (WEF, 2017). German Chancellor Angela Merkel, host leader of the 2017 G20 summit, did not attend WEF in 2017.

The WEF has discussed several issues of importance to the G20. This is reflected not only in speeches by G20 leaders but also in publications – for example, the report *Euro, Dollar, Yuan Uncertainties: Scenarios on the Future of the International Monetary System* (WEF, 2012a). A WEF blog reported that on 18 June 2012 President Calderón welcomed the initiative of the B20 Task Force on Green Growth to launch the Green Growth Action Alliance (G2A2) as

> a unique public-private partnership among over 40 energy companies, banks and development finance institutions which will work in close collaboration with the G20 and other governments to develop breakthrough financing models for green growth and target public money to leverage larger private sector investments into green infrastructure projects.
>
> (WEF, 2012b)

This is explored in more detail in the B20 section ahead.

The International Chamber of Commerce (ICC)

Another important actor in G7/G8-G20 relations with the business sector is the International Chamber of Commerce, a major business interest group. ICC's connections with the G7/G8 and the G20 go back to the 1990 Houston G7 summit; since then it has communicated to high officials – including leaders of summit countries – its business priorities and recommendations to the G7, G8 and G20 summits to high officials, including leaders, of summit countries.

The ICC initiated interactions with the G20 in 2008 when the G20 leaders began convening their summits. Prior to the Washington G20 summit, ICC, along with the WTO, presented to G20 governments its analysis of the impact of the global economic crisis on trade finance. As well, ICC proposed to deliver its messages to government leaders and the public through its own network and through the media (*Financial Times*, IHT [*International Herald Tribune*], CNN, BBC and others).

Before the 2009 London summit, ICC Chair Victor K. Fung met host Prime Minister Gordon Brown and submitted business priorities for G20 discussions. Brown 'urged ICC to take the "pole position" as the voice of global business and to communicate its key messages to political leaders and the public in the lead-up to the Summit' (ICC, 2010b).

In 2010, ICC released a statement addressed to the G8 and G20 leaders prior to the Muskoka G8 and Toronto G20 summits, offering recommendations on international trade and investment: calling for resisting protectionism and economic nationalism; asking for the conclusion of the Doha Round multilateral trade negotiations before the end of 2010; calling on leaders to restore trade finance to more normal levels; appealing to them to improve governance of the world economy; and calling for action on climate change and energy, intellectual property and innovation (Hajnal, 2007a, p. 96; ICC, 2010a). Before the Seoul summit, the ICC chair met with South Korean Prime Minister Lee Myung-bak (ICC, 2010b).

Prior to the Cannes G20 summit, ICC issued a useful handbook, *The G20: What It Is and What It Does: A Business Guide* (Kassum, 2011). It provides a description of the G20, its membership and relationship with business and civil society; an analysis of the Washington, London, Pittsburgh, Toronto and Seoul summits and prospects for the Cannes summit; and a discussion of the G20 agenda and decision-making process. In the same year ICC released its Open Markets Index, 'a policy tool which ranks national market performance on openness to trade'. The index showed that of the G20 countries only Germany was in the top 20 countries (ICC, 2011). In 2012 ICC presented global business policy priorities to the G20 leaders for the Los Cabos summit. The ICC stated, 'It's our responsibility to ensure that the G20 takes into account global business priorities in their deliberations. As the everyday practitioners of the global economy, we need to make sure that the voice of world business is heard' (ICC, 2012c).

In 2012, the ICC's G20 Advisory Group collaborated with the B20 task forces (see ahead) and met with World Trade Organization (WTO) officials to push forward multilateral trade negotiations. Shortly after the Los Cabos summit, the ICC noted with satisfaction, 'The G20 final communiqué, issued on 19 June at the close of the Summit, took into account recommendations that had been delivered to the G20 by several business organizations, including ICC, on behalf of global business' (ICC, 2012a). Also in 2012, ICC published the first edition of its periodic (annual or semi-annual) *G20 Business Scorecard* (ICC, 2012b). (The latest edition at the time of writing is the sixth, issued in December 2016.) This series is explored in more detail in Chapter 8.

In 2013, the ICC prepared six policy papers, as well as messages for policymakers and, in cooperation with WEF, reports and recommendations on business policy for the G20 process (ICC, 2013b). At the end of the year, ICC issued its evaluation of the St Petersburg summit, *ICC Summary of the St. Petersburg G20 Leaders' Declaration*, in which it noted with approval that

> for the first time, the G20 created a special session for 'social partners' within the framework of the G20 Leaders [*sic*] Summit. While the meeting was voluntary to the heads of government, the 'semi-official' meeting represented a significant step forward in the G20's recognition of the role of international business.
>
> (ICC, 2013a)

In 2014, in addition to its usual recommendations to G20 leaders, ICC released *Global Survey of Business Policy Priorities for G20 Leaders* (ICC, 2014). In 2016 it issued a critical *Summary of the Hangzhou G20 Leaders' Communiqué* (ICC, 2016c) and, in an example of ICC interaction with the G20 below the summit level, in the same year it published *Six Steps to Energy Sustainability and Security* for the G20 Energy Ministers (ICC, 2016b).

The Business Summit (B20)

The business sector's relationship with the G20 has been even closer than it was with the G7/G8 before the launch of the leaders'-level G20 summits in November 2008. G8 and G20 business summits started convening around the official summits earlier in 2008. In April of that year a G8 Tokyo Business Summit addressed a statement to the G8 leaders before their Hokkaido summit. These B7 events continue to function.

The first G20-related B20 convened on 25–26 June 2010, with two senior business leaders from each G20 country meeting at the request of the Canadian Prime Minister (host of the Toronto G20 summit) and Finance Minister with the objective of obtaining advice from business leaders on the economic issues on the G20 agenda and building business support for G20 policy objectives. In Toronto, the B20 discussed current business conditions, fiscal exit strategies, financial sector regulation, innovation, trade and investment liberalization, and development. Entrepreneurship and the growth of small business were also on the agenda.

The B20 characterizes itself as

> an integral part of the G20 process, representing the entire G20 business community. [Its] mission . . . is to support the G20 through consolidated representation of interests, concrete policy proposals, and expertise. Furthermore, the B20 promotes dialogue among policymakers, civil society, and business at the international level. . . . In the B20, business representatives from the . . . G20 develop joint recommendations and advocate specific policy actions across the entire G20 agenda. In addition, the B20 organizes a number of events and provides a platform for exchanges with governments and other stakeholders of the G20 process. Like the G20, the B20 is a perennial process with working activities and events during the . . . year.
>
> (B20, 2017a)

At the end of the 2010 Toronto B20, John Manley, President and Chief Executive Officer of the Canadian Council of Chief Executives, who chaired the meeting, released a chair's summary on economic and fiscal challenges, market uncertainty, financial regulation, trade and investment, innovation and entrepreneurship, reflecting the B20 agenda. The B20 also issued a background document on small- and medium-sized enterprises (SMEs), *The SME Finance Challenge* (Canada, 2010). The B20 was clearly not a genuine civil society event, providing further evidence of the separateness of the business sector and civil society; it reflected G20 government ties with the business sector. The final documents even took the form of official G20 supporting documentation.

The host government of the Seoul G20 summit integrated the B20 (which met for its second summit on 11–12 November 2010, overlapping with the G20 summit of 10–11 November). President Lee Myung-bak of the Republic of Korea invited 120 top Korean and international business leaders to the B20, underlining the strong role of the private sector in economic recovery and emphasizing public-private partnerships. The results of this government-business dialogue fed into the G20 summit. The official Korean G20 summit website (no longer accessible) provided a link to the B20 website.

The Cannes B20, also referred to as 'Business 20', met on 1–3 November 2011, preceding and coinciding with the official G20 summit. It was prepared by MEDEF, the largest employers' association in France, mandated by President Nicolas Sarkozy to come up with proposals for the leaders' summit. Business organizations from all G20 countries took part in the preparations. On 2 November Sarkozy met with B20 representatives at the Elysée Palace. The WEF and the ICC had convened panels to develop their own recommendations for the G20. The B20 consolidated all these proposals, gathered in a final report that addressed the following business sector priorities: adjusting global governance to strengthen confidence; unlocking the levers of economic growth; and ensuring that the benefits of growth are shared in a sustainable fashion. The report's 46 recommendations dealt with: global economic policy imperatives; financial regulation; the international monetary system; commodities and raw materials; development and food security; employment and its social dimensions; anti-corruption; trade and investment; information and communications technology (ICT) and innovation; global governance issues; energy; and green growth (B20, 2011). The B20 also issued a joint statement with the 2011 L20 labour summit (B20-L20, 2011; see Chapter 6 for more information on the L20). The G20 Cannes *Communiqué* welcomed the outcomes of the B20 and the L20 (G20, 2011c).

The close association between the business sector and the official G20 was strengthened further at Los Cabos. The B20 convened there on 17–18 June, bringing together some 150 CEOs and Presidents of major businesses from the 19 G20 member countries, with heads of various international organizations (including the International Monetary Fund [IMF], World Bank and the Organisation for Economic Co-operation and Development [OECD]) also participating. On 19 June, the chairs of B20 task forces met with G20 officials over breakfast.

The task forces comprised chief executives of leading companies, government officials, representatives of international governmental organizations (IGOs) and business fora, and selected NGOs. For example, the Task Force on Food

Security in 2012 was co-chaired by the CEOs of Unilever (UK) and Grupo Bimbo (Mexico) and counted among its members the CEOs of Nestlé (Switzerland), Monsanto, DuPont and PepsiCo (US) as well as high officials of the UN and the OECD, and the head of Oxfam Great Britain. The 2012 government liaison of this task force was the Coordinator of International Affairs, Secretariat of Agriculture, Livestock, Rural Development, Fisheries and Food of Mexico.

The WEF was the lead organization of this task force and of four other task forces: Green Growth, Employment, Improving Transparency and Anti-Corruption, and Financing for Growth and Development. The lead organization of the Task Force on Trade and Investment was the ICC; that of the Task Force on ICT and Innovation and the Task Force on Advocacy and Impact was McKinsey & Co (B20, 2012b). Both the composition and the leadership of the task forces vividly illustrate the close collaboration of major businesses and business interest groups.

The fact that President Calderón gave the opening address at the Los Cabos B20 is another indicator of the degree of closeness of the G20 to business; government leaders are fond of mingling with big business executives, and the two types of actors need each other. The B20 discussed the following, among other issues: outlook of the world economy; transparency and anti-corruption; green growth; employment; trade and investment; financing for growth and development; food security; financial inclusion; and innovation (B20, 2012c). The B20 presented detailed recommendations for global economic recovery and growth (B20, 2012a). The Los Cabos *Declaration* explicitly acknowledged the contribution of the B20 and L20, as had the leaders at Cannes (G20, 2012j). The *Declaration* specifically welcomed the G2A2 of the B20, which would increase the use of public resources (e.g., development assistance and taxes) to leverage private investment in key sectors (Alexander, 2012). Alexander and Fuhr (2012) explore the dimensions of public-private partnership in more depth, focusing on resource-related sectors and green growth.

In his end-of-summit press conference, President Calderón expressed his gratitude 'for the participation of the young people, think tanks, members of labor organizations and civil society, businesspeople and academics who shared their ideas in the various forums of this summit', and singled out the B20 for its crucial contribution 'to achieving concrete agreements for growth and development'. The B20, on its part, hailed the establishment of 'closer links with the G20 decision-making process, including regular briefings of G20 sherpas and establishing government liaisons to each [B20] task force' (Ramírez, 2012, p. 16). Once again, the final B20 documents appeared as official G20 supporting documentation, even bearing the same logo as the official G20 summit.

In addition to offering advice to the G20, the B20 has also taken on an important role in monitoring the fulfilment of G20 commitments. To this end, the B20 launched a 'performance dashboard', with input from the WEF, ICC, the McKinsey Global Institute and others (Enter the B20, 2012). The ICC (2012b) compiled a *G20 Business Scorecard*, assessing the performance of G20 countries. (See the 'International Chamber of Commerce' section earlier.)

The Russian host government of the 2013 St Petersburg summit mounted an outreach programme as varied as that of the Los Cabos summit. It involved a Business 20 (in addition to broad civil society outreach). The B20 under the Russian Presidency first met in Moscow on 12 December 2012. Also in Moscow, the B20 convened its summit on 20–21 June. Its recommendations to the G20 appeared as a detailed 'White Book' (B20, 2013a). Another report prepared by the B20 Dialogue Efficiency Task Force examines the efficiency of the B20-G20 dialogue (B20, 2013b). The 2013 B20 created its own website, www.b20russia.com/en, whose content is still accessible, but it does not appear to have had any new items added since early in 2014.

In preparation for the 2014 Brisbane G20 summit, the B20 held its summit in Sydney and issued 20 recommendations, 'mostly new structural reform measures that would deliver on the G20 growth target and form a blueprint for sustainable economic growth in the medium term'. They covered (1) structural flexibility through the promotion of more efficient and productive supply chains, infrastructure and labour markets; (2) free movement of goods, services, labour and capital across borders; (3) consistent and effective market regulation; and (4) integrity and credibility in commerce so as to avoid corruption (B20, 2014, p. 2).

In 2015, the B20's priorities moved to align with those of the Turkish G20 Presidency: continuity, inclusivity and connectivity. The B20's recommendations to the G20 included:

- asking the G20 to ratify and implement the Trade Facilitation Agreement; implement completely its global financial reform agenda; improve the consultation process in that reform agenda; and implement the G20 High Level Principles on Beneficial Ownership; and calling on G20 members to correct imbalances in investment principles and strategies, and develop and finance programs to reduce skills mismatches in view of rapid changes in technology and innovation;
- calling on G20 members to make labour markets more dynamic and inclusive, so as to advance employment opportunities; increase youth employment and female labour-force participation; making data on SME creditworthiness more transparent in order to reduce risk associated with SME lending; enhance SMEs' access to alternative financing; providing support to SMEs to comply with international standards and improve their access to international markets; and incorporating a five-year universal broadband connection target into G20 Member Growth Strategies improving SMEs' access to the digital economy;
- recommending that G20 members should improve the global trade system for the emerging digital economy; initiate G20-wide entrepreneurs' visa programs; reaffirm the standstill commitment and roll back protectionist measures; develop and adopt a comprehensive digital environment for customs procedures and cross-border automated clearance systems in all G20 countries within five years; digitalize public procurement systems, develop high-level reporting mechanisms, and incentivize business compliance programs

for public procurement processes; reduce corruption and improve efficiency of trade; and promote integrity in public procurement by instituting digital systems, high-level reporting mechanisms, and incentivizing business compliance programs (B20, 2015b).

In 2016, the B20 published 20 recommendations to the G20 leaders for their summit in Hangzhou. These included, among others:

- implementing programs such as the SMART (Sustainable innovation, Massive public platform, Accessible network, Revolutionary reform, and Technological innovation) initiative to encourage entrepreneurship and innovation;
- promoting the creation of financial instruments to facilitate infrastructure investment;
- enhancing the catalytic role of multilateral development banks and institutions in enabling private-sector infrastructure investment;
- facilitating the development of green financing and investment markets;
- stimulating financial inclusion by embracing digital technology innovation;
- optimizing global financial regulations to support growth;
- strengthening intergovernmental cooperation against corruption, and supporting the building of capacity for stronger anti-corruption compliance;
- strengthening the multilateral trading system and eliminating new protectionist measures while rolling back existing measures to enable trade growth;
- endorsing the concept of the Electronic World Trade Platform to incubate cross-border electronic trade (e-trade) rules and aid e-trade development;
- facilitating the inclusion of SMEs into global value chains;
- removing structural barriers to increase youth employment, and implementing initiatives to raise the participation rate of women in the labour force;
- enhancing policies to assess and reduce skill mismatches and capability gaps in the workforce; and
- strengthening national, regional and global initiatives to enhance infrastructure interconnectivity.

(B20, 2016)

In 2017, the B20 had the following task forces: Trade and Investment; Energy, Climate, & Resource Efficiency; Financing Growth and Infrastructure; Digitalization; and Employment and Education. In addition, the B20 had two cross-thematic groups: Responsible Business Conduct and Anti-Corruption; and Small and Medium-Sized Enterprises; as well as a health initiative and an initiative on the Compact with Africa. On 21–22 December 2016 there was a B20 conference in Berlin, bringing together all task forces and other groups. The B20 issued policy recommendations to the G20 in the following areas, corresponding with the German agenda around the themes of resilience, sustainability and responsibility:

- under 'Building Resilience': trade as an engine for inclusive growth; digitalization for all; and financial systems as a pillar of resilience and economic growth;

- under 'Improving Sustainability': advancing climate protection and resource efficiency; and investment in future-oriented growth;
- under 'Assuming Responsibility': promoting open, dynamic, and inclusive labour markets; and enabling responsible business conduct.

(B20, 2017c)

The B20 has developed an elaborate structure. In 2017 it was headed by a chair to lead 'the B20 process and represents the B20 vis-à-vis governments, the international business community and the public at large; [an] Executive Committee . . . which . . . takes fundamental decisions concerning B20 by consensus and instructs the B20 [s]herpa . . . , [an] Outreach Committee [and a] Business Advisory Caucus' (B20, 2017d). On 2 and 3 May 2017, the B20 held its summit in Berlin, bringing together some 700 representatives from business, government, civil society and international organizations. Chancellor Angela Merkel also attended.

Mirroring the official G20 process, the B20 has a leadership troika corresponding to the current year's, past year's and next year's G20 Presidency. As Argentina assumed the 2018 G20 Presidency, the German B20 handed over to its Argentine counterpart.

Writing in 2016, Jens Martens deems the B20 to be 'the most visible symbol of corporate engagement' with the G20. He further asserts that the 'B20 and the International Chamber of Commerce (ICC) claim success in influencing G20 decision-making in various impact reports and G20 Business Scorecards, leading to the conclusion that the G20 is increasingly responsive to the priority recommendations put forward by them' (Martens, 2016). A year later, Martens published a longer study, *Corporate Influence on the G20: The Case of the B20 and Transnational Business Networks*, in which he found that

> the comparison of business recommendations and G20 communiqués shows a large proportion of overlapping positions and common language. . . . This indicates the high degree of direct or indirect influence that corporate actors exert on shaping the agenda and the discourse of the G20.
>
> (Martens, 2017)

The Young Entrepreneurs' Summit

A 'Young Entrepreneurs' Summit' (G20YES; later also called YESG20 and YEA20), hosted by the Canadian Youth Business Foundation, met in Toronto in June 2010 for two days, representing young entrepreneurs of the G20 countries. The Canadian government considered this gathering an official G20 event. The G20YES communiqué, which included a declaration, was presented to the leaders of the B20, which used G20YES's recommendations in its own deliberations. Building on the Toronto meeting, G20YES next met in November 2010 in Incheon, Korea, where YEA's *Charter* was adopted on 9 November. It envisions

> a network that, through its discussions with governments, the media, the public and each other, champions the cause of young entrepreneurs at the local,

> national and international level . . . [YEA is] an alliance of organizations from industrialized and developing economies that makes measurable progress towards its goal of a world where an increasing number of entrepreneurs grow businesses, create jobs, change lives and ensure future economic prosperity . . . [and is] a recognized body that exists as part of the official G20 process and is able to engage, contribute to and impact the findings of the G20 to raise awareness and address the issues of emerging entrepreneurs across the globe.
>
> (G20 YEA, 2010)

The group met again on 31 October–2 November 2011 in Nice, France. Prior to this occasion, on 13 October, President Sarkozy met with representatives of the French participants of YESG20. A year later, G20YES met at Los Cabos, Mexico, in 2012, to discuss 'the policy and regulatory changes needed to foster entrepreneurship in the G20 countries' (G20YES, 2012). On 15–17 June 2013, the G20 Young Entrepreneurs' Alliance (G20 YEA) held its summit in Moscow. Its recommendations were conveyed to the 2013 B20 (G20 YEA, 2013). It next met on 18–22 July 2014 in Sydney, Australia; 7–9 September 2015 in Istanbul (where its communiqué was endorsed by the Turkish G20 Presidency); and 8–10 September 2016 in Beijing (where its theme was 'Disruptive Innovation and Smart Entrepreneurship'). The 2017 G20 YEA summit met in Berlin on 15–17 June, bringing together some 500 young entrepreneurs from the G20 countries. They discussed the implications of digital trends (including digital platforms, the 'internet of things' and virtual reality and artificial intelligence) for future business. (More information about the YEA can be found at www.g20yea.com/index.php/summits.)

Private philanthropy

Private philanthropy, related to business, plays a role in providing resources in tandem with governments, including G20 governments. The Bill and Melinda Gates Foundation committed over $1 billion for maternal and child health at the Muskoka G8 summit. In the case of the G20, the Gates Foundation supports two implementing organizations of the G20 financial inclusion initiative: the Consultative Group to Assist the Poor (CGAP; see ahead) and the Alliance for Financial Inclusion (AFI). Culpeper (2012, p. 2) reports that the 'Foundation's 2010 Strategy Brief lists grants in the "policy" area of $35 million to AFI and $23.8 million to CGAP'. The Gates Foundation has also supported the G20's AgResults initiative launched at the Los Cabos summit to improve food security for the poor, and the Agricultural Market Information System (AMIS). (AMIS was created by the G20 Agriculture Ministers' forum's meeting in Paris in September 2011.)

The Gates Foundation has also given grants to G20-related research and advocacy. For example, in 2016 it awarded US$100,000 to Renmin University of China Education Foundation in Beijing to support the financial inclusion Forum in China prior to the Hangzhou G20 summit (Gates Foundation, 2016).

CGAP is a group of donors from 16 countries, 11 multilateral development organizations and five private foundations. Culpeper (2012, p. 2) asserts that '[m]uch of the G20's thinking about financial inclusion has sprouted from the work of CGAP in the past 16 years; its technical assistance, policy work and research. Moreover . . . CGAP is one of the three key implementing agencies for the G20's initiative' on financial inclusion.

Another philanthropy relevant to the G20 is the F20 Platform (F20) comprising some 45 foundations and philanthropic organizations from around the world. Their main interests are climate change and sustainable development. They aim 'to be part of the solution on climate change by building bridges between civil society, business and politics within the G20 countries and beyond' (F20, 2017).

The role of individual 'philanthropic celebrities', notably Bill Gates, arguably has some similarities with issues on which civil society, too, advocates for action. That aspect, therefore, is discussed in the 'Celebrities' section of Chapter 6.

Conclusion

The business sector has proven to be very influential with the G20, to apparent mutual benefit. This relationship has become ever closer in the course of the G20's evolution. Aldo Caliari of the Center of Concern and Nancy Alexander of the Heinrich Böll Foundation (2012) offer a critical examination of the increasingly close G20-B20 'alliance', detailing the potential benefits and risks of this relationship. To maximize impact on the G20, the business community – particularly the B20 – has used consultation with G20 officials, including host leaders, conducted preparations in a timely manner, and worked to ensure continuity of business links with the G20. All this, with the combined and coordinated effort and resources of the B20, the ICC and the WEF, provide powerful evidence of the role and impact of the private sector on the agenda of the G20.

References

Alexander, N., 2012. *What Are the Pros and Cons of Public-Private Partnerships (PPPs) as a Means to Achieve Food Security, Expanded Infrastructure Investment and Green Growth?* Instituto Matías Romero. www.academia.edu/14434806/The_Pros_and_Cons_of_Public-Private_Partnerships_PPPs_as_a_means_to_achieve_food_security_expanded_infrastructure_investment_and_green_growth [Accessed: 8 January 2018].

Alexander, N. and Fuhr, L., 2012. *Privatizing the Governance of 'Green Growth'*. 26 November. www.boell.de/en/content/privatizing-governance-green-growth [Accessed: 8 January 2018].

Australia. Prime Minister, 2014. *Australia's Vision for the G20*. 23 January. www.weforum.org/agenda/2014/01/vision-g20/ [Accessed: 11 February 2017].

B20, 2011. *Final Report with Appendices*. Cannes. November. www.g20.utoronto.ca/b20/B20-2011-report.pdf [Accessed: 8 January 2018].

B20, 2012a. *B20 Global Business Leaders Announce Their Prioritized Recommendations for Global Economic Recovery and Growth*. May. www.prnewswire.com/news-releases/b20-global-business-leaders-announce-their-prioritized-recommendations-for-global-economic-recovery-and-growth-155411765.html [Accessed: 9 January 2018].

B20, 2012b. *B20 Task Force Recommendations: Final Report*. Los Cabos: Boell. 11 May. us.boell.org/sites/default/files/downloads/FINAL_11_May_B20_Task_Force_Recommendations.pdf [Accessed: 6 January 2018].

B20, 2012c. *Program*. 17–18 June. b20.org/documentos/B20_Program_20120615.pdf [Accessed: 9 September 2012].

B20, 2013a. *B20-G20 Partnership for Growth and Jobs: Recommendations from Business 20*. www.b20russia.com/B20_WhiteBook_web.pdf [Accessed: 9 January 2018].

B20, 2013b. *From Toronto to St Petersburg: Assessing G20-B20 Engagement Effectiveness: Draft Report*. www.hse.ru/data/2013/06/24/1287462471/G20-B20_engagement_effectiveness_report_full.pdf [Accessed: 9 January 2018].

B20, 2014. *Driving Growth and Jobs: B20 Policy Recommendations to the G20*. www.g20.utoronto.ca/b20/B20-2014-recommendations.pdf [Accessed: 26 November 2017].

B20, 2015b. *Summary of B20 Recommendations*. g20.org.tr/engagement-groups/business-20-b20 [Accessed: 26 November 2017].

B20, 2016. *Policy Recommendations to the G20 Released to the Public*. en.b20-china.org/mediacenter/article/334 [Accessed: 26 November 2017].

B20, 2017a. *About B20*. www.b20germany.org/the-b20/about-b20/ [Accessed: 25 November 2017].

B20, 2017c. *B20 Germany Recommendations Summary*. May. www.b20germany.org/nc/documents/recommendations-summary/ [Accessed: 25 November 2017].

B20, 2017d. *Structure*. www.b20germany.org/nc/the-b20/structure [Accessed: 25 November 2017].

B20-L20, 2011. *B20-L20 Joint Statement*. November. www.ilo.org/wcmsp5/groups/public/-dgreports/-dcomm/documents/meetingdocument/wcms_166713.pdf and www.g20.utoronto.ca/2011/2011-b20-l20-en.pdf [Accessed: 9 January 2018].

Bill & Melinda Gates Foundation, 2016. Renmin University of China Education Foundation. *How We Work: Grant*. www.gatesfoundation.org/How-We-Work/Quick-Links/Grants-Database/Grants/2016/07/OPP1155157 [Accessed: 8 December 2017].

Caliari, A. and Alexander, N., 2012. Selected Highlights of Business-20 (B20) Draft Recommendations to the G20. *G20 Update*, 12 June, pp. 8–10.

Canada, 2010. *Backgrounder: The SME Finance Challenge*. 26 June. www.canada.ca/en/news/archive/2010/06/backgrounder-sme-finance-challenge.html [Accessed: 9 January 2018].

Canada. Prime Minister's Office, 2010. *Statement by the Prime Minister of Canada at the World Economic Forum*. Davos, Switzerland. 28 January. www.g8.utoronto.ca/summit/2010muskoka/harper-davos.html [Accessed: 9 January 2018].

Culpeper, R. 2012. *The Role of the G20 in Enhancing Financial Inclusion*. February. us.boell.org/sites/default/files/downloads/Culpeper_G20_Financial_Inclusion.pdf [Accessed: 8 January 2018].

Enter the B20; Business and Geopolitics, 2012. *The Economist*, 403(8788), p. 72.

F20, 2017. *F20: Home*. [online]. www.foundations-20.org/ [Accessed: 8 December 2017].

G20, 2011c. *Final Communiqué [of the] G20 Leaders' Summit, Cannes*. 4 November. www.g20.utoronto.ca/2011/2011-cannes-communiqué-111104-en.html [Accessed: 24 October 2017].

G20, 2012j. *G20 Leaders Declaration*. 19 June. www.g20.utoronto.ca/2012/2012-0619-loscabos.pdf [Accessed: 26 September 2017].

G20 Young Entrepreneurs' Alliance, 2010. *Our Charter*. www.g20yea.com/index.php/our-charter [Accessed: 5 December 2017].

G20 Young Entrepreneurs' Alliance, 2013. *G20 Young Entrepreneurs Conveyed Their Recommendations to the Chief of Business 20*. en.g20russia.ru/news/20130618/781458795.html [Accessed: 9 January 2018].

G20YES, 2012. *G20 YES Mexico*. 2–5 June. Los Cabos. www.g20yea.com/index.php/summits [Accessed: 9 January 2018].

Hajnal, P.I., 2007a. *The G8 System and the G20: Evolution, Role and Documentation*. Global Finance Series. Aldershot: Ashgate.

International Chamber of Commerce, 2010a. *Business and the World Economy: ICC Statement on Behalf of World Business to the Heads of State and Government Attending the G8 and G20 Summits in Canada*. 25–27 June. www.iccwbo.org/ Advocacy-Codes-and-Rules/Document-centre/2010/Business-and-the-worldeconomy/ [Accessed: 8 September 2012].

International Chamber of Commerce, 2010b. *Why ICC?: A Legacy in Working with the G8–G20*. www.iccwbo.org/Global-influence/G20/ICC-and-G8-G20/Why-ICC – a-legacy-in-working-with-the-G8-G20/ [Accessed: 8 September 2012].

International Chamber of Commerce, 2011. *G20 Countries Fail to Lead in Trade Openness, ICC Index Indicates*. Geneva. 16 December. iccwbo.org/media-wall/news-speeches/g20-countries-fail-to-lead-in-trade-openness-icc-index-indicates/ [Accessed: 6 January 2018].

International Chamber of Commerce, 2012a. *Business Bolstered by G20 Progress in Los Cabos*. 28 June. https://iccwbo.org/media-wall/news-speeches/business-bolstered-by-g20-progress-in-los-cabos/ [Accessed: 7 January 2018].

International Chamber of Commerce, 2012b. *G20 Business Scorecard*. June. cdn.iccwbo.org/content/uploads/sites/3/2016/11/2012-ICC-G20-Business-Scorecard-high-resolution.pdf [Accessed: 24 November 2017].

International Chamber of Commerce, 2012c. *ICC Delivers Global Business Priorities to G20, Rates Progress as Incomplete*. Los Cabos. 18 June. iccwbo.org/media-wall/news-speeches/icc-delivers-global-business-priorities-to-g20-rates-progress-as-incomplete/ [Accessed: 6 January 2018].

International Chamber of Commerce, 2013a. *ICC summary of the St. Petersburg G20 Leaders' Declaration*. 12 September. cdn.iccwbo.org/content/uploads/sites/3/2016/11/ICC-summary-of-St-Petersburg-G20-Leaders-Declaration.pdf [Accessed: 24 November 2017].

International Chamber of Commerce, 2013b. *St Petersburg G20 Business Summit*. iccwbo.org/Global-influence/G20/ICC-and-G8-G20/St-Petersburg-G20-Business-Summit/ [Accessed: 10 October 2013].

International Chamber of Commerce, 2014. *Global Survey of Business Policy Priorities for G20 Leaders*. cdn.iccwbo.org/content/uploads/sites/3/2016/11/ICC-survey-results-Global-survey-of-business-policy-priorities-for-G20-leaders-2014.pdf [Accessed: 24 November 2017].

International Chamber of Commerce, 2016b. *Six Steps to Energy Sustainability and Security for the G20 Energy Ministers*. cdn.iccwbo.org/content/uploads/sites/3/2016/11/Six-steps-to-energy-sustainability-and-security.pdf [Accessed: 24 November 2017].

International Chamber of Commerce, 2016c. *Summary of the Hangzhou G20 Leaders' Communiqué*. cdn.iccwbo.org/content/uploads/sites/3/2016/11/ICC-summary-of-the-Hangzhou-G20-Leaders-communiqué-6-September-2016.pdf [Accessed: 24 November 2017].

Kassum, J., 2011. *The G20: What It Is and What It Does: A Business Guide*. ICC Publication, 730E. Paris: International Chamber of Commerce.

Martens, J., 2016. Corporate influence on the G20. *Just Governance blog*. March. just-governance.boellblog.org/2017/03/22/corporate-influence-on-the-g20-by-jens-martens/ [Accessed: 8 December 2017].

Martens, J., 2017. *Corporate Influence on the G20: The Case of the B20 and Transnational Business Networks*. Berlin/Bonn/New York: Heinrich Böll Stiftung; Global Policy Forum. March. www.boell.de/sites/default/files/corporate_influence_on_the_g20.pdf?dimension1=ds_g20_en [Accessed: 8 December 2017].

Mexico. Presidencia de la República, 2012a. *Global Economic Crisis: Role and Challenges of the G20*. [Spanish]. 26 January. www.g20.utoronto.ca/2012/2012-120126-calderon-es.html [Accessed: 10 January 2018].

Russia. Prime Minister, 2013. *Group of Twenty Is Becoming More Effective*. 23 January. en.g20russia.ru/news/20130123/781165516.html [Accessed: 12 January 2018].

Turkey. Prime Minister, 2014. *Turkish G20 Presidency Priorities for 2015*. www.g20.utoronto.ca/2015/141201-turkish-priorities.html [Accessed: 13 February 2017].

World Economic Forum, 2010. *Seoul G20 Summit: Priorities and Challenges, Davos Forum Special Address by Lee Myung-bak, President of the Republic of Korea*. Davos, Switzerland. 28 January. www.g20.utoronto.ca/2010/lee-davos.pdf [Accessed: 6 January 2018].

World Economic Forum, 2012a. *Euro, Dollar, Yuan Uncertainties: Scenarios on the Future of the International Monetary System*. World Scenario Series. June. www20.iadb.org/intal/catalogo/PE/2012/10462.pdf [Accessed: 10 January 2018].

World Economic Forum, 2012b. *President Calderón: Green Growth Public Private Partnerships*. www.weforum.org/agenda/2012/06/president-calderon-green-growth-public-private-partnerships/ [Accessed: 6 January 2018].

World Economic Forum, 2017. *Opening Plenary with Xi Jinping, President of the People's Republic of China*. 17 January. www.weforum.org/events/world-economic-forum-annual-meeting-2017/sessions/opening-plenary-davos-2017 [Accessed: 11 February 2017].

6 Relations with civil society

This chapter examines and analyzes the evolving relationship of the Group of Twenty (G20) with not-for-profit civil society organizations (CSOs) and coalitions. It begins with a clarification of the concept of civil society, followed by a brief history of civil society involvement with the G7/G8 and the G20. Next, it surveys the kinds of CSOs that interact with the G20; identifies modes of this interaction; and considers the motivations for, and range of, civil society engagement with the G20. The chapter also examines the question of civil society's influence on the G20 and whether and how civil society and G20 governments have benefited from their engagement. Finally, the chapter reviews factors helping or hindering civil society influence on the G20, and concludes that mutual benefits accrue from this interaction; that civil society has had some positive impact on G20 processes, accountability and agenda emphasis (if not on agenda-setting); and that official G20 acknowledgement of civil society does not necessarily indicate major impact on G20 outcomes. Thus, civil society's influence has not yet reached its full potential.

Introduction

The concept of civil society as used in this chapter needs clarification at the outset. The following explanation makes no attempt at theoretical definitions. These have been amply explored in the literature – for example, by Jan Aart Scholte (2011a), quoted in the next paragraph.

Civil society denotes not-for-profit groups of citizens engaging in collective action around particular public issues of concern. It is a 'political space where associations of citizens seek, from outside political parties, to shape societal rules' through collective action in 'groups that share concerns about, and mobilise around, a particular problem of public affairs' (Scholte, 2011a, p. 34). This includes formally structured non-governmental organizations (NGOs) as well as social movements, campaigns and coalitions of citizen groups. Civil society associations are very diverse, ranging in size, geographic extent, ideological orientation, aims, strategies and tactics.

DOI: 10.4324/9781351266802-7

Civil society's summit experience

As discussed in Chapter 1, the G20 began at the level of Finance Ministers and Central Bank Governors in 1999 in response to the 1997–98 Asian-Latin American financial crisis. It took the financial and economic crisis that became global in 2008 to spur the leaders'-level meeting. In response to the crisis, then-US President George W. Bush convened the first G20 summit meeting in Washington, DC, on 14–15 November 2008. Like the G20 governments themselves, civil society was not well prepared initially for this development; yet CSOs were already aware of the leaders' G20 and engaged in early action around the first G20 summit. Fuller and more sophisticated and varied civil society action was quick to develop; this learning process has unfolded much faster (both on the civil society side and the official G20 side) than had been the case with the G7/G8. By the time of the second summit (London, April 2009), CSOs were ready to respond with a wider range of activities: a conference on human rights, development and the environment; street demonstrations; and other action.

At the third, Pittsburgh, summit (September 2009), the leaders proclaimed the forum to be the major coordinating body for their economic and financial issues, thus taking over the original part of the G7/G8's brief. The fourth, Toronto, G20 summit (26–27 June 2010) followed on the heels of the Muskoka G8 summit (25–26 June), requiring simultaneous but differentiated civil society responses. As CSOs learned more of the G7/G8-G20 dynamic, they have fostered more sophisticated relationships with the two fora.

The 2010 Seoul summit in November, the fifth such meeting, marked an important expansion of the G20 agenda by embracing development and financial safety nets and, more tentatively, climate. These new developments brought more opportunities for CSO action. With further broadening of the agenda, these opportunities are likely to increase.

In 2011, with France holding both the G8 and G20 Presidency, CSOs interacted with the G8 summit in Deauville in late May as well as the G20 summit in Cannes in early November. At Cannes, the ambitious French G20 agenda included: reform of the international monetary system; addressing currency instability; strengthening crisis management mechanisms; combating commodity price volatility; limiting energy price fluctuations; development and climate funding; innovative financing; and global governance reform. This plethora of issues presented both a challenge and an opportunity for CSOs, although, in the event, the Greek debt crisis claimed the centre of attention.

The two summits in 2012 convened in different countries: the G8 at the Camp David US presidential retreat on 18–19 May (immediately followed by the NATO summit in Chicago on 19–21 May); the G20 leaders met in Los Cabos, Mexico, on 18–19 June, so the two 'G' summits were once again fairly closely spaced, presenting CSOs with yet another challenge. There was more breathing space between the Lough Erne (Northern Ireland) G8 and St Petersburg G20 summits (17–18 June and 5–6 September 2013, respectively).

The year 2014 was unusual: the G8 summit originally scheduled for 4–5 June in Sochi, Russia, was cancelled because Russia's membership was suspended over its actions in Crimea; that year's (now G7) summit was convened in Brussels, Belgium, on the same dates set for Sochi. Exceptionally, it was hosted (but not chaired) by the EU. The G20 summit met in Brisbane, Australia, on 15–16 November 2014, with full civil society involvement.

The 2015 summits of the 'Gs' were again fairly far apart, with the G7 leaders meeting on 7–8 June at Schloss Elmau in Germany and the G20 leaders on 15–16 November in Antalya, Turkey. There was less time in 2016 between the 26–27 May G7 summit in Ise-Shima, Japan, and the 4–5 September Hangzhou (China) G20 summit, and even shorter time in 2017 between the Taormina, Italy, G7 summit on 26–27 May and the Hamburg G20 summit on 7–8 July. The 2018 summits were again scheduled with more time in between: the G7 in Charlevoix, Canada, on 8–9 June and the G20 on 30 November–1 December in Buenos Aires, Argentina.

The coexistence of the G7/G8 and G20 poses a problem for civil society. For CSOs this has implications for available resources and expertise, and uncertainty as to whether and how particular agenda items are likely be dealt with by the G7 or the G20. Which summit to focus on: the G7, the G20 or simultaneously both? This double demand on civil society resources will persist as long as both 'Gs' survive and continue meeting in the same year. Add to this the need for CSOs to be present at other major international conferences as well. The questions may be asked: Is this all worth the expense and effort? Does the potential impact on the G7/G8-G20 justify it? Is the value of media exposure worth it? Growing civil society attention to the G20 at the expense of the G7/G8 has been indicative of changing CSO priorities, but CSOs need to remain aware of the continuing influence of the G7.

Beyond the summits, civil society has also recognized the important role of sub-summit G20 entities and has interacted with several such bodies. For example, 78 French and international CSOs addressed a letter to the chairs of the G20 Anti-Corruption Working Group on 11 February 2011, offering recommendations and civil society cooperation with the working group. In the same year a group of economists addressed a letter to the G20 Finance Ministers, ahead of their October meeting, urging them to take effective action to curb excessive speculation on food commodities, which results in higher food prices and increases global poverty. Joint research, conducted by the think-tanks African Economic Research Consortium, Brookings Institution, Development Finance International and New Rules for Global Finance, led to the publication *The Financial Stability Board: Unlocking the Black Box* (New Rules, 2012a). In 2017 the Heinrich Böll Stiftung North America issued a critical analysis of the *Compact with Africa*, a German initiative endorsed by the G20 leaders at the Hamburg summit (Keil, 2017).

Types of CSOs interacting with the G20 and their aims

There is a remarkable range of civil society organizations interacting with the G20. The concerns of civil society groups are equally diverse: poverty, peace and disarmament, development, environment and climate change, human rights, gender issues, health, education, financial regulations and many others. Faith-based groups, labour unions, research institutes, think-tanks and academies of science are also included under the broad umbrella of civil society (Scholte, 2011b).

Four special groups may be considered as outside 'civil society' as that term is employed in this book: the business sector; the related but not synonymous private philanthropies and foundations; celebrities; and parliamentarians. A good case can be made to exclude the private sector from civil society because the former's objectives, *modus operandi* and close ties with governmental and intergovernmental bodies – including the G20 – are quite distinct from those of non-profit civil society associations. But if the business sector were included among CSOs, the overall civil society impact on the G7/G8 and G20 would increase greatly. The G20-business sector relationship is the subject of Chapter 5, which also covers the role of private philanthropies. The following section outlines the role of the other two groups.

Celebrities

Although not strictly civil society actors, celebrities may be considered here because they frequently support civil society objectives of social and economic justice. Celebrities play a variety of roles. Cooper (2008a) examines and analyzes the roles such personalities play in diplomacy.

In the G7/G8-G20 context, rock stars Bono and Bob Geldof staged 'Live 8' concerts around the world before the 2005 Gleneagles G8 summit. Their engagement with the G7/G8 and now the G20 has included their long-standing association with the advocacy group ONE/DATA (Debt, AIDS, Trade, Africa) (Bono still is a board member). Following the tradition of co-editing major newspapers before previous G8 summits, Bono and Geldof were guest editors of the 10 May 2010 issue of Canada's national newspaper, *The Globe and Mail*. The entire issue – assembled by specially assigned reporters, columnists, photographers and guest contributors – was devoted to Africa (Bono and Geldof, 2010).

Bill Gates played a celebrity role in the G20 at Cannes and (less so) in Los Cabos. At Cannes, he presented a report to the G20 leaders, with substantial proposals on development, health and domestic resource mobilization (Gates, 2011). The report was the result of careful preparation that included consultations with CSOs and other stakeholders. The ideas in the report were potentially helpful to the G20, particularly on development. The G20 referenced Bill Gates's recommendations in the *Final Declaration*: 'We discussed a set of options for innovative financing highlighted by Mr Bill Gates' (G20, 2011b). There was, however, no collective G20 follow-up of the recommendations after Cannes. Before the Los Cabos summit, Gates (2012) wrote a letter to President Calderón, emphasizing the importance of health, food and development. Gates and Calderón also appeared as panellists at the World Economic Forum in January of that year. The relationship with celebrities poses a dilemma for NGOs. Some CSOs welcome such high-profile support while other CSOs are concerned about the risk of celebrities stifling the voices of civil society itself. Argentine President Macri, host of the 2018 Buenos Aires G20 summit, held discussions at the World Economic Forum with Bill and Melinda Gates and other prominent personalities (G20, 2018b).

Parliamentarians

Parliaments, as legislative bodies, are outside civil society. But they are crucial in ensuring democratic accountability of elected governments, and are potential interlocutors for civil society. As this assemblage is not itself an official body, some may consider it a CSO. For several years, a parliament-related group has met quite regularly: the G8 Parliamentarians' Group of speakers of legislatures of G8 countries.

An example of civil society engagement with this process occurred when the Halifax Initiative (defunct since 2015) and other CSOs organized three parliamentary roundtables in Ottawa on 20, 26 and 27 April 2010 around the time of the G20 Finance Ministers' meeting in Washington, DC, the G8 Development Ministers' meeting in Halifax and the Africa Partnership Forum meeting in Toronto. The roundtables discussed climate change and climate financing, the financial crisis and the UN Millennium Development Goals (MDGs) – all of which were on the agenda of the G8 and G20 summits (Halifax Initiative, 2010a). Other 2010 parliamentary events between the Toronto and Seoul G20 summits included a meeting of the speakers of the lower houses of parliaments of G8 countries in Ottawa on 9–12 September; and a consultation, also in Ottawa, of G20 parliamentary speakers on 2–5 September. G20 parliament speakers met again in Seoul, 18–20 May 2011, in Riyadh, 24–26 February 2012, and in Mexico City, 4–5 April 2013 (see www.g20.utoronto.ca/speakers.html).

Due to Russia's suspension from the G8 and the latter's reverting to G7, no parliamentary meeting took place in 2014. In 2015, with Germany's G7 Presidency, a parliamentary conference was organized in Berlin on 16–17 April, prior to the Schloss Elmau G7 summit (Troszczynska-van Genderen, 2015, p. 14). G7/G20 parliamentarians' conferences have continued to meet annually; the fifteenth such meeting took place in Rome on 8–9 September 2017.

Civil society associations

As can be expected in the case of the G20, which began with a financial and economic focus and is still largely economic and financial, CSOs (including think-tanks) with relevant expertise have played an important role in interacting with the G20. Examples are the Reinventing Bretton Woods Committee (which works for a stable international financial architecture and monetary system), the New Rules for Global Finance coalition and the Peterson Institute of International Economics.

Other civil society groups realized quickly the broader implications of the financial and economic crisis and have taken action vis-à-vis the G20. With the G20 agenda expanding to development, trade, climate financing, food security and gender issues, it was natural for an increasing range of CSOs to become active in advocating, responding to and otherwise interacting with the G20. These CSOs include anti-poverty groups and campaigns (e.g., the Jubilee Movement, the Make Poverty History and the Global Call for Action against Poverty campaigns); labour union organizations (e.g., the International Trade Union Confederation); climate- and environment-centred CSOs (e.g., the Climate Action Network, the World Wide Fund for Nature [WWF] and Greenpeace); human rights NGOs (e.g., Amnesty International and Human Rights Watch); development NGOs (e.g., Oxfam, Save the Children, ActionAid and World Vision); and CSOs advocating on a whole range of issues in the purview of the G7/G8 and the G20 – for example, the G8/G20 Global Working Group formed in 2010 (now a Google group; see groups.google.com/group/globalG8-G20). The working group prepared common lobbying positions on a set of policy demands vis-à-vis the G8 and the G20. A similar group, the G7 Global Task Force, was formed in 2015. The InterAction coalition, based in Washington, DC, comprises over 180 NGOs.

Several think-tanks have focused exclusively, partly or occasionally on the G20 as an institution – for example, the Centre for Global Studies (until 2012 when its mandate changed), the Centre for International Governance Innovation, the Brookings Institution, Chatham House, the G20 Research Group, the Peterson Institute for International Economics, the Friedrich-Ebert-Stiftung and the Heinrich Böll Stiftung North America. Still other CSOs have interacted with the G20, such as faith-based groups (World Vision and many others). Some CSOs have focused on other social and political issues; the FIM Forum for Democratic Global Governance (no longer active) and Transparency International are examples.

In 2012 the Mexican host government took advantage of CSO expertise by convening a 'Think-20' meeting. In a related development, the Council of Councils, established by the Council of Foreign Relations in 2012, brings together major foreign policy think-tanks, more or less reflecting G20 membership. The inaugural conference of this network took place on 12–13 March 2012 in Washington, DC (Council on Foreign Relations, 2012a); the seventh annual conference met on 6–8 May 2018, focusing on the following themes: trade without Trump; the challenge from Iran; geopolitical implications of new technology; and strengthening effective climate change action (see www.cfr.org/councilofcouncils/events.html).

The Think Tanks and Civil Societies Program of the University of Pennsylvania publishes the annual *Global Go To Think Tank Index Report*, which focuses on think-tanks, including those in G20 and BRICS countries. The eleventh annual edition (McGann, 2018) ranks think-tanks in the following categories: top think-tank of the year; top think-tanks by region, by area of research and by special achievements.

National science academies have also been involved in the G7/G8-G20 nexus; for example, in 2012, national academies from 15 countries (Brazil, Canada, China, France, Germany, India, Indonesia, Italy, Japan, Mexico, Morocco, Russia, South Africa, the UK and the US – known jointly as 'G-Science') issued three joint statements addressed to the G8 and the G20: on the linkage of energy and water; on natural and technology-originated disasters; and on emissions and sinks of greenhouse gases (Royal Society, 2012a, 2012b, 2012c). In 2017, science academies of the G20 countries called for G20 action on improving global health, highlighting global health challenges and the threat posed to the global economy (Royal Society, 2017). Their joint statement was delivered to German Chancellor Angela Merkel.

Although women, through NGOs and mass campaigns, have long engaged the G7/G8 and the G20 on the environment, development, health, human rights and other global issues of concern, women's groups as such had more limited interaction with the G7/G8 and G20 in earlier years. Writing in 2008, Dobson argued that gender equity and women's issues had not figured in a major way on the G8 agenda. Later, Kulik and Kirton (2012) painted a more encouraging picture. On a more sobering note, the public opinion firm TrustLaw conducted a poll in the same year on the situation of women in G20 member countries (19 countries, as the European Union is the twentieth member) and found that the best country in which to be a woman was Canada and the worst was India. In addition to Canada, Germany, the UK, Australia and France were in the top five (TrustLaw, 2012). Women's groups have met in alternative summits for several years and now meet annually and interact with the G20 host government as an engagement group (see ahead). Gender issues have then risen to prominence at recent G7 and G20 summits, and women's G7- and G20-related coalitions have become a firm part of the summit process, as discussed ahead.

Indigenous groups have had a smaller and more tentative relationship with the G7/G8 and the G20 – for example, an alternative summit in 2008, limited dialogue with the Mexican summit hosts in 2012 and Canadian government consultation including indigenous representatives leading up to the 2018 Charlevoix G7 summit. There have also been indigenous protests and demonstrations around summits – for example, in Australia in 2014.

Youth groups have been active since the 2005 Gleneagles G8 summit when the J8 (Junior 8) forum first met, although the 'civil society' status of this initiative is problematic as it was then organized by the United Nations Children's Fund (UNICEF) – an international governmental organization (IGO) – and the G8 host government. Some subsequent youth summits (parallel with G7/G8 and G20 summits) were co-organized or hosted by host governments as well. As with the case of women's groups, G7/G8- and G20-related youth events, too, have now become a firm part of the summit process.

Some CSOs divide their attention between the G7/G8 and the G20 but, despite the still unclear distinction between the functions of the two fora and the shifting agenda of the G20, civil society focus is also evolving. Civil society groups have tended to concentrate their activities in the G7/G8 and G20 summit host country and as close as possible to the actual summit venue. CSOs from other parts of the world, particularly from the global South, often lack sufficient resources to travel to those locations. Moreover, visas or entry permits have been denied for some summits to a number of NGO activists. Although some citizen groups from Africa have been active vis-à-vis the G7/G8 and the G20 in recent years, civil society presence around the summits is likely to remain predominantly local, including domestic affiliates of large international CSOs. And civil society from the global South is often represented by diaspora groups residing in the summit country. It is worth noting here that business and labour associations are funded better (the B20 much better) than other engagement groups (these are discussed later in this chapter) so that they do not face the same constraints as the other groups.

What motivates CSOs to engage with the G20? The answer is as varied as the CSOs themselves. Briefly, they wish to promote social and economic justice, including the alleviation of poverty and inequality; development in the global South (and pockets of the impoverished Far North and other marginalized populations); reduction of the North-South gap; action on climate change, infectious diseases, child and maternal health and mortality; improved education opportunities; just solutions to trade problems and improved human rights, including the rights of women. Recognizing the interconnectedness of international diplomacy, CSOs do not limit their activities to G7/G8 and G20 summits; they bring the same concerns and demands to other major international negotiations at the UN, the WTO, the Bretton Woods institutions and elsewhere.

But different civil society groups have diverging views on what constitutes social and economic justice, and they use a variety of tactics, depending on the type and orientation of particular CSOs. They are also conscious of their impact on official policies and on governance. As importantly, they usually seek media exposure. Finally, more radical groups aim to change political and economic systems – for example, by replacing capitalism with another system.

Stages in the evolution of civil society-G7/G8-G20 relations

Although some local civil society approaches to the G7 were made as early as 1976, the first years of summitry saw little interaction. This history can be divided into six phases:

- Phase I (1975–80): the beginning and early years of the relationship. During this period, which may be called 'mutual ignorance' or 'mutual non-recognition', G7 leaders did not recognize CSOs as potential interlocutors, and civil society, by and large, did not yet realize the power and importance of the G7.
- Phase II (1981–94): one-sided recognition. During this time, civil society acknowledged the G7 but CSOs still had not reached the G7's consciousness. As the agenda of the G7 expanded from the original macroeconomic focus, NGOs began to see this group of powerful states as legitimate targets both for lobbying and for opposing. Advocacy, alternative summits and demonstrations became common.
- Phase III (1995–97): mutual recognition. Starting with the 1995 Halifax G7 summit, the G7, too, began to recognize and acknowledge civil society.
- Phase IV (1998–2001): well-established, systematic G8 contacts with civil society. Beginning with the first true G8 summit in Birmingham in 1998, civil society gradually became stronger and more sophisticated in its relationship with the G8.
- Phase V (2002–2013): regularized relationship. Starting with the 2002 Kananaskis summit, both the NGO world and official summit hosts expected and have been willing – with some exceptions – to interact with each other, with the non-state groups eventually called 'outreach groups'.

- Phase VI (2014 to the present): more formally structured relationship. Starting with the 2014 Brisbane G20 summit, these interlocutors have been termed 'engagement groups'. For the G7, in 2017, they were: B7 (business – not a civil society group), C7 (civil society), S7 (science), T7 (think-tanks), W7 (women), Y7 (youth) and L7 (labour). For the G20, Argentina (2018) has: B20 (business), C20 (civil society), L20 (labour), S20 (science), T20 (think-tanks), W20 (women) and Y20 (youth).

Civil society learned well the lessons of its relationship with the G7/G8. With the establishment of the G20 at the leaders' level, interaction developed at a much faster pace. The 'mutual ignorance' phase did not occur between CSOs and the G20; civil society groups recognized the importance of the G20 leaders' forum from its inception in 2008.

Mutual recognition began with the London G20 summit, where civil society sophistication was already evident. Regularized interaction was established at the Toronto summit, and firmed up the same year at the Seoul summit. It continued strongly at all subsequent summits, with an expanding assemblage of what came to be called G20 'engagement groups'. The 2018 Buenos Aires summit website, g20.org/en/g20-argentina/engagement-groups, lists the following such groups: B20, which was the first engagement group recognized as such at the 2010 Toronto summit (not a civil society group – see Chapter 5); C20, formally established by the Russian Presidency in 2013 (but there were earlier civil society meetings with G20 officials starting around the 2009 Pittsburgh summit); L20, formally recognized in 2011 under the French Presidency (but labour groups met with G20 leaders as early as 2008); S20, which first became a formal engagement group in 2017 under Germany's Presidency (however, science academies had engaged with the 'Gs' for several years); T20, initiated by the Mexican Presidency in 2012 but a forerunner activity had already taken place before the 2009 London summit; W20, initiated by the Turkish Presidency in 2015; and Y20.

However, some important groups are missing from the official engagement groups:

- indigenous representatives, despite the major contributions these populations can make to understanding and respecting the environment and to the preservation and sustainable use of natural resources; as well, they would be justified and qualified to take action to redress inequality;
- faith leaders, who can bring a moral dimension to global governance; and
- sub-state entities (US states, provinces in other countries, businesses) that are essential to the fight against climate change.

The absence of such groups from official G20 interlocutors can be attributed to various factors: despite considerable indigenous presence in several G20 countries (including Australia, Brazil, Canada, Japan, Mexico, Russia and the US), there is no consensus among the G20 leaders about accepting indigenous contributions to G20 deliberations. Although religious leaders have met regularly for many years to discuss and propose G7/G8-G20 action on a number of issues, such as environment and climate, peace and security and inequality, the G20 has not seen fit to include an 'F20' (Faith 20) in their engagement groups. Nor has the G20 found a way to benefit from the knowledge and willingness of sub-state actors as official interlocutors.

An example of the principles of civil society-G20 interaction is that the Mexican host government of the Los Cabos summit outlined the following principles as a basis for its outreach to civil society: permanent dialogue and openness; transparency; inclusiveness; gender diversity; and incorporation of civil society concerns in G20 discussions. In its outreach to civil society, the Mexican government especially emphasized NGOs in Latin America and in the troika countries (in 2012 France, Mexico and Russia). Russian CSOs were fully engaged in this process (Alexander, 2012; email to author, 30 July).

On its part, the civil society association G8/G20 Global Working Group (which later became inactive) presented its guiding principles of dialogue with the G20 on civil society priorities in 2012: development, growth and inequality, food security, transparency and anti-corruption (G8/G20 Global Working Group, 2012).

Types of civil society action around the G20 summits

The G7/G8 and the G20 have both been cognizant of the problem of legitimacy. Establishing and maintaining relations with the global community enhances that legitimacy, and civil society, as part of that community, plays an important role in this process. Successful interaction improves the legitimacy of both CSOs and the G7/G8-G20, increasing the potential of civil society impact on the summits, and can be of mutual benefit.

Over the history of G7/G8-G20 summits, CSOs have had multifaceted interaction with the 'Gs'. The following section highlights and analyzes several types of civil society activities: dialogue, evaluation and monitoring, policy papers, alternative summits, petitions, street demonstrations and other kinds of action. Cooper (2013) argues that the G20-CSO interaction exhibits both similarities to and distinctive differences from the G8-civil society template.

Dialogue

There was some civil society awareness of the implications of the G20's first summit in Washington. Just before the summit, labour union leaders from all the G20 countries met with several G20 leaders and other officials, and with the heads of the IMF and the World Bank; these included Brazilian President Luiz Inacio Lula da Silva and the Prime Ministers of Japan (Taro Aso) and Australia (Kevin Rudd). This dialogue followed earlier labour union meetings with Gordon Brown in the UK and with the Spanish and French leaders in their home countries. They discussed the international labour union movement's 'Washington Declaration', which called for a coordinated recovery plan for the economy, the reregulation of global financial markets, a new international system of economic governance and a strategy to combat growing inequality around the world. The International Trade Union Confederation (ITUC) is the lead union group in such contacts (ITUC, 2008).

Preceding the second G20 summit in April 2009, NGO representatives from various countries convened a conference in the summit city of London on 23–25 February with the theme 'From Crisis to a Just and Sustainable World Economy'. The conference was organized by the development-, human rights– and environment-centred campaign Rights and Humanity. Although this was not a consultation as such, the host government took note of it on its official summit website (no longer accessible). Another indicator of the host's willingness to engage the public appeared some time before the summit, on 30 January, when the UK government announced that the official website would provide a gateway to inform the public and encourage comment and debate; the website subsequently made good on this undertaking (G20, 2009b). Two months later, the Prime Minister addressed faith leaders and NGO representatives at St Paul's Cathedral on the necessity of global economic rules based on common values, and the need for G20 leaders to make decisions on the global economy in the interests of everybody (G20, 2009e). On 14 March, the British consulate in Istanbul hosted a roundtable meeting to discuss the London G20 summit.

By the time of the Pittsburgh G20 summit, civil society interaction with G20 officials developed further. It involved dialogue, a people's summit, policy papers and demonstrations. In one example of dialogue, the US-based civil society umbrella group InterAction organized meetings with G20 officials.

The back-to-back Muskoka G8 and Toronto G20 summits in June 2010 were preceded by a series of dialogue sessions between civil society groups and G8-G20 officials. These included a 'Civil G8', a videoconference with the Canadian host sherpa team and separate consultations on maternal, newborn and child health. This last had significant influence on host Prime Minister Stephen Harper's centrepiece of the G8 summit, even though civil society input was not explicitly acknowledged.

The Seoul summit saw considerable civil society activity, including consultations with expert NGOs. The first 'Civil G20' met before the summit, and other NGO (including trade union) consultations were held with the Korean sherpa and other government officials. Significantly, the Korean government put a senior official in charge of civil society relations.

At the Cannes summit, some 100 NGOs and civil society coalitions were represented at the press centre at the Palais des Festivals, among them major NGOs, such as Oxfam, WWF, ONE and World Vision, French CSOs, such as CCFD-Terre Solidaire and Coordination SUD, the US-based civil society umbrella group InterAction, and others. On 2 November 2011 President Sarkozy met with representatives of the 'Labour 20' (L20) at the Elysée Palace for a working lunch. This L20, not to be confused with the earlier L20 proposal to establish the G20 on the leaders' level (for which see Chapter 7), took place on 3–4 November 2011. The L20 issued a joint statement with the B20 (Business Summit), in an example of stakeholder cooperation between the private sector and the trade union segment of civil society (B20-L20, 2011).

CSOs held several dialogue sessions with officials before, during and after the Los Cabos summit. On 16 June, the session was hosted by the Mexican government and attended by the host country's ministers of foreign affairs, of the economy, and of agriculture, livestock and rural development, fisheries and food. The host government received civil society recommendations addressed to the G20 leaders and noted with approval that CSOs helped enrich the G20 development agenda on priorities like food security, funding for infrastructure projects, inclusive green growth and strengthening nutritional security for at-risk populations. On the same day, several NGOs participated in the 'Rethinking the G20: Designing the Future' forum, hosted by President Calderón. Three more such sessions were held, on 17, 18 and 19 June, two with the participation of the Mexican chair of the Development Working Group (DWG). In terms of CSO access to officials and extent of official outreach, the Mexican summit arguably outshone previous G20 summits, but the quality and content of consultations in 2012 were generally not as good as they might have been. For instance, it would have been useful for CSOs to receive background papers from the Mexican government in advance, in order to provide better context for the consultations. A number of such papers were prepared; for example, for the G20 working groups. Nor did the Mexican government reveal policy options under consideration (Alexander, 2012; interview with author, 4 June; email to author, 30 July). However desirable and ideal, G20 transparency has not generally gone as far as prior sharing of detailed background information with CSOs.

On the first day of the Los Cabos summit, New Rules for Global Finance held a seminar on G20 transparency and participation. On the latter issue, the seminar explored these questions: How effective is the participation of CSOs in G20 processes? Do these groups 'have sufficient access to information about the Summit's policy agenda to participate in informed and constructive ways?' Are there 'opportunities for meaningful consultation in advance of the final decision-making processes?' (New Rules, 2012b).

The first instance of indigenous connection with the G20 occurred in 2012, when the Mexican host government invited representatives of the UN's Permanent Forum on Indigenous Issues to attend part of the Los Cabos summit – where food security figured prominently on the leaders' agenda – to present their position on the right to food (UN ESC, 2012). Prior to the summit, a meeting was held with the participation of Mexican farmers', peasants' and indigenous people's organizations and representatives of the Mexican government, as well as the FAO and OECD. They concentrated on food security. While praiseworthy, it is not clear how effectively this step will promote meaningful indigenous participation in global governance, given the lukewarm or antagonistic attitude of several G20 countries towards their indigenous peoples.

Civil G8

A dialogue process named 'Civil G8' began during Russia's G8 Presidency in 2006. It was preceded by long, careful preparations – and this timeliness is important because attempts at last-minute intervention are too late. This event was organized with impressive resources and substantial support from the Russian host government. The 'Civil G8' and 'Civil G7' have been repeated yearly ever since, but more modestly and with fewer resources.

Consultation with the Canadian G20 host sherpa team

The Montreal-based civil society think-tank FIM Forum for Democratic Global Governance pioneered a consultation with the Canadian G20 host sherpa and his team prior to the Toronto G20 summit (for a brief assessment of this consultation, see Make Poverty History, 2010). FIM built on its experience of initiating a similar dialogue at the 2002 Kananaskis G8 summit between the Canadian host government and three other G8 governments on the one hand and civil society representatives from countries of the North and South on the other side. FIM's cumulative G8 experience is examined by Nigel Martin (2008). The 2010 dialogue involved, on the official side, the Canadian G20 host sherpa, the finance sous-sherpa and others. Twenty civil society leaders from around the world participated. The focus was on 'accountability of the G20 to the citizens of the world'. Apart from the Istanbul roundtable discussion in 2009, the Ottawa dialogue was the first such major event in the G20 setting. It gave civil society representatives from North and South a voice that called on the G20 to 'deepen democratization of global governance institutions, processes, and decision-making' (Tandon and Martin, 2010) Martin and Tandon (2014, pp. 137–160) later analyzed this relationship in greater detail.

The consultation also covered macroeconomic policy issues, stimulus measures 'for the transformation of national and global economies into "green economies that eradicate poverty"', food security, employment, 'clear and transparent regulation of global financial flows' and reform of the governance of international financial institutions, including 'open, transparent, global, professional, and competitive procedures for recruitment of heads of these institutions' (Tandon and Martin, 2010). These ideas seem to have found at least some resonance among G20 officials.

G8-G20 stakeholder videoconference with the Canadian host sherpa team

The Canadian host sherpa for the Muskoka G8 and Toronto G20 summits and his team held a videoconference with G8 and G20 stakeholders – including civil society representatives – on 19 June 2010. The face-to-face meeting with CSO representatives took place at the Department of Foreign Affairs and International Trade in Ottawa; other groups participated by simultaneous video link from McGill University in Montreal, the Liu Institute for Global Issues at the University of British Columbia and the Munk School of Global Affairs at the University of Toronto.

Participants asked the sherpas questions first on items on the G8 agenda (particularly development, and peace and security), and then on the G20 agenda (mainly on the financial and economic crisis and aspects of recovery). In their responses the sherpa team members stressed the importance of consultation and dialogue with NGOs and other stakeholders, and pointed out that accountability was a centrepiece of the Muskoka summit. The replies of the officials did not fully answer civil society criticisms of non-delivery or partial delivery of prior G8 commitments. The officials maintained their view that a clear division of labour remained between the G8 and the G20.

Civil G20

A CSO-G20 dialogue – the first such consultation termed 'Civil G20' – took place on 15 October 2010 in Incheon, South Korea. It was hosted by the G20 Presidential Committee for the G20 Summit in cooperation with the Global Call to Action against Poverty (GCAP) Korea campaign. Over 100 representatives from 34 NGOs from 40 countries participated. The consultation covered trade, reform of financial regulations and international financial institutions, development and G20 governance. The Civil G20's recommendations were delivered to the sherpas, who elaborated on the G20 agenda and, in an important development, called for active cooperation with NGOs (Choi, 2010).

On 30 September 2011, a pre-Cannes summit dialogue, presented as a 'Civil G20', was hosted by the French Ministry of Foreign Affairs. Because this consultation was called on very short notice and was not carefully prepared, French and international NGO attendance was limited. As this session was held at the same time as an official sherpa meeting, several sherpas made only a brief appearance, in order not to miss the official negotiations. There was no real 'Civil G20' dialogue with G20 sherpas before the Los Cabos summit, only several seminars and fora (discussed elsewhere in this chapter). This failure to facilitate a real Civil G20 in 2012 may have been due to G20 officials' negative experience with such meetings before Seoul and Cannes: the format of those two was good but the result was seen as not very effective by the sherpas and participating NGOs alike. The Mexican summit hosts therefore attempted to deliver a better and more effective process and approach in 2012 (Ruthrauff, 2012; email to author, 23 July).

In an earlier meeting, 59 representatives from 51 Mexican and international CSOs held a 1.5-hour dialogue on 23 February in Mexico City with the following Mexican government officials concerned with the G20: the Minister of Foreign Affairs, the G20 sherpa, another Ministry of Foreign Affairs official responsible for outreach to civil society, the G20 representative of the Ministry of Finance, and 15 other officials from various ministries. CSO delegates gave presentations on: guiding principles of G20 dialogue with civil society; food security; development; growth and inequality; and transparency and anti-corruption. The officials welcomed civil society proposals, promised to share some proposals with their peers from other G20 countries, and cautioned that some NGO recommendations had more to do with national policies than with the G20 as a whole. Officials accordingly encouraged CSOs to try to influence their own parliaments and regulators (G8/G20 Global Working Group, 2012; email to author, 2 March).

This was *realpolitik* at play, but nonetheless discouraging. Thus, the results of this consultation were mixed.

The Russian-hosted G20 summit convened in St Petersburg on 5–6 September 2013. The Russian G8/G20 NGOs Working Group took a leading role in a Civil G20 process around the St Petersburg G20 summit. The stated goal of this initiative was

> [t]o provide national and regional civil society organizations with information about ways of cooperation within the scope of G20; to involve all interested organizations in discussion [of] issues covered by the G20; and to develop a joint platform for a dialogue during Civil G20 meeting in 2013 between civil society and policy-makers in Russia and the other G20 countries.
>
> (Russian G8/G20, 2012)

A Civil 20 conference took place in Moscow on 11–13 December 2012, with the participation of 140 representatives of NGOs, academics and think-tanks from 20 countries. The programme, entitled 'G20 Civil Society Vision for the Russian Presidency', focused on civil society's role in the global political dialogue, CSO expectations from the Russian Presidency, accountability and other issues. The 'Civil20 summit was held on 13–14 June 2013 in Moscow; it prepared recommendations for the G20 leaders' (Civil 20, 2013). It proposed that 'further Civil 20 efforts be focused on drawing up general principles of collaboration between the state and civil society in G20 countries' and stated that 'civil society should be autonomous from the state' (Civil 20, 2013).

The 2014 C20 in Australia addressed a number of recommendations to the G20 on inequality and inclusive growth, protection of the environment and addressing climate change, decent work and gender equality. It welcomed 'civil society's inclusion as a permanent engagement group within the G20' and asserted that this relationship is 'central to the legitimacy of the G20' (Civil 20, 2014).

In 2015, the C20 in Turkey issued a communiqué, *A World Economy That Includes All*. The four central issues, some carried over from the previous year, were: inclusive growth, gender equality, governance (focusing on international taxation and anti-corruption) and sustainability. It addressed recommendations to the G20 on these issues (Civil 20, 2015).

The 2016 C20, meeting in Qingdao, China, on 5–6 July, brought together representatives from 54 countries and regions. Their discussion focused on poverty eradication, green development and innovation, emphasizing civil society's role in these efforts 'as forerunner, communicator, supervisor and facilitator'. It put forward the expectation of 'equal and sufficient attention from each and every G20 Presidency in the years to come' and recommended a troika structure, mirroring that of the G20, to ensure continuity, communication and coordination among the past, current and future year's C20 (Civil 20, 2016).

In 2017, 200 representatives from 45 countries participated in the C20 summit process. Their working groups developed recommendations on the following priority topics: agriculture; environment and water issues; global health; inequality;

international financial system reform; responsible investment and the private sector; and climate and energy sustainability. The C20 held its summit in Hamburg C20 on 18–19 June, two weeks before the G20 summit. Civil society enjoyed very good access to German Chancellor Angela Merkel, as well as to sherpas and other officials of other G20 countries. They presented the recommendations to the Chancellor, who then held a one-hour dialogue with four representatives of Oxfam International, Global Trade Watch, the German NGO VENRO and the German NGO Forum on Environment and Development (Ruthfauff and Cadwallader, 2017).

Other consultations

A group of NGOs concerned with maternal, newborn and child health (one of the focal points of the Muskoka G8 summit) held separate consultations with government officials early in 2010. This dialogue, with the participation of NGOs with impressive expertise in the relevant fields, resulted in exchanges useful to both government officials and the NGOs. Details of these consultations have not been released publicly but, judging from the prominent attention to these issues at Muskoka and the significant (albeit relatively modest) G8 commitments, these expert NGOs have influenced the G8, even though such influence was not explicitly acknowledged in summit documents. Governments cannot readily provide this type of expertise; they need civil society input.

In the G20 context, prior to the London summit, representatives of a few think-tanks, notably the Centre for Global Studies and the Peterson Institute of International Economics, met with Prime Minister Gordon Brown and his officials (including the sherpa team and officials from the Treasury and other ministries), and presented ideas on injecting a large amount of money into the IMF, specifically via an SDR allocation. Other issues, such as financial regulation, were also discussed. That Brown stayed at the meeting for an hour is indicative of his interest in and receptivity to think-tank input. This expert contribution arguably played a role in G20's $1 trillion boost of IMF resources – an example of civil society impact on the G20 (Truman, 2012; interview with author, 5 June; email to author, 15 August; Smith, Carin, and Heap, 2012; interviews with author, 7–8 August; emails to author, 15–16 August). Another instance of civil society impact occurred in 2014 when Transparency International (TI) 'successfully influenced the Anti-Corruption Action Plan 2016–2017 . . . and the G20 High Level Beneficial Ownership Principles'. The Principles might not have been agreed to without TI's advocacy. TI was also invited to B20 meetings (Murphy, 2018; email to author, 16 April).

Before the Seoul summit, consultations took place again, besides those with the 'Civil G20'. For example, in October, Korean and international civil society representatives, including those from GCAP, held a workshop on the subject of G20 and development as part of the preparations for the Seoul summit. In addition to civil society discussions, the workshop featured the Korean sherpa, who presented his government's position on the major agenda items for the summit.

Separately, labour union leaders secured bilateral talks on a high level with G20 leaders themselves; these were held before the G20 summit. This type of engagement gives the unions unusual direct access to the leaders. The content and results of this and similar high-level consultations tend not to be made publicly available. NGOs and G20 officials also consulted in other parts of the world before the Seoul summit. For example, civil society representatives met with the Russian, Japanese and German sherpas or their assistants in the respective countries to discuss the forthcoming G20 summit and exchange views.

Prior to the Cannes summit, President Sarkozy met with representatives of the Club of Madrid on 9 September at the Elysée Palace for a working lunch discussing the priorities of the French Presidency. He also held a working meeting on 2 November with NGO representatives. Other NGO meetings with sherpas took place as well.

Later G20 presidencies have also held dialogue sessions with other interlocutors in addition to the official engagement groups. For example, on 6 April 2017 the German Federal Ministry for Economic Affairs and Energy organized a multistakeholder conference, 'Digitalisation: Policies for a Digital Future' in Düsseldorf, in the run-up to the G20 Digital Ministers' meeting.

Think-tanks (T20)

Precursors of G7 and G20 think-tanks began many years ago:

> From the early 1980s, some research (and sometimes private) institutions organised 'pre-summits' that gathered with the support of governments, experts, businessmen, bankers, intellectuals, scholars, economists and national and international civil servants who provided transnational reflections about the topics that would be discussed by the G7.
>
> (Bonhomme, 2014, p. 106)

In the lead-up to the Los Cabos G20 summit, 22 experts from 19 think-tanks from around the world gathered on 27–28 February in Mexico City for a 'Think-20' meeting – the first such consultation in G20 history, although not all G20 countries were represented. The objective of the Mexican host government was to make the G20 dialogue as open, transparent, innovative and inclusive as possible and, through dialogue, to gather practical and innovative ideas for improving the G20 processes and policies. The meeting was initiated by the Mexican host government and organized by the Mexican Council on Foreign Relations with other think-tanks. Mexican G20 sherpa Lourdes Arandes participated (her former chief, Andrés Rozental, played an important part in initiating the Think-20 process), along with former Canadian Prime Minister Paul Martin and others. Participants discussed Mexico's summit priorities:

> economic stability and structural reforms for growth and employment; strengthening the financial system and fostering financial inclusion to

> promote economic growth; improving the international financial architecture; enhancing food security; addressing commodity price volatility; promoting sustainable development and green growth; and fighting against climate change.

The Think-20 submitted its report and recommendations to the Mexican G20 Presidency. The Think-20 consultation took place in a cooperative spirit; the group worked well together, setting aside different ideological dispositions and thematic emphases. The Mexican sherpa and her team were respectful of this engagement with the group. This dialogue, however, would have been more productive had the Mexican government provided background papers and policy options, in order to provide better context for the discussions. Participants came away with a generally positive impression of the Think-20. Some sherpas, however, were not then in favour of the idea to make the Think-20 a regular part of the summit process (Alexander, 2012; interview with author, 4 June; email to author, 30 July).

The Russian host government's outreach programme for St Petersburg included a T20 (along with the C20, Y20 and L20, plus B20). The T20 met, for the second time, on 11 December 2012. This meeting discussed: economic growth, macroeconomic issues and fiscal sustainability; trade and foreign direct investment; and sustainable development (G20, 2012aa).

In the Australian G20 Presidency year, 2014, the T20 continued to be active. Its policy recommendations covered: the G20 economic and finance process; trade liberalization; investment and infrastructure financing; and development. The Turkish T20 in 2015 focused on: macroeconomic coordination and financial stability; trade and investment for development; inclusivity and competition; and infrastructure financing and sustainable development. It convened a summit in Antalya in November.

The 2016 T20 summit met on 29–30 July in Beijing with the theme 'Building New Global Relationships: New Dynamics, New Prospects'. Its policy recommendations centred around: global economic growth; global financial governance; international trade and investment cooperation; inclusive and sustainable development; and G20 governance.

In 2017 the T20 produced 20 policy proposals on the following issues: digitalization; the 2030 Agenda for Sustainable Development, climate policy and finance; G20 and Africa; global inequality and social cohesion; forced migration; ending hunger and sustainable agriculture; financial resilience; trade and investment; circular economy; international cooperation in tax matters; and resilience and inclusive growth (T20, 2017, p. 3). These recommendations were developed by the various T20 task forces. The T20 summit met on 29–30 May in Berlin.

A follow-up 'Global Solutions Summit: A G20/G7 Think Tank Initiative for Global Governance', hosted by Germany but in the stream of the Argentine G20 Presidency, convened in Berlin on 28–29 May 2018. It addressed major G20 topics, including the future of work and education, international tax cooperation, climate action, infrastructure for sustainable development, food security, international economic governance, multilateralism, democracy and the rule of law, gender equity, migration and other important global issues. High-profile speakers included Chancellor Angela Merkel and several Nobel laureates (Global Solutions, 2018). A follow-up Global Solutions Summit is set to take place on 18–19 March 2019 in Berlin.

The most powerful idea behind regular consultations between civil society and the G20 is not the particular type of dialogue (Civil G20, think-tanks and others) but rather the regular relationship and the continuous flow of ideas among CSOs as well as between CSOs – before, during and after summits. The precise makeup of CSO presence for any given event is not of great importance, as long as a group with the relevant expertise is brought together. This process generally worked well at subsequent summits. Civil society impact on actual summit outcomes is difficult to gauge; for such impact on any initiative, there has to be a convergence of all forces, including consensus within the G20 itself (Bradford, 2012; interviews with author, 5 June and 30 July).

Monitoring and evaluation

CSOs play an important role in holding the G7/G8 and G20 accountable for fulfilling their promises. A number of NGOs, including academic and NGO-centred think-tanks, have initiated systematic evaluations either across a range of issues or concentrating on specific sectors – for instance, development. Examples include the G7/G8 and G20 Research Groups at the University of Toronto, New Rules for Global Finance, the ONE (formerly Debt AIDS Trade Africa (DATA) group), the InterAction coalition and Transparency International. Along with monitoring and evaluation by other actors – and self-assessment by the G7/G8 and G20 – civil society's role in this type of activity is explored in more detail in Chapter 8.

Policy papers

These are another means for CSOs to influence the G8 and G20 on pressing global issues. One example is a Friedrich-Ebert-Stiftung study published in December 2009 which noted that the rapid rescue of the global financial system spurred by the G20 leaders, national governments, central banks and IFIs had not been accompanied by equally vigorous efforts to reform global financial governance. The authors called for full transparency and accountability in the global economic system; underlined the need for radical reforms of domestic and international financial institutions; and argued for a socially responsible and democratic global economic system (Rude and Burke, 2009).

Another policy paper appeared in January 2010, with the title *What's Missing in the Response to the Global Financial Crisis?* It builds on the 19–20 October 2009 conference that followed the Pittsburgh G20 summit and was co-hosted by the Halifax Initiative, the North-South Institute, the University of Ottawa and the School of International Development and Global Studies. The paper included recommendations to the June 2010 G8 and G20 summits on the international financial system and IFIs (Halifax Initiative, 2010b).

An NGO based in the Philippines, IBON International, released a paper in October 2010 with a title somewhat similar to the foregoing, *What Is Missing in the G20 Agenda? Redressing Structural Imbalances for Equity, Justice and Sustainability*. The paper detailed the imbalances in the global economy: 'inequality between capital-owners and wage-earners, between high finance and the real economy, between developed and developing countries, and the democratic deficit in institutions of global economic governance'. It characterized these imbalances as 'systemic failures of the neoliberal development model' (Quintos, 2010, p. 2). The paper found the G20 response inadequate and proposed policy alternatives to the G20 agenda.

Also in 2010, Oxfam produced a policy brief, *The Making of a Seoul Development Consensus: The Essential Development Agenda for the G-20*. It advocates for growth that reduces inequality, for more ambitious G20 action on the climate crisis and for the right to food. The paper also recommends ways to deliver the development consensus (Oxfam, 2010). One of the key documents of the Seoul summit is the *Seoul Development Consensus for Shared Growth*. It is not clear whether Oxfam's earlier use of this phrase influenced the G20 in focusing on and choosing as the title the *Seoul Development Consensus* or whether Oxfam had prior knowledge of this likely outcome of the summit (G20, 2010e). Oxfam International published a report before the Los Cabos summit on inequality and environmental degradation (Oxfam, 2011, 2012b). In 2013 Oxfam issued *Cracks in Tax: A Plan of Action: Joint Recommendations to the G20 and OECD for Tackling Base Erosion and Profit Shifting* (Oxfam, 2013a). This policy brief is the result of the collaboration of 34 CSOs. An important paper is *The G20 and Gender Equality*, produced jointly with Heinrich Böll Stiftung North America (Oxfam and Heinrich Böll Stiftung North America, 2014),

InterAction has been preparing policy briefs and policy papers on G7/G8 and G20 issues almost every year since 2005. These are strong, thoughtful, well-focused examples of the way civil society can best address G7/G8-G20 officials (although these are addressed mostly to the US government, whose officials have expressed interest; see www.interaction.org/resources). For example, in 2018 InterAction issued recommendations and background information on the following G20-related topics: anti-corruption; early childhood development; food security and nutrition; gender equality; global health; responsible business conduct; and climate, energy and infrastructure sustainability (InterAction and G7/G20 Advocacy Alliance, 2018).

Heinrich Böll Stiftung North America has published several policy papers, including *The G20: Playing Outside the Big Tent: Implications for Rio+20* by Nancy Alexander and Peter Riggs (2012). They compare the development agendas of the Los Cabos G20 summit and the subsequent UN 'Rio+20' conference, and offer recommendations on G20 accountability and transparency, development financing, and the G20 Development Action Plan. A more recent example is *The Plan for a Better World: The G20 and the 2030 Agenda for Sustainable Development* by Marie-Louise Abshagen (2016). Böll's main information vehicle, however, is a portal, 'G20 in Focus' (us.boell.org/searching/contents/g20%20in%20 focus). As well, Böll issues the 'Just Governance' blog series, which includes a number of G20-related postings (us.boell.org/searching/contents/just%20 governance).

Transparency International issues the *G20 Position Paper* series. A2017 example is *Clean Supply Chains*, which advocates that all G20 countries adhere to the OECD Guidelines for Multinational Enterprises, in order to follow comprehensive anti-corruption programmes and protect whistleblowers (TI, 2017).

Alternative summits

Alternative or parallel summits convened by civil society groups have a long tradition in CSO relations with the G7/G8 and now with the G20. The first such alternative summit, called 'Popular Summit', took place around the time of the 1981 Ottawa (Montebello) G7 summit. Such events are another form of democratic activity through which CSOs, if they choose to engage, can influence the G8 and the G20. Some parallel summits collaborate with G8 or G20 officials and have transmitted recommendations to such officials. This can be considered a form of consultation. Alternative summits that reject dialogue with the G8 and G20 can still demand the rectification of harmful effects of G8 and G20 action or inaction.

People's summits

In the G20 context, a 'people's summit', sponsored by educators and peace- and social justice-oriented advocacy groups, met in Pittsburgh in September 2009, with more than 700 participants. Signalling local official endorsement, the Pittsburgh City Council issued a proclamation supporting the event, which discussed economic, social and political problems worldwide. This gathering, in the *altermondialiste* tradition, issued a vision statement, *Another World Is Possible*, voicing the following ideals: elimination of hunger and poverty; an end to racism; rights and dignity of labour; empowerment of women; education for all; adequate health care as a basic human right; safe and inclusive communities; an end to war; human rights of refugees, immigrants, the disabled and other vulnerable groups; and preservation of the planet's ecosystem (The Peoples' Summit, 2009). Also in 2009, the 'Put People First' coalition of labour unions and development, climate change and faith-based groups held a 'G20 Counter Conference' on jobs, justice and a safer climate on 7 November in London and St Andrews (the venue of the G20 Finance Ministers' and Central Bank Governors' meeting) (Put People First, 2009).

In 2010, the 'People's Summit: Building a Movement for a Just World' in Toronto on 18–20 June, just before the G8-G20 summits in Canada, discussed: global justice (defined by the organizers as 'a struggle against the global expansion of corporate and national imperialism in order to build a better world based on equity, respect and dignity'); environment and climate change (land, water, climate change, resource use, pollution and food security issues); human rights and civil liberties; economic justice (alternatives to neo-liberalism: 'community control over resources, resistance to free trade, anti-poverty organizing, taxing the rich to support the poor'); 'building the movement'; and 'hold[ing] Canada accountable for its policies and practices at home and abroad' (website no longer accessible). This alternative summit did not wish to engage with the 'official' G8 and G20. The Toronto Community Mobilization Network, one of the participating groups, focused on street protests and other action, ranging from peaceful demonstrations to confrontation with authorities and their symbols.

Before the Seoul G20 summit, major Korean CSOs organized a series of events culminating in a people's summit held on 8–10 November, during the 6–12 November 'Joint Action Week'. It was hosted by the People's G20 Response Preparation Committee. The agenda covered financial regulation and taxation on speculative capital; decent work and basic labour rights; the environment and climate change; trade agreements alternative to those under neoliberal policies; food security and agriculture; democracy and human rights; poverty and development; forced migration; peace and security; gender and G20; cultural diversity and intellectual property rights; and public services.

At the margins of the Cannes summit, on 1–4 November 2011, an alternative summit named 'alter-forum' or Forum of the Peoples (Forum des Peuples) met in Nice, with over 40 CSOs participating, including trade unions and social movements. This *altermondialiste* event began with a large demonstration in Nice, with the slogan 'people first, not finance'. This was followed by workshops and discussions around six themes (or rather slogans): Enough of Inequality and Austerity; Life, Not the Stock Market; Change the System, Not the Planet; Do Not Play Games with Our Food; The Indignant, the Revolutionaries and Solidarity; They Are 20, We Are Billions. The main organizing body was Coordination SUD, a French umbrella group of CSOs. The forum closed with a press conference (Coordination SUD, 2011).

A 'Summit of the People' ('Cumbre de los Pueblos frente al G20') convened in Mexico City on 12–15 June and in La Paz, Baja California Sur, Mexico, on 16–19 June 2012, coinciding with and extending beyond the Los Cabos G20 summit. This people's summit brought together CSOs from Mexico and 30 other countries. It was preceded by an 'International Seminar on Alternatives to G20', held in Mexico City on 14–15 June; it featured a panel called 'Illicit Flows of Capital, Financial Transaction Tax and Tax Havens'. The agenda included: democratic alternatives for a new legitimacy; governance, corruption and financial regulation; alternatives to financial policies of banks and speculators, a financial transaction tax and illicit flows of capital; workers against structural adjustment under neoliberal politics; and alternatives to free trade. The people's summit issued an anti-capitalist, anti-G20 declaration.

A counter-summit was held in St Petersburg on 3–4 September 2013, just before the G20 summit. It issued a declaration, asserting that '[t]he G20 is not legitimate, democratic or transparent' and that it 'continues promoting failed neoliberal policies' (Trew, 2013).

On 12–14 November 2014 a people's summit, 'Visioning Another World', was held in Brisbane, Australia. It was 'a three-day festival of symposiums, idea sharing, art, creative activities, education and action, . . . [including] discussion panels and workshops on topics pertaining to austerity, food security, democracy, the environment and feminism' (Moore, 2014). An Alternative G20 Summit met in Istanbul in 2015. (As far as can be determined, there was no similar gathering in 2016.)

The year 2017 saw a 'Global Solidarity Summit', meeting in Hamburg on 5–6 July. It brought together 77 groups, initiatives and organizations and featured panel discussions and workshops, with the keynote speech by Vandana Shiva. The summit argued that '[t]he G20 defends a system that boosts social inequality' and promised to 'point out the links between the global problems and discuss alternatives that can provide a solution' (Global Solidarity Summit, 2017).

Religious leaders' summits

Are religious groups an integral part of civil society? Karen Hamilton (2010, p. 308) answers in the affirmative: 'faith communities are not only a part of civil society but are also grounded in divine imperatives to be so for the sake of the world's peoples and indeed for the sake of the globe itself'. A case can thus be made for including these faith groups in the wide range of civil society activities around the G8/G20 summits.

The first such event was convened at Lambeth Palace in London just before the 2005 Gleneagles G8 summit. Subsequent faith leaders' summits met: in 2006 in Moscow; in 2007 in Cologne; in 2008 in Sapporo and another one in Kyoto and Osaka; in 2009 in Rome; in 2010 in Winnipeg, Canada.

The 2010 gathering brought together 80 senior leaders of religions and faith-based organizations from more than 20 countries of all regions of the world, representing Aboriginal, Bahá'í, Buddhist, Christian, Hindu, Jewish, Muslim, Shinto and Sikh traditions. Thirteen youth delegates also participated, and a number of observers were present. It was the culmination of a year-and-a-half-long process under the aegis of an Interfaith Partnership. The religious summit's final statement, *A Time for Inspired Leadership and Action* (World Religions Summit, 2010), urged the G8 and G20 political leaders to: alleviate poverty and injustice; promote care for the Earth and its environment; attend to the needs of the most vulnerable, especially children; and halt the arms race, reduce nuclear weapons and support a culture of peace and the rule of law. It asked for a transparent and effective dialogue between international organizations and faith communities. The statement was presented to a minister of the Canadian government (host of that year's G8 and G20 summits), who promised to pass it on to Prime Minister Harper (see Hajnal, 2010b, for more detail).

The next religious summit convened in 2011 in Bordeaux, France. The Bordeaux meeting's statement addressed the global macroeconomic situation, global governance, climate change, development and peace. The 2012 Washington meeting's statement advocated for: economic justice; food, health and human security; and poverty reduction. These statements, too, were intended for transmission to the respective year's G8 and G20 summits (Bordeaux Religious Summit, 2011; Joint Religious Coordination, 2012). On 5 April 2013, 80 religious leaders wrote to G8 leaders, 'urging them to keep promises on foreign aid and to "help to create an environment that encourages the conditions for inclusive, equitable and sustainable economic growth"' (ENS Staff, 2013).

The next interfaith summit met under the aegis of the G20 Interfaith Forum in Gold Coast, Australia, on 16–18 November 2014; it called for stronger economic growth and employment outcomes, global economic resilience, and elimination of hunger and poverty. The 16–18 November 2015 Istanbul summit ('Religion, Harmony and Sustainable Development') discussed a number of issues, including refugee relief, peace and sustainable communities, business and economic development, decent employment, health and well-being, the environment, women and dialogue among civilizations. The last topic was central in Beijing on 30 August–1 September 2016. The summit's theme was 'Dialogue among Civilizations and Community of Common Destiny for All Mankind'. The theme of the Potsdam, Germany, gathering on 15–17 June 2017 was 'religion, sustainable development, and the refugee crisis'. The next interfaith summit is scheduled for Buenos Aires on 26–28 September 2018.

Each religious summit issues a report or statement. For detailed information on these summits see www.g20interfaith.org. For an analysis of faith leaders' summits, see Steiner (2018), who assesses religious diplomacy vis-à-vis the G8, G7 and G20 and the potential of moral influence on globalization. As noted earlier, the G20 has not yet accepted the faith leaders' summits (F20) as engagement partners.

Other alternative summits

On one (and so far the only) occasion in G7/G8-G20 summit history, a four-day Indigenous Peoples' Summit was held in Sapporo, Japan, ahead of the G8 summit in 2008, with participants from five continents and the Pacific region. The meeting released the *Nibutani Declaration*, which spelled out various concerns of indigenous peoples and addressed 22 proposals to the G8 (Lewallen, 2008). Although no other indigenous peoples' summit has yet taken place, aboriginal peoples have been represented in various other CSO activities; and there has been limited dialogue (see earlier) in 2012 with the Mexican hosts of the Los Cabos G20 summit and in 2018 with the Canadian hosts of the Charlevoix G7 summit.

G8/G20 university summits (meetings of University Presidents) began in Sapporo, Japan, in 2008 and have met annually since: in Turin and Palermo, Italy, in 2009, in Vancouver, Canada, on 20–22 May 2010 (for the first time, with participants from the G8 and G20 countries). The three themes in 2010 were sustainable energy, sustainable health and sustainable higher education. The group issued a declaration and a statement of action. A related G8 university students' summit was held on 1–3 May in Banff, Alberta; it issued its own statement of action (website no longer accessible). The following year, on 15 February, the University Summit, organized in Dijon by Bourgogne Franche-Comté Universités (2011), issued its statement for transmission to the G20 leaders. In some respects, the science academies' meeting series (discussed elsewhere) can be considered the successor to these university summits.

G7/G8 and G20 youth summits are often co-sponsored by the host governments so they are not always purely civil society events, as noted earlier. Preceded by the J8 or Junior 8 youth forum at Gleneagles in 2005, youth summits have met annually since 2006, in turn in St Petersburg (G8), Berlin (G8), Yokohama (G8), Milan (G8) and Paris (G20), Vancouver (G20/G8) and again in Paris (G20/G8). In 2010, an event called 'My Summit 2010' was co-hosted by the government of Canada and the NGO Global Vision. The G8 portion met in Huntsville in the Muskoka area on 23–25 June during the G8 summit and discussed the same themes as the G8 summit itself. The G20 segment took place on 26–27 June, at the time of the Toronto G20 summit. For that event, university students from each of the 19 member countries of the G20 (the EU as such was not represented) were selected in their home countries. The Canadian government and the students' countries of origin shared the costs. Selection was largely based on the students' interest in economic and political affairs, and the programme of the youth summit had a strong business flavour. During the two-day event, one student from each delegation was given the opportunity to meet with the G20.

The 2011 G8 & G20 Youth Summits event, organized by the group Youth Diplomacy and held under the aegis of the French presidency of the G20 and the G8, met on 29 May–3 June. The G8 portion concentrated on diplomatic and security issues, while the G20 segment focused on finance and economics, governance, environment and development. Youth delegates from G20 countries met with high officials and issued a communiqué, which was presented to the French Presidency (G8 & G20 Youth Summits, 2011).

In the lead-up to the 2012 G20 summit, the Mexican government invited 128 university students representing youth from around the world to participate in 'Y20 Mexico'. This youth forum, held in Puebla, Mexico, on 9–11 May, produced the *Y20 Puebla Agreement*, presented to President Felipe Calderón on 11 May at his official residence, to be shared at the summit with his fellow leaders. The *Puebla Agreement* addressed youth concerns with: economic stability and financial inclusion; youth employment; international trade; sustainable development, green growth and climate change; food security and commodity price volatility; global governance and strengthening multilateral organizations; and the future of the G20. It offered a number of recommendations to the G20 leaders (G20, 2012ag). Earlier in 2012, the organization Young Americans for Diplomatic Leadership hosted a youth summit at George Washington University in Washington, DC (G8 & G20 Youth Summits, 2011).

The Y20 Russia 2013 Summit (youth summit) met on 18–21 June in St Petersburg. Subsequent youth summits were convened in Sydney (12–15 July 2014), Istanbul (15–21 August 2015), Shanghai (27–29 July) and Berlin (2–8 June 2017). The next Y20 is scheduled for 13–18 August 2018 in Córdoba, Argentina.

A Gender Justice Summit was held in 2010 under the aegis of Oxfam Canada. And for the third year in a row, the G(irls) 20 (young women aged 18–20, representing each G20 member plus the African Union) met in the summit host country (in 2012 in Mexico), with an agenda similar to that of the G20. Their mandate was to empower girls and women politically to work for economic development, political stability and social change. Also in 2012, a forum, 'The G20 from a Feminist Perspective', organized by the telephone workers' union of Mexico, took place on 13 June in Mexico City. The G(irls) 20 has continued to meet annually. The latest (eighth) meeting took place in Munich, Germany; its agenda was similar to that of the G20 (but with an emphasis on female labour force participation): the digital economy, energy and climate change, and migration. For further information, see girls20.org.

Far from G8 and G20 summit venues, the 'Poor People's Summit' ('Sommet des pauvres') has been meeting in Mali for over ten years, centred on the lives and needs of the poorest countries and occasionally addressing statements to G8 or G20 leaders. For example, in 2011 such a summit, called 'Forum des peuples', met for four days in Niono, Mali, in late October, opposing the official G20 Cannes summit in the *altermondialiste* spirit – against neo-liberalism and with a Southern perspective. Participants came from Benin, Burkina Faso, Niger, Togo, Côte d'Ivoire, Namibia, the Democratic Republic of the Congo, Haiti, France, Belgium and other countries. The forum had five broad themes: agriculture, mining, the situation of the peasants and food sovereignty; macroeconomic policies; governance; social economy and equitable trade; and mobilization, resistance and revolution (Niono dit non au G20!, 2011). This type of alternative summit seems not to have had subsequent meetings.

Demonstrations and other action

Protests and other street demonstrations have been a recurring feature around summits since the G7 Ottawa/Montebello summit. In the G20 context, there was little protest at the Washington summit, only several hundred peaceful street demonstrators. But before the London summit 35,000 people marched in Hyde Park in central London under the theme 'Put People First'; they demanded more and better jobs, and climate justice and action. During the G20 summit itself, protests were organized by the 'G20 Meltdown' group and others, stressing a number of concerns, including the Iraq War, globalization, human rights and climate change. These, too, were largely peaceful but the police overreacted, resulting in serious injury of an innocent non-protester, Ian Tomlinson, who happened to be in the wrong place. He later died (Dobson, 2011).

The Pittsburgh summit also saw street protests. Among the organizers were the 'Bail Out the People' movement, the 'tcktcktck' climate justice campaign, the 'Pittsburgh G20 Resistance Project' and others. Despite fears of violence, these protests were largely peaceful around the summit venue, but outside of the area there were some skirmishes and road blocks (Dobson, 2011).

The Toronto street scene was tumultuous in June 2010. The People's Summit (discussed earlier) was accompanied by a number of demonstrations, most of them peaceful but a few less so. The grassroots, radically oriented Community Mobilization Network staged a range of activities: the 21–24 June 'Themed Days of Resistance' focused on justice for migrants, income equality, community control over resources, gender justice, rights for the disabled, environmental and climate justice, and justice for indigenous peoples. These events led to 'Days of Action' in opposition to the G8 and G20: a feminist picnic on 25 June; a 'Free the Streets' march and a forum; a march with the theme 'People's First: We Deserve Better'; and another march, 'Get off the Fence'. Some of these actions were prepared in advance; others occurred spontaneously during the summits. The stated aim of the Mobilization Network (also referred to as 'G20 Convergence') was 'to challenge, disrupt and abolish the G8/G20'. This radical approach went further than non-engagement with the G8 and G20. Cooper (2013) posits a dichotomy of delivery-oriented vs. resistance-oriented civil society approaches to the G20.

Inevitably, radical tactics lead to confrontation with police and other security authorities. Is such activity a mark of an 'uncivil society'? 'Uncivil society' is a problematic concept. Clearly, terrorist or racist groups, such as Al-Qaeda, Daesh (ISIS) or the Ku Klux Klan, qualify for the 'uncivil' designation, and so do transnational organized crime, drug cartels, money launderers, paedophile networks and those engaged in human trafficking (Scholte, 2011a). Some analysts would also class anarchists, especially violent anarchists, in this group. Former UN Secretary-General Kofi Annan used the term 'uncivil society' in his discussion of the seamy side of globalization, in particular illicit drug trafficking and transnational organized crime (UN GA, 1999). The Globalization Studies Network held a conference on this topic in 2008; its partial proceedings were subsequently published (GSN, 2008; Heine and Thakur, 2011).

What did such radical protests achieve? They challenged the G20, but did not disrupt it and certainly did not abolish it. Nonetheless, they claimed victory: by organizing 'Toronto's community struggles against the impact of colonial, capitalist policies that seek to weaken us everyday'; through the 'nearly 40,000 people [who] took to the streets, gathered in discussion, watched movies, set up a tent city, danced and fought'; by marching in the 'thousands against colonization and for Indigenous sovereignty', through supporting 'actions . . . for Environmental Justice . . ., for Income Equity and Community Control Over Resources . . ., for Gender Justice and Disability Rights . . ., for Migrant Justice and an End to War and Occupation'; by the Days of Action; by ensuring (as the Mobilization Network claimed) 'that actions with conflicting tactics took place separately'; and by continuing the demonstrations in the face of being 'followed, intimidated, arrested . . . [and] infiltrated'.

Such claims of victory are not persuasive, and the strident rhetoric of the Mobilization Network put off many people. Some of these actions did indeed highlight issues of social and economic justice, but unfortunately such actions were conflated with disruptive activities, wanton destruction of property and other 'uncivil' acts. It is hard to see this as a victory. It could be argued that if the aim of the Mobilization Network was to garner maximum media attention, it achieved that – but to the detriment of the peaceful majority of civil society focusing on important messages on poverty, the environment and other burning global issues. As could be expected, confrontations occurred between protesters and security personnel, including in areas where demonstrations had been officially permitted. No deaths resulted but there were injuries and around 1,100 arrests or detentions (the majority of those arrested or detained were quickly released). In the years following the Toronto summit there have been more than half a dozen inquiries and lawsuits involving the event, including police behaviour; legal repercussions have continued up to 2018 (Perkel, 2018).

Before the Seoul summit, South Korea passed a special law banning all demonstrations in the period 8–12 November within a 2-kilometer radius of the summit venue, which was surrounded by 2-metre-high fences (Lee Sees Peer . . ., 2010; Nam, 2010). But there were rallies elsewhere in Seoul. On 7 November, South Korean activists, including labour campaigners, chanted songs and slogans outside city hall, surrounded by thousands of riot police. According to police estimates, 20,000 people participated; according to the organizers, there were 40,000. This discrepancy has occurred with many other demonstrations in the past; the pattern of police underestimation contrasted with organizers' overestimation leads one to suspect that the true numbers are between the two extremes. The rally was mostly peaceful, except for some small scuffles with riot police, some of whom used pepper spray against the protesters. Six Filipino activists (one of whom had taken part in the Civil G20 in Seoul) who planned to participate in the protest were refused entry permits to South Korea ([J.M.] Lee, 2010). On 11 November, the first day of the summit, South Korean labour and civic groups, along with international activists, marched through downtown Seoul to protest against the G20. The march, called 'Put People First! Korean People's G-20 Response Action', was organized by 83 CSOs. Once again, organizers estimated 10,000 people, while police reckoned about 3,500. The protesters demanded job stability, fair distribution of wealth, the annulment of free trade agreements, and the withdrawal of South Korean troops from Afghanistan. This was a summit of generally peaceful protests, with only a few people arrested (Whittington, 2010, p. A2).

Several demonstrations took place around the Cannes summit, with thousands of participants. They advocated for the financial transaction tax ('Robin Hood tax'), better protection of the environment and fair labour laws, among other causes. The largest of these street demonstrations took place in Nice on 1 November, at the start of the Forum of the Peoples. A couple of days later, several hundred activists marched to the nearby Monaco border to protest tax havens for the rich. Some 12,000 security personnel were deployed around the Riviera, including in Cannes, where the G20 leaders were meeting. Some protests also took place around the time of the 2012 Los Cabos summit, in La Paz, Mexico, in connection with the People's Summit held there.

Subsequent G20 summits generated protest, including instances of radical action: Brisbane, Antalya and especially Hamburg, where there were several protests against capitalism, climate polices and globalization and other G20 positions. The protests included an event with the slogan 'Welcome to Hell', attended by some 12,000 people. Another protest, 'Block G20 – Colour the Red Zone', featured some participants attempting to breach the restricted area. Several cars were set on fire. Protesters included those from the violent Black Bloc. Police (some 20,000 of whom were deployed throughout the summit) used tear gas, pepper spray and water cannons. According to Hamburg Police, 476 officers were injured, at least 186 protesters were arrested and 225 were detained during the protests (see, for example, Al Jazeera, 2017; Fox, 2017; Oltermann, 2017).

Chancellor Merkel expressed respect for peaceful protesters but 'condemned "in the strongest possible terms" the "unfettered violence and unrestrained brutality" . . . during the riots that accompanied the summit in Hamburg' (Germany, 2017).

A different type of civil society action involves issue-specific campaigns. For example, before the Los Cabos summit, CSOs spearheaded by Oxfam continued the long tradition of advocating a financial transaction tax (FTT) by staging a 'global week of action' for the 'Robin Hood tax' on 15–22 May 2012. This tax – of less than half of 1 per cent on speculative financial transactions conducted online – would be used for poverty alleviation and similar causes. The idea began in the 1970s, floated by Nobel-laureate economist James Tobin; it was initially referred to as 'Tobin tax'. Despite some early supporters, it took many years to gather enough momentum. By 2012, it attracted such high-profile backers as Desmond Tutu, Bill Gates, French President François Hollande, Al Gore and the Vatican (Murray, 2012). Yet, the FTT still has not garnered unanimity in the G20, in the face of many member governments resisting the idea.

Petitions

Petitions are another common peaceful tactic of CSOs. In March 2010, the Make Poverty History coalition and other Canadian and global CSOs launched the AT THE TABLE campaign. They called for concrete action by the G8 and G20 summits on poverty, climate change, and economic recovery for all. The campaign aimed to convince as many people as possible to sign a declaration with those three objectives. The campaign also initiated a 'flat leader photo petition' with cut-out images of G8 leaders to serve as interlocutors for civil society supporters.

A similar type of action unfolded before the Seoul summit, in the form of a letter to the Korean President, asking him to put in place a civil society consultation along the lines of the B20. This letter was drafted by the Global Campaign for Climate Action, a coalition of environmental, development, labour and faith-based groups. Such an initiative, if ever acted on by the G20, would greatly raise the profile and increase the impact of civil society. But in the event, the G20-B20 relationship remains much closer.

A third example: the Mexican civil society umbrella group Coalición Mexicana frente al G-20 (Mexican Coalition on the G20) addressed a letter to Mexican government officials, proposing a public debate between social movements and G20 governments during the Los Cabos summit (Coalición Mexicana frente al G-20, 2012b). As far as is known, such a debate did not materialize.

G20 acknowledgement and other indicators of potential civil society impact

Just as the official G7, in its early years, was slow to acknowledge civil society, the official G20 did not immediately do so. Civil society, on its part, was first to interact with the G7. The civil society-G20 nexus has played out in a similar manner. A few specific examples of civil society impact are mentioned earlier in this chapter.

Indicators of official acknowledgement of civil society include G20 documents when they mention CSOs or NGOs, and other explicit forms of official appreciation of the role of civil society. The final document of the Washington summit, the *Declaration of the Summit on Financial Markets and the World Economy*, did not refer to civil society at all; neither did President Bush in his end-of-summit press conference. This ignoring of civil society continued at the second G20 summit in London, where neither the summit's communiqué – *The Global Plan for Recovery and Reform* – nor the two accompanying annexes – *Declaration on Delivering Resources through the International Financial Institutions* and *Declaration on Strengthening the Financial System* – mentioned civil society.

The Pittsburgh summit saw the beginnings of G20 leaders' explicit acknowledgement of civil society. The *Leaders' Statement* refers to NGOs (in a multi-stakeholder setting) in supporting the most vulnerable on food security. On the role of jobs in economic recovery, the leaders called upon the ILO 'to convene its constituents and NGOs to develop a training strategy' (G20, 2009c). President Obama, in his end-of-summit press conference, did not specifically refer to civil society except in answering a reporter's question about protesters (US, 2009).

The Toronto *G20 Summit Declaration* (2010a) did not mention NGOs or civil society. The shorter document, *Principles for Innovative Financial Inclusion*, referred only obliquely to civil society among 'other stakeholders': 'Create an institutional environment with clear lines of accountability and coordination within government; and also encourage partnerships and direct consultation across government, business and other stakeholders' (G20, 2010c).

The *Seoul Summit Leaders' Declaration* did not refer to civil society but the more detailed *Seoul Summit Document* declared,

> We recognize, given the broad impact of our decisions, the necessity to consult with the wider international community. We will increase our efforts to conduct G20 consultation activities in a more systematic way, building on constructive partnerships with international organizations, in particular the UN, regional bodies, civil society, trade unions and academia.
>
> (G20, 2010d, p. 17)

The *Seoul Development Consensus for Shared Growth* (Annex I (G20, 2010e, p. 2) of the *Seoul Summit Document*) calls for 'engaging the private sector and civil society' in efforts to enhance growth, reduce poverty, improve human rights and create decent jobs. In Annex III (G20, 2010f, p. 3), the *G20 Anti-Corruption Action Plan*, the leaders undertake to 'combat corruption . . . by working with industry and civil society to identify vulnerabilities in commercial transactions . . ., with the goal of recommending multi-stakeholder initiatives for improvements in propriety, integrity and transparency'.

The Cannes summit's *Final Declaration: Building Our Common Future: Renewed Collective Action for the Benefit of All* states that on food security, '[w]e agreed to mobilize the G20 capacities to address these key challenges, in close cooperation with all relevant international organisations and in consultation with producers, civil society and the private sector'; and on fighting corruption and on governance the leaders commit to provide for civil society participation (G20, 2011b). By contrast, the final *Communiqué* (G20, 2011c) and *The Cannes Action Plan for Growth and Jobs* (G20, 2011a) make no reference to civil society, with the exception of the *Communiqué* mentioning the Bill Gates report, as detailed earlier. French President Sarkozy, in a 19 May 2011 letter to the President of the (French) Académie des sciences, Alain Carpentier, acknowledged the importance of the proposals of the academies; this followed Sarkozy's earlier meeting with representatives of the academies on 24 March 2011, and is an indicator of the potential high-level impact of such contributions.

The Mexican host government of the Los Cabos G20 summit showed its readiness to engage non-state actors before and during the summit; as mentioned earlier, it appointed a Special Representative of the Mexican G20 presidency, charged with 'exchanging views with groups not directly represented in the Group [of 20], such as non-member countries, international organizations, civil society with particular emphasis on young people, academia, and the business community, among others'.

On civil society, the Mexican government expressed the view that representatives of an organized and globalized civil society offer complementary views on various issues on the G20 agenda. The government was of the opinion that the participation of Mexican and international NGOs – embodying the principles of diversity, representation, transparency and access to information – were of key importance during the Mexican presidency of the G20 and in the lead-up to the Los Cabos summit.

Thus, significant steps were taken for a well-organized consultation process with non-state actors.

The Los Cabos *G20 Leaders Declaration* welcomed progress and new recommendations on food security and commodity price volatility, acknowledging civil society and business-sector input. On anti-corruption, the leaders welcomed the role of civil society and business in the review process of the UN Convention against Corruption. More broadly, the leaders 'thank[ed] international organizations . . . as well as civil society, for their input into the G20 process' and acknowledged that '[t]heir reports and recommendations have provided valuable inputs to G20 discussions, in areas ranging from sustainable development to financial regulation' (G20, 2012j, p. 14). *The Los Cabos Growth and Jobs Action Plan*, however, made no mention of civil society. The broader G20 system also took note of civil society; for example, the DWG acknowledged that '[t]he active and open outreach policy promoted by the Mexican Presidency with relevant governmental and non-governmental organizations, as well as with the private sector, contributed to the enrichment of the Group's aims and deliberations' and welcomed 'Mexico's initiative in hosting an international seminar with civil society on the G20 development agenda' (G20 Development Working Group, 2012, p. 1). This one-day seminar was organized on 7 May by the Mexican foreign ministry, with mostly Mexican NGOs attending, albeit with CSOs with headquarters in Europe and the US overrepresented in terms of leadership at the event. Because the seminar took place immediately after the DWG meeting, it involved DWG members reporting back to participating CSOs with no opportunity for the CSOs to advise the DWG (Alexander, 2012; interview with author, 4 June; email to author, 30 July).

President Calderón, in his end-of-summit press conference, expressed his gratitude to young people, think-tanks, labour organizations and civil society, business people and academics for their ideas in the various fora of the summit. He declared the Los Cabos meeting to have been the most open and inclusive G20 summit. Yet, the impression of several NGO participants and observers at these seminars and fora was that these events had but minimal impact on the summit outcome.

Naylor (2012), too, concludes that

> in absolute terms civil society's inclusion [at Los Cabos] remained limited. CSOs remained relatively marginalized in the summit process, particularly compared to the . . . B20. While the B20, Think20, Rethinking20, L20, Y20, G(irls)20 and Trade20 all involved formal and substantive events, the CS20 did not. CS20 constituted little more than a short-hand term to refer to the [Mexican] presidency's engagement with civil society – an especially sharp contradistinction to the B20, which amounted to a two-day parallel summit of business leaders at the Los Cabos Hilton.

Several documents of subsequent summits refer to civil society's role, including a commitment at St Petersburg, in the *G20 Leaders' Declaration*, to continue 'to expand engagement and partnerships with stakeholders, including non-G20 countries . . ., international organizations, the private sector and civil society' in implementing the development agenda (G20, 2013f, p. 22). At the 2014 Brisbane summit the leaders, in their *Communiqué*, 'thank[ed] the Business 20, Civil Society 20, Labour 20, Think 20 and Youth 20 for their important contribution to the G20's work' (G20, 2014f, p. 5). In the following year, at Antalya, the *G20 Leaders' Communiqué* again 'thank[ed] the G20 engagement groups, namely Business 20, Civil Society 20, Labour 20, Think 20 and Youth 20 for their important contributions . . ., welcome[d] the establishment of the Women20 and look[ed] forward to its active contributions' in the future (G20, 2015a, p. 12). At the Hangzhou summit, the *G20 Action Plan on the 2030 Agenda for Sustainable Development* stated that the *High Level Principles on the Implementation of the 2030 Agenda* would include 'support [for] international development partnerships that engage governments, private sector, civil society, academia and international organizations' (G20, 2016d, p. 2). Several documents of the 2017 Hamburg summit mention civil society: the *G20 Hamburg Climate and Energy Action Plan for Growth*; the *Hamburg Update: Taking Forward the G20 Action Plan on the 2030 Agenda for Sustainable Development*; the *G20 High Level Principles on Combatting Corruption related to Illegal Trade in Wildlife and Wildlife Products* (annexed to the *G20 Leaders Declaration*); the *G20 Initiative '#eSkills4Girls': Transforming the Future of Women and Girls in the Digital Economy* (another annex to the *G20 Leaders Declaration*; the *G20 Resource Efficiency Dialogue*); and the *G20 Anti-Corruption Action Plan 2017–2018*.

Conclusions

The analysis presented in this chapter leads to several conclusions. To begin with, both the G7/G8 and the G20 have been mindful of the problem of their legitimacy. Establishing and maintaining successful relations with the global community enhance legitimacy, and civil society, as part of the global community, plays an important role in this process. This is of mutual benefit as it increases the legitimacy of both CSOs and the G7/G8-G20.

What constitutes successful interaction? There are various factors at play. First, both CSOs and G7/G20 governments must be willing to engage with each other in a meaningful, serious and substantive manner, rather than just staging ritualistic meetings and garnering mere pro-forma G20 acknowledgement of civil society's role. Both parties need to give sustained attention to such engagement, and both should share information in a transparent manner.

One of the most important mechanisms of engagement is consultation. This can take place at various levels, between CSO representatives and G7 and G20 sherpas or other officials or with ministers and working groups, occasionally with G7/G20 leaders themselves, and sometimes with parliamentarians of G7 and G20 countries. Such dialogue can benefit governments by making them aware of civil society's concerns and by using the expertise of NGOs to add to the governments' own knowledge base. These interchanges facilitate exposure of officials to the voice of civil society, including from the global South. On the other side, consultations provide CSOs with an opportunity to learn first-hand about government priorities and approaches and about what is or is not possible to accomplish politically.

Each summit is the result of long, careful preparation culminating in the actual meeting of the leaders. Successful CSOs are aware of the importance of timing, and they, too, start their preparations early, building their knowledge of the sherpa, ministerial and working-group process. Timeliness enhances the benefit to both CSOs and governments from the engagement. Thorough knowledge of the official summit preparatory process, including sherpa and other sub-summit meetings, is equally important to CSOs. Civil society has developed impressive, detailed understanding of the process, but the short interval between some successive summits (e.g., between Cannes and Los Cabos) makes it much more challenging for CSOs to prepare adequately.

When CSOs focus on issues that are also on the G7 or G20 agenda, they are likely to find officials more receptive; this increases civil society's potential influence. Nonetheless, it is also intrinsically important for NGOs to advocate on other issues not yet on the official agenda. Receptivity to civil society may vary not just by the host country of G7/G8-C20 summits but also by the government in power. Kamila Szczepanska (2018) explores this pattern in the context of G7/G8 summits held in Japan.

Systematic, transparent monitoring and evaluation of G7 and G20 commitments and delivery are a crucial component of accountability. (This theme is explored in Chapter 8.) CSOs have consistently called for greater accountability of G20 commitments and the fulfilment of those commitments. Civil society's experience in monitoring and evaluating G7/G8-G20 performance in an efficient and continuous manner is beneficial to 'G' governments and to the global community alike. Considerable progress has been made from the early reluctance of the G20 to do this in a transparent manner to more recent undertakings of meaningful, systematic monitoring of what the G20 has promised and what it has delivered or failed to deliver. G7 and G20 governments, too, have an important role in self-assessment, and there are promising developments in this area. If done in a transparent and efficient manner, this benefits the global community and governments themselves.

Policy papers are also useful in conveying civil society concerns and priorities to broader society and, optimally, to G7 and G20 officials. And alternative summits, when they choose to engage with the G7 and G20, can also have an accountability benefit.

Consultations, alternative summits, policy papers, petitions and participation in peaceful demonstrations all benefit civil society itself. G20 acceptance of regular, systematic consultations with CSOs is a particularly significant advance. Such dialogue can increase (and occasionally has increased) civil society influence on G20 processes and negotiations. In addition, all these processes build consensus and solidarity within civil society itself.

The difficult question of what impact civil society has had on the G7/G8 and G20 can be answered at least partially. CSOs have generally not succeeded in getting the G7/G8 or G20 to include on their agenda issues that the leaders do not wish to include, but CSOs have helped raise the importance of certain issues already on the agenda – as shown, for example, by the maternal, newborn and child health initiative at the Muskoka G8 summit, placed at the centre largely due to civil society push. CSOs also played a role in raising the profile of development in the G20. Another example of civil society impact is the consultation of the host leader and his team with expert think-tank representatives prior to the London G20 summit on infusion of resources into the IMF and financial regulation. This presupposes the host government's receptivity to such a step. These examples point up the beneficial effect of the convergence of CSO and government interest. Prior to the Los Cabos summit, government representatives consulted think-tanks for their expertise, recognizing the benefits of such interchange (this is true even when the source of the expertise is not explicitly recognized). A third example of CSO impact occurred during the 2014 Brisbane summit cycle when Transparency International succeeded in influencing the *2015–16 Anti-Corruption Action Plan* and the *G20 High-Level Principles on Beneficial Ownership Transparency*, both of which were developed by the G20 Anti-Corruption Working Group and endorsed by the leaders at their Brisbane summit.

Much work remains to be done both by CSOs and G20 governments to reach the full potential of civil society's impact on issues of global importance. Ideally, civil society's influence would be greatly enhanced if the G20 accorded CSOs the same status that it has bestowed on the business sector. Meanwhile, increasing G20 initiatives towards multi-stakeholder partnerships of governments, international organizations, the private sector and civil society are encouraging and helpful.

References

Abshagen, M.-L., 2016. *The Plan for a Better World: The G20 and the 2030 Agenda for Sustainable Development*. Heinrich Böll Stiftung North America. 30 November. us.boell.org/2016/11/30/plan-better-world-g20-and-2030-agenda-sustainable-development [Accessed: 17 April 2018].

Alexander, N. and Riggs, P., 2012. *The G20: Playing Outside the Big Tent: Implications for Rio+20*. Washington: Heinrich Böll Stiftung North America. June. us.boell.org/2012/06/08/g20-playing-outside-big-tent [Accessed: 27 March 2018].

Al Jazeera, 2017. *Hamburg Protests Turn Violent as G20 Summit Kicks Off*. 7 July. www.aljazeera.com/news/2017/07/hamburg-protests-turn-violent-g20-summit-kicks-170707115823579.html [Accessed: 4 May 2018].

B20-L20, 2011. *B20-L20 Joint Statement*. November. www.ilo.org/wcmsp5/groups/public/-dgreports/-dcomm/documents/meetingdocument/wcms_166713.pdf and www.g20.utoronto.ca/2011/2011-b20-l20-en.pdf [Accessed: 9 January 2018].

Bonhomme, N., 2014. Between political messages and public expectations: G7 summits in French and US public opinion (1975–1985). In: E. Mourlon-Druol and F. Romero, eds. *International Summitry and Global Governance: The Rise of the G7 and the European Council, 1974–1991*. Cold War History Series. London and New York: Routledge. pp. 92–114.

Bono and Geldof, R., 2010. The African century. *The Globe and Mail*, Special issue, 9 May.

Bordeaux Religious Summit, 2011. *Statement of the Bordeaux Religious Leaders Summit*. www.g8.utoronto.ca/interfaith/2011-interfaith-leaders-en.pdf [Accessed: 27 March 2018].

Bourgogne Franche-Comté Universités, 2011. *Welcome to University Summit 2011*. www.univ-fcomte.fr/download/partage/document/actualite/lettre-flash/10-ufc-lettre10.pdf [Accessed: 27 March 2018].

Choi, J.S., 2010. Civil G20 dialog held in Incheon. *Korea.net*, 19 October. www.socialwatch.org/sites/default/files/2010-M-CiviL_G20_dialog.pdf [Accessed: 1 May 2018].

Civil 20, 2012. *Civil20 Proposals for the Russian Presidency in the G20*. December. g20civil.com/newsg20/1326/ [Accessed: 14 January 2013].

Civil 20, 2013. *Civil20 Address to the G20 Leaders*. civil-20.org/c20–2013-russia/ [Accessed: 25 April 2018].

Civil 20, 2014. *Australian C20 Summit communiqué*. civil-20.org/c20–2014-australia/ [Accessed: 25 April 2018].

Civil 20, 2015. *C20 Turkey Communiqué. A World Economy That Includes All*. civil-20.org/c20–2015-turkey/ [Accessed: 25 April 2018].

Civil 20, 2016. *Communiqué of Civil Society 20 China 2016*. civil-20.org/c20–2016-china/ and http://web.archive.org/web/20160907123353/www.g20.org/English/Documents/Current/201607/t20160706_2885.html [Accessed: 25 April 2018].

Coalición Mexicana frente al G-20, 2012b. *G:20 [sic] Cumbre del Capital, Anticapitalismo y Altermundismo*. Conversaciones sobre el G-20. 21 May. www.coaliciong20.org/?s=Carta+dirigida+al+presidente+pro+tempore+&x=0&y=0 [Accessed: 12 August 2012].

Cooper, A.F., 2008a. *Celebrity Diplomacy*. Boulder: Paradigm Publishers.

Cooper, A.F., 2013. Civil Society relationships with the G20: An extension of the G8 template or distinctive pattern of engagement? *Global Society: Journal of Interdisciplinary International Relations*, 27(2), pp. 179–200.

Coordination SUD, 2011. *Alter-forum de Nice: Les peuples d'abord, pas la finance!* 4 November. www.coordinationsud.org/actualite/alter-forum-de-nice-les-peuples-d'abord-pas-la-finance/ [Accessed: 13 April 2018].

Council on Foreign Relations, 2012a. *CFR Convenes 'Council of Councils' Linking Leading Foreign Policy Institutes from around the World*. 9 March. www.cfr.org/news-releases/cfr-convenes-council-councils-linking-leading-foreign-policy-institutes-around-world?co=C039201 [Accessed: 13 April 2018].

Dobson, H., 2011. The G8, the G20, and civil society. In: P. Savona, J.J. Kirton and C. Oldani, eds. *Global Financial Crisis: Global Impact and Solutions*. Farnham: Ashgate. pp. 245–260.

ENS Staff, 2013. Global religious leaders call on G8 to 'strike at causes of poverty'. *Episcopal News Service*, 5 April. episcopaldigitalnetwork.com/ens/2013/04/05/global-religious-leaders-call-on-g8-to-strike-at-causes-of-poverty/ [Accessed: 2 May 2018].

Fox, K., 2017. *Rallies, Riots And Raves: Hamburg's Three Days of G20 Protests*. CNN. 18 August. www.cnn.com/2017/07/08/europe/g20-protests/index.html [Accessed: 3 May 2018].

G8/G20 Global Working Group, 2012. *Civil Society Statements to the Mexican Government*. 22–24 February. www.g20mexico.org/images/stories/docs/dgvosc/sc20/eng/key_messages_g20_meeting.pdf [Accessed: 31 July 2012].

G8 & G20 Youth Summits, 2011. *Final Communiqué*. 3 June. www.youthpolicy.org/wp-content/uploads/library/2011_G8G20_Youth_ communiqué_Eng.pdf [Accessed: 8 June 2018].

G20, 2009b. *Join the debate ahead of the London Summit*. 30 January. webarchive.nationalarchives.gov.uk/20090505130642/http://londonsummit.gov.uk/en/media-centre/articles-and-publications/join-debate-press-release [Accessed: 8 June 2018].

G20, 2009c. *Leaders Statement: The Pittsburgh Summit*. 25 September. www.g20.utoronto.ca/2009/2009 communiqué0925.html [Accessed: 24 October 2017].

G20, 2009e. *Prime Minister Urges Values-Based Rules for Economy*. 31 March. webarchive.nationalarchives.gov.uk/20090402183547/http://londonsummit.gov.uk/en/media-centre/latest-news/?view=News&id=15662522 [Accessed: 8 June 2018].

G20, 2010a. *The G-20 Toronto Summit Declaration*. 27 June. www.g20.utoronto.ca/2010/to-communiqué.html [Accessed: 24 October 2017].

G20, 2010c. *Principles for Innovative Financial Inclusion*. 27 June. www.g20.utoronto.ca/2010/to-principles.html [Accessed: 26 September 2017].

G20, 2010d. *Seoul Summit Document*. www.g20.utoronto.ca/2010/g20seoul-doc.pdf [Accessed: 24 October 2017].

G20, 2010e. *The Seoul Summit Document–ANNEX I: Seoul Development Consensus for Shared Growth*. www.g20.utoronto.ca/2010/g20seoul-consensus.pdf [Accessed: 8 June 2018].

G20, 2010f. *The Seoul Summit Document, Annex III: G20 Anti-Corruption Action Plan*. www.g20.utoronto.ca/2010/g20seoul-anticorruption.pdf [Accessed: 8 June 2018].

G20, 2011a. *The Cannes Action Plan for Growth and Jobs*. 4 November. www.g20.utoronto.ca/2011/2011-cannes-action-111104-en.html [Accessed: 24 October 2017].

G20, 2011b. *Cannes Summit Final Declaration: Building Our Common Future: Renewed Collective Action for the Benefit of All*. 4 November. www.g20.utoronto.ca/2011/2011-cannes-declaration-111104-en.html [Accessed: 24 October 2017].

G20, 2011c. *Final Communiqué [of the] G20 Leaders' Summit, Cannes*. 4 November. www.g20.utoronto.ca/2011/2011-cannes-communiqué-111104-en.html [Accessed: 24 October 2017].

G20, 2012j. *G20 Leaders Declaration*. 19 June. www.g20.utoronto.ca/2012/2012-0619-loscabos.pdf [Accessed: 26 September 2017].

G20, 2012aa. *Think-20 Summary Report by Co-Chairs*. December. en.g20russia.ru/docs/think_20/summary_report.html [Accessed: 8 June 2018].

G20, 2012ag. *Y20 Puebla Agreement*. 9–11 May. www.younglead.eu/wp-content/uploads/2012/12/2012_Y20 pdf [Accessed: 8 June 2018].

G20, 2013f. *G20 Leaders' Declaration*. 6 September. www.g20.utoronto.ca/2013/Saint_Petersburg_Declaration_ENG.pdf [Accessed: 8 September 2017].

G20, 2014f. *G20 Leaders' Communiqué*. 15–16 November. www.g20.utoronto.ca/2014/brisbane_g20_leaders_summit_ communiqué.pdf [Accessed: 3 October 2017].

G20, 2015a. *G20 Leaders' Communiqué*. 15–16 November. www.g20.utoronto.ca/2015/151116-communiqué.pdf [Accessed: 3 October 2017].

G20, 2016d. *G20 Action Plan on the 2030 Agenda for Sustainable Development*. 8 September. www.g20.utoronto.ca/2016/g20-action-plan-on-2030-agenda.pdf [Accessed: 5 February 2017].

G20, 2018b. *Macri Drives G20 Agenda in Davos*. 24 January. www.g20.org/en/news/macri-drives-g20-agenda-davos [Accessed: 5 April 2018].

G20 Development Working Group, 2012. *2012 Progress Report of the Development Working Group*. www.g20.utoronto.ca/2012/2012-0619-dwg.pdf [Accessed: 13 November 2017].

Gates, W., 2011. *Innovation with Impact: Financing 21st Century Development*. Cannes. www.gatesnotes.com/Development/G20-Report-Innovation-with-Impact [Accessed: 13 April 2018].

Gates, W., 2012. *Letter to President Felipe Calderón Hinojosa*. 13 June. www.g20civil.com/upload/iblock/ec0/Bill%20Gates%20pre-G20%20Letter%20to%20President%20Calderon.pdf [Accessed: 29 July 2012].

Germany. Bundeskanzlerin, 2017. *Angela Merkel on Riots in Hamburg*. www.bundeskanzlerin.de/Content/EN/Artikel/2017/07_en/2017-07-03-sicherheit-hamburg_eng.html [Accessed: 7 May 2018].

Globalization Studies Network, 2008. *Uncivil Society*. Waterloo, Canada: Centre for International Governance Innovation. 25–27 August. www.cigionline.org/events/globalization-studies-network-conference-uncivil-society [Accessed: 13 April 2018].

Global Solidarity Summit, 2017. *Welcome to the Global Solidarity Summit!* solidarity-summit.org/en/ [Accessed: 2 May 2018].

Global Solutions, 2018. *Global Solutions Summit 2018*. registration.global-solutions.international [Accessed: 2 May 2018].

Hajnal, P.I., 2010b. *The World Religions Summit 2010: Interfaith Leaders in the G8 Nations: Notes of an Observer*. www.g8.utoronto.ca/evaluations/2010muskoka/hajnal-faith.html [Accessed: 14 April 2018].

Halifax Initiative, 2010a. *Parliamentary Roundtables on the G8/G20 Agendas*. www.halifaxinitiative.org/content/parliamentary-roundtables-g8g20-agendas [Accessed: 14 April 2018].

Halifax Initiative, 2010b. *What's Missing in the Response to the Global Financial Crisis?* www.halifaxinitiative.org/content/conference-whats-missing-response-global-financial-crisis [Accessed: 14 April 2018].

Hamilton, K., 2010. Inspired leadership: Civil Society's contribution to G8 and G20 summitry. In: J.J. Kirton and M. Koch, eds. *G8 & G20: The 2010 Canadian Summits*. Toronto: Newsdesk Media Group and the G20 Research Group. p. 308.

Heine, J. and Thakur, R. eds., 2011. *The Dark Side of Globalization*. Tokyo: United Nations University Press.

InterAction and G7/G20 Advocacy Alliance, 2018. *2018 G20 Summit Recommendations*. G20 Policy Paper. March. reliefweb.int/sites/reliefweb.int/files/resources/G20-Policy-Paper-2018.pdf [Accessed: 14 May 2018].

International Trade Union Confederation, 2008. *G20 Trade Union Leaders Meet with IFIs, Heads of State and Call for Vigorous Action to Counter the Global Economic Crisis*. 15 November. www.ituc-csi.org/g20-trade-union-leaders-meet-with.html [Accessed: 8 June 2018]. The Washington Declaration (2008) is accessible at: www.ituc-csi.org/IMG/pdf/0811t_gf_G20.pdf.

Joint Religious Coordination for the G8 and G20 Summits, 2012. *2012 Religious Leaders' Statement for the G8 and G20 Summits*. Georgetown University's Berkley Center for Religion, Peace & World Affairs. repository.berkleycenter.georgetown.edu/120517FinalStatementJRLCS.pdf [Accessed: 15 April 2018].

Keil, K., 2017. *The G20 Compact with Africa: Innovation Partnership or Business as Usual?* Heinrich Böll Stiftung North America. 13 December. us.boell.org/2017/12/13/g20-compact-africa-innovative-partnerships-or-business-usual [Accessed: 6 April 2018].

Kulik, J. and Kirton, J.J., 2012. *At the G8 Camp David Summit, Where Are the Women? Everywhere!* 20 May. www.g8.utoronto.ca/evaluations/2012campdavid/kulik-kirton-women.html [Accessed: 15 April 2018].

Lee, J.M., 2010. Activists in South Korea rally against G-20 summit; police fire pepper spray. *Associated Press Newswire*, 7 November.

Lee Sees Peer Pressure Enforcing G20 Deal, 2010. *Korea Herald*, 8 November. view.koreaherald.com/kh/view.php?ud=20101107000251&cpv=0 [Accessed: 2 May 2018].

Lewallen, A., 2008. Indigenous at last! Ainu grassroots organizing and the Indigenous Peoples Summit in Ainu Mosir. *The Asia-Pacific Journal: Japan Focus*, 6(11). japanfocus.org/-ann_elise-lewallen/2971 [Accessed: 2 May 2018].

Make Poverty History, 2010. *Progress in Combating Poverty under Threat: Anti-Poverty Activists Tell G8 Top Policy Makers*. 16 April. archive.makepovertyhistory.ca/en/news/progress-combatting-poverty-under-threat-antipoverty-activists-tell-g8-top-policy-makers [Accessed: 3 August 2012].

Martin, N., 2008. The FIM G8 project, 2002–2006: A case analysis of a project to initiate civil society engagement with the G8. In: J.W.St.G. Walker and A.S. Thompson, eds. *Critical Mass: The Emergence of Global Civil Society*, Waterloo, Canada: Wilfrid Laurier University Press. pp. 183–209.

Martin, N. and Tandon, R., 2014. *Global Governance, Civil Society and Participatory Democracy: A View from Below*. New Delhi: Academic Foundation.

McGann, J.G., 2018. *2017 Global Go To Think Tank Index Report*. Philadelphia: Think Tanks and Civil Societies Program, University of Pennsylvania. 31 January. repository.upenn.edu/think_tanks/13/ [Accessed: 8 June 2018].

Moore, T., 2014. People's Summit a smorgasbord of food for thought. *Brisbane Times*, 12 November. www.brisbanetimes com.au/national/queensland/peoples-summit-a-smorgasbord-of-food-for-thought-20141112-11lcdt.html [Accessed: 2 May 2018].

Murray, L.R., 2012. The Robin Hood tax: Small change for the banks, big change for the U.S. and the world. *The Huffington Post*. 14 May. www.huffingtonpost.com/liz-ryan-murray/the-robin-hood-tax_b_1513664.html [Accessed: 8 June 2018].

Nam, Y.S., 2010. Police thwart fiery protest amid massive G20 security alert. *Agence France Presse*, 10 November.

Naylor, T., 2012. *Civil Society Inclusion at Los Cabos 2012*. 26 June. www.g20.utoronto.ca/analysis/120626-naylor.html [Accessed: 19 April 2018].

New Rules for Global Finance, 2012a. *The Financial Stability Board: Unlocking the Black Box*. www.new-rules.org/what-we-do/fsb-unlocking-the-black-box [Accessed: 19 April 2018].

New Rules for Global Finance, 2012b. *Promises of the G20 Process: Prospects for Advancing Transparency and Accountability*. 18 June. www.new-rules.org/events/3-nr-event/391-promises-of-the-g20 [Accessed: 28 November 2017].

Niono dit non au G20! [Niono Says No to the G20!], 2011. *Journal du Mali*. 31 October. www.journaldumali.com/2011/10/31/niono-dit-non-au-g20/ [Accessed: 8 June 2018].

Oltermann, P., 2017. Arrests and injuries as Hamburg gripped by mass anti-G20 protests. *The Guardian*, 7 July. www.theguardian.com/world/2017/jul/07/g20-protests-hamburg-altona-messehalle [Accessed: 4 May 2018].

Oxfam, 2010. *The Making of a Seoul Development Consensus: The Essential Development Agenda for the G-20*. Oxfam Briefing Note. 11 October. www.oxfam.org/sites/www.oxfam.org/files/bn-making-seoul-consensus-g20-111010-en.pdf [Accessed: 19 April 2018].

Oxfam, 2011. *Not a Game: Speculation vs. Food Security: Regulating Financial Markets to Grow a Better Future*. Oxfam Issue Briefing. 3 October. www.oxfam.org/sites/www.oxfam.org/files/ib-speculation-vs-food-security-031011-en.pdf [Accessed: 19 April 2018].

Oxfam, 2012b. *Left behind by the G20? How Inequality and Environmental Degradation Threaten to Exclude Poor People from the Benefits of Economic Growth*. Oxfam Briefing Paper, No. 157. 19 January. www.oxfam.org/sites/www.oxfam.org/files/bp157-left-behind-by-the-g20-190112-en.pdf [Accessed: 19 April 2018].

Oxfam, 2013a. *Fixing the Cracks in Tax: A Plan of Action: Joint Recommendations to the G20 and OECD for Tackling Base Erosion and Profit Shifting*. Policy Brief. www.oxfam.org/sites/www.oxfam.org/files/fix-the-cracks-in-tax.pdf [Accessed: 19 April 2018].

Oxfam and Heinrich Böll Stiftung North America, 2014. *The G20 and Gender Equality*. Oxfam Briefing Paper 183. 14 July. https://d1tn3vj7xz9fdh.cloudfront.net/s3fs-public/file_attachments/the_g20_and_gender_equality_en.pdf [Accessed: 20 April 2018].

The Peoples' Summit, 2009. *Another World Is Possible*. Pittsburgh. 22 September. www.peoplessummit.com/page/peoples-summit [Accessed: 6 August 2012].

Perkel, C., 2018. Testimony to begin at hearing into Toronto G20 civil lawsuit. *The Globe and Mail*, 4 February. www.theglobeandmail.com/news/national/testimony-to-begin-at-hearing-into-toronto-g20-civil-lawsuit/article37847995/ [Accessed: 15 May 2018].

Post Globalization Initiative, 2013. *St Petersburg Counter Summit Opposes US Plans*. 13 September. www.pglobal.org/news/548/ [Accessed: 10 October 2013].

Put People First, 2009. *G20 Counter Conference Report and Audio*. www.putpeoplefirst.org.uk/2009/12/put-people-first-g20-counter-conference-report-and-audio [Accessed: 6 August 2012].

Quintos, P., 2010. *What Is Missing in the G20 Agenda? Redressing Structural Imbalances for Equity, Justice and Sustainability*. IBON International. 8 October. iboninternational.org/sites/ibon/files/resources/ibon_g-20_policy_brief_2010.pdf [Accessed: 19 April 2018].

The Royal Society, 2012a. *Building Resilience to Disasters of Natural and Technological Origin*. 10 May. royalsociety.org/uploadedFiles/Royal_Society_Content/policy/publications/2012/2012–05–10-G-Science-Resilience.pdf [Accessed: 24 April 2018].

The Royal Society, 2012b. *Energy and Water Linkage: Challenge to a Sustainable Future*. 10 May. royalsociety.org/uploadedFiles/Royal_Society_Content/policy/publications/2012/2012–05–10-G-Science-Energy.pdf [Accessed: 24 April 2018].

The Royal Society, 2012c. *Improving Knowledge of Emissions and Sinks of Greenhouse Gases*. 10 May. royalsociety.org/uploadedFiles/Royal_Society_Content/policy/publications/2012/2012–05–10-G-Science-Emission.pdf [Accessed: 24 April 2018].

The Royal Society, 2017. *Science Academies Call for G20 Action on Improving Global Health*. 22 March. royalsociety.org/news/2017/03/science-academies-call-for-g20-action-on-improving-global-health/ [Accessed: 10 April 2018].

Rude, C. and Burke, S., 2009. *Towards a Socially Responsible and Democratic Global Economic System: Transparency, Accountability and Governance*. Dialogue on Globalization Briefing Paper 15. New York: Friedrich-Ebert-Stiftung. library.fes.de/pdf-files/bueros/usa/06778–20091105.pdf [Accessed: 24 April 2018].

Russian G8/G20 NGOs Working Group, 2012. *Join Civil G20*. www.g20civil.com/g20civil-society/join.php [Accessed: 10 August 2012].

Ruthfauff, J. and Cadwallader, E., 2017. Civil 20 Summit: The World We Want. *InterAction*, [blog]. 29 June. www.interaction.org/newsroom/blog/civil-20-summit-world-we-want [Accessed: 25 April 2018].

Scholte, J.A., 2011a. Global governance, accountability and civil society. In: J.A. Scholte, ed. *Building Global Democracy? Civil Society and Accountable Global Governance*. Cambridge: Cambridge University Press. pp. 8–41.

Scholte, J.A., 2011b. Introduction. In: J.A. Scholte, ed. *Building Global Democracy? Civil Society and Accountable Global Governance*. Cambridge: Cambridge University Press. pp. 1–7.

Steiner, S.M., 2018. *Moral Pressure for Responsible Globalization: Religious Diplomacy in the Age of the Anthropocene*. International Studies in Religion and Society, V.30. Boston: Brill.

Szczepanska, K., 2018. Toward inclusive global governance? Japanese civil society, the state, and G7/8 summitry, 2000–2016. *Global Governance: A Review of Multilateralism and International Organizations*, 24(2), pp. 211–228.

T20, 2017. *20 Solution Proposals for the G20 from the T20 Engagement Group*. www.t20germany.org/wp-content/uploads/2017/07/20_Solutions_for-the_G20_17-7.pdf [Accessed: 1 May 2018].

Tandon, R. and Martin, N., 2010. *Civil Society Dialogue with the Host Sherpa to the Toronto 2010 G20 Summit: Communiqué*. 21 June. www.g8.utoronto.ca/evaluations/2010muskoka/fim-sherpas.pdf [Accessed: 24 April 2018].

Transparency International, 2017. *Clean Supply Chains*. G20 Position Paper. January. files.transparency.org/content/download/2143/13584/file/2017_G20PositionPaper_SupplyChains_EN.pdf [Accessed: 20 April 2018].

Trew, S., 2013. *Declaration of the G20 Counter-Summit*. The Council of Canadians. 7 September. www.canadians.org/blog/declaration-g20-counter-summit [Accessed: 25 April 2018].

Troszczynska-van Genderen, W., 2015. *G7 Summit in Schloss Elmau: A Tighter Agenda, with Wider Impact?* European Parliament. Directorate-General for External Policies. www.europarl.europa.eu/RegData/etudes/IDAN/2015/549041/EXPO_IDA(2015)549041_EN.pdf [Accessed: 10 April 2018].

TrustLaw, 2012. *G20 Countries. The Worst and Best for Women.* 13 June. news.trust.org/item/20120613010100-sk134/?source=spotlight [Accessed: 25 April 2018].

United Nations. Economic and Social Council. 11th Session, 2012. *Half-Day Discussion on the Rights of Indigenous Peoples to Food and Food Sovereignty.* (E/C.19/2012/L.10). 14 May. www.un.org/press/en/2012/hr5092.doc.htm [Accessed: 8 June 2018].

United Nations. General Assembly. 54th Session, 1999. *Official Records*, Supplement No. 1: *Report of the Secretary-General on the Work of the Organization.* (A/54/1).

United States. President, 2009. *Remarks by President Obama at G20 Closing Press Conference.* 25 September. https://obamawhitehouse.archives.gov/the-press-office/remarks-president-g20-closing-press-conference [Accessed: 8 June 2018].

Whittington, L., 2010. Relatively speaking, a G20 summit of love. *Toronto Star*, 14 November, p. A2.

World Religions Summit, 2010. *A Time for Inspired Leadership and Action.* 2010 Interfaith Leaders' Summit. 23 June. www.faithchallengeg8.com/pdfs/2010%20Interfaith%20Statement%20-%20English.pdf [Accessed: 25 April 2018].

7 Reforming the ‘Gs’

Proposals, achievements, interactions, challenges

This chapter surveys and analyzes proposals to reform the G7/G8 and G20, discusses reforms already achieved, and assesses the complex relationship between the G7/G8 and the G20. It examines a variety of reform proposals ranging from membership changes and agenda development to institutional restructuring and improvement of processes; analyzes the relationship between the G7/G8 and the G20; looks at groups and initiatives closely related to the G7/G8 and G20; outlines various potential trajectories of the G7/G8 and the G20; reviews challenges for the G7/G8 and the G20 as they face the future; and presents overall conclusions.

Introduction

Both the G7/G8 and the G20 were formed in response to crises, as discussed in Chapter 1. But, despite its flexibility and significant achievements over its 43-year history, the G7/G8 remains rooted in an earlier era. It has not responded adequately to changing political and economic realities, in particular the emergence of crucial new actors outside the G7/G8 framework and their growing significance in global governance. Without the full participation of major emerging-economy countries, which are systemically important players, appropriate initiatives and action in response to global problems cannot be taken. Some have argued that even wider participation than the G20 is needed to address global challenges of the environment and climate change, development, poverty, food, health, financial architecture and regulation, and security issues, including terrorism.

Many reform proposals have been offered over the decades of the G7/G8’s existence, ranging from abolishing it to expanding or reducing its membership, rationalizing its processes, expanding or contracting its agenda, increasing its representativeness and legitimacy, replacing it with a new body, supplementing it with additional bodies, and making institutional changes, including the establishment of a permanent secretariat. Leaders of the G7/G8 had for many years expressed their wish to stage smaller, more intimate and more focused summit meetings, with fewer officials in attendance and fewer media correspondents around (Hajnal, 2007b, 2007c; Kirton, 2008a).

Many such proposals have merit, including those supported by high-level advocates, notably former Canadian Prime Minister Paul Martin, who pressed

DOI: 10.4324/9781351266802-8

resolutely for the establishment of the 'L20' or Leaders' 20, likely with the same initial membership as the pre-existing G20 Finance Ministers' and Central Bank Governors' forum. Complete integration of China, India, Brazil, Mexico and South Africa (a group initially known as the 'G5' or 'Outreach 5') with the G8 to form a G13 was another proposal that gained currency for a time. However, for such far-reaching reform of the G7/G8 to become reality, it needed to be not only promoted by the advocates of change but also agreed upon and endorsed by consensus of the incumbent leaders of the G7/G8. This remained true with the emergence in November 2008 of the G20 leaders' forum alongside the continuing Finance Ministers' G20 and various other sub-summit groups.

In their review of G20 reform literature, Kharas and Lombardi (2012, p. 7) have grouped contributions into those addressing the broad G20 and those dealing with the G20's sectoral aspects. As an example of the former approach, they cite several authors, including Suominen and Dadush (2012), who argue 'that the main role of the G-20 is that of mediator [rather than a decision-making body], so as to protect common interests in an increasingly globalized economy'. They also cite Vestergaard and Wade (2011), who propose a leaders'-level Global Economic Council, which would 'oversee . . . the work of the Bretton Woods institutions' and would be in a position 'to combine effectiveness . . . and legitimacy' (Kharas and Lombardi, 2012, p. 7); and Ocampo and Stiglitz (2012), who argue along similar lines but would place the United Nations (UN), the Bretton Woods institutions and the WTO under the oversight of such a council. As examples of the sectoral approach, Kharas and Lombardi cite Eric Helleiner (2012) on financial regulation, and Lombardi (2011, p. 153) and Mistral (2012) on the international monetary system and IMF reform.

Proposals to reform the G7/G8

Early reform proposals concerned membership size and composition, agenda changes, and institutional and procedural aspects. Hajnal (2007b, 2007c) and Hajnal and Panova (2012) review these in greater detail. The 1998 Birmingham G8 summit, notably, undertook several innovations in participation, format and agenda, and officially integrated Russia into the club, turning it from G7 to G8. Birmingham was a leaders-only meeting; Foreign and Finance Ministers met separately in London a week before the summit – rather than participating along with the leaders as they had done at previous summits – to prepare for the summit and to deal with issues not on the leaders' agenda. This made it possible to achieve greater informality than at previous summits, enabling the leaders to spend considerable time together and concentrate on topics they themselves wished to discuss. As well, it had a more focused agenda than earlier summits. This more limited agenda also reduced the volume of documentation, although this effect proved to be inconsistent after Birmingham (Bayne, 2005b).

This internal reform became established practice, but it did not satisfy critics. Shortly after Birmingham, Jeffrey Sachs (1998) proposed transforming the G8 into a G16, comprising the G8 plus eight developing countries. Sachs listed democratic governance as the major criterion of membership in this expanded club, arguing that the core developing-country candidates should be Brazil, India, South Korea and South Africa, to be joined 'soon [by] a democratic Nigeria'. In his view, a 'development agenda' should guide this new body, including: global financial markets and international financial reform; conditionality and foreign aid; reform of the international assistance programme; and an end to the debt crisis.

After the tumultuous 2001 Genoa G8 summit, the *Financial Times* (2001, p. 18) questioned whether 'G8 summits should exist and, if so, in what form', and noted that 'summits have worked best when the leaders have had a chance to be separate from their national entourages . . . and when there has been a crisis to try to sort out'. The article concluded that there 'should have been . . . a commitment to hold the next G8 only when there is a burning topic to discuss'. The terrorist attacks of 11 September 2001, which took place mere months after the summit, thrust security more prominently into the international consciousness, placing it firmly on the G8 agenda. In the post-9/11 era, security for the leaders became paramount for summit host countries. Many G7/G8 summits since have met at remote venues, including the 2018 Charlevoix (Canada) G7 summit. This has had the advantage of easier security but also the disadvantage of the leaders meeting far from the media, the public and civil society. Yet, remote locale did not prevent protesters, rock stars and the Make Poverty History campaign from making their presence felt.

The think-tank Shadow G-8 of distinguished individuals with high-level previous summit experience, led by C. Fred Bergsten of the Peterson Institute of International Economics, was launched in 2000 on the premise that 'recent G-8 summits have not fulfilled their potential'. It saw the need for summits to 'reform their methodology and adopt agendas that effectively address the sweeping changes in global economic and security affairs that characterize the early years of the new century' (Bergsten and Montbrial, 2003, p. 4). Given that G8 leaders have had a difficult time reforming themselves, this question was raised: Why not start a new group in which the heads of systemically important countries could meet and get to know one another? (Shadow G-8 member, 2004; interview with the author, 1 December.) (The Shadow G-8 functioned until 2006; in 2007 a different 'Shadow G8' appeared briefly, under the leadership of the Nobel-laureate economist Joseph E. Stiglitz.)

The L20 initiative

One of the most important reform ideas to expand the G8 leaders' forum was the proposal to turn the G20 Finance Ministers' forum (which had existed since 1999) into a leaders'-level group of 20, an 'L20'. In a paper predating this initiative, Shadow G-8 member Wendy Dobson (2001, pp. 23–29) noted that the challenges to leaders had changed since the Cold War days, when the G7 was first established, and asserted that a 'G-3 or G-7 "directorate" [was] no longer acceptable . . . consensus among a wider group [was required]'. She envisioned two scenarios to build on the precedent of the G20 Finance Ministers' forum: convening functional groups of ministers from G20 countries on systemic problems, such as climate change, North-South issues, and trade and poverty alleviation, as well as expanding leaders' meetings to include all G20 countries. In the interest of efficient management, this leaders' body would need a steering committee with revolving membership. This new body would not replace the G8 but would meet periodically before or after G8 summits.

The L20 idea was taken up by Paul Martin, who, in his previous post as Finance Minister (prior to assuming prime ministership of Canada), had been the first to chair the Finance Ministers' and Central Bank Governors' G20. In 2005, he made the case for an expanded leaders'-level forum and introduced the term 'L20'. He reviewed and analyzed the circumstances of the emergence and functioning of the Finance Ministers' G20; discussed the need for a similar forum for political leaders; and outlined the L20's possible composition, initial agenda, potential role and relations with existing multilateral organizations (Martin, 2005).

Building on this framework, the Centre for International Governance Innovation (CIGI) and the Centre for Global Studies (CFGS) (both think-tanks headquartered in Canada, respectively in Waterloo and at the University of Victoria) examined the ramifications of this potential transformation of the Finance Ministers' G20 into the L20. They sought to answer several questions: What are the issues? What would be the appropriate design for a successful L20 acceptable to the leaders? What is the best route to attaining consensus to establish the L20 summit process? Such a new L20, if successful, would be more broadly representative than the G8, bringing to the table systemically important developing countries (notably China, India and Brazil) and other countries with emerging economies. It would focus on priorities at the highest level, transcending national bureaucracies, and would be an institution enjoying legitimacy in promoting fiscal, social and environmentally responsible policies; it would also address the efficiency gap, and would be a catalyst for and guide to broader reforms of global governance. One of the aims of the CIGI/CFGS project was to broaden the understanding of the initiative among the G8 and prospective L20 member countries by including academics and practitioners from each nation. The resulting book, *Reforming from the Top: A Leaders' 20 Summit*, is a comprehensive study of the proposal and its contents and context, including an examination of receptivity to this idea by the South, and a discussion of the modalities of achieving the L20: having an L20 replace the G7/G8 through a 'giant leap'; incrementally increasing the membership of the G8 through a G9 and G10 to an eventual L20 (the incremental approach, however, did not have much traction in the leadership of the G20); or, alternatively, creating an L20 that would operate alongside a continuing G8 (English, Thakur and Cooper, 2005). Another work, by Peter Heap (2008), *Globalization and Summit Reform: An Experiment in International Governance*, provides an accessible shorter account of these proposals.

Other reform proposals

Peter B. Kenen, Jeffrey Shafer, Nigel Wicks and Charles Wyplosz (2004) traced the evolution of international economic and financial cooperation and concluded that its machinery was becoming obsolete, notwithstanding the G7's record of negotiating joint positions and exerting its influence in the Bretton Woods institutions. They recommended the creation of new structures: making room for new players (e.g., by streamlining European representation in the G7 and in the IMF Executive Board); establishing a new G4 comprising the US, the euro zone, Japan and China to deal with exchange rate problems and adjustments; convening an Independent Wise Persons Review Group to examine existing institutions and groups, including the G7; and establishing a new Council for International Financial and Economic Cooperation with 15 or fewer members, to set the agenda and provide strategic direction for the international financial system and to oversee multilateral institutions of international economic cooperation. This council would include the systemically important countries, represented at the Finance Ministers' level. The heads of the UN, IMF, World Bank and WTO would be invited to the council's meetings.

In April 2007, just such a group, the G20 Eminent Persons Group on Global Financial Governance, was established by the G20 Finance Ministers and Central Bank Governors. Its mandate calls for reviewing international financial and monetary systems and financial architecture and governance, including the role of international financial institutions. The group is to report, with recommendations, to the G20 Finance Ministers and Central Bank Governors by the time of the IMF/World Bank Group's 2018 annual meetings (G20, 2017p).

Edwin Truman (2005) of the Peterson Institute for International Economics suggested disbanding the G7/G8 and moving many of its policy coordination functions to the G20. He argued that this strengthening of the G20 would be a major step in rationalizing the institutions of international economic cooperation. At that time he saw the US and the euro area as leaders of this strengthened G20. At the same time, he also envisioned policy coordination of the US and the euro area as an 'informal G2'. Seven years later, however, Truman (2012) cautioned that the

> G-20's accomplishments are in danger of unraveling, because [its members] have failed to implement their Seoul agreement on reform of the International Monetary Fund (IMF) [in order to] enhance the role of the emerging market and developing countries, and help to cement the commitment of those countries to the global system.

It is the lack of political will on the part of G20 leaders that gets in the way of IMF reform: although quota reform has been agreed, with deeper reform on the way, this is linked to the structure of the IMF Executive Board, and some G20 countries resist Board reform. European overrepresentation and the US Congress blocking meaningful Board reform are illustrations of the problem. As a way to get past this hurdle, Kharas and Lombardi (2012, pp. 12–13) propose 'a path for reforming both the G-20 and the IMF . . . in a mutually reinforcing way'. Their proposal calls for an IMF Ministerial Council that would accomplish several goals:

> [It] would strengthen political support for the pursuit of the IMF's own mandate . . . be a formal decision-making body . . . [it would] require support at

> the highest political level . . . [and] if the G-20's finance ministers and central bank governors were to meet as members of . . . [such a] Ministerial Council . . ., [then] universal representation and legitimacy . . . would add to the 'systemic' character of the G-20. . . . The Ministerial Council would have a full mandate from the IMF's 188 country members to discuss and decide on issues related to the international monetary system and international macroeconomic policies.

The reform of IMF quotas and governance was approved on 15 December 2010 by the IMF Board of Governors in order to effect, according to the IMF, a major realignment in the ranking of quota shares that better reflects global realities, and a strengthening in the Fund's legitimacy and effectiveness. At long last, the reform package became effective on 26 January 2016, representing the doubling of total quotas and a major realignment of quota shares (IMF, 2016d). On 5 December 2016 the IMF Board of Governors called on the Executive Board to aim for completing the next review by spring (or fall at the latest) of 2019.

The 'finance G2' concept was explored by Shadow G-8 chair C. Fred Bergsten, who argued that the euro zone and the US needed a new G2 mechanism not only to monitor and consult on the evolution of the dollar-euro exchange rate but, more ambitiously, also to develop a new G2 monetary regime. This G2 would not be a substitute for the G7 and would function informally and without even public announcement of its existence and activities (Bergsten, 2005; Bergsten and Koch-Weser, 2004). Weinrichter (2000) offered a variation of this proposal, advocating the replacement of the G7 with a 'G3' of the US, Japan and the euro area.

In 2004, Stephen Roach of Morgan Stanley recommended a new architecture for economic policy coordination, noting that the global economy was in need of major steps for rebalancing. One of these steps would replace the G7 with a new G5 consisting of the US, the euro zone, Japan, the UK and China. This would be a charter-based organization with a permanent staff, embracing all aspects of global economic imbalances. Like the proposal by Kenen and his colleagues, Roach's ideas did not account for the non-economic agenda of the G7/G8 – the environment, security, global health and other transnational issues.

Colin I. Bradford (2005b, p. 5) of the Brookings Institution argued that the existing 'institutional framework for dealing with contemporary global challenges does not match the scope, scale and nature of the challenges themselves'. One aspect of this mismatch is the G8 and the broader G8 system. Given the considerable reluctance to institute major reform and expansion of the G8 into a true L20, Bradford suggested adding a few regular core members (China, India, Brazil and South Africa being the leading candidates) to the G8 – turning it into a G12 – and allocating six additional places to other countries that would participate on a rotating basis, depending on particular issues on the agenda. Earlier, Bradford and Linn (2004) had discussed three reasons for upgrading the Finance Ministers' and Central Bank Governors' G20 to a leaders'-level summit: the shifting of demographic and economic balance towards emerging-market economies; the need for more representative global governance; and the role of emerging economies in global economic crises and responses to such crises. More recently, Cooper and Thakur (2013, p. 19) pointed out a good reason for having formed the G20: 'the growing misalignment of global structural reconfigurations – of economic weight, military power and diplomatic clout – with the distribution of membership and decision-making authority in the institutions of global governance . . . [This] provide[s] considerable logic for institutional reform'.

Former Canadian diplomat George Haynal (2005, p. 261) made the case for a 'G-XX' – a more comprehensive and representative summit process, where 'XX' does not necessarily stand for '20' but implies that the number of members is an open question. He argued that such a more inclusive summit 'would express the changing nature and balance of power and assist our shared institutions to function better by providing them with the appropriate political direction'. Haynal suggested that new global issues, as well as missing linkages among international institutions, could be addressed by a 'G-XX'. He identified the core membership of the G-XX: the existing G8; China, India, South Africa, Brazil and possibly Mexico; and representation from Africa, the Middle East, Southeast Asia, the Americas and the former Soviet bloc. He envisioned the G-XX as functioning alongside the G8, not replacing it.

Anders Åslund (2006), of the Peterson Institute of International Economics, proposed that China, India, Brazil and South Africa be invited as full members, thus transforming the G8 into a more representative G12. Just two days before the 2006 St Petersburg G8 summit, it was reported that then British Prime Minister Tony Blair had intended to call for making China, India, Brazil, South Africa and Mexico full-fledged members, turning the G8 into the G13, building on the 'G8+5' formula established at the 2005 Gleneagles G8 summit (Elliott and Wintour, 2006). Zbigniew Brzezinski (2009) suggested the creation of two informal groupings: an expanded G8 alongside a G2 of the US and China, such a G2 being the most relevant mechanism to deal best with world issues.

Another reform proposal was offered by the UN General Assembly's Commission of Experts on Reforms of the International Monetary and Financial System, established in October 2008 and headed by Joseph Stiglitz. The Commission's mandate was to study the reform of international financial institutions and to create a coordinated approach to global financial structures in need of drastic overhaul. The Commission's report was issued at the end of March 2009; its recommendations included the creation of a new, elected Global Economic Coordination Council, which, as a part of the UN, would meet annually at the head-of-state level and would be a democratically representative alternative to the G20. The proposed Council would be independent of the Security Council and would have 20 to 25 members (UN News Service, 2009; Harvey, 2009). Following this initiative, the General Assembly convened a Conference on the World Financial and Economic Crisis and Its Impact on Development in New York on 24–26 June 2009. The conference produced a set of proposals accepted by consensus and later endorsed by the General Assembly (UN GA, 2009).

Shortly after the first G20 leaders' summit in November 2008, the *Guardian* wrote that the G20 'summit effectively sounded the death knell for the exclusive club of rich nations represented by the G8' (Elliott, 2008). In 2009, Paul Martin (p. 24) asserted, 'The [2009 London] G20 summit . . . confirms that the G8's days as the world's steering committee have drawn to a close. Yet the world cannot afford a vacuum. Only a successful G20 will fill the void'. The host of the London G20 summit, UK Prime Minister Gordon Brown, 'has been a leading advocate of the G20 format, arguing that the old G8 club of rich, industrial countries was no longer acceptable for directing world affairs' (Parker, 2009, p. 4). Brown thus added his voice to those of several fellow G8 leaders calling for a more representative forum of global governance.

Some G8 countries have been less than enthusiastic about reforming the G8 and the G20. For example, Russia (then still a member of the G8) acknowledged the importance of its membership in both fora, but saw the UN system as principal actors of global governance, with the G8 and G20 playing a secondary, supportive role (Hajnal and Panova, 2012, p. 72). With its suspension from the G8 in 2014, Russia, if anything, is less likely to care about the G7. Some also consider it equally unclear whether China, India and Brazil 'see the G-20 as more of an efficacious venue in which to pursue their interests than the UN is'. Yet, leadership by these countries in the G20 is necessary (Hampson and Heinbecker, 2011, p. 307). Indeed, four years later Fan He (2015, pp. 37–38) argues that '[t]he coming two years [2015–16] will be an important period in the evolution of the G20' and that

> China feels far more at ease at the G20 than in other forums like the G8. It has always been very supportive and is more willing to shoulder greater responsibilities in the international community. China needs the G20 and the G20 needs China. When China assumes the Presidency [in late 2015, to extend to 2016], it should seek to strike a fine balance between developed and developing countries, which will greatly boost the credibility of the G20.

As the L20 project evolved, the prospective agenda for this new leaders' forum was carefully considered. Potential topics foreseen by the L20 think-tanks, as well as in other proposals for a G20, included, among other issues, global health and global security. Yet, what actually sparked the convening of the first G20 summit was the financial crisis that became global in 2008.

At the time of the London G20 summit, there were some signs of agenda expansion in light of linkages of trade, development and other matters with the core financial and economic issues. But it was the 2010 Seoul summit that placed development firmly on the G20 agenda. Commitment to strengthen global financial safety nets was also an important achievement at Seoul, which was taken up by the IMF (Paul Martin, 2018; telephone interview with the author, 25 February). Food security and commodity price volatility figured prominently on the agenda of the 2012 Los Cabos summit; the other agenda items (mostly carry-overs from previous summits but with differing emphases) were: economic stabilization and structural reforms for growth and employment; strengthening the financial system and encouraging financial inclusion; reforming the international financial architecture in an interconnected world; and promoting sustainable development and green growth and fighting against climate change. The Syrian crisis inevitably claimed the leaders' attention at the 2013 St Petersburg summit, adding security to the G20 agenda.

That topic, particularly the use of chemical warfare, was discussed at the leaders-only dinner during the summit as well as at the hastily convened meeting of ten of the G20 Foreign Ministers. But the prepared economic agenda was also adhered to: growth, jobs, financial inclusion, financial regulation and investment. The 2014 Brisbane summit focused on stimulating growth and creating jobs, building a resilient global economy, and strengthening global economic institutions (including IMF and Financial Stability Board reform). Within those parameters, the following themes were discussed: investment, infrastructure, trade and competition, unemployment and job creation, poverty, development, financial regulation, taxation, anti-corruption, energy and climate change. Several of these topics were carried over from earlier summits. That they left the door open for further G20 initiatives in these areas is shown by the priorities of Turkey for the 2015 G20 summit, focusing on 'three I's': inclusiveness, implementation and investment for growth (Turkey. PM, 2014).

The 2016 Hangzhou summit's agenda centred on four 'I's' (adding one to the three Antalya 'I's': innovative, invigorated, interconnected and inclusive world economy). China placed strong emphasis on development, which had been a major theme of earlier summits since Seoul in 2010. In 2017, the Hamburg summit's three pillars of the agenda were: ensuring stability, improving viability for the future, and accepting responsibility. Under these rubrics the German host country included a number of economic issues, such as trade and investment, sustainable global supply chains and an open and resilient financial system, but added digital transformation, health-related items, women's empowerment and climate, as well as the German initiative that launched the G20 Africa Partnership.

Expanding the agenda is difficult. Reasons for this, as noted by Heinbecker (2011a), include: continuing slow economic recovery; lack of consensus by the leaders on how to spur sustainable recovery and growth; and diverging views on developing a broader agenda. Such lack of consensus was evident at the St Petersburg discussions; only 11 countries signed on to the special statement on Syria: Australia, Canada, France, Italy, Japan, Republic of Korea, Saudi Arabia, Spain, Turkey, the UK and the US (US White House, 2013). Edwards (2013) characterized the outcome of the Syria discussions as 'unfortunate. It will also serve as a cautionary example for future summits when there might be temptations to expand the G20 agenda into the political domain. This is not a happy precedent'. Also on Syria, Risto Penttilä (2013), in an opinion piece in the *New York Times*, advanced the argument that the St Petersburg summit 'will be remembered as the meeting where the G-20 took over the role of the United Nations Security Council'.

The lack of G20 consensus came into sharp focus at the 2017 Hamburg summit, where the US, having announced its withdrawal from the Paris climate agreement, openly broke with the rest of the G20. The Americans found their country an outlier, with the other 19 G20 members affirming their adherence to the Paris

Agreement and their continuing efforts to implement it. Trade, particularly trade protectionism, was another contentious issue, but here the leaders found wording that avoided singling out the dissenting position of the US.

Linn (2012, pp. 9–10) notes that '[l]egacy issues . . . now crowd the agenda . . . [Yet, the] agenda needs to maintain continuity with the past and demonstrate follow-through on previous commitments'. Therefore he argues that the G20 'agenda needs to focus on issues where leaders feel interested and challenged, on issues where they can make a difference, and on issues where it is critical that they learn about each other's perspectives'.

Edwin Truman also sees agenda growth as problematic, and asserts that any expansion should be well defined (Truman, 2012; interview with the author, 5 June). The forum 'Rethinking G20: Designing the Future', held on 16 June 2012, just ahead of the Los Cabos summit, examined some of these concerns; the summit host, Mexican President Calderón, participated in some sessions. But Martin (2013, p. 734) asserts that 'while . . . the G20 must set its priorities, there can be no upfront restrictions placed on its scope . . . [A]s the G8's role becomes more and more limited, there can be no issue of global concern that is not within the G20's purview'. Similarly, Fan He (2015, p. 37) argues that '[a]ll long-term issues with global governance and multilateral organisations should be on the G20 agenda'.

Gnath and Schmucker (2015, p. 33), on the other hand, argue that 'the G20 should stop placing themes like growth through investment and structural reform at the centre of its agenda in the future and instead focus on topics that can only be solved at the international level and on which the forum can contribute direct added value'. They add that better continuity is needed when drawing up the summit agenda; to that end, they call for strengthening the troika system to enable past, present and future presidencies to shape the agenda for three consecutive years.

Thomas Bernes (2018; telephone interview with the author, 12 January) argues that the G20 has moved away from the original tight focus group, and is suffering from lack of focus and is drifting a bit.

In contrast with those who decry G20 'agenda creep', Paul Martin asserts that 'the G20 does not have the luxury of dealing only with a self-defined portion of globalization'. He adds that the G20 needs to deal with the threat of terrorism, the spread of disease, implications of climate change, food security and mass migration (Blanchfield, 2016). He amplifies this point by emphasizing the need for G20 cooperation on cyber security and the health of oceans, which are under serious threat.Moreover, he considers the demographic and economic implications of migration, highlighting two examples – Canada, a country which needs immigrants to contribute to society and the economy; and Africa, where there is a growing gap between population growth and job creation:

> More than 10 million young Africans enter the work force each year, yet the continent creates only about three million jobs annually. That gap heralds a future of poverty and migration that will reverberate around the world. The only way to keep this from happening is to invest in infrastructure and

> guarantee job growth and living conditions that will enable them to stay where they want to stay – at home.
>
> (Martin, 2017, p. 1)

The G20 has made a significant start in addressing this through the *Compact with Africa*, a German initiative at the Hamburg summit. The G20 should build on this initiative (Martin, 2017; telephone interviews with the author, 10 January and 25 February 2018).

It is important to note, however, that at its core the G20 is still driven by an economic agenda. Other issues must be significant enough to connect with that agenda. In fact, climate change, infectious diseases, gender issues, migration and other agenda accretions have been anchored to the economic agenda.

Another question should be raised here: what has not been on the G7/G20 agenda? Women, for a long time, were missing from G7/G8 deliberations. This has begun to change; Julia Kulik (2012) notes that leaders at the G8 Camp David summit

> included in their communiqué strong references to the rights of women and girls. It has yet to be determined whether the G20, with more than double the female representation at [the 2012] Los Cabos summit than at its [2008] Washington [s]ummit start, will highlight women, girls and gender issues as important to global economic stability or any other summit priorities or themes.

By November 2015 Kulik (2015) observed that '[b]etween the first summit in 2008 and the most recent in 2014, the G20 has made 10 commitments on or related to gender equality'. She then called for greater accountability on these commitments. In 2016, the Hangzhou summit *Leaders' Communiqué*, para. 6, under the heading 'inclusiveness', undertook to

> work to ensure that our economic growth serves the needs of everyone and benefits all countries and all people including in particular women, youth and disadvantaged groups, generating more quality jobs, addressing inequalities and eradicating poverty so that no one is left behind.
>
> (G20, 2016k)

The 2017 Hamburg summit took further steps to promote or support women's empowerment, women's entrepreneurship and girls' education. Hamburg initiatives included better access for women to education, labour markets and capital, all spelled out in the *G20 Leaders' Declaration*. The declaration also announced the launching of the Business Women Leaders' Task Force to 'bring together business women from G20 countries to examine ways to increase women's participation in the economy and . . . make recommendations at next year's summit on the implementation of G20 commitments regarding the economic empowerment of women' (G20, 2017g). The leaders in Hamburg also launched the #eSkills4Girls initiative to create opportunities and equal participation for women and girls in the digital economy. This indicates that gender issues are now a continuing G20 process. Moreover, the declaration expresses support for the human rights of vulnerable migrant women.

The G7 has also stepped up its involvement in gender equality and protection of migrant and refugee women. This was explicit in the 2017 Taormina G7 summit. Women featured prominently on the agenda of the G7 Charlevoix G7 summit in 2018, gender issues being one of five main summit teams set by the Canadian host government.

Indigenous issues have largely escaped summit attention both in the G7/G8 and the G20. Human rights inside member countries are usually considered to be *ultra vires* for the 'Gs' in many countries; that includes women's and indigenous peoples' human rights. Martin (telephone interviews with the author, 10 January and 25 February 2018) notes that there is an international awakening to these issues; a clear indication of this is the *United Nations Declaration on the Rights of Indigenous Peoples* (UNDRIP). Several G20 countries (including Australia, Brazil, Canada, Japan, Mexico, Russia and the US) have indigenous populations. He argues that the G20 should find a way to deal with indigenous issues. Canada is keenly interested in indigenous issues, but, as host of the Charlevoix summit, it was aware that these issues would not achieve G7 consensus. This is unfortunate, as indigenous peoples have much to contribute, notably to the climate change debate, with their closeness to and appreciation of the environment.

Vadim Lukov (2010, p. 63), in an article with a Russian focus, comments on the G20's dilemma in the post-crisis period:

> The main problem for the G-20 is the preservation of the forum's unity at the stage of the post-crisis development of the global economy. The situation of an acute common danger that existed one to one and a half years ago provided a strong incentive for unity. At present the different speed of the development of national economies also predetermines different views of matters related to the implementation of the Framework for Strong, Sustainable, and Balanced Growth, as well as different approaches toward the pace of scaling down anti-crisis measures. In this situation, the G-20 badly needs a consolidating long-term program for a period after the global crisis.

Lukov's position is part of the debate on turning the G20 from a 'crisis committee' to a 'steering committee' (discussed ahead).

Before the Seoul summit, Barry Carin (2010) recommended that the G20 address the matter of institutionalizing its membership, as well as rotation of Presidency and process of preparation. He further suggested the need for a secretariat to monitor G20 commitments; firmer processes of outreach and consultations with the business sector and civil society; and that the concerns of non-member developing countries should be considered.

Elsewhere he and several of his colleagues (Carin, Heinbecker, Smith and Thakur, 2010, pp. 3, 8) suggested that this objective could be accomplished through a 'non-secretariat' which would be non-bureaucratic, headed by three sherpas corresponding to the troika rotation (previous, current and next host country) and aided by high-level staff released for three years by the troika countries. Such a 'non-secretariat' could be located in the country holding the G20 Presidency. It would provide technical and other support in summit preparation, follow-up monitoring and implementation, and management of relations with non-G20 countries and organizations. This solution would deal with the dual challenge of need for preparation and follow-up on the one hand, and the G20's 'antipathy for formal bureaucracy' on the other. Carin (2011b) fleshes out this idea with an imaginative fictional conversation of French President Sarkozy – aided by a time machine held in secret in the basement of the Louvre – with philosopher Lao Tzu, strategist Sun Tzu and Clio, the muse of history.

Payne (2014, p. 82) elaborates on the idea of a secretariat, to remedy the G20's 'fundamental lack of permanence'. He calls for 'a modest, but permanent, secretariat headed by an experienced international civil servant or ex-politician as Secretary-General'. He would also incorporate the existing troika into this 'more effective G20 executive, composed of the previous, current and next heads of governments convening the summit'. The idea of a secretariat (or a 'non-secretariat') is an interesting example of potential institutional innovation. It is brought up from time to time by certain member countries, but has not found consensus among the leaders.

In another innovation, the Mexican host government, for the first time in G20 summitry at the Los Cabos summit, publicized the division of work (operative since the Washington summit but not publicly announced previously) into a finance track (focusing on financial and economic issues) and a sherpa track (focusing on political, non-financial issues – e.g., employment, agriculture, energy, the fight against corruption and development). Some have expressed concern about this split – for example, Carin suggests that this is an artificial distinction; most sherpa-track items have significant finance-track implications and will have to be ratified by the finance track (Carin, 2012; email to author, 19 November). However, subsequent summit hosts have continued this approach, and work division into these two tracks has become established practice.

Groups and initiatives related to the G7/G8 and G20

Several groupings have arisen in response to the G7/G8 and the G20. This section focuses on four of these, one historical and the other three continuing entities. They are: the G5, the BRICS and the Global Governance Group plus the Major Economies Forum on Energy and Climate. The Heiligendamm/L'Aquila Process (HAP), which was created by the G8, rather than being an outside body formed in response to the G8, is therefore discussed in Chapter 3. (The G20 relationship with the IMF is analyzed in Chapter 4.)

The G5

Five major developing countries (Brazil, China, India, Mexico and South Africa) were invited to attend specific parts of summit meetings, starting with the 2003

Evian G8 summit. They were first referred to as the (G8) '+5' at Gleneagles. In the run-up to the Heiligendamm summit in 2007, the German hosts changed the designation to 'Outreach 5' (O5). The five countries formed their own 'G5' around the time of the 2008 Hokkaido summit. The Japanese and German hosts, respectively, of the Hokkaido and Heiligendamm summits, accepted the 'G5' designation. Host leader Angela Merkel, in preparation for the German-hosted G8 Heiligendamm summit, announced at the World Economic Forum in Davos in January 2007 the wish to deepen the integration of the 'O5' into the summit process. G8 receptivity to the G5 was uneven: they were not invited to the US-hosted Sea Island summit in 2004; Russian President Putin invited them only to the tail end of the 2006 St Petersburg G8 summit; and Japan, the host of the Hokkaido summit, was again less welcoming (Bayne, 2011a). With the growing importance of the G20 and the BRICS group, the G5 countries' connection with the G8 lost relevance (Hajnal and Panova, 2012; Kirton, 2015a).

G8 members varied in their degree of acceptance of the G5 as partners. The G5 countries, on their part, were lukewarm about their relationship with the G8. The much-reduced engagement of the G5 countries with the G8 showed the preference of the five for the G20, in which they are full members and which is a forum embracing diverse systems of government. The G5 faced a dilemma between the attraction of membership in the powerful G8 club and problems arising from association with the Western- or Northern-dominated G8. Their identity as developing countries played a part in this. As indicated earlier, the G8 connection with the G5 became irrelevant with the ascendancy of the G20 and BRICS (Hajnal and Panova, 2012).

The BRICS group

The acronym BRIC was coined by James O'Neill of Goldman Sachs in 2001. It denoted Brazil, Russia, India and China as the most dynamic and systemically important developing countries. BRIC became a reality in 2009 and, starting on 18 February 2011, South Africa officially became part of this group of emerging economies, forming BRICS and embracing the former '+5' countries, except Mexico. BRIC/BRICS was inspired by or arose in response to the G20 and remains related to it.

O'Neill (2012, p. 24) recalls how he 'had the good luck of dreaming up the odd acronym "BRIC" to describe the rising economic importance of Brazil, Russia, India and China'. (See also Keating, 2012, p. 25.) Although BRICS countries' interests diverge on several issues (e.g., trade), they are closer on other issues, such as foreign investment autonomy. They share their relative positions as 'established regional powers with aspirations to global influence' (Desai, 2012, p. 27).

Table 7.1 shows the dates and places of BRIC/BRICS leaders' meetings. They have been convened since 2009 (starting in 2011 as BRICS). In addition to regular annual meetings, leaders have also met (usually informally) at the margins of G20 summits.

At Los Cabos in 2012, just before the summit, they issued a statement on 'most of the key issues at the G20 summit – the euro crisis, global economic growth,

Table 7.1 BRICS Leaders' Summits

Date	*Venue*	*Comments*
16 Jun. 2009	Yekaterinburg, Russia	(BRIC) 1st regular summit
15 Apr. 2010	Brasilia, Brazil	(BRIC) 2nd regular summit
14 Apr. 2011	Sanya, China	(First time as BRICS) 3rd regular summit
3 Nov. 2011	Cannes, France	On margins of G20 summit
29 Mar. 2012	New Delhi, India	4th regular summit
18 Jun. 2012	Los Cabos, Mexico	On margins of G20 summit
25–27 Mar. 2013	Durban, South Africa	5th regular summit
5 Sep. 2013	St Petersburg, Russia	Informal meeting, on margins of G20 summit
15–16 Jul. 2014	Fortaleza, Brazil	6th regular summit
15 Nov. 2014	Brisbane, Australia	Informal meeting, on margins of G20 summit
8–9 Jul. 2015	Ufa, Russia	7th regular summit
15 Nov. 2015	Antalya, Turkey	Informal meeting, on margins of G20 summit
15–16 Oct. 2016	Goa, India	8th regular summit
4 Sep. 2016	Hangzhou, China	Informal meeting, on margins of G20 summit
7 Jul. 2017	Hamburg, Germany	Informal meeting, on margins of G20 summit
3–5 Sep. 2017	Xiamen, China	9th regular summit
25–27 Jul. 2018	Johannesburg, South Africa	10th regular summit

Source: BRICS Research Group (2017).

IMF resources and reform, and development, including investment in infrastructure and in the social sphere' and made some commitments to contribute funds to the IMF intended to mitigate the euro crisis (Kirton and Bracht, 2012). Ahead of the St Petersburg summit, they issued a media note on challenges and vulnerabilities in the global economy, monetary policies of developed economies, IMF reform and other issues of concern (India PIB, 2013).

At their Fortaleza summit, the leaders signed an agreement establishing the New Development Bank, with headquarters in Shanghai and with an initial capital of US$100 billion. They also signed a treaty establishing the Contingent Reserve Arrangement, also with an initial US$100 billion (BRICS RG, 2014). In a sense, these two new financial institutions will be BRICS counterparts of the World Bank and perhaps partly of the IMF.

At Brisbane in 2014 the BRICS leaders declared that 'the agreements establishing the New Development Bank (NDB) and the Contingent Reserve Arrangement (CRA) brought BRICS cooperation to a fundamentally new level with the creation of instruments to contribute to the stability of the international financial system' (BRICS RG, 2015b). At their Ufa, Russia, meeting they issued several documents, including a declaration, an action plan and a *Memorandum of Understanding on Cooperation with the New Development Bank* (BRICS RG, 2015c). The theme of the 2016 Goa summit, as stated in the *Goa Declaration*, was 'Building

Responsive, Inclusive and Collective Solutions' – a clever acronym synonymous with the group's own acronym. The leaders took a five-pronged approach: institution-building to further develop BRICS cooperation; implementation of previous summit decisions; integration of cooperation mechanisms; innovation – that is, new cooperation mechanisms on government-to-government; and continuation of existing cooperation mechanisms. In terms of institutionalization, the *Goa Action Plan* reveals that a broad system and network had evolved, somewhat mirroring the development of the G20 system: ministerial meetings, working groups, seminars and outreach (mostly to business). The 2017 Xiamen summit undertook to: intensify cooperation and development in the BRICS countries; enhance communication and coordination to improve global economic governance in order to 'foster a more just and equitable international economic order'; work for regional peace and stability; 'embrace cultural diversity and promote people-to-people exchanges'; and increase 'popular support for BRICS cooperation through deepened traditional friendships' (BRICS IC, 2017).

BRIC(S) countries have held an expanding range of ministerial-level meetings: Agriculture, Finance, Foreign Affairs, Trade, Education, Science, Energy, Environment, Labour and Employment, Culture, Disaster Management, Health and Industry Ministers, as well as migration authorities. Detailed information is available at brics.utoronto.ca.

Kulik (2014) cites three schools of thought about BRICS. The first 'views the G20 as a forum that has enhanced the role and influence of the BRICS countries in international forums (Luckhurst, 2013)'. The second argues that 'alliances within the G20 arose in a non-traditional ad hoc way and the lack of a BRICS alliance within the G20 is due to issue-specific divergence (Schirm, 2012; Stuenkel, 2012)'. And the 'third school of thought sees the BRICS as an emerging power alliance in multilateral frameworks but with limitations (Keukleire and Hooijmaaijers, 2014)'.

Along similar lines to the first school of thought, Cooper (2014, pp. 92, 94–95) notes that the 'elevated status accorded to BRICS' was confirmed 'in the rotation of the presidency of [the Finance Ministers'] G20 . . . to India in 2002, China in 2005, South Africa in 2007, and Brazil in 2008'. Cooper adds that 'the BRICS provides the big rising powers a diplomatic space that can act among other activities as a lobby or caucus group in tandem with the G7/8'.

Sainsbury (2015, p. 9) offers a more negative assessment. He asserts that BRICS, along with the reinvented G7 and the MITKA group (which consists of Mexico, Indonesia, Turkey, Korea and Australia), has 'the potential . . . to work against global economic cooperation and impede achievement of the necessary compromises that advance international issues, making the task of future G20 presidents harder'.

Examining the G7/G8's relationships with emerging powers, Kirton (2015a, p. 129) argues that the G7/G8 has adapted to the challenges of the developing-country G5, the Major Economies Forum, the Heiligendamm/L'Aquila Process and BRICS. The G7/G8 has accomplished this by shifting to global outreach through working major multilateral organizations and with smaller developing countries. He further argues that 'neither BRICS, with their still fragile economies, nor the G20 with its still restricted agenda . . . can substitute for the global governance contribution that the G7 makes'.

The Global Governance Group (3G)

The 3G emerged at the London G20 summit, where certain non-member countries were invited as observers. At the initiative of Vanu Gopala Menon, Singapore's permanent representative to the UN, meetings were called to create a channel for discussing and conveying the views of non-G20 UN member countries on global governance to the G20, with the objective of strengthening the UN and making the G20 more inclusive. The 3G is an informal coalition established at UN Headquarters in New York. Its members are: Bahamas, Bahrain, Barbados, Botswana, Brunei Darussalam, Chile, Costa Rica, Finland, Guatemala, Jamaica, Kuwait, Liechtenstein, Luxembourg, Malaysia, Monaco, Montenegro, New Zealand, Panama, Peru, Philippines, Qatar, Rwanda, San Marino, Senegal, Singapore, Slovenia, Switzerland, United Arab Emirates, Uruguay and Vietnam (Singapore. MFA, 2013). They represent all regions of the world.

The 3G holds annual ministerial meetings on the sidelines of the UN General Assembly. The tenth such meeting was convened in New York on 22 September 2017 (Singapore. MFA, 2017).

Cooper (2014, p. 100) addresses the matter of fair representation in the G20, asking, 'Can the G20 not only speak for the rest of the world but also impose its will on countries that do not belong to the group?' The 3G has tried to address this issue. Citing Iftekhar Ahmed Chowdhury (2010), Cooper (2014, p. 101) notes that the 3G 'sought to build a more equitable relationship between the G20 and non-G20 countries'. Using skilful strategies since its formation, 'the 3G made its own mechanisms valuable, even indispensable, to both the G20 and the UN' (Cooper, 2014, p.102).

Cooper and Momani (2014, p. 226) further develop this concept by focusing on issues of legitimacy of the G20 process and the important contribution of the 3G, arguing that '[t]he 3G in practice effectively bridged the efficiency of the G-20 with the legitimacy of the UN members' by acting as a key intermediary of the two institutions.

The Major Economies Forum on Energy and Climate

The Major Economies Forum on Energy and Climate (first called Major Emitters Meeting, then Major Economies Meeting) was launched in March 2009 at the initiative of the US government. Its original mandate was 'to facilitate a candid dialogue among major developed and developing economies . . . and advance the exploration of concrete initiatives and joint ventures that increase the supply of clean energy while cutting greenhouse gas emissions' (MEF, 2009). The following countries, plus the European Union, participated in MEF: Australia, Brazil, Canada, China, France, Germany, India, Indonesia, Italy, Japan, Republic of Korea,

Mexico, Russia, South Africa, the UK and the US. In preparation for the UN Copenhagen climate conference in December 2009, Denmark and the UN also participated. MEF leaders met on 9 July 2009 in L'Aquila, Italy, alongside the G8 summit held there; leaders' representatives had met 24 times by September 2016.

MEF established a 'Global Partnership' to promote low-carbon technologies and a ministerial forum – which first met in 2010 – focusing on energy efficiency, clean energy, integration and human capacity. It has launched several action plans; for example, on clean energy, solar energy, and carbon capture, use and storage. MEF had a secretariat within the US Department of State. With the end of the Obama Presidency and the succession of the Trump administration, the forum ceased to exist after a final ministerial meeting on 16 November 2016 (Japan MOFA, 2016). In September 2017, Canada, the EU and China revived the work of the Forum under a new name, Ministerial on Climate Action (MoCA), with representatives from 34 major economies (G20 members and non-members) (Climate Home, 2017; Pacific Institute, 2017).

What future for the G7/G8 and the G20?

There are various trajectories along which the mutual roles of the G7/G8 and the G20 in global governance may develop. The reform proposals reviewed and analyzed in this chapter allow several alternative scenarios to be sketched.

Expansion or reduction of the G7/G8

Past proposals along this line have included, among others, Sachs's 1998 'G16' formula incorporating the G8 plus eight developing countries with democratic governance. Brzezinski's 2009 idea also called for an expanded G8 which would co-exist with a G2 of the US and China as most relevant to geopolitical realities. Others called on the G8 to absorb the G5 as full members. Silvio Berlusconi, the host of the L'Aquila summit, also invited Egypt to participate in the G8+G5 part of the discussions, and even characterized the result as the G14.

European overrepresentation has been a contentious matter all along, with four EU members plus the EU itself as permanent participant in the G7/G8. But this has proved to be a non-starter with the leaders, so the membership has remained constant. However, with Russia's suspension as G8 member in 2014 in response to its actions in Ukraine, the forum has again become G7. While the door to resuming Russia's membership remains notionally open subject to a reversal of its policies, such a development seems unlikely at present. Two G7 summits convened in 2014: a special summit at The Hague on 24 March and a regular G7 summit in Brussels on 4–5 June (hosted for the first time, but not chaired, by the European Union) (European Council, 2014). Germany assumed the G7 Presidency on 29 June 2014 and hosted the G7 summit at Schloss Elmau in Garmisch-Partenkirchen on 7–8 June 2015. With that summit, regular annual rotation of the G7 summit Presidency has resumed, with subsequent summits in Ise-Shima, Japan, 26–27 May 2016, Taormina, Italy, 26–27 May 2017, and Charlevoix, Canada, 8–9 June 2018.

Coexistence of the G7/G8 and the G20

Observers have long been seized with this thorny issue. Examples are Dobson's 2001 formulation cited earlier and, later, a joint article written just before the London G20 summit by Prime Ministers Gordon Brown of the UK and Silvio Berlusconi of Italy (Brown and Berlusconi, 2009). Some leaders, notably Presidents Obama and Sarkozy, who had previously been sceptical of the G8, preferring the G20, came to accept the advantages of continuing both fora. With the 2008 financial and economic crisis and its aftermath, '[a]ny international mechanism for dealing with the crisis had to include the emerging powers as equal partners' (Bayne, 2011a, p. 251). Others have viewed the G7/G8-G20 relationship in three dimensions: competition, coexistence or cooperation, where competition may imply either the continued existence of the G8 alongside the G20 or the eventual replacement of the G7/G8 by the G20 (Stanley Foundation, 2011; Schmucker and Gnath, 2011a; Kirton, 2013a). Cooper and Thakur (2013, p. 14) assert that '[i]n some of its characteristics the G20 is both a rival and a successor to the G8'.

Cooper and Schrumm (2011) highlight the problems of the G8's self-selected status, democratic deficit and inability to deliver effectively on some of its commitments. They contrast this with the comparative advantage of the G20, which engages a much more representative group of countries and operates in a global and interregional manner. However, they also point to constraints that the G20 faces: difficulty of maintaining the commitment of all G20 leaders; problems of the G20's composition notwithstanding its good representativeness; and questions about whether the G20 can successfully expand its economic mandate. They conclude with the optimal scenario of collaboration, not competitiveness, between the G8 and the G20.

Another aspect of G7/G8-G20 coexistence was the relationship between the G20 and the continuing (and until 2014 the only) G7 component (without Russia) of the G8 system: the G7 Finance Ministers' and Central Bank Governors' forum. Gordon Smith (2011c) pinpointed a fundamental problem with this arrangement:

> When the G7 meets instead of, or even at the same time as, the G20, what are the excluded countries to think? . . . The G20 was all about abolishing antechambers. Nonetheless . . . the G7 perpetuates antechambers (and implicitly slights the 'G13') with no clear explanation as to why. What is at stake is the future of global governance writ large – institutions, leaders and the balance between sovereignty and managing global interdependence.

Among the reasons for continued coexistence of the G7/G8 and G20 is the fact that leaders find it more comfortable and consensual to meet in a smaller, more homogenous forum than the much larger G20. Bayne (2014, p. 36) asserts that 'the G20 is much less of a personal instrument for the participating leaders than the G7' and the G20 'can never replicate the compactness and flexibility of its long-lived predecessor'. Reynolds (2014, p. 21), writing about the G7/G8, states that '[t]he evolution of the G7/8 process . . . should be understood as a constant struggle between the two forms of summitry – . . . the highly personal . . . and the institutionalized'. Many G7 and G20 officials, however, see the G7 and the G20 not as competitors but as parallel institutions. Dries Lesage (2015) argues along somewhat similar lines.

As for overlapping agenda items, what would help is 'that the G8 stay out of any issues destined for the G20' so as not to seem to pre-discuss or, worse, pre-resolve issues on the agenda of the G20 (Smith, 2011c). Yet, as the 2012 Camp David and 2013 Lough Erne G8 summits as well as the 2014 Brussels, 2015 Schloss Elmau, 2016 Ise-Shima, 2017 Taormina and 2018 Charlevoix G7 summits show, leaders will discuss any pressing issues they choose; in addition to the security agenda, Camp David took up economic issues (the euro zone crisis) as well as food security (both of which were also on the agenda of the Los Cabos G20 summit). UK Prime Minister David Cameron (2012) indicated that he wanted 'to see the G8 taking a broader approach to development' and to deal with security, prosperity and growth at its 2013 Lough Erne summit. The agenda did indeed include security as well as economic issues (growth, jobs, etc.) and tax-related items, both of which featured on the 2013 St Petersburg G20 summit, too. Russia, originally to be the host of the 2014 Sochi G8 summit, set its priorities on the fight against drugs, anti-terrorism, conflict resolution, disaster management and global health security (G20, 2014h). But the Sochi summit was not to be. Instead, at Brussels, having suspended Russia's G8 membership, the G7 leaders at their summit focused on the global economy, energy, climate change and development, and security issues (Ukraine, Syria, Libya, Mali, Central African Republic, Iran, North Korea, the Middle East, Afghanistan and the South China Sea). They condemned Russia's violation of Ukraine's sovereignty (the cause of Russia's suspension from the G8) (G7, 2014). The agenda at the Schloss Elmau G7 summit focused on the UN's post-2015 Sustainable Development Goals and on climate protection, in anticipation of the Paris conference in December of that year. Health issues, quality of jobs and women's role in the workforce were also on the agenda – Ebola and infectious diseases were discussed at the G20 as well in Brisbane in 2014. The 2016 Ise-Shima summit took up various economic, taxation and other issues that are also of concern to the G20. In 2017, the Taormina G7 and Hamburg G20 summits both discussed climate change – also a main topic in 2018 at the G7 in Charlevoix and the G20 in Buenos Aires. Jobs, too, were on the agenda of both 2018 summits.

Focusing on a crucial difference between the G7/G8 and the G20, Fan He (2015, p. 38) asserts that '[a] Cold War mindset and zero-sum game approach would jeopardise, and be poisonous to, G20 cooperation. One only has to look at how geopolitical conflicts tarnished the G8. A similar failure within the G20 would be unacceptable for its membership'. This strengthens the argument in favour of the diversity that characterizes the G20.

The G20's evolving agenda has been a subject of considerable debate. A 2011 conference on the future of the G8 and the G20 suggested the following criteria for additional topics for the G20: a clear need for collective action; a crisis at hand; a vacuum of leadership; lack of capability of other international bodies to set action on the issue in question; and prospects for a positive outcome. The conference debated whether the G20 should keep to its narrower economic and financial focus or expand their agenda in response to pressures. A practical constraint for G20 leaders is the relatively short time to address too many complex issues during a given summit (Heap, 2011).

Replacement of the G7/G8 by the G20

This was the preferred scenario of the L20 project (although it acknowledged two other possible trajectories: incremental expansion of the G8 and coexistence of the G8 and the L20). Edwin Truman's 2005 formulation also advocated such an outcome. More recently, Heinbecker (2011b, p. 237) considered it 'very likely that the G20 will ultimately absorb the G8'. Similarly, Timothy Garton Ash (2011) observes that

> the G8 is an anachronistic survival of the old, Cold War west . . . [The G20] is a grouping much more appropriate to the economic, political and cultural realities of the 21st century. [I]t would be better to roll the G8 into the G20 and [make] the G20 more serious and more effective than it is now.

Kirton (2013c, p. 10) cites various schools of 'replacers' – those that hold that with the emergence of the G20 the G7/G8 would 'fade away as an effective central forum'.

Is there a similarity between recent developments in the G7/G8 versus the G20 and the early history of the G7? The latter grew out of a series of G5 (France, Germany, Japan, the UK and the US) Finance Ministers' meetings (not to be confused with the G5 developing countries group discussed earlier), which later evolved into leaders' summits, first as G6 in 1975, then as G7 (with Canada) from 1976 to 1997, as G8 with Russia starting in 1998, and, as of 2014, G7 again, without Russia. The original G5 leaders met on the margins of the 1976 Puerto Rico G7 summit. The G5 Finance Ministers' forum survived in tandem with the summits until 1987, when it faded away, yielding its place to the G7 Finance Ministers' forum. G7 leaders continued to meet at the time of summits until the 2002 Kananaskis G8 summit. The G20 forum has functioned at both the Finance Ministers' and the leaders' levels, with a system gradually embracing other sub-summit bodies. It is conceivable that some version of the G5-G7-G8 progression could once again play out. The reversion of the G8 to G7 in 2014 may, however, point the opposite way: the leaders at Brussels restated their common values (which are quite distinct from those of the more diverse G20) and may well wish to continue this relatively like-minded, more democratic and more intimate forum alongside the G20. As well, consensus on certain security and other matters is easier to achieve in the G7 than in the G20. Despite the challenge confronting the G7 and the G20 by Trump's US, both fora are determined to survive and are likely to do so as long as the leaders wish it.

Replacement of the G7/G8 by some other group or G7/G8 coexistence with such groupings

Among the proposals along these lines is that of Kenen, Shafer, Wicks and Wyplosz (2004), which called for the streamlining of European representation in the G7 by establishing a G4 of the US, the euro zone, China and Japan. This would have included a substantial part of the G8 but left out Canada, Russia and the UK. Stephen Roach's 2004 proposal was a variation on this theme; it would establish a new G5 with the US, the euro zone, China, Japan and the UK, thus leaving Canada and Russia out in the cold. Other variations have included Colin Bradford's G12 or G18, and Åslund's G13 (the G8+G5) or G12, without Mexico (Bradford, 2005b; Åslund, 2006). George Haynal's 'G-XX' posits a 'G' of the G8, plus the G5 (possibly without Mexico) and an indeterminate number of others from Africa, the Middle East, Southeast Asia and other regions. This forum would co-exist with the G8 (Haynal, 2005). An interesting variation on this theme was the 2009 proposal of the Stiglitz panel that would establish a council of 20 to 25 members under the aegis of the UN (UN GA, 2009).

The G2 concept

This has been raised in various proposals over the years. For example, Edwin Truman (2005) envisioned a G2 of the US and the euro zone, to co-exist with the G20. Bergsten (2005) argued along the same lines. Later the US and China were mentioned as a G2 configuration (Brzezinski, 2009). These proposals imply acknowledgement of a long-established process of bilateral and plurilateral negotiations that have become routine around the G7/G8, and now the G20, summits – and beyond the summits. The World Economic Forum (2012a) has used the US-China G2 concept in the context of monetary rebalancing.

Variable geometry

This scenario involves the G8 (now G7) continuing as the core of discussions while leaving room for wider participation, depending on the topic on the agenda and involving various combinations of the G7/G8, the earlier G5, the then-Major Economies Forum, the past Heiligendamm/L'Aquila Process, BRICS and other groupings. On 2 April 2009, Italian Foreign Minister Franco Frattini wrote an open letter to the Rome newspaper *Il Messaggero* advocating just such a process. He argued, 'thanks both to its format and to its method, the structure of the G8 summit is still extremely valid today and . . . its flexibility will allow it to spawn an advanced and strategic model in support of world governance'. He then stated that the La Maddalena (later changed to L'Aquila) G8 summit 'will be a clear illustration of a variable geometry structure based on the dossiers under consideration'. Thus, he forecast that the summit would begin with 'an initial meeting of the "historic core" group of countries', and that this would be followed by a joint discussion of items on the summit agenda by the G8 and the G5 plus Egypt.

Finally, there would be a meeting which 'will be opened up to a representative group of African countries as well'. He added, 'It is policy goals, more than anything else that should suggest the formats'. This 'evolved' G8, as he termed this format, would be able 'to respond to real political-economic needs in a rapidly changing world' (Frattini, 2009).

Cooper and Schrumm (2011) recall that the L'Aquila summit did indeed involve different combinations of leaders to discuss specific topics – for example, trade, climate, food and aid. But they assert that 'the practice of variable geometry cannot be sustained over the long term'. They cite Davis and Schrumm (2009) on variable geometry resulting in 'problems of inclusivity by putting labels on these various formats . . . [whereas] some countries straddle various categories'. Yet, it is conceivable that some form of variable geometry may be used for pragmatic reasons.

Cooper (2014, p. 101) points to the use of variable geometry by the 3G group (see earlier) vis-à-vis the G20. It did so by arguing 'that small [non-member] countries should have access to the G20 on a functional basis'. This was achieved, for example, by some 3G countries that have become members of the Financial Stability Board.

In practice, variable geometry has operated at summits, expressed, for example, by non-G20 invited members In 2016, the Chinese host invited to the Hangzhou summit Chad (representing the African Union), Egypt, Kazakhstan, Laos (representing ASEAN), Senegal (representing NEPAD) and 'permanent guest' Spain, plus Singapore and Thailand to increase regional representation. In addition, administrative heads of the following IGOs were also invited: Financial Stability Board, ILO, IMF, OECD, UN, World Bank, WTO and WHO. The relevance of particular stakeholders varies from issue to issue. The area where a G20 summit is held is also part of this consideration.

A 'G-Zero' world

Ian Bremmer and Nouriel Roubini (2011, p. 2) argue that the G20, rather than being at the centre of global economic and political governance, is becoming a source of disarray and disagreement among its members. They assert that, with the easing of the global financial and economic crisis, the G20 is a scene of diverging and competing national values among the member states. They further argue that there is no viable alternative, whether a G2, a G3 or other 'G'-type grouping. They conclude that '[w]e are now living in a G-Zero world, one in which no single country or bloc of countries has the political and economic leverage – or will – to drive a truly international agenda'. Bremmer elaborates on this idea in a 2012 book, *Every Nation for Itself: Winners and Losers in a G-zero World.* This, curiously, is echoed by Trump's National Security Strategy (2017, p. 55), which is 'guided by principled realism . . . because it acknowledges the central role of power in international politics, affirms that sovereign states are the best hope for a peaceful world'. This 'America first' strategy extols competition (and cooperation from a position of strength), embraces US military, cyber and energy dominance and emphasizes national interests rather than interdependence, strength rather than persuasion.

Challenges for the G7

Perhaps the greatest challenge the G7 faces is to maintain its relevance and legitimacy in the context of coexistence with the much more representative G20. A particular challenge is how to achieve better coordination with G20 and how to avoid duplication of effort. For example, when there is agenda overlap between the G8 and the G20 – as in the case of confronting Ebola and other infectious diseases or climate and gender issues – it is essential to tailor the approaches so that each 'G' concentrates on what it can do best.

The G7 must recognize that on overarching global issues the G20 is more relevant, more equitable and more legitimate. Examples are climate change and the environment, where no meaningful action can be taken without China, India and other major emerging countries as equal partners; or, on energy or security it is curious to try to act without the participation of Russia – notwithstanding political developments. Similarly, the G7 must avoid pretensions of leadership extending to other areas not represented in its membership.

Accountability is a continuing challenge for both the G7 and the G20. Both have made progress in improving accountability, but broader and deeper action is needed; so is continuing commitment to be answerable for their actions and inactions.

Challenges for the G20

The dichotomy of efficiency versus representativeness/legitimacy has been a constant in debates: the smaller the group, the more efficient it is likely to be – but smaller groups lack adequate representativeness. Some observers consider the G20 summit too unwieldy to be efficient, notwithstanding the fact that it is much more representative of geopolitical realities than the G7/G8. Callaghan (2014, p. 116) considers it '[t]he great strength of the G20 . . . [in that] it brings together leaders from the major developed and emerging markets and provides the potential for them to make progress on some intractable global issues'. The G7/G8 is often cited approvingly for the like-mindedness of its leaders. But as Cooper and Thakur (2013, p. 12) observe, 'Lacking political like-mindedness, [the G20] will be animated more by pragmatism and problem-solving than by ideology and social cohesion'.

Even the G20 is not completely representative – to achieve that, it would, at the extreme, have to grow to the universality of the UN with its 193 member states (previously, when the UN had 192 members, this was sometimes referred to as the notional 'G192') with the attendant further erosion of efficiency. Payne (2014, p. 82) asserts that because the 'marginal majority' remains unrepresented in the G20, the latter 'is always going to be an elite club, or steering committee'.

Creative proposals to bridge this gap include institutionalizing G20 participation by the UN Secretary-General as well as the African Union. The latter is important because Africa remains underrepresented by having South Africa as the only G20 member from that vast continent. Had Nigeria improved its governance, it might well have made it when the initial membership of the Finance Ministers' and Central Bank Governors' G20 was set up in 1999 (which then carried over to the leaders' 20). Martin (2013) points out the problem with the idea of South Africa representing all of Africa, and writes that remedying African underrepresentation would be the only exception (because Africa is the only continent without adequate regional representation) to reluctance to open the Pandora's Box of G20 membership.

Another problem related to efficiency is that G20 summits regularly feature a much larger number of people actually present in the room – sometimes as many as 50 or more, counting the leaders, Finance Ministers, invited heads of state or government, representatives of IGOs, and high officials and other support personnel (many G20 countries have large delegations). This militates against smooth functioning and the kind of informality in the G7/G8 where more or less like-minded leaders engage in meaningful discussion, sometimes on a first-name basis. Payne (2014, p. 82), too, argues that the commonality of the G7/G8 'cannot be expected to work in the same way at the level of twenty (or more) member states' coming from diverse backgrounds.

Can these numbers be reduced? One partial way out (supported by some G20 leaders but opposed by others) may be taken from the practice of the G7/G8 where, starting with the Birmingham G8 summit, leaders were no longer accompanied by their Finance and Foreign Ministers at summits.

Proliferation of meetings leading up to summits is another problem. Callaghan (2014, p. 111) notes that the Australian host government website listed '69 separate events in the lead-up to the Brisbane [summit]'. He asserts that 'the G20 has become a large and expensive process'.

Gilman (2015, p. 52) argues that it would make more sense if leaders met only when absolutely needed, and 'revert to the earlier model of regular G20 ministerial meetings to get the job done'. He asserts that the 'modest achievements' of G20 summits beginning with Seoul in 2010 could have been attained 'as well or even more effectively at the ministerial level'. Yet, it is difficult to see how the leaders' G20 could revert to a much more limited role, especially given the requirements of global governance on a high level.

The G20's legitimacy – connected to but not synonymous with representativeness – has been debated ever since the establishment of the forum at the leaders' level – as has the legitimacy of the G7/G8 all along. Paola Subacchi and Stephen Pickford (2011) examine the legitimacy versus efficiency dynamic. They ask whether expansion of G20 membership would increase legitimacy and conclude that since any expansion of membership would be politically contentious, there are other ways to increase legitimacy: through better representativeness via members taking on representation of a constituency of non-member states; involving non-members on particular issues; establishing a permanent secretariat; and, most of all, improving transparency and accountability.

Could the G20 be transformed from a 'crisis committee' or 'crisis responder' to a 'steering committee'? This challenge was seen as a desirable outcome, among others, by Lukov (2010), Subacchi and Pickford (2011), Woods (2011), Bradford and Lim (2011c) and Martin (2011b, 2013).

The question is fraught. Crises arise periodically. The Seoul, Cannes and Los Cabos summits were preoccupied with the worsening sovereign debt crisis in the euro zone – a crisis that lasted for several years with implications for the global economy. The Syrian crisis required a great deal of the leaders' attention at the 2013 St Petersburg summit (in 2014 it was taken up by the G7), and the Ebola outbreak in Africa entered the agenda of the 2014 Brisbane summit. Migration and refugee movements are another example of an enduring crisis.

According to Nicholas Bayne (2011a, in an interview with the author's research assistant, G. Clinton, 25 October), the test for the G20 will be whether it can move on to other subjects rather than focusing exclusively on each crisis. Resilience, ability and will on the part of the leaders are required to achieve this change of orientation for the G20. If the G20 gets bogged down in crises, they may become yet another less useful and less effective global group.

Yet, some observers claim that the G20 is already a steering committee, at least in the sense that it remits an increasing range of tasks to other actors. The Hamburg summit, for example, asked several organizations, including the OECD, FSB, WTO, the World Bank Group and other multilateral development banks, the IMF, ILO, IOM and UNHCR, to develop policies and prepare reports. Earlier, Grenville (2014, p. 39) argued that 'the G20 . . . [could] develop over time its role as a ginger group and steering committee for some of these more specialised international agencies', although '[w]henever this is suggested[,] there is understandable pushback from two quarters: from these international agencies themselves, and from smaller countries not directly represented at the G20'.

Martin (2013, p. 729) asserted that the G20's success as a steering committee lies

> in its ability to respond to two challenges: first, can it improve the way globalization works for everyone whether they are at the G20 or not . . . [and s] econd, can it limit the contagion that appears to be the inevitable consequence of the interdependence of nations?

Writing after the Cannes summit, Giovanni Grevi (2011, pp. 1–2, 4) stated that the 2009 Pittsburgh summit had 'triggered the incremental, and contested, transformation of the crisis management committee into a global steering board tasked with addressing the root causes of the crisis by tackling global economic imbalances'. He argued, however, that at Cannes the G20 'atrophied as a global steering board' and has become '[n]either a steering board, nor a crisis management committee [but] . . . seems to have entered an identity crisis'. His way out of this dilemma: 'the . . . G20 should continue to invest in a third critical function, namely a pathfinding role for institutional innovation and normative convergence'. Concluding along the same lines as Bayne, Grevi asserted that the key to this is leadership by those G20 members prepared to provide it.

Edwin Truman adds that the G20 is not yet very good at crisis management; it does better at crisis prevention (Truman, 2012; interview with the author, 5 June). Andrew Cooper (2012) develops this idea further; he places the G20 beyond the crisis committee-steering committee framework and considers the G20 to have become a global focus group for its individual member countries and for its constituent groups, such as BRICS. Callaghan (2014, p. 112), on the other hand, argues that 'the first two G20 summits succeeded in stemming the 2008 financial crisis and prevented it from becoming more severe . . . [but] as for recent G20 summits, the general narrative is that the best days of the G20 are behind it, and that was in its role as a crisis responder'. Cooper (2014, pp. 105–107), in a reassessment, notes that '[t]he G20 has not remained a static entity . . . [and asserts that it] has lost momentum, caught between the roles of a crisis committee and a putative steering committee . . . [Thus] the G20 is a pivotal indication of the state of global governance'.

The argument, however, can be made that the crisis committee-steering committee framework is an unnecessary dichotomy. In practice, the G7/G8 and the G20 have evolved to be both: dealing with crises as they occur and attempting crisis management, and, on the other hand, acting as a steering committee on many issues. German Chancellor Angela Merkel, host of the 2015 Schloss Elmau G7 summit, reasons along somewhat similar lines: 'this G7 summit is about much more than crisis diplomacy. As has been the case ever since the format was established, it is . . . also an opportunity to discuss the global economic situation' (Merkel, 2015, p. A15). More recently, Martin (telephone interview with the author, 10 January 2018) pointed out that there was no contradiction between the crisis committee and the steering committee functions. An example: Gordon Brown's efforts around the time of the 2009 London summit to restrict protectionism were clearly a crisis prevention measure, as without the success of those efforts the 2008 recession could have become a depression. And when the G20 turned the Financial Stability Forum into a much stronger Financial Stability Board (a steering committee measure), regulatory reform of the banking system would not have been possible. The need for both functions continues. In fact, Martin would like to see the FSB transformed into a treaty-based international organization.

Another type of challenge for the G20 lies in domestic constraints of its members. These are analyzed succinctly by Gordon Smith (2012):

> The US presidential election year [during which Americans are unlikely to] support . . . major institutional reform . . . [;] the European Union . . . [which is] still . . . [struggling with] its own financial and economic problems, and [the fact that] European leaders are little inclined to confront their glaring overrepresentation in the decision-making mechanisms of key international organizations; . . . [and finally that] China is in the midst of an economic pause, and is trying to navigate a very sensitive political period as it nears the decennial domestic handover of power.

In his report prepared for the Cannes summit, UK Prime Minister David Cameron (UK PM, 2011, p. 19) addressed the following key aspects of G20 governance: the need for political consensus; enhanced economic policy coordination; strengthening financial sector governance; filling gaps in the governance of global trade; developing more effective global standards; and achieving greater coherence in global governance in the broad sense. To these ends, Cameron made a number of specific proposals for the G20: on the leaders' role, on engaging other actors, improving its working practices and accountability; and ensuring that the G20 and other global institutions work together more effectively. The report observes that 'there is a spectrum of options for increasing the G20's capacity, culminating in a permanent Secretariat with a policy function'. G20 leaders were not uniformly receptive to the latter idea; when it re-emerges from time to time, they are unable to reach consensus.

A new challenge for both the G7 and G20 is posed by the statements and actions of US President Donald Trump. His stance and behaviour, particularly around the 2018 Charlevoix G20 summit, cast doubt on previous assumptions about the unanimous like-mindedness of the G7 leaders. Disagreements among G7/G8 members have arisen in the past – usually privately – but at Charlevoix there was an open split between the US and the other six leaders on climate, trade and some other issues. In addition, the US President called for reinstatement of Russia's membership – also a 'red line' that the other six members refused to cross. Immediately after the summit, Trump disavowed his endorsement of the communiqué which had been agreed by G7 consensus. A larger question is whether the US under Trump shares the G7's values first enunciated at the first (G6) summit at Rambouillet in 1975 and subsequently reaffirmed, most recently at the 2014 Brussels G20 summit.

In the case of the G20, cohesion of members is held together not by common values but by common interests. But in Hamburg, too, there was an open split on climate between the US and the other 19 G20 members. The 2018 Buenos Aires summit may well see a similar divergence on trade protectionism. Will the 'Trump effect' cause irreparable harm to the G7 and the G20 or will it prove to be a temporary phenomenon?

Conclusion

Over the years of existence of the G7/G8, then the G20, many have predicted or prescribed the path that these two fora could or should follow. Possible trajectories include: the expansion of the G7/G8 to reflect changing geopolitical realities; continued coexistence of the G7/G8 with the G20; the G20 replacing the G7/G8; another group replacing the G7/G8, or G7/G8 coexistence with such groups; the 'G2' of the US and China asserting supremacy in global governance; variable geometry of summitry, involving different countries and IGOs depending on the issue discussed and the venue of the summit; and a 'G-Zero' world in which no one country or group of countries can set the global agenda. So far, it is G7-G20 coexistence as parallel institutions has prevailed.

Complex relationships of the G7/G8 and G20 with formal IGOs having major roles in global governance, particularly the UN and the IMF/World Bank, must be part of whatever future the G7/G8 and G20 face. The G7 and the G20 should continue to define and develop their mutual relationship. As part of those efforts, it useful to keep in mind a crucial difference between the G20 on one hand and IGOs on the other: while the latter represent their official constituencies, the former operates independently.

Reform proposals and projections have ranged in scope and kind. Some have addressed the composition of the G7/G8 and G20, through increasing, reducing or otherwise changing membership. Others have involved institutional changes, including whether and how to establish a secretariat (which would provide better continuity and a more rational process but would carry the risk of bureaucratization).

The dichotomy of representativeness versus efficiency has been an enduring concern. On the one hand the G20, as a major actor of global governance, must include all systemically significant countries as members, and on the other hand it must consider the risk of reduced efficiency if membership (or the size of delegations in the room) exceeds a certain number. The G20 will have to come to grips with this dilemma. Representativeness in the G7/G8 is even more inadequate as they exclude a number of systemically important countries.

Expanding or contracting the G20 agenda is another fraught point, posing the challenge of staying within capacity as narrowly conceived or taking leadership on all major global issues, not just financial and economic ones. While the G20 continues to be driven by an economic agenda, other significant issues connect with, and can be anchored in, that agenda – for example, climate change, infectious diseases, gender issues, migration and refugee issues.

A related question is the need to transform the G20 from a 'crisis committee' to a more steady 'steering committee', despite (or because of) periodic crises that must be dealt with – or, rather, the need to acknowledge the reality that the G20 is both a crisis committee and a steering committee. Preventing or managing crises often calls for a G20 steering function.

To sum up, the 'Gs' face multiple challenges: a complex and dynamic relationship between the G7/G8 and the G20; proposals for membership expansion or reduction; agenda broadening or restriction; relationships with non-member countries and international organizations; institutional changes and procedural innovation; and domestic constraints of members. Questions remain: will one or both of the G7/G8 and G20 survive? If so, in what form, membership and mandate, and with a narrower or broader agenda? Will the G20 be able to continue to be both a 'steering committee' and a 'crisis committee'? The answers ultimately lie in the pressure and influence of various actors, unfolding events and changing global priorities, and in the decisions of incumbent leaders of the G7/G8 and the G20.

References

Ash, T.G., 2011. If Obama really wants to lead us to a free world, he should abolish the G8. *The Guardian*, 25 May.

Åslund, A., 2006. Russia's challenges as chair of the G-8. In: *Policy Briefs in International Economics*, March, PB06–3. Washington, DC: Peterson Institute for International Economics. www.iie.com/publications/pb/pb06-3.pdf [Accessed: 24 February 2018].

Bayne, N., 2005b. *Staying Together: The G8 Summit Confronts the 21st Century*. Aldershot, UK: Ashgate.

Bayne, N., 2011a. The decline of the G8 summit and lessons for the G20. In: N. Bayne and S. Woolcock, eds. *The New Economic Diplomacy: Decision-Making and Negotiation in International Economic Relations*. 3rd ed. Global Finance Series. Farnham: Ashgate. pp. 249–262.

Bayne, N., 2014. The foundations of summitry. In: E. Mourlon-Druol and F. Romero, eds. *International Summitry and Global Governance: The Rise of the G7 and the European Council, 1974–1991*. Cold War History Series. London and New York: Routledge. pp. 23–38.

Bergsten, C.F., 2005. The Euro and the Dollar: Toward a Finance G-2? In: A.S. Posen, ed. *The Euro at Five: Ready for a Global Role?* Washington, DC: Institute for International Economics. pp. 27–46.

Bergsten, C.F. and de Montbrial, T., 2003. Letter of transmittal to the leaders of the G-8 member countries. In: Peterson Institute of International Economics, ed. *Restoring G-8 Leadership of the World Economy*. Washington, DC. pp. 4–5. www.iie.com/publications/papers/g8-2003.pdf [Accessed: 22 February 2018].

Bergsten, C.F. and Koch-Weser, C., 2004. The G-2: A new conceptual basis and operating modality for transatlantic economic relations. In: W. Weidenfeld et al., eds. *From Alliance to Coalitions: The Future of Transatlantic Relations*. Gütersloh, Germany: Bertelsmann Foundation. pp. 237–250.

Blanchfield, M., 2016. Former PM Martin: G20 should help beyond economic troubles. *Macleans*, 29 March. www.macleans.ca/news/canada/former-pm-martin-g20-should-help-beyond-economic-troubles/ [Accessed: 22 February 2018].

Bradford, C.I., 2005b. *Global Governance for the 21st Century*. Paper prepared for the Brookings Institution and The Centre for International Governance Innovation Governance. www.brookings.edu/wp-content/uploads/2016/06/20051024bradford.pdf [Accessed: 22 February 2018].

Bradford, C.I. and Lim, W.H., 2011c. Introduction: Toward the consolidation of the G20: From crisis committee to global steering committee. In: C.I. Bradford and W.H. Lim, eds. *Global Leadership in Transition: Making the G20 More Effective and Responsive*. Washington, DC: Brookings Institution Press with Korean Development Institute. pp. 1–10.

Bradford, C.I. and Linn, J.F., 2004. Global economic governance at a crossroads: Replacing the G-7 with the G-20. *Brookings Institution Policy Brief* #132, April. www.brookings.edu/papers/2004/04globaleconomics_colin-i-bradford-jr.aspx [Accessed: 24 February 2018].

Bremmer, I., 2012. *Every Nation for Itself: Winners and Losers in a G-Zero World*. New York: Portfolio/Penguin.

Bremmer, I. and Roubini, N., 2011. A G-zero world: The new economic club will produce conflict, not cooperation. *Foreign Affairs*, 90(2), pp. 2–7.

BRICS Research Group, 2014. *The 6th BRICS Summit: Fortaleza Declaration*. 15 July. www.brics.utoronto.ca/docs/140715-leaders.html [Accessed: 13 March 2018].

BRICS Research Group, 2015a *BRICS Information Centre*. www.brics.utoronto.ca [Accessed: 23 February 2018].

BRICS Research Group, 2015b. *Media Note on the Informal Meeting of BRICS Leaders on the occasion of the G20 Summit in Brisbane*. 15 November. www.brics.utoronto.ca/docs/141115-brisbane.html [Accessed: 23 February 2018].

BRICS Research Group, 2015c. *Memorandum of Understanding on Cooperation with the New Development Bank*. 9 July. www.brics.utoronto.ca/docs/150709-NDB-memorandum-en.html [Accessed: 28 February 2017].

BRICS Research Group, 2017. *BRICS Leaders Xiamen Declaration*. 4 September. www.brics.utoronto.ca/docs/170904-xiamen.html [Accessed: 23 February 2018].

Brown, G. and Berlusconi, S., 2009. *Three Commitments for Global Recovery*. 19 February. webarchive.nationalarchives.gov.uk/20090505181721/www.number10.gov.uk/Page18340 [Accessed: 24 February 2018].

Brzezinski, Z., 2009. The group of two that could change the world. *Financial Times*, 14 January, p. 9.

Callaghan, M., 2014. International economic summits: Are they worth the effort? *Caribbean Journal of International Relations & Diplomacy*, 2(3), pp. 43–60.

Cameron, D., 2012. I will get things done at the G8 Summit. *Politics Home*, 18 May. archive.li/xZqOQ [Accessed: 23 February 2018].

Carin, B., 2010. *The Future of the G20 Process*. Seoul G20 Commentaries. Waterloo, Canada: Centre for International Governance Innovation. November. www.cigionline.org/sites/default/files/barry_carin_commentary.pdf [Accessed: 22 February 2018].

Carin, B., 2011a. A G20 'non-secretariat': President Nicolas Sarkozy's conversation with philosopher Lao Tzu, Strategist Sun Tzu, and Clio, the muse of history. In: C.I. Bradford and W.H. Lim, eds. *Global Leadership in Transition: Making the G20 More Effective and Responsive*. Washington, DC: Brookings Institution Press with Korean Development Institute. pp. 275–282.

Carin, B., 2011b. *No Fairy Tale at the Cannes G20 Summit*. Waterloo, Canada: Centre for International Governance Innovation. 7 November. www.cigionline.org/publications/no-fairy-tale-cannes-g20-summit [Accessed: 16 January 2018].

Carin, B., Heinbecker, P., Smith, G. and Thakur, R., 2010. *Making the G20 Summit Process Work: Some Proposals for Improving Effectiveness and Legitimacy*. CIGI G20 Paper No. 2. June. Waterloo, Canada: Centre for International Governance Innovation. www.cigionline.org/sites/default/files/g20_no2_1.pdf [Accessed: 22 February 2018].

Climate Home, 2017. China, EU and Canada to take lead on climate at Montreal meeting. *Climate Home News*. 13 September. www.climatechangenews.com/2017/09/13/china-eu-canada-take-lead-climate/ [Accessed: 19 March 2018].

Cooper, A.F., 2012. *The G20 as the Global Focus Group: Beyond the Crisis Committee/Steering Committee Framework*. G20 Information Centre. www.g20.utoronto.ca/analysis/120619-cooper-focusgroup.html [Accessed: 24 February 2018].

Cooper, A.F., 2014. The G20 and contested global governance: BRICS, middle powers and small states. *Caribbean Journal of International Relations & Diplomacy*, 2(3), pp. 87–109.

Cooper, A.F. and Momani, B., 2014. Re-balancing the G-20 from efficiency to legitimacy: The 3G coalition and the practice of global governance. *Global Governance: A Review of Multilateralism and International Organizations*, 20(2), pp. 213–232.

Cooper, A.F. and Schrumm, A., 2011. Reconciling the Gs: The G8, the G5, and the G20 in a world of crisis. In: P. Savona et al., eds. *Global Financial Crisis: Global Impact and Solutions*. Farnham: Ashgate. pp. 229–244.

Cooper, A.F. and Thakur, R., 2013. *The Group of Twenty (G20)*. Global Institutions Series. New York: Routledge.

Davis, R. and Schrumm, A., 2009. *Is the G8's Variable Geometry Sustainable?* https://www.cigionline.org/publications/g8s-variable-geometry-sustainable [Accessed: 24 November 2018].

Desai, N., 2012. What interests do the BRICS countries share? In: M. Larionova and J.J. Kirton, eds. *BRICS New Delhi Summit 2012: Stability, Security and Prosperity*. Toronto: Newsdesk Media Group. pp. 26–27. www.brics.utoronto.ca/newsdesk/BRICS-2012.pdf [Accessed: 23 February 2018].

Dobson, W., 2001. Broadening participation in G-7 summits. In: G-8 Preparatory Conference, *Toward Shared Responsibility and Global Leadership: Recommendations for the G-8 Genoa Summit from the G-8 Preparatory Conference*. Turin, Italy: Peterson Institute for International Economics. pp. 23–29.

Edwards, L.J., 2013. *The St. Petersburg Summit: Obama's Futile Quest for Support on Syria Overshadowed the Summit's Economic Successes*. G20 St. Petersburg Rapid Response. Waterloo, Canada: Centre for International Governance Innovation. 10 September. www.cigionline.org/publications/st-petersburg-summit-obamas-futile-quest-support-syria-overshadowed-summits-economic [Accessed: 22 February 2018].

Elliott, L., 2008. This summit signalled the passing of the exclusive club of wealthy nations. *The Guardian*, 11 December.

Elliott, L. and Wintour, P., 2006. Blair wants developing nations in new G13 to help secure key deals. *The Guardian*, 13 July, p. 15.

English, J., Thakur, R. and Cooper, A.F. eds., 2005. *Reforming from the Top: A Leaders' 20 Summit*. Tokyo: United Nations University Press.

European Council, 2014. *Brussels G7 Summit*. 4–5 June. www.european-council.europa.eu/en/meetings/international-summit/2014/06/04-05/ [Accessed: 23 March 2018].

For slimmer and sporadic summits, 2001. *Financial Times*, 23 July, p. 18.

Frattini, F., 2009. Summits of the 'big' countries growing in importance but the G8 continues to play a strategic role. *Il Messaggero*, 2 April. www.esteri.it/MAE/EN/Sala_Stampa/ArchivioNotizie/Interviste/2009/04/20090402_articoloFrattini_Vertici.htm [Accessed: 11 February 2014].

G7, 2014. *The Brussels G7 Summit Declaration*. www.g8.utoronto.ca/summit/2014brussels/declaration.html [Accessed: 24 February 2018].

G20, 2014h. *Sergei Lavrov on the priorities of Russia's G8 Presidency 2014*. en.g8russia.ru/news/20140121/983200521.html [Accessed: 8 February 2014].

G20, 2016k. *G20 Leaders' Communiqué*. 5 September. www.g20.utoronto.ca/2016/160905-communiqué.html [Accessed: 4 October 2017].

G20, 2017g. *G20 Leaders' Declaration*. 8 July. www.g20.utoronto.ca/2017/2017-G20-leaders-declaration.html [Accessed: 4 October 2017].

G20, 2017p. *Terms of Reference, G20 Eminent Persons Group on Global Financial Governance*. www.iai.it/sites/default/files/g20-ep-terms-of-reference.pdf [Accessed: 9 January 2018].

Gilman, M., 2015. A world without G20 summits. In: M. Larionova and J.J. Kirton, eds. *The G8-G20 Relationship in Global Governance*. Farnham, UK: Ashgate. pp. 45–54.

Gnath, K., and Schmucker, C., 2015. Group with a cause: There is no alternative to the G20 but it does need reform. *The G20 at the End of 2014. G20 Monitor*, 15, pp. 32–35. www.lowyinstitute.org/files/g20-at-the-end-of-2014.pdf [Accessed: 24 February 2018].

Grenville, S., 2014. Where is the G20 at end-2014? *The G20 at the End of 2014. G20 Monitor*, 15, pp. 39–40. www.lowyinstitute.org/files/g20-at-the-end-of-2014.pdf [Accessed: 23 February 2018].

Grevi, G., 2011. *The G20 after Cannes: An Identity Crisis*. FRIDE Policy Brief, No. 105. November. Madrid: Fundación para las Relaciones Internacionales y el Diálogo Exterior. www.fride.org/download/PB_105_G20_after_Cannes.pdf [Accessed: 23 February 2016].

Hajnal, P.I., 2007b. *Summitry from G5 to L20: A Review of Reform Initiatives*. Centre for International Governance Innovation. Working Paper, No. 20. www.cigionline.org/publications/summitry-g5-l20-review-reform-initiatives [Accessed: 21 February 2018].

Hajnal, P.I., 2007c. Reform of the G7, G8 and G20. In: P.I. Hajnal, ed. *The G8 System and the G20: Evolution, Role and Documentation*. Aldershot: Ashgate. pp. 159–177.

Hajnal, P.I. and Panova, V., 2012. The future role and reform of the G8. In: M. Larionova, ed. *The European Union in the G8: Promoting Consensus and Concerted Actions for Global Public Goods*. Farnham: Ashgate. pp. 65–81.

Hampson, F.O. and Heinbecker, P., 2011. The 'new' multilateralism of the twenty-first century. *Global Governance: A Review of Multilateralism and International Organizations*, 17(3), pp. 299–310.

Harvey, M., 2009. UN panel calls for council to replace G20. *Financial Times*, 23 March, p. 2.

Haynal, G., 2005. Summitry and governance: The case for a G-XX. In: D. Carment et al., eds. *Canada among Nations 2004: Setting Priorities Straight*. Montreal and Kingston: McGill-Queens University Press. pp. 261–274.

He, F., 2015. Back on track. *The G20 at the End of 2014. G20 Monitor*, 15, pp. 36–38. www.lowyinstitute.org/files/g20-at-the-end-of-2014.pdf [Accessed: 24 February 2018].

Heap, P.C., 2008. *Globalization and Summit Reform: An Experiment in International Governance*. New York and Ottawa: Springer; International Development Research Centre.

Heap, P.C., 2011. *The New Geometry of Global Summitry: The Future of the G20 (and the G8): Conference Report*. Waterloo, Canada: Centre for International Governance Innovation. 25 May. www.cigionline.org/sites/default/files/conference_report_1.pdf [Accessed: 24 February 2018].

Heinbecker, P., 2011a. *The Future of the G20 and Its Place in Global Governance*. CIGI G20 Papers, No. 5. Waterloo, Canada: Centre for International Governance Innovation. 27 April. www.cigionline.org/sites/default/files/g20no5.pdf [Accessed: 24 February 2018].

Heinbecker, P., 2011b. The United Nations and the G20: Synergy or dissonance? In: C.I. Bradford and W.H. Lim, eds. *Global Leadership in Transition: Making the G20 More Effective and Responsive*. Washington, DC: Brookings Institution Press with Korean Development Institute. pp. 236–245.

Helleiner, E., 2012. The limits of incrementalism: The G-20, the FSB, and the international regulatory agenda. *Journal of Globalization and Development*, 2(2).

India. Press Information Bureau. Prime Minister's Office, 2013. *Media Note on the Informal Meeting of BRICS Leaders ahead of the G20 Summit in St. Petersburg*. 5 September. pib.nic.in/newsite/erelease.aspx?relid=99138 [Accessed: 24 February 2018].

International Monetary Fund, 2016d. *Historic Quota and Governance Reforms Become Effective*. Press Release 16/25. 27 January. www.imf.org/en/news/articles/2015/09/14/01/49/pr1625a [Accessed: 25 February 2018].

Japan. Ministry of Foreign Affairs, 2016. *Ministerial Meeting of the Major Economies Forum on Energy and Climate (MEF)*. www.mofa.go.jp/ic/ch/page25e_000103.html [Accessed: 19 March 2018].

Keating, J.E., 2012. More than BRICs in the Wall. *Foreign Policy*, 192, p. 25. www.foreignpolicy.com/articles/2012/02/27/more_than_brics_in_the_wall?page=0,0 [Accessed: 3 February 2014].

Kenen, P.B., et al., 2004. *International Economic and Financial Cooperation: New Issues, New Actors, New Responses*. London: Centre for Economic Policy Research.

Kharas, H. and Lombardi, D., 2012. *The Group of Twenty: Origins, Prospects and Challenges for Global Governance*. Global Economy and Development. Washington, DC: Brookings Institution. www.brookings.edu/wp-content/uploads/2016/06/g20-global-governance-kharas-lombardi.pdf [Accessed: 30 January 2018].

Kirton, J.J., 2008a. *The Case for G8 Reform*. Lecture delivered at Chuo University, Tokyo. 26 June. www.g8.utoronto.ca/scholar/kirton_reform_080629.pdf [Accessed: 24 February 2018].

Kirton, J.J., 2013a. The future of G20 governance. In: J.J. Kirton, ed. *G20 Governance for a Globalized World*. Farnham: Ashgate. pp. 373–390.

Kirton, J.J., 2013c. Introduction. In: J.J. Kirton, ed. *G20 Governance for a Globalized World*. Farnham: Ashgate. pp. 3–26.

Kirton, J.J., 2015a. Going global: The G8's adaptation to rising powers. In: T. van de Graf and D. Lesage, eds. *Rising Powers and Multilateral Institutions*. Houndmills, UK: Palgrave Macmillan. pp. 117–131.

Kirton, J.J. and Bracht, C., 2012. *The BRICS Big Boost for the G20 Los Cabos Summit Success*. 18 June. www.brics.utoronto.ca/analysis/brics-g20-2012.html#appendix [Accessed: 23 February 2018].

Kulik, J., 2012. *Where Are Women at G20 Summits: Almost Nowhere*. 29 November. www.g20.utoronto.ca/analysis/120619-kulik-women.html [Accessed: 12 February 2017].

Kulik, J., 2014. *A BRICS Alliance within the G20? Assessing the Performance of BRICS Members*. Paper prepared for the Seminario Internacional Sobre Potencias Intermediarias, Belo Horizonte, Brazil, 12 September.

Kulik, J., 2015. *G20 Gender Policy Accountability*. 13 November. www.g20.utoronto.ca/analysis/151113-kulik.html [Accessed 12 February 2017].

Lesage, D., 2015. The G7/8 and G20: Parallel paths to pragmatic partnership. In: M. Larionova and J.J. Kirton, eds. *The G8-G20 Relationship in Global Governance*. Global Governance Series. Farnham, UK: Ashgate. pp. 35–44.

Linn, J.F., 2012. Whither the G-20: Proposals for a focused agenda. In: Brookings Institution. *The G-20 Los Cabos Summit 2012: Bolstering the World Economy amid Growing Fears of Recession*, Washington, DC. pp. 9–10. www.brookings.edu/wp-content/uploads/2016/06/g20_full-report.pdf [Accessed: 22 February 2018].

Lombardi, D., 2011. The international monetary system through the lens of emerging Asia. In: K. Dervis, M. Kawai and D. Lombardi, eds. *Asia and Policymaking for the Global Economy*. Washington, DC: Brookings Institution Press and Asian Development Bank Institute. pp. 151–181.

Lukov, V., 2010. G-20 and G-8 in search of solutions: Global problems of economy and society. *International Affairs: A Russian Journal*, 56(5), pp. 58–67.

Major Economies Forum on Energy and Climate, 2009. *Description/Purpose*. www.majoreconomiesforum.org/about/descriptionpurpose.html [Accessed: 17 January 2015].

Martin, N., 2005. Not representative, but still legitimate. *Alliance*, 10(2), pp. 16–17.

Martin, P., 2007. Breaking deadlocks in global governance: The L-20 proposal. *Global Governance: A Review of Multilateralism and International Organizations*, 13(3), pp. 301–305.

Martin, P., 2009. Key challenges. In: J.J. Kirton and M. Koch, eds. *The London Summit 2009: Growth, Stability, Jobs*. London: Newsdesk Media Group. pp. 24–25. www.g20.utoronto.ca/g20london2009.html [Accessed: 22 February 2018].

Martin, P., 2011b. The G20: From global crisis responder to global steering committee. In: C.I. Bradford and W.H. Lim, eds. *Global Leadership in Transition: Making the G20 More Effective and Responsive*. Washington, DC: Brookings Institution Press with Korean Development Institute. pp. 13–15.

Martin, P., 2013. The G20: From global crisis responder to steering committee. In: A.F. Cooper et al., eds. *The Oxford Handbook of Modern Diplomacy*. Oxford: Oxford University Press. pp. 729–744.

Martin, P., 2016. Speech to the Academic Council on the United Nations System conference hosted in collaboration with the International Commission of Jurists. *Canada in Global Affairs*. 29–30 March.

Martin, P., 2017. To Curb the Migrant Crisis, the World Must Invest in Africa. *The World Post*, 19 December. www.washingtonpost.com/news/theworldpost/wp/2017/12/19/investment-africa/?utm_term=.81aa4dce030e [Accessed: 22 February 2018].

Merkel, A., 2015. Why the G7 Summit must go beyond crisis diplomacy. *The Globe and Mail*, 3 June, p. A15.

Mistral, J., 2012. The G-20 and the reform of the international monetary system. *Journal of Globalization and Development*, 2(2).

Ocampo, J.A. and Stiglitz, J.E., 2012. From the G-20 to a global economic coordination council. *Journal of Globalization and Development*, 2(2).

O'Neill, J., 2012. Building BRICS: From conceptual category to rising reality. In: M. Larionova and J.J. Kirton, eds. *BRICS New Delhi Summit 2012: Stability, Security and Prosperity*. Toronto: Newsdesk Media Group. pp. 24–25. www.brics.utoronto.ca/newsdesk/BRICS-2012.pdf [Accessed: 23 February 2018].

Pacific Institute for Climate Solutions, 2017. Canada, EU, China filling climate diplomacy gap. *The Climate Examiner*. 29 November. theclimateexaminer.ca/2017/11/29/canada-eu-china-filling-climate-diplomacy-gap/ [Accessed: 19 March 2018].

Parker, G., 2009. Heads agree to New York reunion. *Financial Times*, 3 April, p. 4.

Payne, A., 2014. Steering into the great uncertainty: The G20 as global governance. *Caribbean Journal of International Relations & Diplomacy*, 2(3), pp. 73–85. journals.sta.uwi.edu/iir/index.asp?action=downloadArticle&articleId=494&galleyId=419 [Accessed: 22 February 2018].

Penttilä, R., 2013. The G-20's rising clout. *The New York Times*, 4 September.

Reynolds, D., 2014. Twentieth century summitry and the G7 process. In: E. Mourlon-Druol and F. Romero, eds. *International Summitry and Global Governance: The Rise of the G7 and the European Council, 1974–1991*. Cold War History Series. London and New York: Routledge. pp. 11–23.

Roach, S., 2004. How to fix the world. *Global Economic Forum*, Morgan Stanley, December, pp. 9–10.

Sachs, J., 1998. Global capitalism: Making it work. *The Economist*, 348(8085), pp. 23–25.

Sainsbury, T., 2015. Policies for the Turkish 2015 G20 presidency: Walking a tightrope of G20 relevancy. *The G20 at the End of 2014. G20 Monitor*, 15, pp. 5–26. www.lowyinstitute.org/files/g20-at-the-end-of-2014.pdf [Accessed: 24 February 2018].

Schmucker, C. and Gnath, K., 2011a. From the G8 to the G-20: Reforming the global economic governance system. In: C. Herrmann and J. Terhechte, eds. *European Yearbook of International Economic Law*, vol. 2. Berlin: Springer. pp. 389–402. (Also appeared as GARNET Working Paper 73/09, Brussels, January 2010 www.g20.utoronto.ca/biblio/7310.pdf [Accessed: 24 February 2018].)

Singapore. Ministry of Foreign Affairs, 2013. *Statement by H.E. Karen Tan, Permanent Representative of Singapore to the United Nations, on behalf of the Global Governance Group (3G) at the Briefing on the Outcome of the G20 Saint Petersburg Summit*. 9 September. www.mfa.gov.sg/content/mfa/overseasmission/newyork/nyemb_statements/global_governance_group/2013/201309/press_20130909.html [Accessed: 24 February 2018].

Singapore. Ministry of Foreign Affairs, 2017. *Press Statement by the Global Governance Group (3G) on Its Tenth Ministerial Meeting in New York*. 22 September. www1.mfa.gov.sg/Newsroom/Press-Statements-Transcripts-and-Photos/2017/09/Press-Statement-by-the-Global-Governance-Group-3G-on-its-Tenth-Ministerial-Meeting-in-New-York-on-22 [Accessed: 24 February 2018].

Smith, G.S., 2011c. Getting the context right: Essential to assuring G20's success. In: M. Brem, ed. *Prescriptions for the G20: The Cannes Summit and Beyond*, Waterloo, Canada: Centre for International Governance Innovation. www.cigionline.org/publications/getting-context-right-essential-assuring-g20s-success [Accessed: 23 February 2018].

Smith, G.S., 2012. The evolving role of the G20. In: *Perspectives on the G20: The Los Cabos Summit and Beyond*, pp. 30–31. Waterloo, Canada: Centre for International Governance Innovation. www.cigionline.org/publications/evolving-role-g20 [Accessed: 24 February 2018].

Stanley Foundation, 2011. *How Are Key 21st-Century Powers Arranging Themselves: For Competition, Coexistence, or Cooperation?* Policy Dialogue Brief. Muscatine, Iowa: Stanley Foundation. 6–8 June. www.stanleyfoundation.org/publications/pdb/21stCenturyPowersPDB811.pdf [Accessed: 26 September 2017].

Subacchi, P. and Pickford, S., 2011. *Legitimacy vs Effectiveness for the G20: A Dynamic Approach to Global Economic Governance*. Chatham House Briefing Paper IE BP 2011/01. London: Chatham House. October. www.chathamhouse.org/sites/files/chathamhouse/1011bp_subacchi_pickford.pdf [Accessed: 24 February 2018].

Suominen, K. and Dadush, U., 2012. Is there life for the G-20 beyond the global financial crisis? *Journal of Globalization and Development*, 2(2).

Truman, E.M., 2005. The Euro and prospects for policy coordination. In: A.S. Posen, ed. *The Euro at Five: Ready for a Global Role?* Washington, DC: Institute for International Economics. pp. 47–85. www.piie.com/publications/chapters_preview/3748/04iie3748.pdf [Accessed: 22 February 2018].

Truman, E.M., 2012. The G-20 is failing. *Foreign Policy*, 12 April. foreignpolicy.com/2012/04/12/the-g-20-is-failing/ [Accessed: 30 January 2018].

Turkey. Prime Minister, 2014. *Turkish G20 Presidency Priorities for 2015*. www.g20.utoronto.ca/2015/141201-turkish-priorities.html [Accessed: 13 February 2017].

United Kingdom. Prime Minister, 2011. *Governance for Growth: Building Consensus for the Future*. November. webarchive.nationalarchives.gov.uk/20130109092234/www.number10.gov.uk/wp-content/uploads/2011/11/GovernanceForGrowth_acc.pdf [Accessed: 26 September 2017].

United Nations. General Assembly. 63rd Session, 2009. *Outcome of the Conference on the World Financial and Economic Crisis and Its Impact on Development: Resolution Adopted by the General Assembly*. 13 July. (A/RES/63/303).

United Nations News Service, 2009. *Global Finance Structures Must Be Revamped, Says UN Expert Panel*. 26 March. https://news.un.org/en/story/2009/03/295182 [Accessed: 24 November 2018].

United States. President, 2017. *National Security Strategy of the United States of America*. December. www.whitehouse.gov/wp-content/uploads/2017/12/NSS-Final-12-18-2017-0905-2.pdf [Accessed: 9 February 2018].

United States. White House. Office of the Press Secretary, 2013. *Joint Statement on Syria*. 6 September. www.whitehouse.gov/the-press-office/2013/09/06/joint-statement-syria [Accessed: 6 October 2017].

Vestergaard, J. and Wade, R., 2011. The G-20 has served its purpose and should be replaced. *Journal of Globalization and Development*, 2(2).

Weinrichter, N., 2000. The world monetary system and external relations of the EMU: Fasten your seatbelts! *European Integration Online Papers* (EIoP), 4(10). 27 August. eiop.or.at/eiop/texte/2000–010.htm [Accessed: 22 February 2018].

Woods, N., 2011. The impact of the G20 on global governance: A history and prospective. In: C.I. Bradford and W.H. Lim, eds. *Global Leadership in Transition: Making the G20 More Effective and Responsive*. Washington, DC: Brookings Institution Press with Korean Development Institute. pp. 36–47.

World Economic Forum, 2012a. *Euro, Dollar, Yuan Uncertainties: Scenarios on the Future of the International Monetary System*. World Scenario Series. June. www20.iadb.org/intal/catalogo/PE/2012/10462.pdf [Accessed: 10 January 2018].

8 Monitoring and evaluating G20 performance

This chapter reviews and analyzes the monitoring and evaluation of the G20's performance – an important aspect of accountability. It first introduces the concept of accountability and applies it to the G20. It then examines the role of civil society (including think-tanks), international governmental organizations (IGOs) and the G20 itself in monitoring and evaluating the performance and fulfilment of G20 promises. Another key aspect of accountability, consultation or dialogue, is covered in Chapters 4 (IGOs), 5 (the business sector) and 6 (civil society). The third dimension, transparency, is discussed in Chapters 9 (documentation) and 10 (other sources of information). The fourth component, redress for harmful action or deleterious effects of inaction, is largely absent due to the informal, non-treaty-based nature of the G20, which precludes it from the option of enforcement or other remedy.

Introduction

Monitoring and evaluating the performance of the G20 (as has also been the case with the G7/G8) are essential elements of accountability. The concept of accountability is complex and much debated. This chapter uses the definition developed by Jan Aart Scholte (2011a): accountability, in particular democratic accountability, means that an actor is answerable for its actions or inactions to all those affected by such actions and inactions. Put another way, accountability 'is a condition and process whereby an actor answers for its conduct to those whom it affects. . . . If A takes an action that impacts upon B, then by the principle of accountability A must answer to B for that action and its consequences' (Scholte, 2011a, p. 16). Accountability may be considered to have four main aspects or manifestations: transparency, consultation, evaluation and correction or redress. Obtaining redress or remedy for inaction or wrong action is problematic in the G20, given its nature as an informal institution not based on a treaty. But this has not stopped civil society and other stakeholder groups from advocating remedies for unjust or unfair action (or lack of necessary action) on the part of the G20. Further questions arise concerning accountability: Accountability for what? Accountability to whom? Accountability by what means, what mechanisms? What is democratic accountability?

As with the G7/G8, the G20 too can be held accountable for its actions and inactions on all issues in its purview: financial and economic cooperation or coordination; sustainable development, green growth, anti-corruption, climate change

DOI: 10.4324/9781351266802-9

financing, global health, gender equality and so forth. (For a G7/G8-related discussion of this aspect, see Hajnal, 2011a.) It owes that accountability to the governments and citizens of member states, including all citizens of the European Union (which is a member of the G20), the broader global community (including marginalized populations), their peer G20 leaders, ministers and sub-summit bodies (internal accountability), and international financial institutions and the financial markets. The G20 also expects and requires accountability on the part of other stakeholders, especially the Bretton Woods institutions (mutual accountability).

G7/G8 and G20 accountability has been of persistent concern to civil society organizations (CSOs), including think-tanks, business groups, the media, some G7/G8 and G20 member governments and to the G7/G8 and then the G20 itself, both of which have recognized that much of their claim to legitimacy rests on the fulfilment of their promises. Often there is a gap between rhetoric and delivery. Due to the diversity of the G20's membership, accountability (democratic, transparent accountability) in that forum is more problematic than in the G7/G8. Although progress has been made, much remains to be done.

Dirk Willem Te Velde (2012, p. 3) argues that the G20 should use its comparative advantage on 'strong, sustainable and balanced growth . . . to broaden its development work to explicitly cover the economic implications of . . . [its] core actions in fiscal, financial, trade, exchange rate, and environmental policies for non-G20 countries'. He further proposes that

> accountability and compliance assessments of the G20 in the area of development . . . [should not only] include but go beyond the MYAP [the Seoul Multi-Year Action Plan on Development], to gain a better understanding of how the full range of G20 actions is being perceived in non-G20 countries.

This speaks to the 'accountability to whom' question. Te Velde further asserts that 'the current approach of the G20 in development is neither fully accountable to those it aims to help nor broad enough to focus on areas in which it has a clear, comparative advantage' (Te Velde (2012, p. 3). This, in turn, addresses part of the 'democratic accountability' challenge.

The role of civil society

Looking back to the G7 and G8, one finds that several CSOs (including think-tanks) evaluated the performance of this forum from before the G8 itself began self-evaluation.

For example, the G7 Research Group at the University of Toronto has released reports of compliance with summit commitments since 1996. These are based on publicly available sources, mostly from precise wording in the text of the principal documents of each summit but also using media reports and other public information. These annual compliance reports have assessed G7/G8 compliance with its commitments – for example, compliance with commitments made by the 2016 Ise-Shima G7 summit during the period 29 May 2016–20 May 2017. This report identified 342 commitments and selected 19 priority commitments from that total. These covered the following issues: climate change (Paris Agreement), regional security, international cyber stability, health, terrorism, Syrian refugees, food security and nutrition, gender issues, development, crime and corruption, Ukraine, trade, macroeconomics and non-proliferation of weapons of mass destruction (some of these are broken down into subcategories, thus totalling 19) (G7 Research Group, 2017).

The G20 Research Group, in collaboration with the Center for International Institutions Research of the Russian Presidential Academy of National Economy and Public Administration (RANEPA), and before that with the International Organizations Research Institute at the National Research University Higher School of Economics (HSE), in Moscow, has prepared similar reports since the first, 2008, G20 summit in Washington, DC, but its first full study of the G20's compliance covered 2010 Toronto G20 summit commitments during 28 June–31 October 2010. The most recent such report, tracking commitments of the 2016 Hangzhou summit, identifies 213 commitments from which the following 19 were selected for analysis: macroeconomics, innovation, tax of development, corruption, fossil fuel subsidies, climate change, trade protectionism, e-commerce, the 2030 Agenda on Sustainable Development, female labour participation, migration and refugees, terrorism, technologies and innovation, financial regulation, tax base erosion and profit shifting, energy efficiency, trade growth, investment and corporate governance (G20 Research Group, 2017). Table 8.1 provides the final compliance scores for the Hangzhou summit.

The commitments are defined on the basis of methodology summarized in the report just cited (and also detailed by Ella Kokotsis, 2006, p. 6):

> The methodology uses a scale from −1 to +1, where +1 indicates full compliance with the stated commitment, −1 indicates a failure to comply or action taken that is directly opposite to the stated goal of the commitment, and 0 indicates partial compliance or work in progress, such as initiatives that have been launched but are not yet near completion and whose results can therefore not be assessed. Each member assessed receives a score of −1, 0 or +1 for each commitment . . . . [T]he scores in the tables have been converted to percentages, where −1 equals 0% and +1 equals 100%.
>
> (G20 Research Group, 2017, p. 6)

The Research Group, illustrating the importance of the compliance exercise to G20 governments, cites the following comment of former British Prime Minister David Cameron, made at the 2012 Los Cabos summit:

> The University of Toronto . . . produced a detailed analysis to the extent of which each G20 country has met its commitments since the last summit . . . I think this is important: we come to these summits, we make these commitments, we say we are going to do these things and it is important that there is an organisation that checks up on who has done what.
>
> (G20 Information Centre, 2015)

Table 8.1 2016 G20 Hangzhou Summit Final Compliance Scores by Issue and Member

		Argentina	*Australia*	*Brazil*	*Canada*	*China*	*France*	*Germany*	*India*	*Indonesia*	*Italy*	*Japan*	*Korea*	*Mexico*	*Russia*	*Saudi Arabia*	*South Africa*	*Turkey*	*United Kingdom*	*United States*	*European Union*	*Average*	
1	Macroeconomics: Growth policy tools	0	+1	+1	+1	+1	0	+1	+1	0	+1	+1	+1	+1	+1	+1	+1	0	+1	0	+1	+0.75	88%
2	Innovation	+1	+1	+1	+1	+1	+1	+1	+1	+1	+1	+1	+1	+1	+1	+1	0	+1	0	+1	+1	+0.90	95%
3	Development: Tax administration	+1	+1	+1	+1	+1	+1	+1	+1	+1	+1	+1	+1	+1	+1	0	+1	+1	+1	+1	+1	+0.95	98%
4	Corruption	+1	+1	+1	+1	+1	+1	+1	0	+1	0	0	+1	−1	0	0	−1	−1	+1	0	0	+0.35	68%
5	Energy: Fossil fuel subsidies	0	−1	−1	−1	0	+1	−1	0	0	−1	−1	0	0	−1	−1	−1	−1	−1	−1	−1	−0.60	20%
6	Climate change	+1	+1	0	+1	+1	+1	+1	0	0	0	+1	0	+1	0	0	0	0	+1	−1	+1	+0.45	73%
7	Trade: Anti-protectionism	+1	+1	0	+1	+1	0	0	0	+1	0	0	0	0	+1	−1	0	0	0	0	+1	+0.30	65%
8	Trade: E-commerce	+1	+1	0	+1	+1	+1	+1	+1	+1	0	0	+1	0	+1	0	0	+1	+1	−1	+1	+0.60	80%
9	2030 Agenda on Sustainable Development	+1	+1	+1	+1	+1	+1	+1	+1	0	0	+1	+1	+1	+1	+1	+1	+1	0	+1	+1	+0.85	93%
10	Employment: Gender	0	0	0	+1	0	0	0	0	0	0	+1	0	0	+1	0	0	0	+1	0	+1	+0.25	63%
11	Migration and refugees	+1	0	+1	+1	0	0	+1	0	+1	+1	+1	0	0	0	0	0	+1	0	0	+1	+0.45	73%
12	Financial regulation: Terrorism	+1	+1	−1	+1	+1	+1	+1	+1	+1	+1	0	+1	0	+1	+1	0	+1	+1	+1	+1	+0.75	88%
13	Knowledge diffusion and technology transfer	+1	+1	+1	+1	+1	+1	+1	+1	+1	+1	+1	+1	+1	+1	+1	+1	+1	+1	+1	+1	+1.00	100%

14	Financial Sector Reform Agenda	0	+1	+1	+1	0	0	+1	+1	0	0	+1	0	0	0	+1	0	0	0	+1	+1	+0.45	73%
15	Base erosion and profit shifting	0	+1	+1	0	+1	+1	+1	+1	0	0	+1	+1	+1	+1	0	+1	0	0	+1	+1	+0.65	83%
16	Energy efficiency	+1	+1	+1	+1	0	−1	+1	0	0	−1	+1	+1	+1	+1	+1	+1	0	0	+1	+1	+0.55	78%
17	Trade: Lowering trade costs	0	+1	+1	+1	+1	+1	+1	+1	+1	0	+1	+1	+1	+1	+1	+1	0	0	+1	+1	+0.80	90%
18	Investment	0	+1	+1	+1	+1	+1	+1	+1	0	+1	+1	+1	+1	+1	+1	+1	+1	+1	+1	+1	+0.90	95%
19	Corporate governance	+1	+1	+1	+1	+1	+1	+1	+1	+1	+1	+1	+1	+1	+1	+1	+1	+1	+1	+1	+1	+1.00	100%
		+0.63	+0.79	+0.58	+0.84	+0.74	+0.63	+0.79	+0.63	+0.53	+0.32	+0.68	+0.68	+0.53	+0.68	+0.42	+0.37	+0.37	+0.47	+0.42	+0.84	+0.60	80%
		82%	89%	79%	92%	87%	82%	89%	82%	76%	66%	84%	84%	76%	84%	71%	68%	68%	74%	71%	92%	80%	

Source: G20 Research Group (2017). Reproduced by permission of the Research Group.

A different approach to evaluation was developed by two foremost scholars of summitry, Robert Putnam and Nicholas Bayne (Putnam and Bayne, 1987; Bayne, 1997, 2005b). They used an alphabetical grading system that assessed G7/G8 summits on the basis of cooperative achievements of the leaders, specifically in terms of four types of policy coordination: mutual enlightenment – that is, sharing information about national policy directions; mutual reinforcement – that is, helping one another to pursue desirable policies in the face of domestic resistance; mutual adjustment – that is, seeking to accommodate or ameliorate policy divergencies; and mutual concession – that is, agreeing on a joint package of national policies designed to raise the collective welfare (Putnam and Bayne, 1987, p. 260).

They presented a letter grade from the highest 'A' to the lowest 'E' for summits from 1975 to 1986. In 1997 Bayne updated the Putnam scale, yielding higher marks for the 1989–94 summits than was the case for the 1981–88 summits but lower than for the first summits from 1975–80. In late 1998 Bayne updated and revised the score to cover the years 1975 through 1998. Still later, Bayne (2005b, pp. 12–13) again updated the grades for all summits from 1975 to 2004 and described in detail his method of assessing summit performance, the subjects assessed, and the grading system using six criteria (previously he had used only five, omitting 'solidarity'):

- leadership: 'how far the G8 summit was able to exercise the political authority'.
- effectiveness: 'the summits' ability to reconcile the tensions between different pressures on the member governments'.
- solidarity: were 'all the G8 countries committed to the decisions taken at the summit, so that they could be fully implemented'?
- durability: does 'the agreement reached at the summit produce a lasting solution to the problem'?
- acceptability: have 'the solutions reached at the summit commanded the support not only of the G8 members but also of the world community as a whole'?
- consistency: have 'G8 decisions in one policy area, such as finance, fitted in with the policies the G8 adopted on other subjects, like trade or development'?

Judith Cherry and Hugo Dobson (2012, pp. 366, 368–370) applied the Putnam/Bayne criteria to the G20, with some modifications, in assessing the results of the 2010 Seoul summit. They found that on the leadership criterion, the Korean Presidency achieved a mixed record of making progress on some 'legacy issues' and advancing some new issues, especially on development. On effectiveness, the Korean host government 'compromised on the promotion of its own agenda in order to facilitate a statement on which fellow summiteers could agree' (Cherry and Dobson 2012, p. 368). As for solidarity, all leaders were able to 'claim victory' on certain issues such as currency, but pressures remained on regional identity. On durability, the leaders made a good contribution in initiating the transition of the G20 from 'crisis committee' to 'steering committee'. On acceptability, Cherry and Dobson see increased outreach to non-G20 actors as positive. On consistency, tensions remained between a limited agenda and a more ambitious one. Finally, on domestic political enhancement (a criterion added to the Putnam/Bayne matrix on the basis of work by John Kirton; see ahead), Korea was able to advance its national interests while promoting collective leadership progress, and the expectation that subsequent summit leaders will seek a similar balance between the domestic and the collective benefit.

Kirton (2015b), Co-director of the G20 Research Group, has developed the following alphabetical scoring scheme to assess overall summit performance, which is somewhat reminiscent of the Bayne grading scheme:

A+	Striking, standout, historic
A	Very strong (London 2009, St Petersburg 2013)
A−	Strong (Washington 2008, Pittsburgh 2009, Toronto 2010, Los Cabos 2012)
B+	Significant
B	Substantial (Seoul 2010, Cannes 2011, Brisbane 2014, Antalya 2015)
B−	Solid
C	Small
D	Very small
F	Failure

As Kirton called the 2017 Hamburg summit one of 'significant success', it would receive a B+ grade (Kirton, 2017b), but a strong (A−) on counter-terrorism.

In 2012 the International Organisations Research Institute (IORI), Higher School of Economics, National Research University (Moscow), and the G20 Research Group released a *Report on Mapping G20 Decisions Implementation*. The report analyzes the implementation of commitments made by G20 members at their summits in the following areas: structural reforms and overcoming imbalances; reform of international financial institutions; financial markets regulation; and development. The analysis includes infrastructure, private investment, job creation, human resource development, trade, financial inclusion, growth with resilience, food security, domestic resource mobilization and knowledge sharing (International Organisations Research Institute and G20 Research Group, 2012). Nancy Alexander and Aldo Caliari (2013) produced a critical commentary on this report.

Kirton and Larionova (2018) include in their book *Accountability for Effectiveness in Global Governance* several contributions on aspects of G7-G20 accountability. They deal with climate change (Chapter 5), gender equality (Chapter 6), regional security (Chapter 7), comparison of the G7, G20 and BRICS (Chapter 9), other aspects of the Research Group's compliance reports (Chapters 10 and 11) and the ICC *G20 Business Scorecard* (Chapter 12).

The G7/G8 and G20 Research Groups' compliance reports are useful (especially when commitments on recurring agenda items are assessed, allowing examination of a time series), and they are often cited in the media and elsewhere, at times to bolster the record of certain member countries. Yet they, like other methods of assessment, have some limitations. While some commitments are measurable, observers have pointed out the problem of numerically quantifying commitments that are expressed in texts. Another limitation specific to one element of the report is that 'on fiscal consolidation, the text holds only the "advanced economies" of the G20 accountable . . . the average for this commitment was therefore calculated based on this group of 10 and not the G20 as a whole' (G20 Research Group, 2012a, p. 11).

Other CSOs have identified G20 summit commitments and assessed G20 performance. For example, in January 2010 the civil society coalition New Rules for Global Finance produced a draft document providing an overview of the G20's financial agenda; the G20's financial commitments to the IMF and multilateral development banks; its directives to international financial institutions; and the creation of the Financial Stability Board (FSB). It also tracked the G20's progress in stabilizing and rebuilding the international financial system (Hersh, 2010). On the first day of the 2012 Los Cabos summit, New Rules held a seminar on G20 transparency and participation. On transparency (as a component of accountability), the seminar addressed the question 'What is the G20's record on delivering on its promises?' (New Rules, 2012b). In 2013 New Rules released its *Global Financial Governance & Impact Report*, assessing and comparing the governance performance of the G20, FSB, IMF, Organization of Economic Co-operation and Development (OECD), the United Nations (UN) and the World Bank in terms of accountability/transparency and inclusivity, and how governance affects the impact of these institutions on development, and on global population and on the poorest (New Rules, 2013). Focusing on inequality, New Rules (2016) produced a joint report with the Friedrich-Ebert-Stiftung, *How Global Financial Institutions Impact Inequality: A Workshop to Strengthen Understanding, Assessment & Reporting*, which similarly assesses the roles of the IMF, World Bank, OECD, UN, G20 and FSB.

An example of a different approach is provided by the US civil society umbrella group InterAction, which has developed scorecards for G20 summits. These scorecards measure commitments in G20 communiqués and other documents against prior policy recommendations of the InterAction G7/G20 Advocacy Alliance. The latest scorecard covers the following issues dealt with by the 2017 Hamburg summit: anti-corruption; jobs and employment; the refugee crisis; responsible business conduct; infrastructure, energy and climate sustainability; and women's economic empowerment. This is one example of how these scorecards monitor and evaluate summits: on jobs and employment prior to the Hamburg summit, InterAction recommended that the G20 '[a]lign action with commitments to . . . operationalize the G20 Action Plan on the 2030 Agenda for Sustainable Development' (Inter Action, 2017, p. 6). The G20 leaders, in their *Hamburg Update: Taking Forward the G20 Action Plan*, stated, 'In taking forward the G20 Action Plan and building on our past commitments, the *Hamburg Update* reflects the priorities of the German presidency – resilience, sustainability, responsibility – and continues G20 efforts of leading by example to implement the 2030 Agenda'. As a specific commitment, the *Hamburg Update* commits thus: 'We will further establish a voluntary peer learning mechanism on the 2030 Agenda, to ensure continuous improvement of our approaches and to be able to share our experiences and lessons learned with other countries worldwide' (G20, 2017j).

ONE, an advocacy CSO particularly concerned with development and Africa, has issued annual DATA (Debt, AIDS, Trade, Africa) reports since the 2005 Gleneagles G8 summit, in order to monitor implementation of G8 promises of assistance to developing countries. Earlier reports evaluated

> whether a country was 'on track' or 'off track' to deliver its . . . total development assistance commitment . . . [but the 2010 edition stipulates] a robust assessment of donors' Gleneagles commitments . . . along three . . . indices: . . . commitment, which judges [the level of] ambition of the donor's original promise in terms of volume and relative to the size of its economy; . . . delivery, based not just on . . . [the] portion of the Gleneagles commitment . . . delivered but on what the actual assistance delivered was between 2004 and 2010, both in volume terms and in terms of growth as a share of GNI; [and] . . . each donors' action plans for its future partnership with Africa and whether targets are in place for the post-Gleneagles era.
>
> (ONE, 2010, p. 12)

The 2010 report notes that 'recently, the role of the G8 *vis-à-vis* other members of the G20 and even beyond has come into question' (ONE, 2010, p. 7). Accordingly, this edition of the report analyzes G8 and G20 performance in terms of: governance and accountability; equitable and sustainable economic growth; and 'smart aid' investments in programmes which have already delivered 'real and measurable results'. The report has a prescriptive aspect:

> G20 and other leaders must also consider how they can develop a positive, proactive agenda for poverty reduction and development that moves beyond aid to incorporate trade and investment policy, enhances accountability and ensures the voices of the poorest are heard.
>
> (ONE, 2010, p. 31)

Looking ahead, the report notes that 'the G20 can be an important forum for coordination among developing countries, emerging donors and traditional, developed country donors' (ONE, 2010, p. 211).

The 2012 edition recalls that these reports have

> held the world's wealthiest countries accountable for their commitments to the world's poorest countries. For the . . . [previous] six years, [they have] tracked progress against the Gleneagles commitments made by the G7 in 2005. however, with those commitments expiring in 2010, key donors such as the United States, Canada and Japan no longer have overall official development assistance (ODA) targets.
>
> (ONE, 2012, p. 5)

The annual DATA reports retain their focus on Africa and continue to highlight G7 and G20 initiatives and shortfalls. The 2017 report carries the subtitle *Financing for the African Century*. It tracks the ODA performance of G7 countries and also comments on the G20's role. It notes that '[t]he new G20 Partnership with Africa – particularly the Compact with Africa initiative, which is focused on increasing private sector investment – and the African Union's roadmap for harnessing the demographic dividend have a vital role to play'. It asserts, however, that the Compact (as well as the European External Investment Plan) 'require[s] better coordination, scaling up and implementation'. Further, ONE calls on the G20 'to double official development finance (ODF) to Africa by 2020, from approximately $60 billion in 2015 to $120 billion' (ONE, 2017, pp. 8, 14, 26).

The DATA reports are based mostly on statistics derived from the OECD DAC online databases (see stats.oecd.org). These data are considered highly reliable, but they tend to be up to a year late, so the DATA reports necessarily reflect a time lag. The DATA reports detail the rationale for using these databases but also acknowledge problems and challenges of using the statistics.

Katharine Keil of the Heinrich Böll Stiftung North America (2017) focuses on an important initiative of the Hamburg summit, the Compact with Africa. She asks whether the Compact will address African development challenges, rapid population growth and outward migration. She criticizes the way the Compact (particularly its use of public-private partnerships) approaches infrastructure development for working against social and environmental protections and risking sustainability in African countries.

Kirton (2012) has applied his matrix of six 'Ds' for assessing G20 patterns of performance: domestic political management ('the way the leaders use their summit presence and performance for managing their politics and policy back home'), deliberation ('measured . . . by the length of time the leaders spend together . . . [and] by the number of documents the leaders collectively issue'), direction-setting ('the affirmation or invention of principles and norms'), decision-making ('producing collective commitments with precision and obligation designed to bind the members'), delivery ('of the decisions, or the compliance of the members with the summit commitments their leaders make') and development of global governance ('developing global governance in its institutional or architectural form, both within and outside the G20 system') (Kirton, 2012, pp. 1–2). It would be helpful if a future scholar or group were to continue to build on the Cherry/Dobson and Kirton schemes when assessing G20 achievements at future summits.

The role of the business sector

Business groupings, as major stakeholders, have taken an interest in G20 accountability. The Business 20 (or Business Summit; see Chapter 5 for details) has not only given advice to the G20; it also took on a role in monitoring the fulfilment of G20 commitments. To this end, the B20 launched a 'performance dashboard, with input from the World Economic Forum (WEF), the International Chamber of Commerce (ICC), the McKinsey Global Institute and others' (Enter the B20,

2012, p. 72). This later became the annual *SDG Index and Dashboards Report*, which publishes a detailed report card for country performance on the Agenda 2030 and the Sustainable Development Goals (SDGs). It was launched in 2017 and is produced by the Sustainable Development Solutions Network (SDSN) and the Bertelsmann Stiftung. The report rates the performance of countries, including the G20 members, on their promises on SDGs and the 2030 Agenda. The 2017 report uses the following 17 indicators: poverty headcount ratio at $1.90/day; projected poverty headcount ratio at $1.90/day in 2030; births attended by skilled health personnel; universal health coverage tracer; HIV infections; death rate from non-communicable diseases; death rate from household and ambient pollution; access to bank account or mobile-money service (% of adult population); logistics performance index; top three university rankings; number of scientific and technical journal articles per capita; rent burden (% of disposable income); e-waste (kg/capita); production-based SO2 emissions (kg/capita); nitrogen production footprint; effective carbon rate; marine sites, mean protected area (%); terrestrial sites, mean protected area (%); freshwater sites, mean protected area; slavery score; and health and education spending (SDSN and Bertelsmann, 2017, p. 7).

The business interest group International Chamber of Commerce issues an annual *G20 Business Scorecard*, assessing the performance of G20 countries in various sectors: the 2014 *Scorecard* focused on trade and investment; financing for growth and development; energy and environment; and anti-corruption. In 2015 the focus was on trade; infrastructure and investment; financing growth; human capital; anti-corruption; energy and environment; and global tax reform. The sixth edition of the *Scorecard* covers Hangzhou summit commitments in the following areas: trade and investment; financing growth; infrastructure; employment; anti-corruption; SME (small and medium enterprises) development; and energy and environment. The report concludes that

> the G20 is deepening attention to an ever-widening scope of global policy challenges . . . the Summit Communiqué and associated reports and guidelines give . . . evidence to the steady progress G20 Leaders are achieving between Summits, increasingly fulfilling the moniker of 'global steering committee'.
>
> (ICC, 2016a, p. 3)

The *Scorecard* 'compares global business recommendations with G20 commitments. [It . . . aims] to generate scores from the recommendations and categorical responses, which can be used to track performance and monitor progress' (Te Velde, 2012, p. 8). The ICC uses a three-step scale: poor, fair and good. Because the sectors examined vary from year to year, the result is somewhat inconsistent. Still, this is an interesting business-oriented view of G20 performance.

> The overall score of 2.3 (out of 3) across the seven major policy groups evaluated in . . . [the 6th] edition of the Scorecard marks the highest overall score since ICC began its monitoring. Despite the positive overall trend, progress is uneven

> across the seven major groupings, which includes three GOOD, three FAIR and one POOR score. The mixed scores highlight several notable advancements on business priorities, but also that room for improvement still exists.
>
> (ICC, 2016a, p. 6)

The role of the G20 and international organizations

The G7/G8 came to recognize its accountability obligations in a concrete way rather late, with accountability reports starting with the Muskoka G8 summit. This happened much faster in the G20's case. One way the latter forum has moved towards greater accountability is through commissioning a series of IMF reports for the G20 Mutual Assessment Process (MAP), with the World Bank and other IGOs also playing a role (IMF, 2010a; World Bank, 2010). MAP was launched by the 2009 Pittsburgh G20 summit as a crucial component of the *Framework for Strong, Sustainable and Balanced Growth* (G20, 2009c). Although MAP has an important accountability dimension, it is an essential component of broader G20-IMF cooperation; therefore it is discussed more fully in Chapter 4.

In their *Toronto Summit Declaration* (2010a, pp. 2, 20) the G20 leaders stated, 'We are determined to be accountable for the commitments we have made, and have instructed our Ministers and officials to take all necessary steps to implement them fully within agreed timelines'. They fleshed this out in a more specific commitment:

> We pledged to support robust and transparent independent international assessment and peer review of our financial systems through the IMF and World Bank's Financial Sector assessment Program and the FSB peer review process. . . . International assessment and peer review are fundamental in making the financial sector safer for all.

The Seoul summit took a further accountability step, stating in the *Leaders' Declaration*, 'We will continue to monitor and assess ongoing implementation of the commitments made today and in the past in a transparent and objective way. We hold ourselves accountable. What we promise, we will deliver' (G20, 2010b, p. 3). The more detailed and specific *G20 Seoul Summit Document* reaffirmed the leaders' undertakings. On corruption:

> the G20 will hold itself accountable for its commitments. Beyond our participation in existing mechanisms of peer review for international anti-corruption standards, we mandate the Anti-Corruption Working Group to submit annual reports on the implementation of our commitments to future Summits for the duration of the anti-Corruption Action Plan.
>
> (G20, 2010d, p. 17)

On development, Annex 1 of the *Summit Document* stated, 'Implementation of G20 action on development should be monitored through an adequate accountability framework' (G20, 2010e, p. 2). The *Supporting Document* consists entirely of a table of policy commitments by G20 members, to facilitate subsequent monitoring and evaluation (G20, 2010g).

The IMF (in collaboration with the OECD, World Bank, ILO and UNCTAD) prepared several MAP-related analyses and assessments as input for the G20 Action Plan launched at the Cannes summit: one of these is an Accountability Report on G20 members' progress in implementing policy commitments since the Seoul summit (IMF, 2011a). (Not all of these reports have been released to the public, leaving a gap in transparency and democratic accountability.) The *Cannes Action Plan for Growth and Jobs* 'draws on the IMF Staff's independent assessments of the root causes of . . . imbalances and recommended policies to address them' (G20, 2011a).

The Los Cabos summit took a further step. Through *The Los Cabos Growth and Jobs Action Plan* (G20, 2012m), which includes an *Accountability Assessment Framework*, the leaders agreed to use third-party evaluations, especially by the IMF, in moving forward with the *Los Cabos Accountability Framework*. The peer review is to include reports by the IMF, OECD, FSB, the World Bank, ILO, UNCTAD and WTO. The *Framework* 'will be used to prepare reports on progress in meeting past commitments, which will inform the development of future action plans and domestic policies' (p. 7). The *Framework also* mandates 'short progress reports prepared for Ministerial meetings and regular Annual Accountability assessments for Ministers, Governors and Leaders' – an example of internal accountability. The *Framework* thus establishes a regular, systematic process of assessments to 'provide critical input to inform the range of concrete policy commitments that should be included in the G-20 Action Plans' (G20, 2012m, pp. 7, 8). The 2013 St Petersburg summit produced the rather full and important *Saint Petersburg Accountability Report on G20 Development Commitments* and the *St. Petersburg Accountability Assessment*, issued as an annex to the *St. Petersburg Action Plan* (G20, 2013k, 2013d).

The MAP report prepared for the Los Cabos summit, *Toward Lasting Stability and Growth: Umbrella Report for G-20 Mutual Assessment Process*, includes an annex providing 'enhanced accountability assessments' (IMF, 2012d, p. 2). (See also www.imf.org/external/np/g20/map2012.htm, which lists annexes and other information.) The enhanced assessment portion is of special interest in the context of evaluation of G20 performance; it concludes that although members have made progress in implementing their policy commitments in the *Cannes Action Plan* in financial policy, fiscal policy, monetary and exchange rate policies, and structural reform, they need to take further action on financial sector reform, sound public finances, rebalancing global demand, and employment and growth. This shows some improvement in transparency, although, as the reports are based on national statistics, which are not equally reliable for all G20 countries, the report is less useful than it could be. Another marked innovation is the Los Cabos release of *Policy Commitments by G20 Members* (G20, 2012r). In September 2013, the IMF issued for the G20 *Imbalances and Growth: Update of Staff Sustainability Assessments for G-20 Mutual Assessment Process* (IMF, 2013a). It was prepared in accordance with the Los Cabos 2012 decision to produce biennial assessments to identify large and persistent imbalances against indicative guidelines.

The 2014 Brisbane summit issued *The Brisbane Accountability Assessment* with the objective of assessing progress towards sustainable and balanced growth, and progress on previous commitments concerning fiscal, monetary, exchange rate and structural reform. The report, which includes country-by-country assessments, concludes that 'G-20 members have made progress towards their commitments across all policy areas . . . [but that] the G-20 has still not achieved its goal of strong, sustainable, and balanced global growth'. The report further promises that

> [o]ver the next year the G-20 will monitor progress towards the Commitments members put forward in Growth Strategies, adapt the Accountability Assessment process to gauge implementation of these measures and the two per cent ambition, and present another Accountability Assessment at the 2015 Summit in Turkey.
>
> (G20, 2014b, p. 10)

In Turkey, there were two sub-summit accountability reports (described ahead).

The *Hangzhou Comprehensive Accountability Report on G20 Development Commitments* discusses the G20 development agenda and the role of the Development Working Group and the role of the G20 Presidency; analyzes the implementation of G20 development commitments; discusses outreach to non-G20 stakeholders and linkages to other G20 work streams; and makes conclusions on lessons learned, with recommendations (G20, 2016p). The *G20 Hamburg Action Plan* refers to the 2017 accountability assessment and confirms that '[w]e have in place a comprehensive framework for monitoring implementation, which includes a member-led . . . assessment by the . . . IMF, the OECD and the World Bank Group'. It further observes that

> G20 members have continued to make progress on the implementation of their Brisbane, Antalya and Hangzhou commitments. These efforts have so far led us to achieve more than half of our collective growth ambition [but notes that s]lower-than-expected implementation means it is likely that our collective growth ambition will be achieved later than originally anticipated. Importantly, however, the longer-term impact on G20 collective GDP of measures members will have implemented as part of the growth strategy exercise will exceed 2 per cent.
>
> (G20, 2017f, p. 2)

The 2017 accountability assessment is further discussed ahead, under the Framework Working Group.

The MAP, led by the IMF, has continued its multi-year work. In 2018, the IMF issued a fact sheet providing a guide to navigate the global recovery and describing building blocks of the *Framework of Strong, Sustainable, and Balanced*

Growth (IMF, 2018). More details on the IMF's role vis-à-vis the G20 may be found at www.imf.org/external/np/g20/index.htm.

Commitments to accountability have also been made by several sub-summit G20 entities – the counterpart of the G20 leaders' accountability to sub-summit bodies. For example, the Finance Ministers and Central Bank Governors, at their 4–5 November 2012 meeting, stated,

> We have . . . made progress in strengthening our Accountability Assessment framework by agreeing on a set of measures to inform our analysis of our fiscal, monetary and exchange rate policies. We will consider a range of indicators and approaches to assess spillover effects, progress towards commitments on structural reforms, and our collective achievement of strong, sustainable and balanced growth.
>
> (G20 Finance Ministers, 2012)

At the working group/expert group level, the G20 Development Working Group (DWG), in its report to the leaders at the Cannes summit, promised, 'We will monitor progress on the reduction of the global average cost [of remittances] through the World Bank, including on actions undertaken in reaching the quantitative target' (G20 DWG, 2011, p. 12). The working group has also expressed its willingness to contribute further to the area on regional and global trade in cooperation with IGOs:

> We would welcome an invitation from the African Union and the African Development Bank to jointly review progress at their annual meeting. This could include assessing the support we are providing at different levels, including to the national level and to the Regional economic Communities and how best to strengthen that support.
>
> (G20 DWG, 2011, p. 4)

In their 2012 report to G20 leaders at Los Cabos, the DWG undertook to 'report back on progress by the end of 2012' on inclusive green growth (G20 DWG, 2012, p. 3). The Los Cabos *Leaders Declaration* (G20, 2012j, p. 11) 'invite[d] the Development Working Group to explore putting in place a process for ensuring assessment and accountability for G20 development actions by the next Summit'. The DWG duly prepared its accountability assessment on development commitments to the St Petersburg summit; this assessment forms part of the *Saint Petersburg Accountability Report on G20 Development Commitments*. In it, the DWG examined

> 67 commitments originating from the Seoul MYAP and 2011–2012 Leaders' Declarations relevant to the DWG's work. The DWG assessed progress in the nine pillars of the MYAP and in inclusive green growth. This process examined implementation, identified lessons learned, drew conclusions and determined next steps for the G20 development agenda.
>
> (G20, 2013k, pp. 6–7)

The *Hamburg Annual Progress Report on G20 Development Commitments* recalls that

> [i]n 2014 an Accountability Framework was adopted to structure a transparent accountability process. According to this framework, every three years a Comprehensive Accountability Report (CAR) of the DWG shall be prepared, the last of which [the *Hangzhou Accountability Assessment*] was completed in 2016. In the years in between, the DWG publishes an Annual Progress Report.
> (G20, 2017i, p. 6)

The G20 Framework for Strong, Sustainable and Balanced Growth Working Group (Framework Working Group) has also made accountability one of its priorities for 2013. It promised to '[f]urther enhance the Accountability Assessment Process' by:

- '[e]xamin[ing] how to assess progress against structural reform commitments and the implications of policy spillovers';
- turning to 'outside experts/academics to assess overall progress towards SSB [Strong, Sustainable, and Balanced] growth . . . [thereby obtaining] an additional perspective on the issue, supplementing the work of the IMF, World Bank, OECD and other IFIs [international financial institutions], without jeopardizing the country-led nature of the exercise';
- '[p]repar[ing] a report on overall progress towards SSB growth, drawing on experts' report (if provided) and inputs from IFIs';
- The working group also undertook to '[a]ssess members' progress against past policy commitments . . . based on a peer-review process'.

(G20 Framework, 2012, p. 1)

As follow-up, the working group released its 2014 *Brisbane Accountability Assessment*, 2015 *Antalya Accountability Assessment* and 2016 *Hangzhou Accountability Assessment*. In its 2017 *Hamburg Accountability Assessment*, which is referenced in the *G20 Hamburg Action Plan*, the working group 'takes stock of the G20's progress towards strong, sustainable, balanced and inclusive growth since the 2016 Leaders' Summit in Hangzhou' (G20 FWG, 2017, p. 1). The report gives a general assessment of G20 economic performance in four areas of sustainable, balanced and inclusive growth. The report then assesses G20 members' delivery on past commitments to promote sustainable, balanced and inclusive growth. It concludes that

> [s]ince the Brisbane Summit, substantial progress has been made with the implementation of members' growth strategy commitments [and that a] lthough implementation to date falls short of what had originally been anticipated, the growth strategy measures are expected to deliver a significant longer-term positive impact to the G20's collective GDP exceeding 2 per cent . . . [and] G20 members continue to make progress on a number of

> collective fiscal, monetary and exchange rate commitments, and further efforts will continue to be important, including in the implementation of the G20 growth strategies.
>
> (G20 FWG, 2017, p. 14)

The working group acknowledges the contributions of the IMF, OECD, the World Bank Group and other international organizations. A recent example of the work of the IMF and the OECD in this area is the report *Quantifying the Implementation and Impact of G-20 Members' Growth Strategies*.

Post-summit reactions and other shorter assessments

CSOs, the media and scholarly observers often express their immediate reaction at the end of each summit. Although this is not systematic evaluation, it is of interest because it conveys the liveliness of 'hot pursuit' and offers comparisons, particularly in the case of civil society. Some examples follow, illustrating the generally critical views of civil society groups, with some acknowledgements of positive outcomes.

The G20 scorecards of the InterAction coalition (discussed earlier) serve as an example of this approach. The scorecards compare commitments contained in the documents of the G20 summit that has just met with 'asks' announced before that summit. Similarly, in earlier years, the ONE organization also compared its pre-summit 'asks' with summit outcomes. For example, after the Cannes G20 summit, ONE prepared a detailed policy analysis of the summit's final documents (Röder, 2011; email to author, 10 November). This assessed results in the following policy areas: agriculture and food security; infrastructure; inclusive growth; transparency and accountability, and innovative finance. After the Los Cabos summit, ONE's reaction included faint praise and criticism: 'Good Intentions Continue at G20, But Promises on Development Are Not Being Kept'; 'G20 Is Getting a Reputation for Over-Promising and Under-Delivering' (Powell, 2012b, 2012a).

Oxfam International has been among the major NGOs observing and commenting on G20 summits for years. After the Hamburg summit it annotated the *G20 Leaders' Declaration* in light of Oxfam's priorities: inequality, climate change, the 'Four Famines' crises and other issues (the four famines in 2017 were those in South Sudan, Northern Nigeria, Yemen and Somalia). This analysis by annotation is an interesting direct comparison of statements in the G20 text with Oxfam's criticism and advocacy. For example, the *Declaration* states, 'We are resolved to tackle common challenges to the global community, including terrorism, displacement, poverty, hunger and health threats, job creation, climate change, energy security, and inequality including gender inequality, as a basis for sustainable development and stability' (G20, 2017g, p. 2). Oxfam's comment is

> The Hamburg communiqu[é] mentions it briefly as one in a list of challenges to the global community. But yet the G20 fail to detail any substantive steps they will take to tackle this challenge. To tackle inequality the current

> economic system needs to change fundamentally, but the G20 are clearly happy with business as usual.
>
> (Oxfam, 2017, p. 2 comments)

On climate change, Oxfam is more positive in assessing the 19 G20 members' explicit commitment to action in the face of US withdrawal from the Paris Agreement. The *Declaration* states, 'We take note of the decision of the United States of America to withdraw from the Paris Agreement . . . The Leaders of the other G20 members state that the Paris Agreement is irreversible' (G20, 2017g, p. 10).

Oxfam's comment:

> The G20 has proven that President Trump is increasingly isolated in his crusade to prop up the fossil fuel industry and abandon the Paris Agreement . . . World leaders from the 19 countries of the G20 have today demonstrated their commitment to the Paris agreement that is integral to modernising the global economy, securing prosperity and stability. The commitment to implement the Paris Agreement is critical news for the world's poorest and vulnerable countries and communities as they build climate resilience and advance towards clean, sustainable economies.
>
> (Oxfam, 2017, p. 10 comments)

On the eve of the Hamburg summit, the L20 (Labour 20) trade union group issued a statement calling for 'policies to ensure coordinated action to create quality jobs for the future, reduce inequality to achieve the Sustainable Development Goals and meet the commitments in the Paris Agreement' (L20, 2017). The L20 had a positive assessment of the Hamburg *G20 Leaders' Declaration* in which it addressed the abuses of human rights and labour standards in global supply chains. On the issue of quality jobs for the future, the L20 found that 'the G20 commitment to employment [was] weak' and further noted that 'G20 leaders have not taken on board the policy implications from the stunning lack of wage dynamics that is holding back growth across different parts of the world'. L20 also called for 'further discussion at the G20 to help advance a new progressive policy agenda on trade and investment agreements'. Finally, it asserted that 'The promise by all the world's leaders of a zero-poverty zero-carbon world, underscored by global agreements on the sustainable development goals and climate, should be led by the G20 with the major share of global population and wealth' (L20, 2017).

Some NGO activists and observers of the G20 scene remarked earlier on the G20's seeming inability to balance the need for austerity, in particular in some Western countries, with the need for strategic investment in job creation. Another criticism was that the G20 High Level Panel on Infrastructure made recommendations that showed little regard for the climate or the natural environment despite the heavy focus on energy and transport. This approach to growth was seen as short-sighted and damaging to the future of the planet (Alexander, 2012; email to author, 29 November).

Academic and other observers have also offered brief assessments of G20 performance, either immediately following a summit or at other times. For example, Edwin Truman asserted that '[t]he G20 has failed on follow-through on the Seoul agreement on IMF reform' (Truman, 2012; interview with author, 5 June; Truman, 2012). Hampson and Heinbecker (2011, p. 304) remarked that G20 members 'were effective in cooperating to stabilize financial markets, coordinate regulatory reform, and launch a global economic stimulus' but were less successful in resolving problems of current accounts, trade and budget imbalances.

After the Los Cabos summit, Colin Bradford (2012b) commented on the significance of the broad engagement of various actors (officials, think-tanks, the business sector and others), and concluded that 'G20 summitry is a human undertaking full of aspiration and hope, grounded in reality and constraints. It is real; it is not a pretense. It is a huge effort to do what can feasibly be done to create a better world – one that is better than it would be without the G20 summit'. In a brief analysis of the St Petersburg summit, Kirton (2013d) had high praise for its results overall. James A. Haley (2012a) of the Centre for International Governance Innovation (CIGI) emphasized the importance of the leaders' endorsement of the revised mandate of the FSB as an 'incremental step on the road to building the governance structures for global capital'.

In a more recent example, Kirton (2017b) assessed the Hamburg summit as one of significant success. He praised host leader Angela Merkel's decision to 'start the summit with a leaders-only retreat . . . encourag[ing] leaders to engage in a free, flowing, frank, interactive way, rather than reading prepared scrip[t]s'. On the contentious climate issue, Kirton noted that

> private deliberations [at the summit] were often animated by an intense debate [between] Trump . . . and newly elected French president Emmanuel Macron, who, in traditional French fashion at such summits, led the expression of a hard-line, antithetical approach to the U.S. president, but now one centered on international economic openness and cooperation and strong collective climate change control with the Paris Agreement at its core.

Also commenting on the Hamburg summit, James Haley (2017) of CIGI delivered a more severe verdict:

> Despite the much-improved economic conjuncture . . . the German chancellor's challenge as chair of the G20 was perhaps more daunting than that faced by leaders nine years ago . . . because the challenge today is not the risk of dysfunctional financial markets; rather, it is the risk of dysfunctional international cooperation. And, remarkably, almost inconceivably, the biggest source of this risk is the president of the United States.

Haley noted the 'key topics that proved contentious in the final G20 communiqué: climate change and international trade' and added that 'Trump's withdrawal from the Paris climate accord can, in some respects, be likened to the US Senate's refusal following World War I to ratify the United States' entry into the League of Nations'. On trade, Haley added, 'If the United States is no longer engaged as a responsible partner, it would be more difficult to keep the rules-based trading system that has been built and which has served the global economy so well over the past 70 years or so. That is the real danger'.

Media outlets tend to report extensively prior to and during the summits, focusing on major challenges for the G20, its often spotty record of achievement, leaked draft documents, street demonstrations and the bilateral meetings taking place on the margins of the summits. They report less fully after the summits, when attention quickly shifts to other events. These pieces do not constitute systematic assessment but can still add interesting insights. For example, Larry Elliott (2012b, pp. 1–2) of the *Guardian* delivered a harsh assessment of the G20:

> There were high hopes for the G20 when it met for the first time in Washington in November 2008. Then, the conclave of the big nations proved they were up to the challenge of responding collectively and decisively, if not with lasting success, to the contraction in the global economy . . . Anybody expecting the G20 to pull another rabbit out of the hat now simply hasn't been paying attention. Leaderless and at odds over what needs to be done, it has taken the G20 less than four years to become as redundant as the G8 it was supposed to replace.

Some examples of immediate press reactions after the Hamburg summit follow: Erlanger and his co-authors (2017, p. A1) write in the *New York Times* that '[w]orld leaders struck a compromise on Saturday to move forward collectively on climate change without the United States, declaring the Paris accord "irreversible" while acknowledging President Trump's decision to withdraw from the agreement'. They note that 'the other 19 members of the group broke explicitly with Mr. Trump in their embrace of the international deal, signing off on a detailed policy blueprint outlining how their countries could meet their goals in the pact'. They further observe that '[d]ifferences between the United States and other nations on climate, trade and migration made for a tricky summit meeting, which unfolded amid large protests that sometimes turned violent'.

Lawrence Summers (2017, p. 11), former US Treasury Secretary and one of the two founding fathers (with Canada's Paul Martin) of the G20, comments that 'the content of the [Hamburg] communiqué . . . [is] a confirmation of the breakdown of international order that many have feared since the election of Donald Trump'. He recalls that

> [t]he existence of the G20 as an annual forum arose from a common belief of major nations that there was a global community with common interests in peace, mutual security, prosperity and economic integration and the containment of threats even as there was competition between nations in the security and economic realms.

Specifically, he asserts that '[t]he US is now isolated on the question of how to deal with the long run security threat of climate change. It has forced the G20 to back away from previous commitments to rejecting protectionism'.

Conclusion

Monitoring and evaluation constitute a key component of accountability for any institution, including the G20. Since the formation of the leaders' G20 at the summit level in 2008, several groups have engaged in assessing the G20's performance and monitoring the fulfilment of its undertakings. Civil society organizations (including think-tanks) have played an important role, often building on their previous experience assessing the record of the G7/G8. Prominent among these is the G20 Research Group, with its regular series of compliance reports; the Heinrich Böll Foundation; New Rules for Global Finance, which has tracked the G20's progress in stabilizing and rebuilding the international financial system; Interaction, which has identified key G20 commitments and called for greater G20 transparency and consistent and specific indicators of progress; and the advocacy group ONE, which has assessed G8 and G20 performance on governance and accountability; sustainable economic growth; and measurable results.

The business sector has also taken an active interest in monitoring and evaluation. Two examples are the B20 (Business 20), which has launched a 'performance dashboard', and the International Chamber of Commerce, which has devised a *G20 Business Scorecard* to assess the performance of G20 countries on trade and investment, green growth, transparency and anti-corruption, and financing for growth and development.

The G20 itself has increasingly recognized the crucial role of accountability in gauging progress and building legitimacy. It initiated the Mutual Assessment Process (MAP), through commissioning a series of IMF reports, with the World Bank and other IGOs also playing a role. (MAP reports address accountability, but they also assess a number of other aspects of the G20-IMF relationship.) Although based on self-reporting and peer review, with possible built-in biases (e.g., various degrees of reliability of national statistics), this is a major step forward.

Te Velde (2012, p. 3) suggested the following four options for the G20 to improve its accountability in the development area:

> (1) a 'careful independent assessment of the MYAP, producing . . . scorecards . . . on . . . compliance and effectiveness'; (2) 'a broader assessment of . . . the G20 in the role of development: identifying governance gaps, providing policy direction, putting a spotlight on issues, knowledge sharing, trust building and developing standards'; (3) making 'explicit . . . [the G20's] role on improving PCD [policy coherence in development], . . . undertak[ing] impact assessments . . . on . . . small, poor and vulnerable economies'; and (4) 'coordinat[ing] the growth plans of G20 and non-G20 countries and assess[ing] how G20 actions support these [italics removed]'.

The diverse methods used by civil society groups, the business sector, international organizations and the G20 itself to assess G20 performance all have strengths and weaknesses, but monitoring and evaluation, when well-designed and performed systematically, carefully and consistently, contribute to enhancing the accountability of the G20. Good incremental progress has been made but more remains to be done.

References

Alexander, N. and Caliari, A., 2013. *Commentary on the Report: 'Mapping G20 Decisions Implementation'*. Washington, DC: Heinrich Böll Stiftung. January. us.boell.org/2013/02/01/commentary-report-mapping-g20-decisions-implementation-group-20 [Accessed: 27 March 2018].

Bayne, N., 1997. Changing patterns at the G7 summit. *G7 Governance*, 1 May. www.g8.utoronto.ca/governance/gov1/ [Accessed: 1 May 2018].

Bayne, N., 2005b. *Staying Together: The G8 Summit Confronts the 21st Century*. Aldershot, UK: Ashgate.

Bradford, C.I., 2012b. *View from the Ground at the Los Cabos Summit*. 22 June. www.cigionline.org/publications/view-ground-los-cabos-summit [Accessed: 27 March 2018].

Cherry, J. and Dobson, H., 2012. 'Seoul-searching': The 2010 G-20 Seoul summit. *Global Governance: A Review of Multilateralism and International Organizations*, 18(3), pp. 363–381.

Elliott, L., 2012b. The world watches Europe. *The Guardian Weekly*, 22–28 June, pp. 1–2.

Enter the B20; Business and Geopolitics, 2012. *The Economist*, 403(8788), p. 72.

Erlanger, S., Smale, A., Friedman, L. and Hirschfeld Davis, J., 2017. Leaders pledge climate action, without Trump. *The New York Times*, 9 July, p. A1.

G7 Research Group, 2017. *2016 G7 Ise-Shima Summit Final Compliance Report, 29 May 2016 to 20 May 2017*. 25 May. www.g8.utoronto.ca/evaluations/2016compliance-final/2016-g7-compliance-final.pdf [Accessed: 11 May 2018].

G20, 2009c. *Leaders Statement: The Pittsburgh Summit*; and Annexes: *Core Values for Sustainable Economic Activity; G20 Framework for Strong, Sustainable, and Balanced Growth*. 25 September. www.g20.utoronto.ca/2009/2009communiqué0925.html [Accessed: 24 October 2017].

G20, 2010a. *The G-20 Toronto Summit Declaration*. 27 June. www.g20.utoronto.ca/2010/to-communiqué.html [Accessed: 24 October 2017].

G20, 2010b. *The G20 Seoul Summit Leaders' Declaration*. 12 November. www.g20.utoronto.ca/2010/g20seoul.pdf [Accessed: 28 November 2017].

G20, 2010d. *Seoul Summit Document*. www.g20.utoronto.ca/2010/g20seoul-doc.pdf [Accessed: 24 October 2017].

G20, 2010e. *The Seoul Summit Document–ANNEX I: Seoul Development Consensus for Shared Growth*. www.g20.utoronto.ca/2010/g20seoul-consensus.pdf [Accessed: 8 June 2018].

G20, 2010g. *Supporting Document*. 12 November. www.canadainternational.gc.ca/g20/assets/pdfs/2010%20-%20Seoul%20Summit%20Supporting_Document.pdf [Accessed: 24 November 2012].

G20, 2011a. *The Cannes Action Plan for Growth and Jobs*. 4 November. www.g20.utoronto.ca/2011/2011-cannes-action-111104-en.html [Accessed: 24 October 2017].

G20, 2012j. *G20 Leaders Declaration*. 19 June. www.g20.utoronto.ca/2012/2012-0619-loscabos.pdf [Accessed: 26 September 2017].

G20, 2012m. *The Los Cabos Growth and Jobs Action Plan*. 19 June. www.g20.utoronto.ca/2012/2012-0619-loscabos-actionplan pdf [Accessed: 24 October 2017].

G20, 2012r. *Policy Commitments by G20 Members*. 19 June. www.g20.utoronto.ca/2012/2012-0619-loscabos-commitments.pdf [Accessed: 24 October 2017].

G20, 2013d. *Annex 4: St. Petersburg Accountability Assessment*. 5 September. en.g20russia.ru/load/783047169 and www.g20.utoronto.ca/2013/Accountabilty_Assessment_FINAL.pdf [Accessed: 28 November 2017].

G20, 2013k. *Saint Petersburg Accountability Report on G20 Development Commitments*. www.g20.utoronto.ca/2013/Saint_Petersburg_Accountability_Report_on_G20_Development_Commitments.pdf [Accessed: 29 September 2017].

G20, 2014b. *The Brisbane Accountability Assessment*. 14 November. www.g20.utoronto.ca/2014/2014_accountability_assessment_report.pdf [Accessed: 16 February 2017].

G20, 2016p. *Hangzhou Comprehensive Accountability Report on G20 Development Commitments*. 14 September. www.g20.utoronto.ca/2016/hangzhou-accountability-development.pdf [Accessed: 16 February 2017].

G20, 2017f. *G20 Hamburg Action Plan*. 8 July. www.g20.utoronto.ca/2017/2017-g20-hamburg-action-plan-en.pdf [Accessed: 17 October 2017].

G20, 2017i. *Hamburg Annual Progress Report on G20 Development Commitments*. www.g20.utoronto.ca/2017/2017-g20-hamburg-annual-progress-report-en.pdf [Accessed: 23 May 2018].

G20, 2017j. *Hamburg Update: Taking Forward the G20 Action Plan on the 2030 Agenda for Sustainable Development*. 8 July. www.g20.utoronto.ca/2017/2017-g20-hamburg-update.html [Accessed: 19 June 2018].

G20 Development Working Group, 2011. *2011 Report of the Development Working Group*. www.g20.utoronto.ca/2011/2011-cannes-dwg-111028-en.pdf [Accessed: 2 July 2018].

G20 Development Working Group, 2012. *2012 Progress Report of the Development Working Group*. www.g20.utoronto.ca/2012/2012-0619-dwg.pdf [Accessed: 13 November 2017].

G20 Finance Ministers and Central Bank Governors, 2012. *Communiqué of Ministers of Finance and Central Bank Governors of the G20: Mexico City*. 5 November. www.g20.utoronto.ca/2012/2012-121105-finance-en.html [Accessed: 2 July 2018].

G20 Framework for Strong, Sustainable, and Balanced Growth Working Group, 2012. *Proposal: Framework Working Group's 2013 Work Plan*. 1 November. en.g20.ria.ru/load/780982134 [Accessed: 2 July 2018].

G20 Framework Working Group, 2017. *Hamburg Accountability Assessment*. July. www.bundesfinanzministerium.de/Content/DE/Downloads/G20-Dokumente/Hamburg_Genannte_Berichte/Hamburg-Accountability-Assessment.pdf;jsessionid=12EB87C5BE442AD772C029650E938AE8?__blob=publicationFile&v=2 [Accessed: 22 May 2018].

G20 Information Centre, 2015. *2014 Brisbane G20 Summit Final Compliance Report*. 14 November. www.g20.utoronto.ca/compliance/2014brisbane-final/index.html [Accessed: 22 February 2017].

G20 Research Group, 2012a. *2011 Cannes G20 Summit Final Compliance Report: 4 November 2011 to 1 June 2012*. 16 June. www.g20.utoronto.ca/compliance/2011cannes-final/2011-g20-compliance-final.pdf [Accessed: 13 April 2018].

G20 Research Group, 2017. *2016 Hangzhou G20 Summit Final Compliance Report, 6 September 2016 to 6 July 2017*. 23 October. www.g20.utoronto.ca/compliance/2016hangzhou-final/2016-g20-final-compliance.pdf [Accessed: 11 May 2018].

Hajnal, P.I., 2011a. Civil society and G8 accountability. In: J.A. Scholte, ed. *Building Global Democracy? Civil Society and Accountable Global Governance*. Cambridge: Cambridge University Press. pp. 182–205.

Haley, J.A., 2012a. *Los Cabos Summit: Incremental Steps on the Road to Globalizing the Regulation of Capital*. 20 June. www.cigionline.org/articles/los-cabos-summit-incremental-steps-road-globalizing-regulation-capital [Accessed: 14 April 2018].

Haley, J.A., 2017. *Strains on Display in Hamburg Reflect Diverging Paths*. 8 July. www.cigionline.org/articles/strains-display-hamburg-reflect-diverging-paths [Accessed: 1 June 2018].

Hampson, F.O. and Heinbecker, P., 2011. The 'new' multilateralism of the twenty-first century. *Global Governance: A Review of Multilateralism and International Organizations*, 17(3), pp. 299–310.

Hersh, A.S., 2010. *Draft: Monitoring Commitments and Compliance of the G20 Framework for Strong, Sustainable, and Balanced Growth*. 13 January. www.new-rules.org/storage/documents/g20-fsb-imf/g20_matrix.pdf [Accessed: 14 April 2018].

InterAction, 2017. *2017 G20 Hamburg, Germany Summit Scorecard*. www.interaction.org/sites/default/files/2017%20G20%20Summit%20scorecard.pdf [Accessed: 15 May 2018].

International Chamber of Commerce, 2016a. *ICC G20 Business Scorecard*, 6th ed. December. cdn.iccwbo.org/content/uploads/sites/3/2017/01/ICC-G20-Business-Scorecard-December-2016.pdf [Accessed: 17 May 2018].

International Monetary Fund, 2010a. *G-20 Mutual Assessment Process: Alternative Policy Scenarios*. www.imf.org/external/np/g20/pdf/062710a.pdf [Accessed: 18 January 2018].

International Monetary Fund, 2011a. *G-20 Mutual Assessment Process: From Pittsburgh to Cannes: IMF Umbrella Report*. IMF Staff Reports for the G-20 Mutual Assessment Process. www.imf.org/external/np/g20/pdf/110411.pdf [Accessed: 24 October 2017].

International Monetary Fund, 2012d. *Toward Lasting Stability and Growth: Umbrella Report for G-20 Mutual Assessment Process*. www.imf.org/external/np/g20/pdf/map2012/umbrella.pdf [Accessed: 24 October 2017].

International Monetary Fund, 2013a. *Imbalances and Growth: Update of Staff Sustainability Assessments for G-20 Mutual Assessment Process*. September. www.imf.org/external/np/g20/pdf/map2013/map2013.pdf [Accessed: 3 July 2018].

International Monetary Fund, 2018. *The G20 Mutual Assessment Process (MAP)*. 8 March. www.imf.org/en/about/factsheets/sheets/2016/07/27/15/48/g20-mutual-assessment-process-map [Accessed: 2 July 2018].

International Organisations Research Institute and G20 Research Group, 2012. *Mapping G20 Decisions Implementation: How G20 Is Delivering on the Decisions Made*. Draft Report. December. Higher School of Economics, National Research University and Munk School of Global Affairs, University of Toronto. www.hse.ru/data/2012/12/13/1301054564/Mapping_G20_Decisions_Implementation_full_report.pdf [Accessed: 15 April 2018].

Keil, K., 2017. *The G20 Compact with Africa: Innovation Partnership or Business as Usual?* Heinrich Böll Stiftung North America. 13 December. us.boell.org/2017/12/13/g20-compact-africa-innovative-partnerships-or-business-usual [Accessed: 5 June 2018].

Kirton, J.J., 2012. *How the G20 Has Escaped Diminishing Returns*. Paper prepared for the conference 'International Co-Operation in Times of Global Crisis: Views from G20 Countries', Higher School of Economics, Moscow, 18–19 October.

Kirton, J.J., 2013d. *A Summit of Very Substantial Success: G20 Governance of the Global Economy and Security at St. Petersburg*. 6 September. www.g20.utoronto.ca/analysis/130906-kirton-performance.html [Accessed: 15 April 2018].

Kirton, J.J., 2015b. *Kirton Scoring Scheme*. 16 November. www.g20.utoronto.ca/analysis/scoring.html [Accessed: 22 February 2017].

Kirton, J.J., 2017b. *A Summit of Significant Success: The G20 at Hamburg*. 11 July. www.g20.utoronto.ca/analysis/170711-kirton-performance.html [Accessed: 14 May 2018].

Kirton, J.J. and Larionova, M. eds., 2018. *Accountability for Effectiveness in Global Governance*. Global Governance Series. London and New York: Routledge.

Kokotsis, E., 2006. *G8 Compliance Coding and Reference Manual*. Toronto: G8 Research Group. www.g8.utoronto.ca/evaluations/compliance_manual_2006.pdf [Accessed: 15 April 2018].

L20, 2017. *Global Unions Reaction to Hamburg G20 Summit*. 11 July. www.ituc-csi.org/global-unions-reaction-to-hamburg?lang=fr [Accessed: 3 July 2018].

New Rules for Global Finance, 2012b. *Promises of the G20 Process: Prospects for Advancing Transparency and Accountability*. 18 June. www.new-rules.org/events/3-nr-event/391-promises-of-the-g20 [Accessed: 28 November 2017].

New Rules for Global Finance, 2013. *Global Financial Governance & Impact Report*. new-rules.org/storage/documents/global_financial_governance__impact%20report_2013%20.pdf [Accessed: 19 April 2018].

New Rules for Global Finance and Friedrich-Ebert-Stiftung, 2016. *How Global Financial Institutions Impact Inequality: A Workshop to Strengthen Understanding, Assessment & Reporting*. www.new-rules.org/storage/documents/Workshop-Report-How-Global-Financial-Institutions-Impact-Inequality-FINAL.pdf [Accessed: 14 May 2018].

ONE, 2010. *The DATA Report: Monitoring the G8 Promise to Africa*. www.one.org/report/2010/en/downloads/DR2010.pdf [Accessed: 23 November 2012].

ONE, 2012. *2012 DATA Report: Europe's African Promise*. 6 July. one.org.s3.amazonaws.com/pdfs/data_report_2012_en.pdf [Accessed: 19 April 2018].

ONE, 2017. *2017 DATA Report: Financing for the African Century*. 28 August. one.org.s3.amazonaws.com/pdfs/one_data_report_2017_en.pdf [Accessed: 15 May 2018].

Organisation for Economic Co-Operation and Development and International Monetary Fund, 2017. *Quantifying the Implementation and Impact of G-20 Members' Growth Strategies*. www.oecd.org/g20/summits/hamburg/Quantifying-the-Implementation-of-Growth-Strategies-2017.pdf [Accessed: 11 November 2017].

Oxfam, 2017. *Oxfam G20 Communiqué Analysis*. 8 July. https://d1tn3vj7xz9fdh.cloudfront.net/s3fs-public/file_attachments/oxfam_g20_communiqué_analysis_0.pdf [Accessed: 25 May 2018].

Powell, J., 2012a. *G20 Is Getting a Reputation for Over-Promising and Under-Delivering*. ONE Blog. 21 June. www.one.org/international/blog/g20-is-getting-a-reputation-for-over-promising-and-under-delivering/ [Accessed: 19 April 2018].

Powell, J., 2012b. *Good Intentions Continue at G20, But Promises on Development Are Not Being Kept*. ONE Blog. 20 June. www.one.org/international/blog/good-intentions-continue-at-g20-but-promises-on-development-are-not-being-kept/ [Accessed: 19 April 2018].

Putnam, R.D. and Bayne, N., 1987. *Hanging Together: Cooperation and Conflict in the Seven-Power Summits*. rev. ed. Cambridge, MA: Harvard University Press.

Scholte, J.A., 2011a. Global governance, accountability and civil society. In: J.A. Scholte, ed. *Building Global Democracy? Civil Society and Accountable Global Governance*. Cambridge: Cambridge University Press. pp. 8–41.

Summers, L.H., 2017. Donald Trump's alarming G20 performance. *Financial Times*, 10 July, p. 11.

Sustainable Development Solutions Network and Bertelsmann Stiftung, 2017. *SDG Index and Dashboards Report 2017: Global Responsibilities*. July. www.sdgindex.org/assets/

files/2017/2017-SDG-Index-and-Dashboards-Report – full.pdf [Accessed: 17 May 2018].

Te Velde, D.W. coord., 2012. *Accountability and Effectiveness of the G20's Role in Promoting Development*. Paper prepared for Workshop on an Accountability Mechanism for G20 Development Commitments, Bali, Indonesia. London: Overseas Development Institute, 3 October. www.odi.org.uk/publications/6859-accountability-effectiveness-g20s-role-promoting-development [Accessed: 24 April 2018].

World Bank, 2010. *G20 and Global Development: Report Prepared by Staff of the World Bank for G20 Growth Framework and Mutual Assessment Process*. siteresources.worldbank.org/DEC/Resources/G20Framework&MAP-WBReport-TorontoSummit-2.pdf [Accessed: 18 January 2018].

9 G20 documentation

This chapter examines the pattern, subject matter, preparation and dissemination of documents of the G20 summits, the G20 Finance Ministers' and Central Bank Governors' forum as well as other G20 ministerial meetings and such sub-summit entities as working groups and task forces. It shows how documents reflect G20 deliberations and initiatives, and indicates how lower-level documents feed into higher levels of the G20 hierarchy. The chapter also includes a survey of documents submitted to the G20 by external actors, and a discussion of the issue of transparency of the G20. Sources of information other than documentary material are discussed in Chapter 10.

Introduction

The G20 system has generated a large number of documents in the course of its work at the level of summits, ministerial fora, working groups, task forces and other sub-summit bodies. This public documentation is the principal source of information about the G20 and its activities. Because the G20 lacks a secretariat to gather, disseminate and analyze the document output, there is a clear need for systematic assessment of this source material.

Collective documents of the G20 are products of consensus. When leaders are at their best and show political will, they can achieve consensus on ambitious initiatives and agreements, even if, at times, the document may be expressed in obscure terms that require reading between the lines. When a more ambitious consensus cannot be reached, the resulting document (or parts of it) reflects the lowest common denominator or, rarely, an open statement of disagreement. Similar compromises characterize G20 documents at the sub-summit level.

Underlying public documentation are the actual negotiations of the G20 leaders and sub-summit bodies. These remain largely private and confidential, with little or no access by the public. This has a bearing on transparency, which is discussed later in this chapter.

G20 summit documents

Documentation varies greatly from summit to summit. Most documents are accessible on the G20 Information Centre website (see www.g20.utoronto.ca)

DOI: 10.4324/9781351266802-10

and, temporarily, on the dedicated websites of host governments (the latter are discussed later in this chapter). Collective documents of the G20 summits can be grouped in the following categories: communiqués and declarations; action plans; reports on policy commitments of G20 members; reports of ministers to the G20 leaders; reports of international governmental organizations (IGOs) and other reports, commissioned by the G20; discussion papers and other supporting documents. Communiqués, declarations, action plans and other collective documents of the leaders are adopted by consensus. Discussion papers, supporting documentation and some other types of lesser documents are the responsibility of the host government. The host leaders' press statements, while also reflecting the sense of the G20 as a whole, express the particular leader's priorities and emphases.

Communiqués and declarations

These are the principal documents of each summit. Their subjects span the array of G20 concerns and reflect the summit agenda, ranging from financial and economic matters to reforming and strengthening international financial institutions, regulating banks and financial markets, promoting sustainable development, 'green growth', trade and investment, jobs, energy, food security, inclusion, accountability, climate change, corruption, terrorism and health. (Agenda evolution is discussed in Chapter 2.) The term denoting this type of document varies somewhat from summit to summit.

Washington 2008: *Declaration of the Summit on Financial Markets and the World Economy*

The *Declaration* (G20, 2008) documents that the inaugural G20 summit identified the root causes of the financial crisis that led to the emergence of the leaders'-level G20; reviewed actions already taken by G20 countries; agreed on economic stimulus measures to be taken; set down common principles for financial market reform and regulation; pledged to increase resources of international financial institutions (IFIs); reaffirmed the leaders' commitment to the reform of the Bretton Woods institutions and to an open global economy; and charged ministers and experts with the elaboration of action plans.

London 2009: *Leaders' Statement*, *Declaration on Strengthening the Financial System* and *Declaration on Delivering Resources through the International Financial Institutions*

This summit achieved substantial results in dealing with the continuing economic and financial crisis, urging coordinated fiscal stimulus measures by member countries, and agreeing to treble financial resources available to the IMF (to US$750 billion) and take other important steps, including new Special Drawing Rights (SDR) allocations and trade finance support. The *Declaration on Strengthening the Financial*

System (G20, 2009a) turned the Financial Stability Forum into the Financial Stability Board with an expanded mandate.

Pittsburgh 2009: *Leaders' Statement* with the annexed *Core Values for Sustainable Economic Activity*

The *Statement* (G20, 2009c) included undertakings to restore growth and jobs, strengthen financial supervision and regulation, strengthen global financial institutions (including IMF and World Bank quota reforms), resist protectionism and promote global trade and investment, and ensure 'a fair and sustainable recovery for all'.

Toronto 2010: *G-20 Toronto Summit Declaration* and *Principles for Innovative Financial Inclusion*

The *Declaration* (G20, 2010a) documents the leaders' commitment 'to taking concerted actions to sustain the recovery, create jobs and to achieve stronger, more sustainable and more balanced growth'. The leaders also undertook to 'at least halve deficits by 2013 and stabilize or reduce government debt-to-GDP ratios by 2016' – a pledge that later proved elusive. The leaders continued to call for financial sector reform and, importantly, established the Development Working Group.

Seoul 2010: *Leaders' Declaration* and *Seoul Summit Document*

Signalling agenda expansion to embrace development issues, these documents are a testament to the leaders' commitment by annexing the *Multi-year Action Plan on Development* and the *Seoul Development Consensus for Shared Growth* (see ahead).

Cannes 2011: *Cannes Summit Final Declaration* (subtitled *Building Our Common Future: Renewed Collective Action for the Benefit of All*) and *G20 Leaders Summit: Final Communiqué*

The *Final Declaration* (G20, 2011b) deals with: employment and social protection; capital flows; crisis management; IMF surveillance; financial sector regulation; tax havens; and other issues. The *Communiqué* (G20, 2011c) reflects the leaders' concern with: growth and jobs; social inclusion; international monetary system reform; financial sector reform; commodity prices and the promotion of agriculture; energy markets and climate change; development; trade and protectionism; corruption; and global governance.

Los Cabos 2012: *G20 Leaders Declaration*

The *Declaration* (G20, 2012j) focuses on: economic stabilization and global recovery; employment and social protection; trade; international financial architecture, including a reiteration of commitment to IMF quota and governance reform by 2012; financial inclusion (this includes an endorsement of the G20 Basic Set of financial inclusion indicators);

food security and commodity price volatility; green growth; and corruption.

St Petersburg 2013: *G20 Leaders' Declaration* and *G20 5th Anniversary Vision Statement*

This *Declaration* (G20, 2013f) covers a wide variety of issues: the global economy (including the G20 Framework for Strong, Sustainable and Balanced Growth); quality jobs; financing for investment; multilateral trade; base erosion and profit shifting, tax avoidance, tax transparency and automatic exchange of information; international financial architecture; financial reregulation; financial inclusion, financial education and consumer protection; development for all; sustainable energy policy and resilience of commodity markets; fight against climate change; and fight against corruption. It also has a tax annex (see Annex 4; G20, 2013d). The *Vision Statement* (G20, 2013e) reaffirms the role of the G20 as the premier forum for their members' international economic cooperation, and the leaders' previous economic and financial commitments.

Brisbane 2014: *G20 Leaders' Communiqué*

The *Communiqué* (G20, 2014f) focused on lifting the level of growth, creating quality jobs, building a stronger and more resilient global economy, and strengthening global economic institutions and energy markets; and fighting corruption. The summit also issued the *G20 Leaders' Brisbane Statement on Ebola* (G20, 2014e), marking agenda expansion to health issues.

Antalya 2015: *G20 Leaders' Communiqué*

The *Communiqué* (G20, 2015a) centred on strengthening the economic recovery, including investment; enhancing resilience in international financial architecture, international taxation, and anti-corruption; buttressing sustainability in development, energy, and climate change financing; enhancing inclusiveness; and the refugee crisis. The summit issued a separate *G20 Statement on the Fight against Terrorism* (G20, 2015b), focusing on the terrorist attacks in Paris on 13 November and in Ankara on 10 October 2015 and thus testifying to the G20's new emphasis on security issues.

Hangzhou 2016: *G20 Leaders' Communiqué*

The *Communiqué* (G20, 2016k) emphasized a new path for growth, robust international trade and investment, and inclusive and interconnected development, the development agenda building on earlier summits, particularly those since the 2010 Seoul summit. This ambitious agenda included: maintaining the momentum of economic recovery; lifting mid- to long-term growth potential; more effective and efficient global economic and financial governance; improving the international financial architecture; financial sector reform; green finance; improving the international tax regime, and implementing consensus on anti-corruption. Further concerns were: trade and investment cooperation; support for the multilateral trading system; promoting the growth of global trade and inclusive and integrated global value chains; and enhancing cooperation and coordination on global investment policy. The summit paid particular attention to implementing the UN's 2030 Agenda for Sustainable Development, optimizing development cooperation, building infrastructure and connectivity, promoting an accessible, affordable and sustainable energy supply, increasing employment, improving food security and nutrition, mobilizing climate finance, eradicating poverty, and supporting industrialization in African and other developing countries. The *Annex to G20 Leaders' Communiqué* (G20, 2016a) contains a number of agreed documents (a term first used at Hangzhou), including the *G20 Blueprint on Innovative Growth* and various action plans and reports (see ahead).

Hamburg 2017: *G20 Leaders' Declaration*

The *Declaration* (G20, 2017g) was built on three pillars: (1) ensuring stability, (2) improving viability for the future and (3) accepting responsibility. The detailed agenda focused on a larger number of issues: sharing the benefits of globalization (including a prosperous global economy; trade and investment; excess capacities; sustainable global supply chains; digital transformation; and boosting employment); building resilience (open and resilient financial system; enhancing the international financial architecture; working for international tax cooperation and financial transparency; safeguarding against health crises, strengthening health systems; and combating antimicrobial resistance); improving sustainable livelihoods (energy and climate issues – the most contentious section – sustainable development; women's empowerment; food security, water sustainability and rural youth employment; and resource efficiency and marine litter); the new G20 Africa Partnership; coordination and cooperation on displacement and migration; and fighting corruption. Gender issues and the digital economy were newly emphasized priorities at Hamburg. The summit also issued a *G20 Leaders' Statement on Countering Terrorism* (G20, 2017h) that included: implementing international commitments and enhancing cooperation; fighting the financing of terrorism; and countering radicalization and the use of the Internet for terrorist purposes. As was the case at Hangzhou, several agreed documents (action plans, initiatives and reports) were released in Hamburg.

Action plans

These are important documents and can include supporting Annex documents which focus on selected issues (which can be found at g20.utoronto.ca/summits) that flesh out the more general provisions of the communiqués and declarations. The Washington summit's *Action Plan to Implement Principles for Reform* is attached to the *Declaration*. The Pittsburgh *Framework for Strong, Sustainable, and Balanced Growth* is related to this category. The Seoul summit produced the *Multi-year Action Plan on Development* and the *G20 Anti-Corruption Action Plan*, both annexed to the *Seoul Summit Document*, as is the *Seoul Development Consensus for Shared Growth*. At Cannes, the *Cannes Action Plan for Growth and Jobs* was released. The Los Cabos summit issued *The Los Cabos Growth and Jobs Action Plan* (G20, 2012m), which addresses fiscal and financial imbalances, and their effect on growth, employment and confidence.

The *St. Petersburg Action Plan* (G20, 2013j) deals with the state of the global economy; recovery and near-term risks; and strong, sustainable and balanced growth (including fiscal sustainability and structural reforms). This *Action Plan* has four annexes: Annex 1 on medium-term fiscal strategies of the advanced-economy countries (G20, 2013a); Annex 2 on strategies of emerging-market economies to promote fiscal sustainability (G20, 2013b); Annex 3 on country-specific reform commitments (MAP policy templates, G20, 2013c); and Annex 4, the St Petersburg accountability assessment of progress achieved on past commitments and new commitments since the Los Cabos summit. The 2014 Brisbane summit issued the *Financial Inclusion Action Plan* and the *Brisbane Action Plan* (on strong, sustainable and balanced growth), the *G20 Plan to Facilitate Remittance Flows* and the *G20 Energy Efficiency Action Plan*, among others.

The 2015 Antalya summit produced the following action plan–type documents, appended to the *G20 Leaders' Communiqué*: *Antalya Action Plan* for strengthening the global economic recovery and fostering strong, sustainable and balanced growth (including comprehensive growth strategies, strengthening the recovery and lifting growth potential); additional action plans included, among others, the *G20 Action Plan on Food Security and Sustainable Food Systems*, the *Multilateral Development Banks Action Plan to Optimize Balance Sheets*, the *G20 Leaders' Call on Inclusive Business*, the *G20/OECD Principles of Corporate Governance*, the *G20 Joint Action Plan on SME* (small and medium enterprises) *Financing* (with the Global Partnership for Financial Inclusion and the G20 Investment and Infrastructure Working Group) and the *G20 Energy Access Action Plan*.

The 2016 Hangzhou summit again issued a large number of action plans and similar documents: *Blueprint on Innovative Growth*; *New Industrial Revolution Action Plan*; *G20 Digital Economy Development and Cooperation Initiative*; the *Hangzhou Action Plan*; *G20 2016 Innovation Action Plan*; *G20 Anti-Corruption Action Plan, 2017–2018*; *G20 New Industrial Revolution Action Plan*; *G20 Action Plan on the 2030 Agenda for Sustainable Development*; *G20 Growth Strategy*; and the *G20 High-Level Principles on Cooperation on Persons Sought for Corruption and Asset Recovery*.

The 2017 Hamburg summit issued, annexed to the *Leaders' Declaration*, the *G20 Hamburg Climate and Energy Action Plan for Growth*, the *Women Entrepreneurs Financing Initiative* (under World Bank trusteeship), the *G20 Hamburg Action Plan* (which sets out the G20's strategy for achieving strong, sustainable, balanced and inclusive growth), the *G20 Action Plan on Marine Litter*, the *G20 Initiative for Rural Youth Employment* and the *G20 Initiative '#eSkills4Girls'* (on the future of women and girls in the digital economy). Related to an earlier action plan, the leaders at Hamburg also issued the *Hamburg Update: Taking Forward the G20 Action Plan on the 2030 Agenda for Sustainable Development*, which follows on the 2016 Hangzhou G20 summit's *G20 Action Plan on the* [UN's] *2030 Agenda for Sustainable Development* with the intention that it would be regularly updated according to the lessons learned and the priorities of G20 presidencies.

G20 leaders' remits to sub-summit entities and other organizations

Some examples are as follows:

- The St Petersburg Strategic Framework for the G20 Anti-Corruption Working Group (G20, 2013l), which sets out the mandate and tasks of the working group.
- The Seoul Summit Document (G20, 2010d), which asks: the IMF to submit a progress report on quota and governance reforms to the G20 Finance Ministers and Central Bank Governors; the FSB and the OECD to report to the next (Cannes) summit on consumer finance protection; and the Global Marine Environment Protection (GMEP) Experts Sub-Group to report on progress with the help of other stakeholders.
- The *G20 Hamburg Action Plan* (G20, 2017f), which asks the Financial Stability Board and the OECD to prepare a progress report on tax transparency and information exchange to the G20 Finance Ministers and Central Bank Governors by early 2018. The *Action Plan* also asks the Global Partnership for Financial Inclusion (GPFI) to develop a roadmap for sustainable and responsible financial inclusion of forcibly displaced persons by 2018.

Reports on policy commitments of G20 members

The Seoul summit issued a detailed table, 'Policy Commitments by G20 Members', the first G20 summit to do so. The Los Cabos summit released its version of policy commitments. Annex 3 to the *St. Petersburg Action Plan* is a MAP template of G20 members' policy commitments. These compilations represent significant aspects of G20 accountability.

The Brisbane summit's 2014 *Accountability Assessment Report* outlines progress on G20 commitments on macroeconomic and structural reform. Also in 2014 the ILO, OECD and the World Bank Group submitted their report, *G20 Labour Markets: Key Challenges and Policy Responses*. The Antalya summit, similarly, received the *Antalya Accountability Assessment*, prepared by the G20 Framework Working Group, reviewing progress on achieving the objectives of strong, sustainable and balanced growth. The *Hangzhou Accountability Assessment* continues along the same lines. The *Hamburg Update* refers to the *G20 Action Plan on the* [UN's] *2030 Agenda for Sustainable Development* and affirms the intention to make 'collective and concrete G20 actions more visible' (G20, 2017j). Also in Hamburg, the G20 Development Working Group released its *Hamburg Annual Progress Report on G20 Development Commitments* (G20 Development Working Group, 2017). The report used input by other G20 working groups, the OECD and other international organizations.

Reports of ministers to the G20 leaders

G20 ministerial fora produce a number of reports, studies and action plans. Some are issued along with summit documents (others are not issued as summit documents but as documents of ministers' meetings) – for example:

- G20 Finance Ministers and Central Bank Governors. *G20 Action Plan to Support the Development of Local Currency Bond Markets*, 15 October 2011.
- G20 Finance Ministers and Central Bank Governors. *G20 Principles for Cooperation between the IMF and Regional Financing Arrangements*, 15 October 2011.
- G20 Finance Ministers and Central Bank Governors. *G20 Coherent Conclusions for the Management of Capital Flows Drawing on Country Experiences*, 15 October 2011.
- *G20 Labour and Employment Ministers' Conclusions*, 26–27 September 2011.
- *Labour and Employment Ministers' Conclusions*, 18 May 2012.
- G20 Agriculture Ministers. *Ministerial Declaration: Action Plan on Food Price Volatility and Agriculture*, 23 June 2011.
- G20 Agriculture Vice Ministers/Deputies Meeting, *Report*, 18 May 2012.
- *Joint Statement of the Finance Ministers and Central (National) Bank Governors of the Customs Union and Common Free Market Zone Member Countries, for the G20 Leaders' Summit in Saint Petersburg*, 27 August 2013.

The 23 October 2010 Gyeongju communiqué of G20 Finance Ministers and Central Bank Governors is illustrative of the importance of ministerial documents. It represents a breakthrough because the ministers and governors agreed at that meeting to 'shifts in [IMF] quota shares to dynamic EMDCs [emerging-market developing countries] and to underrepresented countries of over 6%, while protecting the voting share of the poorest, which we commit to work to complete by the annual Meetings in 2012' (G20 Finance Ministers and Central Bank Governors, 2010, p. 2). Moreover, Gyeongju serves as an example of ministerial documents that are prepared in fulfilment of tasks assigned to these groups by G20 leaders, and, in turn, feed into eventual documents of the summits. The leaders, in their Seoul *Declaration* (G20, 2010b, p. 2), stated,

> In Gyeongju, our Finance Ministers and Central Bank Governors called on the IMF to provide an assessment as part of the MAP on the progress toward external sustainability and the consistency of fiscal, monetary,

financial sector, structural, exchange rate and other policies. In light of this, the first such assessment, to be based on the above mentioned indicative guidelines, will be initiated and undertaken in due course under the French Presidency.

Reports of working groups and other sub-summit bodies submitted to leaders

Some examples are as follows:

- [2011] *First Monitoring Report of the G20 Anti-Corruption Working Group to G20 Leaders on Individual and Collective Progress Made by G20 Countries in the Implementation of the Seoul Action Plan.*
- *Global Partnership for Financial Inclusion: Report to the Leaders*, 5 November 2011.
- *2011 Report of the Development Working Group*, 28 October.
- *2012 Progress Report of the Development Working Group*, 19 June.
- *G20 Anti-Corruption Working Group Progress Report*, September 2013.
- *G20 Development Working Group Accountability Framework*, 5 September 2014.
- G20 Framework Working Group. *Antalya Accountability Assessment*, 2015.
- G20 Digital Economy Task Force. *G20 Digital Economy. Development and Cooperation Initiative*, 5 September 2016.
- G20 Framework Working Group (2016a). *Enhanced Structural Reform Agenda*, 14 September.
- G20 Development Working Group (2016p). *Hangzhou Comprehensive Accountability Report on G20 Development Commitments*, 14 September.
- G20 Anti-Corruption Working Group (ACWG) (2016). *G20 Anti-Corruption Implementation Plan 2017–2018*, 4 November.

Like ministerial documents, those of working groups and similar bodies are the results of instructions, requests or initiatives of a higher body in the G20 hierarchy. They feed into the deliberations of ministers and, at times, of the leaders. An example is the Development Working Group, which, in its 2012 *Progress Report*, states,

> We have advanced significantly in the implementation of previous agreements under the Seoul Multi-Year Action Plan . . ., and identified new actions to enhance concerted efforts in support of developing countries, particularly LICs . . . [The working group promises to] continue to flesh out the linkages between the different streams of our work, in order to make the most of the synergies between them, and aim towards a more holistic approach to development cooperation. This is particularly important in terms of the agreed priorities of infrastructure, food security and inclusive green growth.
>
> (G20 Development Working Group, 2012, p. 1)

Reports of the Financial Stability Board to G20 leaders or Finance Ministers and Central Bank Governors

The following examples can be found on the Financial Stability Board's website (www.fsb.org/publications):

- *FSB Report on the Overview of Progress in the Implementation of the G20 Recommendations for Strengthening Financial Stability*. 4 November 2011.
- *Overview of Progress in the Implementation of the G20 Recommendations for Strengthening Financial Stability*. 19 June 2012.
- *A Narrative Progress Report on Financial Reform: Report of the Financial Stability Board to G20 Leaders*. 30 August 2013.
- *Update on Financial Regulatory Factors Affecting the Supply of Long-Term Investment Finance*. 16 September 2014.
- *Implementation and Effects of the G20 Financial Regulatory Reforms*. 9 November 2015.
- *Progress Report to G20 on the FSB Action Plan to Assess and Address the Decline in Correspondent Banking*. 25 August 2016.
- *Framework for Post-Implementation Evaluation of the Effects of the G20 Financial Regulatory Reforms*. 3 July 2017.

Reports of international governmental organizations (IGOs) and others, commissioned by G20 leaders or ministers

Examples are as follows:

- Bank for International Settlements, Basel Committee on Banking Supervision (see www.bis.org/bcbs/publications.htm)
    - *Report to G20 Leaders on Basel III Implementation*. June 2012.
    - *Report to G20 Finance Ministers and Central Bank Governors on Basel III Implementation*. October 2012.
    - *Report to G20 Finance Ministers and Central Bank Governors on Monitoring Implementation of Basel III Regulatory Reform*. April 2013.
    - *Reducing Excessive Variability in Banks' Regulatory Capital Ratios: A Report to the G20*. November 2014.
    - *Finalising Post-crisis Reforms: An Update; A Report to G20 Leaders*. November 2015.
    - 'Economic Resilience: A Financial Perspective'; note submitted to the G20. 7 November 2016.
    - *Implementation of Basel Standards: A Report to G20 Leaders on Implementation of the Basel III Regulatory Reforms*. July 2017.
- Organisation for Economic Co-operation and Development (see www.oecd.org)
    - *Beating the Crisis: The Role of the OECD and G20*. 2011.

- *The History of the OECD and the G20*. 2012.
- *Boosting Jobs and Living Standards in G20 Countries: A Joint Report by the ILO, OECD, IMF and the World Bank*. June 2012.
- *G20/OECD High-Level Principles on Long-Term Investment Financing by Institutional Investors developed by the OECD Task Force on Institutional Investors and Long-Term Financing*. September 2013.
- OECD. Secretary-General. *Strengthening Global Growth: The G20 Brisbane Summit's Challenges and Contributions*. Brisbane, 13 November 2014.
- *G20/OECD Principles of Corporate Governance*. 30 November 2015.
- OECD. Secretary-General. *Report to G20 Finance Ministers*. Chengdu, China, 23–24 July 2016.
- OECD. Secretary-General. *Report to G20 Leaders*. 20 July 2017.
- *G20 Global Displacement and Migration Trends Report 2017*.

- International Monetary Fund (see www.imf.org/external/np/g20/index.htm)
  - *Note by the Staff of the International Monetary Fund on Stocktaking of the G-20 Responses to the Global Banking Crisis*. 13–14 March 2009.
  - *G-20 Mutual Assessment Process – IMF Staff Assessment of G-20 Policies*. October 2010.
  - *Macroprudential Policy Tools and Frameworks: Update to G20 Finance Ministers and Central Bank Governors*. 14 February 2011.
  - *Progress Report on the G-20 Data Gaps Initiative: Status, Action Plans, and Timetables*. September 2012.
  - *IMF Update on Global Prospects and Policy Challenges*. St Petersburg, 5–6 September 2013.
  - *Growth-Friendly Fiscal Policy*. 2014.
  - *Time to Act on the G-20 Agenda: The Global Economy Will Thank You*. Blog by Managing Director Christine Lagarde. 2015.
  - *Group of Twenty IMF Surveillance Note: G-20 Finance Ministers and Central Bank Governors' Meetings in Shanghai, China: IMF Note on Global Prospects and Policy Challenges*. 26–27 February 2016.
  - *G-20 Report on Strong, Sustainable and Balanced Growth*. October 2017.

Other supporting documents

These include discussion papers and documents on priorities of the host government – for example:

- *Discussion Paper: Mexico's Presidency of the G-20*. January 2012.
- *Global Economic Crisis: Role and Challenges of the G20*. 26 January 2012.
- *Priorities of Russia's G20 Presidency in 2013*. 2013.
- *G20 2014: Overview of Australia's Presidency*. 1 December 2013.
- *Turkey's 2015 G20 Priorities for 2015*, 1 December 2014.

- *G20 Summit 2016, China.* 1 December 2015.
- *Priorities of the 2017 G20 Summit.* 1 December 2016.

Besides collective documents of G20 summits, there are other types of closely related public information released at the summits – for example, transcripts or webcasts of press conferences.

Transcripts or webcasts of press conferences

Particularly interesting are press conferences at the end of the summits – of the host leader and his or her peers – for example:

- *Conférence de presse du Président de la République à l'issue du Sommet du G20 de Cannes.* 4 November 2011.
- *The VIIth G20 Leaders' Summit Concludes.* 19 June 2012 [not a full transcript].
- *Press Statement by President Felipe Calderón to Mark the End of the G20 Summit.* 19 June 2012.
- *Vladimir Putin's News Conference following the G20 Summit.* 6 September 2013.
- *Press Conference [of] Australia's Prime Minister Tony Abbott.* 16 November 2014.
- *President Xi Jinping['s] Closing Speech.* 5 September 2016.
- *Together We Can Achieve More* [Chancellor Angela Merkel's press conference at the end of the Hamburg summit]. 8 July 2017.

Press conferences of leaders other than the summit host are good indicators of the position of members of the G20. Such press conferences of leaders (and this includes the summit host) allow media representatives to ask probing questions, provided the leader is willing to answer. The answers can reveal additional information not reflected in official summit documents.

Outside communications addressed to the G20

These come from NGOs and coalitions, business groups or individuals – for example:

- L20 (Labour20): *Statement to the G20 Summit.* June 2012.
- G8/G20 Global Working Group: *Civil Society Statements to the Mexican Government.* 22–24 February 2012.
- Gates, W.: *Innovation with Impact: Financing 21st Century Development.* November 2011.
- Gates, W.: *Letter to President Felipe Calderón Hinojosa.* 13 June 2012.
- Joint Religious Coordination for the G8 and G20 Summits: *2012 Religious Leaders' Statement for the G8 and G20 Summits.*

- B20: *B20* (Business 20) *Task Force Recommendations: Final Report*. 11 May 2012.
- B20-G20 *Partnership for Growth and Jobs: Recommendations from Business 20*. 5–6 September 2012.
- *Civil20 Recommendations to the G20*. 19 June 2017.

Official briefings

G20 officials give media briefings at summits; these are not always reflected in press releases but serve as background information. As well, the host country issues a number of minor documents for the information of the attending media before and during summits. These include items such as notices of upcoming briefings and photo opportunities, and a detailed media handbook that gives information on the composition of official delegations, hotel assignments for the delegations, location of briefing rooms in the media centre, and schedules of the leaders' meetings (this last is subject to change due to the progress of the leaders' negotiations and, as the case may be, unexpected events that interfere with the schedule). The frequency of such briefings and the countries giving briefings varies from summit to summit.

Other types of information released during summits

G20 summits are good opportunities for two, three or more assembled leaders to meet privately to discuss common concerns and, at times, come to mutual understanding or agreement. For example, during the Los Cabos summit, President Obama met with his Russian counterpart, Vladimir Putin. Australian Prime Minister Tony Abbott met with the leaders of Spain, Italy, Brazil and Indonesia during the Brisbane summit. At the Antalya summit, Turkish host leader Recep Tayyip Erdoğan met with US President Barack Obama and German Chancellor Angela Merkel met with Vladimir Putin to discuss Ukraine and Syria. The following year in Hangzhou, Obama again met Putin (on Syria), and Merkel met Erdoğan (on migration, Syria and German-Turkish relations) and French president François Hollande (on the future of the EU, among other concerns). At the Hamburg summit, there was a much-discussed two-hour bilateral meeting between US President Donald Trump and Putin – the first meeting of the two. Reportedly, Trump questioned Putin about Russian meddling in the 2016 US election, which the latter denied; Putin, on his part, wanted an end to or the easing of Western sanctions against Russia. Syria was another topic of the meeting (Davis, Sanger and Thrush, 2017, p. A1).

The participants usually issue brief statements on such meetings; these tend to be carried as news releases on the official website of the summit but then disappear from public view when the official summit site is no longer active.

From time to time, documents are released jointly by the G20 leaders and invited heads of non-G20 countries or international organizations. These also tend to appear as news releases during the summits on the official summit websites.

Preparing and distributing the communiqué and other summit documents

For both the G8 and the G20, the preparation of the communiqué and action plans is a long and complex process. The sherpas play a crucial role in developing and shaping these documents, which go through many drafts in the year leading up to the summit. This is done through regular communication with the leaders, fellow sherpas and various experts, including a series of meetings during the year (under the German Presidency, between the 2016 Hangzhou summit and the 2017 Hamburg summit, the sherpas met four times, with a follow-up meeting after the summit, on 9–10 November). During this process the sherpas are guided by the priorities and political constraints of all the G20 leaders. Preparation of the communiqué and action plans begins once the summit host finalizes the agenda early in the year of the leader's G7/G8 or G20 Presidency. The initial document is a skeletal, outline version, setting out the concept and tone of the forthcoming summit. The draft then develops gradually until, by the start of the summit, it becomes practically the full communiqué (perhaps with a few square-bracketed words and phrases whose removal requires discussion of the leaders themselves).

The final communiqué is adopted by consensus of the leaders, as is the case with G20 declarations and communiqués (discussed later in this chapter). Setting a new precedent, US President Donald Trump, immediately after the 2018 Charlevoix G7 summit, disavowed his earlier approval of the agreed communiqué. What is the significance of that withdrawal of endorsement? Unlike a binding international agreement, which may be abrogated by a state that previously signed and ratified it, the G7 communiqué is an informal document which presumably still embodies G7 consensus.

In earlier years of summitry, telegrams, letters, faxes, couriers and the occasional diplomatic pouch were the means of communication among sherpas, in addition to face-to-face meetings. For the G7/G8, the process also involved the preparation of thematic papers dealing with individual topics on the summit agenda and briefing books bringing together voluminous confidential reports, letters and other documentation.

With the advent and rapid development of information and communication technology, the means of communication changed radically. In the case of the G20, there is very little use of letters, couriers and faxes. Instead, voluminous exchanges of email messages, teleconferencing and some videoconferencing have become common practice. The term 'thematic papers' has given way to 'building blocks' for individual themes of the forthcoming summit. Host countries have also stepped up the use of web-based intranet restricted to the sherpas. Briefing books (confidential comprehensive collections of background documents, talking points and issue briefs for the use of each G20 leader and their high officials), formerly in paper form, are now created, maintained and generally kept electronically. Whatever the method, sherpa communications and other internal communications remain confidential and unavailable to the public.

Most public documents released at the summit are made available to the attending media, although increasingly less on paper and more through open websites. These are also accessible to the public as long as the website remains active (see further discussion ahead, in the section on transparency).

G20 ministerial documents

In addition to ministerial reports to the G20 leaders (discussed earlier), various G20 ministerial fora have issued documents. Communiqués of ministers are the major documents of this type. These, as is the case for summits, tend to be adopted by consensus. Several ministerial fora also produce reports, seminar or conference proceedings and various studies. Arguably the most voluminous output is that of the G20 Finance Ministers and Central Bank Governors, not surprisingly because of the long history of that forum; as of 2017, some 40 meetings have each issued communiqués.

Besides the Finance Ministers' forum, other fora emerged after the establishment of the G20 summit. Some examples of ministerial documents follow (these can be found at www.g20.utoronto.ca under Finance Ministers and Central Bank Governors and under Other Ministerial Meetings):

- *Financial Sector Regulation and Supervision (Backgrounder)*. Berlin, 15–16 December 1999.
- *Agenda for Growth: Progress Report*. Boca Raton, Florida, 7 February 2004.
- *G8 Finance Ministers' Conclusions on Development*. London, 10–11 February 2005.
- *The G-20 Statement on Reforming the Bretton Woods Institutions*. Xianghe, Hebei (China), 15–16 October 2005.
- *G8 Finance Ministers' Statement on Access to Energy Services for the Millennium Development Goals*. St Petersburg, 9–10 June 2006.
- *G20 Labour and Employment Ministers' Recommendations to G20 Leaders*. Washington, DC, 21 April 2010.
- *G20 Labour and Employment Ministers' Conclusions*. Paris, 27 September 2011.
- *Ministerial Declaration [and] Action Plan on Food Price Volatility and Agriculture*. Paris, 23 June 2011.
- *G20 Ministerial Meeting on Development: Communiqué*. Washington, DC. 23 September 2011.
- G20 Tourism Ministers. *T.20 Initiative*. 2012. Under the auspices of the United Nations World Tourism Organization.
- G8-G20 Ministers of Culture and Intellectual Property ('Cultural G8-G20'). *Sommet culturel sur la création à l'ère numérique*. Avignon, 18 November 2011.
- *The Informal Meeting of G20 Foreign Ministers Concludes*. Los Cabos, 20 February 2012.

- G20 Trade Ministers. *Condensed Version of the Press Conference held by the Minister of Economy, Bruno Ferrari, to Present the Conclusions of the G20 Trade Ministerial Meeting*. Puerto Vallarta, Mexico. April 2012.
- G20 Labour and Employment Ministers and Finance Ministers. *Communiqué*. Moscow, 19 July 2013.
- G20 Agriculture Ministers. *Final Communiqué*. Istanbul, 8 May 2015.
- G20 Energy Ministers. *Communiqué*. Beijing, 29 June 2016.
- G20 Health Ministers. *Declaration: Together Today for a Healthy Tomorrow*. Berlin, 20 May 2017.
- G20 Digital Economy Ministerial Conference. *Declaration: Shaping Digitalisation for an Interconnected World*. Düsseldorf, 7 April 2017.

Earlier communiqués and some other reports are accessible at www.g20.utoronto.ca/ministerials.html. Summit host countries' official websites, as long as they remain active, also carry past communiqués and other reports.

Occasionally, ministers release statements without a formal meeting. For example, the G20 Finance Ministers (2012), in support of European policy initiatives on the euro zone crisis, issued a statement, *The G20 Welcomes Major Policy Actions in Europe*, on 29 June 2012. Such statements are usually agreed to by teleconferencing or videoconferencing.

Ministers also issue joint statements with IGOs. One such statement, by the G20 Finance Ministers/Central Bank Governors and the IMF's International Monetary and Financial Committee, concerns IMF resources (IMF, 2012b).

Documents of G20 working groups, task forces and similar sub-summit entities

In addition to reports submitted to the G20 leaders or ministers and issued as documents of the summits (discussed earlier), various G20 sub-summit bodies have issued other reports and documents. Examples follow:

- G20 Trade Finance Experts Group. *Report*. August 2009.
- Energy Experts Group. *Report to Leaders on the G20 Commitment to Rationalize and Phase Out Inefficient Fossil Fuel Subsidies*. June 2010.
- G20 Study Group on Commodities. *Report of the G20 Study Group on Commodities*. November 2011.
- Development Working Group. *2012 Progress Report*. 19 June 2012.
- G20 Study Group on Financing for Investment. *G20 Workplan on Financing for Investment: Study Group's Findings and Ways Forward*. July 2013.
- Anti-Corruption Working Group. *G20 2014: Brisbane Anti-Corruption Update*. November 2014.
- G-20 Framework Working Group. *Antalya Accountability Assessment*. 2015.
- G20 Framework Working Group. *Enhanced Structural Reform Agenda*. 14 September 2016.

- Global Partnership for Financial Inclusion. *G20 Financial Inclusion Action Plan (FIAP) 2017*. 6 July 2017.

Documents of seminars and workshops (co-)organized by the G20

The G20, at various levels, has organized a number of workshops, conferences and seminars over the years, often in collaboration with IGOs or individual governments. The proceedings of these events are sometimes released by the G20 itself; in other instances they are published by IGOs or the government hosting the event. Examples follow:

- *G-20 Workshop on Developing Strong Domestic Financial Markets*, Ottawa, 26–27 April 2004.
- *G-20 Workshop on Demographic Challenges and Migration*, Sydney, Australia, 27–28 August 2005
- *Proceedings of a Conference on Demography and Financial Markets*, Sydney, Australia, 23–25 July 2006. Treasury and Reserve Bank of Australia.
- *Proceedings of the G20 Workshop on Competition in the Financial Sector*, Bali, 16–17 February 2008. Organized by the Bank of Indonesia and the Banco de Mexico.
- *G20 Workshop on the Global Economy: Causes of the Crisis: Key Lessons*, Mumbai, India, 24–26 May 2009. Co-hosted by the Reserve Bank of India and the Bank of England.
- *Effective Financial Market Regulation after Pittsburgh: Achievements and Challenges: International Conference*. Berlin, 19–20 May 2010.
- *Korea-FSB [Financial Stability Board] Financial Reform Conference: An Emerging Market Perspective*, Seoul, 2–3 September 2010.
- G20-OECD Conference: Joining Forces against Corruption: G20 Business and Government. *Conference Summary and Conclusions*. Paris, 21 October 2011.
- *Seminar on 'Giving International Finance an Adequate Architecture'*. 18 January 2012.
- High-Level Public-Private Sector IIF [Institute of International Finance]. *G-20 Seminar 'The Financial Inclusion: From Principles to Action'*. Washington, DC, 22 April 2012.
- G20 Seminar on Green Growth. *Agenda*. Paris, 22 May 2012.
- Seminar on Regional Financial Arrangements: RFA's Role in International Financial Architecture and Their Cooperation with the IMF. *Overview*. 17 April 2013.
- G20 Small and Medium Enterprises Workshop. *Final Report*. Riyadh, Saudi Arabia, 11–12 March 2014. Hosted by Saudi Arabia as part of Australia's 2014 G20 Presidency.
- G20 Global Forum on Migration & Development-Global Migration Group. *G20-GFMD-GMG Joint Event*. Izmir, Turkey, 3 June 2015.

- Forum on Tax Administration. *Communiqué*. Beijing, 13 May 2016.
- International Conference on the Prevention of Radicalization, 13–15 November 2017.

The issue of transparency

Accountability, as discussed in Chapter 8, can be seen as having four dimensions: consultation, monitoring and evaluation, transparency and the availability of redress (Scholte, 2011a). Here this concept is applied to the G20: consultation or dialogue is examined in Chapters 4 (IGOs), 5 (the business sector) and 6 (civil society), and evaluation is explored in Chapter 8. Redress for inadequate accountability is problematic in the G20, which is not a treaty-based entity and therefore lacks machinery for enforcement. This section discusses the dimension of transparency.

As indicated at the beginning of this chapter, public documents of the G20 are the end product of summits and sub-summit bodies. The underlying negotiations remain largely private and confidential, with little or no access for the public. Although more and more documents are now released to the public, thereby increasing transparency, this does not extend to revealing the primary sources that provide the full content of G20 in-camera discussions and the whole slew of supporting documentation generated by and available to G20 insiders in member governments. In the case of the early years of the G7, such material is, by and large, eventually opened in official archives, but, in the case of G20 archives, this is problematic, as discussed in the next section.

The occasional researcher or persistent journalist may succeed in gaining privileged access to records of negotiations of certain heads of state and government, or ministers. Official off-the-record briefings during summits occasionally allow a glimpse of some useful inside information. Where national legislation allows, access-to-information requests are another option, but that process tends to be slow and the outcome not always positive. But all this does not amount to systematic, full information. However desirable complete transparency may be, basic confidentiality is a necessary part of summit and government diplomacy – and, on occasion, quiet diplomacy initiatives between civil society and G20 officials.

Memoirs of former high officials (leaders and ministers) of the G20 help partly fill this transparency gap. (See also Chapter 10.) For example, former UK Prime Minister Gordon Brown's 2010 book *Beyond the Crash* gives a detailed account of how the leaders' dinners and agreements and disagreements were among the participants. And former Canadian Prime Minister Paul Martin's 2008 memoir, *Hell or High Water: My Life in and out of Politics*, throws much light on the antecedents and establishment of the G20.

The transparency problem extends to the ever-increasing number of reports commissioned by the G20. Although many of these are now public, quite a few remain unavailable to citizens. For example, the IMF (with the OECD, World Bank, ILO and UNCTAD) produced several analyses and assessments related to the G20's Mutual Assessment Process (MAP): an 'umbrella report' that summarizes the component reports and offers a scenario for collective action by the G20; an accountability report on G20 members' progress in implementing policy commitments since the 2010 Seoul summit; a MAP report analysing member countries' medium-term macroeconomic and policy frameworks; and sustainability reports for seven G20 countries (China, France, Germany, India, Japan, the UK and the US) (IMF, 2011a). Not all of these reports have been released to the public, leaving a transparency gap (G20, 2011a). Some of these G20-commissioned reports themselves address aspects of transparency – for example, the OECD report, *Global Forum on Transparency and Exchange of Information for Tax Purposes*, cited earlier in this chapter.

Civil society and other groups have long advocated greater accountability and stronger transparency in particular. For example, the New Rules for Global Finance group (2012b) dealt with this question in *Promises of the G20 Process: Prospects for Enhanced Transparency and Accountability*. Another example is the NGO Transparency International, which has published its influential annual *Corruption Perception Index* since 1995 (see www.transparency.org/research/cpi/overview).

Draft documents

Draft communiqués and other draft documents are not officially distributed but are sometimes leaked to the media or civil society and other groups either before or at the summits. For example, a version of the leaked draft of the *Toronto Summit Declaration* (www.g20.utoronto.ca/2010/to-leakedcommuniqué.html) was published by the *Toronto Sun* newspaper, and excerpts of the draft G20 declaration of the Cannes G20 summit were released by a branch of Reuters (reutersreprints.com). A draft *Leaders' Communiqué* of the 2015 Antalya summit can be seen at www.g20.utoronto.ca/2015/151116-draft-communiqué.pdf. Although such leaked documents may make a small dent in one aspect of transparency, it should be noted that, as there are many successive drafts, one leaked document is just a snapshot of the moment.

These leaks can cause problems for the leaders; for example, as the host of the 2009 London summit, UK Prime Minister Gordon Brown (2010, p. 120) recalled,

> Unfortunately, our work hit a big snag when, a few days before the G20 met, the draft communiqué was leaked to a German magazine. Luckily, the leaked version did not involve the figures that would have added up to $1 trillion [to IMF resources]. That huge total was still under wraps, because I was determined it should surprise and shock the market.

The problem of archival research

Unlike in the case of the G7/G8, a forum that goes back to 1975, research based on detailed source material for the G20 in official archives is not yet possible (for a discussion, and examples, of archives of the early G7, see Hajnal, 2007a). Official archives – in countries where they are well organized and well maintained – are accessible to the public after the passage of (usually) 30 years.

However, in G20 countries that have freedom-of-information legislation, access requests can yield good results. Using a Canadian example, the following is indicative of what is contained in archival sources. It relates to the 2016 Hangzhou G20 summit and reflects Canada's positions and priorities. Documents obtained by an Access to Information and Privacy (ATIP) request under Canada's *Access to Information Act* include these sources:

- Proposed program elements for the Prime Minister's bilateral visits to China, presented in various iterations.
- 'Scenario and background book', originally classified 'secret'. It contains, among other material, the following parts:
  - draft program;
  - overview scenario;
  - draft Leaders' Declaration;
  - background briefs on the Canadian economic outlook;
- G20 topics:
  - global economy;
  - Framework Working Group for Strong, Sustainable and Balanced Growth;
  - financial regulation;
  - international taxation;
  - trade and investment;
  - excess capacity and production in global markets;
  - G20 development;
  - climate change and green/climate financing;
  - employment;
  - energy;
  - innovation and G20 blueprint on innovative growth;
  - anti-corruption;
  - international financial architecture;
  - tackling antimicrobial resistance in the G20;
  - G20 ministerial meetings in 2016;
  - Brexit fallout and implications;
  - implications of the coup attempt in Turkey; and
  - Global Find replenishment.
- Global issues:
  - countering the financing of terrorism; and global displacement and migration crisis; and
  - G20 country fact sheets.

The summit programme details the summit's working sessions as follows:

1 strengthening policy coordination and breaking a new path for growth;
2 more effective and efficient global economic and financial governance;

3 robust international trade and investment;
4 inclusive and interconnected development; and
5 other issues affecting the world economy.

The programme also includes details regarding travel, private programme elements, entertainment and bilateral side meetings.

Although the released documents are heavily redacted, they contain a wealth of useful information usually not available to the public. They, and similar documents from other G20 countries, when available under freedom-of-information legislation, are a rich repository of source material for research.

The G20, even at the Finance Ministers' and Central Bank Governors' level, is still young. Therefore, an important aspect of transparency is lacking. That is why memoirs of prominent G20 officials – such as Paul Martin's and Gordon Brown's – can serve as good sources of background information not otherwise available to the public.

A related problem involves the use of technology. In recent years, including the earliest years of the Finance Ministers' and Central Bank Governors' G20, communication among G20 officials has quite often been conducted by teleconferencing, videoconferencing and email exchanges. There is often an incomplete or non-existent 'paper trail' to document such exchanges. Although technological advances in preserving digital records have been made, much remains to be done. Thus, even when archives documenting the G20 are eventually opened, the records are likely to be incomplete. This is unfortunate for future researchers and for a full understanding of G20 processes. It should be noted that at least some summits provide a 'listening room' at the venue of the leader's discussions, available to officials of G20 members. Such officials could make their own recordings – again, these are not available to the public.

The problem of elusive websites

G7/G8 summit host countries began establishing websites in 1995, with the Halifax G7 summit. This practice has been continued by the G20 Finance Ministers' and Central Bank Governors' forum since its inception in 1999. Once the leaders'-level G20 summits began in 2008, each summit host government launched its dedicated website for the duration of its year of G20 Presidency, and sometimes kept up the site longer.

These official websites have varied greatly in richness of content, ease of navigation and the kind of information made (or not made) available. With the increasing sophistication of technology, official websites have added multimedia features, social media access and so forth. But, as discussed ahead, most of these sites have proved to be temporary, only to disappear completely or, once a country's Presidency was over, to be partially absorbed by the host's website for a particular ministry or other administrative unit. Invariably, in the process content has become lost, scattered or otherwise difficult or impossible to access. This represents loss of transparency, whether by technological fiat or political decisions.

The website of the G20 Information Centre at the University of Toronto, www.g20.utoronto.ca, was designed and has been maintained to serve as a permanent, authoritative source of G20-related documentary and other material, so that it continues to serve public information needs and thus transparency. However, for all its richness, this site cannot completely fill the gap caused by the host government's elusive websites by preserving the entire content of those sites. A number of IGOs, think-tanks and other groups have created G20-related websites. Such sites are discussed in Chapter 10.

The following brief review traces the fate of host governments' G20 websites. It also indicates where 'lost' content may be accessed. The US website for the 2008 Washington summit is no longer available, but a few key documents remain accessible at other government sites – for example, on an archival web page of the White House, georgewbush-whitehouse.archives.gov/infocus/financialmarkets, which states, 'This is historical material, "frozen in time". The web site is no longer updated and links to external web sites and some internal pages will not work'.

The UK site for the 2009 London summit is no longer active. Selected documents are accessible elsewhere – for example, at The National Archives website in the UK Government Web Archive section, webarchive.nationalarchives.gov.uk/*/www.g20.org.

The US website for the 2009 Pittsburgh summit is no longer live either. The State Department site keeps some summit-related information available at https://2009-2017.state.gov/e/eb/ecosum/pittsburgh2009/index.htm. Similarly, the Canadian website for the 2010 Toronto summit is no longer available. The Department of Global Affairs maintains an archival website for the G20 at international.gc.ca/world-monde/international_relations-relations_internationales/g20, but it covers only the 2015–17 G20 summits.

The Korean website for the 2010 Seoul summit likewise is no longer active. Residual information may be available on other Korean government websites. The French website for the 2011 Cannes summit, similarly, is no longer accessible. The same is true of the Mexican official website for the Los Cabos summit, but during its year of G20 Presidency, 2012, the Mexican government subsumed the previously distinct www.g20.org website, which originated in 1999 with the establishment of the G20 Finance Ministers' and Central Bank Governors' forum. That original www.g20.org site contained a great deal of useful, detailed information and links to the full text not only of all ministerial communiqués but also of a number of reports and studies. This amalgamation of the site for the G20 leaders has reduced a formerly higher level of transparency. Subsequent G20 host countries continued the practice of incorporating the www.g20.org site on assuming the G20 Presidency; for example, with the assumption of Argentine Presidency on 1 December 2017, the site is now maintained by the new host country.

There are archival websites for the following more recent G20 summits: St Petersburg 2013: www.g20russia.ru; Antalya 2015: g20.org.tr; and Hangzhou 2016: www.g20chn.org/English/China2016. These vary in completeness of coverage, and it is difficult to predict how long they will remain available. It is to be hoped that future summit host countries will continue to preserve at least the essential content of their official summit information.

Official websites of summit host countries generally link to major documents of previous summits. Some sites group such documents together while others merge them with other, non-summit G20 documents; for example, the Argentine summit website provides the texts of major summit documents from 2008 on, at www.g20.org/en/g20/timeline.

Conclusion

Public documents released by G20 leaders' summits, ministerial fora, working groups and other sub-summit bodies are the principal source of information on the G20 and its activities. Declarations, communiqués, action plans and other major collective documents express consensus of the G20 (while others represent the emphases of the host leader). Other documents include reports commissioned by the G20 from international organizations and other entities. Major documents of summits are the end result of careful preparation by sherpa teams, who regularly consult with their leaders, counterparts from other G20 members and, to some extent, other actors during the year-long process leading to the summit. They are then subject to the final imprimatur of the leaders, and thus they embody G20 decisions and initiatives and give expression to summit results.

Actual negotiations around the summit table (and at ministerial and some working group meetings) and sherpa communications are usually confidential and, in the interest of diplomacy, necessarily so. This has a bearing on transparency, an important aspect of accountability. Of the many commissioned reports, most are available but some remain unavailable to the public. Opacity is sometimes breached somewhat by leaked documents and confidential briefings. Unlike the archives of G7 countries, which are now open to researchers for the early summits, archives of the G20 members will long remain closed and, even when eventually opened, are unlikely to be as complete a record as in the case of the G7. Memoirs of high-level summit officials are another window on summit preparations and conduct. Volatility of government websites and their content – whether caused by technological or political decisions – is yet another obstacle to transparency.

Documents of sub-summit G20 entities are largely prepared in fulfilment of tasks assigned to these groups by higher bodies in the G20 hierarchy. In turn, these documents feed into eventual summit documents.

Public documents released by G20 summits, ministerial fora and other sub-summit bodies are the principal source of information available to researchers and the wider community on the G20 and its activities. But much information remains out of bounds to the public, due either to the confidential nature of diplomatic negotiations or to inadvertent or overzealous custodians of information. Overall transparency of the G20 has increased but there are persistent and newly arising obstacles that need to be remedied whenever possible.

References

Brown, G., 2010. *Beyond the Crash: Overcoming the First Crisis of Globalization*. New York and London: Free Press.

Davis, J.H., Sanger, D.E. and Thrush, G., 2017. Trump questions Putin on election meddling at eagerly awaited encounter. *The New York Times*, 7 July, p. A1.

G20, 2008. *Declaration: Summit on Financial Markets and the World Economy* and *Action Plan to Implement Principles for Reform*. Washington, DC. 15 November. www.g20.utoronto.ca/2008/2008declaration1115.html [Accessed: 24 October 2017].

G20, 2009a. *Declaration on Strengthening the Financial System and Declaration on Delivering Resources through the International Financial Institutions*. London. 2 April. www.g20.utoronto.ca/2009/2009ifi.pdf and www.g20.utoronto.ca/2009/2009delivery.pdf [Accessed: 28 November 2017].

G20, 2009c. *Leaders Statement: The Pittsburgh Summit*. 24–25 September. www.g20.utoronto.ca/2009/2009communiqué0925.html [Accessed: 24 October 2017].

G20, 2010a. *The G-20 Toronto Summit Declaration*. 27 June. www.g20.utoronto. ca/2010/to-communiqué.html [Accessed: 24 October 2017].

G20, 2010b. *The G20 Seoul Summit Leaders' Declaration*. 12 November. www.g20.utoronto.ca/2010/g20seoul.pdf [Accessed: 28 November 2017].

G20, 2010d. *Seoul Summit Document*. www.g20.utoronto.ca/2010/g20seoul-doc.pdf [Accessed: 24 October 2017].

G20, 2011a. *The Cannes Action Plan for Growth and Jobs*. 4 November. www.g20.utoronto.ca/2011/2011-cannes-action-111104-en.html [Accessed: 24 October 2017].

G20, 2011b. *Cannes Summit Final Declaration: Building Our Common Future: Renewed Collective Action for the Benefit of All*. 4 November. www.g20.utoronto.ca/2011/2011-cannes-declaration-111104-en.html [Accessed: 24 October 2017].

G20, 2011c. *Final Communiqué [of the] G20 Leaders' Summit, Cannes*. 4 November. www.g20.utoronto.ca/2011/2011-cannes-communiqué-111104-en.html [Accessed: 24 October 2017].

G20, 2012j. *G20 Leaders Declaration*. 19 June. www.g20.utoronto.ca/2012/2012-0619-loscabos.pdf [Accessed: 26 September 2017].

G20, 2012m. *The Los Cabos Growth and Jobs Action Plan*. 19 June. www.g20.utoronto.ca/2012/2012-0619-loscabos-actionplan.pdf [Accessed: 24 October 2017].

G20, 2013a. *Annex 1: St. Petersburg Fiscal Templates: G-20 Advanced Economies*. en.g20russia.ru/load/783139442 and www.g20.utoronto.ca/2013/Annex_1_-_St_Petersburg_Fiscal_Strategies___AEs___FINAL.pdf [Accessed: 28 November 2017].

G20, 2013b. *Annex 2: St. Petersburg Fiscal Templates: G-20 Emerging Economies*. en.g20russia.ru/load/783047026 and www.g20.utoronto.ca/2013/Annex_2_-_St_Petersburg_Fiscal_Strategies___EMEs_FINAL.pdf [Accessed: 28 November 2017].

G20, 2013c. *Annex 3: MAP Policy Templates for all G20 Countries*. en.g20russia.ru/load/783046978 and www.g20.utoronto.ca/2013/Annex_3_MAP_Policy_Commitments_by_Members_September_5.pdf [Accessed: 28 November 2017].

G20, 2013d. *Annex 4: St. Petersburg Accountability Assessment*. en.g20russia.ru/load/783047169 and www.g20.utoronto.ca/2013/Accountabilty_Assessment_FINAL.pdf [Accessed: 28 November 2017].

G20, 2013e. *G20 5th Anniversary Vision Statement*. September. www.g20.utoronto.ca/2013/G20_5th_Anniversary_Vision_Statement.pdf [Accessed: 29 September 2017].

G20, 2013f. *G20 Leaders' Declaration*. 6 September. www.g20.utoronto.ca/2013/Saint_Petersburg_Declaration_ENG.pdf [Accessed: 8 September 2017].

G20, 2013j. *St. Petersburg Action Plan.* www.g20.utoronto.ca/2013/St_Petersburg_Action_Plan.pdf [Accessed: 8 September 2017].

G20, 2013l. *St. Petersburg Strategic Framework for the G20 Anti-Corruption Working Group.* en.g20russia.ru/load/783345715 [Accessed: 28 November 2017].

G20, 2014e. *G20 Leaders' Brisbane Statement on Ebola.* www.g20.utoronto.ca/2014/g20_leaders_brisbane_statement_ebola.pdf [Accessed: 3 October 2017].

G20, 2014f. *G20 Leaders' Communiqué.* www.g20.utoronto.ca/2014/brisbane_g20_leaders_summit_communiqué.pdf [Accessed: 3 October 2017].

G20, 2015a. *G20 Leaders' Communiqué.* www.g20.utoronto.ca/2015/151116-communiqué.pdf [Accessed: 3 October 2017].

G20, 2015b. *G20 Statement on the Fight against Terrorism.* www.g20.utoronto.ca/2015/151116-terrorism.pdf [Accessed: 3 October 2017].

G20, 2016a. *Annex to G20 Leaders' Communiqué.* 5 September. www.g20.utoronto.ca/2016/160905-annex.html [Accessed: 4 October 2017].

G20, 2016k. *G20 Leaders' Communiqué.* 5 September. www.g20.utoronto.ca/2016/160905-communiqué.html [Accessed: 4 October 2017].

G20, 2017f. *G20 Hamburg Action Plan.* 8 July. www.g20.utoronto.ca/2017/2017-g20-hamburg-action-plan-en.pdf [Accessed: 17 October 2017].

G20, 2017g. *G20 Leaders' Declaration.* 8 July. www.g20.utoronto.ca/2017/2017-G20-leaders-declaration.html [Accessed: 4 October 2017].

G20, 2017h. *G20 Leaders' Statement on Countering Terrorism.* 7 July. www.g20.utoronto.ca/2017/170707-counterterrorism.html [Accessed: 4 October 2017].

G20. Anti-Corruption Working Group, 2016. *G20 Anti-Corruption Implementation Plan 2017–2018.* 4 November. bit.ly/2mtztee [Accessed: 24 February 2017].

G20. Development Working Group, 2012. *2012 Progress Report of the Development Working Group.* www.g20.utoronto.ca/2012/2012-0619-dwg.pdf [Accessed: 13 November 2017].

G20 Development Working Group (2016p). *Hangzhou Comprehensive Accountability Report on G20 Development Commitments*, 14 September. http://www.g20.utoronto.ca/2016/hangzhou-accountability-development.pdf [Accessed: 27 November 2018].

G20. Development Working Group, 2017. *Hamburg Annual Progress Report on G20 Development Commitments.* June. www.g20.utoronto.ca/2017/2017-g20-hamburg-annual-progress-report-en.pdf [Accessed: 17 October 2017].

G20 Finance Ministers, 2012. *The G20 Welcomes Major Policy Actions in Europe.* 29 June. www.g20.utoronto.ca/2012/2012-0629-finance.pdf [Accessed: 28 November 2017].

G20 Finance Ministers and Central Bank Governors, 2010. *Communiqué.* Gyeongju, Republic of South Korea. 23 October. www.g20.utoronto.ca/2010/g20finance101023.pdf [Accessed: 28 November 2017].

G20 Framework Working Group, 2016a. *Enhanced Structural Reform Agenda.* 14 September. www.mofa.go.jp/files/000185875.pdf [Accessed: 24 February 2017].

Hajnal, P.I., 2007a. *The G8 System and the G20: Evolution, Role and Documentation.* Global Finance Series. Aldershot: Ashgate.

International Monetary Fund, 2011a. *G-20 Mutual Assessment Process: From Pittsburgh to Cannes: IMF Umbrella Report.* IMF Staff Reports for the G-20 Mutual Assessment Process. www.imf.org/external/np/g20/pdf/110411.pdf [Accessed: 24 October 2017].

International Monetary Fund, 2012b. *Joint Statement by the International Monetary and Financial Committee and the Group of 20 Finance Ministers and Central Bank Governors on IMF Resources.* Washington, DC. 20 April. Press Release 12/144. www.imf.org/external/np/sec/pr/2012/pr12144.htm [Accessed: 28 November 2017].

New Rules for Global Finance, 2012b. *Promises of the G20 Process: Prospects for Advancing Transparency and Accountability*. 18 June. www.new-rules.org/events/3-nr-event/391-promises-of-the-g20 [Accessed: 28 November 2017].

Scholte, J.A., 2011a. Global governance, accountability and civil society. In: J.A. Scholte, ed. *Building Global Democracy? Civil Society and Accountable Global Governance*. Cambridge: Cambridge University Press. pp. 8–41.

10 Other sources of information

In addition to public documents released by the G20 summits and ministerial and other sub-summit bodies (which are discussed in Chapter 9), various other important information sources are available about the G20. This chapter highlights and analyzes several types of such sources: think-tanks and foundations, non-governmental organizations (NGOs) and business groups focusing on the G20; memoirs of prominent former G20 participants; writings about the role of member countries and regions; and websites and social media. The chapter also gives a brief account of academic theses and dissertations, and creative works dealing with the G7/G8 and G20. Contributions by international governmental organizations are covered in Chapters 4 and 9. The problem of archival research related to the G20 is discussed in Chapter 9.

Introduction

There is a growing body of publications about the G20 and related issues. These range from scholarly analyses to compilations of texts; government publications, including parliamentary reviews in summit countries; reports and position papers by NGOs and business groups; memoirs and other writings by prominent former summit participants; reference works of various types; reportage and analysis in newspapers, journals, radio and television; and social media.

Some media accounts are of high quality, based on knowledgeable reporting; prominent examples are the *Financial Times* of London, which follows economic and other summit-related issues the year round and is thus well placed to interpret and analyze fast-breaking news at the summits; and other newspapers of record (the *New York Times*, the *Guardian*, *Le Monde* and others). Other media personnel are often dispatched to the summit by their news organizations simply because they are posted nearby and thus available at lower cost; their work can be uneven. Still others are merely interested in photo opportunities or in 'lifestyle' reporting. Moreover, mainstream media reporting often focuses more on protests and other spectacular events or activities than on the substance of the summits. As well, media attention span can be short. Bernes (2013) writes, 'Two days after the official communiqué was released, the St Petersburg G20 Summit has virtually

DOI: 10.4324/9781351266802-11

disappeared from media commentary. It is quickly becoming the most forgettable of the eight G20 summits held to date'.

Think-tanks and foundations

A number of academic and other think-tanks have studied and analyzed various aspects and activities of the G20. This section describes several such groups.

The Brookings Institution (www.brookings.edu) is a Washington-based, not-for-profit think-tank focusing on research for solving local, national and global problems. Brookings has published widely on the G20 – for example, Bradford and Lim, *Global Leadership in Transition: Making the G20 More Effective and Responsive* (2011b); *The G-20 and Central Banks in the New World of Unconventional Monetary Policy* (2013), written for the Think 20 and comprising chapters by authors from most G20 countries; Derviş Kamal and Peter Drysdale (2014), *The G-20 Summit at Five: Time for Strategic Leadership*; and a blog post by Homi Kharas (2017), 'The G-20 Steadily Progresses'.

Bruegel (www.bruegel.org), a Brussels-based European think-tank, focuses on international economics. Its members are governments of EU countries as well as international corporations and institutions. The G20 is among its main topics of interest. Examples of Bruegel papers are: Angeloni (2011), *The Group of G20: Trials of Global Governance in Times of Crisis*; Angeloni and Pisani-Ferry (2012), *The G20: Characters in Search of an Author*; and Sait Akman (2017), *Key Policy Options for the G20 in 2017 to Support an Open and Inclusive Trade and Investment System*. For some years, Bruegel also produced the *Bruegel G20 Monitor*, with scholarly comment before or after G20 summits and ministerial meetings.

The Centre for Global Studies at the University of Victoria, Canada (www.globalcentres.org), until its mandate changed in 2012, focused on collaborative, policy-oriented research on the impact of globalization on global governance, finance, the environment, security and sustainable development. An example of G20-related publications was a 2011 conference presentation by the Centre's former Director, Gordon Smith, *Getting the Context Right: Essential to Assuring G20's Success* (Smith, 2011c).

The Centre for International Governance Innovation (CIGI) (www.cigionline.org) is a think-tank based in Waterloo, Canada, focusing on global governance in areas of the global economy, global security and politics, and international law, including G20-related issues. CIGI has issued a series of reports, papers and articles on the G20. Some examples are: *Making the G20 Summit Process Work: Some Proposals for Improving Effectiveness and Legitimacy*, by Barry Carin, Paul Heinbecker, Gordon Smith and Ramesh Thakur (2010); *Prescriptions for the G20: The Cannes Summit and Beyond*, edited by Max Brem; Paul Heinbecker (2011a), *The Future of the G20 and Its Place in Global Governance*; Paul Martin (2015), *Strengthening the Multilateral Institutions: A G20 Priority*; and R. Andreas Kraemer (2017), *The G20 and Building Global Governance for 'Climate Refugees'*.

Chatham House (Royal Institute of International Affairs) (www.chathamhouse.org) was founded in 1920. The mission of this venerable institution is 'to help build a sustainably secure, prosperous and just world, through informed debate, independent analysis, new policy ideas, and outreach to audiences' (Chatham House, 2018). Chatham House has held conferences and seminars and produced a number of authoritative papers and other contributions on the G20 and its issues. Two examples of publications are a 2009 report, written by Paola Subacchi and Monsarrat (2009), *New Ideas for the London Summit: Recommendations to the G20 Leaders*, and a 2011 working paper, written by Paola Subacchi and Stephen Pickford, *Legitimacy vs Effectiveness for the G20: A Dynamic Approach to Global Economic Governance*. A recent example of a Chatham House conference is 'Argentina: Political Change and the G20 Presidency', held on 5 June 2018. Another event, scheduled for 23 October 2018, will be 'The G20@10: Benefits, Limitations and the Future of Global Club Governance'.

The Club de Madrid (www.clubmadrid.org) is a group of former heads of state and government from a wide range of countries. Their aim is to bring change for institutional and leadership strengthening, development and the well-being of citizens. This group interacted with the host governments of the 2010 Seoul and 2011 Cannes G20 summits. It prepared a report for the Korean government ahead of the Seoul summit, *The G20's Role in the Post-Crisis World: Final Report* (Club de Madrid, 2010). In 2011 the Club prepared recommendations for French President Sarkozy prior to the Cannes G20 summit, on food security, innovative financing for development, and energy. The Club's members discussed the recommendations in a working lunch with Sarkozy at the Elysée Palace on 9 September. The final report for 2011 was released in time for the Cannes summit (Club de Madrid, 2011). On 30 April 2012 the Club organized a roundtable in Mexico City on the post-crisis world and green growth. It dealt with resources and population growth; green cities; and taxation and fossil fuel subsidies. The main theme of the Club's 2013 annual conference (31 October) was 'Jobs and Inclusive Growth'. A policy dialogue was organized by the Club on 7–8 December 2013 in Coolum Beach Queensland, Australia, with the title 'Societies That Work: Jobs for Inclusive Growth: A Call to the G-20' (Club de Madrid, 2013). *A New Paradigm for Sustainable Development?* (2017) is a product of the Club's Working Group on Environmental Sustainability and Shared Societies; the report has several references to the G20's role.

The US-based Council on Foreign Relations (CFR) launched a project in 2012, bringing together similar foreign policy institutions for discussing global governance issues. The first conference of this new Council of Councils took place on 12–13 March 2012 in Washington, DC. It focused on global governance and multilateral cooperation. Membership of the Council of Councils roughly reflects G20 membership. Its seventh annual conference convened on 6–8 May 2018, with emphasis on trade, Iran, new technologies and climate change (see www.cfr.org/councilofcouncils/events.html).

The Friedrich-Ebert-Stiftung is a German non-profit foundation that 'focuses on the core ideas and values of social democracy – freedom, justice and solidarity' (Friedrich-Ebert-Stiftung, 2012, see https://www.fesdc.org/about/friedrich-ebert-stiftung). Its work involves: political education, think-tanks, international cooperation, support for youth, and preservation of the collective memory of social democracy. Headquartered in Bonn and Berlin, it has regional offices in Germany and offices in several other countries. It has held workshops and conferences and issued publications about the G20. Examples of its G20-related publications are: Rude and Burke (2009), *Towards a Socially Responsible and Democratic Global Economic System: Transparency, Accountability and Governance*; Detlef J. Kotte (2011), *G-20 Two Years after the Crisis: Back to Business as Usual?*; and Ngaire Woods (2018), *When Uncle Sam Stays at Home*.

The G7 Research Group was formed at the University of Toronto in 1987 in the run-up to the 1988 Toronto G7 summit. This 'is a global network of scholars, students and professionals in the academic, research, media, business, non-governmental, governmental and intergovernmental communities who follow the work of the G7, the G8 and related institutions'. Its 'mission [is] to serve as the world's leading independent source of information, analysis and research on the G7/8' (G7 Information Centre, 2018).

Beginning in 1999, the Group's work has included G20-related activities; in early 2008, the separate G20 Research Group was launched, functioning alongside the continuing G8 Research Group (as it then was). Over the years, the two groups have expanded their membership and activities, as well as the level and geographical location of participants. The groups' activities include research and analysis, conferences and seminars, teaching, an extensive publication programme, and the G7 and G20 Information Centre websites managed by the University of Toronto Library. The G7 Information Centre (www.g8.utoronto.ca) and G20 Information Centre (www.g20.utoronto.ca) are permanent, authoritative and comprehensive repositories of available collective documents of the G7, G8 and G20 summits and ministerial and other related documents from the beginning of summitry, including links to materials from and about these fora, as well as a great deal of other material: texts of or links to scholarly publications; analytical studies produced by members of the group; seminar and conference papers; information on research and publications; an online finding aid to the University of Toronto/Trinity College Graham Library's G7/G8 and G20 Research Collections; and extensive links to governmental, international organization and civil society websites relevant to the G7/G and G20 systems. A related project is the BRICS Information Centre, with its own website (www. brics.utoronto.ca).

The Global Summitry Project at the Munk School of Global Affairs (2012) is also a part of the University of Toronto (see globalsummitryproject.com. s197331.gridserver.com). The project's objective is to 'promote . . . examination and research into global governance and the architecture of the contemporary global order'. It publishes the journal *Global Summitry: Politics, Economics and Law in International Governance* (academic.oup.com/globalsummitry), issued at irregular intervals under the Oxford University Press imprint on behalf of the Global Summitry Project and the Rotman School of Business of the University of Toronto. In addition, the project produces the series Global Summitry Reports.

Both the journal and the reports include G20-related items from time to time. Examples are: Gregory Chin and Hugo Dobson (2015), 'China's Presidency of the

G20 Hangzhou: On Global Leadership and Strategy'; Axel Berger and Simon J. Evenett (2018), 'The Trump-Induced G20 Stress Test on Trade: Did the German Presidency Pass?', and Blagovesta Tacheva (2013), *Global Health Governance: Challenges, Efforts, and the G20.*

The Heinrich Böll Stiftung (www.boell.org), with headquarters in Berlin and offices in a number of countries, is a not-for-profit foundation whose concerns include democracy, education and culture, ecology, economic and social issues, and international politics. Its Washington office (us.boell.org) has a portal, 'G20 in Focus' (2018, www.boell.de/en/g20-germany-2017), as well as the *Just Governance* blog series, which includes a number of G20-related postings (justgovernance.boellblog.org) and the 'B20 Dossier', which focuses on the business sector. Examples of their publications are: *The G20: Playing Outside the Big Tent: Implications for Rio+20* (Alexander and Riggs, 2012); Alexander, Schuele and Löschmann (2016) *The G7 and G20 in the Global Governance Landscape*; Löschmann and Alexander (2016), *The Solar System of G20: Engagement Groups*; Katharina Keil (2017), *The G20 Compact with Africa: Innovative Partnerships or Business as Usual?*; and Alexander (2018b), *The Priorities of Argentina's G20 Presidency.*

The Interaction Council (interactioncouncil.org) was established in 1983. Its members are some former heads of state and government of a number of countries; they convene annual plenary meetings and issue policy recommendations on: peace and security, economic development, environment and ecology, arms control and disarmament, and religion and universal ethical standards. The Council has created high-level expert groups on its areas of focus. In the past, some recommendations were addressed to the G7 and G8 leaders; more recently, the Council's annual communiqués refer occasionally to the G20. For example, the *Final Communiqué* of the 2011 plenary meeting notes that '[w]hile a coordinated approach by the G20 has prevented a depression, the financial crisis is not yet over' and encourages 'implementation of the agreements reached at the G20 Summit in Pittsburgh in 2009' (Interaction Council, 2011). The 2012 *Final Communiqué* argues that '[t]he G20 has replaced the G8 in managing global challenges, especially the financial crisis' and recommends that 'the G20 continue to take the predominant leadership role that it took during the early days of the financial crisis' (Interaction Council, 2012).

The Peterson Institute for International Economics (www.piie.com) is a prestigious not-for-profit research institution in the area of international economic policy, including G7/G8-G20-related matters. Examples of its publications are: Edwin M. Truman (2011), *G-20 Reforms of the International Monetary System: An Evaluation*; a 20 October 2011 testimony before the US Senate by C. Fred Bergsten, the Institute's founding Director, entitled *An Action Plan for the G-20*; 'The G-20 Is Failing' (US, Congress, 2011), *Foreign Policy*, 12 April (also by Truman, 2012); Luiz Awazu Pereira da Silva's 2013 remarks at a conference, *From Currency Wars to Policy Peace under the G-20*; Jan Zilinsky and Cathleen Cimino-Isaacs (2016), *Slow Trade Growth and the G20 Response*; and Sean Miner (2016), *What Can China Accomplish with Its G-20 Presidency?*

The Stanley Foundation (www.stanleyfoundation.org) is a not-for-profit foundation created in 1956. It focuses on multilateralism, a rules-based international system, peace and security and other global challenges. The G8 and the G20 were among its areas of interest in earlier years. Examples of publications are: *Shifting Coalitions and Potential Blocs for Asian and Pacific Leadership in the G-20* (2012); *The G-20 and Food Security: What Is the Right Agenda?*, by Sophia Murray (2013); and Joshua Busby (2013), *The G-20 and Climate Change: Beyond Goal Setting at Brisbane.*

Other civil society studies and policy papers

Apart from think-tanks and not-for-profit foundations (which are part of the broad spectrum of civil society), NGOs and other civil society organizations (CSOs) issue publications and releases on the G20. Examples follow:

- IBON International, 2010. *What Is Missing in the G20 Agenda? Redressing Structural Imbalances for Equity, Justice and Sustainability.* 8 October, by Paul Quintos.
- Oxfam, 2010. *The Making of a Seoul Development Consensus: The Essential Development Agenda for the G-20.* Oxfam Briefing Note. 11 October.
- Oxfam, 2012b. *Left Behind by the G20? How Inequality and Environmental Degradation Threaten to Exclude Poor People from the Benefits of Economic Growth.* Oxfam Briefing Paper, No. 157. 19 January.
- G20 Research Group, 2017. *2016 Hangzhou G20 Summit Final Compliance Report, 6 September 2016 to 6 July 2017.*
- New Rules for Global Finance, 2012b. *Promises of the G20 Process: Prospects for Enhanced Transparency and Accountability.* 18 June.
- New Rules for Global Finance, 2013. *Global Financial Governance & Impact Report 2013: Tax Rule-Making Bodies*, by Jo Marie Griesgraber.
- G20 Interfaith Summit, 2017b. *Religion, Sustainable Development, and the Refugee Crisis.*
- G20 Update, 2012. *Ingredients for a Successful G20 Presidency: A Civil Society Perspective.* 14 (December) by John Ruthrauff and Robert Lovelace.
- Overseas Development Institute, 2012. *Accountability and Effectiveness of the G20's Role in Promoting Development: Analysis, Views, Annotated Bibliography and Workshop Report.* Paper prepared for the Workshop on an Accountability Mechanism for G20 Development Commitments, Bali, Indonesia, 3 October, coordinated by Dirk Te Velde.
- InterAction and G7/G20 Advocacy Alliance, 2018. *2018 G20 Summit Recommendations.* G20 Policy Paper.

The business sector

The business sector and groups representing business interests have been actively involved in dialogue and advocacy with the G20. (See Chapter 5 for more detail.)

This is reflected by their publications, some of which are presented here as examples.

Before the Cannes G20 summit, the International Chamber of Commerce published a short handbook describing the G20 and its membership, and its relationship with business and civil society; and analysing the Washington, London, Pittsburgh, Toronto and Seoul G20 summits. It also sketched the prospects for the Cannes summit and discussed the G20 agenda and decision-making process (Kassum, 2011). In 2014, the ICC produced the *Global Survey of Business Policy Priorities for G20 Leaders*. The ICC also weighed in with its evaluations of G20 performance with its *G20 Business Scorecard* series; the sixth (2016a) edition covers 2016.

The B20 or 'Business 20' is an influential business interest group that has convened its parallel summits at the time of G20 summits since June 2010. This forum has privileged access to G20 leaders and officials, and has exerted considerable influence on G20 deliberations and decisions. Its 2017 recommendations illustrate their activities: *B20 Germany Recommendations Summary*.

The World Economic Forum is a highly influential and exclusive business interest group that is interested in all aspects of global governance, including G7/G8 and G20 issues. It has been the preferred venue for G7/G8 and G20 leaders to unveil their agenda for the forthcoming summit. One of its 2012 publications is *Euro, Dollar, Yuan Uncertainties: Scenarios on the Future of the International Monetary System* (World Scenario Series, June 2012a). A more recent example is the Chinese President's 2017 keynote address, *Opening Plenary with Xi Jinping, President of the People's Republic of China* (World Economic Forum, 2017).

Memoirs

Memoirs of former leaders, ministers and other officials of the G20 are useful sources of inside information and personal observations. For example, former Canadian Prime Minister and former Finance Minister Paul Martin's 2008 memoir, *Hell or High Water: My Life in and out of Politics*, describes the antecedents and establishment of the G20, at both the ministers'/central bank governors' and leaders' levels. Former UK Prime Minister Gordon Brown's 2010 book, *Beyond the Crash*, provides details of the leaders' dinners and working sessions and explains the dynamics, agreements and disagreements among the participants. Former UK Prime Minister Tony Blair's 2010 memoir, *A Journey: My Political Life*, is also useful. By contrast, George W. Bush's book, *Decision Points*, pays scant attention to the G20 despite the fact that he convened the first G20 summit in Washington in 2008. Two former French Prime Ministers, Nicolas Sarkozy (2016) and François Hollande (2018), published memoirs, entitled respectively *La France pour la vie* and *Les leçons du pouvoir*, which include reminiscences of 'G' summits.

Other former leaders will likely have something to say about the G20 summits that met during their tenure, particularly the summits that they hosted. Angela Merkel (likely after her time in government ends) bears watching, as do Vladimir Putin of Russia, Stephen Harper of Canada and other former political leaders.

G20-related writings about the role of member countries and regions

There is a growing body of literature focusing on the role and position of individual members and regions in the G20. Some examples follow, covering the majority of G20 countries:

- Acharya, A. 'Can Asia Lead? Power Ambitions and Global Governance in the 21st Century', in *International Affairs*.
- Alexander, N. *The G20, Latin America, and the Future of Regional Integration.*
- Bowles, P. 'ASEAN and the G8: Potentially Productive Partners or Two Ships Passing in the Night?', in *Emerging Powers in Global Governance: Lessons from the Heiligendamm Process.*
- Callaghan, M. *Playbook for the G20 Brisbane Summit.*
- Gnath, K., and Schmucker, C. *L'Allemagne et les 'clubs G'* [Germany and the 'G' Clubs].
- He, A. *The Dragon's Footprints: China in the Global Economic Governance System under the G20 Framework.*
- Hermawan, Y.P., Sriyuliani, W., Hardjowijono, G.H. and Tanaga, S. *The Role of Indonesia in the G-20: Background, Role and Objectives of Indonesia's Membership.*
- Huigens, J. and Niemann, A. *The EU within the G8: A Case of Ambiguous and Contested Actorness.*
- Kirton, J.J. *China's G20 Leadership.*
- Lee, D.H. *The G20 in Korea's Diplomacy.*
- Lins, M.A.D.T., and Silva, P. 'Brazil and the G20: Recent Development Strategy and Strength among 'New' Emerging Economies', in *G20: Perceptions and Perspectives for Global Governance.*
- Persini, C. ed. *G20: les enjeux de la présidence française.*
- Vickers, B. 'South Africa: Global Reformism, Global Apartheid, and the Heiligendamm Process', in *Emerging Powers in Global Governance: Lessons from the Heiligendamm Process.*

Additionally, the 2010 special issue of *Studia Diplomatica* had a number of examples of such literature:

- Chin, G. *The Emerging Countries and China in the G20: Reshaping Global Economic Governance. The Future of the G8 and G20.*
- Debaere, P. *The Output and Input Dimension of the European Representation in the G20. The Future of the G8 and G20.*
- Larionova, M. *Is It G8 or G20? For Russia, of Course, It's Both. The Future of the G8 and G20.*
- Lesage, D., and Kaçar, Y. *Turkey's Profile in the G20: Emerging Economy, Middle Power and Bridge-Builder. The Future of the G8 and G20.*
- Wright, T. *The United States and the G20. The Future of the G8 and G20.*

An important undertaking of CIGI, the National Perspectives on Global Leadership (NPGL) project, was launched in April 2009 and ran until 2012. Under the leadership of Colin Bradford, NPGL worked with

> leading think tanks in a dozen G20 countries to observe how national publics perceive[d] their leaders at global summits, as seen through the lens of leading media outlets in each of their capitals. Their findings . . . [were] published online as short, interpretive commentaries under the general title NPGL Soundings.
>
> (CIGI, 2011, p. 7)

> The NPGL Soundings series covered the following G8 and G20 summits (some covered more than one summit): London (G20), L'Aquila (G8), Pittsburgh (G20), Muskoka (G8), Toronto (G20), Seoul (G20), Cannes (G20) and Los Cabos (G20).
>
> (CIGI, 2012)

Theses and dissertations on the G7, G8 and G20

Various topics associated with the G7/G8 and G20 have stimulated academic work resulting in master's theses and doctoral dissertations. Some examples follow:

- Baker, A., 2000. *The Politics of G7 Co-operation in the 1990s: Global Finance, Macroeconomic Policy and Multi-dimensional Diplomacy*. DPhil dissertation. Belfast: University of Ulster.
- Böhm, E., 2013. *Die Sicherheit des Westens: Entstehung und Funktion der G7-Gipfel* [Western security: Development and function of the G7 summit]. Oldenbourg Verlag. PhD dissertation, Marburg: Philipps-Universität Marburg.
- Brokest, E., 2016. *Dissent Denied: Public Order Policing and the Criminalization of Protest at the 2010 Toronto G20*. Master's thesis (Canadian studies and indigenous studies). Peterborough, Canada: Trent University.
- Cao L.J., 2004. *Ba Guo Ji Tuan Yan Jiu Cong G7 Dao G8* [Research on the G8: From G7 to G8]. PhD dissertation (international relations). Beijing: Party School of the Central Committee of the Communist Party of China.
- Debaere, P., 2014. *Internal EU Coordination for the G7, G8 and G20*. Ghent University.
- Gingras, A.T., 2010. *Pre-emptive Peace: Collective Security & Rogue States in the 21st Century*. [Includes analyses of the G8 and its Foreign Ministers' forum and the idea of a G20 Foreign Ministers' forum.] Master's thesis. Uppsala: Uppsala Universitet, Dept. of Peace and Conflict Research.
- Kamel, M., 2015. *International Monetary and Financial Negotiations in Times of Crises: The G20 Leaders' Summits (2008–2011)*. University of Cambridge.
- Von Kleestein, M., 2014. *G7, G8 und G20. Internationale Organisationen und deren Rollenverständnis*. Stuttgart: Hochschule für Wirtschaft und Umwelt Nürtingen-Geislingen.

- Kokotsis, E., 1998. *National Compliance with G7 Environment and Development Commitments, 1988–1995*. PhD dissertation (political economy). Toronto: University of Toronto.
- Lees, N.D.M., 2013. *The Evolution of International Inequality: Justice, Order and North-South Relations from the NIEO to the G20*. University of Oxford.
- Li S.C., 2011. *Quan Qiu Zhi Li Shi Ye Xia De G20 Yan Jiu* [G20 research from the perspective of global governance]. PhD (international relations). Shanghai Social Science Institute.
- Panova, V., 2005. *Deiatel'nost' Mekhanizmov Mnogostoronnego Vzaimodeistviia v Sfere Predotvrashcheniia i Uregulirovaniia Konfliktov (na Primere 'Bol'shoi Vos'merki'), 1991–2004 Gody*. [The G8 and its role in conflict management, 1991–2004]. PhD dissertation (history of international relations and foreign policy). Moscow: MGIMO University.
- Scherrer, A., 2007. *La production normative du G8 face à la 'criminalité transnationale organisée' (1989–2005): la force du discours, le poids de l'expertise* [Normative action of the G8 vis-à-vis international organized crime]. PhD dissertation (political science and international relations). Paris: Institut d'Etudes politiques [Sciences Po].
- Xu T., 2010. *Quan Qiu Qi Hou Zhi Li Zhong De Fei Zheng Shi Guo Ji Ji Zhi Yan Jiu: Yi Ba Guo Ji Tuan Wei Li* [The informal international institution in global climate governance: The case of the G8]. PhD dissertation (international relations). Shanghai: Shanghai International Studies University.

Creative works about or around G8 and G20 summits

G8 and G20 summits have inspired some works of fiction (books, plays and films), art exhibitions and other creative works, with greater or lesser actual connection to the summits. Some examples are as follows:

- *Girl in the Café*. A 2005 film by British screenwriter Richard Curtis. Its plot, enlivened by depictions of NGO advocacy and love interest, is a semi-fictional depiction of the 2005 Gleneagles G8 summit. In this film, the summit takes place in Reykjavik, Iceland.
- Hurd, Douglas. 1998. *The Shape of Ice*. London: Little, Brown. The plot of this novel, written by the former UK Foreign Secretary, unfolds during the tenure of a fictitious UK Prime Minister, including his role at a notional G8 summit in Halifax. (The only 'G' summit in Halifax was the 1995 G7 summit.)
- Jenkell, Laurence. 2011. *Jenkell, parcours: sculptures en plein Coeur de Cannes*. Exhibition catalogue of the French sculptor, whose style mixes pop art and new realism. This exhibition consisted of colourful 2-metre-high free-standing sculptures of sweets wrapped in the images of flags of each G20 member, including the EU, as well as of each invited country (United Arab Emirates, Spain, Ethiopia, Equatorial Guinea and Singapore).
- Rankin, Ian. 2006. *The Naming of the Dead*. London: Orion. A murder mystery with the Gleneagles summit as background.

- Taylor, Tommy. *You Should Have Stayed Home.* A 2011 play about the G20 street protests in Toronto, adapted by the playwright from his notes posted on Facebook following his arrest and detention during the Toronto summit. The Facebook entry was entitled 'How I Got Arrested and Abused at the G20 in Toronto, Canada'.
- Vicari, Daniele. *Diaz: Don't Clean Up This Blood.* A 2013 film about the 2001 Genoa G8 protests.

G20 host countries have produced elaborate entertainment for the leaders and their spouses, as well as (sometimes) separate programmes for the attending media. These are designed to put forward the best in culture and way of life of the host country. For example, the hosts of the 2016 Hangzhou summit staged 'Impressions of West Lake', an outdoor musical performed at Hangzhou's scenic attraction, West Lake. The musical is based on the Legend of White Snake, an old Chinese folk story. It was directed by the renowned Zhang Yimou, who was also involved in the opening ceremony of the 2008 Beijing Olympics. The German hosts of the 2017 Hamburg summit chose the Great Concert Hall of the city's new Elbphilharmonie. The programme featured the Hamburg State Philharmonic Orchestra, directed by Kent Nagano. They played Beethoven's Ninth Symphony, Opus 125. The entertainment programmes, as well as the summit handouts to attending media personnel, can be viewed as the host country's efforts at self-legitimation. This aspect of the G20 (and G7) is explored by Gronau (2015).

Websites and web content

G7 and G8 summit host countries have created official websites since the 1995 Halifax G7 summit. The G20 Finance Ministers' and Central Bank Governors' forum has had a website since its beginning (1999), and this practice has been continued by host governments of each leaders' summit beginning with 2008, although, starting in 2012, the G20 summit hosts' official websites have subsumed the separate ministerial sites, with some loss of content. These official websites are discussed in Chapter 9.

A number of international governmental organizations, some non-G20 member governments, think-tanks and other civil society groups and business interest groups have websites dedicated to the G20 or other web content reflecting G20 information, scholarship, analysis or advocacy. Many examples of text available on those websites are cited in Chapters 4 (IGOs), 5 (business) and 6 (civil society).

Some examples are given ahead.

Engagement groups

- B20 (business sector): www.b20argentina.info is the latest version of the website. It has copious information about this G20 engagement group: organizational structure, list of past and future events, sectoral task forces, news releases, and papers, reports and statements.

- C20 (civil society): The website civil-20.org contains information on its current working groups, list of events, news items, papers, statements and communiqués, and contact information.
- L20 (labour organizations): www.l20argentina.org is the latest incarnation of its website. It has information about the labour groups and their priorities, statement, reports and other documents, news items and contact information.
- S20 (academies of sciences): Its website, www.s20argentina.org, provides information about its leadership, structure, programmes, speakers and chairs, and contact information.
- T20 (think-tanks): includes on the latest version of its website, t20argentina.org, information about its task forces and team leaders, documents, policy briefs, and the usual contact information.
- W20 (women): This G20 engagement group also has its website, w20argentina.com, including focus topics, events, news, international and national dialogue, and past and current publications.
- The final G20 engagement group in Argentina is the Y20 (youth). Its website, youth20.org, provides information on the priorities of this forum of young leaders. It also has links to reports and other publications.

International governmental organizations

The International Monetary Fund's web page, *IMF and the Group of Twenty* (www.imf.org/external/np/g20), provides information on the IMF's relations and activities with the G20. It includes references to principal documents of G20 at both the leaders' and Finance Ministers and Central Bank Governors' levels, and the IMF's related activities, with links to relevant documents – for example, the Managing Director's statements to summits, staff reports under the Mutual Assessment Process (see Chapter 8 for details) and pre-summit surveillance notes on global economic prospects.

The OECD has a web page (www.oecd.org/g20) devoted to its relations with, and work for, the G20. The page includes a brief history of OECD-G20 relations, and links to major recent reports that the organization prepared for the G20, related other reports, speeches and articles, and further information.

Other IGOs have substantial G20-related information – for example, the UN, the World Bank, and the Bank for International Settlements. See Chapters 4 and 9 for details.

Social media use during the 2017 Hamburg G20 summit

The author thanks Gillian Clinton for researching and writing this section

Social media are variously defined as interactive, Internet-based communities that facilitate the creation and sharing of information and other forms of expression

(Tech Terms, 2017; Wikipedia, 2017). For nearly a decade, G7/G8 and G20 summit hosts have been reaching out to stakeholders and the general public using a changing variety of social media platforms.

The 2017 G20 summit, held in Hamburg, Germany, on 7–8 July, provided links from its website to five social media platforms: Twitter, YouTube, RSS Feeds, Facebook and Instagram. Unlike the German G7 summit of 2015, Flickr was not included. For this section, 'snapshots' of online activity were taken during the summit as well as ten days before and after the event.

Prior to the summit, the website (g20.org) included links to dialogues with the engagement groups: Business20, Civil20, Labour20, Science20, Women20, Think20 and Youth20. On the actual summit dates, the website posted photos, podcasts, articles and speeches related to attendees and their activities. Daily summaries were provided covering events and accomplishments. Declarations and associated documents as well as the final summary, *The Outcomes of the G20 Summit*, listing ten achievements (Germany, 2017), were posted afterwards.

Apart from the website, most of the German government's social media activity took place on Twitter (@RegSprecher) and Facebook (www.facebook.com/Bundesregierung). Tweets were fed directly to the German federal government's Facebook page. Twitter enables short messages, often including links to more detailed text or image posts, to be tagged by topic and easily shared. Prior to the summit, the feed consisted primarily of police posts regarding security and safety as well as some from the local telephone company regarding communications. 'Hamburg police at one point issued a statement via Twitter in which they clarified that reports of the employment of nuclear weapons in the city were taken from a satirical news website' (Oltermann, 2017). Tweets were primarily in German, with some translated into English and retweeted. Many tweets were accompanied by photos, which was not always the case in the early years. G20-related topics throughout Twitter were primarily identified by #G20, #Merkel and #G20Summit.

During the summit, the vast majority of tweets by the public were in English, using #G20 or #G20Summit, and referenced US President Trump – usually in a negative context. Furthermore, #G20 was in the top 100 trending hashtags on Twitter, with thousands of tweets per hour. However, within a few days of the summit's ending, almost all references to it ceased.

The German federal government's (Bundesregierung) Facebook page posted G20 videos as well as lists (in German and English) for fact-checking 'false news' (*Faktencheck*). During the summit, the page featured a number of images (captioned in both English and German) and videos (in German). Posts and comments were predominantly in German with some in English, although the automatic translation feature was active and fairly accurate. Post-summit, the Bundesregierung page was still posting discussions about the value of the G20 and other summits. Specific topics included global health, occupational safety and photos of attendees. Another interest-based social networking platform, Google+, had hundreds of G20-related posts by individuals during and for some time after the summit. These ranged from images of the riots and their aftermath to such analyses of the summit results as *G20 Leaves Three Billion People Out in the Cold,* which links to a geopolitical weblog (globalgeopolitics.net/ggnarc/2017/07/18/g20-leaves-three-billion-people-out-in-the-cold). There were even posts by aircraft enthusiasts extolling the variety of planes 'spotted' at Hamburg airport due to the summit.

The federal government's YouTube video-sharing channel was not used much by the G20 host, although there were several thousand summit-related videos on the main YouTube site posted by news services, such as the BBC, as well as the public. The German government posted only three German-language videos during the conference, which received several hundred views each at the time (quite low for this medium).

An RSS feed was linked to the main G20 website but appeared to be about 12–24 hours behind in getting information out and provided only one to two feeds per day, which focused on such things as the Spouses' Programme and summaries of each day's discussion topics. Two additional posts were made summarizing summit outcomes.

The German government's mobile phone image-sharing platform on Instagram was used during the summit to display informal photographs with descriptive text in German and English. Viewer comments were primarily in German.

There was some limited use of other forms of social media, such as podcasts (digital audio/video broadcasts) – several official German-language posts and many news podcasts covered the G20 summit on such sites as US National Public Radio (NPR), Canada's CBC, the BBC and private stations within Germany. In addition, there was a page on Wikipedia, the online, open-access encyclopaedia, entitled '2017 G20 Hamburg Summit', which contained images of all the participants as well as links to other Wikipedia pages with details about each person or organization. A Results section has been added and what were formerly the Agenda topics, such as Women's Economic Empowerment or Refugees and European Migrant Crisis, have now been filled in with summaries. Another section covered the protests, including a chronology, and there were links to over 60 references to articles and websites covering various aspects of the summit.

Social media use by G20 participants

The German federal government made available to the participants and accredited observers a Social Media Area, which facilitated professional social media reporting, including a live-stream studio and technician. The ability for the staff of world leaders to upload live events proved popular and many leaders had their one-on-one meetings linked to their Facebook or YouTube sites. As well, over half of the heads of state were tweeting about both the main meetings and their one-on-one side meetings.

The following G20 members do not appear to use social media at all: China, Japan, South Korea, Saudi Arabia, Turkey and South Africa. Italy made minimal use of Twitter and Facebook. Russia appeared to prefer Facebook, while Brazil, the EU, France, India, the UK and the US primarily used Twitter. Argentina, Australia, Canada, Germany, Indonesia and Mexico used both equally.

Social media use by G20 protesters

NGO protesters ranged from organizations such as Greenpeace and Oxfam – Greenpeace issued press releases on its website documenting its actions while Oxfam issued both press releases and communiqués analysing the summit – to militant anarchists, whose demonstration was called 'Welcome to Hell' and whose mostly German-language website included *An Anarchist Guide to the 2017 G20 Summit in Hamburg* (CrimethInc, 2017), with an overview of planned demonstrations. In addition, 170 organizations banded together as G20: Not Welcome and included representatives of Germany's socialist parties, trade unions and Communist Party. They had their own website (g20-protest.info) with links to newsletters beforehand and an information sheet containing maps, contact information (including access to a legal team in the event the protester was arrested), a schedule of demonstrations, and Facebook (@g20 international) and Twitter (@NoG20_Inter) accounts.

Conclusion

Although public documents released by the G20 summits and ministerial and other sub-summit bodies are the main primary sources of public information on that forum, they must be supplemented by other important information sources about the G20: the output of think-tanks and foundations, NGOs and business groups interested in the G20; memoirs of prominent former G20 participants; works about the role of member countries and regions; websites and social media; and academic theses and dissertations. Some films, plays, books and works of fine art have chosen as their subject or background the G7, G8 and G20; they afford a view through a creative lens. All such sources have important research potential for gaining a fuller understanding of the G20 and its context and activities.

References

Akman, S., et al., 2017. *Key Policy Options for the G20 in 2017 to Support an Open and Inclusive Trade and Investment System*. 3 April. bruegel.org/2017/04/key-policy-options-for-the-g20-in-2017-to-support-an-open-and-inclusive-trade-and-investment-system [Accessed: 11 June 2018].

Alexander, N., 2018a. *Just Governance* [blog]. justgovernance.boellblog.org/ [Accessed: 15 August 2018].

Alexander, N., 2018b. *The Priorities of Argentina's Presidency*. 5 January. us.boell.org/2018/01/05/priorities-argentinas-g20-presidency [Accessed: 3 August 2018].

Alexander, N. and Riggs, P., 2012. *The G20: Playing Outside the Big Tent: Implications for Rio+20*. Washington: Heinrich Böll Stiftung North America. June. us.boell.org/2012/06/08/g20-playing-outside-big-tent [Accessed: 27 March 2018].

Alexander, N., Schuele, W. and Löschmann, H., 2016. *The G7 and G20 in the Global Governance Landscape*. 30 November. us.boell.org/2016/11/30/g7-and-g20-global-governance-landscape [Accessed: 15 June 2018].

Angeloni, I., 2011. *The Group of G20: Trials of Global Governance in Times of Crisis*. Bruegel Working Paper 2011/12. bruegel.org/2011/12/the-group-of-g20-trials-of-global-governance-in-times-of-crisis/ [Accessed: 27 March 2018].

Angeloni, I. and Pisani-Ferry, J., 2012. *The G20: Characters in Search of an Author*. Bruegel Working Paper. March. bruegel.org/2012/03/the-g20-characters-in-search-of-an-author/ [Accessed: 27 March 2018].

Berger, A. and Evenett, S.J., 2018. The Trump-Induced G20 Stress Test on trade: Did the German presidency pass? *Global Summitry: Politics, Economics and Law in International Governance*. 17 May. academic.oup.com/globalsummitry/advance-article-abstract/doi/10.1093/global/guy002/4999066?redirectedFrom=fulltext [Accessed: 3 August 2018].

Bernes, T.A., 2013. *Ho Hum . . . On to Brisbane*. G20 St Petersburg Rapid Response. Waterloo, Canada: Centre for International Governance Innovation. 9 September. www.cigionline.org/publications/ho-humon-brisbane [Accessed: 6 July 2018].

Blair, T., 2010. *A Journey: My Political Life*. London: Hutchinson.

Bradford, C.I. and Lim, W.H. eds., 2011b. *Global Leadership in Transition: Making the G20 More Effective and Responsive*. Washington, DC: Brookings Institution Press with Korean Development Institute.

Brem, M. ed., 2011b. *Prescriptions for the G20: The Cannes Summit and Beyond*. Waterloo, Canada: Centre for International Governance Innovation. www.cigionline.org/series/prescriptions-g20-cannes-summit-and-beyond [Accessed: 13 April 2018].

Brookings Institution, 2013. *Think Tank 20: The G-20 and Central Banks in the New World of Unconventional Monetary Policy*. August. www.brookings.edu/research/think-tank-20-the-g-20-and-central-banks-in-the-new-world-of-unconventional-monetary-policy/ [Accessed: 13 April 2018].

Brown, G., 2010. *Beyond the Crash: Overcoming the First Crisis of Globalization*. New York and London: Free Press.

Busby, J., 2013. *The G-20 and Climate Change: Beyond Goal Setting at Brisbane*. December. www.stanleyfoundation.org/publications/other/BusbyGg20ClimateChangeBeyondGoalsSettingBrisbane.pdf [Accessed: 19 June 2018].

Bush, G.W., 2010. *Decision Points*. New York: Crown Publishers.

Carin, B., Heinbecker, P., Smith, G. and Thakur, R., 2010. *Making the G20 Summit Process Work: Some Proposals for Improving Effectiveness and Legitimacy*. CIGI G20 Paper No. 2. June. Waterloo, Canada: Centre for International Governance Innovation. www.cigionline.org/sites/default/files/g20_no2_1.pdf [Accessed: 22 February 2018].

Centre for International Governance Innovation, 2012. *National Perspectives on Global Leadership during the Los Cabos G20 Summit*. Soundings Series No. 7. 27 July. www.cigionline.org/publications/national-perspectives-global-leadership-during-los-cabos-g20-summit [Accessed: 13 April 2018].

Centre for International Governance Innovation and Brookings Institution, 2011. *National Perspectives on Global Leadership: Summitry and Public Perceptions*. Soundings Series. www.cigionline.org/sites/default/files/npglv2_0.pdf [Accessed: 15 August 2018].

Chatham House, 2018. *Our Mission*. www.chathamhouse.org/about/mission [Accessed: 15 August 2018].

Chin, G. and Dobson, H., 2015. China's presidency of the G20 Hangzhou: On global leadership and strategy. *Global Summitry: Politics, Economics and Law in International Governance*, 1(2), pp. 151–170. academic.oup.com/globalsummitry/article/1/2/151/2363169 [Accessed: 14 June 2018].

Club de Madrid, 2010. *The G20's Role in the Post-Crisis World: Final Report*. Seoul: Club de Madrid; FRIDE; Government of Korea. www.clubmadrid.org/wp-content/uploads/2017/10/G20_FINAL_REPORT.pdf [Accessed: 13 April 2018].

Club de Madrid, 2011. *The G20's Role in the Post-Crisis World: Briefing Book*. Madrid: Club de Madrid. www.clubmadrid.org/img/secciones/G20-France_Report_2011.pdf [Accessed: 21 May 2012].

Club de Madrid, 2013. *Societies That Work: Jobs for Inclusive Growth: A Call to the G-20*. www.clubmadrid.org/policy-dialogue/2013/ [Accessed: 11 June 2018].

Club de Madrid, 2017. *A New Paradigm for Sustainable Development?* www.clubmadrid.org/wp-content/uploads/2017/11/Shared_Societies-Report-13.pdf [Accessed: 11 June 2018].

CrimethInc, 2017. *An Anarchist Guide to the 2017 G20 Summit in Hamburg: With a Review of Previous G8 and G20 Protests*. 26 June. crimethinc.com/2017/06/26/an-anarchist-guide-to-the-2017-g20-summit-in-hamburg-with-a-review-of-previous-g8-and-g20-protests [Accessed: 7 August 2018].

Friedrich-Ebert-Stiftung, 2012. *Friedrich-Ebert-Stiftung*. www.fesdc.org/about/friedrich-ebert-stiftung/ [Accessed: 13 April 2018].

G7 Information Centre, 2018. *About the G7 and G8 Research Group*. www.g8.utoronto.ca/about/index.html [Accessed: 14 June 2018].

G20 Research Group, 2017. *2016 Hangzhou G20 Summit Final Compliance Report, 6 September 2016 to 6 July 2017*. 23 October. www.g20.utoronto.ca/compliance/2016hangzhou-final/2016-g20-final-compliance.pdf [Accessed: 11 May 2018].

G20 Interfaith Forum, 2017b. *Interfaith Summit: Religion, Sustainable Development and the Refugee Crisis*. www.g20interfaith.org/content/g20-interfaith-summit-2017-potsdam [Accessed: 15 August 2018].

Germany, Bundesregierung, 2017. *The Outcomes of the G20 Summit: Tangible Progress Made*. 12 July. www.bundesregierung.de/Content/EN/Artikel/2017/07_en/2017-07-11-g20-10-erfolge_en.html [Accessed: 7 August 2018].

Global Summitry Project and Rotman School of Business. *Global Summitry: Politics, Economics, and Law in International Governance*. Oxford: Oxford University Press. academic.oup.com/globalsummitry [Accessed: 3 August 2018].

Gronau, J., 2015. *Die Selbstlegitimation internationaler Institutionen. G8 und G20 im Vergleich*. Frankfurt am Main and New York: Campus.

Heinbecker, P., 2011a. *The Future of the G20 and Its Place in Global Governance*. CIGI G20 Papers, No. 5. Waterloo, Canada: Centre for International Governance Innovation. 27 April. www.cigionline.org/sites/default/files/g20no5.pdf [Accessed: 11 June 2018].

Heinrich Böll Stiftung, 2018. *G20 in Focus*. www.boell.de/en/g20-germany-2017 [Accessed: 15 August 2018].

Heinrich Böll Stiftung North America, 2012a. *Business 20 (B-20) Dossier*. www.boell.org/web/group_of_20-B20-Dossier.html [Accessed: 29 December 2012].

Heinrich Böll Stiftung North America, 2012b. *G20 Dossier*. www.boell.org/web/group_of_20.html [Accessed: 29 December 2012].

Hollande, F., 2018. *Les leçons du pouvoir*. Paris: Stock.

InterAction Council, 2011. *Final Communiqué: 29th Annual Plenary Meeting*. 29–31 May. www.interactioncouncil org/publications/29th-annual-plenary-meeting [Accessed: 3 August 2018].

InterAction Council, 2012. *Final Communiqué*. 10–12 May. www.interactioncouncil.org/publications/30th-annual-plenary-meeting [Accessed: 15 June 2018].

InterAction and G7/G20 Advocacy Alliance, 2018. *2018 G20 Summit Recommendations*. G20 Policy Paper. March. reliefweb.int/sites/reliefweb.int/files/resources/G20-Policy-Paper-2018.pdf [Accessed: 14 May 2018].

International Chamber of Commerce, 2014. *Global Survey of Business Policy Priorities for G20 Leaders*. cdn.iccwbo.org/content/uploads/sites/3/2016/11/ICC-survey-results-Global-survey-of-business-policy-priorities-for-G20-leaders-2014.pdf [Accessed: 24 November 2017].

International Chamber of Commerce, 2016a. *ICC G20 Business Scorecard*, 6th ed. December. cdn.iccwbo.org/content/uploads/sites/3/2017/01/ICC-G20-Business-Scorecard-December-2016.pdf [Accessed: 17 May 2018].

Kamal, D. and Drysdale, P., 2014. *The G-20 Summit at Five: Time for Strategic Leadership*. Washington, DC: Brookings Institution Press.

Kassum, J., 2011. *The G20: What It Is and What It Does: A Business Guide*. ICC Publication, 730E. Paris: International Chamber of Commerce.

Keil, K., 2017. *The G20 Compact with Africa: Innovation Partnership or Business as Usual?* Heinrich Böll Stiftung North America. 13 December. us.boell.org/2017/12/13/g20-compact-africa-innovative-partnerships-or-business-usual [Accessed: 5 June 2018].

Kharas, H., 2017. The G-20 steadily progresses. *Future Development*, [blog]. 11 July. www.brookings.edu/blog/future-development/2017/07/11/the-g-20-steadily-progresses/ [Accessed: 11 June 2018].

Kotte, D.J., 2011. *G-20 Two Years after the Crisis: Back to Business as Usual?* International Policy Analysis. Berlin: Friedrich-Ebert-Stiftung. October. library.fes.de/pdf-files/iez/08568.pdf [Accessed: 15 April 2018].

Kraemer, R.A., 2017. *The G20 and Building Global Governance for 'Climate Refugees'*. Policy Brief 107. May. www.cigionline.org/sites/default/files/documents/PB%20 no.107web.pdf [Accessed: 11 June 2018].

Löschmann, H. and Alexander, N., 2016. *The Solar System of G20: Engagement Groups*. 9 December. us.boell.org/2016/12/09/solar-system-g20-engagement-groups [Accessed: 15 June 2018].

Martin, P., 2008. *Hell or High Water: My Life in and out of Politics*. Toronto: McClelland & Stewart.

Martin, P., 2015. *Strengthening the Multilateral Institutions: A G20 Priority*. 2 November. www.cigionline.org/publications/strengthening-multilateral-institutions-g20-priority-0 [Accessed: 11 June 2018].

Miner, S., 2016. *What Can China Accomplish with Its G-20 Presidency?* 22 June. piie.com/blogs/china-economic-watch/what-can-china-accomplish-its-g-20-presidency [Accessed: 18 June 2018].

Munk School of Global Affairs, 2012. *Global Summitry Project*. University of Toronto. munkschool.utoronto.ca/program/global-summitry-project and globalsummitryproject.com [Accessed: 19 April 2018].

Murray, S., 2013. *The G-20 and Food Security: What Is the Right Agenda? Policy Analysis Brief*. Muscatine, Iowa: Stanley Foundation. March. www.stanleyfoundation.org/publications/pab/MurphyPAB313.pdf [Accessed: 19 April 2018].

New Rules for Global Finance, 2012b. *Promises of the G20 Process: Prospects for Advancing Transparency and Accountability*. 18 June. www.new-rules.org/events/3-nr-event/391-promises-of-the-g20 [Accessed: 28 November 2017].

New Rules for Global Finance, 2013. *Global Financial Governance & Impact Report*. new-rules.org/storage/documents/global_financial_governance__impact%20 report_2013%20.pdf [Accessed: 19 April 2018].

Oltermann, P., 2017. Arrests and injuries as Hamburg gripped by mass anti-G20 protests. *The Guardian*, 7 July.

Oxfam, 2010. *The Making of a Seoul Development Consensus: The Essential Development Agenda for the G-20.* Oxfam Briefing Note. 11 October. www.oxfam.org/sites/www.oxfam.org/files/bn-making-seoul-consensus-g20-111010-en.pdf [Accessed: 19 April 2018].

Oxfam, 2012b. *Left behind by the G20? How Inequality and Environmental Degradation Threaten to Exclude Poor People from the Benefits of Economic Growth.* Oxfam Briefing Paper, No. 157. 19 January. www.oxfam.org/sites/www.oxfam.org/files/bp157-left-behind-by-the-g20-190112-en.pdf [Accessed: 19 April 2018].

Pereira da Silva, L.A., 2013. *From Currency Wars to Policy Peace under the G-20.* Peterson Institute for International Economics. Washington, DC. www.piie.com/publications/papers/pereira20130402.pdf [Accessed: 19 April 2018].

Quintos, P., 2010. *What Is Missing in the G20 Agenda? Redressing Structural Imbalances for Equity, Justice and Sustainability.* IBON International. 8 October. iboninternational.org/sites/ibon/files/resources/ibon_g-20_policy_brief_2010.pdf [Accessed: 19 April 2018].

Rude, C. and Burke, S., 2009. *Towards a Socially Responsible and Democratic Global Economic System: Transparency, Accountability and Governance.* Dialogue on Globalization Briefing Paper 15. New York: Friedrich-Ebert-Stiftung. library.fes.de/pdf-files/bueros/usa/06778–20091105.pdf [Accessed: 24 April 2018].

Ruthrauff, J. and Lovelace, R. 2012. Ingredients for a successful G20 presidency: A civil society perspective. *G20 Update.* 14 December.

Sarkozy, N., 2016. *La France pour la vie.* Paris: Plon.

Smith, G.S., 2011c. Getting the context right: Essential to assuring G20's success. In: M. Brem, ed. *Prescriptions for the G20: The Cannes Summit and Beyond.* Waterloo, Canada: Centre for International Governance Innovation. www.cigionline.org/publications/getting-context-right-essential-assuring-g20s-success [Accessed: 23 February 2018].

Stanley Foundation, 2012. *Shifting Coalitions and Potential Blocs for Asian and Pacific Leadership in the G-20.* Policy Dialogue Brief. September. www.stanleyfoundation.org/publications/pdb/ShanghaiPDB1112.pdf [Accessed: 24 April 2018].

Subacchi, P. and Monsarrat, A., 2009. *New Ideas for the London Summit: Recommendations to the G20 Leaders.* Chatham House Report; Chatham House and Atlantic Council Report. London: Chatham House. March. www.chathamhouse.org/publications/papers/view/109022 [Accessed: 24 April 2018].

Subacchi, P. and Pickford, S., 2011. *Legitimacy vs Effectiveness for the G20: A Dynamic Approach to Global Economic Governance.* Chatham House Briefing Paper IE BP 2011/01 London: Chatham House. October. www.chathamhouse.org/sites/files/chathamhouse/1011bp_subacchi_pickford.pdf [Accessed: 24 February 2018].

Tacheva, B., 2013. *Global Health Governance: Challenges, Efforts, and the G20.* Global Summitry Reports. globalsummitryproject.com.s197331.gridserver.com/blog/global-summitry-report/global-health-governance-challenges-efforts-and-the-g20/ [Accessed: 14 June 2018].

The Tech Terms Computer Dictionary, 2017. *Social Media.* techterms.com/definition/social_media [Accessed: 24 July 2017].

Te Velde, D.W. coord., 2012. *Accountability and Effectiveness of the G20's Role in Promoting Development.* Paper prepared for Workshop on an Accountability Mechanism for G20 Development Commitments, Bali, Indonesia, 3 October. [London: Overseas Development Institute.] www.odi.org.uk/publications/6859-accountability-effectiveness-g20s-role-promoting-development [Accessed: 24 April 2018].

Truman, E.M., 2011. *G-20 Reforms of the International Monetary System: An Evaluation.* Policy Brief 11–19. Washington: Peterson Institute for International Economics. November. www.iie.com/publications/pb/pb11-19.pdf [Accessed: 25 April 2018].

Truman, E.M., 2012. The G-20 is failing. *Foreign Policy*, 12 April. foreignpolicy.com/2012/04/12/the-g-20-is-failing/ [Accessed: 30 January 2018].

United States. Congress. Senate. Committee on Banking, Housing and Urban Affairs, 2011. *An Action Plan for the G-20: Testimony before the Hearing 'The G-20 and Global Economic and Financial Risks'*, Bergsten, C.F.; and Urban Affairs Subcommittee on Security and International Trade and Finance. 20 October. www.piie.com/publications/testimony/testimony.cfm?ResearchID=1960 [Accessed: 15 August 2018].

Wikipedia, 2017. *Social Media.* en.wikipedia.org/wiki/Social_media [Accessed: 24 July 2017].

Woods, N., 2018. When Uncle Sam stays home. *International Politics and Society.* 26 February. www.ips-journal.eu/regions/global/article/show/when-uncle-sam-stays-at-home-2601 [Accessed: 14 June 2018].

World Economic Forum, 2012a. *Euro, Dollar, Yuan Uncertainties: Scenarios on the Future of the International Monetary System.* World Scenario Series. June. www20.iadb.org/intal/catalogo/PE/2012/10462.pdf [Accessed: 10 January 2018].

World Economic Forum, 2017. *Opening Plenary with Xi Jinping, President of the People's Republic of China.* 17 January. www.weforum.org/events/world-economic-forum-annual-meeting-2017/sessions/opening-plenary-davos-2017 [Accessed: 11 February 2017].

Zilinsky, J. and Cimino-Isaacs, C., 2016. *Slow Trade Growth and the G20 Response.* 8 March. piie.com/blogs/trade-investment-policy-watch/slow-trade-growth-and-g20-response [Accessed: 18 June 2018].

Conclusion

The G20 is a plurilateral forum of discussion, policy debate and political initiatives and decisions. It meets at the highest level at leaders' summits, and on a more technical level in ministerial fora and working groups and other sub-summit entities. It arose, at both the Finance Ministers'/Central Bank Governors' level (in 1999) and at the leaders' level (in 2008), in response to the economic and financial crises which existing institutions were unable to address adequately. The G20 brings together systemically important developed and emerging-economy countries from across regions of the world which, collectively, represent 85 per cent of gross world product, three-quarters of global trade and two-thirds of the world's population. This reflects the shift of the balance of power from advanced market-economy countries to major emerging countries, which made it imperative to include both kinds of actors as equals, in contrast with the G7 of mostly Western developed countries. Political leadership and commitment at the highest level were preconditions for establishing the G20 as a powerful global governance institution.

The G20 is an informal group, or network, and a relatively non-bureaucratic institution. Unlike formally constituted and structured international governmental organizations (IGOs), it is not based on a founding charter and lacks a permanent secretariat. At their 2009 Pittsburgh summit, the leaders proclaimed the G20 to be the premier forum for their international economic cooperation. Although the G20's composition – unlike that of the G7, the institution that created it – has remained constant since its inception at the ministerial level in 1999, membership has often been a contentious issue, with the dichotomy of representativeness versus effectiveness being of persistent concern. Yet, the G20 has been transformed from a rather *ad hoc* gathering into a more permanent institution, with an incrementally growing agenda moving from the initial exclusive focus on economic and financial issues to include development, food security, climate, anti-corruption, global health, cyber security, gender equity and other topics. The agenda has been marked by both continuity and innovation.

The leaders' summits are at the apex of the G20 but they are underpinned by subsidiary bodies. The first of these, the G20 Finance Ministers' and Central Bank Governors' forum (created by the G8 leaders), was the first component of the gradually evolving broader G20 system, preceding the summits by almost a decade and continuing to operate alongside the summits. Since the beginning of

DOI: 10.4324/9781351266802-12

the G20 summits, a varying number of other ministerial fora as well as working groups and similar sub-summit entities have been formed, the Financial Stability Board being a particularly important building block. Some of these bodies hold regular periodic meetings while others have been convened on an *ad hoc* basis. Some cease activities when completing their tasks or simply fade away, while others continue for many years. These sub-summit entities may well be the most important practical parts of the work of the G20; they, alongside with the leaders' personal representatives (sherpas), are essential in supporting and supplementing the leaders' work on specific issues and tasks.

The G20 system, however important it may be, constitutes just one face of global governance as a whole. The G20 maintains a strong relationship with various kinds of other actors: non-member states, IGOs and engagement groups, including the business sector and civil society. This nexus is necessary and mutually beneficial to the G20 and its interlocutors. Non-member states, IGOs and engagement groups often attend G20 summits and ministerial and task force meetings, using those opportunities to contribute to outcomes to a greater or lesser degree.

Among IGOs, the Bretton Woods institutions (the International Monetary Fund and the World Bank) enjoy a privileged relationship with the G20. They participate in G20 summits, ministerial meetings and working groups. They and other IGOs (especially the United Nations [UN], the Organisation for Economic Co-operation and Development [OECD] and the Bank for International Settlements [BIS] and its Basel Committee) offer analysis, policy proposals and performance evaluations, thereby enhancing the legitimacy of the G20. IGOs, particularly the UN, are a way to make the universal voice of the unrepresented heard in the G20. The G20, for its part, when it is able to reach consensus, provides political impetus on the highest level, facilitating progress in the IGOs. The G20 can also be the source of new resources – for example, for the IMF and various global initiatives. Mutual information-sharing is another action that has aided progress in both the G20 and the IGOs.

Similarly, the G20 relationship with the business sector has resulted in mutual benefit to both actors. Powerful business interest groups, such as the World Economic Forum (WEF), the International Chamber of Commerce (ICC), the Business 20 (B20) and the Young Entrepreneurs' Alliance (YEA), and private philanthropies are vital to the G20, and they have used their clout strategically to exert strong influence on the G20.

The G20's relationship with not-for-profit civil society organizations (CSOs) has been more complex. The tremendous diversity of CSOs (which include NGOs, coalitions and movements, think-tanks, academic institutions and other groups) has manifested itself in a range of activities, including consultations, monitoring and evaluation, the preparation of reports, policy papers and petitions, and staging alternative summits and street demonstrations. A number of factors influence success in this interaction: mutual willingness of specific CSOs and G20 governments to engage with each other (some G20 host countries have been more receptive than others); careful preparation; understanding of the G20 system and its processes; timeliness of interventions; and expertise brought to bear. The civil society-G20 nexus has brought about some mutual benefits, but civil society's impact on the G20 (notwithstanding a few notable exceptions) has yet to reach its full potential.

Monitoring and evaluating the G20's performance are key aspects of accountability. Here, too, CSOs, IGOs and business groups have been engaged actively, using a variety of methods. The G20 itself has become involved in monitoring and evaluating its own performance and fulfilment of its promises through accountability reports, which have become routine at summits and at the sub-summit level. The Mutual Assessment Process (MAP) is a major step forward in assessing progress, through a series of IMF reports, with other IGOs also contributing to the exercise. The diverse methods used by civil society groups, the business sector, IGOs and the G20 itself to monitor and evaluate G20 performance all have strengths and weaknesses, but they all contribute to enhancing the accountability of the G20. Good incremental progress has been made but more remains to be done.

Efforts to reform, improve, replace or abolish the G20 (and before that the G7 and G8) began almost as soon as these fora came into being. Reform proposals and projections have ranged widely in scope and kind. Some have addressed the composition of the G7/G8 and G20, through increasing, reducing or changing membership. Others have suggested institutional changes, including whether and how to establish a secretariat. Expanding or contracting the G20 agenda has also been much discussed, as has the need to transform the G20 from a 'crisis committee' to a 'steering committee' or the reality of parallel operation of these two modes. The G20's evolving relationship with the G7/G8, IGOs, business groups and CSOs and proposals from a variety of other sources have all played a part in these efforts. Many have predicted or prescribed the path that the G7/G8 and G20 could or should follow. Possible trajectories envisioned have included: the expansion of the G7/G8 to reflect changing geopolitical realities; continued coexistence of the G7/G8 with the G20; the G20 replacing the G7/G8; some other group replacing the G20, or the G20 coexisting with such groups; variable geometry of summitry, involving different countries depending on the issue discussed; and a 'G-Zero' world in which no one country or group of countries can set the global agenda. In actual fact, the G7-G20 coexistence as parallel institutions has prevailed thus far.

The G7/G8 and the G20 have both faced major challenges. Complex relationships of the G7/G8 and G20 with formal IGOs as major global governance institutions must be part of the future of the G7 and G20, and the G7 and the G20 should continue to define and develop their mutual relationship.

Publicly available information generated by and about the G20 system is the best way for experts as well as the general public to understand this forum. Documents released by G20 summits, ministerial fora and other sub-summit bodies are the principal source of information on the G20 and its activities, even though they do not fully reflect the content and extent of actual proceedings. Much remains out of bounds to the public, due either to the confidential nature of diplomatic negotiations or to actions or inactions of the custodians of information. This is an important element of transparency of the G20, which has increased on the whole, but there are persistent as well as new obstacles that need to be remedied whenever possible, given the contrasting need for informing the public and preserving necessary confidentiality in the conduct of diplomacy.

Other types of sources about the G20 round out public information found in documents: various individual works and media accounts about the G20; think-tanks focusing on G20 research and sometimes advocacy; memoirs of prominent present and former G20 participants; academic theses and dissertations; creative works; websites; and social media. Such sources constitute, to a greater or lesser extent, important additional material; they need to be incorporated in research in order to gain fuller understanding of the G20 and its activities.

During its history thus far, the G20 has proven itself to be an important and necessary component of the complex global governance network of institutions and various other actors. Despite the somewhat uncertain path ahead, it is likely to continue, as long as leaders consider it as an appropriate forum for addressing major global issues, concerns and tasks that call for common action.

Bibliography

This bibliography not only contains entries referenced in the text of the book but also aims to provide an extensive bibliography of information generated by the G20 (and the G7/G8 where relevant), and works about the G20, including G7/G8/G20 reform.

Web addresses and links (URLs): websites tend to appear, change or disappear, often without warning. URLs cited in this bibliography and throughout the book were accurate and active at the time of access unless otherwise noted.

Books, shorter writings and publications in series

Abshagen, M.-L., 2016. *The Plan for a Better World: The G20 and the 2030 Agenda for Sustainable Development.* Heinrich Böll Stiftung North America. 30 November. us.boell.org/2016/11/30/plan-better-world-g20-and-2030-agenda-sustainable-development [Accessed: 17 April 2018].

Alagh, Y.K., Nathan, D., Sharma, A.N., Rustagi, P. and Shrotria, S., 2012. *The G20, the Seoul Development Consensus and India: A Report.* [With financial support from the International Labour Office through the ILO-Korea Partnership Program] http://www.g20.utoronto.ca/biblio/SDC_India.pdf [Accessed: 22 November 2018].

Alexander, N., 2011a. *The G20, Latin America, and the Future of Regional Integration.* New York: Heinrich Böll Stiftung North America. July. us.boell.org/2011/06/17/g20-latin-america-and-future-regional-integration [Accessed: 27 March 2018].

Alexander, N., 2011b. *The G20: 'Maestro' of the Development Finance World? Implications of the G20's Development Action Plan for Efforts to Democratize Global Governance and Achieve Sustainable Development.* New York: Heinrich Böll Stiftung North America. July. us.boell.org/2011/06/21/g20-maestro-development-finance-world-group-20 [Accessed: 27 March 2018].

Alexander, N., 2011c. *Introduction to the G20.* Washington, DC: Heinrich Böll Stiftung North America. June. www.boell.org/web/group_of_20-651.html [Accessed: 21 May 2012].

Alexander, N., 2012. *What Are the Pros and Cons of Public-Private Partnerships (PPPs) as a Means to Achieve Food Security, Expanded Infrastructure Investment and Green Growth?* Instituto Matías Romero. www.academia.edu/14434806/The_Pros_and_Cons_of_Public-Private_Partnerships_PPPs_as_a_means_to_achieve_food_security_expanded_infrastructure_investment_and_green_growth [Accessed: 8 January 2018].

Alexander, N., 2017. *IMF and World Bank: Marching to a G20 Tune?* 24 October. us.boell.org/2017/10/24/imf-and-world-bank-marching-g20-tune [Accessed: 15 December 2017].

Alexander, N., 2018a. *Just Governance* [blog]. justgovernance.boellblog.org/ [Accessed: 15 August 2018].

Alexander, N., 2018b. *The Priorities of Argentina's Presidency*. 5 January. us.boell.org/2018/01/05/priorities-argentinas-g20-presidency [Accessed: 3 August 2018].

Alexander, N. and Caliari, A., 2013. *Commentary on the Report: 'Mapping G20 Decisions Implementation'*. Washington, DC: Heinrich Böll Stiftung. January. us.boell.org/2013/02/01/commentary-report-mapping-g20-decisions-implementation-group-20 [Accessed: 27 March 2018].

Alexander, N. and Fuhr, L., 2012. *Privatizing the Governance of 'Green Growth'*. 26 November. www.boell.de/en/content/privatizing-governance-green-growth [Accessed: 8 January 2018].

Alexander, N. and Riggs, P., 2012. *The G20: Playing Outside the Big Tent: Implications for Rio+20*. Washington: Heinrich Böll Stiftung North America, June. us.boell.org/2012/06/08/g20-playing-outside-big-tent [Accessed: 27 March 2018].

Alexander, N., Schuele, W. and Löschmann, H., 2016. *The G7 and G20 in the Global Governance Landscape*. 30 November. us.boell.org/2016/11/30/g7-and-g20-global-governance-landscape [Accessed: 15 June 2018].

Alexandroff, A.S. ed., 2008a. *Can the World Be Governed? Possibilities for Effective Multilateralism*. Waterloo, Canada: Wilfrid Laurier University Press.

Alexandroff, A. and Cooper, A. eds., 2010. *Rising States, Rising Institutions: Challenges for Global Governance*. Washington, DC: Brookings Institution Press.

Alexandroff, A., Shorr, D. and Wang, Z.B., 2010. *Leadership and the Global Governance Agenda: Three Voices*. Waterloo, Canada: Centre for International Governance Innovation, Stanley Foundation and China Institutes of Contemporary International Relations. June. www.cigionline.org/publications/leadership-and-global-governance-agenda-three-voices [Accessed: 27 March 2018].

Angeloni, I., 2011. *The Group of G20: Trials of Global Governance in Times of Crisis*. Bruegel Working Paper 2011/12. bruegel.org/2011/12/the-group-of-g20-trials-of-global-governance-in-times-of-crisis/ [Accessed: 27 March 2018].

Angeloni, I. and Pisani-Ferry, J., 2012. *The G20: Characters in Search of an Author*. Bruegel Working Paper. March. bruegel.org/2012/03/the-g20-characters-in-search-of-an-author/ [Accessed: 27 March 2018].

Antkiewicz, A., Cooper, A.F. and Shaw, T.M., 2006. *Economic Size Trumps All Else? Lessons from BRICSAM*. CIGI Working Paper, No. 12. December. Waterloo, Canada: Centre for International Governance Innovation. www.cigionline.org/publications/economic-size-trumps-all-else-lessons-bricsam [Accessed: 27 March 2018].

B20, 2011. *Final Report with Appendices*. Cannes: November. www.g20.utoronto.ca/b20/B20-2011-report.pdf [Accessed: 8 January 2018].

B20, 2012a. *B20 Global Business Leaders Announce Their Prioritized Recommendations for Global Economic Recovery and Growth*. May. www.prnewswire.com/news-releases/b20-global-business-leaders-announce-their-prioritized-recommendations-for-global-economic-recovery-and-growth-155411765.html [Accessed: 9 January 2018].

B20, 2012b. *B20 Task Force Recommendations: Final Report*. Los Cabos: Boell. 11 May. us.boell.org/sites/default/files/downloads/FINAL_11_May_B20_Task_Force_Recommendations.pdf [Accessed: 06 January 2018].

B20, 2012c. *Program*. 17–18 June. b20.org/documentos/B20_Program_20120615.pdf [Accessed: 9 September 2012].

B20, 2013a. *B20-G20 Partnership for Growth and Jobs: Recommendations from Business 20*. www.b20russia.com/B20_WhiteBook_web.pdf [Accessed: 9 January 2018].

B20, 2013b. *From Toronto to Saint Petersburg: Assessing G20-B20 Engagement Effectiveness: Draft Report*. www.hse.ru/data/2013/06/24/1287462471/G20-B20_engagement_effectiveness_report_full.pdf [Accessed: 9 January 2018].

B20, 2014. *Driving Growth and Jobs: B20 Policy Recommendations to the G20*. www.g20.utoronto.ca/b20/B20-2014-recommendations.pdf [Accessed: 26 November 2017].

B20, 2015a. *B20 Policy Achievements: Assessment of Alignment with the Antalya G20 Leaders' Communiqué*. 17 November. www.g20.utoronto.ca/b20/B20-2015-Policy-Acheivements.pdf [Accessed: 11 February 2017].

B20, 2015b. *Summary of B20 Recommendations*. g20.org.tr/engagement-groups/business-20-b20 [Accessed: 26 November 2017].

B20, 2016. *Policy Recommendations to the G20 Released to the Public*. en.b20-china.org/mediacenter/article/334 [Accessed: 26 November 2017].

B20, 2017a. *About B20*. www.b20germany.org/the-b20/about-b20/ [Accessed: 25 November 2017].

B20, 2017b. *About the G20* www.b20germany.org/the-b20/about-g20/ [Accessed: 17 July 2018].

B20, 2017c. *B20 Germany Recommendations Summary*. May. www.b20germany.org/nc/documents/recommendations-summary/ [Accessed: 25 November 2017].

B20, 2017d. *Structure*. www.b20germany.org/nc/the-b20/structure [Accessed: 25 November 2017].

B20-L20, 2011. *B20-L20 Joint Statement*. November. www.ilo.org/wcmsp5/groups/public/ – dgreports/-dcomm/documents/meetingdocument/wcms_166713.pdf and www.g20.utoronto.ca/2011/2011-b20-l20-en.pdf [Accessed: 9 January 2018].

Baker, A., 2000b. *The Politics of G7 Co-operation in the 1990s: Global Finance, Macroeconomic Policy and Multi-dimensional Diplomacy*. DPhil. University of Ulster, Belfast.

Baker, A., 2006. *The Group of Seven: Finance Ministries, Central Banks and Global Financial Governance*. New York: Routledge.

Bast, E., Kretzmann, S., Krishnaswamy, S. and Romine, T., 2012. *Low-Hanging Fruit: Fossil Fuel Subsidies, Climate Finance, and Sustainable Development*. Washington: Heinrich Böll Stiftung, with Oil Change International and Natural Resources Defense Council. June. www.boell.de/en/ecology/climate-energy-policy-paper-fossil-fuel-subsidies-14818.html [Accessed: 27 March 2018].

Bayne, N., 2000. *Hanging in There: The G7 and G8 Summit in Maturity and Renewal*. Ashgate: Aldershot.

Bayne, N., 2001. *Concentrating the Mind: Decision-Making in the G7/G8 System*. Promoting Conflict Prevention and Human Security: What Can the G8 Do? www.g8.utoronto.ca/conferences/2001/rome/bayne-conflict.pdf [Accessed: 27 March 2018].

Bayne, N., 2005b. *Staying Together: The G8 Summit Confronts the 21st Century*. Aldershot, UK: Ashgate.

Bayne, N. and Woolcock, S. eds., 2011. *The New Economic Diplomacy: Decision-Making and Negotiation in International Economic Relations*. 3rd ed. Global Finance Series. Farnham: Ashgate.

Bénassy-Quéré, A., Lahrèche-Révil, M. and Mignon, V., 2006. *World Consistent Equilibrium Exchange Rates*. CEPII Working Paper, No. 2006–20. Paris: Centre d'Études prospectives et d'informations internationales. www.piie.com/publications/pb/pb07-4/benassy.pdf [Accessed: 27 March 2018].

Bénassy-Quéré, et al., 2011. *Réformer le système monétaire international* [Reforming the International Monetary System]. Rapports du CAE [Conseil d'Analyse économique]. Paris: Documentation française.

Ben Hammouda, H. and Sadni-Jallab, M., 2011. *Le G20 et des défis de la gouvernance globale*. Bruxelles: De Boeck.

Bergsten, C.F., 2004. *The G-20 and the World Economy*. Speech to the Deputies of the G-20, Leipzig, Germany, March 4. www.iie.com/publications/papers/bergsten0304-2.htm [Accessed: 27 March 2018]. See also *World Economics*, 5(3), pp. 27–36.

Bergsten, C.F. and Henning, C.R., 1996. *Global Economic Leadership and the Group of Seven*. Washington, DC: Institute for International Economics.

Bernes, T.A., 2010. *IMF Reform: An Agenda for the G20 Summit*. Seoul G20 Commentaries. Waterloo, Canada: Centre for International Governance Innovation. November. www.cigionline.org/publications/imf-reform-agenda-g20-summit [Accessed: 27 March 2018].

Bernes, T.A., 2013. *Ho Hum . . . on to Brisbane*. G20 St Petersburg Rapid Response. Waterloo, Canada: Centre for International Governance Innovation. 9 September. www.cigionline.org/publications/ho-humon-brisbane [Accessed: 6 July 2018].

Blair, T., 2010. *A Journey: My Political Life*. London: Hutchinson.

Blakers, M., 2013. *An Introduction to the G20: The Australian Presidency in Context*. 1 February. us.boell.org/2013/01/01/introduction-g20-australian-presidency-context [Accessed: 27 March 2018].

Böhm, E., 2013. *Die Sicherheit des Westens: Entstehung und Funktion der G7-Gipfel* [Western Security: Development and Function of the G7 Summit]. Oldenbourg Verlag. PhD. Marburg: Philipps-Universität Marburg.

Bordeaux Religious Summit, 2011. *Statement of the Bordeaux Religious Leaders Summit*. www.g8.utoronto.ca/interfaith/2011-interfaith-leaders-en.pdf [Accessed: 27 March 2018].

Bosshard, P., 2012. *Infrastructure for Whom? A Critique of the Infrastructure Strategies of the Group of 20 and the World Bank*. May. Berkeley, CA: International Rivers. www.internationalrivers.org/sites/default/files/attached-files/infrastructure_for_whom_report.pdf [Accessed: 27 March 2018].

Bourgogne Franche-Comté Universités, 2011. *Welcome to University Summit 2011*. www.univ-fcomte.fr/download/partage/document/actualite/lettre-flash/10-ufc-lettre10.pdf [Accessed: 27 March 2018].

Bradford, C.I., 2005b. *Global Governance for the 21st Century*. Paper prepared for the Brookings Institution and The Centre for International Governance Innovation Governance. www.brookings.edu/wp-content/uploads/2016/06/20051024bradford.pdf [Accessed: 22 February 2018].

Bradford, C.I. ed., 2011b. *National Perspectives on Global Leadership During the Cannes G20*. Soundings Series No. 6. Waterloo, Canada: Centre for International Governance Innovation and Washington: Brookings Institution. www.cigionline.org/publications/national-perspectives-global-leadership-during-cannes-g20 [Accessed: 27 March 2018].

Bradford, C.I. ed., 2011c. *National Perspectives on Global Leadership Soundings Series: Summitry and Public Perceptions*. CIGI Papers. Waterloo, Canada: Centre for International Governance Innovation and Washington: Brookings Institution. www.cigionline.org/publications/npl-soundings-series-summitry-and-public-perceptions-0 [Accessed: 27 March 2018].

Bradford, C.I. ed., 2012a. *National Perspectives on Global Leadership during the Los Cabos G20 summit*. Soundings Series No. 7. Waterloo, Canada: Centre for International Governance Innovation and Washington: Brookings Institution. www.cigionline.org/publications/national-perspectives-global-leadership-during-los-cabos-g20-summit [Accessed: 27 March 2018].

Bradford, C.I., 2012b. *View from the Ground at the Los Cabos Summit*. 22 June. www.cigionline.org/publications/view-ground-los-cabos-summit [Accessed: 27 March 2018].

Bradford, C.I. and Lim, W.H., 2010. *Toward the Consolidation of the G20 Summits: From Crisis Committee to Global Steering Committee*. Seoul and Washington, DC: Korea Development Institute and Brookings Institution. www.cigionline.org/articles/toward-consolidation-g20-summits-crisis-committee-global-steering-committee [Accessed: 27 March 2018].

Bradford, C.I. and Lim, W.H. eds., 2011b. *Global Leadership in Transition: Making the G20 More Effective and Responsive*. Washington, DC: Brookings Institution Press with Korean Development Institute.

Brem, M. comp., 2011a. *The G20 Agenda and Process: Analysis and Insight by CIGI Experts*. CIGI Special Report. Waterloo, Canada: Centre for International Governance Innovation. March. www.cigionline.org/publications/g20-agenda-and-process-analysis-and-insight-cigi-experts [Accessed: 13 April 2018].

Brem, M. ed., 2011b. *Prescriptions for the G20: The Cannes Summit and Beyond*. Waterloo, Canada: Centre for International Governance Innovation. www.cigionline.org/series/prescriptions-g20-cannes-summit-and-beyond [Accessed: 13 April 2018].

Bremmer, I., 2012. *Every Nation for Itself: Winners and Losers in a G-Zero World*. New York: Portfolio/Penguin.

BRICS Research Group, 2012. *BRICS Official Documents and Meetings*. www.brics.utoronto.ca/docs/index.html [Accessed: 13 April 2018].

BRICS Research Group, 2014. *The 6th BRICS Summit: Fortaleza Declaration*. 15 July. www.brics.utoronto.ca/docs/140715-leaders.html [Accessed: 13 March 2018].

BRICS Research Group, 2015a. *BRICS Information Centre*. www.brics.utoronto.ca [Accessed: 23 February 2018].

BRICS Research Group, 2015b. *Media Note on the Informal Meeting of BRICS Leaders on the Occasion of the G20 Summit in Brisbane*. 15 November. www.brics.utoronto.ca/docs/141115-brisbane.html [Accessed: 23 February 2018].

BRICS Research Group, 2015c. *Memorandum of Understanding on Cooperation with the New Development Bank*. 9 July. www.brics.utoronto.ca/docs/150709-NDB-memorandum-en.html [Accessed: 28 February 2017].

BRICS Research Group, 2017. *BRICS Leaders Xiamen Declaration*. 4 September. www.brics.utoronto.ca/docs/170904-xiamen.html [Accessed: 23 February 2018].

Brookings Institution, 2008. *The G20 Financial Summit: Seven Issues at Stake*. Washington, DC. November. www.brookings.edu/research/the-g-20-financial-summit-seven-issues-at-stake/ [Accessed: 13 April 2018].

Brookings Institution, 2012a. *About Us*. www.brookings.edu/about-us/ [Accessed: 13 April 2018].

Brookings Institution, 2012b. *The G-20 Los Cabos Summit 2012: Bolstering the World Economy amid Growing Fears of Recession*. June. www.brookings.edu/multi-chapter-report/the-g-20-los-cabos-summit-2012-bolstering-the-world-economy-amid-growing-fears-of-recession/ [Accessed: 13 April 2018].

Brookings Institution, 2013. *Think Tank 20: The G-20 and Central Banks in the New World of Unconventional Monetary Policy*. August. www.brookings.edu/research/think-tank-20-the-g-20-and-central-banks-in-the-new-world-of-unconventional-monetary-policy/ [Accessed: 13 April 2018].

Brown, G., 2010. *Beyond the Crash: Overcoming the First Crisis of Globalization*. New York, London: Free Press.

Brzezinski, Z., 2004. *The Choice: Global Domination or Global Leadership*. New York: Basic Books.

Bush, G.W., 2010. *Decision Points*. New York: Crown Publishers.

Callaghan, M., Bradford, C., Carin, B., Skilling, D. and Thirlwell, M., 2012. *G20 Monitor: Challenges Facing the G20 in 2013*. No. 1. December. www.lowyinstitute.org/publications/challenges-facing-g20-2013 [Accessed: 13 April 2018].

Camdessus, M., Lamfalussy, A. and Padoa-Schioppa, T., 2011. *La réforme du système monétaire international: une approche coopérative pour le vingt-et-unième siècle* [Reform of the International Monetary System: A Cooperative Approach for the Twenty-First Century]. Paris: Présidence de la République.

Cao, L.J., 2004. *Ba Guo Ji Tuan Yan Jiu Cong G7 Dao G8* [Research on the G8: From G7 to G8]. PhD. dissertation (international relations). Beijing: Party School of the Central Committee of the Communist Party of China.

Carin, B., 2010. *The Future of the G20 Process*. Seoul G20 Commentaries. Waterloo, Canada: Centre for International Governance Innovation. November. www.cigionline.org/sites/default/files/barry_carin_commentary.pdf [Accessed: 22 February 2018].

Carin, B., 2011b. *No Fairy Tale at the Cannes G20 Summit*. Waterloo, Canada: Centre for International Governance Innovation. 7 November. www.cigionline.org/publications/no-fairy-tale-cannes-g20-summit [Accessed: 16 January 2018].

Carin, B., 2013. *St. Petersburg G20 and Progress on International Economic Governance*. 20 September. www.cigionline.org/publications/st-petersburg-g20-and-progress-international-economic-governance [Accessed: 13 April 2018].

Carin, B., Heinbecker, P., Smith, G. and Thakur, R., 2010. *Making the G20 Summit Process Work: Some Proposals for Improving Effectiveness and Legitimacy*. CIGI G20 Paper No. 2. June. Waterloo, Canada: Centre for International Governance Innovation. www.cigionline.org/sites/default/files/g20_no2_1.pdf [Accessed: 22 February 2018].

Center of Concern, 2012. A bottom-up approach to righting financial regulation. *The Group of 20, Financial Regulation and Human Rights*, (4). www.cesr.org/sites/default/files/G20_and_Financial_Regulation_0.pdf [Accessed: 23 November 2018].

Centre for Global Studies, 2006a. *Next Steps: Breaking Global Deadlocks*. www.l20.org/nextsteps.php [Accessed: 6 July 2012].

Centre for Global Studies, 2006b. *L20 Findings: Outcomes and Conclusions*. www.l20.org/findings.php [Accessed: 6 July 2012].

Centre for International Governance Innovation, 2012. *National Perspectives on Global Leadership during the Los Cabos G20 Summit*. Soundings Series, No. 7. 27 July. www.cigionline.org/publications/national-perspectives-global-leadership-during-los-cabos-g20-summit [Accessed: 13 April 2018].

Centre for International Governance Innovation and Brookings Institution, 2011. *National Perspectives on Global Leadership: Summitry and Public Perceptions*. Soundings Series. www.cigionline.org/sites/default/files/nplv2_0.pdf [Accessed: 15 August 2018].

Chatham House, 2018. *Our Mission*. www.chathamhouse.org/about/mission [Accessed: 15 August 2018].

Chen, D., 2008. *Building up a Cooperative & Co-Progressive Community: China's Asia Strategy towards 2020*. Shanghai: Shanghai Institutes for International Studies. www.siis.org.cn/sh_yj_cms//upics/20081022151524lEW9.PDF [Accessed: 21 May 2012].

Chen, D.X., Schlager, C. and Zhang, H.B., 2015. *Zhong Guo Yu Er Shi Guo Ji Tuan* [China and the G20]. Shanghai: Shanghai People's Publishing House.

Chen, X.J., 2006. *Zhong Guo Yu Ba Guo Ji Tuan* [China and the G8]. Beijing: Current Affairs Press.

Chin, G., 2011. *Benefit Sharing for the French G20: The Role of Asia*. Waterloo, Canada: Centre for International Governance Innovation. 17 February. www.cigionline.org/publications/benefit-sharing-french-g20-role-asia [Accessed: 13 April 2018].

Choe, W.I., 2010. *The Role of Korea in G20 Process and the Seoul Summit*. Paper prepared for an international conference on 'G20 Seoul Summit: From Crisis to Cooperation', Organized by the Korea Association of Negotiations Studies. Seoul, 20 May.

Chongyang Institute for Financial Studies, Renmin University of China, 2013. *Who Will Govern the New World? The Present and Future of the G20*. Beijing: Social Sciences Academic Press. [Also available in Chinese.]

Chowdhury, I.A., 2010. *The Global Governance Group ('3G') and Singaporean Leadership: Can Small Be Significant?* ISAS Working Paper, No. 108. 19 May. www.isas.nus.edu.sg/ISAS%20Reports/ISAS_Working_Paper_108_-_Email_-_The_Global_Governance_Group_19052010134423.pdf [Accessed: 28 February 2017].

Civil 20, 2012. *Civil20 Proposals for the Russian Presidency in the G20*. December. g20civil.com/newsg20/1326/ [Accessed: 14 January 2013].

Civil 20, 2013. *Civil20 Address to the G20 Leaders*. civil-20.org/c20–2013-russia/ [Accessed: 25 April 2018].

Civil 20, 2014. *Australian C20 Summit Communique*. civil-20.org/c20–2014-australia/ [Accessed: 25 April 2018].

Civil 20, 2015. *C20 Turkey Communiqué: A World Economy That Includes All*. civil-20.org/c20–2015-turkey/ [Accessed: 25 April 2018].

Civil 20, 2016. *Communiqué of Civil Society 20 China 2016*. civil-20.org/c20–2016-china/ andhttp://web.archive.org/web/20160907123353/www.g20.org/English/Documents/Current/201607/t20160706_2885.html [Accessed: 25 April 2018].

Clapp, J., 2011. *How to Add Value to the G20 Agriculture Ministers' Meeting*. Waterloo, Canada: Centre for International Governance Innovation. www.cigionline.org/publications/how-add-value-g20-agriculture-ministers-meeting [Accessed: 13 April 2018].

Clapp, J. and Martin, S., 2011. *The G20 Agricultural Action Plan: Changing the Course of Capitalism?* Waterloo, Canada: Centre for International Governance Innovation. www.cigionline.org/publications/g20-agricultural-action-plan-changing-course-capitalism [Accessed: 13 April 2018].

Clinton, W., 2005. *My Life*. New York: Vintage.

Club de Madrid, 2010. *The G20's Role in the Post-Crisis World: Final Report*. Seoul: Club de Madrid and FRIDE and Government of Korea. www.clubmadrid.org/wp-content/uploads/2017/10/G20_FINAL_REPORT.pdf [Accessed: 13 April 2018].

Club de Madrid, 2011. *The G20's Role in the Post-Crisis World: Briefing Book*. Madrid: Club de Madrid. www.clubmadrid.org/img/secciones/G20-France_Report_2011.pdf [Accessed: 21 May 2012].

Club de Madrid, 2017. *A New Paradigm for Sustainable Development?* www.clubmadrid.org/wp-content/uploads/2017/11/Shared_Societies-Report-13.pdf [Accessed: 11 June 2018].

Commission on Global Governance, 1995. *Our Global Neighbourhood: The Report of the Commission on Global Governance*. New York: Oxford University Press.

Cooper, A.F., 2007. *The Logic of the B(R)ICSAM Model for G8 Reform*. CIGI Policy Brief in International Governance, No. 1. May. Waterloo, Canada: Centre for International Governance Innovation. www.cigionline.org/publications/logic-bricsam-model-g8-reform [Accessed: 13 April 2018].

Cooper, A.F., 2008a. *Celebrity Diplomacy*. Boulder: Paradigm Publishers.

Cooper, A.F., 2012. *The G20 as the Global Focus Group: Beyond the Crisis Committee/Steering Committee Framework*. G20 Information Centre. www.g20.utoronto.ca/analysis/120619-cooper-focusgroup.html [Accessed: 24 February 2018].

Cooper, A.F. and Antkiewicz, A. eds., 2008. *Emerging Powers in Global Governance: Lessons from the Heiligendamm Process*. Waterloo, Canada: Wilfrid Laurier University

Press and Centre for International Governance Innovation. Also available in Chinese 2008: *Quan Qiu Zhi Li Zhong De Xin Xing Guo Jia* [Emerging Powers in Global Governance]. Shanghai: Shanghai People's Publishing House.

Cooper, A.F. and Bradford, C.I., 2010. *The G20 and the Post-Crisis Economic Order*. CIGI G20 Paper No. 3. Waterloo, Canada: Centre for International Governance Innovation. June. www.cigionline.org/publications/g20-and-post-crisis-economic-order [Accessed: 13 April 2018].

Cooper, A.F. and Fues, T., 2005. *L20 and ECOSOC Reform: Complementary Building Blocks for Inclusive Global Governance and a More Effective UN*. Briefing Paper, 6/2005. Bonn: Deutsches Institut für Entwicklungspolitik (DIE).

Cooper, A.F. and Schrumm, A., 2009. *Moving the G20 Forward: From Private Wrongs to Public Goods*. Waterloo, Canada: Centre for International Governance Innovation. www.cigionline.org/publications/moving-g20-forward-private-wrongs-public-goods [Accessed: 23 February 2018].

Cooper, A.F. and Schwanen, D. eds., 2009. *Flashpoints for the Pittsburgh Summit*. CIGI Special G20 Report. 24–25 September. Waterloo, Canada: Centre for International Governance Innovation. www.cigionline.org/publications/flashpoints-pittsburgh-summit [Accessed: 13 April 2018].

Cooper, A.F. and Thakur, R., 2013. *The Group of Twenty (G20)*. Global Institutions Series. New York: Routledge.

Coordination SUD, 2011. *Alter-forum de Nice: Les peuples d'abord, pas la finance!* 4 November. www.coordinationsud.org/actualite/alter-forum-de-nice-les-peuples-d'abord-pas-la-finance/ [Accessed: 13 April 2018].

Council on Foreign Relations, 2012a. *CFR Convenes 'Council of Councils' Linking Leading Foreign Policy Institutes from Around the World*. 9 March. www.cfr.org/news-releases/cfr-convenes-council-councils-linking-leading-foreign-policy-institutes-around-world?co=C039201 [Accessed: 13 April 2018].

Council on Foreign Relations, 2012b. *The 'Council of Councils' Inaugural Conference*. March. www.cfr.org/content/publications/attachments/CoC-Inaugural-Conference-Meeting-Note-Final.pdf [Accessed: 28 December 2012].

CrimethInc, 2017. *An Anarchist Guide to the 2017 G20 Summit in Hamburg: With a Review of Previous G8 and G20 Protests*. 26 June. crimethinc.com/2017/06/26/an-anarchist-guide-to-the-2017-g20-summit-in-hamburg-with-a-review-of-previous-g8-and-g20-protests [Accessed: 7 August 2018].

Culpeper, R., 2000. *Systemic Reform at a Standstill: A Flock of 'Gs' in Search of Global Financial Stability*. Critical Issues in Financial Reform: Latin-American/Caribbean and Canadian Perspectives, Munk Centre for International Studies, University of Toronto, 1–2 June. www.g8.utoronto.ca/scholar/culpeper2000/index.html [Accessed: 13 April 2018]. (Also available as Culpeper, R., 2003. Systemic reform at a standstill: A flock of 'Gs' in search of global financial stability. In: A. Berry and G. Indart, eds. *Critical Issues in International Financial Reform*. New Brunswick, NJ and London: Transaction Publishers, pp. 203–236.)

Culpeper, R., 2012. *The Role of the G20 in Enhancing Financial Inclusion*. February. us.boell.org/sites/default/files/downloads/Culpeper_G20_Financial_Inclusion.pdf [Accessed: 8 January 2018].

Daniels, J.P., 1993. *The Meaning and Reliability of Economic Undertakings, 1975–1989*. New York: Garland Publishing.

Davis, R. and Schrumm, A., 2009. *Is the G8's Variable Geometry Sustainable?* https://www.cigionline.org/publications/g8s-variable-geometry-sustainable [Accessed: 24 November 2018].

Desai, S., 2006. *Expanding the G8: Should China Join?* Foreign Policy Centre. fpc.org.uk/publications/expanding-the-g8-should-china-join/ [Accessed: 13 April 2018].

Dillon, J., 2009. *G20 Rehabilitates IMF, Marginalizes UN*. Kairos Policy Briefing Paper, No. 17. 22 April. www.kairoscanada.org/kairos-briefing-paper-17-g20-rehabilitates-imf-marginalizes-un [Accessed: 13 April 2018].

Dobson, H., 2007. *The Group of 7/8*. New York: Routledge.

Dobson, H., 2008. *Where Are the Women at the G8?* www.g8.utoronto.ca/scholar/dobson-2008.html [Accessed: 1 May 2018].

Edwards, J., Kemp, J. and Sestanovich, S., 2006. *Russia's Wrong Direction: What the United States Can and Should Do*. Task Force Report. March. New York: Council on Foreign Relations. www.cfr.org/iran/russias-wrong-direction/p9997 [Accessed: 13 April 2018].

Edwards, L.J., 2013. *The St. Petersburg Summit: Obama's Futile Quest for Support on Syria Overshadowed the Summit's Economic Successes*. G20 St. Petersburg Rapid Response. Waterloo, Canada: Centre for International Governance Innovation. 10 September. www.cigionline.org/publications/st-petersburg-summit-obamas-futile-quest-support-syria-overshadowed-summits-economic [Accessed: 22 February 2018].

Eichengreen, B. and Baldwin, R. eds., 2008. *What G20 Leaders Must Do to Stabilise Our Economy and Fix the Financial System*. A VoxEU.org Publication. London: Centre for Economic Policy Research. November. voxeu.org/content/what-g20-leaders-must-do-stabilise-our-economy-and-fix-financial-system [Accessed: 13 April 2018].

English, J., Thakur, R. and Cooper, A.F. eds., 2005. *Reforming from the Top: A Leaders' 20 Summit*. Tokyo: United Nations University Press.

F20, 2017. *F20: Home*. [online] www.foundations-20.org/ [Accessed: 8 December 2017].

Fakir, S., 2012. *The G20's Energy Infrastructure Plans for Africa: What Is Missing?* Cape Town. June. us.boell.org/2012/06/01/g20s-energy-infrastructure-plans-africa-what-missing [Accessed: 13 April 2018].

Fardoust, S., Kim, Y.B. and Paz Sepulveda, C. eds., 2010. *Postcrisis Growth and Development: A Development Agenda for the G20*. Washington, DC: World Bank.

Fitoussi, J.P., Stiglitz, J.E. and the Paris Group, 2011. *The G20 and Recovery and Beyond: An Agenda for Global Governance for the Twenty-First Century*. OFCE ebook. February. www.ofce.sciences-po.fr/pdf/documents/ebook2011.pdf [Accessed: 13 April 2018].

Fratianni, M., Kirton, J.J., Rugman, A.M. and Savona, P. eds., 2005. *New Perspectives on Global Governance: Why America Needs the G8*. Global Finance Series. Farnham: Ashgate.

Fratianni, M., Salvatore, D. and Savona, P. eds., 1999. *Ideas for the Future of the International Monetary System*. Reprinted from *Open Economies Review*, 9. Special Supplement. Boston: Kluwer Academic Publishers.

Freytag, A., Kirton, J.J., Sally, R. and Savona, P., 2011. *Securing the Global Economy: G8 Global Governance for a Post-Crisis World*. Global Finance Series. Farnham: Ashgate.

Friedrich-Ebert-Stiftung, 2012. *Friedrich-Ebert-Stiftung*. www.fesdc.org/about/friedrich-ebert-stiftung/ [Accessed: 13 April 2018].

Fues, T. and Wolff, P. eds., 2010. *G20 and Global Development: How Can the New Summit Architecture Promote Pro-Poor Growth and Sustainability?* Bonn: German Development Institute [Deutsches Institut für Entwicklungspolitik]. www.g20.utoronto.ca/biblio/GDI_G20_Korea-2010.pdf [Accessed: 13 April 2018].

G7 Information Centre, 2018. *About the G7 and G8 Research Group*. www.g8.utoronto.ca/about/index.html [Accessed: 14 June 2018].

G7 Research Group, 2017. *2016 G7 Ise-Shima Summit Final Compliance Report, 29 May 2016 to 20 May 2017*. 25 May. www.g8.utoronto.ca/evaluations/2016compliance-final/2016-g7-compliance-final.pdf [Accessed: 11 May 2018].

G8 Research Group, 2012. *2011 Deauville G8 Summit Final Compliance Report*. 18 May. www.g7.utoronto.ca/evaluations/2011compliance-final/2011g8finalcompliance.pdf [Accessed: 15 June 2018].

G8 Research Group, 2013. *2012 Camp David G8 Summit Final Compliance Report*. 14 June. www.g8.utoronto.ca/evaluations/2012compliance/2012compliance.pdf [Accessed: 15 June 2018].

G8/G20 Global Working Group, 2012. *Civil Society Statements to the Mexican Government*. 22–24 February. www.g20mexico.org/images/stories/docs/dgvosc/sc20/eng/key_messages_g20_meeting.pdf [Accessed: 31 July 2012].

G20 Information Centre, 2013. *G20 Ministerial and Deputies Meetings*. www.g20.utoronto.ca/ministerials.html [Accessed: 27 November 2017].

G20 Information Centre, 2015. *2014 Brisbane G20 Summit Final Compliance Report*. 14 November. www.g20.utoronto.ca/compliance/2014brisbane-final/index.html [Accessed: 22 February 2017].

G20 Information Centre, 2017a. *G20 Business Summit/B20*. www.g20.utoronto.ca/b20/index.html [Accessed: 13 February 2017].

G20 Information Centre, 2017b. *G20 Meetings of Finance Ministers and Central Bank Governors and Deputies Official Documents*. www.g20.utoronto.ca/ministerials.html [Accessed: 7 February 2017].

G20 Information Centre, 2018a. *G20 Meetings of Finance Ministers and Central Bank Governors and Deputies Official Documents*. www.g20.utoronto.ca/ministerials.html [Accessed: 17 August 2018].

G20 Information Centre, 2018b. *G20 Summits*. www.g20.utoronto.ca/summits/index.html [Accessed: 8 August 2018].

G20 Interfaith Forum, 2017. *InterFaith Summit: Religion, Sustainable Development and the Refugee Crisis*. www.g20interfaith.org/content/g20-interfaith-summit-2017-potsdam [Accessed: 15 August 2018].

G20 Research Group, 2010. *2010 G20 Toronto Summit Final Compliance Report: 28 June 2010 to 29 October 2010*. 14 November. www.g20.utoronto.ca/analysis/2010toronto-101114.pdf [Accessed: 13 April 2018].

G20 Research Group, 2012a. *2011 Cannes G20 Summit Final Compliance Report: 4 November 2011 to 1 June 2012*. 16 June. www.g20.utoronto.ca/compliance/2011cannes-final/2011-g20-compliance-final.pdf [Accessed: 13 April 2018].

G20 Research Group, 2012b. *Mapping G20 Decisions Implementation: How G20 Is Delivering on the Decisions Made; Draft Report*. December. Toronto; Moscow: G20 Research Group and International Organisations Research Institute and Higher School of Economics, National Research University. www.hse.ru/data/2012/12/13/1301054564/Mapping_G20_Decisions_Implementation_full_report.pdf [Accessed: 13 April 2018].

G20 Research Group, 2013. *2012 Los Cabos G20 Summit Final Compliance Report: 20 June 2012 to 30 July 2013*. 4 September. www.g20.utoronto.ca/compliance/2012loscabos-final/ [Accessed: 13 April 2018].

G20 Research Group, 2016. *2015 G20 Antalya Summit Final Compliance Report*. 10 December. www.g20.utoronto.ca/compliance/2015antalya-final/index.html [Accessed: 15 February 2017].

G20 Research Group, 2017. *2016 Hangzhou G20 Summit Final Compliance Report, 6 September 2016 to 6 July 2017*. 23 October. www.g20.utoronto.ca/compliance/2016hangzhou-final/2016-g20-final-compliance.pdf [Accessed: 11 May 2018].

G20 Update (Monthly Newsletter), August 2010. Heinrich Böll Stiftung. www.boell.de/en/2014/02/11/g20-update-archive [Accessed: 13 April 2018].

G20YES, 2012. *G20 YES Mexico*. Los Cabos. 2–5 June. www.g20yea.com/index.php/summits [Accessed: 9 January 2018].

G20 Young Entrepreneurs' Alliance, 2010. *Our Charter*. www.g20yea.com/index.php/our-charter [Accessed: 5 December 2017].

G20 Young Entrepreneurs' Alliance, 2013. G20 *Young Entrepreneurs Conveyed Their Recommendations to the Chief of Business 20*. en.g20russia.ru/news/20130618/781458795.html [Accessed: 9 January 2018].

Gacs, D., Sada, A. and Zissis, C., 2012. *Mexico and the G20: Rethinking Global Economic Balance*. Mexico City. 13 March. Council of the Americas Seminar. www.as-coa.org/articles/mexico-and-g20-rethinking-global-economic-balance [Accessed: 13 April 2018].

Gao, H.H., 2016. *Er Shi Guo Ji Tuan Yu Quan Qiu Jing Ji Zhi Li* [The G20 and Global Economic Governance]. Beijing: China Social Sciences Press.

Gates, W., 2011. *Innovation with Impact: Financing 21st Century Development*. Cannes. www.gatesnotes.com/Development/G20-Report-Innovation-with-Impact [Accessed: 13 April 2018].

Gates, W., 2012. *Letter to President Felipe Calderón Hinojosa*. 13 June. www.g20civil.com/upload/iblock/ec0/Bill%20Gates%20pre-G20%20Letter%20to%20President%20Calderon.pdf [Accessed: 29 July 2012].

Germain, R.D., 2001b. *Reforming the International Financial Architecture: The New Political Agenda*. International Studies Association. Chicago, IL. 20–24 February. www.g8.utoronto.ca/scholar/germain2001/Germain_G20.pdf [Accessed: 13 April 2018].

Gingras, A.T., 2010. *Pre-Emptive Peace: Collective Security & Rogue States in the 21st Century*. Master's thesis. Uppsala: Uppsala Universitet, Dept. of Peace and Conflict Research.

The Girl in the Café, 2005. [DVD] Directed by David Yates. UK: Tightrope Pictures.

G(irls)20 Summit, 2012a. *Communiqué of the 2012 G(irls)20 Summit*. www.girls20summit.com/wp-content/uploads/2012-MEXICO-COMMUNIQUE_FINAL.pdf [Accessed: 6 August 2012].

G(irls)20 Summit, 2012b. *What Do We Do?* girls20.org/about/ [Accessed: 13 April 2018].

Global Solutions, 2018. *Global Solutions Summit 2018*. registration.global-solutions.international [Accessed: 2 May 2018].

Global Summitry Project and Rotman School of Business. *Global Summitry: Politics, Economics, and Law in International Governance*. Oxford: Oxford University Press. academic.oup.com/globalsummitry [Accessed: 03 August 2018].

Globalization Studies Network, 2008. *Uncivil Society*. Waterloo, Canada: Centre for International Governance Innovation. 25–27 August. www.cigionline.org/events/globalization-studies-network-conference-uncivil-society [Accessed: 13 April 2018].

Gnath, K., 2010. *A Group's Architecture in Flux: The G8 and the Heiligendamm Process*. RSCAS Working Paper 2010/06. San Domenico di Fiesole, Italy: Robert Schuman Centre for Advanced Studies, European University Institute. www.g20.utoronto.ca/biblio/RSCAS_2010_06.pdf [Accessed: 14 April 2018].

Gnath, K. and Reimers, N., 2009. *Die G8-Gipfelarchitektur im Wandel: Neue Herausforderungen an globales Regieren am Beispiel von Indiens wirtschaftlichem Aufstieg* [G8 Summitry in Flux: New Challenges for Global Governance Exemplified by India's Economic Rise]. DGAP Analyse, 6. June. www.g8.utoronto.ca/scholar/gnath-reimers.pdf [Accessed: 14 April 2018].

Gnath, K. and Schmucker, C., 2010. *Der Gipfel in Seoul: Nach der Einigung zur IWF-Reform Stehen Weitere Wichtige Entscheidungen auf der Agenda der G20* [The Summit in Seoul: After Agreeing on IMF Reform, The G20 Faces Further Important

Decisions]. DGAP Analyse Kompakt, 8. November. www.g20.utoronto.ca/biblio/2010-08_Schmucker_Gnath.pdf [Accessed: 14 April 2018].

Gnath, K. and Schmucker, C., 2011. *L'Allemagne et les 'clubs G'* [Germany and the 'G Clubs']. Note du Cerfa, 85. Paris: Comité d'études des relations franco-allemandes. May. www.g20.utoronto.ca/biblio/IFRI_noteducerfa85clubsgfr.pdf [Accessed: 14 April 2018]. Also available in German: *Deutschland und die G-Clubs*. www.g20.utoronto.ca/biblio/IFRI_noteducerfa85gclubsde.pdf [Accessed: 14 April 2018].

Goldman Sachs Global Economics Group, 2007. *BRICs and Beyond*. November. www.goldmansachs.com/our-thinking/archive/archive-pdfs/brics-book/brics-full-book.pdf [Accessed: 14 April 2018].

Grevi, G., 2011. *The G20 after Cannes: An Identity Crisis*. FRIDE Policy Brief, No. 105. Madrid: Fundación para las Relaciones Internacionales y el Diálogo Exterior. November. www.fride.org/download/PB_105_G20_after_Cannes.pdf [Accessed: 23 February 2016].

Griffith-Jones, S., Helleiner, E. and Woods, N. eds., 2010. *The Financial Stability Board: An Effective Fourth Pillar of Global Economic Governance?* CIGI Special Report. Waterloo, Canada: Centre for International Governance Innovation. June. www.cigionline.org/publications/financial-stability-board-effective-fourth-pillar-global-economic-governance [Accessed: 14 April 2018].

Gronau, J., 2015. *Die Selbstlegitimation internationaler Institutionen. G8 und G20 im Vergleich*. Frankfurt am Main and New York: Campus.

Gronau, J. and Schneider, S., 2009. *Metaphorical Concepts and the Discursive Construction of Legitimacy: The Discursive Framing of International Governance Arrangements*. American Political Science Annual Conference. Toronto. 5 October.

Hajnal, P.I., 2007a. *The G8 System and the G20: Evolution, Role and Documentation*. Global Finance Series. Aldershot: Ashgate.

Hajnal, P.I., 2007b. *Summitry from G5 to L20: A Review of Reform Initiatives*. Centre for International Governance Innovation. Working Paper, No. 20. www.cigionline.org/publications/summitry-g5-l20-review-reform-initiatives [Accessed: 21 February 2018].

Hajnal, P.I., 2008. *Gruppa Vos'mi i Gruppa Dvadtsati: Evoliutsiia, Rol' i Dokumentatsiia*. Moscow: Logos.

Hajnal, P.I., 2010a. *Ba Guo Ji Tuan Ti Xi Yu Er Shi Guo Ji Tuan: Yan Jin, Jue Se Yu Wen Xian* [The G8 System and the G20]. Shanghai: Shanghai Ren Min Chu Ban She [Shanghai People's Publishing House].

Hajnal, P.I., 2010b. *The World Religions Summit 2010: Interfaith Leaders in the G8 Nations: Notes of an Observer*. www.g8.utoronto.ca/evaluations/2010muskoka/hajnal-faith.html [Accessed: 14 April 2018].

Hajnal, P.I., 2014. *The G20: Evolution, Interrelationships, Documentation*. Farnham: Ashgate.

Haley, J.A., 2012a. *Los Cabos Summit: Incremental Steps on the Road to Globalizing the Regulation of Capital*. 20 June. www.cigionline.org/articles/los-cabos-summit-incremental-steps-road-globalizing-regulation-capital [Accessed: 14 April 2018].

Haley, J.A. ed., 2012b. *Perspectives on the G20: The Los Cabos Summit and Beyond*. Waterloo, Canada: Centre for International Governance Innovation. June. www.cigionline.org/publications/perspectives-g20-los-cabos-summit-and-beyond [Accessed: 14 April 2018].

Halifax Initiative, 2010a. *Parliamentary Roundtables on the G8/G20 Agendas*. www.halifaxinitiative.org/content/parliamentary-roundtables-g8g20-agendas [Accessed: 14 April 2018].

Halifax Initiative, 2010b. *What's Missing in the Response to the Global Financial Crisis?* www.halifaxinitiative.org/content/conference-whats-missing-response-global-financial-crisis [Accessed: 14 April 2018].

Heap, P.C., 2008. *Globalization and Summit Reform: An Experiment in International Governance*. New York and Ottawa: Springer; International Development Research Centre. *Provides an accessible account of the L20 proposals (see English and Thakur 2005).*

Heap, P.C., 2011. *The New Geometry of Global Summitry: The Future of the G20 (and the G8): Conference Report*. Waterloo, Canada: Centre for International Governance Innovation. 25 May. www.cigionline.org/sites/default/files/conference_report_1.pdf [Accessed: 24 February 2018].

Heinbecker, P., 2011a. *The Future of the G20 and Its Place in Global Governance*. CIGI G20 Papers, No. 5. Waterloo, Canada: Centre for International Governance Innovation. 27 April. www.cigionline.org/sites/default/files/g20no5.pdf [Accessed: 11 June 2018].

Heine, J. and Thakur, R. eds., 2011. *The Dark Side of Globalization*. Tokyo: United Nations University Press.

Heinrich Böll Stiftung, 2018. *G20 in Focus*. www.boell.de/en/g20-germany-2017 [Accessed: 15 August 2018].

Heinrich Böll Stiftung North America, 2012a. *Business 20 (B-20) Dossier*. www.boell.org/web/group_of_20-B20-Dossier.html [Accessed: 29 December 2012].

Heinrich Böll Stiftung North America, 2012b. *G20 Dossier*. www.boell.org/web/group_of_20.html [Accessed: 29 December 2012].

Heinrich Böll Stiftung North America, 2012c. *G20 Fundamentals*. www.boell.org/web/group_of_20-G20_Fundamentals.html [Accessed: 13 May 2013].

Helleiner, E., 2010b. *The Financial Stability Board and International Standards*. CIGI G20 Paper, No. 1. Waterloo, Canada: Centre for International Governance Innovation. June. www.cigionline.org/publications/financial-stability-board-and-international-standards [Accessed: 14 April 2018].

Helleiner, E., 2010c. *Lasting Legacy on Financial Regulatory Reform*. Seoul G20 Commentaries. Waterloo, Canada: Centre for International Governance Innovation. November. www.cigionline.org/publications/lasting-legacy-financial-regulatory-reform [Accessed: 14 April 2018].

Helleiner, E. and Pagliari, S., 2008. *Towards the G20 Summit: From Financial Crisis to International Regulatory Reform*. CIGI Policy Brief No. 9. Waterloo, Canada: Centre for International Governance Innovation. November. www.cigionline.org/publications/towards-g20-summit-financial-crisis-international-regulatory-reform [Accessed: 14 April 2018].

Helleiner, G.K., 2001. *Developing Countries, Global Financial Governance and the Group of Twenty: A Note*. Toronto: University of Toronto. fpif.org/developing_countries_global_financial_governance_and_the_group_of_twenty/ [Accessed: 14 April 2018].

Hermawan, Y.P., Sriyuliani, W., Hardjowijono, G.H. and Tanaga, S., 2011. *The Role of Indonesia in the G-20: Background, Role and Objectives of Indonesia's Membership*. G-20 Research Project. (Jakarta: Friedrich-Ebert-Stiftung Indonesia Office in cooperation with Department of International Relations, Parahyangan University). May. library.fes.de/pdf-files/bueros/indonesien/08365.pdf [Accessed: 14 April 2018].

Hersh, A.S., 2010. *DRAFT: Monitoring Commitments and Compliance of the G20 Framework for Strong, Sustainable, and Balanced Growth*. 13 January. www.new-rules.org/storage/documents/g20-fsb-imf/g20_matrix.pdf [Accessed: 14 April 2018].

Hillman, J., 2010. *Saving Multilateralism: Renovating the House of Global Economic Governance for the 21st Century*. Brussels Forum Paper Series. Washington, DC: German

Marshall Fund of the United States. 4 March. brussels.gmfus.org/publications/jennifer-hillman-renovating-house-global-economic-governace-21st-century-new-european [Accessed: 22 February 2018].

Hofmeister, W. and Vogt, S., 2011. *G20: Perceptions and Perspectives for Global Governance*. Singapore: Konrad Adenauer Stiftung. 19 October. www.kas.de/wf/en/33.29099 [Accessed: 14 April 2018].

Hollande, F., 2018. *Les leçons du pouvoir*. Paris: Stock.

Huigens, J. and Niemann, A., 2009. *The EU within the G8: A Case of Ambiguous and Contested Actorness*. EU Diplomacy Papers, 5/2009. Bruges: College of Europe. www.g8.utoronto.ca/scholar/huigensneimann.pdf [Accessed: 24 October 2017].

Hurd, D., 1998. *The Shape of Ice*. London: Little, Brown.

InterAction, 2010. *The G20 and Development: A New Era (updated)*. reliefweb.int/sites/reliefweb.int/files/resources/4513928080F35D68492577BC0009F071-Full_Report.pdf [Accessed: 14 April 2018].

InterAction, 2011. *G20 Summit Policy Paper: Recommendations for Cannes Summit*. September. www.interaction.org/document/g20-summit-policy-paper-recommendations-cannes-summit [Accessed: 15 April 2018].

InterAction, 2012a. G20 *Background Policy Brief: Accountability: It's Time for a G20 Commitment*. March. www.scribd.com/document/85242171/g20-Background-Brief-Final-Accountability-3-5-12 [Accessed: 15 April 2018].

InterAction, 2012b. *Background Policy Brief: Anti-Corruption*. February. www.interaction.org/sites/default/files/5649/G20%20Background%20brief%20FINAL%20ANTI-CORRUPTION%202-27-2012%20(updated)_0.pdf [Accessed: 4 August 2012].

InterAction, 2012c. *G20 Background Policy Brief: Financial Inclusion*. March. www.scribd.com/document/85241207/g20-Background-Brief-Final-Financial-Inclusion-3-5-2012 [Accessed: 15 April 2018].

InterAction, 2012d. *G20 Background Policy Brief: Food Security, Agriculture and Nutrition*. March. www.scribd.com/document/85242666/G20-Background-Brief-FINAL-FS-AG-N-3-5-2012 [Accessed: 15 April 2018].

InterAction, 2012e. *G20 Background Policy Brief: Green Growth and Climate Change*. March. www.scribd.com/document/93504189/g20-Background-Brief-Final-Green-Growth-3-5-2012-0 [Accessed: 15 April 2018].

InterAction, 2012f. *G20 Leaders Declaration Scorecard*. 22 August. www.interaction.org/sites/default/files/5524/G20%20Declaration%20SUMMARY%20%20scorecard%20CHART%208-15-12.pdf [Accessed: 23 November 2012].

InterAction, 2012g. *Los Cabos G20 Summit: InterAction Scorecard and Summaries of Selected Documents and Reports*. August. osf.org.za/wp-content/uploads/2015/08/G20-Leaders-Declaration-scorecard.pdf [Accessed: 15 April 2018].

InterAction, 2012h. *Recommendations for Los Cabos, Mexico Summit*. February. www.interaction.org/sites/default/files/G20%20Policy%20Paper%202-14-12%20FINAL_0.pdf [Accessed: 15 April 2018].

InterAction. 2017. *2017 G20 Summit Recommendations* [of the] *G7/G20 Advocacy Alliance (U.S.) Hamburg, Germany*. G20 Policy Paper. February. https://www.interaction.org/document/2017-g20-summit-recommendations [Accessed: 17 May 2018].

InterAction Council, 2011. *Final Communiqué: 29th Annual Plenary Meeting*. 29–31 May. www.interactioncouncil.org/publications/29th-annual-plenary-meeting [Accessed: 3 August 2018].

InterAction Council, 2012. *Final Communiqué*. 10–12 May. www.interactioncouncil.org/publications/30th-annual-plenary-meeting [Accessed: 15 June 2018].

InterAction and G7/G20 Advocacy Alliance, 2018. *2018 G20 Summit Recommendations*. G20 Policy Paper. March. reliefweb.int/sites/reliefweb.int/files/resources/G20-Policy-Paper-2018.pdf [Accessed: 14 May 2018].

International Chamber of Commerce, 2010a. *Business and the World Economy: ICC Statement on Behalf of World Business to the Heads of State and Government Attending the G8 and G20 Summits in Canada*. 25–27 June. www.iccwbo.org/Advocacy-Codes-and-Rules/Document-centre/2010/Business-and-the-world-economy/ [Accessed: 8 September 2012].

International Chamber of Commerce, 2010b. *Why ICC?: A Legacy in Working with the G8-G20*. www.iccwbo.org/Global-influence/G20/ICC-and-G8-G20/Why-ICC-a-legacy-in-working-with-the-G8-G20/ [Accessed: 8 September 2012].

International Chamber of Commerce, 2011. *G20 Countries Fail to Lead in Trade Openness, ICC Index Indicates*. Geneva. 16 December. iccwbo.org/media-wall/news-speeches/g20-countries-fail-to-lead-in-trade-openness-icc-index-indicates/ [Accessed: 6 January 2018].

International Chamber of Commerce, 2012a. *Business Bolstered by G20 Progress in Los Cabos*. 28 June. https://iccwbo.org/media-wall/news-speeches/business-bolstered-by-g20-progress-in-los-cabos/ [Accessed: 7 January 2018].

International Chamber of Commerce, 2012b. *G20 Business Scorecard*. June. cdn.iccwbo.org/content/uploads/sites/3/2016/11/2012-ICC-G20-Business-Scorecard-high-resolution.pdf [Accessed: 24 November 2017].

International Chamber of Commerce, 2012c. *ICC Delivers Global Business Priorities to G20, Rates Progress as Incomplete*. Los Cabos. 18 June. iccwbo.org/media-wall/news-speeches/icc-delivers-global-business-priorities-to-g20-rates-progress-as-incomplete/ [Accessed: 6 January 2018].

International Chamber of Commerce, 2013a. *ICC Summary of the St. Petersburg G20 Leaders' Declaration*. 12 September. cdn.iccwbo.org/content/uploads/sites/3/2016/11/ICC-summary-of-St-Petersburg-G20-Leaders-Declaration.pdf [Accessed: 24 November 2017].

International Chamber of Commerce, 2013b. *St Petersburg G20 Business Summit*. iccwbo.org/Global-influence/G20/ICC-and-G8-G20/St-Petersburg-G20-Business-Summit/ [Accessed: 10 October 2013].

International Chamber of Commerce, 2014. *Global Survey of Business Policy Priorities for G20 Leaders*. cdn.iccwbo.org/content/uploads/sites/3/2016/11/ICC-survey-results-Global-survey-of-business-policy-priorities-for-G20-leaders-2014.pdf [Accessed: 24 November 2017].

International Chamber of Commerce, 2016a. *ICC G20 Business Scorecard*, 6th ed. December. cdn.iccwbo.org/content/uploads/sites/3/2017/01/ICC-G20-Business-Scorecard-December-2016.pdf [Accessed: 17 May 2018].

International Chamber of Commerce, 2016b. *Six Steps to Energy Sustainability and Security for the G20 Energy Ministers*. cdn.iccwbo.org/content/uploads/sites/3/2016/11/Six-steps-to-energy-sustainability-and-security.pdf [Accessed: 24 November 2017].

International Chamber of Commerce, 2016c. *Summary of the Hangzhou G20 Leaders' Communiqué*. cdn.iccwbo.org/content/uploads/sites/3/2016/11/ICC-summary-of-the-Hangzhou-G20-Leaders-Communique-6-September-2016.pdf [Accessed: 24 November 2017].

International Organisations Research Institute and G20 Research Group, 2012. *Mapping G20 Decisions Implementation: How G20 Is Delivering on the Decisions Made*. Draft Report. December. Higher School of Economics, National Research University and Munk School of Global Affairs, University of Toronto. www.hse.ru/data/2012/12/13/1301054564/Mapping_G20_Decisions_Implementation_full_report.pdf [Accessed: 15 April 2018].

Jaffrelot, C., 2011. *La France, le G20 et les 'pays émergents': un nouvel équilibre des pouvoirs?* Document de travail. Institut Choiseul. January. www.institutmontaigne.org/publications/la-france-le-g20-et-les-pays-emergents-un-nouvel-equilibre-des-pouvoirs [Accessed: 15 April 2018].

Jenkell, L., 2011. *Jenkell/Parcours: sculptures en plein coeur de Cannes*. Quimper: Editions.

Jenkins, P. and Subacchi, P., 2011. *Preventing Crises and Promoting Economic Growth: A Framework for International Policy Cooperation.* Joint Chatham House-CIGI Report. Waterloo, Canada and London: Centre for International Governance Innovation; Chatham House. April. www.cigionline.org/publications/special-report-preventing-crises-and-promoting-economic-growth [Accessed: 15 April 2018].

Joint Religious Coordination for the G8 and G20 Summits, 2012. *2012 Religious Leaders' Statement for the G8 and G20 Summits.* Georgetown University's Berkley Center for Religion, Peace & World Affairs. repository.berkleycenter.georgetown.edu/120517FinalStatementJRLCS.pdf [Accessed: 15 April 2018].

Jokela, J., 2011. *The G-20: A Pathway to Effective Multilateralism?* Chaillot Paper, No. 125. Paris: European Union, Institute for Security Studies. 21 April. www.iss.europa.eu/content/g-20-pathway-effective-multilateralism [Accessed: 15 April 2018].

Kaiser, K., Kirton, J.J. and Daniels, J. eds., 2000. *Shaping a New International Financial System: Challenges of Governance in a Globalizing World.* Aldershot: Ashgate.

Kamal, D. and Drysdale, P., 2014. *The G-20 Summit at Five: Time for Strategic Leadership.* Washington, DC: Brookings Institution Press.

Kassum, J., 2011. *The G20: What It Is and What It Does: A Business Guide*. ICC Publication, 730E. Paris: International Chamber of Commerce.

Keil, K., 2017. *The G20 Compact with Africa: Innovation Partnership or Business as Usual?* Heinrich Böll Stiftung North America. 13 December. us.boell.org/2017/12/13/g20-compact-africa-innovative-partnerships-or-business-usual [Accessed: 5 June 2018].

Kenen, P.B., et al., 2004. *International Economic and Financial Cooperation: New Issues, New Actors, New Responses*. London: Centre for Economic Policy Research.

Kharas, H. and Lombardi, D., 2012. *The Group of Twenty: Origins, Prospects and Challenges for Global Governance*. Global Economy and Development. Washington, DC: Brookings Institution. www.brookings.edu/wp-content/uploads/2016/06/g20-global-governance-kharas-lombardi.pdf [Accessed: 30 January 2018].

Kirton, J.J., 1999. *What Is the G20?* Adapted from *The G7, China and the International Financial System*. International Think Tank Forum on 'China in the Twenty-First Century'. China Development Institute. 10–12 November. www.g8.utoronto.ca/g20/g20whatisit.html [Accessed: 15 April 2018].

Kirton, J.J., 2004. *Getting the L20 Going: Reaching out from the G8*. Prepared for workshop 'G20 to Replace the G8: Why Not Now?', sponsored by the Brookings Institution, Peterson Institute for International Economics, and the Centre for Global Governance, Washington, DC. 22 September. www.g8.utoronto.ca/scholar/kirton2004/kirton_040922.html [Accessed: 15 April 2018].

Kirton, J.J., 2005a. From G7 to G20: Capacity, leadership and normative diffusion in global financial governance. In: ISA (International Studies Association), *Dynamics of World Politics: Capacity, Preferences and Leadership*. Honolulu, Hawaii. 1–5 March. www.g8.utoronto.ca/scholar/kirton2005/kirton_isa2005.pdf [Accessed: 18 October 2017].

Kirton, J.J., 2008a. *The Case for G8 Reform*. Lecture delivered at Chuo University, Tokyo. 26 June. www.g8.utoronto.ca/scholar/kirton_reform_080629.pdf [Accessed: 24 February 2018].

Kirton, J.J., 2010c. *The G20, the G8, the G5 and the Role of Ascending Powers*. Prepared for the seminar on 'Ascending Powers and the International System', Instituto Matías Romero, Secretaria de Relaciones Exteriores, Mexico City, 13–14 December, and for publication in *Revista Mexicana de Politica Exterior*. 27 December. www.g20.utoronto.ca/biblio/kirton-g20-g8-g5.pdf [Accessed: 15 April 2018].

Kirton, J.J., 2012. *How the G20 Has Escaped Diminishing Returns*. Paper prepared for the conference 'International Co-operation in Times of Global Crisis: Views from G20 Countries', Higher School of Economics, Moscow, 18–19 October.

Kirton, J.J., 2013b. *G20 Governance for a Globalized World*. Farnham: Ashgate.

Kirton, J.J., 2013d. *A Summit of Very Substantial Success: G20 Governance of the Global Economy and Security at St. Petersburg*. 6 September. www.g20.utoronto.ca/analysis/130906-kirton-performance.html [Accessed: 15 April 2018].

Kirton, J.J., 2015b. *Kirton Scoring Scheme*. 16 November. www.g20.utoronto.ca/analysis/scoring.html [Accessed: 22 February 2017].

Kirton, J.J., 2016. *A Summit of Significant Success: G20 Leaders at the 2016 Hangzhou Summit*. 7 September. www.g20.utoronto.ca/analysis/160907-kirton-performance.html [Accessed: 22 February 2017].

Kirton, J.J., 2017a. *China's G20 Leadership*. Global Governance Series. London and New York: Routledge.

Kirton, J.J., 2017b. *A Summit of Significant Success: The G20 at Hamburg*. 11 July. www.g20.utoronto.ca/analysis/170711-kirton-performance.html [Accessed: 14 May 2018].

Kirton, J.J. and Bracht, C., 2012. *The BRICS Big Boost for the G20 Los Cabos Summit Success*. 18 June. www.brics.utoronto.ca/analysis/brics-g20-2012.html#appendix [Accessed: 23 February 2018].

Kirton, J.J., Bracht, C. and Rasmussen, L., 2012. *Implementing the G20 Seoul Development and Employment Commitments: An Assessment*. 29 October. www.g20.utoronto.ca/biblio/SDC_Assessment.pdf [Accessed: 15 April 2018].

Kirton, J.J. and Koch, M. eds., 2008a. *The G20 Cannes Summit 201: A New Way Forward*. London: Newsdesk Communications.

Kirton, J.J. and Koch, M. eds., 2008b. *G20 São Paulo/Brazil Summit 2008: Growth, Innovation, Inclusion: The G20 at Ten*. London: Newsdesk Communications.

Kirton, J.J. and Koch, M. eds., 2009a. *G20: The London Summit 2009: Growth, Stability, Jobs*. London: Newsdesk Communications.

Kirton, J.J. and Koch, M. eds., 2009b. *G20: The Pittsburgh Summit 2009: Sustaining Global Recovery*. London: Newsdesk Communications.

Kirton, J.J. and Koch, M. eds., 2010a. *G8-G20: The Canadian Summits: Recovery and New Beginnings*. London: Newsdesk Communications.

Kirton, J.J. and Koch, M. eds., 2010b. *The G20 Seoul Summit 2010: Shared Growth beyond Crisis*. London: Newsdesk Communications.

Kirton, J.J. and Koch, M. eds., 2011. *G20: The Cannes Summit: A New Way Forward*. London: Newsdesk Media.

Kirton, J.J. and Koch, M. eds., 2012. *G20: The Mexico Summit: The Quest for Growth and Stability*. London: Newsdesk Media.

Kirton, J.J. and Kulik, J., 2012a. *The Shortcomings of the G20 Los Cabos Summit*. Toronto: G20 Research Group. 27 June. www.g20.utoronto.ca/analysis/120627-kirton-kulik-shortcomings.html [Accessed: 24 October 2017].

Kirton, J.J. and Kulik, J., 2012b. *A Summit of Significant Success: G20 Los Cabos Leaders Deliver the Desired Double Dividend*. Los Cabos: G20 Research Group. 19 June. www.g20.utoronto.ca/analysis/120619-kirton-success.html [Accessed: 24 October 2017].

Kirton, J.J. and Larionova, M. eds., 2012. *BRICS New Delhi Summit 2012: Stability, Security and Prosperity*. London: Newsdesk Communications.

Kirton, J.J. and Larionova, M. eds., 2018. *Accountability for Effectiveness in Global Governance*. Global Governance Series. London and New York: Routledge.

Kirton, J.J., Larionova, M. and Savona, P. eds., 2010. *Making Global Economic Governance Effective: Hard and Soft Law Institutions in a Crowded World*. Aldershot: Ashgate.

Kirton, J.J. and von Furstenberg, G. eds., 2001. *New Directions in Global Economic Governance: Managing Globalization in the Twenty-First Century*. Aldershot: Ashgate.

Kokotsis, E., 1998. *National Compliance with G7 Environment and Development Commitments, 1988–1995*. Ph.D. (political economy). Toronto: University of Toronto.

Kokotsis, E., 1999. *Keeping International Commitments: Compliance, Credibility, and the G7, 1988–1995*. New York: Garland Publishing.

Kokotsis, E., 2006. *G8 Compliance Coding and Reference Manual*. Toronto: G8 Research Group. www.g8.utoronto.ca/evaluations/compliance_manual_2006.pdf [Accessed: 15 April 2018].

Konrad Adenauer Stiftung, 2012. *[4th] G20 Conference on Global Economic Cooperation: Views from G20 Countries*. 8–9 October. www.kas.de/indien/en/publications/32350/ [Accessed: 15 April 2018].

Koplow, D., 2012. *Phasing Out Fossil-Fuel Subsidies in the G20: A Progress Update*. Oil Change International. June. priceofoil.org/wp-content/uploads/2012/06/FIN.OCI_Phasing_out_fossil-fuel_g20.pdf [Accessed: 15 April 2018].

Kotte, D.J., 2011. *G-20 Two Years after the Crisis: Back to Business as Usual?* International Policy Analysis. Berlin: Friedrich-Ebert-Stiftung. October. library.fes.de/pdf-files/iez/08568.pdf [Accessed: 15 April 2018].

Kraemer, R.A., 2017. *The G20 and Building Global Governance for 'Climate Refugees'*. Policy Brief 107. May. www.cigionline.org/sites/default/files/documents/PB%20no.107web.pdf [Accessed: 11 June 2018].

Kulik, J., 2012. *Where Are Women at G20 Summits: Almost Nowhere*. 29 November. www.g20.utoronto.ca/analysis/120619-kulik-women.html [Accessed: 12 February 2017].

Kulik, J., 2014. *A BRICS Alliance within the G20? Assessing the Performance of BRICS Members*. Paper prepared for the Seminario Internacional Sobre Potencias Intermediarias, Belo Horizonte, Brazil, 12 September.

Kulik, J., 2015. *G20 Gender Policy Accountability*. 13 November. www.g20.utoronto.ca/analysis/151113-kulik.html [Accessed: 12 February 2017].

Kulik, J. and Kirton, J.J., 2012. *At the G8 Camp David Summit, Where Are the Women? Everywhere!* 20 May. www.g8.utoronto.ca/evaluations/2012campdavid/kulik-kirton-women.html [Accessed: 15 April 2018].

L20 [Labour 20], 2012. *L20 Statement to the G20 Summit*. June. www.g20.utoronto.ca/2012/2012-l20-en.pdf [Accessed: 15 April 2018].

L20 [Labour 20], 2013. *TUAC-ITUC Evaluation of the G20 Saint-Petersburg Summit Outcomes*. 6 September. en.g20russia.ru/load/783171459 [Accessed: 15 April 2018].

L20, 2017. *Global Unions Reaction to Hamburg G20 Summit*. 11 July. www.ituc-csi.org/global-unions-reaction-to-hamburg?lang=fr [Accessed: 3 July 2018].

Larionova, M. ed., 2007. *Problemy Effektivnosti i Reformy Sistemy Mezhdunarodnykh Mnogostoronnikh Institutov* [Problems of Effectiveness and Reform of the System of

International Multilateral Institutions]. Moscow: International Organizations and International Cooperation Institute. Higher School of Economics.

Larionova, M. ed., 2010b. G-X Summitry. *International Organizations Research Journal*, 5(31). Moscow: International Organizations Research Institute, Higher School of Economics.

Larionova, M. ed., 2012a. *The European Union in the G8: Promoting Consensus and Concerted Actions for Global Public Goods*. Farnham: Ashgate.

Larionova, M. ed., 2012d. *Razdelenie Truda kak Osnova Povysheniia Effektivnosti Mnogostoronnikh Mekhanizmov Global'nogo Upravleniia* [Division of Labour as a Foundation for Increasing the Effectiveness of Multilateral Mechanisms of Global Governance]. Moscow: Publishing House of the Higher School of Economics.

Larionova, M. and Kirton, J.J. eds., 2015. *The G8-G20 Relationship in Global Governance*. Global Governance Series. Farnham: Ashgate.

Lee, D., 2009. *The G20 in Korea's Diplomacy*. Munk Centre for International Studies. University of Toronto. 6 November. www.g20.utoronto.ca/events/lee-091106.html [Accessed: 15 April 2018].

Leifso, D., Bradford, C.I., Carin, B., Smith, G. and Jenkins, P., 2011. *Challenges and Opportunities for the French Presidency: The G20–2011 and Beyond*. CIGI-IFRI Conference Report March. Waterloo, Canada: Centre for International Governance Innovation. www.cigionline.org/publications/challenges-and-opportunities-french-presidency-g20-2011-and-beyond [Accessed: 15 April 2018].

Lesage, D. ed., 2010a. *The Future of the G8 and G20*. Special issue of *Studia Diplomatica*, 63(2).

Li, J.P., Li, M.R. and Zhao, X.L., 2014. *Er Shi Guo Ji Tuan Guo Jia Chuang Xin Jing Zheng Li Fa Zhan Bao Gao (2013–2014)*. [Report on the G20 National Innovation Competitive Development (2013–2014)]. Beijing: Social Sciences Academic Press.

Li, S.C., 2011. *Quan Qiu Zhi Li Shi Ye Xia De G20 Yan Jiu* [G20 Research from the Perspective of Global Governance]. PhD. (international relations). Shanghai Social Science Institute.

Lombardi, D., Jenkins, P., Siklos, P., Bernes, T.A., Schadler, S. Carin, B. and Smith, G., 2013. *Priorities for the G20: The St. Petersburg Summit and Beyond*. Waterloo, Canada: Centre for International Governance Innovation. www.cigionline.org/publications/priorities-g20-st-petersburg-summit-and-beyond [Accessed: 15 April 2018].

Löschmann, H. and Alexander, N., 2016. *The Solar System of G20: Engagement Groups*. 9 December. us.boell.org/2016/12/09/solar-system-g20-engagement-groups [Accessed: 15 June 2018].

Lukov, V., 2004. *'Gruppa Vos'mi : Uchebnoe Posobie* [The Group of Twenty: A Textbook]. Moscow: Nauchnaia Kniga.

Make Poverty History, 2010. *Progress in Combating Poverty under Threat: Anti-Poverty Activists Tell G8 Top Policy Makers*. 16 April. archive.makepovertyhistory.ca/en/news/progress-combatting-poverty-under-threat-antipoverty-activists-tell-g8-top-policy-makers [Accessed: 3 August 2012].

Martens, J., 2016. Corporate influence on the G20. *Just Governance blog*. March. just-governance.boellblog.org/2017/03/22/corporate-influence-on-the-g20-by-jens-martens/ [Accessed: 8 December 2017].

Martens, J., 2017. *Corporate Influence on the G20: The Case of the B20 and Transnational Business Networks*. March. Berlin, Bonn and New York: Heinrich Böll Stiftung; Global Policy Forum. www.boell.de/sites/default/files/corporate_influence_on_the_g20.pdf?dimension1=ds_g20_en [Accessed: 8 December 2017].

Martin, N. and Tandon, R. eds., 2014. *Global Governance, Civil Society and Participatory Democracy: A View from Below*. New Delhi: Academic Foundation.

Martin, P., 2006. *Speaking Notes for the Right Honourable Paul Martin P.C., M.P.: Annual Meeting of the Development and Peace Foundation*. Dresden, Germany. 8 June.

Martin, P., 2008. *Hell or High Water: My Life in and out of Politics*. Toronto: McClelland & Stewart.

Martin, P., 2015. *Strengthening the Multilateral Institutions: A G20 Priority*. 2 November. www.cigionline.org/publications/strengthening-multilateral-institutions-g20-priority-0 [Accessed: 11 June 2018].

Martinez-Diaz, L., 2007. *The G20 after Eight Years: How Effective a Vehicle for Developing-Country Influence?* Global Economy and Development Working Papers, No. 11. Washington, DC: The Brookings Institution. 17 October. www.brookings.edu/research/the-g-20-after-eight-years-how-effective-a-vehicle-for-developing-country-influence/ [Accessed: 15 April 2018].

McGann, J.G., 2018. *2017 Global Go to Think Tank Index Report*. Philadelphia: Think Tanks and Civil Societies Program, University of Pennsylvania. 31 January. repository.upenn.edu/think_tanks/13/ [Accessed: 8 June 2018].

Mistral, J., 2011b. *Le G20 et la nouvelle gouvernance économique mondiale* [The G20 and New Global Economic Governance]. Cahiers du Cercle des économistes. Paris: Presses Universitaires de France.

Moschella, M., 2011. *Delegation to and Discretion for the Financial Stability Board and the G20: Transaction Costs or Legitimacy Concerns?* GARNET Working Paper 73/09. Brussels. February. www.garnet-eu.org/fileadmin/documents/working_papers/7510.pdf [Accessed: 25 January 2013].

Munk School of Global Affairs, 2012. *Global Summitry Project*. University of Toronto. munkschool.utoronto.ca/program/global-summitry-project and globalsummitryproject.com [Accessed: 19 April 2018].

Murray, S., 2013. *The G-20 and Food Security: What Is the Right Agenda? Policy Analysis Brief*. Muscatine, Iowa: Stanley Foundation. March. www.stanleyfoundation.org/publications/pab/MurphyPAB313.pdf [Accessed: 19 April 2018].

Naylor, T., 2012. *Civil Society Inclusion at Los Cabos 2012*. 26 June. www.g20.utoronto.ca/analysis/120626-naylor.html [Accessed: 19 April 2018].

Nayyar, D. ed., 2002. *Governing Globalization: Issues and Institutions*. New Delhi: Oxford University Press.

New Rules for Global Finance, 2012a. *The Financial Stability Board: Unlocking the Black Box*. www.new-rules.org/what-we-do/fsb-unlocking-the-black-box [Accessed: 19 April 2018].

New Rules for Global Finance, 2012b. *Promises of the G20 Process: Prospects for Advancing Transparency and Accountability*. 18 June. www.new-rules.org/events/3-nr-event/391-promises-of-the-g20 [Accessed: 28 November 2017].

New Rules for Global Finance, 2012c. *Revised FSB Charter: Shift toward Improved Transparency and Inclusion*. www.new-rules.org/news/program-updates/411-revised-fsb-charter-shift-toward-improved-transparency-and-inclusion and www.new-rules.org/storage/documents/revised_fsb_charter_with_annotations.pdf [Accessed: 19 April 2018].

New Rules for Global Finance, 2013. *Global Financial Governance & Impact Report*. new-rules.org/storage/documents/global_financial_governance__impact%20report_2013%20.pdf [Accessed: 19 April 2018].

New Rules for Global Finance and Friedrich-Ebert-Stiftung, 2016. *How Global Financial Institutions Impact Inequality: A Workshop to Strengthen Understanding, Assessment &*

Reporting. www.new-rules.org/storage/documents/Workshop-Report-How-Global-Financial-Institutions-Impact-Inequality-FINAL.pdf [Accessed: 14 May 2018].

ONE, 2010. *The DATA Report: Monitoring the G8 Promise to Africa*. www.one.org/report/2010/en/downloads/DR2010.pdf [Accessed: 23 November 2012].

ONE, 2011. *Policy Analysis [of] G20 [Cannes] Final Documents*. November. webmail.utoronto.ca/imp/view.php?popup_view=1&index=88850&mailbox=INBOX&actionID=view_attach&id=2&mimecache=5c88089d62672737f0f4c7a0bc7f0708 [Accessed: 25 November 2012].

ONE, 2012. *2012 DATA Report: Europe's African Promise*. 6 July. one.org.s3.amazonaws.com/pdfs/data_report_2012_en.pdf [Accessed: 19 April 2018].

ONE, 2014. *The 2014 Data Report: Fighting Poverty and Financing Africa's Future*. one-org.s3.amazonaws.com/us/wp-content/uploads/2014/10/One_DATA_Report-2014-9-19-14-RGB.pdf [Accessed: 22 February 2017].

ONE, 2017. *2017 DATA Report: Financing for the African Century*. 28 August. one.org.s3.amazonaws.com/pdfs/one_data_report_2017_en.pdf [Accessed: 15 May 2018].

O'Neill, J., 2009. *Some Advice for the G20*. Global Economics Paper No. 181. Goldman Sachs Global Economics, Commodities and Strategy Research. 20 March. www.goldmansachs.com/our-thinking/archive/some-advice-for-g20.pdf [Accessed: 19 April 2018].

O'Neill, J. and Hormats, R., 2004. *The G8: Time for a Change*. Global Economics Paper, No. 112 Goldman Sachs. 3 June.

Oxfam, 2010. *The Making of a Seoul Development Consensus: The Essential Development Agenda for the G-20*. Oxfam Briefing Note. 11 October. www.oxfam.org/sites/www.oxfam.org/files/bn-making-seoul-consensus-g20-111010-en.pdf [Accessed: 19 April 2018].

Oxfam, 2011. *Not a Game: Speculation vs. Food Security: Regulating Financial Markets to Grow a Better Future*. Oxfam Issue Briefing. 3 October. www.oxfam.org/sites/www.oxfam.org/files/ib-speculation-vs-food-security-031011-en.pdf [Accessed: 19 April 2018].

Oxfam, 2012a. *G20 Fails 1 Billion Hungry People Worldwide*. 19 June. www.oxfam.org/en/grow/pressroom/pressrelease/2012-06-19/g20-fails-1-billion-hungry-people-worldwide [Accessed: 19 April 2018].

Oxfam, 2012b. *Left behind by the G20? How Inequality and Environmental Degradation Threaten to Exclude Poor People from the Benefits of Economic Growth*. Oxfam Briefing Paper, No. 157. 19 January. www.oxfam.org/sites/www.oxfam.org/files/bp157-left-behind-by-the-g20-190112-en.pdf [Accessed: 19 April 2018].

Oxfam, 2013a. *Fixing the Cracks in Tax: A Plan of Action: Joint Recommendations to the G20 and OECD for Tackling Base Erosion and Profit Shifting*. Policy Brief. www.oxfam.org/sites/www.oxfam.org/files/fix-the-cracks-in-tax.pdf [Accessed: 19 April 2018].

Oxfam, 2013b. *Oxfam Verdict on the G20 Russia Summit*. 6 September. www.oxfam.org/en/pressroom/pressrelease/2013-09-06/oxfam-verdict-g20-summit-russia [Accessed: 19 April 2018].

Oxfam and Heinrich Böll Stiftung North America, 2014. *The G20 and Gender Equality*. Oxfam Briefing Paper 183. 14 July. https://d1tn3vj7xz9fdh.cloudfront.net/s3fs-public/file_attachments/the_g20_and_gender_equality_en.pdf [Accessed: 20 April 2018].

Panova, V., 2005. *Deiatel'nost Mekhanizmov Mnogostoronnego Vzaimodeistviia v Sfere Predotvrashcheniia i Uregulirovaniia Konfliktov (na Primere 'Bol'shoi Vos'merki'), 1991–2004 Gody* [The G8 and Its Role in Conflict Management, 1991–2004]. PhD. (history of international relations and foreign policy). Moscow: MGIMO University.

Peñaloza Mendez, A. and Pérez-Rocha, M., 2011. *G20: Confusión sobre la Caracterización de la Actual Crisis* [G20: Confusion about the Current Crisis]. New York: Heinrich Böll

Stiftung North America; Institute for Policy Studies; and Red Mexicana de Acción Frente al Libre Comercio, June. us.boell.org/sites/default/files/downloads/6-20-11_FINAL_penaloza_perezrocha_ES_and_EN.pdf [Accessed: 19 April 2018].

Peng, L., 2015. *Er Shi Guo Ji Tuan Fa Zhan Bao Gao (2014–2015)* [Development Report on the G20 (2014–2015)]. Beijing: China Economic Publishing House.

Penttilä, R., 2009. *Multilateralism Light: The Rise of Informal International Governance*. London: Centre for European Reform. www.cer.eu/sites/default/files/publications/attachments/pdf/2011/penttila_essay_july09-1334.pdf [Accessed: 18 July 2018].

The Peoples' Summit, 2009. *Another World Is Possible*. Pittsburgh. 22 September. www.peoplessummit.com/page/peoples-summit [Accessed: 6 August 2012].

Pereira da Silva, L.A., 2013. *From Currency Wars to Policy Peace under the G-20*. Peterson Institute for International Economics. Washington, DC. www.piie.com/publications/papers/pereira20130402.pdf [Accessed: 19 April 2018].

Porter, T., 2000. The G-7, the Financial Stability Forum, the G-20, and the politics of international financial regulation. In: ISA (International Studies Association), *Reflection, Integration, Cumulation: International Studies Past and Future*. Los Angeles, CA. 15 March. www.g20.utoronto.ca/biblio/porter-isa-2000.pdf [Accessed: 18 October 2017].

Postel-Vinay, K., 2011. *Le G20: laboratoire d'un monde émergent*. Nouveaux débats. Paris: Presses de SciencesPo.

Post Globalization Initiative, 2013. *St. Petersburg Counter Summit Opposes US Plans*. 13 September. www.plobal.org/news/548/ [Accessed: 10 October 2013].

Powell, J., 2012a. *G20 Is Getting a Reputation for Over-Promising and Under-Delivering*. ONE Blog. 21 June. www.one.org/international/blog/g20-is-getting-a-reputation-for-over-promising-and-under-delivering/ [Accessed: 19 April 2018].

Powell, J., 2012b. *Good Intentions Continue at G20, But Promises on Development Are Not Being Kept*. ONE Blog. 20 June. www.one.org/international/blog/good-intentions-continue-at-g20-but-promises-on-development-are-not-being-kept/ [Accessed: 19 April 2018].

Putin, V., 2012. *Vladimir Putin on Foreign Policy: Russia and the Changing World*. 27 February. www.globalresearch.ca/vladimir-putin-russia-and-the-changing-world/5477500 [Accessed: 19 April 2018].

Putnam, R.D. and Bayne, N., 1987. *Hanging Together: Cooperation and Conflict in the Seven-Power Summits*. rev. ed. Cambridge, MA: Harvard University Press.

Put People First, 2009. *G20 Counter Conference Report and Audio*. www.putpeoplefirst.org.uk/2009/12/put-people-first-g20-counter-conference-report-and-audio [Accessed: 6 August 2012].

Quintos, P., 2010. *What Is Missing in the G20 Agenda? Redressing Structural Imbalances for Equity, Justice and Sustainability*. IBON International. 8 October. iboninternational.org/sites/ibon/files/resources/ibon_g-20_policy_brief_2010.pdf [Accessed: 19 April 2018].

Rankin, I., 2006. *The Naming of the Dead*. London: Orion.

Robertson, C., 2010. *A Primer to the G8/G20 Toronto and Huntsville Summits*. Calgary, Alberta: Canadian Defence & Foreign Affairs Institute. June. www.cdfai.org/PDF/A%20Primer%20to%20the%20G8G20%20Toronto%20and%20Huntsville%20Summits.pdf [Accessed: 24 June 2012].

Rottier, S. and Véron, N., 2010. *An Assessment of the G20's Initial Action Terms*. Bruegel Policy Contribution 2010/08. aei.pitt.edu/14873/ [Accessed: 24 April 2018].

The Royal Society, 2012a. *Building Resilience to Disasters of Natural and Technological Origin*. 10 May. royalsociety.org/uploadedFiles/Royal_Society_Content/policy/publications/2012/2012–05–10-G-Science-Resilience.pdf [Accessed: 24 April 2018].

The Royal Society, 2012b. *Energy and Water Linkage: Challenge to a Sustainable Future*. 10 May. royalsociety.org/uploadedFiles/Royal_Society_Content/policy/publications/2012/2012–05–10-G-Science-Energy.pdf [Accessed: 24 April 2018].

The Royal Society, 2012c. *Improving Knowledge of Emissions and Sinks of Greenhouse Gases*. 10 May. royalsociety.org/uploadedFiles/Royal_Society_Content/policy/publications/2012/2012–05–10-G-Science-Emission.pdf [Accessed: 24 April 2018].

The Royal Society, 2017. *Science Academies Call for G20 Action on Improving Global Health*. 22 March. royalsociety.org/news/2017/03/science-academies-call-for-g20-action-on-improving-global-health/ [Accessed: 10 April 2018].

Rude, C. and Burke, S., 2009. *Towards a Socially Responsible and Democratic Global Economic System: Transparency, Accountability and Governance*. Dialogue on Globalization Briefing Paper 15. New York: Friedrich-Ebert-Stiftung. library.fes.de/pdf-files/bueros/usa/06778–20091105 pdf [Accessed: 24 April 2018].

Russian G8/G20 NGOs Working Group, 2012. *Join Civil G20*. www.g20civil.com/g20civil-society/join.php [Accessed: 10 August 2012].

Samans, R., Uzan, M. and Lopez-Carlos, A. eds., 2007a. *The International Monetary System, the IMF, and the G20: A Great Transformation in the Making?* World Economic Forum. Basingstoke: Palgrave Macmillan.

Sarkozy, N., 2016. *La France pour la vie*. Paris: Plon.

Savona, P., Kirton, J.J. and Oldani, C. eds., 2011. *Global Financial Crisis: Global Impact and Solutions*. Farnham: Ashgate.

Scherrer, A., 2007. *La production normative du G8 face à la "criminalité transnationale organisée" (1989–2005): la force du discours, le poids de l'expertise* [Normative Action of the G8 *vis-à-vis* International Organized Crime]. PhD (political science and international relations). Paris: Institut d'Etudes politiques [Sciences Po].

Schmidt, H., 2007. *Observations on the Present State of the World: Keynote Speech to the 25th Plenary Session of the InterAction Council*. 21 May. interactioncouncil.org/sites/default/files/pschmidt07.pdf [Accessed: 24 April 2018].

Schmucker, C. and Gnath, K., 2011b. *The Role of the Emerging Countries in the G20: Agenda-Setter, Veto Player or Spectator?* Bruges Regional Integration & Global Governance Papers, No. 2. Bruges: College of Europe; United Nations University, Comparative Regional Integration Studies.

Schulz, N.S., 2011. *The G20: Driving Development behind Closed Doors*. FRIDE Policy Brief, No. 107. December. Madrid: Fundación para las Relaciones Internacionales y el Diálogo Exterior. www.fride.org/download/PB_107_G20_development.pdf [Accessed: 24 April 2018].

Schwanen, D., 2010. *The G20 Framework for Strong, Sustainable and Balanced Growth: A Study in Credible Cooperation*. CIGI G20 Paper, No. 4. Waterloo, Canada: Centre for International Governance Innovation. 22 June. www.cigionline.org/publications/g20-framework-strong-sustainable-and-balanced-growth-study-credible-cooperation [Accessed: 24 April 2018].

Shaw, S., 2017. *From Hamburg to Buenos Aires: Education, Innovation and the Future of Work*. G20 Information Centre. www.g7g20.utoronto.ca/comment/170908-shaw.html [Accessed: 12 September 2017].

Shorr, D., 2011. *Making the G-20 a Reservoir of Global Leadership: A Maximalist Argument*. Policy Analysis Brief. April. www.stanleyfoundation.org/publications/pab/ShorrPAB411.pdf [Accessed: 24 April 2018].

Singapore Institute of International Affairs, 2010. *SIIA Welcomes New 3G Initiative for Small States*. www.siiaonline.org/?q=programmes/insights/siia-welcomes-new-3g-initiative-small-states [Accessed: 4 November 2012].

Slaughter, A.-M., 2004. *A New World Order*. Princeton: Princeton University Press.

Smith, G.S., 2011a. *G7 to G8 to G20: Evolution in Global Governance*. Waterloo, Canada: Centre for International Governance Innovation. CIGI G20 Papers, No. 6. 25 May. www.cigionline.org/sites/default/files/g20no6-2.pdf [Accessed: 7 September 2017].

Stanley Foundation, 2010b. *The United Nations and the G-20: Ensuring Complementary Efforts*. 41st United Nations Issues Conference. Tarrytown, NY. 26–28 March. www.stanleyfoundation.org/publications/report/Issues2010.pdf [Accessed: 16 January 2018].

Stanley Foundation, 2011. *How Are Key 21st-Century Powers Arranging Themselves: For Competition, Coexistence, or Cooperation?* Policy Dialogue Brief. Muscatine, Iowa: Stanley Foundation. 6–8 June. www.stanleyfoundation.org/publications/pdb/21stCenturyPowersPDB811.pdf [Accessed: 26 September 2017].

Stanley Foundation, 2012. *Shifting Coalitions and Potential Blocs for Asian and Pacific Leadership in the G-20*. Policy Dialogue Brief. September. www.stanleyfoundation.org/publications/pdb/ShanghaiPDB1112.pdf [Accessed: 24 April 2018].

Steiner, S.M., 2018. *Moral Pressure for Responsible Globalization: Religious Diplomacy in the Age of the Anthropocene*. International Studies in Religion and Society, vol. 30. Boston: Brill.

Stern, N., 2007. *The Economics of Climate Change: The Stern Review*. Cambridge: Cambridge University Press.

Studer, I. and Contreras, T., 2012. *Assessing the Impact of the Seoul Summit Development Commitments: Case Study Mexico* [With Financial Support from the International Labour Office through the ILO-Korea Partnership Program]. www.g20.utoronto.ca/biblio/SDC_Mexico.pdf [Accessed: 24 April 2018].

Subacchi, P. and Helleiner, E., 2009. *From London to L'Aquila: Building a Bridge between the G20 and the G8*. Briefing Paper. London: Chatham House; Centre for International Governance Innovation. June. www.chathamhouse.org/publications/papers/view/109085 [Accessed: 24 April 2018].

Subacchi, P. and Monsarrat, A., 2009. *New Ideas for the London Summit: Recommendations to the G20 Leaders*. Chatham House Report; Chatham House and Atlantic Council Report. London: Chatham House. March. www.chathamhouse.org/publications/papers/view/109022 [Accessed: 24 April 2018].

Subacchi, P. and Pickford, S., 2011. *Legitimacy vs Effectiveness for the G20: A Dynamic Approach to Global Economic Governance*. Chatham House Briefing Paper IE BP 2011/01. London: Chatham House. October. www.chathamhouse.org/sites/files/chathamhouse/1011bp_subacchi_pickford.pdf [Accessed: 24 February 2018].

Sustainable Development Solutions Network and Bertelsmann Stiftung, 2017. *SDG Index and Dashboards Report 2017: Global Responsibilities*. July. www.sdgindex.org/assets/files/2017/2017-SDG-Index-and-Dashboards-Report-full.pdf [Accessed: 17 May 2018].

T20, 2017. *20 Solution Proposals for the G20 from the T20 Engagement Group*. www.t20germany.org/wp-content/uploads/2017/07/20_Solutions_for-the_G20_17-7.pdf [Accessed: 1 May 2018].

Tacheva, B., 2013. *Global Health Governance: Challenges, Efforts, and the G20*. Global Summitry Reports. globalsummitryproject.com.s197331.gridserver.com/blog/global-summitry-report/global-health-governance-challenges-efforts-and-the-g20/ [Accessed: 14 June 2018].

Tandon, R. and Martin, N., 2010. *Civil Society Dialogue with the Host Sherpa to the Toronto 2010 G20 Summit: Communiqué*. 21 June. www.g8.utoronto.ca/evaluations/2010muskoka/fim-sherpas.pdf [Accessed: 24 April 2018].

Tang Y., 2010. *Quan Qiu Zhi Li Zhong De Fa Da Guo Jia Yu Xin Xing Guo Jia* [Developed Countries and Emerging Countries in Global Governance]. PhD. (international relations). Beijing: China Foreign Affairs University.

Taylor, T., 2011. *You Should Have Stayed Home*. Toronto: Praxis Theatre.

Te Velde, D.W., 2010. *The G-20 Framework for Strong, Sustainable and Balanced Growth: What Role for Low-Income, Small and Vulnerable Countries?* London: Overseas Development Institute. June. www.odi.org.uk/publications/4905-g-20-framework-strong-sustainable-balanced-growth-role-low-income-small-vulnerable-countries [Accessed: 24 April 2018].

Te Velde, D.W. coord., 2012. *Accountability and Effectiveness of the G20's Role in Promoting Development*. Paper prepared for Workshop on an Accountability Mechanism for G20 Development Commitments, Bali, Indonesia, 3 October. [London: Overseas Development Institute.] www.odi.org.uk/publications/6859-accountability-effectiveness-g20s-role-promoting-development [Accessed: 24 April 2018].

Thirlwell, M. and Cook, M., 2006. *Geeing up the G-20*. Policy Brief. Lowy Institute for International Policy. April. www.files.ethz.ch/isn/56361/Thirlwell%20and%20Cook,%20Geeing%20up%20the%20G20%20s.pdf [Accessed: 24 April 2018].

Thomson Reuters, 2013. *The Research & Innovation Performance of the G20 and Its Impact on Decisions Made by the World's Most Influential Economic Leaders*. September. http://sciencewatch.com/sites/sw/files/images/basic/research-innovation-g20.pdf [Accessed: 29 September 2013].

Tietmeyer, H., 1999. *International Cooperation and Coordination in the Area of Financial Market Supervision and Surveillance: Report by Hans Tietmeyer, President of the Deutsche Bundesbank*. 11 February. www.fsb.org/wp-content/uploads/r_9902.pdf [Accessed: 25 April 2018].

Transparency International, 2017. *Clean Supply Chains*. G20 Position Paper. January. files.transparency.org/content/download/2143/13584/file/2017_G20PositionPaper_SupplyChains_EN.pdf [Accessed: 20 April 2018].

Traub, J., 2009. *At the World's Summit: How Will Leading Nations Lead?* Policy Analysis Brief. Muscatine, Iowa: Stanley Foundation. June. www.stanleyfoundation.org/publications/pab/TraubPAB609.pdf [Accessed: 25 April 2018].

Trew, S., 2013. *Declaration of the G20 Counter-Summit*. The Council of Canadians. 7 September. www.canadians.org/blog/declaration-g20-counter-summit [Accessed: 25 April 2018].

Troszczynska-van Genderen, W., 2015. *G7 Summit in Schloss Elmau: A Tighter Agenda, with Wider Impact?* European Parliament. Directorate-General for External Policies. www.europarl.europa.eu/RegData/etudes/IDAN/2015/549041/EXPO_IDA(2015)549041_EN.pdf [Accessed: 10 April 2018].

Truman, E.M., 2011. *G-20 Reforms of the International Monetary System: An Evaluation*. Policy Brief 11–19. Washington: Peterson Institute for International Economics. November. www.iie.com/publications/pb/pb11-19.pdf [Accessed: 25 April 2018].

TrustLaw, 2012. *G20 Countries: The Worst and Best for Women*. 13 June. news.trust.org/item/20120613010100-sk134/?source=spotlight [Accessed: 25 April 2018].

Tussie, D. and Trucco, P., 2009. *The G20 and the Future of Market Regulation*. Policy Brief, 20. Madrid: FRIDE [Fundacion para las Relaciones Internacionales y el Diálogo Exterior]. September. www.fride.org/download/PB20_G20_market_regulation_ENG_sep09.pdf [Accessed: 25 April 2018].

Vestergaard, J., 2011. *The G20 and Beyond. Towards Effective Economic Governance*. Danish Institute for International Studies. 16 March. www.diis.dk/sw106138.asp [Accessed: 25 April 2018].

Vines, D. and Gilbert, C.L. eds., 2004. *The IMF and Its Critics: Reform of Global Financial Architecture*. Cambridge: Cambridge University Press.

Von Furstenberg, G.M., 2000. *Tinkering with the International Financial System and Debt Forgiveness: What Insights Have Surfaced in the G7/IMF Going Forward from Cologne to the Okinawa Summit?* Toronto: University of Toronto G8 Research Group. 21 July. www.g8.utoronto.ca/scholar/furstenberg20000720 [Accessed: 25 April 2018].

Wahl, P., 2012. *The G20: Overestimated and Underperforming: Drawing a Balance of the G20 Achievements: Four Years after the Crash*. Discussion Paper. Berlin: WEED. 15 June. www.networkideas.org/featured-articles/2012/06/the-g20-overestimated-and-underperforming-drawing-a-balance-of-the-g20-achievements-four-years-after-the-crash/ [Accessed: 25 April 2018].

Wang, A., 2016. *China's Coordination of the G20 and BRICS Summits*. 4 September. www.g7g20.utoronto.ca/comment/160904-wang.html [Accessed: 24 February 2018].

Wang, D.Y., 2009. *Ba Guo Ji Tuan Guo Ji Xie Tiao Ji Zhi Yan Jiu* [Research on the G8's Global Coordination Mechanism]. PhD. dissertation. Shanghai: East China Normal University.

Wilson, D. and Purushothaman, R., 2003. *Dreaming with BRICs: The Path to 2050*. Global Economics Paper No. 99. New York: Goldman Sachs. October. www.goldmansachs.com/our-thinking/archive/brics-dream.html [Accessed: 25 April 2018].

Winters, L.A., Wonhyuk, L., Hanmer, L. and Augustin, S., 2010. *Economic Growth in Low Income Countries: How the G20 Can Help to Raise and Sustain It*. Economics Dept. Working Paper Series, 8–2010. Brighton, UK: University of Sussex. www.sussex.ac.uk/economics/documents/wps8-2010-winters.pdf [Accessed: 25 April 2018].

Wolf, M., 2010. *Fixing Global Finance*. Expanded and updated ed. Baltimore: Johns Hopkins University Press.

Woods, N., 2010a. *The G20 Leaders and Global Governance*. GEG Working Paper 2010/59, Global Economic Governance Programme. Oxford University. www.geg.ox.ac.uk/geg-wp-201059-g20-leaders-and-global-governance [Accessed: 25 April 2018].

World Economic Forum, 2007. *Merkel Urges New Dialogue and Closer Atlantic Partnership*. Press Releases. 24 January.

World Economic Forum, 2010. *Seoul G20 Summit: Priorities and Challenges, Davos Forum Special Address by Lee Myung-bak, President of the Republic of Korea*. Davos, Switzerland. 28 January. www.g20.utoronto.ca/2010/lee-davos.pdf [Accessed: 6 January 2018].

World Economic Forum, 2012a. *Euro, Dollar, Yuan Uncertainties: Scenarios on the Future of the International Monetary System*. World Scenario Series. June. www20.iadb.org/intal/catalogo/PE/2012/10462.pdf [Accessed: 10 January 2018].

World Economic Forum, 2012b. *President Calderón: Green Growth Public Private Partnerships*. www.weforum.org/agenda/2012/06/president-calderon-green-growth-public-private-partnerships/ [Accessed: 6 January 2018].

World Economic Forum, 2017. *Opening Plenary with Xi Jinping, President of the People's Republic of China*. 17 January. www.weforum.org/events/world-economic-forum-annual-meeting-2017/sessions/opening-plenary-davos-2017 [Accessed: 11 February 2017].

World Religions Summit, 2010. *A Time for Inspired Leadership and Action*. 2010 Interfaith Leaders' Summit. 23 June. www.faithchallengeg8.com/pdfs/2010%20Interfaith%20Statement%20-%20English.pdf [Accessed: 25 April 2018].

World Vision Canada, 2012. *World Vision Says G20 Finally Puts Nutrition on Its Plate but Fast Delivery Needed for Vulnerable Children*. 19 June. www.newswire.ca/

news-releases/g20-finally-puts-nutrition-on-its-plate-but-fast-delivery-needed-for-vulnerable-children-510396501.html [Accessed: 25 April 2018].

WWF, 2012. *Final G-20 Statement Plagued with Ambiguous Language Fails to Provide Rio+20 Needed Boost*. 20 June. wwf.panda.org/?205307/Final-G-20-statement-plagued-with-ambiguous-language-fails-to-provide-Rio20-needed-boost – WWF [Accessed: 25 April 2018].

Xu, F., 2015. *Er Shi Guo Ji Tuan Ji Zhi Hua Jian She Yan Jiu* [Research on G20 Institutionalization]. Beijing: University of International Business and Economics Press.

Xu, T., 2010. *Quan Qiu Qi Hou Zhi Li Zhong De Fei Zheng Shi Guo Ji Ji Zhi Yan Jiu: Yi Ba Guo Ji Tuan Wei Li* [Research on Informal Mechanisms of Global Climate Governance: The Case of the G8]. PhD. dissertation (international relations). Shanghai: Shanghai International Studies University.

Yan, Q.M. et al. eds., 2013. *Who Will Govern the New World? The Present and Future of the G20*. Beijing: Social Sciences Academic Press. [Also available in Chinese]

Zilinsky, J. and Cimino-Isaacs, C., 2016. *Slow Trade Growth and the G20 Response*. 8 March. piie.com/blogs/trade-investment-policy-watch/slow-trade-growth-and-g20-response [Accessed: 18 June 2018].

Book chapters

Alagh, Y.K., 2005. On sherpas and coolies: The L20 and non-Brahmanical futures. In: J. English, R. Thakur and A.F. Cooper, eds. *Reforming from the Top: A Leaders' 20 Summit*. Tokyo: United Nations University Press. pp. 169–186.

Alexandroff, A.S., 2008b. Enhanced engagement: The Heiligendamm process and beyond. In: A.F. Cooper and A. Antkiewicz, eds. *Emerging Powers in Global Governance: Lessons from the Heiligendamm Process*. Waterloo, Canada: Wilfrid Laurier University Press and Centre for International Governance Innovation. pp. 337–351.

Alexandroff, A.S. and Kirton, J., 2010. The 'great recession' and the emergence of the G20 leaders' summit. In: A. Alexandroff and A. F. Cooper, eds. *Rising States, Rising Institutions: Can the World Be Governed?* Washington: Brookings Institution Press. pp. 177–195.

Bayne, N., 2005a. Do we need the G8 summit? Lessons from the past, looking ahead to the future. In: M. Fratianni, J.J. Kirton, A.M. Rugman and P. Savona, eds. *New Perspectives on Global Governance*. Aldershot, UK: Ashgate. pp. 15–29.

Bayne, N., 2011a. The decline of the G8 summit and lessons for the G20. In: N. Bayne and S. Woolcock, eds. *The New Economic Diplomacy: Decision-Making and Negotiation in International Economic Relations*. 3rd ed. Global Finance Series. Farnham: Ashgate. pp. 249–262.

Bayne, N., 2011b. Plurilateralism and multilateralism: Comparing institutions. In: N. Bayne and S. Woolcock, eds. *The New Economic Diplomacy: Decision-Making and Negotiation in International Economic Relations*. 3rd ed. Global Finance Series. Farnham: Ashgate. pp. 205–230.

Bayne, N., 2014. The foundations of summitry. In: E. Mourlon-Druol and F. Romero, eds. *International Summitry and Global Governance: The Rise of the G7 and the European Council, 1974–1991*. Cold War History Series. London and New York: Routledge. pp. 23–38.

Bayne, N., 2015. 40 years of summits: Addressing global challenges. In: J.J. Kirton, M. Koch and A.S. Freitag, eds. *G7 Germany: The Schloss Elmau Summit, June 2015*. London: Newsdesk Media, Special Supplement, pp. 1–7, 10–15.

Beattie, A., 2011. Successful communications strategy for G20 summits. In: C.I. Bradford and W.H. Lim, eds. *Global Leadership in Transition: Making the G20 More Effective and Responsive*. Washington, DC: Brookings Institution Press with Korean Development Institute. pp. 312–317.

Bergsten, C.F., 2005. The Euro and the Dollar: Toward a Finance G-2? In: A.S. Posen, ed. *The Euro at Five: Ready for a Global Role?* Washington, DC: Institute for International Economics. pp. 27–46.

Bergsten, C.F. and de Montbrial, T., 2003. Letter of transmittal to the leaders of the G-8 member countries. In: Peterson Institute of International Economics. *Restoring G-8 Leadership of the World Economy*. Washington, DC. pp. 4–5. www.iie.com/publications/papers/g8-2003.pdf [Accessed: 22 February 2018].

Bergsten, C.F. and Koch-Weser, C., 2004. The G-2: A new conceptual basis and operating modality for transatlantic economic relations. In: W. Weidenfeld et al., eds. *From Alliance to Coalitions: The Future of Transatlantic Relations*. Gütersloh, Germany: Bertelsmann Foundation. pp. 237–250.

Bernes, T.A., 2011. IMF legitimacy and governance reform: Will the G20 help or hinder? In: C.I. Bradford and W.H. Lim, eds. *Global Leadership in Transition: Making the G20 More Effective and Responsive*. Washington, DC: Brookings Institution Press with Korean Development Institute. pp. 219–223.

Bhushan, A. and Tussie, D., 2010. Widening global governance: Building on the G20. In: North-South Institute, ed. *Canadian Development Report: A Global Crisis of Development*. Ottawa: North-South Institute. pp. 3–17. www.nsi-ins.ca/wp-content/uploads/2012/11/2010-CDR.pdf [Accessed: 25 April 2018].

Bitar, S., 2011. Infrastructure and development: A new area for international cooperation. In: C.I. Bradford and W.H. Lim, eds. *Global Leadership in Transition: Making the G20 More Effective and Responsive*. Washington, DC: Brookings Institution Press with Korean Development Institute. pp. 201–208.

Blustein, P., 2011. A healthy fear factor: The media as action-forcer at summits. In: C.I. Bradford and W.H. Lim, eds. *Global Leadership in Transition: Making the G20 More Effective and Responsive*. Washington, DC: Brookings Institution Press with Korean Development Institute. pp. 318–323.

Bonhomme, N., 2014. Between political messages and public expectations: G7 summits in French and US public opinion (1975–1985). In: E. Mourlon-Druol and F. Romero, eds. *International Summitry and Global Governance: The Rise of the G7 and the European Council, 1974–1991*. Cold War History Series. London and New York: Routledge. pp. 92–114.

Bowles, P., 2008. ASEAN and the G8: Potentially productive partners or two ships passing in the night? In: A.F. Cooper and A. Antkiewicz, eds. *Emerging Powers in Global Governance: Lessons from the Heiligendamm Process*. Waterloo, Canada: Wilfrid Laurier University Press and Centre for International Governance Innovation. pp. 213–231.

Bradford, C.I., 2005a. Anticipating the future: A political agenda for global economic governance. In: J. English, R. Thakur and A.F. Cooper, eds. *Reforming from the Top: A Leaders' 20 Summit*. Tokyo: United Nations University Press. pp. 46–62.

Bradford, C.I., 2008. The United States and summit reform in a transformational era. In: A.F. Cooper and A. Antkiewicz, eds. *Emerging Powers in Global Governance: Lessons from the Heiligendamm Process*. Waterloo, Canada: Wilfrid Laurier University Press and Centre for International Governance Innovation. pp. 307–336.

Bradford, C.I., 2011a. The cultural foundations for the new dynamics of summitry. In: C.I. Bradford and W.H. Lim, eds. *Global Leadership in Transition: Making the G20 More

Effective and Responsive. Washington, DC: Brookings Institution Press with Korean Development Institute. pp. 249–256.

Bradford, C.I. and Lim, W.H., 2011a. Conclusion: Priority innovations and challenges for the G20. In: C.I. Bradford and W.H. Lim, eds. *Global Leadership in Transition: Making the G20 More Effective and Responsive*. Washington, DC: Brookings Institution Press with Korean Development Institute. pp. 324–332.

Bradford, C.I. and Lim, W.H., 2011c. Introduction: Toward the consolidation of the G20: From crisis committee to global steering committee. In: C.I. Bradford and W.H. Lim, eds. *Global Leadership in Transition: Making the G20 More Effective and Responsive*. Washington, DC: Brookings Institution Press with Korean Development Institute. pp. 1–10.

Bradford, C.I. and Linn, J.F., 2007. Summit reform: Toward an L-20. In: C.I. Bradford and J.F. Linn, eds. *Global Governance Reform: Breaking the Stalemate*. Washington, DC: Brookings Institution Press. pp. 77–86.

Bronnert, D., 2011. Making government policy: The G8 and G20 in 2010. In: N. Bayne and S. Woolcock, eds. *The New Economic Diplomacy: Decision-Making and Negotiation in International Economic Relations*. 3rd ed. Global Finance Series. Farnham: Ashgate. pp. 81–91.

Carin, B., 2011a. A G20 'Non-Secretariat': President Nicolas Sarkozy's conversation with Philosopher Lao Tzu, Strategist Sun Tzu, and Clio, the Muse of History. In: C.I. Bradford and W.H. Lim, eds. *Global Leadership in Transition: Making the G20 More Effective and Responsive*. Washington, DC: Brookings Institution Press with Korean Development Institute. pp. 275–282.

Carin, B. and Smith, G., 2005. Making change happen at the global level. In: J. English, R. Thakur and A.F. Cooper, eds. *Reforming from the Top: A Leaders' 20 Summit*. Tokyo: United Nations University Press. pp. 25–45.

Chin, G.T., 2008. China's evolving G8 engagement: Complex interests and multiple identity in global governance reform. In: A.F. Cooper and A. Antkiewicz, eds. *Emerging Powers in Global Governance: Lessons from the Heiligendamm Process*. Waterloo, Canada: Wilfrid Laurier University Press and Centre for International Governance Innovation. pp. 83–113.

Cooper, A.F., 2008b. The Heiligendamm process: Structural reordering and diplomatic agency. In: A.F. Cooper and A. Antkiewicz, eds. *Emerging Powers in Global Governance: Lessons from the Heiligendamm Process*. Waterloo, Canada: Wilfrid Laurier University Press and Centre for International Governance Innovation. pp. 1–18.

Cooper, A.F., 2010a. The G8-G20 partnership. In: J.J. Kirton and M. Koch, eds. *G8-G20: The 2010 Canadian Summits: Recovery and New Beginnings*. London: Newsdesk. pp. 306–307.

Cooper, A.F., 2011b. The G20 and regional dynamics. In: C.I. Bradford and W.H. Lim, eds. *Global Leadership in Transition: Making the G20 More Effective and Responsive*. Washington, DC: Brookings Institution Press with Korean Development Institute. pp. 265–274.

Cooper, A.F. and English, J., 2005. Introduction: Reforming the international system from the top: A Leaders' 20 Summit. In: J. English, R. Thakur and A.F. Cooper, eds. *Reforming from the Top: A Leaders' 20 Summit*. Tokyo: United Nations University Press. pp. 1–24.

Cooper, A.F. and Schrumm, A., 2011. Reconciling the Gs: The G8, the G5, and the G20 in a world of crisis. In: P. Savona et al., eds. *Global Financial Crisis: Global Impact and Solutions*. Farnham: Ashgate. pp. 229–244.

Culpeper, R., 2003. Systemic reform at a standstill: A flock of 'Gs' in search of global financial stability. In: A. Berry and G. Indart, eds. *Critical Issues in International Financial Reform*. New Brunswick, NJ and London: Transaction Publishers. pp. 203–236.

Derviş, K., 2011. Global imbalances and the G20. In: C.I. Bradford and W.H. Lim, eds. *Global Leadership in Transition: Making the G20 More Effective and Responsive*. Washington, DC: Brookings Institution Press with Korean Development Institute. pp. 125–137.

Desai, N., 2012. What interests do the BRICS countries share? In: M. Larionova and J.J. Kirton, eds. *BRICS New Delhi Summit 2012: Stability, Security and Prosperity*. Toronto: Newsdesk Media Group. pp. 26–27. www.brics.utoronto.ca/newsdesk/BRICS-2012.pdf [Accessed: 23 February 2018].

Dluhosch, B., 2001. The G7 and the debt of the poorest. In: J.J. Kirton, J. Daniels and A. Freytag, eds. *Guiding Global Order: G8 Governance in the Twenty-First Century*. The G8 and Global Governance Series. Aldershot: Ashgate. pp. 79–91.

Dobson, H., 2011. The G8, the G20, and civil society. In: P. Savona, J.J. Kirton and C. Oldani, eds. *Global Financial Crisis: Global Impact and Solutions*. Farnham: Ashgate. pp. 245–260.

Dobson, W., 2001. Broadening participation in G-7 summits. In: G-8 Preparatory Conference. *Toward Shared Responsibility and Global Leadership: Recommendations for the G-8 Genoa Summit from the G-8 Preparatory Conference*. Turin, Italy: Peterson Institute for International Economics. pp. 23–29.

Dobson, W., 2008. Global lessons from the 2008 financial crisis. In: Rotman School of Management, ed. *The Finance Crisis and Rescue: What Went Wrong? Why? What Lessons Can Be Learned?* Toronto: University of Toronto Press. pp. 95–106.

Drache, D., 2005. The political economy of dissent: Global publics after Cancún. In: J. English, R. Thakur and A.F. Cooper, eds. *Reforming from the Top: A Leaders' 20 Summit*. Tokyo: United Nations University Press. pp. 121–140.

Fues, T. and Leininger, J., 2008. Germany and the Heiligendamm process. In: A.F. Cooper and A. Antkiewicz, eds. *Emerging Powers in Global Governance: Lessons from the Heiligendamm Process*. Waterloo, Canada: Wilfrid Laurier University Press and Centre for International Governance Innovation. pp. 235–262.

Germain, R.D., 2001a. Financial Stability Board. In: R. Rosecrance, ed. *The New Great Power Coalition: Toward a World Concert of Nations*. New York: Rowman & Littlefield. pp. 50–55.

Germain, R.D., 2011. Financial Stability Board. In: T. Hale and T. Held, eds. *Handbook of Transnational Governance Innovation*. London: Polity Press. pp. 50–55.

Gill, S., 1999. Structural Changes in Multilateralism: The G-7 Nexus and the Global Crisis. In: M. G. Schechter, ed. *Innovation in Multilateralism*. New York: St. Martin's Press. pp. 113–165.

Gilman, M., 2015. A World without G20 Summits. In: M. Larionova and J.J. Kirton, eds. *The G8-G20 Relationship in Global Governance*. Farnham, UK: Ashgate. pp. 45–54.

Gregory, D. and de Almeida, P.R., 2008. Brazil and the G8 Heiligendamm process. In: A.F. Cooper and A. Antkiewicz, eds. *Emerging Powers in Global Governance: Lessons from the Heiligendamm Process*. Waterloo, Canada: Wilfrid Laurier University Press and Centre for International Governance Innovation. pp. 137–161.

Gurría, A., 2005. A Leaders' 20 Summit? In: J. English, R. Thakur and A.F. Cooper, eds. *Reforming from the Top: A Leaders' 20 Summit*. Tokyo: United Nations University Press. pp. 63–71.

Hajnal, P.I., 2007c. Reform of the G7, G8 and G20. In: P.I. Hajnal, ed. *The G8 System and the G20: Evolution, Role and Documentation*. Aldershot: Ashgate. pp. 159–177.

Hajnal, P.I., 2011a. Civil society and G8 accountability. In: J.A. Scholte, ed. *Building Global Democracy? Civil Society and Accountable Global Governance*. Cambridge: Cambridge University Press. pp. 182–205.

Hajnal, P.I. and Panova, V., 2012. The future role and reform of the G8. In: M. Larionova, ed. *The European Union in the G8: Promoting Consensus and Concerted Actions for Global Public Goods*. Farnham: Ashgate. pp. 65–81.

Hamilton, K., 2010. Inspired leadership: Civil Society's contribution to G8 and G20 summitry. In: J.J. Kirton and M. Koch, eds. *G8 & G20: The 2010 Canadian Summits*. Toronto: Newsdesk Media Group and the G20 Research Group. p. 308.

Haynal, G., 2005. Summitry and governance: The case for a G-XX. In: D. Carment et al., eds. *Canada among Nations 2004: Setting Priorities Straight*. Montreal and Kingston: McGill-Queens University Press. pp. 261–274.

Heinbecker, P., 2011b. The United Nations and the G20: Synergy or dissonance? In: C.I. Bradford and W.H. Lim, eds. *Global Leadership in Transition: Making the G20 More Effective and Responsive*. Washington, DC: Brookings Institution Press with Korean Development Institute. pp. 236–245.

Higgott, R., 2005. Multilateralism and the limits of global governance. In: J. English, R. Thakur and A.F. Cooper, eds. *Reforming from the Top: A Leaders' 20 Summit*. Tokyo: United Nations University Press. pp. 72–96.

Huang, W., 2011. Global governance under the G20: A Chinese perspective. In: W. Hofmeister, and S. Vogt, eds. *G20: Perceptions and Perspectives for Global Governance*. Singapore: Konrad Adenauer Stiftung. pp. 41–49. www.kas.de/upload/dokumente/2011/10/G20_E-Book/chapter_5.pdf [Accessed: 29 April 2018].

Kharas, H., 2011. Bringing development into the G20: Overarching themes. In: C.I. Bradford and W.H. Lim, eds. *Global Leadership in Transition: Making the G20 More Effective and Responsive*. Washington, DC: Brookings Institution Press with Korean Development Institute. pp. 165–175.

Kim, H.W., 2011. G20 framework for more sustainable and balanced growth. In: C.I. Bradford and W.H. Lim, eds. *Global Leadership in Transition: Making the G20 More Effective and Responsive*. Washington, DC: Brookings Institution Press with Korean Development Institute. pp. 151–157.

Kirton, J.J., 2001a. The G7/8 and China: Toward a closer association. In: J.J. Kirton, J.P. Daniels and A. Freytag, eds. *Guiding Global Order: G8 Governance in the Twenty-First Century*. The G8 and Global Governance Series. Aldershot, UK: Ashgate. pp. 189–222.

Kirton, J.J., 2001b. The G20: Representativeness, effectiveness and leadership. In: J.J. Kirton, J.P. Daniels and A. Freytag, eds. *Guiding Global Order: G8 Governance in the Twenty-First Century*. The G8 and Global Governance Series. Aldershot, UK: Ashgate. pp. 143–173.

Kirton, J.J., 2001c. Guiding global economic governance: The G20, the G7, and the International Monetary Fund at century's dawn. In: J.J. Kirton and G.M. von Furstenberg, eds. *New Directions in Global Economic Governance: Managing Globalisation in the Twenty-First Century*. The G8 and Global Governance Series. Aldershot, UK: Ashgate. pp. 143–167.

Kirton, J.J., 2005b. Toward multilateral reform: The G20's contribution. In: J. English, R. Thakur and A.F. Cooper, eds. *Reforming from the Top: A Leaders' 20 Summit*. Tokyo: United Nations University Press. pp. 141–168.

Kirton, J.J., 2008b. From G8 2003 to G13 2010? The Heiligendamm process's past, present, and future. In: A.F. Cooper and A. Antkiewicz, eds. *Emerging Powers in Global Governance: Lessons from the Heiligendamm Process*. Waterloo, Canada: Wilfrid Laurier University Press and Centre for International Governance Innovation. pp. 45–79.

Kirton, J.J., 2011a. The G8: Legacy, limitations, and lessons. In: C.I. Bradford and W.H. Lim, eds. *Global Leadership in Transition: Making the G20 More Effective and*

Responsive. Washington, DC: Brookings Institution Press with Korean Development Institute. pp. 16–35.

Kirton, J.J., 2011b. The Group of Twenty. In: T. Hale and T. Held, eds. *Handbook of Transnational Governance Innovation*. London: Polity Press. pp. 55–60.

Kirton, J.J., 2013a. The future of G20 governance. In: J.J. Kirton, ed. *G20 Governance for a Globalized World*. Farnham: Ashgate. pp. 373–390.

Kirton, J.J., 2013c. Introduction. In: J.J. Kirton, ed. *G20 Governance for a Globalized World*. Farnham: Ashgate. pp. 3–26.

Kirton, J.J., 2013e. The systemic hub model of G20 governance. In: J.J. Kirton, ed. *G20 Governance for a Globalized World*. Farnham: Ashgate. pp. 27–52.

Kirton, J.J., 2015a. Going global: The G8's adaptation to rising powers. In: T. van de Graf and D. Lesage, eds. *Rising Powers and Multilateral Institutions*. Houndmills, UK: Palgrave Macmillan. pp. 117–131.

Lesage, D., 2015. The G7/8 and G20: Parallel paths to pragmatic partnership. In: M. Larionova and J.J. Kirton, eds. *The G8-G20 Relationship in Global Governance*. Global Governance Series. Farnham, UK: Ashgate. pp. 35–44.

Lim, W.H., 2011. Sharing knowledge for development. In: C.I. Bradford and W.H. Lim, eds. *Global Leadership in Transition: Making the G20 More Effective and Responsive*. Washington, DC: Brookings Institution Press with Korean Development Institute. pp. 209–216.

Linn, J.F., 2011. How the G20 can break the stalemate in the reform of the multilateral development system: Proposals for action. In: C.I. Bradford and W.H. Lim, eds. *Global Leadership in Transition: Making the G20 More Effective and Responsive*. Washington, DC: Brookings Institution Press with Korean Development Institute. pp. 224–235.

Linn, J.F., 2012. Whither the G-20: Proposals for a focused agenda. In: Brookings Institution. *The G-20 Los Cabos Summit 2012: Bolstering the World Economy amid Growing Fears of Recession*. Washington, DC. pp. 9–10. www.brookings.edu/wp-content/uploads/2016/06/g20_full-report.pdf [Accessed: 22 February 2018].

Lins, M.A.D.T. and Silva, L.P., 2011. Brazil and the G20: Recent development strategy and strength among 'new' emerging economies. In: W. Hofmeister and S. Vogt, eds. *G20: Perceptions and Perspectives for Global Governance*. Singapore: Konrad Adenauer Stiftung. pp. 21–30. www.kas.de/upload/dokumente/2011/10/G20_E-Book/chapter_3.pdf [Accessed: 1 May 2018].

Lombardi, D., 2011. The International Monetary System through the lens of emerging Asia. In: K. Dervis, M. Kawai and D. Lombardi, eds. *Asia and Policymaking for the Global Economy*. Washington, DC: Brookings Institution Press and Asian Development Bank Institute. pp. 151–181.

Lombardi, D., 2012. The G-20, the IMF and the European debt crisis. In: *The G-20 Los Cabos Summit 2012: Bolstering the World Economy amid Growing Fears of Recession*. Washington, DC: Brookings Institution. pp. 7–8. www.brookings.edu/~/media/research/files/reports/2012/6/g20/g20_lombardi.pdf [Accessed: 18 January 2018].

Malan, P.S., 2011. Rebalancing the world economy: The G20's potential role. In: C.I. Bradford and W.H. Lim, eds. *Global Leadership in Transition: Making the G20 More Effective and Responsive*. Washington, DC: Brookings Institution Press with Korean Development Institute. pp. 158–161.

Mann, T., 2011. G20 summitry: Domestic leadership in a polarized and globalized world. In: C.I. Bradford and W.H. Lim, eds. *Global Leadership in Transition: Making the G20 More Effective and Responsive*. Washington, DC: Brookings Institution Press with Korean Development Institute. pp. 299–303.

Martin, N., 2008. The FIM G8 project, 2002–2006: A case analysis of a project to initiate civil society engagement with the G8. In: J.W. St.G. Walker and A.S. Thompson, eds. *Critical Mass: The Emergence of Global Civil Society*. Waterloo, Canada: Wilfrid Laurier University Press. pp. 183–209.

Martin, P., 2009. Key challenges. In: J.J. Kirton and M. Koch, eds. *The London Summit 2009: Growth, Stability, Jobs*. London: Newsdesk Media Group. pp. 24–25. www.g20.utoronto.ca/g20london2009.html [Accessed: 22 February 2018].

Martin, P., 2011a. Financial sector reform and the G20. In: C.I. Bradford and W.H. Lim, eds. *Global Leadership in Transition: Making the G20 More Effective and Responsive*. Washington, DC: Brookings Institution Press with Korean Development Institute. pp. 65–69.

Martin, P., 2011b. The G20: From global crisis responder to global steering committee. In: C.I. Bradford and W.H. Lim, eds. *Global Leadership in Transition: Making the G20 More Effective and Responsive*. Washington, DC: Brookings Institution Press with Korean Development Institute. pp. 13–15.

Martin, P., 2013. The G20: From global crisis responder to steering committee. In: A.F. Cooper et al., eds. *The Oxford Handbook of Modern Diplomacy*. Oxford: Oxford University Press. pp. 729–744.

Maxwell, S., 2011. Laying the foundation for a long-term G20 work program on development. In: C.I. Bradford and W.H. Lim, eds. *Global Leadership in Transition: Making the G20 More Effective and Responsive*. Washington, DC: Brookings Institution Press with Korean Development Institute. pp. 176–190.

Mistral, J., 2011a. The G20 and the challenge of international financial reregulation. In: C.I. Bradford and W.H. Lim, eds. *Global Leadership in Transition: Making the G20 More Effective and Responsive*. Washington, DC: Brookings Institution Press with Korean Development Institute. pp. 86–100.

Murinde, V., 2011. Bank regulation in Africa: From Basel I to Basel II and now at a crossroads. In: C.I. Bradford and W.H. Lim, eds. *Global Leadership in Transition: Making the G20 More Effective and Responsive*. Washington, DC: Brookings Institution Press with Korean Development Institute. pp. 101–121.

Nafey, A., 2008. India and the G8: Reaching out or out of reach? In: A.F. Cooper and A. Antkiewicz, eds. *Emerging Powers in Global Governance: Lessons from the Heiligendamm Process*. Waterloo, Canada: Wilfrid Laurier University Press and Centre for International Governance Innovation. pp. 115–135.

O'Neill, J., 2012. Building BRICS: From conceptual category to rising reality. In: M. Larionova and J.J. Kirton, eds. *BRICS New Delhi Summit 2012: Stability, Security and Prosperity*. Toronto: Newsdesk Media Group. pp. 24–25. www.brics.utoronto.ca/newsdesk/BRICS-2012.pdf [Accessed: 23 February 2018].

Padoan, P.C., 2011. The political economy of global rebalancing and the role of structural reforms. In: C.I. Bradford and W.H. Lim, eds. *Global Leadership in Transition: Making the G20 More Effective and Responsive*. Washington, DC: Brookings Institution Press with Korean Development Institute. pp. 138–150.

Panova, V.V., 2008. Russia and the evolution of the Heiligendamm process. In: A.F. Cooper and A. Antkiewicz, eds. *Emerging Powers in Global Governance: Lessons from the Heiligendamm Process*. Waterloo, Canada: Wilfrid Laurier University Press and Centre for International Governance Innovation. pp. 285–306.

Park, Y.C. and Kim, S.M., 2011. G20 financial regulatory reform: Current status and future challenges. In: C.I. Bradford and W.H. Lim, eds. *Global Leadership in Transition: Making the G20 More Effective and Responsive*. Washington, DC: Brookings Institution Press with Korean Development Institute. pp. 70–85.

Patrick, S., 2011. The G20: Shifting coalitions of consensus rather than blocs. In: C.I. Bradford and W.H. Lim, eds. *Global Leadership in Transition: Making the G20 More Effective and Responsive*. Washington, DC: Brookings Institution Press with Korean Development Institute. pp. 257–263.

Payne, A., 2005. The study of governance in a global political economy. In: N. Phillips, ed. *Globalizing International Political Economy*. Basingstoke: Palgrave Macmillan. pp. 55–81.

Reynolds, D., 2014. Twentieth century summitry and the G7 process. In: E. Mourlon-Druol and F. Romero, eds. *International Summitry and Global Governance: The Rise of the G7 and the European Council, 1974–1991*. Cold War History Series. London and New York: Routledge. pp. 11–23.

Rosecrance, R. and Stein, A.A., 2001. The theory of overlapping clubs. In: R. Rosecrance, ed. *The New Great Power Coalition: Toward a World Concert of Nations*. New York: Rowman & Littlefield. pp. 221–234.

Rubio-Marquez, V., 2009. The G20: A practitioner's perspective. In: L. Martinez-Diaz and N. Woods, eds. *Networks of Influence? Developing Countries in a Networked Global Order*. Oxford: Oxford University Press. pp. 19–37.

Samans, R., Uzan, M. and Lopez-Carlos, A., 2007b. Introduction: The international monetary convention project. In: R. Samans, M. Uzan and A. Lopez-Carlos, eds. *The International Monetary System, the IMF, and the G20: A Great Transformation in the Making?* World Economic Forum. Basingstoke: Palgrave Macmillan. pp. xiii–xxvii.

Schmucker, C. and Gnath, K., 2011a. From the G8 to the G-20: Reforming the global economic governance system. In: C. Herrmann and J. Terhechte, eds. *European Yearbook of International Economic Law*, vol. 2. Berlin: Springer. pp. 389–402. (Also appeared as GARNET Working Paper 73/09, Brussels, January 2010 www.g20.utoronto.ca/biblio/7310.pdf [Accessed: 24 February 2018].)

Scholte, J.A., 2002. Governing global finance. In: D. Held and A. McGrew, eds. *Governing Globalization: Power, Authority and Global Governance*. Malden: Blackwell Publishing. pp. 189–208.

Scholte, J.A., 2011a. Global governance, accountability and civil society. In: J.A. Scholte, ed. *Building Global Democracy? Civil Society and Accountable Global Governance*. Cambridge: Cambridge University Press. pp. 8–41.

Scholte, J.A., 2011b. Introduction. In: J.A. Scholte, ed. *Building Global Democracy? Civil Society and Accountable Global Governance*. Cambridge: Cambridge University Press. pp. 1–7.

Shaw, T., Antkiewicz, A. and Cooper, A.F., 2008. The logic of the B(R)ICSAM model for global governance. In: A.F. Cooper and A. Antkiewicz, eds. *Emerging Powers in Global Governance: Lessons from the Heiligendamm Process*. Waterloo, Canada: Wilfrid Laurier University Press and Centre for International Governance Innovation. pp. 19–44.

Sherman, W., 2011. The G20 takes center stage as a twenty-first century leadership forum. In: C.I. Bradford and W.H. Lim, eds. *Global Leadership in Transition: Making the G20 More Effective and Responsive*. Washington, DC: Brookings Institution Press with Korean Development Institute. pp. 304–311.

Slaughter, A.-M., 2005. Government networks, world order, and the L20. In: J. English, R. Thakur and A.F. Cooper, eds. *Reforming from the Top: A Leaders' 20 Summit*. Tokyo: United Nations University Press. pp. 281–295.

Smith, G.S., 2011b. The G8 and the G20: What relationship now? In: C.I. Bradford and W.H. Lim, eds. *Global Leadership in Transition: Making the G20 More Effective and*

Responsive. Washington, DC: Brookings Institution Press with Korean Development Institute. pp. 48–54.

Smith, G.S., 2011c. Getting the context right: Essential to assuring G20's success. In: M. Brem, ed. *Prescriptions for the G20· The Cannes Summit and Beyond*, Waterloo, Canada: Centre for International Governance Innovation. www.cigionline.org/publications/getting-context-right-essential-assuring-g20s-success [Accessed: 23 February 2018].

Stephens, G., 2010. Information and communication: G8 institutionalization and compliance in the DOT Force. In: J.J. Kirton, M. Larionova and P. Savona, eds. *Making Global Economic Governance Effective: Hard and Soft Law Institutions in a Crowded World*. Farnham: Ashgate. pp. 201–215.

Stokes, B., 2011. Public attitudes in G20 countries. In: C.I. Bradford and W.H. Lim, eds. *Global Leadership in Transition: Making the G20 More Effective and Responsive*. Washington, DC: Brookings Institution Press with Korean Development Institute. pp. 285–298.

Summers, L., 2008. The birth of the G20. In: J.J. Kirton and M. Koch, eds. *G20 São Paulo/Brazil Summit 2008: Growth, Innovation, Inclusion: The G20 at Ten*. London: Newsdesk Communications. pp. 29–31.

Sundaram, J.K., 2011. The G20 and development: From financial stability to sustained growth. In: C.I. Bradford and W.H. Lim, eds. *Global Leadership in Transition: Making the G20 More Effective and Responsive*. Washington, DC: Brookings Institution Press with Korean Development Institute. pp. 191–200.

Truman, E.M., 2005. The euro and prospects for policy coordination. In: A.S. Posen, ed. *The Euro at Five: Ready for a Global Role?* Washington, DC: Institute for International Economics. pp. 47–85. www.piie.com/publications/chapters_preview/3748/04iie3748.pdf [Accessed: 22 February 2018].

Vickers, B., 2008. South Africa: Global reformism, global apartheid, and the Heiligendamm process. In: A.F. Cooper and A. Antkiewicz, eds. *Emerging Powers in Global Governance: Lessons from the Heiligendamm Process*. Waterloo, Canada: Wilfrid Laurier University Press and Centre for International Governance Innovation. pp. 163–191.

Wood, D., 2008. A break with the past or a natural progression? Mexico and the Heiligendamm process. In: A.F. Cooper and A. Antkiewicz, eds. *Emerging Powers in Global Governance: Lessons from the Heiligendamm Process*. Waterloo, Canada: Wilfrid Laurier University Press and Centre for International Governance Innovation. pp. 193–212.

Woods, N., 2011. The impact of the G20 on global governance: A history and prospective. In: C.I. Bradford and W.H. Lim, eds. *Global Leadership in Transition: Making the G20 More Effective and Responsive*. Washington, DC: Brookings Institution Press with Korean Development Institute. pp. 36–47.

Woodward, R., 2008. Why is the OECD involved in the Heiligendamm process? In: A.F. Cooper and A. Antkiewicz, eds. *Emerging Powers in Global Governance: Lessons from the Heiligendamm Process*. Waterloo, Canada: Wilfrid Laurier University Press and Centre for International Governance Innovation. pp. 263–283.

Xue, L. and Zhang, Y.B., 2011. Turning the G20 into a new mechanism for global economic governance: Obstacles and prospects. In: C.I. Bradford and W.H. Lim, eds. *Global Leadership in Transition: Making the G20 More Effective and Responsive*. Washington, DC: Brookings Institution Press with Korean Development Institute. pp. 55–62.

Young, K., 2001. The Basel Committee on Banking Supervision. In: R. Rosecrance, ed. *The New Great Power Coalition: Toward a World Concert of Nations*. New York: Rowman & Littlefield. pp. 39–45.

Yu, Y.D., 2005. China's evolving global view. In: J. English, R. Thakur and A.F. Cooper, eds. *Reforming from the Top: A Leaders' 20 Summit*. Tokyo: United Nations University Press. pp. 187–200.

Articles in periodicals

Acharya, A., 2011. Can Asia lead? Power ambitions and global governance in the 21st century. *International Affairs*, 87(4), pp. 851–869.

Agarwal, M., 2009. Africa, the economic crisis, and international economic governance. *South African Journal of International Affairs*, 16(1), pp. 1–15.

Alexander, N., 2013. The Russian G20 parade begins: The C20, T20, B20, Y20, G(irls)20. *G20 Update*, 15(February), pp. 6–8. us.boell.org/sites/default/files/g20_update_15_en.pdf [Accessed: 1 May 2018].

Alexandroff, A.S., 2010. Stuck in transition: Conflicting ambitions for the G-20's future. *Global Asia: A Journal of the East Asia Foundation*, 5(3), pp. 42–46. www.globalasia.org/v5no3/cover/stuck-in-transition-conflicting-ambitions-for-the-g-20s-future_alan-s-alexandroff [Accessed: 1 May 2018].

Alexandroff, A.S., 2011. The Gx global governance: China faces G20 leadership. *Munk Monitor*, Spring(1), pp. 40–56.

Alexandroff, A.S. and Shorr, D., 2010. What we have learned: 'New foundations for global governance'. *Contemporary International Relations*, 20(5), pp. 30–50.

Allard, P. and Lechervy, C., 2011. Les puissances émergentes et le G20: la musique ou les chaises? *Revue défense nationale*, 741(June).

Altman, R., 2009. The great crash, 2008: A geopolitical setback for the West. *Foreign Affairs*, 88(1), pp. 2–14.

Ash, T.G., 2011. If Obama really wants to lead us to a free world, he should abolish the G8. *The Guardian*, 25 May.

Åslund, A., 2006. Russia's challenges as Chair of the G-8. *Policy Briefs in International Economics*, March, PB06–3. Washington, DC: Peterson Institute for International Economics. www.iie.com/publications/pb/pb06-3.pdf [Accessed: 24 February 2018].

Åslund, A., 2009. The Group of 20 must be stopped. *Financial Times*, 27 November, p. 11.

Axworthy, T., 2007. Eight is not enough at summit. *Toronto Star*, 8 June, p. AA8.

Azambuja, M. de, 2007. Design for a multipolar world. *Global Governance: A Review of Multilateralism and International Organizations*, 13(3), pp. 307–310.

Baker, A., 2000a. The G7 as a global 'Ginger Group': Plurilateralism and four-dimensional diplomacy. *Global Governance: A Review of Multilateralism and International Organizations*, 6(2), pp. 165–189.

Baker, A., 2010. Restraining regulatory capture? Anglo-America, crisis politics and trajectories of change in global financial governance. *International Affairs*, 83(3), pp. 647–663.

Baliamoune, M., 2000. Economics of summitry: An empirical assessment of the economic effects of summits. *Empirica*, 27(3), pp. 295–314.

Ban, K.-M., 2011. The clock is ticking. *International Herald Tribune*, 1 November.

Bayne, N., 1995. The G7 summit and the reform of global institutions. *Government and Opposition*, 30(4), pp. 492–509.

Bayne, N., 1997. Changing patterns at the G7 summit. *G7 Governance*, 1 May. www.g8.utoronto.ca/governance/gov1/ [Accessed: 1 May 2018].

Beattie, A., 1999. New forum to supplement G7 work. *Financial Times*, 27 September, p. 5.

Beattie, A., 2010. The G20: Ad hoc institution faces tough struggle to show it has teeth. *Financial Times*, 11 November, p. 2.

Beeson, M. and Bell, S., 2009. The G-20 and international economic governance: Hegemony, collectivism, or both? *Global Governance: A Review of Multilateralism and International Organizations*, 15(1), pp. 67–86.

Berger, A. and Evenett, S.J., 2018. The Trump-Induced G20 Stress Test on trade: Did the German presidency pass? *Global Summitry: Politics, Economics and Law in International Governance*, 17 May. academic.oup.com/globalsummitry/advance-article-abstract/doi/10.1093/global/guy002/4999066?redirectedFrom=fulltext [Accessed: 3 August 2018].

Bergsten, C.F., 2008. A call for an 'Asian Plaza'. *The International Economy*, 22(2), pp. 12–15, 70–71.

Bezaury, L.A., 2010. The potential of our relations is very big. *International Affairs (Eastview Press)*, 56(2), pp. 193–200.

Bill & Melinda Gates Foundation, 2016. Renmin University of China Education Foundation. *How We Work: Grant*. www.gatesfoundation.org/How-We-Work/Quick-Links/Grants-Database/Grants/2016/07/OPP1155157 [Accessed: 8 December 2017].

Birdsall, N. and de la Torre, A., 2001. Il Washington contentious. *Politica Internazionale*, 29(1/2), pp. 95–103.

Black, D., 2012a. The G8 and Africa: A partial reckoning. *Global Governance: A Review of Multilateralism and International Organizations*, 18(4), pp. 441–447.

Black, D., 2012b. The G8 and Germany's Africa policy: A case of hegemonic mainstreaming. *Global Governance: A Review of Multilateralism and International Organizations*, 18(4), pp. 471–476.

Blanchfield, M., 2016. Former PM Martin: G20 should help beyond economic troubles. *Macleans*, 29 March. www.macleans.ca/news/canada/former-pm-martin-g20-should-help-beyond-economic-troubles/ [Accessed: 22 February 2018].

Bono and Geldof, R., 2010. The African Century. *The Globe and Mail*, Special Issue, 9 May.

Bradford, C.I. and Linn, J.F., 2004. Global economic governance at a crossroads: Replacing the G-7 with the G-20. *Brookings Institution Policy Brief* #132, April. www.brookings.edu/papers/2004/04globaleconomics_colin-i – bradford – jr.aspx [Accessed: 24 February 2018]. Also available in German: Ist die G-8 noch zeitgemäß? Plädoyer für eine Reform der 'Global Economic Governance' mit einer Gestärkten G-20. *Internationale Politik*, 59, pp. 90–95.

Bremmer, I. and Roubini, N., 2011. A G-zero world: The new economic club will produce conflict, not cooperation. *Foreign Affairs*, 90(2), pp. 2–7.

Brown, G. and Berlusconi, S., 2009. *Three Commitments for Global Recovery*. 19 February. webarchive.nationalarchives.gov.uk/20090505181721/www.number10.gov.uk/Page18340 [Accessed: 24 February 2018].

Brzezinski, Z., 1996. Let's add to the G-7. *The New York Times*, 25 June, p. A11.

Brzezinski, Z., 2009. The Group of Two that could change the world. *Financial Times*, 14 January, p. 9.

Caliari, A. and Alexander, N., 2012. Selected highlights of Business-20 (B20) draft recommendations to the G20. *G20 Update*, 12(June), pp. 8–10.

Callaghan, M., 2014. International Economic Summits: Are they worth the effort? *Caribbean Journal of International Relations & Diplomacy*, 2(3), pp. 43–60.

Cameron, D., 2012. I will get things done at the G8 Summit. *Politics Home*, 18 May. archive.li/xZqOQ [Accessed: 23 February 2018].

Cao, L.J., 2003a. Guan yu zhong guo ju jue jia ru ba guo ji tuan de si kao [Reflections on China's refusal to join the G8]. *Shan Tou Da Xue Xue Bao (Ren Wen She Hui Ke Xue Ban)* [Journal of Shantou University (Humanities and Social Sciences)], (3), pp. 10–16.

Cao, L.J., 2003b. Zhong guo jia ru ba guo ji tuan yan jiu [Research on China joining the G8]. *Yan Shan Da Xue Xue Bao (Zhe Xue She Hui Ke Xue Ban)* [Journal of Yanshan University (Philosophy and Social Sciences)], (4), pp. 68–71.

Cao, L.J., 2006. E luo si jia ru qi guo ji tuan dui zhong guo de qi shi [Lessons from Russia's joining the G7]. *Xue Xi Lun Tan* [Tribune of Study], 22(8), pp. 72–74.

Carin, B. and Mehlenbacher, A., 2010. Constituting global leadership: Which countries need to be around the summit table for climate change and energy security? *Global Governance*, 16(1), pp. 21–38.

Chand, S., Morrison, J.S., Piot, P. and Heymann, D.L., 2010. From G8 to G20, is health next in line? *The Lancet*, 23 June, pp. 1–3. c657621.r21.cf2.rackcdn.com/commissioners/lancetg8g20.pdf [Accessed: 1 May 2018].

Chavagneux, C., 2009. Le G20 va-t-il vraiment réguler la finance? [Will the G20 really regulate finances?] *Alternatives économiques*, 285(November).

Cherry, J. and Dobson, H., 2012. 'Seoul-searching': The 2010 G-20 Seoul summit. *Global Governance: A Review of Multilateralism and International Organizations*, 18(3), pp. 363–381.

Chin, G., 2010a. The emerging countries and China in the G20: Reshaping global economic governance. *The Future of the G8 and G20*, special issue of *Studia Diplomatica*, 63(2), pp. 105–123.

Chin, G., 2010b. Remaking the architecture: The emerging powers, self-insuring and regional insulation. *International Affairs*, 86(3), pp. 693–715.

Chin, G. and Dobson, H., 2015. China's presidency of the G20 Hangzhou: On global leadership and strategy. *Global Summitry: Politics, Economics and Law in International Governance*, 1(2), pp. 151–170. academic.oup.com/globalsummitry/article/1/2/151/2363169 [Accessed: 14 June 2018].

Chin, G. and Thakur, R., 2010. Will China change the rules of global order? *The Washington Quarterly*, 33(4), pp. 119–138.

Chodor, T., 2017. The G-20 since the global financial crisis: Neither hegemony nor collectivism. *Global Governance: A Review of Multilateralism and International Organizations*, 23(3), pp. 423–441.

Choi, J.S., 2010. Civil G20 dialog held in Incheon. *Korea.net*, 19 October. www.socialwatch.org/sites/default/files/2010-M-CiviL_G20_dialog.pdf [Accessed: 1 May 2018].

CIVICUS, 2012. *e-CIVICUS*. 595. 20 July. www.civicus.org/index.php/media-center/newsletters [Accessed: 13 April 2018].

Climate Home, 2017. China, EU and Canada to take lead on climate at Montreal meeting. *Climate Home News*. 13 September. www.climatechangenews.com/2017/09/13/china-eu-canada-take-lead-climate/ [Accessed: 19 March 2018].

Collins, A., 2017. Goal setting and governance: Examining the G8 new alliance for food security and nutrition with a gender lens. *Global Governance: A Review of Multilateralism and International Organizations*, 23(2), pp. 205–223.

Cooper, A.F., 2006. Opening up governance from the top: The L20 as a project of 'new multilateralism' and 'new regionalism'. *Korean Journal of International Organizations*, 1(1), pp. 121–133.

Cooper, A.F., 2010b. The G20 as an improvised crisis committee and/or a contested 'Steering Committee' for the world. *International Affairs*, 86(3), pp. 741–758.

Cooper, A.F., 2011a. The G20 and its regional critics: The search for inclusion. *Global Policy*, 2(2), pp. 203–209.

Cooper, A.F., 2013. Civil society relationships with the G20: An extension of the G8 template or distinctive pattern of engagement? *Global Society: Journal of Interdisciplinary International Relations*, 27(2), pp. 179–200.

Cooper, A.F., 2014. The G20 and contested global governance: BRICS, middle powers and small states. *Caribbean Journal of International Relations & Diplomacy*, 2(3), pp. 87–109.

Cooper, A.F. and Antkiewicz, A., 2010. G20 for global governance: Lessons from G8 outreach. *The Future of the G8 and G20*, special issue of *Studia Diplomatica*, 63(2), pp. 91–103.

Cooper, A.F. and Jackson, K., 2007b. Regaining legitimacy: The G8 and the 'Heiligendamm Process'. *CIIA International Insights*, 9 July. www.cigionline.org/articles/regaining-legitimacy-g8-and-heiligendamm-process [Accessed: 1 May 2018].

Cooper, A.F. and Momani, B., 2014. Re-balancing the G-20 from efficiency to legitimacy: The 3G coalition and the practice of global governance. *Global Governance: A Review of Multilateralism and International Organizations*, 20(2), pp. 213–232.

Cooper, H., 2012. Leaders make little headway in solving debt crisis. *The New York Times*, 20 June, p. A3.

Cornelissen, S., 2012. Selling Africa: Japan's G8 politics and its Africa diplomacy. *Global Governance: A Review of Multilateralism and International Organizations*, 18(4), pp. 461–470.

Cui, L.R., 2009. G20 begins to search for new path and windows of opportunities in global governance. *Contemporary International Relations*, 11, pp. 1–3.

da Silva, L.I.L., 2010. The G-20 moment. *New Perspectives Quarterly*, 27(1), pp. 33–34.

Davis, J.H., Sanger, D.E. and Thrush, G., 2017. Trump questions Putin on election meddling at eagerly awaited encounter. *The New York Times*, 7 July, p. A1.

Debaere, P., 2010. The output and input dimension of the European representation in the G20, *The Future of the G8 and G20*, special issue of *Studia Diplomatica*, 63(2), pp. 141–154.

de Guttry, A., 1994. The institutional configuration of the G-7 in the new international scenario. *The International Spectator*, 29(2), pp. 67–80.

Downie, C., 2015. Global energy governance in the G-20: States, coalitions, and crises. *Global Governance: A Review of Multilateralism and International Organizations*, 21(3), pp. 475–492.

Duncan, R., 2008. Bring back the link between gold and the dollar. *Financial Times*, 24 November, p. 11.

East Asia Forum, 2010. Asia and the G20. *East Asia Forum Quarterly*, 2(4). epress.anu.edu.au/wp-content/uploads/2011/05/whole6.pdf [Accessed: 2 May 2018].

Edwards, L., 2011. Missing in action, the G20 must step up at Cannes. *The Globe and Mail*, 3 November, p. A19.

Eichel, H., 2004. Globalisierung gestalten: Die G20 als wichtiges Element der Global Governance [Shaping globalization: The G20 as an important element of global governance]. *Internationale Politik: Deutschlands Führende Aussenpolitische Zeitschrift*, October, pp. 98–102.

Elliott, L., 2008. This summit signalled the passing of the exclusive club of wealthy nations. *The Guardian*, 11 December.

Elliott, L., 2012a. Europe needs to deliver on its fine-sounding rhetoric. *The Guardian*, 20 June.

Elliott, L., 2012b. The world watches Europe. *The Guardian Weekly*, 22–28 June, pp. 1–2.

Elliott, L. and Wintour, P., 2006. Blair wants developing nations in new G13 to help secure key deals. *The Guardian*, 13 July, p. 15.

Engel, U., 2012. The G8 and Germany's Africa policy: A case of hegemonic mainstreaming. *Global Governance: A Review of Multilateralism and International Organizations*, 18(4), pp. 471–476.

Engelbrekt, K., 2015. Mission Creep? The nontraditional security agenda of the G7/8 and the nascent role of the G-20. *Global Governance: A Review of Multilateralism and International Organizations*, 21(4), pp. 537–556.

Engelen, K.C., 2008. Letter from the G20 summit: Rift barely avoided: Letter from the G20 summit. *The International Economy*, 22(4), pp. 10–11.

ENS Staff, 2013. Global religious leaders call on G8 to 'strike at causes of poverty'. *Episcopal News Service*, 5 April. episcopaldigitalnetwork.com/ens/2013/04/05/global-religious-leaders-call-on-g8-to-strike-at-causes-of-poverty/ [Accessed: 2 May 2018].

Enter the B20; business and geopolitics, 2012. *The Economist*, 403(8788), p. 72.

Ferguson, N., 2010. The G-2: Are America and China headed for divorce? *New Perspectives Quarterly*, 27(1), pp. 35–38.

For slimmer and sporadic summits, 2001. *Financial Times*, 23 July, p. 18.

Fratianni, M. and Pattison, J., 2001. International organisations in a world of regional trade agreements: Lessons from club theory. *World Economy*, 24(3), pp. 197–222.

Frattini, F., 2009. Summits of the 'big' countries growing in importance but the G8 continues to play a strategic role. *Il Messaggero*, 2 April. www.esteri.it/MAE/EN/Sala_Stampa/ArchivioNotizie/Interviste/2009/04/20090402_articoloFrattini_Vertici.htm [Accessed: 11 February 2014].

Fues, T., 2007. Global governance beyond the G8: Reform prospects for the summit architecture. *Internationale Politik und Gesellschaft*, 2, pp. 11–24.

Garten, J., 2005. Russia's leadership of the Group of Eight will be farcical. *Financial Times*, 23 June, p. 28.

G-Force: The G7 no longer governs the world economy: Does anyone?, 2004. *The Economist*, 373(8396), p. 72.

Giles, C., 2009. G20 yet to deliver on early promise. *Financial Times*, 9 November, p. 2.

Giles, C., 2011. Meetings yet to reach the peak of achievement. *Financial Times*, 3 November, p. 2.

Global insights: A symposium: Global summit reform and the L-20, 2007. *Global Governance: A Review of Multilateralism and International Organizations*, 13(3), pp. 299–323.

Gnath, K., 2007. Beyond Heiligendamm: The G8 and its dialogue with emerging countries. *Internationale Politik: Global Edition*, 8, pp. 36–39. nbn-resolving.de/urn:nbn:de:0168-ssoar-130936 [Accessed: 2 May 2018].

Gnath, K. and Schmucker, C., 2015. Group with a cause: There is no alternative to the G20 but it does need reform. *The G20 at the End of 2014. G20 Monitor*, 15, pp. 32–35. www.lowyinstitute.org/files/g20-at-the-end-of-2014.pdf [Accessed: 24 February 2018].

Gong, W. and Zhao, C.Z., 2008. Er shi guo ji tuan: 21 shi ji quan qiu zhi li zhong xin? [G20: Center of 21st century global governance?]. *Dang Dai Shi Jie* [The Contemporary World], (6), pp. 27–28.

Grenville, S., 2014. Where is the G20 at end-2014? *The G20 at the End of 2014. G20 Monitor*, 15, pp. 39–40. www.lowyinstitute.org/files/g20-at-the-end-of-2014.pdf [Accessed: 23 February 2018].

Griesgraber, J.M., 2009. Reforms for major new roles of the International Monetary Fund? The IMF post-G-20 summit. *Global Governance: A Review of Multilateralism and International Organizations*, 15(2), pp. 179–185.

Guebert, J., 2010. The G8, G20 and multilateral organizations: Cooperating and collaborating. *The Future of the G8 and G20*, special issue of *Studia Diplomatica*, 63(2), pp. 53–69.

Guerrieri, P., 2010. Multipolar governance and global imbalances. *International Affairs*, 86(3), pp. 681–692.

Haas, R., 2005. Leaders have a flawed Gleneagles agenda. *Financial Times*, 1 July, p. 19.

Hajnal, P.I., 2011b. G20 yu shi min she hui [The G20 and civil society]. *Guo Ji Guan Cha* [International Review], 2, pp. 16–22.

Halimi, S., 2008. What's the G20 for? *Le Monde diplomatique*, translated by B. Wilson, 1 December, p. 1.

Hampson, F.O. and Heinbecker, P., 2011. The 'new' multilateralism of the twenty-first century. *Global Governance: A Review of Multilateralism and International Organizations*, 17(3), pp. 299–310.

Harvey, M., 2009. UN panel calls for council to replace G20. *Financial Times*, 23 March, p. 2.

He, F., 2015. Back on track. *The G20 at the End of 2014. G20 Monitor*, 15, pp. 36–38. www.lowyinstitute.org/files/g20-at-the-end-of-2014.pdf [Accessed: 24 February 2018].

He, X.Q., 2016. China and global energy governance under the G20 framework. *Global Petroleum Economy*, 24(9), pp. 16–24.

Helleiner, E., 2009. Reregulation and fragmentation in international financial governance. *Global Governance: A Review of Multilateralism and International Organizations*, 15(1), pp. 16–22.

Helleiner, E., 2010a. A Bretton Woods moment? The 2007–2008 crisis and the future of global finance. *International Affairs*, 86(3), pp. 619–636.

Helleiner, E., 2012. The limits of incrementalism: The G-20, the FSB, and the International Regulatory Agenda. *Journal of Globalization and Development*, 2(2).

Helleiner, E. and Pagliari, S., 2009. Towards a new Bretton Woods? The first G20 leaders' summit and the regulation of global finance. *New Political Economy*, 14(2), pp. 275–287.

Helleiner, E. and Pagliari, S., 2011. The end of an era in international financial regulation? A postcrisis research agenda. *International Organization*, 65(1), pp. 169–200.

Helleiner, G.K., 2000. *Markets, Politics and Globalization: Can the Global Economy be Civilized?* 10th Raúl Prebisch Lecture: Delivered at the Palais des Nations, Geneva. 11 December. www.unctad.org/en/docs/prebisch10th.en.pdf [Accessed: 18 October 2017]. Abridged version published 2001 in *Global Governance*, 7(3), pp. 243–263.

Helleiner, G.K., 2010. Towards realistic governance reform in international financial institutions. *Global Economy Journal*, 10(3), Article 5.

Hodges, M.R., 1994. More efficiency, less dignity: British perspectives on future role and working of the G-7. *The International Spectator*, 29(2), pp. 141–160.

Ikenberry, G.J., 1993. Salvaging the G-7. *Foreign Affairs*, 72(2), pp. 132–139.

Inoguchi, K., 1994. The changing significance of the G-7 summits. *Japan Review of International Affairs*, 8(1), pp. 21–38.

Jiao Y., 2005. G20 zhong guo cai jing wai jiao qi xin pian [New chapter of China's G20 financial diplomacy]. *Zhong Guo Jing Mao* [China Business Update], 11, p. 28.

Kaluzi, S. 2013. G20 exclusion of African perspectives. *G20 Update*, 15(February), pp. 16–17. us.boell.org/sites/default/files/g20_update_15_en.pdf [Accessed: 2 May 2018].

Kapur, D., 2000. Who gets to run the world? *Foreign Policy*, 121, pp. 44–50.

Keating, J.E., 2012. More than BRICs in the wall. *Foreign Policy*, 192, p. 25. www.foreignpolicy.com/articles/2012/02/27/more_than_brics_in_the_wall?page=0,0 [Accessed: 3 February 2014].

Keukleire, S. and Hooijmaaijers, B., 2014. The BRICS and other emerging power alliances and multilateral organizations in the Asia-Pacific and the Global South: Challenges for the European Union and its view on multilateralism. *Journal of Common Market Studies*, 52(3), pp. 582–599.

Kim, C.J., 2010. Special G20 stamps released. *Korea.net*, 10 November, www.korea.net/NewsFocus/policies/view?articleId=97687 [Accessed: 2 May 2018].

Kirton, J.J., 1994. Exercising concerted leadership: Canada's approach to summit reform. *The International Spectator*, 29(2), pp. 161–176.

Kirton, J.J., 2009. Coexistence, co-operation, competition: G summits. *Aspenia: The Aspen Institute Italia Review*, 14(43–44), pp. 156–162.

Kirton, J.J., 2010a. The future of the G20. *Munk Monitor*, Spring(1), p. 6.

Kirton, J.J., 2010b. The G8-G20 partnership. *The Future of the G8 and G20*, special issue of *Studia Diplomatica*, 63(2), pp. 23–34.

Lagarde, C., 2015. Time to act on the G-20 agenda: The global economy will thank you. *IMFBlog*, 6 February. blogs.imf.org/2015/02/06/time-to-act-on-the-g-20-agenda-the-global-economy-will-thank-you/ [Accessed: 30 January 2018].

Larionova, M., 2010a. Assessing G8 and G20 effectiveness in global governance so far. *Vestnik Mezhdunarodnykh Organizatsii* [International Organizations Research Journal], 5(31), pp. 99–120.

Larionova, M., 2010c. Is it G8 or G20? For Russia, of course, it's both. *The Future of the G8 and G20*, special issue of *Studia Diplomatica*, 63(2), pp. 81–90.

Larionova, M., 2011. Mekhanizmy Podotchetnosti: Vozmozhnosti dlia Povysheniia Legitimnosti 'Gruppy Vos'mi' i 'Gruppy Dvadtsati'? [Accountability mechanisms: Opportunities to increase the legitimacy of the Group of Eight and the Group of Twenty?]. *International Vestnik Mezhdunarodnykh Organizatsii* [Organizations Research Journal], 3(34), pp. 4–9.

Larionova, M., 2012b. From the Mexican to the Russian G20 presidency. *G20 Update*, 13(September), pp. 3–5. publications.hse.ru/mirror/pubs/share/folder/jax65qrt1p/direct/63020446 [Accessed: 2 May 2018].

Larionova, M., 2012c. Novye izmereniia sotrudnichestva 'Gruppy Dvadsati'. [G20 Los Cabos Summit: New dimensions of collaboration]. *Vestnik Mezhdunarodnykh Organizatsii* [International Organizations Research Journal], 3(38), pp. 25–41.

Larionova, M., 2018. Cooperation for growth and development: The G20, BRICS and APEC in the system of international institutions: A piece of good news for global governance. *International Organisations Research Journal*, 33(1), pp. 7–33.

Larionova, M., Rakhmangulov, M., Nagornov, V.A. and Shelepov, A.V., 2012. Problemy upravleniia global'nymi riskami i vozmozhnosti 'Gruppy Dvadsati' [Global risks governance and G20, G8, BRICS capabilities]. *Vestnik Mezhdunarodnykh Organizatsii* [International Organizations Research Journal], 3(38), pp. 42–91.

Lee, D., 2010. From Toronto to Seoul: Evolution of the G20 process. *The Future of the G8 and G20*, special issue of *Studia Diplomatica*, 63(2), pp. 35–51.

Lee, J.M., 2010. Activists in South Korea rally against G-20 summit; police fire pepper spray. *Associated Press Newswire*, 7 November.

Lee Sees Peer Pressure Enforcing G20 Deal, 2010. *Korea Herald*, 8 November. view.koreaherald.com/kh/view.php?ud=20101107000251&cpv=0 [Accessed: 2 May 2018].

Lesage, D., 2007. Globalisation, multipolarity and the L20 as an alternative to the G8. *Global Society*, 21(3), pp. 343–361.

Lesage, D., 2010b. Introduction: The G8 and G20 in flux, under the skilful presidency of Canada and Korea. *The Future of the G8 and G20*, special issue of *Studia Diplomatica*, 63(2), pp. 3–6.

Lesage, D. and Kaçar, Y., 2010. Turkey's profile in the G20: Emerging economy, middle power and bridge-builder. *The Future of the G8 and G20*, special issue of *Studia Diplomatica*, 63(2), pp. 125–140.

Lewallen, A., 2008. Indigenous at last! Ainu grassroots organizing and the Indigenous Peoples Summit in Ainu Mosir. *The Asia-Pacific Journal: Japan Focus*, 6(11). japanfocus.org/-ann_elise-lewallen/2971 [Accessed: 2 May 2018].

Lewis, F., 1991. The 'G-7½' directorate. *Foreign Policy*, 85, pp. 25–40.

Li, L.S., 2016. China's role and influence in the G20 and global governance. *Globalization*, 9, pp. 81–91.

Li, Y. and Gao, T.H., 2016. From G7 to G20: Competing multilateralism and Japan's role in global governance. *Foreign Affairs Commentary: Journal of School of Foreign Affairs*, 5, pp. 109–134.

Li, Y. and Su, X., 2016. New path of American leadership of global economic governance: Comment on China's strategic response. *Contemporary Asia-Pacific*, 2, pp. 58–79.

Liu, H., 2016. Deep reasons for and a re-evaluation of the path of G20 transformation. *Reform*, 7, pp. 96–103.

Liu, H.S., 2014. He Fa Xing, You Xiao Xing Yu Er Shi Guo Ji Tuan Ji Zhi Zhuan Xin [Legitimacy, effectiveness and G20 institutional change]. *International Review*, (3), pp. 128–141.

Liu, H.S., 2016. The expansion of G20 agenda and its effects on institutional effectiveness. *Global Forum*, 3, pp. 7–11.

Liu, H.S., 2017. Er Shi Guo Ji Tuan He Zuo Zhi Li Mo Shi De You Xiao Xing Fen Xi [Effectiveness of the G20's cooperative governance model]. *World Economics and Politics*, (6).

Liu, Z.Y., 2011. Er shi guo ji tuan de jue se zhuan xing yu fa guo ga na feng hui zhan wang [Transformation of the G20's role and prospects for the Cannes Summit]. *Guo Ji Guan Cha* [International Review], (2), pp. 30–36.

Liu, Z.Y., 2015. Er Shi Guo Ji Tuan Ji Zhi Zhuan Xin Yu Zhong Guo De Jue Se [G20 institutional change and China's role]. *Contemporary International Relations*, (7).

Luckhurst, J., 2013. Building cooperation between the BRICS and leading industrialized states. *Latin American Policy*, 4(2), pp. 251–268.

Lukov, V., 2010. G-20 and G-8 in search of solutions: Global problems of economy and society. *International Affairs: A Russian Journal*, 56(5), pp. 58–67.

Make way for the mighty G20, 2004. *The International Economy*, 18(4), p. 6.

Martin, L., 2006. Miles to go before Martin sleeps. *The Globe and Mail*, 1 June, pp. A1, 7.

Martin, N., 2005. Not representative, but still legitimate. *Alliance*, 10(2), pp. 16–17.

Martin, P., 2005. A global answer to global problems: The case for a new leaders' forum. *Foreign Affairs*, 84(3), pp. 2–6.

Martin, P., 2007. Breaking deadlocks in global governance: The L-20 proposal. *Global Governance: A Review of Multilateralism and International Organizations*, 13(3), pp. 301–305.

Martin, P., 2016. Speech to the Academic Council on the United Nations System conference hosted in collaboration with the International Commission of Jurists. *Canada in Global Affairs*, 29–30 March.

Martin, P., 2017. To curb the migrant crisis, the world must invest in Africa. *The World Post*, 19 December. www.washingtonpost.com/news/theworldpost/wp/2017/12/19/investment-africa/?utm_term=.81aa4dce030e [Accessed: 22 February 2018].

Maull, H.W., 1994. Germany at the summit. *The International Spectator*, 29(2), pp. 113–140.

McClellan, A., 2013. The G20's Anti-Corruption Working Group: Its history, achievements, and goals. *G20 Update*, 15(February), pp. 12–14. us.boell.org/sites/default/files/g20_update_15_en.pdf [Accessed: 2 May 2018].

McCormick, D., 2012. Policy makers must see granular level: And get a Plan B. *Financial Times*, 21 June, p. 32.

Mehta, P.B., 2007. Summit reform: The good and the bad news. *Global Governance: A Review of Multilateralism and International Organizations*, 13(3), pp. 311–314.

Merkel, A., 2015. Why the G7 Summit must go beyond crisis diplomacy. *The Globe and Mail*, 3 June, p. A15.

Merlini, C., 1994. The G-7 and the need for reform. *The International Spectator*, 29(2), pp. 5–26.

Mistral, J., 2012. The G-20 and the reform of the international monetary system. *Journal of Globalization and Development*, 2(2).

Moore, T., 2014. People's Summit a smorgasbord of food for thought. *Brisbane Times*, 12 November. www.brisbanetimes.com.au/national/queensland/peoples-summit-a-smorgasbord-of-food-for-thought-20141112-11lcdt.html [Accessed: 2 May 2018].

Mosley, L., 2009. An end to global standards and codes? *Global Governance: A Review of Multilateralism and International Organizations*, 15(1), pp. 9–15.

Murray, L.R., 2012. The Robin Hood tax: Small change for the banks, big change for the U.S. and the world. *The Huffington Post*, 14 May. www.huffingtonpost.com/liz-ryan-murray/the-robin-hood-tax_b_1513664.html [Accessed: 8 June 2018].

Naiman. R., 2001. Gli 'errori' delle istituzioni finanziarie internazionali [The 'errors' of the international financial institutions]. *Politica Internazionale*, 29(1/2), pp. 81–88.

Nam, Y.S., 2010. Police thwart fiery protest amid massive G20 security alert. *Agence France Presse*, 10 November.

Narlikar, A., 2010. New powers in the club: The challenges of global trade governance. *International Affairs*, 86(3), pp. 717–728.

Navarro, C., 2012. Pacific alliance, Group of 20 summits boost Mexico's international prestige. *SourceMex: Economic News & Analysis on Mexico*, 20 June.

Ni, J.J. and Wang, K., 2009. Cong hua sheng dun dao lun dun de G20 feng hui chuan da le shen me xin xi? [What message did the G20 summits convey from Washington to London?]. *Shi Jie Zhi Shi* [World Affairs], (8), pp. 50–51.

Niblett, R., 2012. Beyond Los Cabos. *First Magazine*, June. www.chathamhouse.org/sites/default/files/public/Research/International%20Economics/0612niblett.pdf [Accessed: 17 August 2018].

Niono dit non au G20! [Niono says no to the G20!], 2011. *Journal du Mali*, 31 October. www.journaldumali.com/2011/10/31/niono-dit-non-au-g20/ [Accessed: 8 June 2018].

Nye, J.S., 2010. American and Chinese power after the financial crisis. *The Washington Quarterly*, 33(4), pp. 143–153.

Ocampo, J.A. and Stiglitz, J.E., 2012. From the G-20 to a global economic coordination council. *Journal of Globalization and Development*, 2(2).

Pacific Institute for Climate Solutions, 2017. Canada, EU, China filling climate diplomacy gap. *The Climate Examiner*, 29 November. theclimateexaminer.ca/2017/11/29/canada-eu-china-filling-climate-diplomacy-gap/ [Accessed: 19 March 2018].

Pamfilova, E., 2013. The story of Russia's CivilG8–2006 project. *G20 Update*, 15(February), pp. 3–5. us.boell.org/sites/default/files/g20_update_15_en.pdf [Accessed: 17 August 2018].

Pang, Z.P., 2016. From Ise Shima G7 to Hangzhou G20: Bringing out the importance of global governance. *Contemporary World*, 7, pp. 42–45.

Pang, Z.Y., 2015. China sets strategic analysis of G20 summit agenda. *International Economic Cooperation*. 6, pp. 16–19.

Parker, G., 2009. Heads agree to New York reunion. *Financial Times*, 3 April, p. 4.

Parker, G. and Giles, C., 2012. Hopes of eurozone action rise at G20. *Financial Times*, 20 June, p. 10.

Pauly, L., 2010. Voices from the past: The international politics of financial stability. *Munk Monitor*, Spring, p. 7.

Payne, A., 2010. How many Gs are there in 'global governance' after the crisis? The perspectives of the 'marginal majority' of the world's states. *International Affairs*, 86(3), pp. 729–740.

Payne, A., 2014. Steering into the great uncertainty: The G20 as global governance. *Caribbean Journal of International Relations & Diplomacy*, 2(3), pp. 73–85. journals.sta.uwi.edu/iir/index.asp?action=downloadArticle&articleId=494&galleyId=419 [Accessed: 22 February 2018].

Penttilä, R., 2013. The G-20's rising clout. *The New York Times*, 4 September.

Persaud, A., 2010. The locus of financial regulation: Home versus host. *International Affairs*, 86(3), pp. 637–646.

Politica Internazionale, 2001. [Special G8 issue], 29(1/2), January–April.

Porter, T., 2009. Why international institutions matter in the global credit crisis. *Global Governance: A Review of Multilateralism and International Organizations*, 15(1), pp. 3–8.

Putnam, R.D., 1994. Western summitry in the 1990s: American perspectives. *The International Spectator*, 29(2), pp. 81–94.

Qureshi, Z., 2015. Addressing rising inequality in G20 economies. *Let's Talk Development Blog*. 11 June. blogs.worldbank.org/developmenttalk/addressing-rising-inequality-g20-economies [Accessed: 18 January 2018].

Rachman, G., 2010. A modern guide to G-ology: The clubs that would rule the world. *The Economist: The World in 2010*, pp. 73–74.

Rakhmangulov, M., 2012. Vklad 'Gruppy Dvadsati' v preodolenie disbalansov v mirovoi ekonomike (fiskal'naia konsolidatsiia). [G20 contribution to reducing global imbalances (fiscal consolidation)]. *Vestnik Mezhdunarodnykh Organizatsii* [International Organizations Research Journal], 3, pp. 109–119.

Ren, X., 2016. Zhong Guo Yu Er Shi Guo Ji Tuan: Cong Gui Ze Jie Shou Zhe Dao Gui Ze Zhi Ding Zhe [China and the G20: From rule-taker to rule-maker]. *Zhejiang Social Sciences*, (5).

Renard, T., 2010. G:20: Towards a new world order. *The Future of the G8 and G20*, special issue of *Studia Diplomatica*, 63(2), pp. 7–21.

Reynolds, D., 2009. Summitry as intercultural communication. *International Affairs*, 85(1), pp. 115–127.

Roach, S., 2004. How to fix the world. *Global Economic Forum*, Morgan Stanley, December, pp. 9–10.

The Royal Society, 2011. Science academies issue joint statement ahead of G8 summit in France. *Science News*, 19 May. royalsociety.org/news/2011/science-academies-issue-joint-statements [Accessed: 17 August 2018].

Ruthrauff, J. and Cadwallader, E., 2017. Civil 20 Summit: The world we want. *InterAction*, [blog] 29 June. www.interaction.org/newsroom/blog/civil-20-summit-world-we-want [Accessed: 25 April 2018].

Ruthrauff, J. and Lovelace, R., 2012. Ingredients for a successful G20 presidency: A civil society perspective. *G20 Update*, 14(December).

Sachs, J., 1998. Global capitalism: Making it work. *The Economist*, 348(8085), pp. 23–25.

Sachs, J., 2010. The unaccountable G-8: Lessons for the future. *The International Economy*, 24(3), pp. 42–43.

Sainsbury, T., 2015. Policies for the Turkish 2015 G20 presidency: Walking a tightrope of G20 relevancy. *The G20 at the End of 2014. G20 Monitor*, 15, pp. 5–26. www.lowyinstitute.org/files/g20-at-the-end-of-2014.pdf [Accessed: 24 February 2018].

Schirm, S.A., 2013. Global politics are domestic politics: A societal approach to divergence in the G20. *Review of International Studies*, 39(3), pp. 685–706.

Schneckener, U., 2009. Globales Regieren durch Clubs: Definition, Chancen und Grenzen von Club Governance [The opportunities and limits of global governance by clubs]. *SWP-Aktuell*, p. 47. www.swp-berlin.org/fileadmin/contents/products/aktuell/2009A47_skr_ks.pdf [Accessed: 17 August 2018].

Shkolyar, N., 2010. Made in Mexico: Oil, tequila, etc. *International Affairs (Eastview Press)*, 56(3), pp. 120–129.

Shorr, D. and Wright, T., 2010. The G20 and global governance: An exchange. *Survival*, 52(2), pp. 181–198.

Sidiropoulos, E., 2007. Toward more inclusive informal global governance: A view from South Africa. *Global Governance: A Review of Multilateralism and International Organizations*, 13(3), pp. 315–319.

Slaughter, A.-M., 1997. The real new world order. *Foreign Affairs*, 76(5), pp. 183–197.

Smith, G.S., 2012. The evolving role of the G20. *Perspectives on the G20: The Los Cabos Summit and Beyond*, pp. 30–31. Waterloo, Canada: Centre for International Governance Innovation. www.cigionline.org/publications/evolving-role-g20 [Accessed: 24 February 2018].

Smyser, W.R., 1993. Goodbye, G-7. *The Washington Quarterly*, 16(1), pp. 15–28.

Stanley Foundation, 2010a. The rise of the G-20. *Courier*, Special issue, Spring.

Steiner, S., 2011. Religious soft power as accountability mechanism for power in world politics: The Interfaith leaders' summit(s). *SAGE Open*, 1(3). sgo.sagepub.com/content/1/3/2158244011428085 [Accessed: 17 August 2018].

Steiner, S., 2012. Faith-based accountability mechanism typology: The 2011 Interfaith summit as soft power in global governance. *SAGE Open*, 2(2). sgo.sagepub.com/content/2/2/2158244012450705.full [Accessed: 17 August 2018].

Stephens, P., 1992. Major calls for overhaul of G7 summits. *Financial Times* (London), 10 September, p. 1.

Stephens, P., 2006. Only by reshaping the postwar settlement can it be preserved. *Financial Times*, 24 February, p. 17.

Stiglitz, J.E. and Griffith-Jones, S., 2007. Growth with responsibility in a globalized world: Findings of the Shadow G8. *Dialogue on Globalization*, p. 31. library.fes.de/pdf-files/iez/global/04472.pdf [Accessed: 17 August 2018].

Stuenkel, O., 2012. Can the BRICS co-operate in the G-20? A view from Brazil. South African Institute of International Affairs, Economic Diplomacy Programme. *Occasional Paper*, 123, December. ri.fgv.br/sites/default/files/publicacoes/Can%20the%20BRICS%20Co-operate%20in%20the%20G-20.pdf [Accessed: 24 February 2018].

Subacchi, P., 2010. Who is in control of the international monetary system? *International Affairs*, 86(3), pp. 665–680.

Subacchi, P. and Cooper, A. eds., 2010. Global Economic Governance in Transition. *International Affairs*, 86(3), pp. 607–617 [Special issue].

Summers, L.H., 2007. Summers speaks. *The International Economy*, 21(4), pp. 12–17.

Summers, L.H., 2017. Donald Trump's alarming G20 performance. *Financial Times*, 10 July, p. 11.

Suominen, K. and Dadush, U., 2012. Is there life for the G-20 beyond the global financial crisis? *Journal of Globalization and Development*, 2(2).

Switow, M., 2012. Access and the G8: Hear our voices. *Huffington Post*, 17 May. www.huffingtonpost.com/michael-switow/access-and-the-g8-hear-ou_b_1520027.html [Accessed: 17 August 2018].

Szczepanska, K., 2018. Toward inclusive global governance? Japanese civil society, the state, and G7/8 summitry, 2000–2016. *Global Governance: A Review of Multilateralism and International Organizations*, 24(2), pp. 211–228.

Taylor, I., 2012. Spinderella on Safari: British policies toward Africa under new labour. *Global Governance: A Review of Multilateralism and International Organizations*, 18(4), pp. 449–460.

The trouble with Ms. Merkel, 2012. *The New York Times*, 20 June, p. A28.

Truman, E.M., 2009. Globalization goes into reverse? *Real Time Economic Issues Watch*, 30 January. Washington: Peterson Institute for International Economics. www.peterson-institute.org/realtime/?p=453 [Accessed: 30 January 2018].

Truman, E.M., 2012. The G-20 is failing. *Foreign Policy*, 12 April. foreignpolicy.com/2012/04/12/the-g-20-is-failing/ [Accessed: 30 January 2018].

Ugarteche, O., 2012. Are we moving towards the privatization of international governance? *G20 Update*, 13(September), pp. 9–11. ke.boell.org/sites/default/files/g20_update_13_final_2012–09–191.pdf [Accessed: 17 August 2018].

Van de Graaf, T. and Westphal, K., 2011. The G8 and G20 as global steering committees for energy: Opportunities and constraints. *Global Policy*, 7(2, Supplement 1), pp. 19–30. onlinelibrary.wiley.com/doi/epdf/10.1111/j.1758–5899.2011.00121.x [Accessed: 17 August 2018].

Vestergaard, J. and Wade, R., 2011. The G-20 has served its purpose and should be replaced. *Journal of Globalization and Development*, 2(2).

Vestergaard, J., and Wade, R., 2012. The governance response to the great recession: The 'success' of the G20. *Journal of Economic Issues*, 46(2), pp. 481–490.

Vickers, B., 2006. Heading towards the G-8 St. Petersburg Summit: What's in it for Africa? *Global Insight*, 63(July). www.igd.org.za/publications/global-insight/send/20-global-insight/433-global-insight-63 [Accessed: 17 August 2018].

Vinci Giacchi, A., 2001. Origine del vertice [Origin of the summit]. *Politica Internazionale*, 29(1/2), pp. 31–36.

Von Furstenberg, G M. and Daniels, J.P., 1992. *Economic Summit Declarations, 1975–1989: Examining the Written Record of International Cooperation*. Princeton, NJ: Princeton Studies in International Finance, 72, International Finance Section, Dept. of Economics, Princeton University.

Wang, L.H.,and Gen, Z., 2018. Mei Guo Yu Er Shi Guo Ji Tuan :Ren Zhi Yu Zheng Ce Fan Ying [The United States and the G20: Perception and policy response]. *International Review*, (2).

Weinrichter, N., 2000. The world monetary system and external relations of the EMU: Fasten your seatbelts! *European Integration Online Papers (EIoP)*, 4(10), 27 August. eiop.or.at/eiop/texte/2000–010.htm [Accessed: 22 February 2018].

Whittington, L., 2010. Relatively speaking, a G20 summit of love. *Toronto Star*, 14 November, p. A2.

Whyman, W.E., 1995. We can't go on meeting like this: Revitalizing the G-7 process. *The Washington Quarterly*, 18(3), pp. 149–163.

Williamson, H., 2007. Emerging powers flex muscles to push for more influence on G8. *Financial Times*, 4 July, p. 6.

Wilson, M., 2010. The future of the G8. *Munk Monitor*, Spring, p. 5.

Woods, N., 2010b. Global governance after the financial crisis: A new multilateralism or the last gasp of the great powers? *Global Policy*, 1(1), pp. 51–63. onlinelibrary.wiley.com/doi/10.1111/j.1758–5899.2009.0013.x/pdf [Accessed: 17 August 2018].

Wright, T., 2010. The United States and the G20. *The Future of the G8 and G20*, special issue of *Studia Diplomatica*, 63(2), pp. 71–79.

Wu, X.B., 2010. Understanding the geopolitical implications of the global financial crisis. *The Washington Quarterly*, 33(4), pp. 155–163.

Xu, F., 2014. G20 institutionalization and China's strategic choice: Inquiry into global economic cooperation under the vision of a small group. *Northeast Asia Forum*, 6, pp. 35–45.

Xu, F., 2015. Yin Du De Er Shi Guo Ji Tuan Zhan Lue Ji Qi Dui Quan Qiu Zhi Li De Ying Xiang [India's strategy towards the G20 and global governance]. *South Asian Studies*, (5).

Xu, T., 2011. Kua zheng fu wang luo yu G20 de zhi li mo shi [Inter-governmental networks and G20 governance]. *Guo Ji Guan Cha* [International Review], (2), pp. 23–29.

Xue, L., 2007. Breaking deadlocks in global governance: How to make the L-20 work. *Global Governance: A Review of Multilateralism and International Organizations*, 13(3), pp. 320–323.

Yamashita, H., 2013. The Group of 8 and global peacekeeping, 2004–2010. *Global Governance: A Review of Multilateralism and International Organizations*, 19(3), pp. 333–352.

Yi, M., 2000. Er shi guo ji tuan zai bo lin chang shi [The G20's creation in Berlin]. *Shanghai Wai Mao Xue Yuan Xue Bao* [Journal of Shanghai University of International Business and Economics], 1, p. 7.

Yi, M., 2003. Er shi guo ji tuan qiang diao tui jin shi jie mao zu zhi fa zhan hui he tan pan [The G20 emphasizes promoting the WTO's development round negotiations]. *Shi Jie Mao Yi Zu Zhi Dong Tai Yu Yan Jiu* [Journal of Shanghai University of International Business and Economics], 1, p. 44.

Yu, X., 2009. Cong G20 feng hui kan shi jie jing ji tie xu xin dong xiang [Looking at trends in the global economic system from G20 summits]. *Dang Dai Shi Jie* [The Contemporary World], 5, pp. 53–55.

Yu, Y.D., 2004. Jue qi de zhong guo yu qi guo ji tuan er shi guo ji tuan [Rising China and the G7 and G20]. *Guo Ji Jing Ji Ping Lun* [International Economic Review], 5, pp. 9–12.

Zhan, X.N., 2016. Quan Qiu Tou Zi Zhi Li De Xin Lu Jing: Jie Du Er Shi Guo Ji Tuan Quan Quan Qiu Tou Zi Zhi Dao Yuan Ze [New approach to global investment governance: G20 guiding principles on global investment]. *World Economics and Politics*, (10).

Zhang, G.H., 2016. Lian He Guo, Er Shi Guo Ji Tuan Yu Quan Qiu Fa Zhan Zhi Li [The UN, the G20 and global development governance]. *Contemporary World and Socialism*, (4).

Zhang, H.B., 2015. G20: Global powers competition and cooperation. *Frontiers (People Daily Forum)*, 21, pp. 39–51.

Zhang, W., 2009. Er shi guo ji tuan lun dun feng hui de cheng guo yu nan ti [Results and challenges of the G20 London Summit]. *Guo Ji Zi Liao Xin Xi* [International Data Information], 4, pp. 41–42.

Zhang, W.H. and Gao, Y.R., 2016. G20 transformation: Path and direction, *Chinese Development Observations*, 8, pp. 5–7.

Zhao, Q.S., 2015. Strategic choice of China's participation in G20 global energy governance. *Contemporary Globalism and Socialism*, 6, pp. 132–138.

Zhen, B.X., 2016. Er Shi Guo Ji Tuan Ji Zhi Zhuan Xin:Wen Ti Yu Jie Jue Fang An [G20 institutional change: Problems and solutions]. *China International Studies*, (4).

Zhou, M. and Chen, J., 2016. G20 pushes for global governance systematic reform. *China Foreign Investment*, 19, pp. 50–53.

Zhou, Z.Q., 2016. Achievements and prospects of G20 participation in global energy governance. *Contemporary Economic Discussion*, 1, pp. 50–54.

Zhu, J.J. 2011. G20 ji zhi fei zheng shi xing de qi yuan [Origins of the G20 mechanism's informality]. *Guo Ji Guan Cha* [International Review], 2, pp. 9–15.

Zhu, J.J., 2015. Guo Ji Ji Zhi Jian He Zuo Yu Er Shi Guo Ji Tuan Ji Zhi Zhuan Xin [Regime complex and G20 institutional change]. *Global Review*, (5).

Zhu, J.J., 2016. 2030 Nian Ke Chi Xu Fa Zhan Yi Cheng Yu Er Shi Guo Ji Tuan Ji Zhi Zhuan Xin [2030 agenda for sustainable development and G20 institutional change]. *Global Review*, (4).

Official (governmental and IGO) publications

Australia. Prime Minister, 2014. *Australia's Vision for the G20*. 23 January. www.weforum.org/agenda/2014/01/vision-g20/ [Accessed: 11 February 2017].

Australia. Treasury and Reserve Bank of Australia, 2006. *Demography and Financial Markets: Proceedings of a Conference, Sydney, Australia, 23–25 July*, edited by C. Kent, A. Park and D. Rees. Canberra. 12 October. www.rba.gov.au/publications/confs/2006/pdf/conf-vol-2006.pdf [Accessed: 17 August 2018].

Bank for International Settlements, 2012. *About BIS*. www.bis.org/about/index.htm [Accessed: 19 January 2018].

Bank for International Settlements, 2016. *Identifying and Tracking Financial Risks: BIS Contributions*. 10 June. g20chn.org/English/Documents/Current/201608/P020160811539681780152.pdf [Accessed: 1 February 2018].

Bank for International Settlements. Basel Committee on Banking Supervision, 2010. *Basel III: International Framework for Liquidity Risk Measurement, Standards and Monitoring*. December. www.bis.org/publ/bcbs188.htm [Accessed: 19 January 2018].

Bank for International Settlements. Basel Committee on Banking Supervision, 2012a. *About the Basel Committee*. www.bis.org/bcbs/about.htm [Accessed: 19 January 2018].

Bank for International Settlements. Basel Committee on Banking Supervision, 2012b. *Report to G20 Finance Ministers and Central Bank Governors on Basel III Implementation*. October. www.bis.org/publ/bcbs234.pdf [Accessed: 19 January 2018].

Bank for International Settlements. Basel Committee on Banking Supervision, 2012c. *Report to G20 Leaders on Basel III Implementation*. June. www.bis.org/publ/bcbs220.pdf [Accessed: 19 January 2018].

Bank for International Settlements. Basel Committee on Banking Supervision, 2013. *Progress Report on Implementation of the Basel Regulatory Framework*. www.bis.org/publ/bcbs247.pdf [Accessed: 18 January 2018].

Bank of Indonesia and the Banco de Mexico, 2008. *Proceedings of the G20 Workshop on Competition in the Financial Sector*, Bali. 16–17 February. www.g20mexico.org/images/stories/canalfinan/eventante/05competition.pdf [Accessed: 1 February 2013].

Canada, 2010. *Backgrounder: The SME Finance Challenge*. 26 June. www.canada.ca/en/news/archive/2010/06/backgrounder-sme-finance-challenge.html [Accessed: 9 January 2018].

Canada. Department of Foreign Affairs and International Trade, 2012. *How the G20 Works*. www.canadainternational.gc.ca/g20/about-a_propos/howworks-g20-fonctionnement.aspx?lang=eng&view=d [Accessed: 14 July 2012].

Canada. Prime Minister's Office, 2010. *Statement by the Prime Minister of Canada at the World Economic Forum*. Davos, Switzerland. 28 January. www.g8.utoronto.ca/summit/2010muskoka/harper-davos.html [Accessed: 9 January 2018].

China. President, 2016. *President Xi Jinping['s] Closing Speech*. 5 September. www.g20.utoronto.ca/2016/160905-xi.html [Accessed: 24 February 2017].

De Brouwer, G., 2012. *The Asian Century and the G20: An Australian Perspective on a Changing World*. Department of Foreign Affairs and Trade. dfat.gov.au/people-to-people/foundations-councils-institutes/australia-india-council/programs/Pages/the-asian-century-and-the-g20-an-australian-perspective-on-a-changing-world.aspx [Accessed: 17 August 2018].

De Brouwer, G. and Yeaman, L., 2007. *Australia's G-20 Host Year: A Treasury Perspective*. http://archive.treasury.gov.au/documents/1268/HTML/docshell.asp?URL=03_G-20.asp [Accessed: 17 August 2018].

European Council, 2014. *Brussels G7 Summit*. 4–5 June. www.european-council.europa.eu/en/meetings/international-summit/2014/06/04-05/ [Accessed: 23 March 2018].

Finance Canada, 2017. *G20 Finance Ministers' and Central Bank Governors' Meetings*. [email] Message to P.I. Hajnal. Sent 6 December.

Financial Stability Board, 2010. *Korea-FSB Financial Reform Conference: An Emerging Market Perspective*. Seoul, 2–3 September. www.g20mexico.org/load/780982897 [Accessed: 1 February 2013].

Financial Stability Board, 2011. *FSB Report on the Overview of Progress in the Implementation of the G20 Recommendations for Strengthening Financial Stability*. 4 November. www.financialstabilityboard.org/publications/r_111104.pdf [Accessed: 17 August 2018].

Financial Stability Board, 2012a. *Mandate*. www.fsb.org/about/ [Accessed: 3 October 2017].

Financial Stability Board, 2012b. *Overview of Progress in the Implementation of the G20 Recommendations for Strengthening Financial Stability*. 19 June. www.financialstabilityboard.org/publications/r_120619a.pdf [Accessed: 17 August 2018].

Financial Stability Board, 2016. *Chair's Letter to the G20 Finance Ministers and Central Bank Governors*. 24 July. www.fsb.org/wp-content/uploads/FSB-Chair-letter-to-G20-Ministers-and-Governors-July-2016.pdf [Accessed: 1 February 2018].

France G20, 2011. *Press Kit: Cannes Summit*. 3–4 November. ca.ambafrance.org/IMG/pdf/Livret_Presse_englishG20Cannes.pdf?5222/8eefafee2dbfa42b41ccb18e871827f0314fff75 [Accessed: 17 August 2018].

France. Ministère de la Culture et de la Communication, 2011. *Cultural Summit Avignon*, 17–18 November. https://ifacca.org/en/news/2011/11/18/cultural-summit-avignon-17-and-18-november-2011/ and www.culturecommunication.gouv.fr/Ministere/L-histoire-du-ministere/Archives/Frederic-Mitterrand-2009-2012/Articles-2009-2012/Sommet-culturel-sur-la-creation-a-l-ere-numerique/(language)/fre-FR [Accessed: 27 November 2017].

France. Ministère de l'Économie, des Finances et de l'Industrie, 2011. *G20 Ministerial Meeting on Development: Communiqué*. Washington, DC. 23 September. http://proxy-pubminefi.diffusion.finances.gouv.fr/pub/document/18/11572.pdf [Accessed: 27 November 2017].

France. Présidence de la République, 2008. *Conférence de presse*. 8 January.

G7, 1995. *The Halifax Summit Review of the International Financial Institutions: Background Document, 5: Promoting Financial Stability in a Globalized Economy*. 16 June. www.g8.utoronto.ca/summit/1995halifax/financial/5.html [Accessed: 18 October 2017].

G7, 2014. *The Brussels G7 Summit Declaration*. www.g8.utoronto.ca/summit/2014brussels/declaration.html [Accessed: 24 February 2018].

G7 Finance Ministers and Central Bank Governors, 1999a. *Communiqué*. 20 February. www.g8.utoronto.ca/finance/fm022099.htm [Accessed: 18 October 2017].

G7 Finance Ministers and Central Bank Governors, 1999b. *Statement of G-7 Finance Ministers and Central Bank Governors*. Washington, DC. 25 September. www.g8.utoronto.ca/finance/fm992509state.htm [Accessed: 18 October 2017].

G8, 2009. *The Agenda of the Heiligendamm/L'Aquila Process (HAP)*. 9 July. www.g8.utoronto.ca/summit/2009laquila/2009-g5-g8-2-hap.html [Accessed: 18 October 2017].

G8 Finance Ministers and Central Bank Governors, 1999. *Communiqué*. 20 February. www.g8.utoronto.ca/finance/fm022099.htm [Accessed: 17 August 2018].

G8 Finance Ministers and Central Bank Governors, 2006. *G8 Finance Ministers' Statement on Access to Energy Services for the Millennium Development Goals*. St. Petersburg. 9–10 June. www.g8.utoronto.ca/finance/fm060610_energy.htm [Accessed: 17 August 2018].

G8 & G20 Youth Summits, 2011. *Final Communiqué*. 3 June. www.youthpolicy.org/wp-content/uploads/library/2011_G8G20_Youth_Communique_Eng.pdf [Accessed: 8 June 2018].

G20, 1999. *Communiqué of G-20 Finance Ministers and Central Bank Governors–Berlin, Germany*. 15–16 December. www.g20.utoronto.ca/1999/1999communique.pdf [Accessed: 18 January 2018].

G20, 2002. *Globalisation, Living Standards and Inequality: Recent Progress and Continuing Challenges*. September. www.rba.gov.au/publications/bulletin/2002/sep/pdf/bu-0902-1.pdf [Accessed: 17 August 2018].

G20, 2003. *Economic Reform in This Era of Globalization: 16 Country Cases*. www.g20.utoronto.ca/docs/economicreform.pdf [Accessed: 17 August 2018].

G20, 2004. *G-20 Accord for Sustained Growth*. 21 November. www.g8.utoronto.ca/g20/2004/2004growth.html [Accessed: 17 August 2018].

G20, 2005. *Case Studies: Institution Building in the Financial Sector*. www.g20.utoronto.ca/docs/ [Accessed: 17 August 2018].

G20, 2007. *The Group of Twenty: A History*. www.g20.utoronto.ca/docs/g20history.pdf [Accessed: 18 October 2017].

G20, 2008. *Declaration: Summit on Financial Markets and the World Economy and Action Plan to Implement Principles for Reform*. Washington, DC. 15 November. www.g20.utoronto.ca/2008/2008declaration1115 html [Accessed: 24 October 2017].

G20, 2009a. *Declaration on Strengthening the Financial System and Declaration on Delivering Resources through the International Financial Institutions*. London. 2 April. www.g20.utoronto.ca/2009/2009ifi.pdf and www.g20.utoronto.ca/2009/2009delivery.pdf [Accessed: 28 November 2017].

G20, 2009b. *Join the debate ahead of the London Summit*. 30 January. webarchive.nationalarchives.gov.uk/20090505130642/http://londonsummit.gov.uk/en/media-centre/articles-and-publications/join-debate-press-release [Accessed: 8 June 2018].

G20, 2009c. *Leaders Statement: The Pittsburgh Summit*; and Annexes: *Core Values for Sustainable Economic Activity; G20 Framework for Strong, Sustainable, and Balanced Growth*. 25 September. www.g20.utoronto.ca/2009/2009communique0925.html [Accessed: 24 October 2017].

G20, 2009d. *London Summit: Leaders' Statement*. 2 April. www.g20.utoronto.ca/2009/2009communique0402.pdf [Accessed: 24 October 2017].

G20, 2009e. *Prime Minister Urges Values-Based Rules for Economy*. 31 March. webarchive.nationalarchives.gov.uk/20090402183547/http://londonsummit.gov.uk/en/media-centre/latest-news/?view=News&id=15662522 [Accessed: 8 June 2018].

G20, 2010a. *The G-20 Toronto Summit Declaration*. 27 June. www.g20.utoronto.ca/2010/to-communique.html [Accessed: 24 October 2017].

G20, 2010b. *The G20 Seoul Summit Leaders' Declaration*. 12 November. www.g20.utoronto.ca/2010/g20seoul.pdf [Accessed: 28 November 2017].

G20, 2010c. *Principles for Innovative Financial Inclusion*. 27 June. www.g20.utoronto.ca/2010/to-principles.html [Accessed: 26 September 2017].

G20, 2010d. *Seoul Summit Document.* www.g20.utoronto.ca/2010/g20seoul-doc.pdf [Accessed: 24 October 2017].

G20, 2010e. *The Seoul Summit Document, Annex I: Seoul Development Consensus for Shared Growth.* www.g20.utoronto.ca/2010/g20seoul-consensus.pdf [Accessed: 8 June 2018].

G20, 2010f. *The Seoul Summit Document, Annex III: G20 Anti-Corruption Action Plan.* www.g20.utoronto.ca/2010/g20seoul-anticorruption.pdf [Accessed: 8 June 2018].

G20, 2010g. *Supporting Document.* 12 November. www.canadainternational.gc.ca/g20/assets/pdfs/2010%20-%20Seoul%20Summit%20Supporting_Document.pdf [Accessed: 24 November 2012].

G20, 2011a. *The Cannes Action Plan for Growth and Jobs.* 4 November. www.g20.utoronto.ca/2011/2011-cannes-action-111104-en.html [Accessed: 24 October 2017].

G20, 2011b. *Cannes Summit Final Declaration: Building Our Common Future: Renewed Collective Action for the Benefit of All.* 4 November. www.g20.utoronto.ca/2011/2011-cannes-declaration-111104-en.html [Accessed: 24 October 2017].

G20, 2011c. *Final Communiqué [of the] G20 Leaders' Summit, Cannes.* 4 November. www.g20.utoronto.ca/2011/2011-cannes-communique-111104-en.html [Accessed: 24 October 2017].

G20, 2011d. *G20 Action Plan to Support the Development of Local Currency Bond Markets.* 15 October. www.g20.utoronto.ca/2011/2011-finance-action-plan-currency-111015-en.pdf [Accessed: 17 August 2018].

G20, 2011e. *G20 Coherent Conclusions for the Management of Capital Flows Drawing on Country Experiences.* 15 October. www.g20.utoronto.ca/2011/2011-finance-capital-flows-111015-en.pdf [Accessed: 17 August 2018].

G20, 2011f. *G20 Principles for Cooperation between the IMF and Regional Financing Arrangements.* 15 October. www.g20.utoronto.ca/2011/2011-finance-principles-111015-en.pdf [Accessed: 17 August 2018].

G20, 2011g. *What Is the G20?* www.g20-g8.com/g8-g20/g20/english/what-is-the-g20-/what-is-the-g20-/what-is-the-g20.70.html [Accessed: 23 March 2012].

G20, 2012c. *Calendar.* www.g20.utoronto.ca/2012/2012-loscabos-cal.html [Accessed: 27 November 2017].

G20, 2012e. *Communiqué of Ministers of Finance and Central Bank Governors of the G20.* 5 November. www.g20.utoronto.ca/2012/2012-121105-finance-en.html [Accessed: 27 November 2017].

G20, 2012h. *Financial Inclusion: From Principles to Action.* Washington, DC. 22 April. www.worldbank.org/en/events/2012/04/22/financial-inclusion-from-principles-to-action [Accessed: 7 August 2018].

G20, 2012j. *G20 Leaders Declaration.* 19 June. www.g20.utoronto.ca/2012/2012-0619-loscabos.pdf [Accessed: 26 September 2017].

G20, 2012m. *The Los Cabos Growth and Jobs Action Plan.* 19 June. www.g20.utoronto.ca/2012/2012-0619-loscabos-actionplan.pdf [Accessed: 24 October 2017].

G20, 2012r. *Policy Commitments by G20 Members.* 19 June. www.g20.utoronto.ca/2012/2012-0619-loscabos-commitments.pdf [Accessed: 24 October 2017].

G20, 2012v. *The Sherpas Hold Their Fifth and Final Meeting Under the Mexican Presidency of the G20.* 31 October. globalsummitryproject.com.s197331.gridserver.com/archive/g20–2012_los_cabos1/www.g20mexico.org/index.php/en/press-releases/541-los-sherpas-sostienen-su-quinta-y-ultima-reunion-en-el-marco-de-la-presidencia-mexicana-del-grupo-de-los-veinte.html [Accessed: 27 November 2017].

G20, 2012aa. *Think-20 Summary Report by Co-Chairs*. December. en.g20russia.ru/docs/think_20/summary_report.html [Accessed: 8 June 2018].

G20, 2012ag. *Y20 Puebla Agreement*. 9–11 May. www.younglead.eu/wp-content/uploads/2012/12/2012_Y20.pdf [Accessed: 8 June 2018].

G20, 2013a. *Annex 1: St. Petersburg Fiscal Templates: G-20 Advanced Economies*. en.g20russia.ru/load/783139442 and www.g20.utoronto.ca/2013/Annex_1_-_St_Petersburg_Fiscal_Strategies___AEs___FINAL.pdf [Accessed: 28 November 2017].

G20, 2013b. *Annex 2: St. Petersburg Fiscal Templates: G-20 Emerging Economies*. en.g20russia.ru/load/783047026 and www.g20.utoronto.ca/2013/Annex_2_-_St_Petersburg_Fiscal_Strategies___EMEs_FINAL.pdf [Accessed: 28 November 2017].

G20, 2013c. *Annex 3: MAP Policy Templates for all G20 Countries*. en.g20russia.ru/load/783046978 and www.g20.utoronto.ca/2013/Annex_3_MAP_Policy_Commitments_by_Members_September_5.pdf [Accessed: 28 November 2017].

G20, 2013d. *Annex 4: St. Petersburg Accountability Assessment*. 5 September. en.g20russia.ru/load/783047169 and www.g20.utoronto.ca/2013/Accountabilty_Assessment_FINAL.pdf [Accessed: 28 November 2017].

G20, 2013e. *G20 5th Anniversary Vision Statement*. September. www.g20.utoronto.ca/2013/G20_5th_Anniversary_Vision_Statement.pdf [Accessed: 29 September 2017].

G20, 2013f. *G20 Leaders' Declaration*. 6 September. www.g20.utoronto.ca/2013/Saint_Petersburg_Declaration_ENG.pdf [Accessed: 8 September 2017].

G20, 2013g. [Official logo of the] *Leaders' Summit 2013*. en.g20russia.ru/docs/summit/summit_2013.html [Accessed: 24 October 2013].

G20, 2013h. *Priorities of Russia's G20 Presidency in 2013*. December. en.g20russia.ru/docs/g20_russia/priorities.html [Accessed: 24 October 2017].

G20, 2013i. *The Russian Presidency of the G20: Outline*. en.g20russia.ru/docs/g20_russia/outline [Accessed: 17 August 2018].

G20, 2013j. *St. Petersburg Action Plan*. September. www.g20.utoronto.ca/2013/St_Petersburg_Action_Plan.pdf [Accessed: 8 September 2017].

G20, 2013k. *Saint Petersburg Accountability Report on G20 Development Commitments*. www.g20.utoronto.ca/2013/Saint_Petersburg_Accountability_Report_on_G20_Development_Commitments.pdf [Accessed: 29 September 2017].

G20, 2013l. *St. Petersburg Strategic Framework for the G20 Anti-Corruption Working Group*. en.g20russia.ru/load/783345715 [Accessed: 28 November 2017].

G20, 2014a. *Accountability Assessment Framework Going Forward*. www.g20.utoronto.ca/2014/2015_g20_accountability_assessment_process.pdf [Accessed: 22 February 2017].

G20, 2014b. *The Brisbane Accountability Assessment*. 14 November. www.g20.utoronto.ca/2014/2014_accountability_assessment_report.pdf [Accessed: 16 February 2017].

G20, 2014c. *Brisbane Action Plan*. November. www.g20.utoronto.ca/2014/brisbane_action_plan.pdf [Accessed: 24 January 2017].

G20, 2014d. *The G20 Australia 2014 Logo*. www.g20australia.org/sites/default/files/g20_resources/library/Factsheet-G20%20Logo.pdf [Accessed: 5 September 2017].

G20, 2014e. *G20 Leaders' Brisbane Statement on Ebola*. www.g20.utoronto.ca/2014/g20_leaders_brisbane_statement_ebola.pdf [Accessed: 3 October 2017].

G20, 2014f. *G20 Leaders' Communiqué*. 15–16 November. www.g20.utoronto.ca/2014/brisbane_g20_leaders_summit_communique.pdf [Accessed: 3 October 2017].

G20, 2014g. *Preparing the G20 Brisbane Summit Agenda: An Overview from the Australian Presidency*. www.g20.utoronto.ca/2014/2014-policy-notes.html [Accessed: 20 January 2017].

G20, 2014h. *Sergei Lavrov on the Priorities of Russia's G8 Presidency 2014*. en.g8russia.ru/news/20140121/983200521.html [Accessed: 8 February 2014].

G20, 2014i. *Turkish G20 Presidency Priorities for 2015*. 1 December. www.g20.utoronto.ca/2015/141201-turkish-priorities.html [Accessed: 21 January 2017].

G20, 2015a. *G20 Leaders' Communiqué*. 15–16 November. www.g20.utoronto.ca/2015/151116-communique.pdf [Accessed: 3 October 2017].

G20, 2015b. *G20 Statement on the Fight against Terrorism*. www.g20.utoronto.ca/2015/151116-terrorism.pdf [Accessed: 3 October 2017].

G20, 2015c. *Logo*. g20.org.tr/logo-2/ [Accessed: 5 September 2017].

G20, 2016a. *Annex to G20 Leaders' Communiqué*. 5 September. www.g20.utoronto.ca/2016/160905-annex.html [Accessed: 4 October 2017].

G20, 2016b. *Documents: Current Presidency [China]*. web.archive.org/web/20161105214915/http:/g20.org/English/Documents/Current/index.html [Accessed: 1 February 2018].

G20, 2016c. *G20 2016 Innovation Action Plan*. 5 September. www.g20.utoronto.ca/2016/160905-innovation.html [Accessed: 24 February 2017].

G20, 2016d. *G20 Action Plan on the 2030 Agenda for Sustainable Development*. 8 September. www.g20.utoronto.ca/2016/g20-action-plan-on-2030-agenda.pdf [Accessed: 5 February 2017].

G20, 2016e. *G20 Anti-Corruption Action Plan, 2017–2018*. 27 September. www.g20.utoronto.ca/2016/160905-anticorruption.html [Accessed: 24 February 2017].

G20, 2016f. *G20 Blueprint on Innovative Growth*. 5 September. www.g20.utoronto.ca/2016/160905-blueprint.html [Accessed: 24 January 2017].

G20, 2016g. *G20 Digital Economy Development and Cooperation Initiative*. 5 September. www.g20.utoronto.ca/2016/160905-digital.html [Accessed: 24 February 2017].

G20, 2016h. *G20 Growth Strategies*. 26 September. www.g20.utoronto.ca/2016/growth-strategies.html [Accessed: 24 February 2017].

G20, 2016i. *G20 High-Level Principles on Cooperation on Persons Sought for Corruption and Asset Recovery*. 27 September. www.g20.utoronto.ca/2016/asset-recovery.html [Accessed: 24 February 2017].

G20, 2016j. *G20 Initiative on Supporting Industrialization in Africa and Least Developed Countries*. 27 September. www.g20.utoronto.ca/2016/supporting-industralization.html [Accessed: 24 February 2017].

G20, 2016k. *G20 Leaders' Communiqué*. 5 September. www.g20.utoronto.ca/2016/160905-communique.html [Accessed: 4 October 2017].

G20, 2016l. *G20 New Industrial Revolution Action Plan*. 5 September. www.g20.utoronto.ca/2016/160905-industrial.html [Accessed: 24 February 2017].

G20, 2016m. *G20 Strategy for Global Trade Growth (SGTG)*. 10 July. www.g20.utoronto.ca/2016/160710-trade-annex2.html [Accessed: 24 February 2017].

G20, 2016n. *G20 Summit 2016: China*. 1 December. www.g20.utoronto.ca/2016/xi-151201-en.pdf [Accessed: 21 January 2017].

G20, 2016o. *Hangzhou Action Plan*. 5 September. www.g20.utoronto.ca/2016/160905-action.html [Accessed: 24 February 2017].

G20, 2016p. *Hangzhou Comprehensive Accountability Report on G20 Development Commitments*. 14 September. www.g20.utoronto.ca/2016/hangzhou-accountability-development.pdf [Accessed: 16 February 2017].

G20, 2016q. *Logo*. www.g20chn.org/English/China2016/Logo/index.html [Accessed: 6 September 2017].

G20, 2017a. *About the G20*. www.b20germany.org/the-b20/about-g20/ [Accessed: 8 January 2017].

G20, 2017b. *Argentina's Priorities for the G20 2018 Agenda*. 13 December. www.g20.org/en/news/argentinas-priorities-g20-2018-agenda [Accessed: 20 December 2017].

G20, 2017c. *First Day of the Summit*. www.bundesregierung.de/Content/EN/Artikel/2017/07_en/2017-07-07-gipfel-freitag_en.html?nn=709674 [Accessed: 30 January 2018].

G20, 2017d. *Frequently Asked Questions*. www.g20.org/en/g20/faqs [Accessed: 21 August 2018].

G20, 2017e. *G20: A Meeting at the Highest Level*. www.g20.org/Webs/G20/EN/G20/Participants/participants_node.html;jsessionid=7B39207FA25D764A07156CB149DF27CD.s4t2 [Accessed: 5 September 2017].

G20, 2017f. *G20 Hamburg Action Plan*. 8 July. www.g20.utoronto.ca/2017/2017-g20-hamburg-action-plan-en.pdf [Accessed: 17 October 2017].

G20, 2017g. *G20 Leaders' Declaration*. 8 July. www.g20.utoronto.ca/2017/2017-G20-leaders-declaration.html [Accessed: 4 October 2017].

G20, 2017h. *G20 Leaders' Statement on Countering Terrorism*. 7 July. www.g20.utoronto.ca/2017/170707-counterterrorism.html [Accessed: 4 October 2017].

G20, 2017i. *Hamburg Annual Progress Report on G20 Development Commitments*. www.g20.utoronto.ca/2017/2017-g20-hamburg-annual-progress-report-en.pdf [Accessed: 23 May 2018].

G20, 2017j. *Hamburg Update: Taking Forward the G20 Action Plan on the 2030 Agenda for Sustainable Development*. 8 July. www.g20.utoronto.ca/2017/2017-g20-hamburg-update.html [Accessed: 19 June 2018].

G20, 2017k. *Introductory Statement*. www.g20.org/Content/EN/Artikel/2017/07_en/2017-07-07-eingangsstatement-merkel-g20-en.html [Accessed: 26 September 2017].

G20, 2017l. *The Outcomes of the G20 Summit: Tangible Progress Made*. www.bundesregierung.de/Content/EN/Artikel/2017/07_en/2017-07-11-g20-10-erfolge_en.html?nn=709674 [Accessed: 30 January 2018].

G20, 2017m. *Overview of Argentina's G20 Presidency: Building Consensus for Fair and Sustainable Development*. 1 December. g20.org/sites/default/files/docs/Marco-Conceptual-english.pdf [Accessed: 29 July 2018].

G20, 2017n. *Priorities of the 2017 G20 Summit*. www.g20.utoronto.ca/2017/2016-g20-praesidentschaftspapier-en.pdf [Accessed: 30 January 2017].

G20, 2017o. *Speech by Federal Chancellor Angela Merkel at the G20 Dialogue Forum with Non Governmental Organisations (C20) in Hamburg on 19 June 2017*. www.bundesregierung.de/Content/EN/Reden/2017/2017-06-19-bk-merkel-c20_en.html?nn=709674 [Accessed: 30 January 2018].

G20, 2017p. *Terms of Reference, G20 Eminent Persons Group on Global Financial Governance*. www.iai.it/sites/default/files/g20-ep-terms-of-reference.pdf [Accessed: 9 January 2018].

G20, 2018a. *About the G20: Frequently Asked Questions*. www.g20.org/en/g20/faqs [Accessed: 17 July 2018].

G20, 2018b. *Macri Drives G20 Agenda in Davos*. 24 January. www.g20.org/en/news/macri-drives-g20-agenda-davos [Accessed: 6 April 2018].

G20 Agriculture Ministers, 2011. *Agriculture Ministers' Action Plan on Food Price Volatility and Agriculture*. 22–23 June. www.g20.utoronto.ca/2011/2011-agriculture-plan-en.pdf [Accessed: 17 August 2018].

G20 Agriculture Vice Ministers/Deputies, 2012. *Report*. 18 May. www.g20.utoronto.ca/2012/2012-0518-agriculture.pdf [Accessed: 28 January 2013].

G20. Anti-Corruption Working Group, 2011. *First Monitoring Report of the G20 Anti-Corruption Working Group to G20 Leaders on Individual and Collective Progress Made by G20 Countries in the Implementation of the Seoul Action Plan*. www.mofa.go.jp/policy/economy/g20_summit/2011/pdfs/annex08.pdf [Accessed: 17 August 2018].

G20. Anti-Corruption Working Group, 2015. *Accountability Report*. November. bit.ly/2lHYYuZ [Accessed: 22 February 2017].

G20. Anti-Corruption Working Group, 2016. *G20 Anti-Corruption Implementation Plan 2017–2018*. 4 November. bit.ly/2mtztee [Accessed: 24 February 2017].

G20. Climate Finance Study Group, 2016a. *Report*. June. www.g20.utoronto.ca/2016/2016-promoting-efficient-transparent-provision.pdf [Accessed: 5 October 2017].

G20. Climate Finance Study Group, 2016b. *Toolkit Prepared by Invited IOs*. June. web.archive.org/web/20161020083105/http://g20.org:80/English/Documents/Current/201608/P020160815357624187353.pdf [Accessed: 1 February 2018].

G20. Development Working Group, 2011. *2011 Report of the Development Working Group*. www.g20.utoronto.ca/2011/2011-cannes-dwg-111028-en.pdf [Accessed: 2 July 2018].

G20. Development Working Group, 2012. *2012 Progress Report of the Development Working Group*. www.g20.utoronto.ca/2012/2012-0619-dwg.pdf [Accessed: 13 November 2017].

G20. Development Working Group, 2014. *Accountability Framework*. 5 September. www.g20.utoronto.ca/2014/g20_development_working_group_accountability_framework.pdf [Accessed: 16 February 2017].

G20. Development Working Group (2016p). *Hangzhou Comprehensive Accountability Report on G20 Development Commitments*, 14 September. http://www.g20.utoronto.ca/2016/hangzhou-accountability-development.pdf [Accessed: 27 November 2018].

G20. Development Working Group, 2017. *Hamburg Annual Progress Report on G20 Development Commitments*. June. www.g20.utoronto.ca/2017/2017-g20-hamburg-annual-progress-report-en.pdf [Accessed: 17 October 2017].

G20. Energy Experts Group, 2010. *Report to Leaders on the G20 Commitment to Rationalize and Phase Out Inefficient Fossil Fuel Subsidies*. www.eenews.net/assets/2010/06/28/document_cw_02.pdf [Accessed: 17 August 2018].

G20 Finance Ministers, 2012. *The G20 Welcomes Major Policy Actions in Europe*. 29 June. www.g20.utoronto.ca/2012/2012-0629-finance.pdf [Accessed: 28 November 2017].

G20 Finance Ministers and Central Bank Governors, 1999. *Financial Sector Regulation and Supervision (Backgrounder)*. Berlin. 15–16 December. www.g20.utoronto.ca/1999/1999regulation.htm [Accessed: 17 August 2018].

G20 Finance Ministers and Central Bank Governors, 2005. *The G20 Statement on Reforming the Bretton Woods Institutions*. Xianghe, Hebei, China. 16 October. www.g20.utoronto.ca/2005/2005bwi.pdf [Accessed: 17 August 2018].

G20 Finance Ministers and Central Bank Governors, 2010. *Communiqué*. Gyeongju, Republic of South Korea. 23 October. www.g20.utoronto.ca/2010/g20finance101023.pdf [Accessed: 28 November 2017].

G20 Finance Ministers and Central Bank Governors, 2011. *Communiqué [of the] Meeting*. Washington, DC. 14–15 April. www.g20.utoronto.ca/2011/2011-finance-110415-en.html [Accessed: 18 January 2018].

G20 Finance Ministers and Central Bank Governors, 2012. *Communiqué of Ministers of Finance and Central Bank Governors of the G20*. Mexico City. 5 November. www.g20.utoronto.ca/2012/2012-121105-finance-en.html [Accessed: 2 July 2018].

G20 Finance Ministers and Central Bank Governors, 2016. *Communiqué*. 24 July. www.g20.utoronto.ca/2016/160724-finance.html [Accessed: 15 September 2017]

G20 Finance Ministers and Central Bank Governors, 2017. *Communiqué*. 18 March. www.g20.utoronto.ca/2017/170318-finance-en.html [Accessed: 15 September 2017]

G20 Framework for Strong, Sustainable, and Balanced Growth Working Group, 2012. *Proposal: Framework Working Group's 2013 Work Plan*. 1 November. en.g20.ria.ru/load/780982134 [Accessed: 2 July 2018].

G20 Framework Working Group, 2015. *Antalya Accountability Assessment*. www.g20.utoronto.ca/2015/Accountability-Assessment-Report.pdf [Accessed: 21 August 2018].

G20 Framework Working Group, 2016a. *Enhanced Structural Reform Agenda*. 14 September. www.mofa.go.jp/files/000185875.pdf [Accessed: 24 February 2017].

G20 Framework Working Group, 2016b. *Hangzhou Accountability Assessment*. www.g20.utoronto.ca/2016/hangzhou-accountability-assessment-report.pdf [Accessed: 22 February 2017].

G20 Framework Working Group, 2017. *Hamburg Accountability Assessment*. July. www.bundesfinanzministerium.de/Content/DE/Downloads/G20-Dokumente/Hamburg_Genannte_Berichte/Hamburg-Accountability-Assessment.pdf;jsessionid=12EB87C5BE442AD772C029650E938AE8?__blob=publicationFile&v=2 [Accessed: 22 May 2018].

G20 Global Partnership for Financial Inclusion, 2011. *Report to the Leaders*. 5 November. www.g8.utoronto.ca/g20/2011/2011-cannes-global-partnership-report.pdf [Accessed: 17 August 2018].

G20 Global Partnership for Financial Inclusion, 2012. *Follow Up Report to G20 Leaders*. 19 June. www.ranepa.ru/images/media/g20/2012loscabos/2012-June-Financial-inclusion-Follow-up-report-to-G20-Ledaers.pdf [Accessed: 17 August 2018].

G20 Global Partnership for Financial Inclusion, 2013. *Report to the Leaders*. 5–6 September. www.g20.utoronto.ca/2013/GPFI_Report_to_the_Leaders.pdf [Accessed: 29 September 2017].

G20 High-Level Panel on Infrastructure, 2011. *Recommendations to G20: Final Report*. www.g20-g8.com/g8-g20/root/bank_objects/HLP_-_Full_report.pdf [Accessed: 24 July 2012].

G20 Labour and Employment Ministers, 2010. *G20 Labour and Employment Ministers' Recommendations to G20 Leaders*. Washington, DC. 21 April. www.g20.utoronto.ca/2010/g20lab0421.html [Accessed: 17 August 2018].

G20 Labour and Employment Ministers, 2011. *G20 Labour and Employment Ministers' Conclusions*. Paris. 27 September. www.g20.utoronto.ca/2011/2011-labour-110927-en.html [Accessed: 17 August 2018].

G20 Labour and Employment Ministers, 2012. *G20 Labour and Employment Ministers' Conclusions*. Guadalajara, Mexico. 18 May. www.g20.utoronto.ca/2012/2012-0518-labour.pdf [Accessed: 21 August 2018]

G20 Study Group on Commodities, 2011. *Report of the G20 Study Group on Commodities under the Chairmanship of Mr. Hiroshi Nakaso*. November. www.cmegroup.com/education/files/G20Nakaso-November202011.pdf [Accessed: 21 August 2018].

G20 Trade Finance Experts Group, 2009. *Report: US-UK Chair's Recommendations for Finance Ministers*. August. g20mexico.org/images/stories/canalfinan/gexpert/finanzas/02g20finance.pdf [Accessed: 28 January 2013].

G20 Trade Finance Experts Group, 2010. *Report: Canada-Korea Chair's Recommendations for Finance Ministers*. April. g20mexico.org/images/stories/canalfinan/gexpert/finanzas/01g20finance.pdf [Accessed: 28 January 2013].

G20 Trade Ministers, 2012. *Condensed Version of the Press Conference held by the Minister of Economy, Bruno Ferrari, to Present the Conclusions of the G20 Trade Ministerial Meeting*. Puerto Vallarta, Mexico. April. www.g20mexico.org/index.php/en/speeches/355-version-estenografica-del-mensaje-ofrecido-por-bruno-ferrari-secretario-de-economia-de-mexico-y-presidente-de-la-reunion-ministerial-de-economia-y-comercio-del-g20-durante-la-presentacion-de-las-conclusion [Accessed: 28 January 2013].

G22, 1998. *Summary of Reports on the International Financial Architecture*. Washington, DC. October. www.imf.org/external/np/g22/summry.pdf [Accessed: 18 October 2017].

Germany. Bundesregierung, 2006. *Focuses of the German G-8 Presidency*. G8 Summit 2007: Heiligendamm. 18 November. www.g-8.de/Webs/G8/EN/Agenda/agenda.html [Accessed: 1 February 2013].

Germany. Bundesregierung, 2017. *The Outcomes of the G20 Summit: Tangible Progress Made*. 12 July. www.bundesregierung.de/Content/EN/Artikel/2017/07_en/2017-07-11-g20-10-erfolge_en.html [Accessed: 7 August 2018].

Germany. Federal Ministry of Finance, 2010. *Effective Financial Market Regulation after Pittsburgh: Achievements and Challenges: International Conference*. Berlin. 19–20 May. www.re-define.org/sites/default/files/Programme%2019-20%20May.pdf [Accessed: 21 August 2018].

India. Ministry of Finance, 2012. *The BRICS Report: A Study of Brazil, Russia, India, China, and South Africa with Special Focus on Synergies and Complementarities*. New Delhi: Oxford University Press.

India. Press Information Bureau. Prime Minister's Office, 2013. *Media Note on the Informal Meeting of BRICS Leaders ahead of the G20 Summit in St. Petersburg*. 5 September. pib.nic.in/newsite/erelease.aspx?relid=99138 [Accessed: 24 February 2018].

Institute of International Finance, 2012. *High-Level Public-Private Sector IIF G-20 Seminar: The G-20 Agenda under the Mexican Chairmanship*. Mexico City. 24–25 February. www.g20mexico.org/images/stories/canalfinan/eventante/summary_iif_g20.pdf [Accessed: 1 February 2013].

Inter-American Development Bank, 2012. *The Priorities of Latin America and the Caribbean for the Group of Twenty*. Seminar. Montevideo, Uruguay. 17 March. www.g20mexico.org/images/stories/canalfinan/eventante/seminar_priorities_latin_america_for_the_g20_17032012.pdf [Accessed: 1 February 2013].

International Monetary Fund, 1998. *Reports on the International Financial Architecture*. October. www.imf.org/external/np/g22/ [Accessed: 7 September 2017].

International Monetary Fund, 2006. *A Guide to Committees, Groups, and Clubs: Factsheet*. www.imf.org/external/np/exr/facts/groups.htm [Accessed: 18 October 2017].

International Monetary Fund, 2009. *Note by the Staff of the International Monetary Fund on Stocktaking of the G-20 Responses to the Global Banking Crisis*. 13–14 March. www.imf.org/external/np/g20/pdf/031909b.pdf [Accessed: 15 November 2017].

International Monetary Fund, 2010a. *G-20 Mutual Assessment Process: Alternative Policy Scenarios*. www.imf.org/external/np/g20/pdf/062710a.pdf [Accessed: 18 January 2018].

International Monetary Fund, 2010b. *G-20 Mutual Assessment Process: IMF Staff Assessment of G-20 Policies*. www.imf.org/external/np/g20/pdf/111210.pdf [Accessed: 18 January 2018].

International Monetary Fund, 2011a. *G-20 Mutual Assessment Process: From Pittsburgh to Cannes: IMF Umbrella Report*. IMF Staff Reports for the G-20 Mutual Assessment Process. www.imf.org/external/np/g20/pdf/110411.pdf [Accessed: 24 October 2017].

International Monetary Fund, 2011b. *Review of the Fund's Involvement in the G-20 Mutual Assessment Process*. 13 May. www.imf.org/external/np/pp/eng/2011/051311.pdf [Accessed: 21 August 2018].

International Monetary Fund, 2011c. *Supporting the Development of More Effective Tax Systems: A Report to the G-20 Development Working Group by the IMF, OECD, UN and World Bank*. www.imf.org/external/np/g20/pdf/110311.pdf [Accessed: 15 November 2017].

International Monetary Fund, 2012a. G20 *Agreement on Quotas and Governance*. 18 June. www.imf.org/external/np/exr/faq/quotasgov.htm [Accessed: 21 August 2018].

International Monetary Fund, 2012b. *Joint Statement by the International Monetary and Financial Committee and the Group of 20 Finance Ministers and Central Bank Governors on IMF Resources*. Washington, DC. 20 April. Press Release 12/144. www.imf.org/external/np/sec/pr/2012/pr12144.htm [Accessed: 28 November 2017].

International Monetary Fund, 2012c. *Progress Report on the G-20 Data Gaps Initiative: Status, Action Plans, and Timetables*. Prepared by the Staff of the IMF and the FSB Secretariat. September. www.imf.org/external/np/g20/pdf/093012.pdf [Accessed: 15 November 2017].

International Monetary Fund, 2012d. *Toward Lasting Stability and Growth: Umbrella Report for G-20 Mutual Assessment Process*. www.imf.org/external/np/g20/pdf/map2012/umbrella.pdf [Accessed: 24 October 2017].

International Monetary Fund, 2013a. *Imbalances and Growth: Update of Staff Sustainability Assessments for G-20 Mutual Assessment Process*. September. www.imf.org/external/np/g20/pdf/map2013/map2013.pdf [Accessed: 3 July 2018].

International Monetary Fund, 2013b. *Update on Global Prospects and Policy Challenges*. St. Petersburg. 5–6 September. www.imf.org/external/np/g20/pdf/2013/090513.pdf [Accessed: 15 November 2017].

International Monetary Fund, 2014. *Growth-Friendly Fiscal Policy*. Cairns, Australia. 20–21 September. www.imf.org/external/np/g20/pdf/2014/fiscpolnote.pdf [Accessed: 15 November 2017].

International Monetary Fund, 2015. *Imbalances and Growth: Update of Staff Sustainability Assessments for G-20 Mutual Assessment Process*. October. www.imf.org/external/np/g20/pdf/map2015/map2015.pdf [Accessed: 14 November 2017].

International Monetary Fund, 2016a. *The G20 Mutual Assessment Process (MAP)*. International Monetary Fund Fact Sheet. 21 September. www.imf.org/external/np/exr/facts/g20map.htm [Accessed: 22 February 2017].

International Monetary Fund, 2016b. *Global and Country Risk Assessment at the IMF*. 11 August. g20chn.org/English/Documents/Current/201608/t20160811_3133.html [Accessed: 1 February 2018].

International Monetary Fund, 2016c. *Global Prospects and Policy Challenges: G-20 Finance Ministers and Central Bank Governors' Meetings*. 26–27 February. www.imf.org/external/np/g20/pdf/2016/022616.pdf [Accessed: 15 November 2017].

International Monetary Fund, 2016d. *Historic Quota and Governance Reforms become Effective*. Press Release 16/25. 27 January. www.imf.org/en/news/articles/2015/09/14/01/49/pr1625a [Accessed: 25 February 2018].

International Monetary Fund, 2016e. *International Monetary Fund-World Bank Group Technical Assistance Activities on Public Debt Management in Low Income Countries*. 11 August. g20chn.org/English/Documents/Current/201608/t20160811_3130.html [Accessed: 1 February 2018].

International Monetary Fund, 2016f. *Priorities for Structural Reforms in G-20 Countries*. 22 July. Staff Background Paper for G-20 Surveillance Note. www.imf.org/external/np/pp/eng/2016/072216a.pdf [Accessed: 1 February 2018].

International Monetary Fund, 2016g. *The Role of the SDR: Initial Considerations*. 15 July. Staff Note for the G20. www.imf.org/external/np/pp/eng/2016/072416.pdf [Accessed: 1 February 2018].

International Monetary Fund, 2017a. *Factsheet: IMF Quotas*. 13 October. www.imf.org/About/Factsheets/Sheets/2016/07/14/12/21/IMF-Quotas?pdf=1 [Accessed: 19 January 2018].

International Monetary Fund, 2017b. *G-20 Report on Strong, Sustainable and Balanced Growth: IMF Annual Meetings*. Prepared with input from the OECD. October. www.imf.org/external/np/g20/pdf/2017/100617.pdf [Accessed: 15 November 2017].

International Monetary Fund, 2018. *The G20 Mutual Assessment Process (MAP)*. 8 March. www.imf.org/en/about/factsheets/sheets/2016/07/27/15/48/g20-mutual-assessment-process-map [Accessed: 2 July 2018].

International Trade Union Confederation, 2008. *G20 Trade Union Leaders Meet with IFIs, Heads of State and Call for Vigorous Action to Counter the Global Economic Crisis*. 15 November. www.ituc-csi.org/g20-trade-union-leaders-meet-with.html [Accessed: 8 June 2018]. The Washington Declaration (2008) is accessible at: www.ituc-csi.org/IMG/pdf/0811t_gf_G20.pdf.

Japan. Ministry of Foreign Affairs, 2012. *MOFA: G20 Rotating Presidencies: Regional Groups*. www.mofa.go.jp/policy/economy/g20_summit/2011/annex10.html?b5d444e0 [Accessed: 21 August 2018].

Japan. Ministry of Foreign Affairs, 2016. *Ministerial Meeting of the Major Economies Forum on Energy and Climate (MEF)*. www.mofa.go.jp/ic/ch/page25e_000103.html [Accessed: 19 March 2018].

Korea. Ministry of Strategy and Finance, 2009. *G-20 Workshop on Securing Sustainable Economic Recovery: Chair's Statement*. Seoul. 15–16 November. www.g20mexico.org/images/stories/canalfinan/eventante/03seoul.pdf [Accessed: 1 February 2013].

Major Economies Forum on Energy and Climate, 2009. *Description/Purpose*. www.majoreconomiesforum.org/about/descriptionpurpose.html [Accessed: 17 January 2015].

Major, J. and Gorbachev, M., 1991. *Joint Press Conference Given by the Prime Minister, Mr John Major and the Soviet President, Mr Mikhail Gorbachev*. London, UK. 17 July.

Mexico, 2012. *Discussion Paper: Mexico's Presidency of the G-20*. January. www.g20.utoronto.ca/2012/2012-loscabos-disc-en.pdf [Accessed: 27 November 2017].

Mexico. Ministry of Finance, 2011. *G20 Seminar on 'Current Challenges for Global Economic Growth': Summary*. 12–13 December. www.g20mexico.org/images/stories/canalfinan/eventante/summary.pdf [1 February 2013].

Mexico. Presidencia de la República, 2012a. *Global Economic Crisis: Role and Challenges of the G20*. [Spanish]. 26 January. www.g20.utoronto.ca/2012/2012-120126-calderon-es.html [Accessed: 10 January 2018].

Mexico. President, 2012b. *Remarks made by the President of Mexico, Felipe Calderón Hinojosa, during the G20 Ministers of Foreign Affairs Informal Meeting*. 20 February. www.g20mexico.org/index.php/en/speeches/221-mensaje-al-grupo-del-g20-por-parte-del-presidente-felipe-calderon [Accessed: 24 July 2012].

Mexico. Secretary of Foreign Affairs, 2012. The Role of Mexico in the G20 by Aranda Bezaury, L. *G20 Journals*, 1, 1–39. Mexico City: Matías Romero Institute. http://g20mexico.org/images/stories/docs/cuadernos/G20ceng.pdf [Accessed: 24 July 2012].

Multilateral Development Banks, 2016a. *MDB Response to the G20 Action Plan for MDB Balance Sheet Optimisation.* July. g20chn.org/English/Documents/Current/201608/P020160815361155807206.pdf [Accessed: 1 February 2018].

Multilateral Development Banks, 2016b. *MDBs Joint Declaration of Aspirations on Actions to Support Infrastructure Investment.* August. g20chn.org/English/Documents/Current/201608/P020160815360318908738.pdf [Accessed: 1 February 2018].

Nelson, R., 2009. *The G20 and International Economic Cooperation: Background and Implications for Congress.* Congressional Research Service 7–5700. 9 December.

Organisation for Economic Co-operation and Development, 2009. *Mandate of the Heiligendamm L'Aquila Process Support Unit.* www.oecd.org/document/50/0,3746,en_21571361_40549151_41518322_1_1_1_1,00.html [Accessed: 24 July 2012].

Organisation for Economic Co-operation and Development, 2011a. *Beating the Crisis: The Role of the OECD and G20.* www.oecd.org/document/0/0,3746,en_2649_201185_48964973_1_1_1_1,00.html [Accessed: 19 January 2018].

Organisation for Economic Co-operation and Development, 2011b. *Joining Forces against Corruption: G20 Business and Government: Conference Summary and Conclusions.* Paris. 21 October. www.oecd.org/daf/briberyininternationalbusiness/47715445.pdf [Accessed: 21 August 2018].

Organisation for Economic Co-operation and Development, 2011c. *Price Volatility in Food and Agricultural Markets: Policy Responses: Policy Report.* 2 June. www.oecd.org/dataoecd/40/34/48152638.pdf [Accessed: 21 August 2018].

Organisation for Economic Co-operation and Development, 2012a. *Boosting Jobs and Living Standards in G20 Countries: A Joint Report by the ILO, OECD, IMF and the World Bank.* June. www.oecd.org/eco/productivityandlongtermgrowth/Boosting%20jobs%20and%20living%20standards%20in%20G20%20countries.pdf [Accessed: 18 January 2018].

Organisation for Economic Co-operation and Development, 2012b. *G20/OECD Policy Note on Pension Fund Financing for Green Infrastructure and Initiatives.* June. www.oecd.org/daf/financialmarketsinsuranceandpensions/privatepensions/S3%20G20%20OECD%20Pension%20funds%20for%20green%20infrastructure%20-%20June%202012.pdf [Accessed: 21 August 2018].

Organisation for Economic Co-operation and Development, 2012c. *G20 Seminar on Green Growth: Agenda.* Paris. 22 May. www.g20mexico.org/images/stories/canalfinan/greengrowth/final_annotated_agenda_g20_green_growth_seminar.pdf [Accessed: 1 February 2013].

Organisation for Economic Co-operation and Development, 2012d. *Global Forum on Transparency and Exchange of Information for Tax Purposes: Progress Report to the G20.* June. www.oecd.org/ctp/exchangeofinformation/G20_Progress_Report_June_2012.pdf [Accessed: 21 August 2018].

Organisation for Economic Co-operation and Development, 2012f. *Incorporating Green Growth and Sustainable Development Policies into Structural Reform Agendas.* www.google.com/url?q=www.oecd.org/eco/greeneco/G20_report_on_GG_and_SD_final.pdf&sa=U&ei=nq1mUu7yEcep2gXF5oHgDQ&ved=0CAcQFjAA&client=internal-uds-cse&usg=AFQjCNFqSp15AeLhKE6ZoqH2xS3dDgspzg [Accessed: 21 August 2018].

Organisation for Economic Co-operation and Development, 2012g. *OECD/INFE High-Level Principles on National Strategies for Financial Education.* August. www.oecd.org/finance/financial-education/OECD-INFE-Principles-National-Strategies-Financial-Education.pdf [Accessed: 21 August 2018].

Organisation for Economic Co-operation and Development, 2012h. *Pursuing Strong, Sustainable and Balanced Growth: A Note on Implementation of G20 Structural Commitments*. June. www.oecd.org/eco/productivityandlongtermgrowth/OECD%20G20%20Framework%20Note%20on%20Structural%20Policy%20Implementation%20(12%20June%202012.pdf [Accessed: 21 August 2018].

Organisation for Economic Co-operation and Development, 2012i. *Reports on G20 Trade and Investment Measures*. 31 May. www.oecd.org/daf/internationalinvestment/investmentpolicy/50492978.pdf [Accessed: 21 August 2018].

Organisation for Economic Co-operation and Development, 2012j. *Sustainable Agricultural Productivity Growth and Bridging the Gap for Small Family Farms: Interagency Report to the Mexican G20 Presidency*. 12 June. www.oecd.org/tad/agriculturalpoliciesandsupport/50544691.pdf [Accessed: 21 August 2018].

Organisation for Economic Co-operation and Development, 2014. *G20 Labour Markets: Outlook, Key Challenges and Policy Responses*. Report Prepared by ILO, OECD and the World Bank Group. www.oecd.org/g20/topics/employment-and-social-policy/G20-labour-markets-outlook-key-challenges-and-policy-responses.pdf [Accessed: 10 November 2017].

Organisation for Economic Co-operation and Development, 2016a. *Developments in Investment and Policy Challenges*. June. g20chn.org/English/Documents/Current/201608/t20160815_3148.html [Accessed: 1 February 2018].

Organisation for Economic Co-operation and Development, 2016b. *Developments in Trade and Policy Challenges*. June. g20chn.org/English/Documents/Current/201608/t20160815_3146.html [Accessed: 1 February 2018].

Organisation for Economic Co-operation and Development, 2016c. *G20/OECD Guidance Note on Diversification of Financial Instruments for Infrastructure and SMEs*. September. www.oecd.org/g20/topics/financing-for-investment/G20-OECD-Guidance-Note-Diversification-Financial-Instruments.pdf [Accessed: 1 February 2018].

Organisation for Economic Co-operation and Development, 2016d. *G20/OECD Progress Report on the Implementation of the G20/OECD Principles of Corporate Governance*. August. www.oecd.org/corporate/G20-OECD-Progress-Report-on-Corporate-Governance-Principles.pdf [Accessed: 1 February 2018].

Organisation for Economic Co-operation and Development, 2016e. *The OECD Code of Liberalisation of Capital Movements: Recent Developments*. April. OECD Report to the G20. www.oecd.org/daf/inv/investment-policy/OECD-G20-Note-Code-Review-April-2016.pdf [Accessed: 1 February 2018].

Organisation for Economic Co-operation and Development, 2017a. *2017 G20 Hamburg Summit–OECD's Contributions*. Hamburg, 7–8 July. www.oecd.org/g20/ [Accessed: 21 November 2017].

Organisation for Economic Co-operation and Development, 2017b. *Compendium of Good Practices on the Publication and Reuse of Open Data for Anti-Corruption across G20 Countries: Towards Data-Driven Public Sector Integrity and Civic Auditing*. www.oecd.org/gov/digital-government/g20-oecd-compendium.pdf [Accessed: 11 November 2017].

Organisation for Economic Co-operation and Development, 2017c. *G20 Global Displacement and Migration Trends Report 2017*. www.oecd.org/g20/summits/hamburg/G20-OECD-migration.pdf [Accessed: 11 November 2017].

Organisation for Economic Co-operation and Development, 2017d. *Integrity in Customs: Taking Stock of Good Practices*. Prepared at the request of the G20 Anti-Corruption Working Group. www.oecd.org/gov/ethics/G20-integrity-in-customs-taking-stock-of-good-practices.pdf [Accessed: 11 November 2017].

Organisation for Economic Co-operation and Development, 2017e. *Investing in Climate, Investing in Growth*. Produced in the context of the German G20 presidency. June. www.oecd.org/environment/cc/g20-climate/synthesis-investing-in-climate-investing-in-growth.pdf [Accessed: 21 November 2017].

Organisation for Economic Co-operation and Development, 2017f. *The Next Production Revolution: A Report for the G20*. Prepared at the request of the G20 New Industrial Revolution Task Force by the OECD with input from the United Nations Conference on Trade and Development (UNCTAD) and the United Nations Industrial Development Organisation (UNIDO). www.oecd org/g20/summits/hamburg/the-next-production-revolution-G20-report.pdf [Accessed: 11 November 2017].

Organisation for Economic Co-operation and Development, 2017g. *A Policy Framework to Help Guide the G20 in Its Development of Policy Options to Foster More Inclusive Growth*. Prepared by the OECD and the World Bank Group. July. www.oecd.org/g20/summits/hamburg/OECD-WBG-Policy-Framework-to-help-Gguide-the-G20-in-its-development.pdf [Accessed: 11 November 2017].

Organisation for Economic Co-operation and Development, 2018. *OECD and the G20: About*. www.oecd.org/g20/about.htm [Accessed: 31 January 2018].

Organisation for Economic Co-operation and Development. Secretary-General, 2017a. *Report to G20 Finance Ministers*. Baden-Baden. March. www.oecd.org/tax/oecd-secretary-general-tax-report-g20-finance-ministers-march-2017.pdf [Accessed: 1 February 2018].

Organisation for Economic Co-operation and Development. Secretary-General, 2017b. *Report to G20 Leaders*. Hamburg. July. www.oecd.org/g20/summits/hamburg/oecd-secretary-general-tax-report-g20-leaders-july-2017.pdf [Accessed: 11 November 2017].

Organisation for Economic Co-operation and Development and International Monetary Fund, 2017. *Quantifying the Implementation and Impact of G-20 Members' Growth Strategies*. www.oecd.org/g20/summits/hamburg/Quantifying-the-Implementation-of-Growth-Strategies-2017.pdf [Accessed: 11 November 2017].

Organisation for Economic Co-operation and Development and Russia's G20 Presidency, 2013. *Advancing National Strategies for Financial Education*. www.oecd.org/finance/financial-education/G20_OECD_NSFinancialEducation.pdf [Accessed: 21 August 2018].

Organisation for Economic Co-operation and Development. OECD Task Force on Institutional Investors and Long-Term Financing, 2013. *G20/OECD High-Level Principles of Long-Term Investments Financing by Institutional Investors*. www.oecd.org/daf/fin/private-pensions/G20-OECD-Principles-LTI-Financing.pdf [Accessed: 21 August 2018].

Persini, C. ed., 2011. *G20: les enjeux de la présidence française*. Regards sur l'actualité, 371. Paris: Documentation française. May.

Ramos, G., 2011. G20 and the OECD: Before and beyond the Crisis. *Uluslararası Ekonomik Sorunlar*, 41(11), pp. 7–15. Turkey: Ministry of Foreign Affairs. www.mfa.gov.tr/data/Kutuphane/Yayinlar/EkonomikSorunlarDergisi/Sayi41/sayı%2041_mayis_2011.pdf [Accessed: 21 August 2018].

Reserve Bank of India and the Bank of England, 2009. *G20 Workshop on the Global Economy: Causes of the Crisis: Key Lessons*. Mumbai, India. 24–26 May. www.pdffiller.com/jsfiller-desk6/?projectId=213135944&expId=3726&expBranch=1#9b952d8294654da09efab837e330b508 [Accessed: 21 August 2018].

Russia. President, 2012. *Address by Vladimir Putin on Russia Assuming the G20 Presidency*. 1 December. www.g20.utoronto.ca/2012/2012-putin-1201.html [Accessed: 26 October 2017].

Russia. President, 2013. *Vladimir Putin's News Conference Following the G20 Summit*. 6 September. en.g20russia.ru/news/20130906/782816253.html [Accessed: 21 August 2018].

Russia. Prime Minister, 2013. *Group of Twenty Is Becoming More Effective*. 23 January. en.g20russia.ru/news/20130123/781165516.html [Accessed: 12 January 2018].

Sala-i-Martin, X. and Mohapatra, S., 2002. *Poverty, inequality and the distribution of income in the Group of 20*. Australia. Treasury. Prepared for the G20 Finance Ministers' and Central Bank Governors' meeting in November. www.g20.utoronto.ca/biblio/salaimartin-mohapatra.pdf [Accessed: 21 August 2018].

Singapore. Ministry of Foreign Affairs, 2013. *Statement by H.E. Karen Tan, Permanent Representative of Singapore to the United Nations, on behalf of the Global Governance Group (3G) at the Briefing on the Outcome of the G20 Saint Petersburg Summit*. 9 September. www.mfa.gov.sg/content/mfa/overseasmission/newyork/nyemb_statements/global_governance_group/2013/201309/press_20130909.html [Accessed: 24 February 2018].

Singapore. Ministry of Foreign Affairs, 2016. *Press Statement by the Global Governance Group (3G) on Its Ninth Ministerial Meeting in New York*. 22 September. www1.mfa.gov.sg/Newsroom/Press-Statements-Transcripts-and-Photos/2016/09/Press-Statement-by-the-Global-Governance-Group-3G-on-its-Ninth-Ministerial-Meeting-in-New-York-on-22 [Accessed: 21 August 2018].

Singapore. Ministry of Foreign Affairs, 2017. *Press Statement by the Global Governance Group (3G) on Its Tenth Ministerial Meeting in New York*. 22 September. www1.mfa.gov.sg/Newsroom/Press-Statements-Transcripts-and-Photos/2017/09/Press-Statement-by-the-Global-Governance-Group-3G-on-its-Tenth-Ministerial-Meeting-in-New-York-on-22 [Accessed: 24 February 2018].

Turkey. Prime Minister, 2014. *Turkish G20 Presidency Priorities for 2015*. www.g20.utoronto.ca/2015/141201-turkish-priorities.html [Accessed: 13 February 2017].

United Kingdom, 2009. *The Road to the London Summit: The Plan for Recovery*. www.astrid-online.it/static/upload/protected/UK-G/UK-GOV_road-to-london-summit-2009_18_02_09.pdf [Accessed: 21 August 2018].

United Kingdom. Prime Minister, 2011. *Governance for Growth: Building Consensus for the Future*. November. webarchive.nationalarchives.gov.uk/20130109092234/www.number10.gov.uk/wp-content/uploads/2011/11/GovernanceForGrowth_acc.pdf [Accessed: 26 September 2017].

United Kingdom. Prime Minister, 2012. In fight for open world, G8 still matters. *The Globe and Mail*, 21 November, p. B2.

United Nations, 2004. *A More Secure World: Our Shared Responsibility, Report of the High-Level Panel on Threats, Challenges and Change*. New York: United Nations.

United Nations. Department of Public Information, 2008. *Activities of the Secretary-General in Washington, DC, 14–15 November*. (SG/T/2633). www.un.org/News/Press/docs/2008/sgt2633.doc.htm [Accessed: 16 January 2018].

United Nations. Department of Public Information, 2009a. *Activities of the Secretary-General in United Kingdom, 1–3 April*. (SG/T/2665). www.un.org/News/Press/docs/2009/sgt2665.doc.htm [Accessed: 16 January 2018].

United Nations. Department of Public Information, 2009b. *Premature Exit from Stimulus Efforts Could Put Global Recovery at Risk, Secretary-General Warns in Remarks to G-20 Summit*. 25 September. (SG/SM/12491-ECO/171). www.un.org/News/Press/docs/2009/sgsm12491.doc.htm [Accessed: 16 January 2018].

United Nations. Department of Public Information, 2009c. *Secretary-General Welcomes Pledge of G-20 Leaders to $1.1 Trillion Aid Package*. (SG/SM/12165-ECO/148). www.un.org/News/Press/docs/2009/sgsm12165.doc.htm [Accessed: 16 January 2018].

United Nations. Department of Public Information, 2010a. *Daily Press Briefing by the Office of the Spokesperson for the Secretary-General*. 24 June. www.un.org/press/en/2010/db100624.doc.htm [Accessed: 16 January 2018].

United Nations. Department of Public Information, 2010b. *In Seoul, Secretary-General Says Development Not Side Issue: 'Investing in Development Is Investing in Everyone's Recovery'*. 12 November. (SG/SM/13244-DEV/2848). www.un.org/News/Press/docs/2010/sgsm13244.doc.htm [Accessed: 16 January 2018].

United Nations. Department of Public Information, 2010c. *Secretary-General, in Remarks to Economic and Social Council, Reports Uneven Progress on Millennium Development Goals*. 28 June. (SG/SM/12977-ECOSOC/6431). www.un.org/News/Press/docs/2010/sgsm12977.doc.htm [Accessed: 16 January 2018].

United Nations. Department of Public Information, 2011. *Daily Press Briefing by the Office of the Spokesperson for the Secretary-General*. 3 November. www.un.org/press/en/2011/db111103.doc.htm [Accessed: 16 January 2018].

United Nations. Department of Public Information, 2012. *Secretary-General Outlines Messages He Took to G-20 Summit in Los Cabos, Introduces Mexico's Vice-Minister to Brief General Assembly in Detail*. 31 July. (SG/SM/14438-GA/11265). www.un.org/News/Press/docs/2012/sgsm14438.doc.htm [Accessed: 16 January 2018].

United Nations. Economic and Social Council. 11th Session, 2012. 14 May. *Half-Day Discussion on the Rights of Indigenous Peoples to Food and Food Sovereignty*. (E/C.19/2012/L.10). www.un.org/press/en/2012/hr5092.doc.htm [Accessed: 8 June 2018].

United Nations. General Assembly. 54th Session, 1999. *Official Records*, Supplement No. 1: *Report of the Secretary-General on the Work of the Organization*. (A/54/1).

United Nations. General Assembly. 63rd Session, 2009. *Outcome of the Conference on the World Financial and Economic Crisis and Its Impact on Development: Resolution Adopted by the General Assembly*. 13 July. (A/RES/63/303).

United Nations News Service, 2009. *Global Finance Structures Must Be Revamped, Says UN Expert Panel*. 26 March. https://news.un.org/en/story/2009/03/295182 [Accessed: 24 November 2018].

United Nations News Service, 2013. *At G20 Summit, Ban, UN-Arab League Envoy Push for Political Solution to Syria Crisis*. 5 September. www.un.org/apps/news/story.asp?NewsID=45780&Cr=syria&Cr1=g20#.UnUiORBcyBZ [Accessed: 16 January 2018].

United Nations News Service, 2014. *G-20 Countries Have Political Responsibility to Tackle World's Greatest Challenges–Ban*. 15 November. www.un.org/apps/news/story.asp?NewsID=49348#.WgHs1IhOk2w [Accessed: 7 November 2017].

United Nations. Secretary-General, 2015. *Secretary-General's Remarks at G20 Working Lunch on Development and Climate Change*. 15 November. www.un.org/sg/statements/index.asp?nid=9247 [Accessed: 7 November 2017].

United Nations. Secretary-General, 2015a. *Secretary-General's Press Conference at G20 Summit in Turkey*. 15 November. https://www.un.org/sg/en/content/sg/press-encounter/2015-11-15/secretary-general%E2%80%99s-press-conference-g20-summit-turkey-qa [Accessed: 21 November 2018].

United Nations. Secretary-General, 2016. *Opening Remarks at Press Conference at G20 Summit in China*. 4 September. www.un.org/sg/en/content/sg/speeches/2016-09-04/opening-remarks-press-conference-g20-summit-china [Accessed: 7 November 2017].

United Nations. Secretary-General, 2017. *Activities of Secretary-General in Germany, 7–8 July*. 13 July. (SG/T/3183). www.un.org/press/en/2017/sgt3183.doc.htm, Accessed 7 November 2017].

United Nations World Tourism Organization, 2012. *T.20 Initiative*. http://t20.unwto.org/en [Accessed: 27 November 2017].

United States. Congress. Senate. Committee on Banking, Housing and Urban Affairs, 2011. *An Action Plan for the G-20: Testimony before the Hearing 'The G-20 and Global Economic and Financial Risks'*, Bergsten, C.F.; and Urban Affairs Subcommittee on Security and International Trade and Finance. 20 October. www.piie.com/publications/testimony/testimony.cfm?ResearchID=1960 [Accessed: 15 August 2018].

United States. Department of State, 2012. *G8 Summit 2012*. https://2009-2017.state.gov/e/eb/ecosum/2012g8/index.htm [Accessed: 26 September 2017].

United States. President, 2009. *Remarks by President Obama at G20 Closing Press Conference*. 25 September. https://obamawhitehouse.archives.gov/the-press-office/remarks-president-g20-closing-press-conference [Accessed: 8 June 2018].

United States. President, 2017. *National Security Strategy of the United States of America*. December. www.whitehouse.gov/wp-content/uploads/2017/12/NSS-Final-12-18-2017-0905-2.pdf [Accessed: 9 February 2018].

United States. White House. Office of the Press Secretary, 2013. *Joint Statement on Syria*. 6 September. www.whitehouse.gov/the-press-office/2013/09/06/joint-statement-syria [Accessed: 6 October 2017].

Walter, A., 2011. *Global Economic Governance after the Crisis*. Bank of Korea Working Papers. Seoul: Bank of Korea. January.

World Bank, 2010. *G20 and Global Development: Report Prepared by Staff of the World Bank for G20 Growth Framework and Mutual Assessment Process*. siteresources.worldbank.org/DEC/Resources/G20Framework&MAP-WBReport-TorontoSummit-2.pdf [Accessed: 18 January 2018].

World Bank, 2011. *Mobilizing Climate Finance: A Paper Prepared at the Request of G20 Finance Ministers*. 6 October. www.imf.org/external/np/g20/pdf/110411c.pdf [Accessed: 30 January 2018].

World Bank, 2012a. *G20 Commodities Seminar: Summary*. Los Cabos, Mexico. 5–6 May. G20russia.ru/load/780990537 [Accessed: 21 August 2018].

World Bank, 2012b. *Measuring Financial Inclusion: The Global Financial Inclusion Indicators (GFII)*. go.worldbank.org/MXB6HOJ5U0 [Accessed: 18 January 2018].

World Bank, 2012c. *Measuring Financial Inclusion: The Global Findex Database*. www-wds.worldbank.org/servlet/WDSContentServer/WDSP/IB/2012/04/19/000158349_20120419083611/Rendered/PDF/WPS6025.pdf [Accessed: 21 August 2018].

World Bank, 2012d. *Restoring and Sustaining Growth*. 8 June. siteresources.worldbank.org/DEC/Resources/84797-1320153303397/World_Bank_Repor_for_G20_Framework_June_8_2012.pdf [Accessed: 30 January 2018].

World Bank, 2014. *Report on the Remittance Agenda of the G20*. Prepared for the G20 Australian Presidency. siteresources.worldbank.org/EXTFINANCIALSECTOR/Resources/282884–1400093105293/GPFI_Remittances_Report_Final072014.pdf [Accessed: 10 November 2017].

World Bank, 2016. *Towards a G20 Strategy for Promoting Inclusive Global Value Chains*. Prepared by the OECD, WBG, and the International Trade Centre for submission to the G20 Trade Ministers Meeting, Shanghai, China. 9–10 July. documents.worldbank.org/curated/en/736471473258884274/pdf/108169-WP.pdf [Accessed: 10 November 2017].

World Bank, 2017. *New World Bank Group Facility to Enable More than $1 Billion for Women Entrepreneurship*. 8 July. www.worldbank.org/en/news/press-release/2017/07/08/new-world-bank-group-facility-to-enable-more-than-1-billion-for-women-entrepreneurship [Accessed: 10 November 2017].

World Bank Group, 2011. *Mobilizing Climate Finance: A Paper Prepared at the Request of G20 Finance Ministers*. 6 October. www.imf.org/external/np/g20/pdf/110411c.pdf [Accessed: 21 August 2018].

World Bank Group, 2015. *Global Findex: Measuring Financial Inclusion around the World*. www.worldbank.org/en/programs/globalfindex [Accessed: 17 November 2017].

Websites

Note: All of the websites listed ahead were accessible as of 28 August 2018, unless indicated otherwise.

BRICS Research Group. *BRICS Information Centre*. www.brics.utoronto.ca.

Financial Stability Board. www.fsb.org.

G7 Research Group. *G7 Information Centre*. www.g8.utoronto.ca.

G20 Research Group. *G20 Information Centre*. www.g20.utoronto.ca.

International Monetary Fund. [G20-related web page]. www.imf.org/external/np/g20.

Index

www.ingramcontent.com/pod-product-compliance
Lightning Source LLC
LaVergne TN
LVHW052245200926
848481LV00002B/278

9781032073330